A Grammar of Piedmontese

Grammars and Sketches of the World's Languages

Romance Languages

Editor

Roberta D'Alessandro
(*Utrecht University*)

The titles published in this series are listed at *brill.com/rola*

A Grammar of Piedmontese

A Minority Language of Northwest Italy

By

Mauro Tosco
Emanuele Miola
Nicola Duberti

BRILL

LEIDEN | BOSTON

The Library of Congress Cataloging-in-Publication Data is available online at https:/catalog.loc.gov
LC record available at http://lccn.loc.gov/2023007394

Typeface for the Latin, Greek, and Cyrillic scripts: "Brill". See and download: brill.com/brill-typeface.

ISSN 2352-9342
ISBN 978-90-04-54405-5 (hardback)
ISBN 978-90-04-54429-1 (e-book)

Copyright 2023 by Mauro Tosco, Emanuele Miola and Nicola Duberti. Published by Koninklijke Brill NV, Leiden, The Netherlands.
Koninklijke Brill NV incorporates the imprints Brill, Brill Nijhoff, Brill Hotei, Brill Schöningh, Brill Fink, Brill mentis, Vandenhoeck & Ruprecht, Böhlau, V&R unipress and Wageningen Academic.
Koninklijke Brill NV reserves the right to protect this publication against unauthorized use. Requests for re-use and/or translations must be addressed to Koninklijke Brill NV via brill.com or copyright.com.

This book is printed on acid-free paper and produced in a sustainable manner.

Minority languages are often the subject of today's belittlement;
their loss, the source of tomorrow's bemoaning.
As linguists, we must fight the former to avoid the latter.

∴

Contents

Conventions, Glosses and Symbols XVII
Maps of Place Names in Piedmont Mentioned in the Grammar XXI
List of Maps, Tables and Figures XXV

1 **The Language and Its History, Classification and Variation** 1
   1.1   Overview: Language and Speakers 1
   1.2   Disentangling Classification and Ideology 4
   1.3   The Dialects of Piedmontese: Features and Classification 6
   1.4   The Internal Classification of the Piedmontese Varieties 13
   1.5   Social Varieties in Old Piedmontese 20
   1.6   The Speech of the Piedmontese Jews, Sinti and Waldensians 21
   1.7   A Short Linguistic History of Piedmont 22
       1.7.1 *From the Origins to the 17th Century* 22
       1.7.2 *The 18th Century* 26
       1.7.3 *The 19th Century* 29
       1.7.4 *The Contemporary Age* 31
   1.8   An Outline of Piedmontese Literature 33
       1.8.1 *From the Origins to the 17th Century* 33
       1.8.2 *The 18th Century* 39
       1.8.3 *The 19th Century* 44
       1.8.4 *The Contemporary Scene* 49

2 **Phonetics and Phonology** 58
   2.1   Default Articulation of Phonemes 58
   2.2   Loan Phonemes, Borrowing and Adaptation 65
   2.3   Previous Accounts of the Phonology of Piedmontese 68
   2.4   Phonetic Processes 70
       2.4.1 *Vowels* 70
       2.4.2 *Approximants* 75
       2.4.3 *Final Devoicing* 76
       2.4.4 *Nasals and the Status of* /ŋ/ 78
       2.4.5 *Sibilants* 82
   2.5   Positional Restrictions on the Occurrence of Phonemes 82
       2.5.1 *Consonants* 82
       2.5.2 *Vowels* 83
   2.6   Syllables 83

		2.7	Clusters 84
			2.7.1 *Sequences of Vocoids* 84
			2.7.2 *Consonant Clusters* 87
		2.8	Length 94
		2.9	Stress 94
		2.10	Pitch and Intonation 96
3		**Writing System and Orthography** 101
		3.1	Overview 101
			3.1.1 *Grapheme-Phoneme Correspondences* 101
			3.1.2 *Bigraphemes* 104
			3.1.3 *Allographs* 105
			3.1.4 *Phoneme-Spelling Correspondences* 107
			3.1.5 *Prosthetic* ⟨ë⟩ 107
			3.1.6 *Other Graphic Symbols* 109
		3.2	History 110
			3.2.1 *First Attestations and Fluctuations in the Early Modern Period* 111
			3.2.2 *18th Century Stabilization* 111
			3.2.3 *The* ortografia *moderna* 112
		3.3	Evaluation 113
			3.3.1 *Appropriateness* 113
			3.3.2 *Effectiveness* 115
			3.3.3 *Conclusions* 116
4		**Words, Word Constituents and Word Classes** 117
		4.1	Roots, Stems, Words, Affixes and Clitics 117
			4.1.1 *Roots and Stems* 117
			4.1.2 *Words* 118
			4.1.3 *Affixes* 119
			4.1.4 *Clitics* 120
			4.1.5 *Canonical Form of Words and Palindromes* 121
		4.2	Morphological Mechanisms 122
		4.3	Suppletion 124
		4.4	Syncretism 125
		4.5	Word Classes 125
5		**Nouns** 128
		5.1	Overview 128
		5.2	Gender 131

		5.2.1	*Inherent Gender* 132
		5.2.2	*Gender Inflection* 133
	5.3	Number 134	
	5.4	Derivational Morphology of Nouns 136	
		5.4.1	*Zero-Derivation* 136
		5.4.2	*Suffixal Derivation* 138
		5.4.3	*Prefixation* 146
		5.4.4	*Compound Nouns* 147

6 **Adjectives**   149
   6.1   Overview   149
   6.2   Semantics of Adjectives   149
   6.3   Morphology of Adjectives   151
       6.3.1 *L-ending Adjectives*   154
       6.3.2 *Allomorphic Variation in the Stem*   155
       6.3.3 *Prenominal Position and Syntactically-Governed Allomorphs*   156
   6.4   Comparative Constructions   158
       6.4.1 *Equative and Similative Constructions*   159
       6.4.2 *Superlative and Elative Constructions*   159
   6.5   Adjectives as Nouns   162
   6.6   Derivational Morphology of Adjectives   162
       6.6.1 *Derivational Suffixes*   162
       6.6.2 *Prefixation*   165

7 **Personal Pronouns**   168
   7.1   Overview   168
   7.2   Independent Personal Pronouns   171
       7.2.1 *Independent Status*   171
       7.2.2 *The Exclusive Pronouns*   171
       7.2.3 *Third Persons and Deictic Extensions*   173
       7.2.4 *Use of the Independent Pronouns*   174
       7.2.5 *Use of the Independent Pronouns as Politeness Markers*   176
   7.3   Subject Personal Pronouns   177
   7.4   Non-subject Personal Pronouns: Object and Indirect Object   180
   7.5   Interrogative Subject Clitics   185
   7.6   Reflexive, Reciprocal and Impersonal Personal Pronouns   187
   7.7   Attributive Pronoun   188

		7.8	Lexicalized Verb-Clitic Constructions 189
		7.9	Post-Tonic Vowel Dropping 193
		7.10	Sequences of Clitics 194

8 Grounding and Deixis 198
- 8.1 Overview 198
- 8.2 Determiners and Classifiers 200
  - 8.2.1 *Semantics of the Determiners* 200
  - 8.2.2 *Semantics of the Classifiers* 203
  - 8.2.3 *Morphonology of the Determiners and Classifiers* 206
- 8.3 Deixis 214
  - 8.3.1 *Spatial Frame of Reference* 214
  - 8.3.2 *The Deictics: An Overview* 215
  - 8.3.3 *Spatial Deixis* 216
  - 8.3.4 *The Demonstrative System: Deixis in Grounding* 219
  - 8.3.5 *Adnominal Demonstratives* 219
  - 8.3.6 *Pronominal Demonstratives* 221
  - 8.3.7 *Intersubjective Use and Other Uses of the Demonstratives* 224
- 8.4 Possessives 225

9 Quantifiers 230
- 9.1 Numerals 230
  - 9.1.1 *Cardinals* 230
  - 9.1.2 *Ordinals* 234
  - 9.1.3 *Numerals-Derived Nouns* 235
  - 9.1.4 *A Note on Finger-Counting* 235
- 9.2 Generic Quantifiers 235
- 9.3 Negative Quantifiers 241
- 9.4 Interrogative Quantifiers 242
- 9.5 Quantificational Nouns 243

10 Verbs 245
- 10.1 Semantic Overview 245
  - 10.1.1 *Labiles and Inherent Reflexives* 246
- 10.2 Morphological Overview 248
  - 10.2.1 *Morphological Classes: Previous Studies* 251
  - 10.2.2 *The First Verbal Class* 253
  - 10.2.3 *The Second Verbal Class* 254
  - 10.2.4 *Irregular Verbs* 255

	10.2.5	*The Paradigms* 263
	10.2.6	*Compound Paradigms: An Overview* 275
10.3	Affixes, Allomorphy and Syncretism 276
10.4	Historical and Comparative Notes 278
	10.4.1	*First Person Singular* 279
	10.4.2	*Second Person Singular* 279
	10.4.3	*Third Person Singular* 282
	10.4.4	*First Person Plural* 282
	10.4.5	*Second Person Plural* 283
	10.4.6	*Third Person Plural* 284
	10.4.7	*Beyond Piedmontese* 284
10.5	Moods and Tenses 293
	10.5.1	*Main* 293
	10.5.2	*The Subjunctive* 303
	10.5.3	*The Dubitative* 311
	10.5.4	*The Conditional* 314
	10.5.5	*The Imperative* 316
	10.5.6	*The Infinitive* 318
	10.5.7	*The Gerund* 318
	10.5.8	*The Participle* 322
10.6	Use of the Auxiliaries 325
	10.6.1	*Past: Active* 326
	10.6.2	*Past: Reflexive* 328
	10.6.3	*Passive* 330
10.7	Verbal Derivation 332

11 Verbal Periphrases and Modalities   335
- 11.1   Valency-Increasing Operation, 1: Causative   336
- 11.2   Valency-Increasing Operation, 2: Permissive   338
- 11.3   Valency-Increasing Operation, 3: Middle   339
- 11.4   Modal Verbs   341
- 11.5   Progressive and Continuous   346
- 11.6   Imminential   348
- 11.7   Inchoative   348
- 11.8   Durative   349
- 11.9   Terminative   350
- 11.10 Immediative   351
- 11.11 Iterative   353

12 Adverbs 355
- 12.1 Overview 355
  - 12.1.1 *Terminology and Prototypicality* 358
- 12.2 Predicate Adverbs 360
  - 12.2.1 *Manner Adverbs* 360
  - 12.2.2 *Phasal and Aspectual Adverbs* 362
  - 12.2.3 *Intensity Adverbs* 365
- 12.3 Degree Adverbs and Focalizers 366
- 12.4 Sentence Adverbs 367
  - 12.4.1 *Setting and Directional Adverbials* 367
  - 12.4.2 *Sentence Adverbs* 368
- 12.5 Linking Adverbs 370
- 12.6 Adverb Formation Rules and Productivity 371

13 Prepositions and Prepositional Phrases 373
- 13.1 The Expression of Location and Movement 373
- 13.2 Basic Prepositions 374
  - 13.2.1 *Adessive* a 375
  - 13.2.2 *Inessive* an 376
  - 13.2.3 *Ablative* da 378
  - 13.2.4 *Benefactive* për 383
  - 13.2.5 *Comitative* con 385
  - 13.2.6 *Combinations of Prepositions* 387
- 13.3 Non-basic Prepositions 387
  - 13.3.1 *Superessive* su 388
  - 13.3.2 *Interessive* (an)tra 389
- 13.4 Prepositional Use of Adverbs 390
- 13.5 Attributive Phrases and Binominal Constructions 392
  - 13.5.1 *The Attributive in the Expression of Origin* 392
  - 13.5.2 *The Attributive in Temporal Expressions* 393
  - 13.5.3 *The Attributive as a Marker of Possession* 394
  - 13.5.4 *The Attributive of Inherent Relationship* 394
  - 13.5.5 *The Attributive in the Expression of Material* 395
  - 13.5.6 *The Attributive in Nominalizations* 395
  - 13.5.7 *The Attributive in Quantification* 395
  - 13.5.8 *The Attributive as a Grounder* 397
  - 13.5.9 *The Attributive in the Expression of Categorization* 398
  - 13.5.10 *The Attributive in the Expressive Elative* 399
  - 13.5.11 *Sequences of Attributive Phrases* 400
  - 13.5.12 *Syntactic Properties of Binominal Constructions* 400

CONTENTS XIII

14 **Phrases** 403
    14.1 The Structure of the Noun Phrase 403
    14.2 Grounding and Ordering of Phrases 403
    14.3 Adjectival Phrases 405
    14.4 Temporal Phrases and Telling the Time 412

15 **Clauses** 417
    15.1 Non-verbal Predication 417
        15.1.1 *Bare (Elliptical) Non-verbal Predication* 417
        15.1.2 *Non-verbal Predication with a Copula* 420
    15.2 Declarative Clauses 423
    15.3 Introducing the Ubiquitous *che* 425
    15.4 Bare *che* in Non-verbal Predication 426
        15.4.1 *Exclamative* che 426
        15.4.2 *Quantificational* che ëd 427
    15.5 Relative Clauses 427
    15.6 Imperative Clauses 431
    15.7 Exhortative Clauses 432
    15.8 Mirative and Exclamative Clauses 433
    15.9 Questions 435
        15.9.1 *Polar Questions* 435
        15.9.2 *Tag Questions* 437
        15.9.3 *Negative Questions* 437
        15.9.4 *Constituent Questions* 438
    15.10 The Expression of Atmospheric Events 440

16 **Linkage** 442
    16.1 Coordination 442
        16.1.1 *Conjunction* 442
        16.1.2 *Disjunction* 443
        16.1.3 *Contrast* 444
        16.1.4 *Correlatives* 446
    16.2 Subordination 447
        16.2.1 *Untensed Subordination* 447
        16.2.2 *Subordination with* che *and Use of Tenses* 448
        16.2.3 *Subject and Object Clauses* 454
        16.2.4 *Temporal Clauses* 455
        16.2.5 *Concomitant Temporal Clauses* 456
        16.2.6 *Antecedent Temporal Clauses* 456
        16.2.7 *Clauses Expression Location and Movement* 457

        16.2.8 *Phrases and Clauses Expressing Manner*   457
        16.2.9 *Causal and Final Phrases and Clauses*   457
        16.2.10 *Concessive Phrases and Clauses*   460
        16.2.11 *Conditional Clauses*   461

17 Negation   464

    17.1 Overview   464
    17.2 Sentence Negators   464
        17.2.1 *Other Sentence-Negating Constructions*   468
        17.2.2 *Other Intensifying Negators*   468
    17.3 Negation with Scope over Smaller Units   469
    17.4 Other Negative Items   470
    17.5 Negative Concord   470
    17.6 Holophrastic Negation   473

18 Pragmatics and Discourse   476

    18.1 Information Structure and Sentence Word Order   476
    18.2 Hanging Topics and Clefts   480
    18.3 Discourse Markers   482

19 Piedmontese in a Typological Perspective   489

    19.1 Genealogy and Overview   489
    19.2 Phonology   490
    19.3 Morphosyntax   491
    19.4 Lexical Typology   498
    19.5 Piedmontese, Standard Average European, and Other Romance Languages   499

20 Use, Contact and Care: Codeswitching, Endangerment, Enrichment and Standardization   501

    20.1 Language Ideology through Language Use   501
        20.1.1 *Codeswitching and Borrowing*   503
        20.1.2 *Language Attrition*   504
        20.1.3 *Codeswitched Piedmontese*   505
        20.1.4 *Piedmontese in Other Languages*   509
        20.1.5 *Language Attrition in a Written Dialect*   514
        20.1.6 *Piedmontese in the World Wide Web*   515

20.2	The Long Road toward Resurgence 517	
	20.2.1 *The Orthography: A Resource and a Problem* 517	
	20.2.2 *Ausbauization: Between Tradition, Enrichment, and Standardization* 518	
	20.2.3 *Phraseology, Ausbau and Language Policy* 523	
20.3	Envoi 524	

Appendix: Text 527
References 533
Index of Subjects 566
Index of Languages, Varieties and Language Groups 568
Index of Towns, Villages, and Geographical Terms in Piedmont 569

Conventions, Glosses and Symbols

Conventions

All Piedmontese forms are given in the standard orthography (☞ 3.2.3.) in italics, followed by a phonemic transcription (in slanting brackets when occurring in the running text); a phonetic transcription in square brackets is occasionally added. The original orthography of the sources has been occasionally normalized according to the current rules. The first word of an example and its translation is capitalized only when it is so in the original.

No corpus of Piedmontese is yet available; all examples are drawn from different printed and electronic sources or our own native personal knowledge.

In examples, the orthographic form, the phonemic (as well as, occasionally, its phonetic transcription), and the English translation follow in this order. For morphologically complex words a morpheme-by-morpheme gloss is provided:

i deurbo
i=ˈdørb-u
SBJ.1=open-PRS.1S
'I open'

in which the gloss stands for "First person Subject clitic" and "First person Singular Subject of the verb 'to open' in the Main Present paradigm."

Default categories are unglossed. Thus, the Masculine forms of the Determiner and many Personal Pronouns is left unglossed for gender and number: *ël* /əl/ is "DET" and its Plural *ij* /j/ is "DET\P"—not *"DET\M-P." Likewise, in verbs the Main mood (which is also textually the most frequent) is left unglossed (as shown above).

Grammatical and linguistic terms are capitalized only when defined and described in the grammar—in other words, when they correspond to a category in Piedmontese (e.g, "Noun" and "Subject" are capitalized, "interjection" and "conjunction" are not).

Words and sentences in foreign languages are given in the respective standard orthography; in the case of Italian, they are phonologically transcribed according to the local Piedmontese accent (for an introduction to the phonology of the regional varieties of Italian, cf. Canepari 1980).

The variety described in the volume is contemporary Turinese, i.e., the contemporary Piedmontese koine (☞ 1.7.), understood by all Piedmontese speakers and used whenever necessary, e.g., for the interacactions between Piedmontese speakers that live in different provinces of the region. Notes on local varieties are preceded by the silhouette of Piedmont and are marked by a vertical line on the right.

Literary meanings are given in square brackets, while glosses in the running text and meanings are contained in inverted commas. Unless otherwise indicated, all translations are ours and all online resources were last accessed on Nov. 24, 2022, unless otherwise indicated.

Glosses and Symbols

By and large, glosses follow the *Leipzig Glossing Rules*.[1]

(blank)	word boundary
=	clitic boundary
-	affix boundary
\	precedes the gloss of a non-concatenative morpheme
.	separates elements in a portmanteau morpheme
_	separates elements in lexical glosses
?	dubious or marginal form
*	ungrammatical or unattested form
~	alternates with
→	yields (in phonological and morphological processes)
←	derives from (in phonological and morphological processes)
>	becomes in diachrony
/	minor prosodic boundary
//	major prosodic boundary
↗	interrogative intonation (in transcriptions)
'	main word stress
1	first person
2	second person
3	third person
⟨ ⟩	enclose graphemes

---

1 https://www.eva.mpg.de/lingua/pdf/Glossing-Rules.pdf.

CONVENTIONS, GLOSSES AND SYMBOLS

⟨ ⟩$_{cs}$	enclose codeswitched material
( )	(in the translation of examples) encloses "etic" material absent from the source language and whose presence is required by the target language
[ ]	(in the translation of examples) encloses "emic" material found in the source language and not translated in the target language
☞	points to another section in the grammar
ABL	ablative preposition *da*
ADE	adessive preposition *a*
ATTR	attributive preposition *ëd*
ATTR.PRO	attributive pronoun *ne/na*
ATTR.SUB	attributive subordinator *dont*
BEN	benefactive preposition *për*
C	oral consonant
COND	conditional
COM	comitative and instrumental preposition *con*
DEICT	neutral deictic
DEICT.ADV	adverbial neutral deictic
DEP	dependent
DET	determiner
DIST	distal deictic
DIST.PRO	pronominal distal deictic
DM	discourse marker
DUB	dubitative
EXCL	exclusive form of independent pronoun
F	feminine
GER	gerund
IDP	independent pronoun
IMPF	imperfect
IND	indirect object pronoun
INDEF	indefinite
INE	inessive preposition *an*
INF	infinitive
INT	interrogative subject pronoun
INTER	interessive preposition *antra*
IPV	imperative
M	masculine
N	nasal stop
NEG	negator
NEG.EMPH	emphatic negator

NEG.RES	resumptive negator
OBJ	object pronoun (direct object for all persons, indirect object for 1st and 2nd persons)
P	plural
POSS	possessive
PP	phonetic process
PROX	proximal deictic
PROX.PRO	pronominal proximal deictic
PRS	present
PTCL	participle
PST	past
REFL	reflexive pronoun
REL	relative phrase marker
Q	interrogative intonation (in glosses)
S	singular
SBJ	subject pronoun
SUB	subordinator
SUBJ	subjunctive
SUP	superessive preposition *su*
TAG	tag marker *neh?*
V	vowel

Maps of Place Names in Piedmont Mentioned in the Grammar

These maps provide the location of all the towns in Piedmont mentioned in the grammar. Following current anthropological and linguistic practice, place names are given first in Piedmontese, followed by their official denomination in Italian.

Upon their first occurrence in the grammar, the name in Piedmontese and Italian is reported in a footnote, followed, in case, by the name in Occitan or Franco-Provençal and, finally, the latitude and longitude.

The maps that follow were made using the program Google Earth.

Piedmont

XXII MAPS OF PLACE NAMES IN PIEDMONT MENTIONED IN THE GRAMMAR

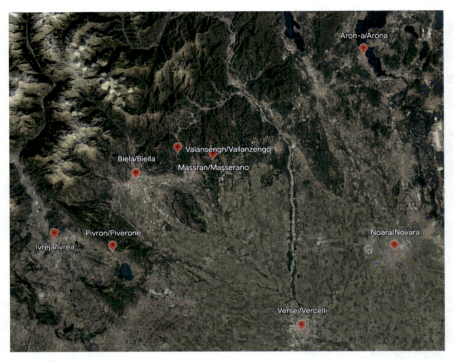

The northeast

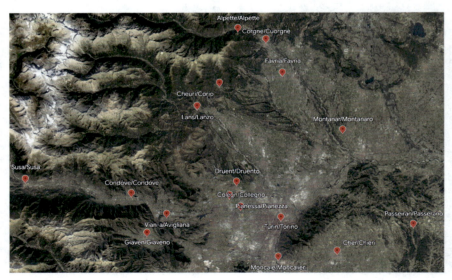

The northwest

MAPS OF PLACE NAMES IN PIEDMONT MENTIONED IN THE GRAMMAR   XXIII

The west

The southwest

XXIV   MAPS OF PLACE NAMES IN PIEDMONT MENTIONED IN THE GRAMMAR

The southeast

Maps, Tables and Figures

Maps

1 The Piedmontese-speaking area and the neighboring languages   3
2 Outcome of Latin CL   8
3 Outcome of Latin CT   12
4 'To cry' in the Piedmontese dialects   15
5 'Woman' in the Piedmontese dialects   16
6 Classification of Piedmontese and transitional varieties   19
7 Piedmont within the Duchy (since 1718 Kingdom) of Savoy   27
8 Map of the States of Savoy in 1839   30
9 The Masculine Determiner in the Piedmontese varieties   207
10 Outcome of Latin Infinitive -ARE in the Piedmontese varieties   253
11 First Singular Main Present of 'to have' in the Piedmontese varieties   260
12 Ending of the 1st Main Present, First Class in the Piedmontese varieties   280

Tables

1 The classification of the Piedmontese dialects according to Biondelli (1853) and a few isoglosses   13
2 Classification of Piedmontese and transitional varieties   18
3 The consonantal phonemes of Piedmontese   58
4 The Piedmontese inventory of consonants according to Soffietti (1949: 17)   68
5 Word-initial two-consonants clusters   90
6 Grapheme-phoneme correspondence in the Piedmontese writing system   102
7 Bigraphemes-phoneme correspondence in the Piedmontese writing system   104
8 Grapheme-phoneme correspondences for phonemes in local dialects   107
9 Relations Orth for Piedmontese   108
10 Appropriateness of the Piedmontese orthography   114
11 Graphical representation of words, clitics, stems and affixes   121
12 Word length and number of phonemes per word   122
13 Suppletion in the Main Present of 'to be' and 'to go' (Subject clitics not included)   124
14 Suppletion in the First Singular Pronouns   124
15 Syncretism in the verb: 'to take,' Main Present   125
16 Syncretism in the Subject clitics   125

17	Inflectional classes of nouns	130
18	Subclasses of Adjectives	152
19	An overview of the Personal Pronouns	170
20	Allomorphs of the Determiners	206
21	Allomorphs of the Classifiers	208
22	Local enlargement of the Attributive with the Determiners	209
23	The adnominal Demonstratives and their gendered and numbered allomorphs	220
24	The pronominal Demonstratives with a spatial adverb	222
25	The Possessives	225
26	Main Present (above) and Main Imperfect (below) of 'to be' and 'to have'	262
27	The two regular Classes of Piedmontese verbs	264
28	First Class irregular Verbs	268
29	Second Class irregular Verbs	270
30	Auxiliary Verbs	274
31	Simple and Compound paradigms of the Verb *rusé* /**ry'ze**/ 'to scold'	276
32	Mood and tense formants	276
33	Formants and affixes: person affixes	277
34	The person affixes at a glance	279
35	N distribution: the (literary) Italian Verb *udire* 'to hear'	285
36	L distribution: the Portuguese Verb *dizer* 'to say'	286
37	L distribution: the Verb *dì* 'to say' in the Piedmontese variety of Viola	286
38	U distribution: the Italian Verb *crescere* 'to grow'	287
39	U distribution: the Piedmontese Verb *soné* 'to play music' and *porté* 'to bring, carry'	287
40	U distribution: the Piedmontese verb *prové* 'to prove' and *durmì* 'to sleep'	288
41	U distribution: the Piedmontese Verb *plé* 'to peel' and *pentné* 'to comb'	288
42	U distribution: the Piedmontese Verb *sëmné* 'to sow'	288
43	The Main Present in the Piedmontese variety of Viola: Verbs *caté* /**ka'te**/ 'to buy,' *pard* /**pard**/ 'to lose,' and *bzé* /**bdze**/ 'to weigh'	290
44	U distribution: the Piedmontese Verb *peisé* 'to weigh'	289
45	The Main Present in the Piedmontese variety of Viola: Verb *dzoé* /**dzwe**/ 'to play games'	290
46	The Main Present in the town variety of ël Mondvì: Verb *porté* /**por'te**/ 'to bring, carry,' *seurte* /**'sørte**/ 'to go out' and *vèghe* /**'væge**/ 'to see'	291
47	L distribution: the Piedmontese Verbs *dé* /**de**/ 'to give' and *fé* /**fe**/ 'to do, make'	291
48	L distribution: the Piedmontese Verbs *sté* /**ste**/ 'to stay' and *andé* 'to go'	292
49	L distribution: the Piedmontese Verbs *podèj* /**pu'dæj**/ 'can' and *vorèj* /**vu'ræj**/ 'to want'	292

MAPS, TABLES AND FIGURES   XXVII

50   A list of regular and irregular Participles   323
51   Perfective auxiliary selection in some varieties spoken in Europe   327
52   The basic prepositions in combination with the Determiners   374
53   Order of elements in the Noun phrase   405
54   Time and tense in subordinate clauses   449
55   Combinations of *se* and a Subject Clitic   461
56   Independent personal Pronouns   492

Figures

1   Language vitality and EGIDS level of Piedmontese   2
2   A page from the Sermons Subalpins (12th century)   34
3   The vocalic phonemes of Piedmontese   59
4   Phonetic processes affecting vowels   71
5   Final devoicing in *lagh* /lag/ 'lake'   77
6   *lagh* /lag/ 'lake' with no final devoicing   77
7   *lait* /lajt/ 'milk,' declarative intonation   96
8   *lait* /lajt/ 'milk,' question   97
9   *lait* /lajt/ 'milk,' rhetoric question implying surprise, disbelief, etc.   97
10   *ij cit a dësmoro ant la cort* /i=ˈtʃit a=ˈdëzmur-u ant=l-a=kurt/ 'the children are playing in the yard' (declarative, neutral statement)   98
11   *ij cit a dësmoro ant la cort?* /i=ˈtʃit a=ˈdëzmur-u ant=l-a=kurt ↗/ 'are the children playing in the yard?'   99
12   *ij cit a dësmoro ant la cort* /i=ˈtʃit a=ˈdëzmur-u ant=l-a=kurt/ '*the children* are playing in the yard'   99
13   *ij cit a dësmoro ant la cort* /i=ˈtʃit a=ˈdëzmur-u ant=l-a=kurt/ 'the children *are* playing in the yard'   100
14   *ij cit a dësmoro ant la cort* /i=ˈtʃit a=ˈdëzmur-u ant=l-a=kurt/ 'the children are playing *in the* yard'   100
15   A feature-geometric representation of the Subject clitics   178
16   A pictorial representation of Adessive *a*   375
17   A pictorial representation of Inessive *an*   376
18   A pictorial representation of Ablative *da*   379
19   A pictorial representation of Ablative *da* in the expression of path   379
20   A pictorial representation of Benefactive and Goal *për* as a perlative   383
21   Declarative intonation   417
22   Interrogative intonation   418
23   *it-ses andait?* ('did you (s) go?')   436
24   *ses-to andait?* ('did you (s) go?')   436

CHAPTER 1

The Language and Its History, Classification and Variation

1.1 Overview: Language and Speakers[1]

Piedmontese (ethnonym *piemontèis* /**pjemuŋˈtæjz**/; ISO 639-3 code: pms) is a Western Romance language spoken in Piedmont, a north-western region of Italy. Along with Lombard, Emilian and Rumagnol it is part of the Gallo-Italic (or Gallo-Italian) languages.[2]

Piedmontese is considered "definitely endangered" in Salminen (2007) and the *Unesco Atlas of the World's Languages in Danger* (Moseley 2010). On the *Expanded Graded Intergenerational Disruption Scale*, Ethnologue places the language at level 7, "shifting."

As is often the case, any estimate of the number of speakers is made particularly impervious by the usual problems of bilingualism and diglossia, use in codeswitching only, etc. The *Unesco Atlas* ventures as many as two million (but adding: a "Compromise figure based on various sources, possibly inflated"). In a similar vein, Allasino (2007: 70–71) estimates 2 million adults who can speak and understand enough Piedmontese while more than another million have some knowledge of it. More limited numbers are proposed by *Ethnologue*, which, after having ventured at least 1,600,000 speakers in Italy, has more recently reduced the number to 700,000, as also suggested by Regis (2012b).

The Italian Census does not report on language, while the Italian National Institute of Statistics (ISTAT) does; in the case of Piedmontese, this would, in any case, be hampered by the unrecognized status of the language by the Italian government, whose language policy for recognized language minorities is regulated by Law No. 482/1999.

---

1 The entire volume is the result of a continuous exchange of ideas between its three authors. However, and for legal and academic Italian purposes only, we hereby state that Nicola Duberti is the author of Chapters 1 and 10, and of the Appendix; Emanuele Miola is the author of Chapters 3, 12, 17, 18, 19 and Section 8.3 of Chapter 8; and Mauro Tosco is the author of Chapters 2, 4, 5, 6, 7, 8 (except for Section 8.3.), 9, 11, 13, 14, 15, 16 and 20.
   We thank Lorenzo Ferrarotti for the maps showing the isoglosses in this and the following chapters and Fabio Gasparini for the spectrograms in Chapter 2, the anonymous reviewers and Roberta D'Alessandro for their insightful comments on a previous draft of this work.
2 Ligurian is also sometimes added to the list.

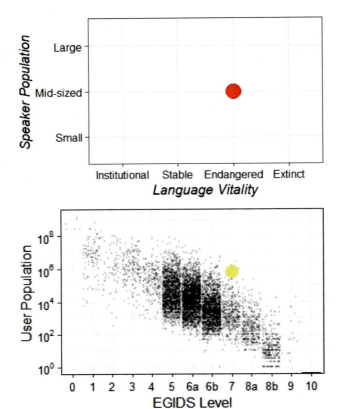

FIGURE 1   Language vitality and EGIDS level of Piedmontese
HTTPS://WWW.ETHNOLOGUE.COM/LANGUAGE/
PMS

Virtually all speakers of Piedmontese are completely bilingual and literate in Italian. Literacy in Piedmontese, on the other hand, is minimal. A small Piedmontese-speaking community (where speakers are bilingual and literate in Spanish) is also present in Argentina.[3]

Map 1. gives the approximate location of Piedmontese and neighboring languages. These are, to the West, Occitan and Franco-Provençal (and nowadays mainly French); to the North, Franco-Provençal and French again but also Walser and Swiss German; to the East, mainly Lombard (and marginally Emil-

---

3 Eugenio Goria (p. c., July 26, 2022), on the basis of his ongoing fieldwork on Argentinian Piedmontese, estimates a few hundred speakers only (semispeakers excluded). Preliminary results are Goria (2015) and Goria (forthcoming). Other data on the Piedmontese of Argentina can be found in Giolitto (2010) and (2016).

THE LANGUAGE AND ITS HISTORY, CLASSIFICATION AND VARIATION 3

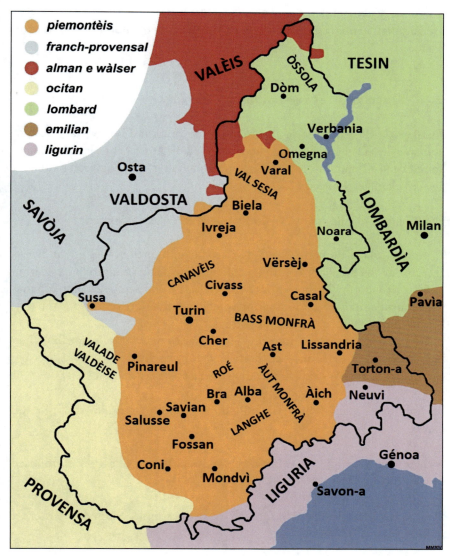

MAP 1   The Piedmontese-speaking area and the neighboring languages (originally in Tosco, Rubat-Borel and Bertolino 2006: 43). Key to language names: piemontèis: Piedmontese; franch-provensal: Franco-Provençal; alman e wàlser: Alemannic varieties, Walser; ocitan: Occitan (alternative glottonym: Provençal); Lombard: Lombard; emilian: Emilian; ligurin: Ligurian. Key to places outside Piedmont (from North to South): Valèis: Valais; Tesin: Ticino; Valdosta: Aosta Valley; Savòja: Savoy; Lombardìa: Lombardy; Provensa: Provence; Liguria: Liguria

ian and Ligurian), and to the South, Ligurian. Many areas that will be labeled "transitional" in our classification (☞ 1.4.) are considered non-Piedmontese on the map.

1.2 Disentangling Classification and Ideology

The genetic classification of Piedmontese beyond (and below) the Western Romance level is hampered by the controversial status of the classification of Romance itself (and the different criteria underlying it). A common (and least nested) classification is probably

Piedmontese < Gallo-Italic < Gallo-Romance < Western < Romance

This proposal has Romance divided in two major branches, Western and Eastern, cutting the Romance continuum along a line running approximately from La Spezia to Rimini (or sometimes between Massa and Senigallia) and separating peninsular Italy to the South from what lies to the North and West (roughly: Northern Italy, France, Spain, and Portugal).

On the contrary, *Ethnologue* divides Romance into three major branches, Italo-Western, Eastern and Southern, and further divides Italo-Western between Italian and Western, again along the La Spezia–Rimini line:

Piedmontese < Gallo-Italic < Gallo-Romance < Western < Italo-Western < Romance

A slightly more complicated but essentially similar classification is proposed by Glottolog:[4]

Piedmontese-Lombard < Gallo-Italian < Northwestern < Shifted < Western < Italo-Western < Romance

In both classifications the Italian linguistic domain north of Peninsular Italy is cut off from Italian and Southern Italian languages and moderately aligned with the languages of France and beyond. Such a view is robustly supported by, e.g., Hull (1982) and, before him, Schmid (1956) and Bec (1970–1971).

---

4 https://glottolog.org/resource/languoid/id/piem1238.

Apart from genetic considerations, the division of the Romance *Sprachraum* along a north-south axis is also supported by the analysis of structural and typological features. Following, among others, La Fauci (1991), Zamboni (1998) and Ledgeway (2020), that area of Romània located North of the La Spezia–Rimini line encompasses French, Occitan, Franco-Provençal, Rhaeto-Romance and Gallo-Italic varieties (among which is of course Piedmontese) and exhibits, for instance, subject clitics/non pro-drop, the development and grammaticalization of the partitive as an obligatory pre-nominal marker, the alternation of Latin HABERE and ESSE as sources for auxiliaries in compound Verb forms, and loss of the synthetic past; southern Romània (i.e., central Italian dialects, Southern varieties spoken in Italy, Sardinian, Ibero-Romance, Dalmatian, and Daco-Romance) are pro-drop, tend to mark the Object (e.g., with Differential Object Marking), generalize a single auxiliary (either form HABERE or from ESSE), and maintain alive the synthetic past.

A different tradition, mainly based on phonetic and lexical features, particularly influential in Italy, is represented, e.g., by Wartburg (1950), Lausberg (1963), Hall (1976), and Pellegrini (1975, 1992), and more recently in Loporcaro (2009). It subsumes Gallo-Italic (and, *a fortiori*, Piedmontese), within all the other Italian varieties of Italy under the label of Italo-Romance, thus following a narrative that is part and parcel of an ideological construal whose establishment harks back to the very rise of dialectology in the 19th-century nation-states of Europe.

This label, in turn, has been thoroughly reviewed in Regis (2020), where its non-cladistic and basically non-linguistic nature becomes apparent. As convincingly argued by Brasca (2021), the very idea of an Italo-Romance group is essentially based upon socio-political and historical reasons. This seems to be admitted, although obliquely, by Loporcaro (2009: 11–12), who argues:

> Why, then, do we call it [Turinese] an Italian dialect, like Sicilian? The answer is in part of a socio-political nature: since the sixteenth century, Turinese has Italian as its roof language and the standardization processes push it insensibly towards a structural homogenisation to Italian. If the duchy of Savoy in the sixteenth century remained totally culturally French, Turinese would now be given a different classification. However, it is not to be thought that classification is a purely conventional operation, made on a political basis and free from linguistic criteria.[5]

---

5   Original: *Perché dunque chiamiamo quest'ultimo [i.e., Turinese] un dialetto italiano, al pari*

In the lines that follow this quote, Loporcaro argues that although French is its roof language today, Corsican is still part of Italo-Romance—here on the basis of linguistic considerations. Therefore, he maintains that Italo-Romance is not a purely sociolinguistic label.

Apart from the use of the questionable concept of "roof language" and a mistake regarding standardization (if anything, the contemporary standardization of Piedmontese aims at *avoiding* Italianisms and Italianization, cf. Tosco 2011a, 2012), in the preceding quote one may note the label "Turinese," which seems to negate the reality of a Piedmontese linguistic unity. All in all, the enterprise aiming to subsume Gallo-Italic within Italo-Romance seems to be a pious attempt to have it both ways: to encompass all the Romance varieties spoken in Italy (or at least, those that have not been granted the coveted status of "minority language") under an Italian coating, to gloss over any close link between Northern Italian languages and varieties abroad (as implicit in the "Western Romance" classification) and at the same time, to deny the ideological underpinnings of the whole operation.

1.3 The Dialects of Piedmontese: Features and Classification

Piedmontese, as any natural language, has a certain degree of diatopic variability in dialects, and therefore within the limits of mutual intelligibility.

Still, the history of the classification of Piedmontese varieties—as that of Piedmontese itself, as sketched in the preceding section—is strictly intertwined, and understandably so, with the linguistic ideologies of the political elites and academic milieus.

In this sense, Piedmontese is a clear example of a "contested language" as intended by Tamburelli and Tosco (2021): a language whose status as a language is beyond doubt from a strictly linguistic point of view but whose full recognition, even academically, is hampered by sociolinguistic and political considerations. All of this is reflected in a certain disinterest, if not outright hostility, by the academia; the lack of academic descriptions was aptly remarked

> del siciliano? La risposta è in parte di natura sociopolitica: il torinese, sin dal Cinquecento, ha come lingua tetto l'italiano e in direzione di un'omologazione strutturale all'italiano lo spingono, insensibilmente, i processi di standardizzazione. Se il ducato di Savoia nel Cinquecento fosse rimasto per intero culturalmente francese, del torinese si darebbe oggi una classificazione diversa. Non bisogna però credere che la classificazione sia operazione puramente convenzionale, su base politica e svincolata da criteri linguistici [translation by Lissander Brasca (2021: 76)].

upon by Berruto (1990–1991: 497): 'Piedmontese lacks full grammatical descriptions, and until now there has been no historical grammar nor a synchronic descriptive grammar.'[6]

Even before the language vs dialect issue, language contestation often starts with the very name of a language: *piemontèis* is the everyday appellation of the language when one is speaking either the supraregional koine (☞ 1.6., 1.7.) or, often, a specific local variety; either *piemontese* or *dialetto* ('dialect') are used when speaking Italian (Regis 2012a: 271).

For one thing, Piedmontese shares with the other languages attested in the Po valley and generally in the North of Italy—the Gallo-Italic languages seen in sections 1.1. and 1.2.—many diachronic features, such as (Savoia 1997: 225–227; Loporcaro 2009: 82–91):
- consonant degemination: GALLINA(M) > *galin-a* /ga'liɲa/ 'hen;' *CAPPELLA(M) > *capela* /ka'pela/ 'chapel,' CARRU(M) > *car/cher* /kar/kær/ 'cart;'
- palatalization of CL and GL, see Map 2.: CLAVE(M) > *ciav* /tʃaw/ 'key;' *GLACIA(M) > *giassa* /'dʒasa/ 'ice;'
- dropping of the Late-Latin/early-Romance ending -U and -OS in nouns and adjectives. Only the Latin First Declension -A and -E endings are kept: MULU(M) > *mul* /myl/ 'mule,' POMU(M) > *pom* /pum/ 'apple,' LUPU(M)/LUPOS > *luv* /lyw/ 'wolf/wolves.'

While the last feature does not concern many varieties of Liguria and Veneto (the latter not belonging to Gallo-Italic), there are a few other synchronic phonological features that can distinguish the Northern Italian varieties labeled Gallo-Italic languages (Biondelli 1853):
- the presence of a near-front close-mid vowel like /ø/ or an open-mid central one like /œ/. In some varieties, as in French, both of them actually do co-occur with a phonemic status, while in many others, among them Piedmontese, they are allophones of a single phoneme: COR > *cheur* /kør/ 'heart,' SOMNIU(M) > *seugn* /søɲ/ 'dream,' NOVA(M) > *neuva* /'nøv-a/ 'new-F', FOCU(M) > *feu* /fø/;
- the presence of a close front vowel such as /y/, normally from Latin or Germanic -U-: CULU(M) > *cul* /kyl/ 'arse,' FUMU(M) > *fum* /fym/ 'smoke.'

Since Biondelli (1853), certain linguistic features have been isolated in order to distinguish Piedmontese from the other Gallo-Italic languages of Northern

---

6 Original: *ël piemonteis a manca ëd descrission sientifiche complete, ancora ancheuj i l'oma nen ni na gramatica stòrica ni na gramàtica descritiva sincrònica.*

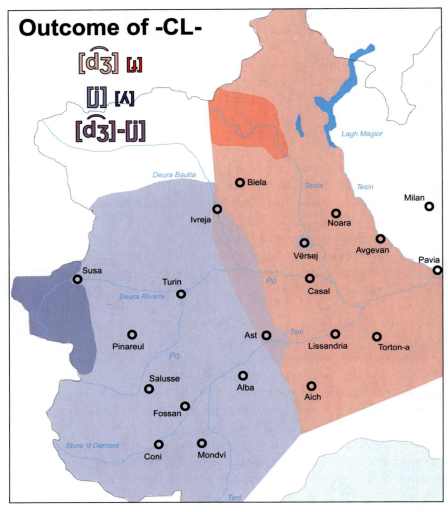

MAP 2   Outcome of Latin CL
         COURTESY OF LORENZO FERRAROTTI

Italy. The same features have naturally been used to divide the Piedmontese linguistic space in many subareas.

A short list of such diachronic features include:

- the phonological rising of /a/ in the Latin Infinitive ending -ARE: koine Piemontese exhibits /ˈe/ in these contexts, e.g., LAXARE > *lassé* /laˈse/ 'to leave,' CAPTARE > *caté* /kaˈte/ 'to buy,' *BULLICARE > *bogé* /buˈdʒe/ 'to move.' This rising distinguishes Piedmontese from other Gallo-Romance languages such as Franco-Provençal and Occitan, where -ARE becomes /ˈar/

(DOC: *laissar* /laj'sar/, *achatar* /atʃa'tar/, *bojar* /bu'dʒar/), but also from Ligurian and Lombard varieties, where -ARE > /'a/. Nevertheless, this feature is not uniformly distributed throughout the territory: many Eastern Piedmontese dialects show /'a/, but /'e/ can be found in some very "Eastern" Ossola dialects (Ferrarotti 2022: 50–54) while /'ar/ is the common ending of Canavzan[7] varieties (Telmon 2001: 76: *lassar, catar, bogiar*; also 'd Min 2015; Tonso 2017; Zörner 1998) and even some High-Piedmontese dialects around Coni[8] display forms in /'a/ sometimes velarized in [ɑ] or [ɒ]: Boves *lassò, catò, bogiò*;

- the raising and fronting of /a/ in the agentive suffixes -ARIU(M): MACELLARIU(M) > *maslé* /maz'le/ 'butcher;' this is more widely distributed over the whole area;
- the dropping of pro-tonic vowels: SEPTIMANAM > *sman-a* /'zmaŋa/ 'week,' MELONE(M) > *mlon* /mluŋ/ 'melon,' TELARIU(M) > *tlé* /tle/ 'loom.' This feature distinguishes Piedmontese from Occitan (*setmana, melon, telier*) but also from Lombard and Ligurian that sometimes keep the unstressed vowels, unlike Emilian varieties, in which vowel dropping is likewise very frequent;
- the evolution CT > /jt/, see Map 3: LACTE(M) > *lait* /lajt/ 'milk,' FACTU(M) > *fait* /fajt/ 'done,' distinguishes Piedmontese from Occitan and Lombard that display CT > /tʃ/ instead. CT > /jt/ is, in fact, attested only in the Western part of Piedmont, including all the Canavzan dialects (except for some Ciusèila valley[9] varieties) as well as the Franco-Provençal varieties, but, as anticipated, barring the Occitan varieties (except for those of the Gess[10] valley). All the Eastern dialects, including the Langhe[11] and the ël Mondvì[12] areas, share the evolution CT > /tʃ/ with Lombard and Occitan and also with dialects of the Tane[13] valley, usually considered Ligurian varieties;

---

7 Canavzan /kanav'zaŋ/ or Canavèis / kana'væjz /, Italian Canavese /kana'veze/ is a wide region in the Northwest of Piedmont, within the province of Turin; it comprises a "higher," mountainous part and a "lower" area to the North of Turin.
8 Coni /'kuni/, Italian Cuneo /'kuneo/ (44°23'22"N 07°32'52"E) a major town in Southwest Piedmont and a provincial capital.
9 Ciusèila /tʃy'zæjla/, Italian Chiusella /kju'zella/.
10 Gess /dʒes/, Italian Gesso /'dʒesso/.
11 Langhe /'laŋge/, Italian Langhe /'lange/ is a hilly region in the southern part of Piedmont within the provinces of Coni and Ast.
12 ël Mondvì /(əl=)muɲd'vi/, Italian Mondovì /mondo'vi/ (44°23'20"N 07°49'05"E) is a major town in Southwest Piedmont.
13 Tani /'tani/, Italian Tanaro /'tanaro/.

- the dropping (or reduction to /i/ or /j/) of etymological intervocalic C and G: URTICA(M) > *urtìa* /yrˈtia/ 'nettle,' FICU(M) > *fi* /fi/ 'fig,' MASTICARE > *mastié* /masˈtje/ 'to chew,' MANICA(M) > *mania* /ˈmanja/ 'sleeve', *MELICA(M) > *melia* /ˈmelja/ 'corn,' BRACAS > *braje* /ˈbraje/ 'trousers,' FURMICA(M) > *furmija* /fyrˈmi(j)a/ 'ant.'[14] This feature is not unique to Piedmontese because it is found in Ladin and Friulian (Bertoni 1916: 87) but not in Ligurian and Lombard, and links Piedmontese directly to Northern or Alpine Occitan, Franco-Provençal and French. Many Eastern dialects display this feature, including traditional Lomellina dialects that are administratively part of Lombardia; nevertheless, some Piedmontese Eastern dialects (particularly those of the Sesia, Stron-a and Séssera[15] valleys) do not exhibit this feature and have a simple sonorization of the etymological velar plosive (Ferrarotti 2019: 267): *melga, formiga*;
- the dropping of etymological intervocalic T and D: BETULLA(M) > *biola* /ˈbjula/ 'birch,' MEDULLA(M) > *miola* /ˈmjula/ 'pith,' *BOTELLOS > *buej* /byˈej/ 'guts,' SCUTELLA(M) > *scoela* /ˈskwela/ 'bowl.' This can barely be taken as a distinctive feature of Piedmontese, at least in siynchrony, since it is partially shared by some Lombard and especially Ligurian dialects. On the other hand, today's Piedmontese koine exhibits many cases of reintegration of the alvealor plosive sound: **bedola* or **medola* are not attested, while *budej* and *scudela* are by far the most common forms (possibly due to Italianization);
- the existence of a velar nasal between vowels and before consonants, like in LUNA(M) > *lun-a* /ˈlyŋa/ 'moon,' FONTANA(M) > *fontan-a* /fuŋˈtaŋa/ 'fountain,' PLENA(M) > *pien-a* /ˈpjæŋ-a/ 'full-F,' LANA(M) > *lan-a* /ˈlaŋa/ 'wool.' Unidentified in all the so-called Gallo-Italic varieties (Lombard, Emilian) and in Occitan alike, it is a specific feature of Piedmontese. Nevertheless, it is shared by Ligurian (Genoese) and it is not uniformly distributed throughout the territory: many Piedmontese dialects, especially those in contact with Occitan, show no trace of it;
- the diphthongitzation of Ĭ and Ē in open syllables: TELA(M) > *tèila* /ˈtæjla/ 'cloth,' PIPERE(M) > *pèiver* /ˈpæjver/ 'pepper,' NIGRUM > *nèir* /ˈnæjr/ 'black,' FRIGIDU(M) > *frèid* /ˈfræjd/ 'cold,' SERA(M) > *sèira* /ˈsæjra/ 'evening.' This feature is unknown to Occitan and Lombard varieties but it is shared by Lig-

---

14 It is worth emphasizing that URTICA(M) and FORMICA(M) show the same evolution /y/ for both U and O: it is a very common phenomenon in the Piedmontese koine, and it takes place especially when unstressed Us or Os are followed by a stressed /i/ vowel: SORTIRE > *surtì* /syrˈti/ 'to exit', MORIRI > *murì* /myˈri/ 'to die', and so on.
15 Sesia, Stron-a and Séssera /ˈsezja, ˈstruŋa, ˈsesera/, Italian Sesia, Strona and Sessera /ˈsezja, ˈstrona, ˈsessera/.

urian and Emilian; on the other hand, it disappears in some subareas, e.g., in the High Piedmontese varieties around Cuneo that display an Occitan-like evolution;
- the reduction to -*o* /u/ of the Third Plural verbal endings -ANT, -ENT, -UNT and -IUNT: > MANDUCANT > (*a*) *mangio* /(a=)'maŋdʒu/, DEBENT > (*a*) *deuvo* /(a=)'døvu/, LEGUNT >, (*a*) *leso* /(a=)'lezu/, VENIUNT > (*a*) *veno* /(a=)'væŋu/ 'they eat/must/read/come.' The same reduction is applied to all Latin proparoxytone nominal endings such as -INEM, -INUM, -ENEM, -ANUM, -ULUM, -IRIS, -OREM: AERUGINE(M) > *ruso* /'ryzu/ 'rust,' PECTINE(M) > *pento* /'pæŋtu/ 'comb,' INCUDINE(M) > *ancuso* /aŋ'kyzu/ 'anvil,' TERMINU(M) > *termo* /'tærmu/ 'field's border,' ASINU(M) > *aso* /'azu/ 'donkey,' IUVENE(M) > *giovo* /'dʒuvu/ 'young,' ORGANU(M) > *òrgo* /'orgu/ 'organ,' TABULU(M) > *tavo* /'tavu/ 'table,' PERICULU(M) > *privo* /'privu/ 'danger,' *WINDULUM > *vindo* /'viŋdu/ 'wool-winder,' *MERCURIS > *mercol* /'mærku(l)/ 'Wednesday,' ARBORE(M) > *erbo* /'ærbu/ 'tree.' This feature is exclusively Piedmontese and widely attested since the 16th century in the works of Alione (Ferrarotti 2019: 68); no other neighboring language displays such an evolution. In Piedmont, on the other hand, it is absent in Canavzan varieties;
- the velarization of /l/ in the etymological string -AL-: ALTU(M) > *àut* /awt/ 'high,' ALTERU(M) > *àutr* /awtr/ 'other,' FALDA(M) > *fàuda* /'fawda/ 'skirt,' FALSU(M) > *fàuss* /faws/ 'false,' GALBINU(M) > *giàun* /dʒawn/ 'yellow,' SALTARE > *sauté* /saw'te/ 'to jump.' This feature is shared by many other languages (including Occitan and medieval French) but it is not equally distributed all over the region: some Piedmontese varieties have just a long /aː/ as Ligurian dialects do: /aːt/, /aːtr/ and so on;
- the merging of CL and LJ into /j/: GENUC(U)LU(M) > *gënoj* /dʒə'nuj/ or *znoj* /znuj/ 'knee,' FENUC(U)LU(M)> *fnoj* /fnuj/ 'fennel,' OC(U)LU(M) > *euj* /øj/ 'eye,' CUNIC(U)LU(M) > *cunij* /ky'nij/ 'rabbit' show exactly the same phoneme of *FOLIA(M) > *feuja* /'føja/ 'leaf,' MELIU(S) > *mej* /mej/ 'better,' FILIU(M) > *fij* /'fij/ 'son' (arc.), TALIARE > *tajé* /ta'je/ 'to cut.' In fact, as we have already seen, this is a very useful feature for classifying different varieties spoken in the territory of Piedmont, since it links very closely all the Western and Southern Piedmontese dialects to Occitan and French, while Eastern varieties (including transitional dialects of the Bormia[16] valley) display a "Lombard" distinction between CL > /tʃ/ or /dʒ/ vs LJ > /j/;
- the First Plural verbal ending /'uma/ (Berruto 1974: 22; Telmon 1988: 473–474) that applies to all inflectional classes, regardless of the form they had in ori-

---

16 Bormia /'burmia/, Italian Bormida /'bormida/.

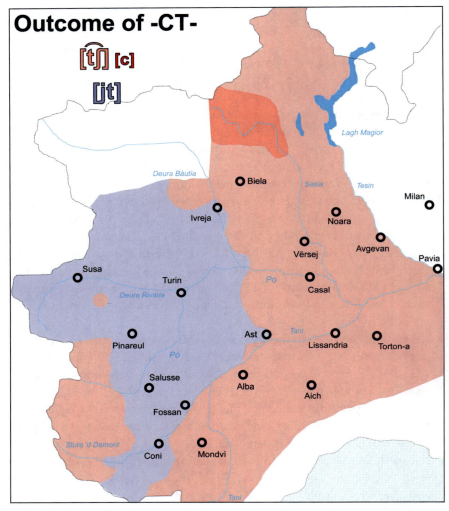

MAP 3   Outcome of Latin CT
COURTESY OF LORENZO FERRAROTTI

gin: CANTAMUS > (*i*) *cantoma* /(i=)kaŋˈtuma/ 'we sing,' PLACEMUS > (*i*) *piasoma* /(i=)pjaˈzuma/ 'we are likeable,' LEGIMUS > (*i*) *lesoma* /(i=)leˈzuma/ 'we read,' FINIMUS > (*i*) *finioma* /(i=)finˈjuma/ 'we finish.' It is widespread and even in very Eastern areas such the Sesia valley and beyond the borders of Piedmont, as in Lomellina, but it is absent in Canavzan dialects.

THE LANGUAGE AND ITS HISTORY, CLASSIFICATION AND VARIATION 13

TABLE 1   The classification of the Piedmontese dialects according to Biondelli (1853) and a few isoglosses

	Piedmontese	Monfrà	Canavzan
1st Class Infinitive	aŋˈde	aŋˈdæ	aŋˈdar
FACTUM	fajt	fattʃ	fæt
/y/ ~ /i/	ˈtyti	tittʃ	ˈtyit
Clitic pronouns ('s/he told me')	a=ˈm=a di=me[a]	o=ˈm=a dittʃ	a=ˈm=a dit
Dubitative ("Future"; 'I'll do')	i=faˈrø/ i=ˈfaraj	i=faˈro	i=faˈru

a   Modern Piedmontese: *a l'ha dime* / a=ˈl=a di=me / (☞ 7.4.).

1.4   The Internal Classification of the Piedmontese Varieties

Biondelli (1853: 471) divided the Piedmontese linguistic space into three macrogroups:
– "Proper" Piedmontese dialects, spoken in the Western part of the region, in direct contact with Occitan dialects spoken in the Alpine valleys;
– Canavzan dialects in the North-East area;
– Monfrà[17] dialects in the South-East.

According to Biondelli (1853: 474), Piedmontese dialects are strongly influenced by the languages of Southern France (i.e., Occitan, but also regional forms of French), while Canavzan dialects have several Lombard features, and Monfrà dialects appear closely connected with Ligurian varieties. The dialect of ël Mondvì and those of the neighboring valleys display features of proper Piedmontese and of the Monfrà dialects, and are a sort of bridge towards Ligurian.

Moreover, Biondelli identified five phonetic and morphosyntactic features that may be used to distinguish these groups (Table 1.1.):
– the first conjugation's infinitive ending;
– the outcome of the Latin cluster CT, as in FACTUM, LACTEM and so on;
– the presence/absence of the phoneme /y/;
– the position of the clitic pronouns;
– the form of the future.

---

17   Monfrà /muŋˈfra/, Italian Monferrato /monferrˈato/ is a hilly area in the Southern and Southeast part of Piedmont within the provinces of Ast and Lissandria.

Much later, we owe to Berruto (1974: 12–13) a proposal dividing Piedmont into five sub-areas:
- the Proper Piedmontese area;
- the Canavzan area;
- the area of Biela;[18]
- the Langhe and Monfrà areas;
- the High Piedmontese area.

This subdivision leaves out many geographic areas, including certain Piedmontese-speaking areas: Vërsèj,[19] Noara,[20] Lissandria[21] are considered not Piedmontese in a strict sense.

More recently, Telmon (2001: 54–80) has much refined and enlarged Berruto's classification with the inclusion of many areas and dialects that Berruto did not consider Piedmontese:
- Turin[22] Piedmontese;
- High Piedmontese;
- varieties of the Monfrà;
- Lissandria varieties;
- Langhe varieties;
- Canavzan varieties;
- Bielèis varieties;
- Vërsèj varieties;
- Sesia Valley's[23] varieties.

Telmon (2001: 66) underlines the existence of some lexical divergences that run through the linguistic space of Piedmont from North to South. Therefore, from the morpho-syntactic point of view these varieties are highly similar, while lexically a Western Piedmontese and an Eastern Piedmontese can be opposed.

---

18   Biela /ˈbjela/, Italian Biella /ˈbjella/ (45°34′N 08°04′E) is a major town in Northern Piedmont and a provincial capital.
19   Vërsèj /vəˈsæj/, Italian Vercelli /verˈtʃelli/ (45°19′N 08°25′E) is a major town in Northeast Piedmont and a provincial capital.
20   Noara /nuˈara/, Italian Novara /noˈvara/ (45°27′N 08°37′E) is a major town in East Piedmont and a provincial capital.
21   Lissandria /liˈsaɲdria/, Italian Alessandria /alesˈsandria/ (44°55′N 08°37′E) is a major town in Southeast Piedmont and a provincial capital.
22   Turin /tyˈriŋ/, Italian Torino /toˈrino/ (45°04′45″N 07°40′34″E) is the major town of Piedmont and its regional capital.
23   The Valsesia /valˈsezja/ (homographous and homophonous in Piedmontese and Italian) is actually a whole group of valleys in the North of Piedmont within the Vërsèj province; it takes its name from the main river, Sesia /ˈsezja/.

THE LANGUAGE AND ITS HISTORY, CLASSIFICATION AND VARIATION 15

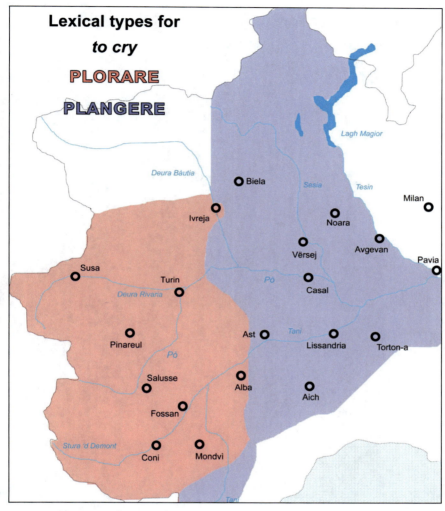

MAP 4 'To cry' in Piedmontese dialects
COURTESY OF LORENZO FERRAROTTI

Such an opposition can be visualized in Maps 4 and 5, regarding, respectively:
– 'to cry' (*pioré* in the West, *pianze* in the East; see also Grassi, Sobrero and Telmon 1997: 128);
– 'woman, wife' (*fomna* /ˈfumna/ in the West, *dòna* /ˈdona/ in the East).
Other cases in which Western (W) varieties lexically contrast with Eastern (E) ones are (Telmon 2001: 66–67):
– W *albicòch* /albiˈkok/ vs E *armognan* /armuˈɲaŋ/ 'apricot;'

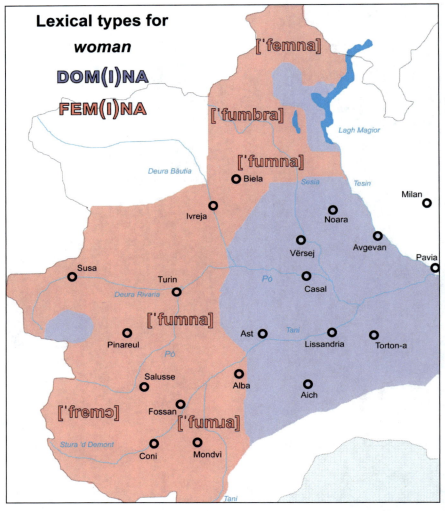

MAP 5   'Woman, wife' in Piedmontese dialects
COURTESY OF LORENZO FERRAROTTI

– W *ambossor* /ambuˈsu(r)/ vs E *tortreu* /turˈtrø/ 'funnel;'
– W *ramassa* /raˈmasa/ vs E *scoa* /skya/ 'broom;'
– W *pom* /pum/ vs E *mèir* /mæjr/ 'apple;'
– W *pruss* /prys/ vs E *pèir* /pæjr/ 'pear;'
– W *sofié* /suˈfje/ vs E *bufé* /byˈfe/ 'to blow;'
– W *pòis* /pojz/ vs E *arbion* /arˈbjuŋ/ 'pea;'
– W *cròch* /krok/ vs E *rampin* /ramˈpiŋ/ 'hook;'
– W *menton* /mæŋˈtuŋ/ vs E *barbaròt* /barbaˈrɔt/ 'chin;'

- W *còj* /koj/ vs E *vèrza* /'værza/ 'cabbage;'
- W *përsëmmo, pnansëmmo* /pər'səmmu, pnaŋ'səmmu/ vs E *erbolent* /ærbu'læŋt/ 'parsley;'
- W *faudal* /faw'dal/, vs E *scossal* /sku'sal/ 'apron' (see also Telmon 2001: 50).

Another classification has more recently been proposed by Ferrarotti (2019: 269–270) on the basis of phonetic features only. Combining the isoglosses for the outcomes of -CT- and -CL-, he divides the Piedmontese linguistic space into three macro-areas:
- Western dialects in which -CL- becomes /j/: VETULUM > VECLU(M) > *vej* /vej/ 'old', and -CT- turns into /jt/: FACTU(M) > *fàit* /fajt/ 'done;'
- Eastern dialects in which -CL- becomes /dʒ/: VETULUM > VECLU(M) > *vegg* /vedʒ/ 'old', and -CT- becomes /tʃ/: FACTU(M) > *facc* /fattʃ/ 'done;'
- Southern dialects where -CL- becomes /j/: VETULUM > VECLU(M) > *vej* /vej/ 'old', and -CT- becomes /tʃ/: FACTU(M) > *facc* /fattʃ/ 'done.'

Such a simplified classification may be easier to manage since many linguistic features used by scholars to divide the linguistic space display an irregular distribution. For instance, the isogloss for the Infinitive ending *-é* ~ *-à* as used in Pellegrini (1977) does not offer a geographical portrait of the real situation on the territory (as, e.g., reported in Ferrarotti 2019: 60).

> *OCLU(M), FOLIU(M): the evolution of Latin -CL- and -LI-
> In Piedmontese, word-internal etymological -CL- and -LI- merged in the approximant palatal sound /j/: *OCLU(M) > *euj* /øj/ 'eye' like FOLIU(M) > *feuj* /føj/ 'sheet.' Piedmontese is not alone in this merging solution, which concerns French and Occitan as well. Some Occitan varieties display different phonemes such as /ʎ/ that was attested in Ancient French as well as in Ancient Piedmontese. The merging is to be understood as a Western phenomenon since a large section of Piedmont, especially in the East is excluded. The most Western point in which these sounds are kept separated is probably Garess[24] in the High Tane Valley, where *OCLU(M) results in *eugio* /'ødʒu/ while FOLIU(M) yields *feujo* /'føju/.

Working on the traditional divide between a Northern and a Southern area, as well as Telmon's opposition of (lexical) Western and Eastern dialects, a more comprehensive list of the Piedmontese varieties runs as follows:

---

24 Garess /ga'res/ (locally /ga'reʃe/), Italian Garessio /ga'ressjo/ (44°12′N 08°01′E).

TABLE 2   Classification of Piedmontese and transitional varieties

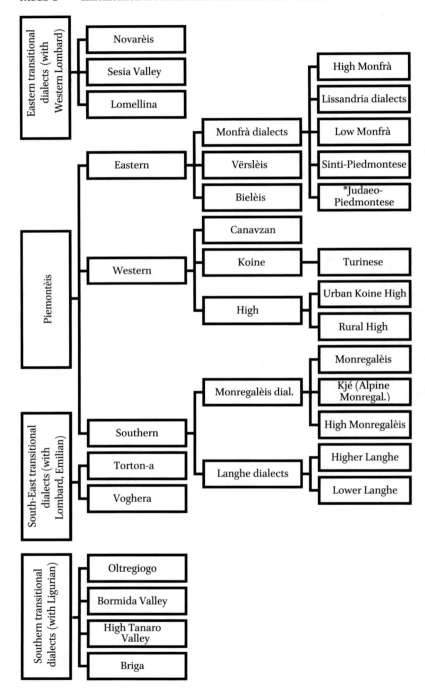

THE LANGUAGE AND ITS HISTORY, CLASSIFICATION AND VARIATION

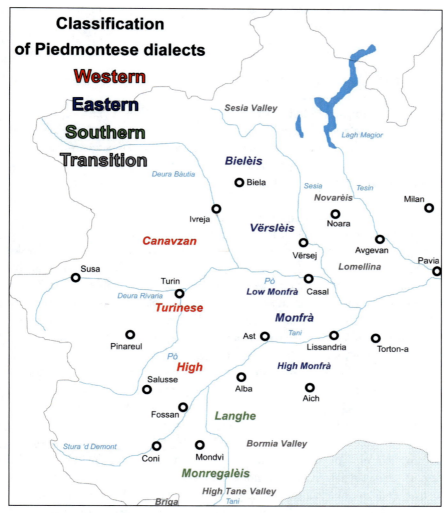

MAP 6   Classification of Piedmontese and transitional varieties
COURTESY OF LORENZO FERRAROTTI

In our classification all Piedmontese varieties fall within one of three groups: North-Eastern, Western, and South-Eastern. The Canavzan and Monregalèis dialects are intermediate between, respectively, the North-Eastern and Western groups, and the Western and South-Eastern group.

Apart from the dialects that fall squarely within the Piedmontese language, there are three transitional areas: in the North-East with Lombard, in the South-East with Lombard, Ligurian, and Emilian varieties, and in the South with Ligurian varieties.

Intermediate varieties with Occitan and Franco-Provençal (as in the Low Val Stura) are not considered here.

1.5 Social Varieties in Old Piedmontese

In the past centuries Piedmontese has always shown a high degree of diastratic variability. It is highlighted, for instance, in Pipino (1783: vi) where the language of the capital, Turin, appears to have at least three different social varieties:
- the Courtier Language, spoken by the Court and the Noblemen;
- the *Volgare* (cf. Clivio 1970b), i.e., Popular Language, spoken by the bourgeoisie;
- the Plebeian Language, spoken by the underclass.

Pipino also exemplifies the differences between these varieties: the nobles, the gentry and the educated people said *sofièt* /su'fjæt/ 'bellows,' *frèsch* /fræsk/ 'fresh,' *vëdd* /vədd/ or *vèd* /væd/ 'he/she sees,' while the bourgeoisie and the underclass said *sofiat* /su'fjat/, *frasch* /frask/, *vad* /vad/; noblemen said *liber* /'libær/, while the underclass said *libër* /'libər/ 'book.' This kind of variability was strictly diastratic because it concerned the population of Turin, no matter what neighborhood they were from. It is noteworthy that in all these cases the upper variant won out and is the only one used nowadays in koine Piedmontese. Quite the contrary happened with the *-ai* vs. *-eu* opposition in the 1st Singular of the Main Present of many verbs, such as *i sai* /i='saj/ vs. *i seu* /i='sø/ 'I know.' In this case, what was apparently the "high" variety, *i seu*, has nowadays disappeared from Turin and is restricted to the South.[25]

The 19th-century scientist, Francesco Baruffi (Billò et al. 2003: 117) provides another example of social variation in a provincial context:[26] in a letter, he remarked that in his native ël Mondvì there were at least two different social, as well as many diatopic, varieties. The population of the higher town, i.e. the aristocrats and higher bourgeois, were used to speaking a strongly 'Turinized' (and Italianized) variety, saying *aqua* /'akwa/ instead of *éva* /'eva/ for 'water,' *su* /sy/ and *giù* /ʤy/ instead of *amont* /a'muŋt/, *aval* /a'val/ for 'up' and 'down,' *palëtta* /pa'lət:a/ and *cassiëtta* /ka'sjətta/ instead of *partà* /par'ta/, and *castà* /kas'ta/ for 'little shovel' and 'small case.' It can be noticed that today the Turinized/Ital-

---

25   Pipino adds another kind of variability, in which he conflates diastratic and diatopic variation, quoting another two varieties of Piedmontese: the Provincial and the Peasant varieties.
26   Giuseppe Francesco Baruffi (ël Mondvì 1801—Turin 1875) was a professor of mathematics and geometry at the University of Turin and a science popularizer.

ianized forms have gained general acceptance and have completely replaced the older forms, while only in the case of 'water' both *aqua* and *éva* continue to be used.

1.6 The Speech of the Piedmontese Jews, Sinti and Waldensians

Two noteworthy varieties of Piedmontese developed during the Modern Age. They are (or have been) spoken by two community-focused groups and they have a few morphological features in common (for instance the Plural *-i* ending of Feminine Nouns whose singular ends in *-a*), even if no link between the two communities is historically documented or even conceivable.

The chronologically older variety is the so-called Judaeo-Piedmontese (*Lason Akodesh*, as its speakers called it; Jochnowitz 1981 and No date a, b; Duberti, Milano and Miola 2015); it was the language spoken by the Jews (*Ebre(v)o* /eb'ræ(w)u/ in Piedmontese) settled in many towns of Piedmont, and it was probably adopted only a generation after their first settlement in the 15th century. It was clearly a *religiolect* influenced by non-Romance varieties, such as Hebrew and Aramaic that provided many adapted and non-adapted loans and even a few morphological features.

The second variety, the Sinti-Piedmontese, is spoken by the Sinti (largely underinvestigated, but cf. Scala 2015), i.e., the Gypsies (*Singher* /'siŋgær/ in Piedmontese) living in Piedmont at least since the beginning of the 17th century. It largely took the place of the Romanī variety spoken in Piedmont at least occasionally by elders. Of course, some Romanī borrowings are commonly used by Sinti-Piedmontese speakers. It has an Eastern Piedmontese orientation, and can be rearranged as an in-group language by simply inserting in the Piedmontese sentence structure a large number of lexical borrowing from the "other" language, when the Sinti do not want *Gadžé* (i.e., non-Sinti) to understand.

The Piedmontese of the Sinti is extremely alive, and today the Sinti community is the only one in Piedmont where all the children have Piedmontese as their first language (Duberti 2010).

Finally, it is worth mentioning that adherents to the Waldensian church (formally a member of the Union of Methodist and Waldesian Churches) have no particular religiolect. Some of them (*Valdèis* /val'dæjz/ in Piedmontese)[27]

---

[27] Just as *Singher* for the Sinti may have a derogatory meaning, a depreciative term originally used for the Valdese and then sometimes extended to the Jews and to all non-practising Catholics is *barbèt* /bar'bæt/.

actively speak Piedmontese and even have it as their own first language; this is true especially in the towns and villages in the lower part of the Waldensian valleys (Germanasca, Chison, Pélis[28]). It is often a Piedmontese variety heavily influenced by the Occitan that occupies the head of the valleys and is historically part of the Waldensian community repertoire along with French. The (formerly) high sociolinguistic position of Piedmontese within the community is also shown by the fact that, among many publications in Occitan, they also published the first translation of the Gospels in Piedmontese using a French-like orthography (Geymet 1834; for a recent survey on these topics, see Rivoira 2020).

1.7 A Short Linguistic History of Piedmont

1.7.1 *From the Origins to the 17th Century*

Piedmont has always been an area of language contact. Latin never ceased to be the established official language of the Duchy of Savoy until the 16th century. Only in 1560, by an edict enacted in Nice, did Duke Emmanuel Philibert impose the use of the *Volgare* language instead of Latin in the Senat of Savoy. The *Volgare* designed to substitute Latin in this edict was clearly intended to be French. But a year later, through a new edict written in Rivoli, the Duke himself made clear that every province should introduce its own *Volgare* language in all the legal affairs: *la langue vulgaire, chaque province la sienne* ('the vernacular language—each province its own').

We can say that 1560 and 1561 are the crucial years for language policy in Piedmont. Even authors such as Marazzini (1984, 1992, 1994), who highlight the links between the territories now called 'Piedmont' and the Tuscan language and see them as much more natural and unavoidable than they may appear in our reconstruction, admit that only in Piedmont did Italian spread as a direct consequence of choices made by the central power, i.e., through an overt language policy (Marazzini 1994: 13).

Duke Emmanuel Philibert (1528–1580) was the first prince of the House of Savoy to choose Italian as his everyday spoken language instead of his native Piedmontese and French. As the Duke himself acknowledged, he was more fluent in Spanish than in Italian; nevertheless, he chose to speak Italian

---

28 Germanasca, Chison, Pélis /dʒerma'naska, ki'zuŋ, 'peliz/, Italian Germanasca, Chisone, Pellice /dʒerma'naska, ki'zone, 'pellitʃe/.

almost continuously (Migliorini 1978: 330–331) in order to Italianize his provinces on the Eastern side of the Alps.

Emmanuel Philibert had been reestablished in his hereditary dominions only a couple of years earlier, in 1559: until then, most of Piedmont had been occupied by the French army and incorporated into the Kingdom of France. The policy of French governors during these years had not been very oppressive and many Piedmontese showed some appreciation for it. As a consequence, the traditional connections with the French language and literature had been strongly reinforced. Ascending to the throne, Emanuel Philibert was compelled to reverse this policy in order to sever as many cultural ties as he could with France. This was obviously not possible in the provinces—such as Savoy or the Aosta Valley—where Franco-Provençal dialects were spoken and French had always been the only *Volgare* used in non-official writings. Emmanuel Philibert wanted the Duchy of Savoy to become a bilingual State, and to do this he needed to reorient the Eastern provinces toward Italian. It was a vast project, in which a very important role was played by the new university of ël Mondvì: here many Italian writers and scholars were invited, together with the most important Italian printers.[29]

Although neither Italian nor French were specifically mentioned in the edicts of 1560 and 1561, Piedmontese—the only *Volgare* really spoken in the whole country—became a subordinated language with no right to enter the official domains. The same fate lay in store for Franco-Provençal—subject to French in Savoy and in the Aosta Valley and to Italian in the Susa and Lans valleys—and for Occitan. As for the latter, for at least two centuries (the 13th and 14th) it spread widely in Piedmont as a written language, since many troubadours attended the courts of the Piedmont states—e.g., the Marquisates of Monfrà, Salusse,[30] Seva[31]—and a few Piedmontese became troubadours themselves, such as Nicolet de Turin (Paterson 2008) and Peire Guilhem de Luserna.[32] It is worth emphasizing that in Medieval Piedmont Occitan was used not only for poetic purposes, but also for administrative acts: e.g., in 1369

---

29 An interesting *Promptuarium* for helping students to translate from *vulgaire* into Latin was printed in 1564 in one of these typographies. Written by the Neapolitan teacher Michele Vopisco, it has been somehow considered the first sample of a Piedmontese dictionary because its *vulgaire* entries, even if written in the Po Valleys koine that Sanga (1990) calls "lingua lombarda," often reflects a strongly Piedmontese form (Gasca Queirazza 1967; Ramello 2004).

30 Salusse /sa'lyse/, Italian Saluzzo /sa'luttso/ (44°39′N 07°29′E) is a major town in Southwest Piedmont.

31 Seva /'seva/, Italian Ceva /'tʃeva/ (44°23′N 08°02′E).

32 See Corpus des Trobadours—Institut d'Estudis Catalans (iec.cat).

some passages in the scrolls from the castellany of ël Mondvì were written in classical Occitan, even if this town never was in an Occitan-speaking area (Cornagliotti 1993: 960).

For this reason, it is not surprising that the first full-bodied text of Piedmontese literature, the *Sermons Subalpins*, probably written between the 12th and 13th centuries, displays many Occitan features (Danesi 1974, 1991; Wolf 1991; Villata 1996). In fact, the language of these twenty-two *Sermons* (preaches) may give the impression of a mixed language, in which Piedmontese features are strictly intertwined with Occitan and even French linguistic ones. Nevertheless, it is traditionally seen as the forerunner of Piedmontese literature, both for its intellectual depth and for its historical early date (Brero 1981: 27–43; Clivio 2002: 21–30).

At that time, Piedmont was surely more closely tied to Provence and to France than to Italy. This is clearly documented in a famous passage by Dante in his *De vulgari eloquentia* (book I, chapter 15, 8):

> *Quare, cribellum cupientes deponere, ut residentiam cito visamus, dicimus Tridentum atque Taurinum nec non Alexandriam civitates metis Ytalie in tantum sedere propinquas quod puras nequeunt habere loquelas; ita quod si etiam quod turpissimum habent vulgare, haberent pulcerrimum, propter aliorum commixtionem esse vere latium negaremus. Quare, si latium illustre venamur, quod venamur in illis inveniri non potest*

> On which account, and in order to survey quickly what is left (for I am anxious to lay down my sieve), I say that Trento and Turin, in my opinion, along with Alessandria, are situated so close to the boundaries of Italy that they could not possibly speak a pure language. So, even if they possessed the most beautiful of vernaculars—and the ones they do have are appalling—I would deny that their speech is truly Italian, because of its contamination by that of others. I conclude, therefore, that if we are hunting an illustrious form of Italian, our prey is not to be found in any of these cities.[33]

The Piedmont cities mentioned by Dante are Turin and Lissandria: both of them are said to be on the borders of Italy, and that is why their languages are so mixed that it is actually impossible to call them "truly Italian." In other

---

33 Translation by Steven Botterill, *De Vulgari Eloquentia* (Cambridge Medieval Classics), Cambridge: Cambridge University Press: 1996; available online at: https://www.danteonline.it/english/opere.asp?idope=3&idlang=UK.

words, the language spoken in the region presently called Piedmont could not be counted among the Italian vernaculars. Their language did not have a name because the word Piedmont did not exist in the Middle Ages; it appears for the first time in the 14th century (Telmon 2001: 3), and at the beginning, it identified only the thin Western belt at the foot of the Alps between the rivers Po and Sangon, and excluded Ast,[34] a town geographically central in modern Piedmont. It is no wonder, then, that Giovan Giorgio Alione, the most relevant Piedmontese writer of the 16th century, wrote

> *el fa ancour sì bon vive an Ast / com a gnun leu de Lombardia*
> Farsa de Nicolao Spranga caligario, vv. 43–44

> *it is still so nice to live in Ast as in no other place in Lombardy.*
> this and all following translations by the authors

In this period, Lombardy meant generically 'lying in the Po valley' and did not imply any linguistic (nor, of course, political) evaluation. It is worth mentioning that in the farces by Alione—published in 1521—the geographic name *Pemont* is found, and it is associated with a language that seems to be the direct ancestor of today's High Piedmontese varieties. Alione's farces are actually multilingual: not only is the Astesan Piedmontese of the 16th century found, but also Western Piedmontese, Lombard, French and Latin. Italian seems to be foreign to the author, since even his compositional models are drawn from French literature (Clivio 2002: 103). The titles of the farces were in Italian,[35] but they were added by the printer rather than written and chosen by the author. Indeed, there was a very close connection between the rise of printing and the establishment of Italian as an official language in Piedmont: Duke Emmanuel Philibert's project mentioned earlier included both the spread of the art of printing and the willingness to Italianize his own Cisalpine provinces. Surely, it is not by chance that the first book printed in Piedmontese, i.e., Alione's farces, came to light in Ast, a place that at that time was *not* under the jurisdiction of the House of Savoy, but a French dominion.

Since the 16th century, the presence of Italian in Piedmont became increasingly important, even if it never did become a widely spoken language until the second half of the 20th century.

---

34 Ast /ast/, Italian /ˈasti/ (44°54′00″N 8°12′25″E) is a major town in central Piedmont and a provincial capital.
35 It could be more correct to label this language "lingua lombarda" in the sense of 'koine of the Po Valley' (Sanga 1990).

Between the 17th and the 18th centuries, on the other hand, a deep transformation of the linguistic landscape took place: Turin, that had been chosen in 1563 as the new capital city of the Duchy of Savoy, experienced a great growth in population between 1650 and 1721, and its ancient High-Piedmontese dialect deeply changed, shifting to what Regis (2012c) has suggested labelling a "primary koine" (see also Siegel 1985) that rapidly spread throughout the whole Piedmontese territory in a movement of "secondary koineization."

1.7.2 *The 18th Century*

During the 18th century, the Turinese koine became a sort of semi-official language that covered all the intermediate domains of use, leaving the lowest ones to the local dialects and the highest ones to French and Italian (and still Latin to some extent).

This is probably the most important century for the Piedmontese koine. In 1713 the House of Savoy acquired the status of Royal House, receiving the crown of the Kingdom of Sicily (1713–1720) and later the crown of the Kingdom of Sardinia. The role of Italian became increasingly more relevant and was established as the official language of the "Italian" parts of the Kingdom (in addition to taking the place of Spanish in Sardinia). The favorable political attitude toward Italian did not imply a crisis for the Piedmontese koine, which acquired an increasingly relevant role in the so-called *Stati Sardi di Terraferma* (Mainland Sardinian States), i.e., Piedmont, Aosta Valley and the County of Nice: people living in the Occitan Valleys, in the newly acquired territories of Vërsej or Noara, as well as in the Franco-Provençal Aosta Valley, used to speak the koine for every out-group interaction or to communicate with civil and military authorities.

The 18th century is primarily an age of great development of the literary production in Piedmontese, mostly in the koine: Fr. Ignassi Isler, author of more than fifty "popular" songs, as well as Ventura Cartiermetre and the physician Edoard Ignassi Calvo were Turinese; Vitòrio Amedeo Borrelli was born in Valensa,[36] Silvio Balbis lived his entire life in Salusse, and the anonymous Pegemade might have come from the South-Western areas between Piedmont and Liguria. The Piedmontese koine was now seen not only as a sort of spoken lingua franca but also as a well-established means of literary expression. It is no wonder that at the end of this century Piedmontese had its first grammatical formalization: in 1783 the Court doctor Morissi Pipin (Italian: Maur-

---

36 Valensa /vaˈlæŋsa/, Italian Valenza /vaˈlentsa/, an Eastern town close to the border with Lombardy (45°01′N 08°39′E).

THE LANGUAGE AND ITS HISTORY, CLASSIFICATION AND VARIATION   27

MAP 7   Piedmont within the Duchy (since 1718 Kingdom) of Savoy
RAYMOND PALMER AT ENGLISH WIKIPEDIA—DOMAIN, HTTPS://COMMONS
.WIKIMEDIA.ORG/W/INDEX.PHP?CURID=12271418

izio Pipino) published a *Gramàtica piemontese*, along with an Anthology of Piedmontese Poetry and a quadrilingual (Piedmontese, Italian, French, and Latin) vocabulary. All of these were dedicated to the French Princess Marie Adelaïde de Bourbon, wife of the future King of Sardinia Carlo Emanuel IV; coming from France, she wanted to learn Piedmontese and used to speak it.

According to Cognasso (1969: 190), learning Piedmontese was actually normal for the acquired members of the Royal House of Savoy because this language was commonly spoken at Court, much more than French and Italian (even if the Court's members were able to speak all three languages; Pipino 1783a: 133). Some historians report that in 1788, while arranging the wedding between the Duke of Aosta (and future King) Vittorio Emanuele I and the Austrian princess Maria Theresa von Absburg-Este, the Savoy sent to Milan (where the Princess was living) Abbot Draghetti with the only aim to teach her Piedmontese. Some months later, Marquis Cacciapiatti assured—in French— the Royal Family that the young princess was able to speak Piedmontese *avec beaucoup de facilité et de grâce* ('with much ease and grace;' Cognasso 1969: 190).

Pipino (1783b: vi–vii), in the introduction to his Vocabulary, gives ample evidence to the fact that Piedmontese was spoken in many different ways (☞ 1.5.). Yet he also identifies Piedmontese and Turinese (the latter a higher variant of the former), proving that the secondary koine had spread throughout the whole territory: he himself was not a Turinese, having been born near Coni in 1739.

Despite the language policy followed from 1560–1561, two centuries later Italian was still *per tutti gli strati sociali una realtà straniera ed aliena* ('a foreign and alien language for every social layer;' Clivio 1984: 269) and Piedmontese had no rivals as a spoken medium. The outstanding Italian poet and tragediograph Vittorio Alfieri, born in Ast in 1749, "when he was seventeen years old did not know French [...] and knew Italian much less" (Metzeltin 1990: 97–98). Even though a noble, he was used to speaking what he later called "gergaccio piemontese" ('bad Piedmontese jargon;' Merlotti 2017: 410) and he had to work hard to learn Italian. He was successful; but obviously Vittorio Alfieri never forgot his mother tongue, as he also wrote a few sonnets in Piedmontese.

As a member of the nobility, he primarily spoke it with other nobles as well as the royalty (e.g., with King Carl Emanuel IV; Merlotti 2017: 410, fn. 64). The English historian Edward Gibbon, in a letter to John Holroyd, emphasizes the use of Piedmontese amongst the noblemen gathered in their parlors: "and a poor Englishman, who can neither talk Piemontois nor play Faro, stands by himself without one of their haughty nobility doing him the honor of speaking to him" (Gibbon 1840: 126; quoted in Regis 2014: 154).

As a result, Pipino explicitly declares that Piedmontese can cover all the domains of use, and also quotes an anonymous poem in which Piedmontese is placed on the same level as Swedish, Portuguese and Dutch; these languages are to Danish, Spanish and German, respectively, as Piedmontese is to Italian.

Things did not change during the Napoleonic period (1802–1814), when Piedmont was annexed to the French Empire and divided in five Departments. The official language was no longer Italian but French; nevertheless, Piedmontese remained the only spoken language.

1.7.3 The 19th Century

After the Restoration (1814) French, which had been the language of the Revolution and the Napoleonic rule, faced progressive marginalization: when taking possession of his restored Kingdom (expanded with the addition of the territories of the former Republic of Genoa) King Vittorio Emanuel I decided that Italian would be the only language used in the army and the bureaucracy, at the expense of French (Cognasso 1969: 316). The choice of Italian was repeatedly reaffirmed many times, not only by the House of Savoy but also by the local *intelligentsia*, which started to endorse the project of a *Risorgimento* in which Piedmont would play a fundamental role. Writing from Turin in 1841, the French ambassador informed his government that in the city's parlors *on decide desormais de parler italien* ('it has now been decided to speak Italian'). Maybe this decision remained, at least within certain limits, a mere stance; in fact, many years later Sir Horace Rumbold, attaché to the British embassy in Turin between 1849 and 1851, in his *Recollections of a Diplomatist* observed: "the Piedmontese ladies would have attained perfection but for two failings—their love for their native dialect and their passion for that indigenous fungus, the white truffle" (Rumbold 1902: 125; quoted in Cognasso 1969: 316 and in Regis 2014:155).

The 19th century is also the age of the Piedmontese Dictionaries:

- the *Dictionnaire Portatif piémontais-français suivi d'un vocabulaire français des termes usités dans les Arts et Métiers, par ordre alphabétique et de matières, avec leur explication*, published in 1814 by Count Luigi Capello di Sanfranco;
- the *Dissionari piemontèis, italian, latin e fransèis* by Fr. Casimiro Zalli was first printed in 1815 and became a *Dizionario piemontese, italiano, latino e francese* in its second revised (and posthumous) 1830 edition;
- the *Vocabolario piemontese-italiano* by Abbot Michele Ponza met with much success and was reedited as many as nine times between its first edition in 1826 and the final edition in 1877. Ponza was a teacher of Italian and his aim was to promote the knowledge of Italian in Piedmont; therefore, his vocabulary excluded both Latin and French and focussed on Italian, his target-language;
- the *Gran Dizionario Piemontese-Italiano* by Count Vittorio Righini di Sant'Albino, which appeared in 1859 and is very rich in lexicon; the author explicitly

MAP 8   Map of the States of Savoy in 1839
DOMAINE PUBLIC, HTTPS://COMMONS.WIKIMEDIA.ORG/W/INDEX.PHP?CURID=488998

declares that his Dictionary was conceived as a medium to help the Piedmontese people improve their skills in Italian;
- the *Nuovo Dizionario Piemontese-Italiano ragionato e comparato alla lingua comune* by Giovanni Pasquali, which had two editions: 1869 and 1870;
- the *Vocabolario piemontese-italiano* by the engineer Giuseppe Gavuzzi, published in 1891, and followed five years later by a *Vocabolario italiano-piemontese* that may be the first sample of a complete reverse dictionary, from Italian to Piedmontese. This is noteworthy: the author does not offer just a medium for learning or improving Italian, but draws up a much more complex project, providing materials to learn or improve Piedmontese for Italian-speaking people.

At this point, the linguistic panorama of Piedmont and Piedmontese was really changing. Around 1870, the decline of French was complete (Clivio 1972: 130) and Italian had definitively acquired an exclusive supremacy, becoming to some extent an actively spoken language, at least in Turin and in some urban contexts amongst the members of the bourgeoisie.

1.7.4 The Contemporary Age

The interference of Italian became even stronger after World War I, when many peasants and workers were compelled to leave their own home and country and had to live together in the trenches with peasants and workers from Sicily, Veneto, Sardinia or Tuscany: apart from the fact that at least some command of Italian was strongly encouraged by the army's hierarchies, the cogent necessities of everyday communication in the army were so strong that they forced many Piedmontese speakers to get used to speaking Italian—more or less fluently (De Mauro 1963).

In his 1933 *Grammatica piemontese*, Arturo Aly-Belfàdel noted some phenomena of interference from Italian, such as the repalatalization of sibilants (Aly Belfàdel 1933: 15). But the process had already started almost immediately after the creation of the Kingdom of Italy (1861), and many evidences of this can be found in the popular novels written in the second half of the Nineteenth Century by authors like Luigi Pietracqua (1832–1901), Mario Leoni (1847–1931), Carolina Invernizio (1858–1916), Carlo Bernardino Ferrero (1866–1924) and Ciro Bolaro (1882–1920). In the novels by these authors, it is already possible to detect most of the phonetic Italian interferences described some decades later by Clivio (1972), such as the reintroduction of voiceless stops in intervocalic position; the repalatalization of sibilants; the reintroduction of protonic vowels in order to break the consonant clusters ruled out by the Italian phonological system; and many syntactic features of Italianization.

Clivio (1972: 128) offers an interesting artificial (but in no way unrealistic) example of the contrast between an Italianized sentence "as it would sound in Turin" ((1)) and "in a kind of 'pure' Piedmontese which can still be heard today" ((2)). The English translation is in ((3)):

(1) *ël fratel dël pëscador a l'ha portà ij vitej a la sorgent për cerché 'd feje bèive prima ch'a tornèissa a gelé l'aqua e guardé s'a-i ero staje dij cerv*

(2) *ël frel dël pëscaor a l'ha portà ij vej (cf AIS VI 1046) a la sorziss për sërché (cf AIS III 636) 'd feje bèive prima ch'a tornèissa a zlé (cf AIS II 383) l'eva e vardé (cf AIS I 6) s'a-i ero staje dij serv*

(3) 'the fisherman's brother led the calves to the spring to try to have them drink before the water could freeze again and to see whether any deer had been there.'

Even if Italianized, Piedmontese remained the mother language of the young generations in rural and urban contexts: in 1924, introducing his exercises of translation from Piedmontese to Italian, the linguist Benvenuto Aronne Terracini advised primary school teachers that these exercises had been conceived not to teach Piedmontese "che gli scolari conoscono già perfettamente" ('that pupils already know perfectly'), but to teach Italian through Piedmontese (Terracini 1924: 3).

The situation underwent a radical change after the social upheavals that invested Turin and the major Piedmontese cities in the 1960s: the rapid development of factories (in Turin strictly connected with the automotive company FIAT and the entire mechanical sector related to it) attracted a huge number of immigrants from Southern Italy and Veneto, and these newcomers (unlike the immigrants in previous decades) were less prone to learn Piedmontese. Moreover, the increasing power of state-controlled media such as the radio and television, in addition to military service for males and generalized compulsory schooling were for the first time effective in imposing a unifying model of culture and society—to be identified with Italian.

The overwhelming weight of the roof language (Regis 2014: 159) yielded a completely new situation: rather than teaching Italian through Piedmontese, the new goal was to preserve Piedmontese from the interference and oppression of Italian. Indeed, in the 1960s the first grammar of Piedmontese completely written in Piedmontese (Brero 1967) appeared, and a few years later the *Dissionari piemontèis* edited by Gianfranco Gribaudo, Pinin Seglie and Sergio Seglie (first published in four books between 1972 and 1975; Gribaudo 1996) followed suit. Camillo Brero's *Vocabolario italiano-piemontese/piemontese-italiano*, first edited in 1976, provided a complete survey of the lexical heritage of Piedmontese useful to a new generation who already knew (even if possibly rather poorly) Italian:

> Times are a-changing and the Piedmontese dictionaries stopped being useful in the old way—to teach the Italian language to whomever had not been so lucky to suck it in their wet nurse's milk. Actually, as today even wet nurses think they will make a great display of dignity if they, for better or worse, speak Tuscan, the Piedmontese have reached the point of struggling with their natural language. Not to mention those children who have been deprived of their natural rights by parents who assume they will pour wisdom into their children if they just protect them from the original sin of their forefathers' language.[37]

37　Brero 1972: viii. Original: *Ij temp a cambio e ij vocabolari piemontèis a l'han finì 'd fé servissi a*

The decline of intergenerational transmission has followed the reduction in the domains of use of Piedmontese. Chapter 20 will be specifically devoted to different levels of language mixing and switching and to revitalization efforts.

1.8 An Outline of Piedmontese Literature

1.8.1 *From the Origins to the 17th Century*

The very first attestations of Piedmontese are found in a few words of debated meaning (Clivio 2002: 17–20) engraved in the churches of Casal Monfrà[38] and Vërsèj and dating back to the late 11th or early 12th century. A few decades later, we find the first testimonies of a true literary use of the local *Volgare* (Brero 1975: 12) due to the pastoral zeal of churchmen. Following the advice of the Council of Tours (Brero 2002: 22), around the year 1000, many preachers had started to translate in *Volgare* the passages from the Scriptures they were going to read during the services. The *Sermons Subalpins* were written with the purpose of helping preachers to organize their sermons for an illiterate audience that had no knowledge of Latin.

The *Sermons Subalpins* date back to the 12th century and have as their model the sermonaries written in Occitan (Clivio 2002: 21). The 22 Piedmontese preaches (also known as *Galloitalische Predigten*, Clivio 2002: 22) are organized following the dates of the liturgical year and form a continuous commentary on the readings. The content of the Scriptures is explained and illustrated through samples of everyday life, legends, proverbs, and tales.

The *Sermons Subalpins* are written in prose, at times rhymed (Brero 1981: 29–30) and in a language rich in Occitan and French features. These features might have been common in the Piedmontese *Volgare* of the 12th century or they may be related to the geographical origin of the manuscript (code D.VI.10 of the National Library of Turin) in an Alpine valley (Gasca Queirazza 1996).

---

    la veja manera: cola ëd mostré la lenga italian-a a chi a l'avìa nen avù 'l boneur d'amprendla con ël làit ëd la bàila. An efet, ancheuj, che 'd cò le bàile a chërdo dë spompé na dignità parland o bin o mal ël toscan, ij piemontèis a son rivà a la mira dë stanté a parlé soa lenga natural. Për nen dì dle masnà tradìe ant sò dirit natural da pare e mare che a chërdo 'd sëmné la sapiensa ant ij fieuj dësfendendje dal pecà original dla lenga dij vej.

38   Casal Monfrà /ka'zal muŋ'fra/ (or Casal dla Paja /d=l-a='paja/ 'of the straw'), Italian Casale Monferrato /ka'zale mon'ferrato/ (45°08′N 08°27′E) is a major town in East Piedmont.

FIGURE 2 A page from the Sermons Subalpins (12th century). Manuscript D.VI.10. at the National University Library in Turin. Full translation in Italian edited by Silvana Delfuoco and Giuseppe Bernardi; transcription edited by Giuliano Gasca Queirazza
TORINO: CENTRO STUDI PIEMONTESI/CA DE STUDI PIEMONTÈIS—CONSIGLIO REGIONALE DEL PIEMONTE: 2004: 321

What follows is a brief sample from the *XIII Sermo in Dominicis Diebus* (Gasca Queirazza 2003: 46) followed by our word-by-word translation in contemporary Piedmontese (1b):

(1) a. *Encor poem entendre que cascun de noi dé garder so coratge e sei meesme per lealtà, per bone ovre, que el no sea vastà per le volp e per li luf, zo son le heretie cogitaciun e li hereti pensement e le male coveitisie, qui vasten l'arma, qui est vigna de Dè e temple. Sì cum dit saint Poil:* Vos estis templum Dei et Spiritus Sancti sedes: *voi sì casa de Dè e seti d'Espirit saint. Lo seti de Déu si est cascauna bona arma, sì cum dit Salomun:* Anima iusti sedes Dei est. Anima peccatorum scabellum pedum eius. *En qual visa est anima iusti sedes Dei? Il meesme Christ lo dit per lo Propheta:* Super humeros iusti requiescit spiritus meus. *Zo est, sore lo cor de bon hom se reposa lo saint Esperit. Or gardem, seignor, que noi siam seti, ó Deus sea e que noi siam en l'orden deil angel qui son apelai throni, sore li quail sè nostre Seignor,* qui est iudex vivorum et mortuorum. Quod ipse prestare dignetur, qui vivit.

b. *Ancora i podoma antende che ciaschedun ëd noi dev guardé sò coragi e guardesse chiel midem për lealtà, për bon-e euvre, ch'a sia nen vastà da le volp e dai luv, visadì le erétiche cogitassion e j' erétich pensament e ij cativ desideri, ch'a vasto l'ànima, ch'a l'é vigna ëd Dé e templ. Parèj coma ch'a dis san Pò:* Vos estis templum Dei et Spiritus Sancti sedes: *voi i seve ca ëd Dé e segi dl'Ëspìrit sant. Ël segi ëd Dé a l'é minca bon-a ànima, parèj coma ch'a dis Salomon:* Anima iusti sedes Dei est. Anima peccatorum scabellum pedum eius. *An qual manera a l'é* anima iusti sedes Dei? *Ël midem Crist a lo dis për mes dël Profeta:* Super humeros iusti requiescit spiritus meus. *Visadì, dzora ël cheur dl'òm bon as arpòsa ël Sant Ëspìrit. Or vardoma, monsù, che noi i sio segi, andoa Dé a staga setà e che noi i sio ant l'órdin dj'àngej ch'a son apelà tròno, dzora ij quaj a stà setà Nosgnor,* qui est iudex vivorum et mortuorum. Quod ipse prestare dignetur, qui vivit.

c. Furthermore, we may understand that each of us has to preserve his courage and be careful with himself through loyalty, through good works, so that he is not spoiled by the foxes and by the wolves; that is to say, the heretic cogitations and the heretic thoughts and the evil desires that spoil the soul, which is God's vineyard and temple. So, as Saint Paul says: *Vos estis templum Dei et Spiritus Sancti sedes:* you are the house of God and the seat of the Holy Ghost. God's seat is each good soul, as Solomon says: *Anima iusti sedes Dei est. Anima peccatorum scabellum pedum eius.* In what way is *anima iusti sedes Dei*? Christ himself says it through the Prophet: *Super humeros iusti requiescit spiritus meus*. That is to say, on the good man's heart the Holy Ghost rests. Now let us mind, sirs, we are a seat, where God may sit and we are in the order of the angels who are called the thrones, upon whom Our Lord is seated, *qui est iudex vivorum et mortuorum. Quod ipse prestare dignetur, qui vivit.*

After the *Sermons Subalpins*, many other samples of early literary use of Piedmontese are strictly related to religion, e.g., the *Passion ëd Versej* (Vitale Brovarone 1978), the *Lamentassion ëd Turin* (Gasca Queirazza 2003: 93), the *Lamentassion ëd Cher* (Gasca Queirazza 2003: 97), the *Làuda ëd la Confratèrnita ëd Salusse* (Gasca Queirazza 2003: 107) and the *Làuda dij Dissiplinà ëd Droné* (Gasca Queirazza 2003: 111). All these religious chants, dating back to the 14th and 15th centuries, are written in verse. They were inspired by sacred songs and poems from Umbria (Central Italy), probably through models drawn up in Lombardy or Veneto. Texts of the same period written in prose are much more interesting in order to understand the actual linguistic features of Piedmontese as spoken in the Middle Ages (Gasca Queirazza 2003: 113 and 123): this is the case of the *Recomendaciones ëd Salusse* and the *Ordinament dij Dissiplinà e dj'Arcomandà ëd Droné*. From the *Recomendaciones ëd Salusse* (Gasca Queirazza 2003: 114) we quote a short passage from the first *recomendacio* (2a) and its translation in modern Piedmontese (2b):

(2) a. *Noe se tornerema devotement al altissim Dè Nostre Segnor Yhesu Crist, dal qual venen tuyt gli bin e tute le gracie, que nos n'à dait gracia en chast beneyt dì de fer questa disciplina, qu'El nos dea gracia che noy la pussem e voglen fer a tuit gli temp de la nostra vita al so los, honor e Gloria e a recordament de la soa sanctissima passion e a esmendament di nostri peccay* [...]
 b. *Noi is vireroma devotament vers l'altissim Dé Nostr Signor Gesù Crist, dal qual a ven-o tùit ij bin e tute le grassie, che a l'ha dane grassia, an cost dì benedet, ëd fé costa dissiplin-a, Chiel an daga grassia che noi la peusso e i veujo fé a tùit ij temp ëd nòstra vita a soa làuda, onor e glòria e an arcòrd ëd soa santìssima passion e an emendament dij nòstri pecà* [...]
 c. We will devotedly turn to the God Most High, Our Lord Jesus Christ, from whom all goods and graces come, who gave us the grace, in this blessed day, to do this discipline, may He give us the grace that we can and want to do for our whole life in order to praise, honour and glorify Him and in memory of His most holy passion and in amendment of our sins [...]

Things take an abrupt change in the 16th century with the first great writer and his unique personality: Giovan Giorgio Alione (1460 or 1470–1529?), born in Ast and author of ten farces first published in 1521 and essentially written in his city dialect, although a few characters speak other languages. Apart from their literary value, Alione's farces are very useful because they exhibit an old Astesan variety and provide rich data about the whole geo-linguistic situation of Piedmont in the past.

In the 17th century, four *Canson Turinèise* were published in appendix to the Turin editions of *I Freschi della villa* by the Emilian writer Giulio Cesare Croce (1550–1609) in 1663 and in 1677. Edited and studied by Clivio (1974), they are written in an older form of Turinese that often does not display the features normally attributed to this variety.

The titles of these four *canzones* are partly in Italian and partly in Piedmontese:
– *Canzone di Madonna Luchina* (modern Piedmontese *Canson ëd madòna Luchin-a*) 'Song of Lady Luchin-a;'
– *La Canson di Disbauchià* (modern Piedmontese *La canson dij dësbaucià*) 'The song of the debauched people;'
– *Canzone della Ballouria* (modern Piedmontese *Canson ëd la baleuria*) 'Revelry's song;'
– *Canson pr 'l Tramué d'San Michel* (modern Piedmontese *Canson për ël tramué 'd San Michel*) 'Song for the move on St. Michael's day.'

We offer as a sample *stanza* 32 from the last one (Clivio 1974: 59), followed by a rewriting in contemporary Piedmontese (in which the poetry's prosody is obviously altered):

(3) a. *S'un volas scrive tuit i msté*
     a gl'sarea d'ampì un'herca
     i saren strac d' tan canté.
     Chi ne völ pi, s'na vogna a cerca:
     pchit e grand
     puolo cantéla
     e pöi slonghéla
     un'autr'tant
   b. *S'un a volèissa scrive tùit ij mësté*
     a-i sarìa da ampì n'erca
     i sarìo strach ëd tant canté.
     Chi ch'a na veul ëd pì, s'na vada an cerca:
     cit e grand
     a peulo cantela

>   *e peui slonghela*
>   *un àutr tant.*
> c. If one should write all the trades
>   there would be so many to fill a sideboard,
>   we would be tired of singing so long.
>   Whoever wants more, go in search:
>   the little and big
>   may sing it
>   and then lengthen it
>   just as much.

These four songs are the first example of the *Tòni*, a literary subgenre (Clivio 2002: 157) which will be extremely successful among all the social classes during the late 17th and the 18th century (☞ 1.7.2.). The *Tòni* was a poetic composition mainly written with a satirical intent, sometimes accompanied by music, often unpublished and circulating in manuscript form. It normally takes the point of view of the lowest social classes, as in the *Tòni dle servente* 'Housekeeper's Toni:' the *Canson ëd madòna Luchin-a* fits into this literary tradition. According to Brero (1981: 75–77), the name 'Tòni' is not to be etymologically connected with a hypocoristic for 'Tony' but with the Spanish word *tono* 'tone,' used to designate a very similar poetic genre (for instance, *los Tonos Castellanos*, built upon texts by Lope de Vega). Both these literary expressions have probably at least one model in common, i.e. the melodic *tonus* of the Gregorian Chant (Brero 1981: 77).

Another important literary work dating back to the 17h century is *Ël cont Piolèt*, a bilingual, three act comedy probably written in the last decade of the century. Its language differs greatly from the language of the four *Canson* and displays almost all the features of the modern koine (Regis 2012: 18). This is probably due to the social membership of its author, the nobleman Carlo Giambattista Tana, Count of Entrèive[39] (Chér[40] 1649–1713 or 1718), but also crucial in this connection is the fact that the comedy was actually published only toward the end of the following century, and more precisely in 1784 (Clivio 2002: 162). In the third scene of the first act, one of the characters in the comedy, Bias, listens in secret to the Roman gentleman Silvio talking with his servant Pippo. They speak Italian, and Bias says:

---

39   Entrèive /enˈtræjve/, Occitan Antràigue /anˈtrajgwue/, Italian Entracque /enˈtrakwe/ (44°15′N 07°24′E), a town close to the French border.

40   Chér /ker/, Italian Chieri /ˈkjeri/ (45°00′45″N 07°49′30″E), a major town in Central Piedmont, not far from Turin.

j'euvr j'orije, e ten scotà
e n'antend gnanca la mità.

I open my ears, and I pledge to listen,
and I cannot even understand half of it.

1.8.2 The 18th Century

The 18th century has been defined as the golden century for literature in Piedmontese (Brero 1975:14), 'Piedmont [...] firmly established itself as a Nation'[41] by the adoption of a common language 'that during the 18th century, transforming itself in koine, had to rise to the function of "national" language, at least in terms of the spoken language' (Clivio 2003b: 169).[42]

The first example of the Piedmontese koine is the 2000-verse poem *L'Arpa Dëscordà*, focused on the siege of Turin in 1705–1706 but published much later, in the last decades of the century (Clivio 2003b: 172). It is attributed to the priest Francesco Antòni Tarizzo ëd Favria.[43]

The first true poet of this century is Ignassi Isler (1699–1778, according to Burdet 2012). He is the author of over fifty *canson* 'songs' that are undoubtedly masterpieces of the genre *Tòni*. Isler, born in Turin to Swiss parents, lived his whole life as a member of the religious order of the *Trinatari Calzati* in the convent of Saint Mary of the Graces (in those times located in the suburbs of Turin but presently downtown). He wrote his poems to provide a large corpus of texts (accompanied by music) for his parishioners, who loved to sing vulgar and trashy lyrics that offended the priest's ears (Brero 1981: 100; Pasero 2013: xii). Isler never published his works, which came to light only posthumously in 1783, and were partially published for the first time in an anthology of Piedmontese poets arranged by the grammarian Morissi Pipin, who altered the original texts in order to make them more polite. The first edition of Isler's complete works dates back to 1799, and the ninth edition was published in 1894, followed by a 1968 edition by Luis Olivé and Andrea Viglòngo and a 2013 edition by Dario Pasé.

Isler is also very interesting philologically because the nine editions of his works published between 1799 and 1894 display many differences (Pasero 2013: xx–xxiii). The situation is further complicated by the presence of thirteen manuscripts (Duberti 2013, 2018) whose text often does not match any of the

---

41   Original: *È questo il secolo in cui il Piemonte [...] si costituisce saldamente in Nazione.*
42   Original: [*quella lingua*] *che nel corso del Settecento, trasformandosi in coinè, doveva assurgere alla funzione di lingua "nazionale", almeno a livello parlato.*
43   Piedmontese and Italian /ˈfavria/ (45°20′N 07°41′E).

editions. The 1968 edition, rather than being a critical one, is often a brilliant personal rielaboration by the two editors (Pasero 2013: xxiii). Only the 2013 edition may be seen as a critical edition.

Written in a very popular variety of Piedmontese, Isler's satirical poems have the lower classes of Turin as their only subject. The author's stylistic code is the grotesque (Girardin 1989: 22) and his many characters from the common people (Giaco Tross, Stevo Brombo, Lucressia Gelofrada, Barba Giròni etc., see Brero 1981: 103) are introduced with their faults, bad habits, sins and diseases—never with their virtues. It would seem that Isler did not recognize any positive element in the *populace* he wrote about: on the other hand, there is not a single verse describing the aristocrats negatively.

Nonetheless, it is hard to say whether Isler is a "classist" in a strict sense. He was a member of the clergy, allied with the aristocracy against the Third State. He sounds misogynist at times, but it is very difficult to evaluate the ideological setting of every single song.

Girardin (1989: 66) concludes his critical essay on Isler writing that his art 'is [...] a meditated, studied, sometimes suffered art, with ambitions that point to the great satirical art and therefore include moral and figurative needs, coupled time after time in a different proportion. In no case could one speak about this art as 'popular', if not in the sense that it was a great success with the public,'[44] and Clivio (2002: 190) agrees with such a statement.

We propose here three quatrains from the *Canson 15*, dating back to 1742. In this song the main character is Barba Giròni, an old man who has just become a father, albeit in old age (Pasero 2013: 126):

> *L'ha na gòj Barba Giròni*
> *ch'a fa 'd sàut com un cravieul:*
> *sui trant agn 'd sò matrimòni*
> *finalment a l'ha avù un fieul.*
>
> *Për piasì ch'lo-lì ha faje*
> *(fur da rije da crëpé)*
> *an sautand s-ciancher le braje*
> *ch'a-j drochero giù sui pé.*

---

44 Original: *a l'é [...] n'art medità, studià, a vire soferta, con d'ambission ch'as arfan a la grand'art satìrica e donca comprensiva d'esigense moraj e icàstiche, cobià via via an proporsion diferente. An gnun cas as podrà parlé 'd s'art coma d'art "popolar", se nen ant ël sens ch'a l'ha avù un gran success da part dël pùblich.*

Òh che bele trebaudëtte
ch'a-j han faje ij seu vësin
con le mòle e le palette
sui paireul e sui bronzin.

Uncle Jerome has such joy
that he jumps like a roe deer:
after around thirty years of marriage
he finally had a child.

Due to the pleasure that it gave him
(it was so funny that you would die with laughter)
jumping he tore his own pants
that fell down to his feet.

Oh what beautiful chiming of celebration
offered him his neighbours
with tongs and shovels
on the cauldrons and the saucepans.

Isler's Piedmontese is very close to the 18th-century koine, keeping at the same time a few basilectal archaic features; among them the use of a Simple Past (i.e., without an auxiliary; ☞ 10.2.6., 10.5.1.3., 10.6.1.), which has since disappeared in Piedmontese and is seen in the verses above in *fur, s-ciancher, drochero*; the plural possessive adjective with metaphony (*ij seu* instead of *ij sò* for 'their;' ☞ 8.4.) and the plural invariable form of the *-l* ending nouns (*paireul* instead of *paireuj*; ☞ 5.3.).

Ventura Cartiermetre's (Turin 1733–1777) *tòni* appear to be completrly different from Isler's. He wrote some *tòni* to express—ironically—the growing malaise of the bourgeoisie and the bad mood of the lower classes living in conditions of poverty and misery (Clivio 2002: 202).

His example was followed, after the French Revolution, by the physician Edoard Ignassi Calv (Edoardo Ignazio Calvo). Born in 1773 in Turin, he died of typhus in 1804 treating the sick in the Turin hospital of Saint John. He was very young when he joined the Jacobin party in 1796, and never changed his political ideas; on the contrary, his rationalistic, anti-traditionalistic and egalitarian approach to both life and science grew and permeated his entire literary production.

Calv wrote many works, but the most important remains the *Fàule moraj* ('Moral Fables'), published in 1802–1803 which contains twelve fairy tales in verse, where the animals represent human characters and express some moral and/or political concept. They are often 'a very bold indictment against the French bad governance and a condemnation of the miseries arising from this bad governance'[45] (Brero and Gandolfo 1967: 399).

The titles of Calvo's "Moral Fables" are:
1. *L'intendent e 'l poj* ('The Mayor and the Louse');
2. *Le sansùe e 'l bòrgno* ('The Leeches and the Blind Man');
3. *Platon e ij pito* ('Plato and the Turkeys');
4. *Ij scalavron e j'avije* ('The Hornets and the Bees');
5. *La passra solitaria e la berta* ('The Lone Flounder and the Magpie');
6. *Ël can e l'òss* ('The Dog and the Bone');
7. an untitled tale about a shepherd who entrusts his flock to an unfaithful servant;
8. *La spa e la lumassa rablòira* ('The Sword and the Slug');
9. *La cioss e le pole* ('The Hen and the Chickens');
10. *Ël balon volant e le grùe* ('The Hot Air Ballon and the Cranes');
11. *Le tre virtù a l'Ostarìa dla Pas* ('The Three Virtues at the Inn' of Peace);
12. *Ij strunej e ij merlo* ('The Starlings and the Blackbirds').

No. 7 is really a short masterpiece. Here is the whole text (quoted from Clivio and Pasero 2004: 49–50):

Ant un 'd coj castej frust ch'a-i stà le masche,
famos ant ij sò temp për soe gran tor,
sgarblà, tut mes distrut, cuvert dë frasche,

për là ant una caverna a-i era ancor,
sotrà an mes al rotam, a la rumenta,
la spa ch'un di portava col gran sgnor;

a l'era mancomal tuta rusnenta,
ma tant, an mes al ruso, un sert barlum
mostrava ancor l'orìgine lusenta.

Rablandse, com a l'é ant ël sò costum,
slongand ij còrn, na lumassa rablòira
a-j é montaje adòss carià 'd bavum.

---

45 Original: *Requisitoria audacissima contro il malgoverno francese e denuncia delle miserie da esso derivanti.*

La spa 's buta a crijé:—Son pa na msòira,
am pijs-to për na ressia o pr'un faussèt,
për n'apia, për na ranza o na tisòira?

Sapia che mi ant ël sécol 'd Bajasèt,
ai temp dël Re Arduin e 'd Carlo Magno,
tajava ij Paladin com 'd ravanèt!—

—E adess,—l'àutra a-j rispond,—mi të scarcagno;
s'i veuj mi it pisso adòss, e con ij còrn,
se mi 'm batèiss con ti, tant it guadagno.—

Sta fàula a dev gaveje 'l capëstorn
a coj ch'a vivo mach pr'ampisse 'd bòria:
buté na pugnà 'd paja drint a 'n forn,

a fà l'istess efet la vòstra glòria.

In one of those crumbling castles where witches live
famous in its times for its big towers
pitted, half-destroyed everywhere, covered by branches,

there was still over there in a cave
buried in the scrap metal, in the garbage,
the sword that the grand lord carried once upon a time;

it was all rusty indeed,
and however, in the rust, a certain glimmer
still showed its shiny origin.

Crawling, as it is its custom,
stretching its horns, a slug
climbs on it full of drool.

The sword starts screaming:—I am not a sickle,
do you take me for a saw or for a pruning knife,
for an axe, for a grass scythe or for some scissors?

You have to know that in Bayazet's century
in the time of King Arduin and of Charlemagne
I used to cut the paladins like they were radishes!–

—And now—the other one replies—I trample you;
If just I want I piss upon you, and by my horns
if I would fight against you, I should overcome you so.–

This tale must remove the conceit
from those people that live just to fill themselves with arrogance:
put a handful of straw into an oven,

your glory has the same effect.

1.8.3   *The 19th Century*

After the Restoration (1815) Piedmont intensified its contacts with the Italian States and became increasingly important for the so-called *Risorgimento*, which had its climax in 1861: in this year Turin, the former capital city of the Principality of Piedmont and later of the Kingdom of Sardinia, became the capital city of the newborn Kingdom of Italy. This role passed very soon to Florence (1865) and finally to Rome (1871).

The spirit of the *Risorgimento*—and its ideological and political exploitation (Brero 1982: 95)—permeated the literary ambience of the century and was particularly important for the two best poets of this age, i.e. Àngel Broferi (Angelo Brofferio) and Norbert Reusa (Norberto Rosa).

The former was deeply involved in political life as an activist and later as a MP of the democratic left. Born in Castelneuv Brusà[46] in 1802, he died in Switzerland in 1866. His *Canson piemontèise* 'Piedmontese Songs' were very successful and had many editions: the first one, in Switzerland in 1839, was followed by another seven editions in the 19th century and eight more in the 20th (Clivio 2002: 320). Many scholars have linked Broferi's work to a supposed inspiration by his contemporary French songwriter Pierre-Jean de Béranger (Brero 1982: 107–108; Clivio 2002: 323). His literary model, nonetheless, was Calv.

Norbert Reusa (Vian-a[47] 1803—Susa[48] 1862), a lawyer and, like his friend Broferi, an MP, displays an altogether different spirit. Despite his involvement in the Risorgimento and his liberal ideas, in his writings he was less inclined to contest the government and the social system, even if his literary models were

---

[46]   Castelneuv Brusà /kastel'nøw bry'z-a/, Italian Castelnuovo Calcea /kastel'nwovo kal'tʃea/ (44°47′N 08°17′E), in the Monfrà area.

[47]   /'vjaɲa/, Italian Avigliana /avi'ʎana/ (45°05′N 07°24′E).

[48]   Susa /'syza/, Italian Susa /'suza/, Franco-provençal Suisa (45°08′N 07°03′E), a town lying in the middle of the Susa Valley connecting Turin to France.

fairly similar to Broferi's (especially Calv), although mitigated by a certain Epicurean philosophy of life (Clivio 2002: 328).

He wrote many poems in Piedmontese (*La vorp e la mascrada* 'The Fox and the Mask,' *La farfala e la lumassa* 'The Butterfly and the Snail,' *Ël ver filòsofo* 'The True Philosopher,' and *Ij piasì* 'The Pleasures,' usually regarded as his masterpiece), until in 1848 he decided to forgo his own language and write only in Italian.

Poetry was not the most popular genre in the 19th century. Indeed journalistic prose and theatre works were. Playwrights like Gioann Tosel (Giovanni Toselli; Coni 1819—Genoa 1886), Federich Garel (Federico Garelli; ël Mondvì 1831—Rome 1885), Tòjo Bersessi (Vittorio Bersezio; Povragn[49] 1828—Turin 1900), Erald Barèt (Eraldo Baretti; ël Mondvì 1846—Rome 1895) enjoyed, with their comedies, a huge success at their time and are often still popular in Piedmont today. The crucial year was 1857 (Clivio 2002: 336): Tosel debuted at Teatro d'Angennes in Turin with his comedy *Cichin-a 'd Moncalé* 'Young Frances from Moncalé,' a parody of the tragedy *Francesca da Rimini* written in Italian by Silvio Pellico on a subject by Dante (Brero 1982: 153).

We will limit ourselves to mentioning some of the best-known comedies: apart from *Cichin-a 'd Moncalé*, *La Lena dël Rociamlon* 'Magdalen from Rociamlon' by Federich Garel, *Le miserie 'd Monsù Travèt* 'Mr. Travet's Miseries' by Tòjo Bersessi and *Ij fastidi d'un grand òm* 'A Great Man's Troubles' by Erald Barèt.

The authors mentioned above were all from the Southern Province of Coni, and their varieties of Piedmontese were sometimes different from Turinese; nevertheless, all their comedies were written in koine and were perfectly intelligible to all Piedmontese speakers. Furthermore, Bersessi's work rapidly went beyond Piedmont's borders, becoming a sort of universal paradigm of some human types, and the word *travèt* entered Italian with the meaning of 'petty clerk.'

The high quality of these literary works has to be considered in a global context of rich theatrical production: Brero (1982: 182–191) reproduced a list of productions performed between 1859 and 1887 and recorded over three hundred comedies.

These remarkable numbers were surpassed by those of the Piedmontese magazines. All published in Turin, they were certainly a unique phenomenon in Italy for a regional language (Clivio 2002: 357). At the same time, the humoristic character of most of them is often evident from their very titles: fully adopting the dominant linguistic ideology, "high" prose and, most of all, non-literary

---

49   Povragn /pu'vraɲ/, Occitan Poranh, Italian Peveragno /peve'raɲo/ (44°20′N 07°37′E).

subjects like politics, economy and society are generally absent—although a few exceptions may be found in the contemporary press (which nevertheless have a much smaller circulation).

The following list (based upon Clivio 2002 and Tesio 1991; updated) provides the names of the magazines in chronological order (and in the writing system they used), with some basic information:

- *Parnas Piemonteis*. Periodicity: annualy. Period of publishing: 1831–1849. Publishers: Alliana (1831), Fodratti (1832–1849);
- *Gasëta 'd Gianduja*. Periodicity: twice weekly (from 1866 to 1867); three times a week (from 1867 to 1868). Period of publishing: 13 May 1866–24 May 1868. Founded by Luigi Pietracqua. Publisher: Tipografia Nazionale di Torino;
- *'L Falabrach*. Periodicity: variable. Period of publishing: not sure. From 1877. On 17 November 1895 it became *'L Falabrach. Giornal dla gent senza fastidi*; publisher: Tipografia Subalpina;
- *'L neuv falabrach, giornal scassa fastidi*. Periodicity: weekly. Period of publishing: from 8 July 1888. Publisher: Baglione;
- *L'falabrach modern, umoristich, satirich, politich, regional*. Periodicity: weekly. Period of publishing: from 11 January 1902 to 1903. Publisher: Tipografia Bosio;
- *L'Aso. Giornal an dialet piemonteis*. Periodicity: weekly. Period of publishing: 1886–1887. Editors: Domenico Beccari and Oreste Mentasti. Publisher: Tipografia Valentino;
- *'L Birichin. Giornal piemonteis satirich, leterari, sportiv, umoristich, social*. Periodicity: weekly. Period of publishing: 1886–1926. Founded by Giacomo Sacerdote. Circulation: 12 thousand copies;
- *La Birichiña. Giornal piemonteis satirich*. Periodicity: weekly. Period of publishing: January 1893-January 1909. Editors: Carlin Tiochet and Carlo Alberto Occhetti;
- *Compare Bonom*. Periodicity: weekly (1889–1893), then twice weekly (1893). Period of publishing: 22 June 1889–13 December 1893. Founded by Luigi Petracqua. Publisher: Tipografia Artale (later Bocca, latest Foa);
- *Gazzetta Subalpina. Compare Bonom*. Periodicity: twice weekly. Period of publishing: 27 December 1893–1895;
- *'L Mul*. Periodicity: weekly. Period of publishing: 1877–1878;
- *'L courê 'd Turin: giornal dij Farfo*. Periodicity: weekly. Period of publishing: 1871–?
- *L'indiscret*. Periodicity: weekly. Period of publishing: 26 December 1891–?
- *'L Bougianen, gazeta turineisa*, later *Il Bougianen. Ilustrassion 'd la capital d'Giandoja*; Periodicity: weekly. Period of publishing: 1878–1890. Editor: Ubaldo Cassone. Publisher: Tipografia Mastrella.

- *Cerea!* Periodicity: weekly. Period of publishing: from March 1908. Publisher: Bianchi.
- *'L Passatemp: romansie piemonteis illustrà.* Periodicity: weekly. Period of publishing: not known. Publisher: Tipografia Borgarelli.
- *Il ritorno di Gironi.* Periodicity: variable. Period of publishing: unknown. Publisher: Tipografia provinciale Marenco, Coni.
- *La sartòira.* Periodicity: weekly. Period of publishing: 1895–? Publisher: Tipografia Industriale.
- *Sartoirëtta. Giornal piemonteis.* Periodicity: variable. Period of publishing: 1895-? Publisher: Tipografia Industriale.
- *'L Caval d'brôns.* Periodicity: weekly. Period of publishing: 1923-? From 1946:
- *'L Caval 'd brons. Portavos dla Famija Turinèisa.* Periodicity: monthly.
- *Ël Tòr. Arvista lìbera dij piemontèis.* Periodicity: weekly. Period of publishing: 1946–1947. Publisher: Nuove Edizioni Italiane, Roma.
- *Musicalbrandé. Arvista piemontèisa.* Periodicity: quarterly. Period of publishing: 1959–1994.
- *Il Codino rosso: rosso ma codino, codino ma rosso.* Periodicity: weekly. Period of publishing: 1924-? Publisher: unknown.
- *Gianduja.* Periodicity: variable. Period of publishing: 1893-? Publisher: Tipografia Origlia, Festa e C.
- *I brandé. Arvista piemontèisa.* Periodicity: bimonthly. Period of publishing: March–May 1927. Publisher: Cecchini. Founded by Pinin Pacòt, Oreste Gallina e Virginio Fiochèt.
- *Il richiamo—I brandé: rivista mensile di letteratura.* Periodicity: monthly. Period of publishing: November 1927-? Publisher: s.t.e.l.b.
- *Ij brandé. Giornal ëd poesìa piemontèisa.* Periodicity: monthly (later once a year). Period of publishing: 1946–
- *Piemontèis ancheuj. Giornal ëd poesìa e 'd coltura piemontèisa.* Periodicity: weekly. Period of publishing: 1982 (number zero); 1983–. Publisher: Centro Studi "Don Minzoni."
- *La slòira.* Periodicity: quarterly. Period of publishing: 1995–. Publisher: Associazione Culturale "La Slòira" (Ivreja[50]).
- *Assion Piemontèisa.* Periodicity: monthly. Period of publishing: 1993–2003. Publisher: Cooperativa Pro Piemonte S.r.l.
- *é!* Periodicity: bimonthly. Period of publishing: 2004–2006 (14 issues). Publisher: Associassion Piemontpress.

---

50   Ivreja /i'vreja/, Italian Ivrea /i'vrea/ (45°27'32"40 N 07°52'22"80 E).

As is evident from this list, most of these magazines were published between the last decades of the 19th century and the first three decades of the 20th century. Some of them—e.g. *'L Birichin*—attained a very large circulation. The same holds for novels in Piedmontese: amongst the regional languages of Italy and France, Piedmontese is probably the only one that can boast a large production of novels. Storytelling in Piedmontese was born as an appendix prose, feuilleton-style, and was strictly linked to the existence of the magazines: the novels were published in volumes only after they came out serially in the magazines. Nevertheless, they often found renewed success in this form, and are still reprinted today by the publishing house Viglongo.

The social context of the novels is usually the urban underclass (and the underworld), sometimes introduced as instruments of social denunciation.

Following Clivio (2002: 362–375) we will mention here only the two most important authors: Luis Pietracqua (Luigi Pietracqua; Voghera[51] 1832—Turin 1901), who wrote inter alia *Don Pipeta l'Asilé* 'Don Pipette the Vinegar Maker' (1867–1868), *Lucio dla Venerìa* 'Lucius from Venaria' (1877), *Lorens ël suicida. Còs val-lo n'òm mort?* 'Laurence, the Suicide. What is a Dead Man Worth?' (1889), *La còca dël gàmber* 'The Gang of the Shrimp' (1890), *Ij misteri 'd Vanchija* 'Vanchiglia's Misteries' (1894); and Carl Bërnardin Fré (Carlo Bernardino Ferrero; Turin 1866–1924), who, on the contrary, took his inspiration from the French novelist Émile Zola and with a realistic mood depicted the shabby life of the *lumpenproletariat* (Clivio 2002: 369) in his novels *La cracia* 'The Scum' (1890), *Ij mort ëd fam* 'The Starving People' (1891), *La bassa Russia* 'The Low Russia' (1891).

To offer an example of Ferrero's very interesting style, we reproduce here—together with its typographic peculiarities—the incipit of *La Cracia* (p. 13 of the 1981 Viglongo edition):

> *Mare Michin, strojassà s'un cadregon d'paja, con i pè apogià sna banchëtta, a piava 'l sò sòlit bròd darè dël fnestrin dla portieria. A l'avìa sui ginoj le* Vite dei Santi: *cola letura a la divertìa motobin. A l'era un dover ch'adempìa tute le dumìniche d'lesne un capitol, e tute le dumìniche ai na dasija na durmià anssima.*
>
> *Già, chila a patìa inmenssament 'l caod, e col dì lì a l'avia sentulo pì che 'l sòlit, përchè a l'avia ancora nen durvì 'l liber che già j'euj a j'ero serasse.*

---

51   Voghera /vuˈgera/, Italian /voˈgera/ (44°59′33″N 09°00′33″E), a major town in the province of Pavia, Lombardy, very close to the Piedmontese borders.

Mother Dominique, sprawled on a big straw sofa, with her feet resting on a bench, was taking her usual nap behind the concierge window. She had on her knees the *Vite dei Santi* ("Lives of the Saints"): that reading amused her very much. Reading a chapter from it was a duty she would performed every Sunday, and every Sunday she used to take a nap upon it.

In fact, she suffered the heat immensely, and that day she felt it more than usual, since even before she opened the book her eyes had already closed.

1.8.4 *The Contemporary Scene*

The contemporary age of Piedmontese literary history began in 1927 with the publication of the first issue of the literary magazine *Ij Brandé*. Around this magazine, a cultural group rapidly formed, taking the name of *Companìa dij Brandé* 'Company of the Andirons.' Its theoretical and practical importance can hardly be overestimated: they were the ones to establish present day Piedmontese orthography (☞ 3.2.3.), and one of their goals was to bring the literary production in Piedmontese to the level of the most famous contemporary European literatures, namely French and Spanish literature. They set out to follow the steps for revitalization of Occitan literature taken by Frédéric Mistral in Southern France, and in fact the first achievement of the *Companìa dij Brandé* was the publication in 1930 of a collection of poetry in honor of Mistral.

The heart and soul of this literary movement was Pinin Pacòt (Italian Giuseppe Pacotto; Turin 1899—Castel d'Anon[52] 1964). He was involved not only in the renewal of Piedmontese literature along with the *Brandé*, but also in the movements promoting the renaissance of a literature in the Occitan from Piedmont: with a few other poets he established in 1961 the Occitan *Escolo dóu Po*, 'The school of the Po river.' His poems were collected in many books: *Arsivòli* 'Reveries' (1926); *Crosiere* 'Crossroads' (1935), *Speransa* 'Hope' (1946), *Gioventù, pòvra amija ...* 'Youth, Poor friend ...' (1954), and *Sèira* 'Evening' (1964).

He is generally considered the most important Piedmontese poet of the 20th century, together with Nino Còsta. Older than Pacòt, Nino Còsta (Turin 1886–1945) had a controversial relationship with the *Companìa*, for both literary and political reasons. He was a Catholic and anti-fascist, while some members of the *Companìa dij Brandé* tried to please the regime; moreover, his poetic style was akin to the atmosphere of the *Birichin*, rather than to the French and Span-

---

52   Castel d'Anon /kasˈtel d=aˈnuŋ/, Italian Castello di Annone /kasˈtello d(i)=anˈnone/ (44°53′N 08°19′E).

ish models that, together with the Italian poet Gabriele D'Annunzio, highly influenced the fictional universe of Pacòt and his *scòla*. For instance, Nino Còsta started writing with a graphic system elaborated by the poet Alberto Viriglio (Turin 1851–1913) in contrast to the earlier writing tradition (Clivio 2002: 414); later, he adopted the Brandé system, and finally went back to the Viriglio system in his last collection. Còsta was much less interested in theoretical and linguistic issues than Pacòt, but his poetic production is much more popular and better known among the Piedmontese.[53] The volumes collecting his poems are *Mamina* 'Mommy' (1922), *Sal e pèiver* 'Salt and Pepper' (1924), *Brassabòsch* 'Ivy' (1928), *Fruta Madura* 'Ripe Fruit' (1931), *Poesìe religiose piemontèise* 'Piedmontese Religious Poems' (1934), *Ròba nòstra* 'Our Stuff' (1938), and *Tempesta* 'Hailstorm' (1946).

Besides Pacòt and Còsta, there are many other poets in Piedmontese contemporary literature. Tesio and Malerba (1990) mention:

- Vincenzo Buronzo; Moncalv Monfrà[54] (1884–1976), the author of two collections of poems written in a Monfrà variety: *Al me pais* 'My Village' (1962) and *Al litaniji di giòbia* 'The Litanies of Thursday' (1977);
- Oreste Gallina (Ël Mango[55] 1898—Arona[56] 1985): among the co-founders of *Ij Brandé*, his collections are *Freidolin-e* 'Meadow Saffron' (1926), *Canta Péro!* 'Sing Peter!' (1933), *Pare e fieul* 'Father and Son' (1946), *Mia tèra* 'My Land' (1960);
- Alfredino Nicòla (Turin 1902–1995), a member of the *Companìa dij Brandé* and founder (1959) of the Piedmontese musical magazine *Musicalbrandé*. He is the author of a very rich poetic production collected in many books: *Penombre* 'Dim Light' (1929), *Primavere* 'Primroses' (1933), *Nìvole* 'Clouds' (1951), *Spers* 'Lost' (1969), *Arcordanse* 'Reminders' (1970), *Stòrie dle valade 'd Lans* 'Stories from Lanzo Valleys' (1970), *Samada* (1982), *Cartolin-e* 'Postcards' (1986), in addition to *Buscaje* 'Splinters of Wood' (without date) and some *Poesìe sparse* 'Scattered Poems' finally collected in two volumes with a critical edition published in 2007;
- Armand Motura (Armando Mottura; Turin 1905–1976), a member of the *Companìa dij Brandé* and the author of many poetry collections, like *Reuse rosse* 'Red Roses' (1947), *Paisagi 'd Val Susa* 'Landscapes of Susa Valley' (1949),

---

53 It may be worth mentioning that one of his poems was publicly quoted by Pope Francis (himself of Piedmontese origins) during his visit in Turin on June 21, 2015.
54 Moncalv Monfrà /muŋˈkalv muŋˈfra/, Italian Moncalvo Monferrato /monˈkalvo monferˈrato/ (45°03′N 08°16′E).
55 Ël Mango /əlˈmaŋgu/, Italian Mango /ˈmango/ (44°41′N 08°09′E).
56 Aron-a /aˈruŋa/, Italian Arona /aˈrona/ (45°45′N 08°33′E), a town on Lake Maggiore.

La patria cita 'The Little Country' (1959), *... e adess pòvr òm?* '... and Now, Poor Man?' (1969), *Vita, stòria bela* 'Life, Beautiful Story' (1973);
- Luis Olivé (Luigi Olivero; Vilastlon[57] 1909—Rome 1995), founder of the magazine *Ël tòr*, is the author of more than a thousand poems in Piedmontese, only partially published in his collections *Roma andalusa* 'Andalusian Rome' (1947), *Sent poesìe* 'A Hundred Poems' (1952), *Ij faunèt* 'The Little Fauns' (1955), *Epicedïon dij mè dódes gat mort* 'Epicedium of My Twelve Dead Cats' (1959), *Rondò dle masche* 'Rondo of the Witches' (1971), *Romanzìe* 'Trimming' (1983);
- Umberto Luigi Ronco (Pamparà[58] 1913—Rome 1997), better known as a futurist painter and author of many poems only very partially published in a single collection titled *Novèmber violagiàun* 'Purple-Yellow November' (1962);
- Dumini Badalin (Domenico Badalin; Turin 1917–1980), whose mother was a native of the Monfrà area and who wrote in this local variety most of his important works, collected in two books: *Listeurji dij Varèj. Poesìe paisan-e dle tère pòvre dël Monfrà* 'The Stories of the Short Valleys. Peasant Poems from the Poor Monferrato Lands' (1978) and *Doe minute për ti. Paròle d'amor sitadin-e e paisan-e për tute j'età* 'Two Minutes for You. City and Country Love Words for Every Age' (1979);
- Barba Tòni Bodrìe (Antonio Bodrero; Frasso[59] 1921—Coni 1999) who wrote poems both in Occitan and in Piedmontese; written in the latter language are *Val d'Inghildon* 'Inghildon Valley' (1974), *Sust* 'Wisdom' (1985) and *Dal prim uch a l'aluch* 'From the First Cry to the Rattle' (2000);
- Giovanni Rapetti (Lissandria 1922–2014), artist and sculptor, whose production in the Lissandria variety remains largely unpublished, except for a few collections, namely *Er fugaron* 'The Big Fire' (1973), *I pas ant l'èrba* 'The Steps in the Grass' (1987), *Ra memòria dra stèila* 'The Memory of the Star' (1993) and finally *Er len-ni an Tani* 'The Moons in the Tani River' (2012);
- Milo Bré (Camillo Brero; Druent[60] 1926—Pianëssa[61] 2018), successor of Pinin Pacòt as the leader of the *Companìa dij Brandé* and well-known for his works on Piedmontese normative grammar as well as on Piedmontese literature, was also a talented poet, publishing books such as *Spluve* 'Sparks' (1949), *Stèile ... steilin-e* 'Stars ... Starlets' (1956), *Breviari dl'ànima* 'A Breviary

---

57 Vilastlon /vila'stluŋ/, Italian Villastellone /villastel'lone/ (44°55′N 07°45′E).
58 Pamparà /pampa'ra/, Italian Pamparato /pampa'rato/ (44°17′N 07°55′E).
59 Frasso /'frasu/, Italian Frassino /'frassino/ (44°34′N 07°17′E).
60 Druent /dry'æŋt/, Italian Druento /dru'ento/ (45°08′N 07°35′E).
61 Pianëssa /pja'nəssa/, Italian Pianezza /pja'nettsa/ (45°06′N 07°33′E).

of the Soul' (1962), *L'ànima mia a s'anàndia* 'My Soul Starts to Move' (1968), *Bin a la tèra e l'àutra bin* 'The Love for the Land and the Other Love' (1977), *Ma 'l sol doman a ven ... Bin e poesìa an lenga piemontèisa* 'But the Sun Will Come Tomorrow ... Prayer and Poetry in the Piedmontese Language' (1986), *E a l'é torna l'alba* 'And It is Dawn Again' (1992), *An brass al sol* 'In the Arms of the Sun' (1996), *Vos ëd l'etern present* 'Voices of the Eternal Present' (2003);

– Carlo Regis (Mondvì 1929–2017), chemist and poet, who published in the Mondvì variety some important collections such as *Cantoma pian* 'Let's Sing Softly' (1960, together with other Mondvì poets), *Mia gent mie montagne* 'My People My Mountains' (1971), *Sinch canson d'amor cantà a doi vos an Piassa* 'Five Love Songs Sung in Two Voices in the Old Town of Mondvì' (1977), *Ël nì dl'ajassa* 'The Magpie's Nest' (1980), *La Gatògna* 'The Cat's Heat' (1985), *Lun-e* 'Moons' (1989), *Bleupom* 'Apple Blue' (1997), *Ël tornidor ëd lun-e* 'The Moons' Turner' (2007);

– Tavo Burat (Ottavio Buratti; Stezà[62] 1932—Biela 2009) was an ecologist and a staunch defender of minority languages and founded, together with Pinin Pacòt, the *Escolo dóu Po* for the renaissance of Occitan culture on the Piedmontese side of the Western Alps. Author of many studies and essays on the regional culture (some of them written in Piedmontese, like *Lassomse nen tajé la lenga* 'Let's Not Have Our Tongue Cut Off,' 2005), Tavo Burat founded the Piedmontese magazine *La Slòira* 'The Plough' and published some interesting poetical works, mostly in the Biela variety, collected in *Prusse mulinere* 'Chickadees' (1960), *Finagi* 'Border Territory' (1979) and finally *Poesìe* (2008);

– Bianca Dorato (Turin 1933–2007) wrote many theatrical works, but is more famous for her poems, principally dedicated to the alpine atmosphere, collected in *Tzantelèina. Canson ëd lus, d'aria e 'd rije d'eva* 'Tzantelèina. Songs of Light, of Air and of the Laughing of the Water' (1984), *Drere 'd lus* 'Pathways of Light' (1990), *Passagi* 'Passage' (1990), *Fiòca e òr* 'Snow and Gold' (1998), *Travërsera* 'Footpath' (2003) and *Signaj* 'Signals' (2006);

– Remigio Bertolino (Montàud dël Mondvì[63] 1948–), whose very particular poetical works (written in his native mountain dialect) were published in many collections, such as *L'eva d'ënvern* 'It Was in Winter' but also 'The Winter Water' (1986), *Sbaluch* 'Dazzle' (1989), *A lum ëd fiòca* 'To the Light of Snow' (1995), *Ël vos* 'The Voices' (2003), *Stanse d'ënvern* 'Winter Rooms' (2006), *La fin dël mond* 'The End of the World' (2013), *Litre d'ënvern* 'Winter Letters' (2015), *Nìvole da prim* 'Spring Clouds' (2019).

---

62 A town in the province of Bergamo, Lombardy.
63 Montàud dël Mondvì /muŋˈtawd d=əl=muŋdˈvi/, Italian Montaldo di Mondovi /monˈ-taldo di=mondoˈvi/ (44°19′N 07°52′E).

In the last decade of the 20th century and in the early 21st century, new poets have started writing and publishing poems, and many others have enriched their previous production. It is not possible to name all of them; we will mention just two local anthologies: Bertolino and Duberti (2007), in French for the Mondvì area, and Garuzzo (2011) for the Lissandria province. Actually, writing in local varieties is distinctly on the increase and is related to the decay of the koine (as aptly remarked by Regis 2012a; ☞ 20.2.2.).

Poetry is surely the most practiced genre in Piedmontese literary history, and this statement is even truer for the contemporary age. This fact was highlighted by Girardin (1995) in a paper dedicated to one of the most relevant prose-writers in Piedmontese: Nino Autelli. Born in Spinëtta Marengh in 1903 and killed for political reasons in the aftermath of the Second World War in 1945, Autelli wrote two collections of traditional Piedmontese tales: *Pan 'd coa* 'Wholemeal Bread' (1931) and *Masnà* 'Children' (1937). From the former, it is worth quoting the beginning of the tale *Gioanin trambla-nen* 'John Tremblenot:'

> *Na vòlta a na dòna l'era naje 'n cit, ch'a l'era nen pì àut che 'l dil mamlin. Chila, però, sicome l'era sensa fieuj, l'é trovasse contenta l'istess e a-j volìa tuta la bin ch'as peul imaginé. Antant a disìa daspërchila: "Con tòch e tocon a dventrà 'd cò chiel n'òm parèj 'd tuti j'àutri" e a l'ha butaje nòm Gioanin.*

> Once upon a time to a woman was born a child, who was no taller than the little finger. But she was happy since she had no other child and she loved him as much as one can imagine. Meanwhile she would say to herself: "By bread pieces and big bread pieces he will become a man just like everyone else" and she named him Little John.

Tavio Còsio (Vilafalèt[64] 1923—ël Mel[65] 1989) was another important author of literary prose. Born in the lowlands, he graduated in chemistry and moved to Ël Mél, a little village in the Varàita Valley, where he set up a pharmacy. Strongly influenced by the poet Barba Tòni Bodrìe and by the traditional oral culture of the valley, he decided to write down the stories his clients and neighbours used to tell him, as well as the stories he had heard from his parents and relatives when he was a child. Thus he published two collections of short stories, *Pere, gramon e lionsa* 'Stones, Spear Grass and Creeping Bent' (1975) and *Sota al chinché* 'Under the Oil Chandelier' (1980); a few years later (1984) he also

---

64 Vilafalèt /vilafaˈlæt/, Italian Villafalletto /villafalˈletto/ (44°33′N 07°32′E).
65 ël Mel /əlˈmel/, Italian Melle /melˈle/ (44°34′N 07°19′E).

collected a few traditional tales of the valley in the Occitan language (*Roche, sarvan e masche* 'Rocks, Wild Men and Witches').

His narrative style is very original and his language rich in loans from Occitan varieties, as is normal for a Western Piedmontese dialect like his.

What follows is an excerpt from the short story *Ij quat frej soldà e sant* 'The Four Brothers, Soldiers and Saints' (*Pere, gramon e lionsa*, 127):

> *Le valade alpin-e 'd Coni a son tuta na sëmnera 'd pilon ch'a fan preuva dla grignor dij viton ën vers ij sò Sant. As ne vëgh ëd vej, d'ëstravej, e 'd neuv trench ën pò daspërtut; ën bass arlongh jë stradon ch'a van an cobia con ij gròss ri 'd montagna, ën brova ai drajòt ch'a meno su ai pasturage, stërmà 'n mes a d'ënvërtoj ëd ronze ch'a smija ch'a veulo travondije, o a la dëscuverta 'n gropa ai chiòt con dalògn la vista dij pich bleu dle crëste o dla pian-a 'nfinìa.*

The Alpine valleys of Coni are all a row of votive pylons that prove the peasants' affection for their Saints. There are old, very old and brand new ones everywhere; down below, all along the streets that go like a couple with the great mountain streams, on the side of the little pathways to the pastures, hidden away between bundles of brambles that seem to swallow them, or outdoors on the back of the little mountain plains, within the distance the sight of the ridges' blue peaks, or of the infinite plain.

A final note on music: popular and folk music in Piedmont have always used a plurality of languages, but Piedmontese got the lion's share since it was spoken by all social classes and was understood by everybody. The most famous collection of such songs is no doubt Nigra (1888), with many songs dating back to at least the 18th century, when a definite musical tradition was established. In that century, the lyrics and music of some older songs such as *La Bërgera, Maria Gioana, La Monfrin-a* were definitely fixed and new songs created: this is the case of *Baron Litron* and *La Bela Carolin*, both closely linked to historical events. Not by chance, it was also in the 18th century when Ignazio Isler (☞ 1.7.2.) authored more than fifty *Canson* that were real songs: their lyrics were regularly accompanied by pieces of music that Isler himself used to write (Pasero 2003: 355; Pasero 2013: xii–xiii).

Traditional Piedmontese songs were collected and transcribed by the musician and musicologist Leone Sinigaglia (Turin 1868–1944), a member of the Jewish community of Turin who died during the Nazi persecutions. Roberto Leydi (Ivreja[66] 1928—Milan 2003) was another well-known Piedmontese ethnomusicologist who collected many traditional songs.

---

66   Ivreja /iv'ræja/, Italian Ivrea /iv'rea/ (45°28′N 07°53′E).

While vaudevilles and similar shows always hosted monologues and music numbers in Piedmontese, in the 1960s Piedmontese artists singing in Piedmontese came to enjoy a nation-wide critical success all over Italy. Gipo (born Giuseppe) Farassino (Turin 1934–2013) was perhaps the most talented and famous of the songwriters, singers and actors using Piedmontese in their artworks. In later years, he was also a politician devoted to fostering an identity sentiment in Piedmont in the ranks of the Lega Nord party, in which he served for a few years as an MP in the Italian and later in the European parliaments. Farassino's poetics were thoroughly examined, e.g., by Tesio (2014: 107–112), while the interesting linguistic pastiche of his lyrics were analyzed by Regis (2002).

As a sample of Piedmontese musical lyrics we propose one of Farassino's most famous and inspired songs: *Ël 6 ëd via Coni* ('6 Coni Street') from the mid-1960s and recorded on the LP *Auguri* (1967). The music is also by Farassino (the lyrics are reproduced according to Brero 1981: 466–467).

Ël 6 ëd via Coni	6 Coni Street
Ël 6 ëd via Coni a l'é na ca veja	6 Coni Street is an old house
che gnanca na vòlta a l'era nen bela.	that even in the past was not beautiful.
Davanti al porton, doe bale 'd ciman	in front of the door two concrete balls
a paravo ij canton dal crep dij carton	protected the gate-posts from the blows of the carriages
ch'a intravo e cariavo jë scart ëd metal	that entered to pick up scrap metal
da cola oficin-a, là an fond a la cort,	from the workshop at the end of the
na cort con le sterne piantà an sël batù.	pebble-strewn courtyard.
D'an mes a sta cort, se ti t'ausse j'euj	If you look, stand in the middle of this courtyard and look up
it vëdde ij pogieuj, carià dë stendùa con tanti tacon.	you see myriad patched clothes hanging out to dry on the railings.
Su ògni pogieul j'é un pàira d'alògg	On each balcony there are two apartments
e un cess an comun; j'é nen na masnà,	and a shared toilet; there are no children around;
j'é mach tant rabel e odor ëd frità.	Just mad chaos and the smell of omelettes.
A l'é pròpe lì, al fond dël prim pian, che son naje mi.	It is right there, at the end of the first floor, that I was born.
Mi i guardo ij pogieuj con cole ringhere carià dë	I look at the balconies with those railings

stendùa,	loaded with hanging clothes,
là al fond ëd la cort a-i é 'l finimond ch'a fà l'oficina	there at the end of the courtyard there is the racket of the workshop
e 'l cel lassù an aria a smija un tendon	and the sky up there looks like a tent
d'un gris così spòrch ch'a crija: "Laveme".	of such dirty gray that it seems to be pleading: "Wash me!"
Am buta vërgògna. Vërgògna ... ma 'd còsa?	I am ashamed. Ashamed ... but of what?
D'esse na sì, an mes a sta cort,	Of being born here, in the middle of this courtyard,
an cole doe stànsie col cess an comun,	in those two rooms with the shared toilet,
i l'hai quasi paura ch'a-i sia quaidun	I am almost afraid that there is someone
che ancora as ricòrda che mi i son nà sì,	who still remembers that I was born here,
paura ch'a-i passa quaidun ch'am conòssa,	afraid that a passerby might recognize me,
dovèj ciamé scusa, dovèj-je conté	and that I'd have to apologize to him, and to explain
ël percome, ël përchè, che ij mé j'ero pòver.	how and why my parents were poor.
Am monta 'l magon e am ven da pioré.	I get a lump in my throat and I feel like crying.
Ma peui àusso j'euj lassù al prim pian,	But then I look up, there on the first floor,
e i vëddo mia mama ... a rij e am fà ciao,	and I see my mother ... she is laughing and says "Hi,"
così, con la man: antlora am ven veuja	like that, and waves: and I feel
ëd core 'nt la strà, fërmé 'l prim ch'a passa,	like running into the street, stopping the first passerby,
crijéje: "Monsù! Ma a lo sa chiel che sì,	and shouting at the top of my voice: "Sir, do you know that it is right here
al 6 ëd via Coni, i son naje mi!?!"	in 6 Coni Street, that I was born?"

In roughly the same years Roberto Balocco (Turin 1941) and Alberto Cesa (Turin 1947–2010) rearranged with the ensemble *Cantovivo* several traditional Piedmontese songs, while from 1959 to 1994 Alfredo Nicola was the director of *Musicalbrandé*, a magazine explicitly devoted to Piedmontese music.

At the beginning of the third millennium, albeit anti-'dialect' bias remains far from gone, local languages all over Italy have gained—at least for some Italians—a new, positive value. The new attitude towards these languages has given rise to "resurgences" of usage, also in rock music, rap, and other genres targeted at young people (Berruto 2002, 2006, 2018; see also Coveri 1996).

Chansonniers such as Gian Maria Testa (Cavlimor[67] 1958—Alba[68] 2016), rappers such as Tito Sherpa and Neekoshy (active since 2021), pop bands such as *Mau mau* (active since 1990), pop-folk artists as *Quinta Rua* (active since 2002) and *Amemanera* (active since 2013), and reggae authors as Laika (active since 2012) have recorded songs or full albums in Piedmontese, partially in the footsteps of Fabrizio De André's 1984 masterpiece *Creuza de mä*, sung entirely in Ligurian. *Mau mau*'s Piedmontese is analyzed by Scholz (1998: 121–158).

Musical comedy, a genre also frequented by Farassino, is kept alive by bands such as *Farinei dla brigna* (active since 1989) and *Trelilu* (active since 1992; Aime, Favole and Milano 2013), while a few comic sketches performed by *Il piemontese moderno* in a Southern dialect have attained a very high number of views on YouTube.

67 Cavlimor /kavli'mur/, Italian /kavallerma'dʒdʒore/ (44°43'N 07°41'E).
68 Piedmontese and Italian Alba /'alba/ (44°42'N 08°02'E).

CHAPTER 2

Phonetics and Phonology

2.1 Default Articulation of Phonemes

Twenty consonantal phonemes are used in Piedmontese. Table 3. shows their default articulation in the absence of allophonic phonological or phonetic processes:

TABLE 3 The consonantal phonemes of Piedmontese

| | Labial |||| Coronal |||||| Velar ||
| | Bilabial || Labiodent. || Dental/alveolar || Palato-alveolar || Palatal || Velar ||
	vd.	vl.	vd.	vl.	vd.	vl.	vd.	vl.	vd.	vl.	vd.	vl.
Plosives												
oral	b	p			d	t					g	k
nasal	m				n				ɲ		ŋ	
Affricates							dʒ	tʃ				
Fricatives			v	f	z	s						
Trill					r							
Approx.												
central	w										j	
lateral					l							

Piedmontese has nine vocalic phonemes, as represented in Figure 3.

The phonetic description of the consonantal and vocalic phonemes of Piedmontese is given below together with their standard orthography (☞ 3.):

[p] a voiceless bilabial stop, fully exploded in every position; it is always writt⟨p⟩, except when it is the result of PP 10. FINAL DEVOICING (☞ 2.4.3.), in whi case it is written ⟨b⟩; it can occur in all positions; e.g.: *pocio* /ˈputʃu/ 'pout; m lar' *sapa* /ˈsapa/ 'hoe;' *sap* /sap/ 'fir-tree'

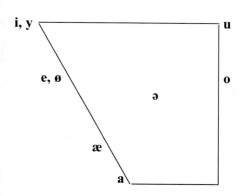

FIGURE 3
The vocalic phonemes of Piedmontese

[t̪] a voiceless dental stop, fully exploded in every position. Dentality will be left unmarked in transcription and plain /t/ will be used. It is always written ⟨t⟩, except when it is the result of PP 10. FINAL DEVOICING (☞ 2.4.3.), in which case it is written ⟨d⟩; it can occur in all positions; e.g.: *tampa* /'tampa/ 'hole, ditch;' *nata* /'nata/ 'cork;' *gat* /gat/ 'cat'

[k] a voiceless velar stop, fully exploded in every position. As in other Romance languages, its orthographic expression is etymological (☞ 3.). In particular, the Piedmontese orthography reflects similar choices in Italian, and has recourse to three different graphemes, according to the rule:
1. ⟨c⟩ / {a, o, u, y, C}   as in: *curt* /kyrt/ 'short (Masculine);' *vaca* /'vaka/ 'cow'
2. ⟨q⟩ / _ wV   *quaj* /kwaj/ 1. 'blister;' 2. 'rennet'
3. ⟨ch⟩ / elsewhere   *chërde* /'kərde/ 'to believe;' *such* /syk/ 'stump, log'

[b] a voiced bilabial stop, fully exploded in every position and devoiced to [p] word-finally in many varieties (among which the koine). It is always written ⟨b⟩ and may occur in every position, but is rare word-finally: *bora* /'bura/ 'waste wool, down;' *saba* /'saba/ 'Saturday'

[d̪] a voiced dental stop, fully exploded in every position and devoiced to [t] word-finally in many varieties (among which the koine; cf. AIS 1578). As in the case of /t/, dentality will be left unmarked and plain /d/ will be used in transcription. This phoneme is always written ⟨d⟩ and can occur in all positions, but it is rare word-finally: *dagné* /da'ɲ-e/[1] 'to drip;' *veder* /'veder/ 'glass;' *anvod* /aŋ'vud/ 'nephew'

---

[1] In this chapter, the transcription follows the same principles as throughout in the grammar

[g] a voiced velar stop, fully exploded in every position; it is rare word-finally, where it is devoiced to [k] in many varieties (among which the koine). Again, its orthographic expression is etymological and has recourse to two different graphemes, according to the rule:
  1. ⟨g⟩/ {a, o, u, y, C}   as in: gavé /ga'v-e/ 'to take out'
  2. ⟨gh⟩/ elsewhere   ghëddo /'gəddu/ 'good manners'

[m] a voiced bilabial nasal stop, always written ⟨m⟩. It can occur in all positions. E.g.: mnis /mniz/ 'garbage'; amis /a'miz/ 'friend;' aram /a'ram/ 'copper'

[n̪] a voiced dental nasal stop. In transcriptions plain /n/ will be used. It is written ⟨nn⟩ in word-final position unless preceded by a glide (where it is rare) and ⟨n⟩ elsewhere. E.g.:
  1. ⟨nn⟩ / _ #   as in: ann /an/ 'year;' brenn /bræn/ 'bran'
  2. ⟨n⟩ / elsewhere   nas /naz/ 'nose'

[ɲ] a voiced palatal nasal stop, orthographically ⟨gn⟩. It can occur in every position, although it is rare word-finally; gnard /ɲard/ 'mincing; looking for wheedlings (said of a child)'; cavagna /ka'vaɲa/ 'basket;' aragn /a'raɲ/ 'spider'

[ŋ] a voiced velar nasal stop whose phonemic status will be discussed at length below and in 3.5.4. It does not appear word-initially. It is orthographically expressed:
  1. ⟨n-⟩ / V_V   as in: cun-a /'kyŋa/ 'crib'
  2. ⟨m⟩ / {b, p}   ambrassé /aŋbra'se/ 'to hug'
  3. ⟨n⟩ / elsewhere   pjen /pjæŋ/ 'full'

[tʃ] a voiceless palato-alveolar affricate; orthographically written:
  1. ⟨cc⟩ / _ #   as in: baricc /ba'ritʃ/ 'squint-eyed'
  2. ⟨c⟩/ _ {e, i, ë}   cesa /'tʃeza/ 'church;' cëmmi /tʃəm'mi/ 'to smoulder'
  3. ⟨ci⟩ / elsewhere   ciòca /'tʃoka/ 'bell'

---

but no morphological glosses are given in order not to encumber reading. E.g., the gloss of dagné /da'ɲ-e/ 'to drip' is 'drip-INF'.

PHONETICS AND PHONOLOGY 61

[ʤ] a voiced palatoalveolar affricate; orthographically written:
1. ⟨gg⟩ / _ # as in: *magg* /maʤ/ 'May'
2. ⟨g⟩ / _ {e, i, ë} *givo* /'ʤivu/ 'cockchafer; (cigarette) butt'
3. ⟨gi⟩ / elsewhere *gieugh* /ʤøg/ 'play, game'

[f] a voiceless labiodental fricative, consistently written ⟨f⟩ and occurring in any position, but rare word-finally. Eg.: *fi* /fi/ 'fig;' *scufia* /'skyfja/ 'head-dress, cap;' *tuf* /tyf/ 'sultriness'

[s] a voiceless alveolar sibilant fricative, rendered orthographically either with ⟨s⟩ or ⟨ss⟩:
1. ⟨ss⟩ / { #, V_V, _j } as in: *pess* /pes/ 'piece' (cf. below *pes* 'worse')
   rossa /'rus-a/ 'red (Singular Feminine)'
   ressia /'resja/ 'saw'
2. ⟨s⟩ / elsewhere *sal* /sal/ 'salt'

[v] a voiced labiodental fricative, consistently written ⟨v⟩ and occurring in any position. E.g.: *vagné* /va'ɲe/ 'to win;' word-finally it usually shifts to /w/ (see below): *luv* /lyv ~ lyw/ 'wolf'

[z] a voiced alveolar sibilant fricative; its orthographical expression is ⟨s⟩ word-finally and between vowels (i.e., the opposite of /s/) and ⟨z⟩ word-initially. It is a much rarer phoneme than its voiceless counterpart:
1. ⟨s⟩ / { #, V_V} as in: *pes* /pez/ 'worse' (cf. above *pess* 'piece')
   reusa /'røza/ 'rose'
2. ⟨z⟩ / elsewhere *zenziva* /zæŋ'ziva/ '(dental) gum'

[r] more commonly a voiced alveolar trill, orthographically ⟨r⟩. E.g.: *ronza* /'runza/ 'blackberry bush.' It often has a uvular point of articulation, either trill [ʀ] or fricative [ʁ]. The uvular articulation carries no regional or social stigma—and the uvular fricative may even be classy (or snobby).

The approximant alveolar /ɹ/

Piedmontese dialects often display a richer phonological inventory than the koine's. They may have phonemes unknown to the koine but widely attested in other Gallo-Italic, Occitan or French varieties, such us /ʎ/, /ʃ/, /ʒ/, and so on. On the other hand, many Southern varieties from the Monfrà to Monregalèis valleys show a phoneme completely unknown to the surrounding languages (except in some Ligurian dialects): an approximant alveolar ⟨ř⟩ /ɹ/ (Telmon 2001: 74). Berruto (1974: 32) describes this pronunciation as 'non-vibrant,' and discusses its phonological status vs. both /r/ and /l/. The functional efficiency of the minimum phonological pair /r/~/ɹ/ is not very high; still, a few minimal pairs occur: *sra* /sra/ 'closed' vs. *sřa* /sɹa/ '(it) will be' (the two homophonous and homographic *sarà* in common Piedmontese), and *pla* /pla/ 'bald' (the same in common Piedmontese, written *pla*) vs. *přa* /pɹa/ 'meadow' (elsewhere *pra* /pra/), or, still, *maria* /ma'ria/ 'bad' (Feminine) vs. *Mařia* /ma'ɹia/ 'Mary.' In this phoneme both intervocalic etymological L and R merge: PALA(M) > *pařa* /'paɹa/ 'shovel,' and FERIA(M) > *feřa* /'feɹa/ 'fair,' SCHOLA(M) > *scòřa* /'skɔɹa/ 'school' and SCALA(M) > *scařa* /'skaɹa/ 'stairs' like MATRE(M) > *mařa* /'maɹe/ 'mother.' It can be noted that, although often written ⟨ř⟩ by local poets and lexicographers of Southern varieties, many others use to write simply *pala, fera, scòla, scala, mare* according to the etymological origin and following the orthography of the corresponding forms in the koine.

[w]   a rounded labial-velar central voiced approximant; a rare phoneme (and somehow of dubious phonemic status) that does not appear word-initially, it is written ⟨u⟩, especially after ⟨q⟩ and, inconsistently, ⟨o⟩ when preceding /a/: *quand* /kwaŋd/ 'when;' *vidoa* /'vidwa/ 'widow'. Word-finally it may sometimes be written ⟨v⟩: *ciav* /tʃaw/ 'key'

[j]   a rounded palatal central voiced approximant, written ⟨i⟩ before a stressed vowel and ⟨j⟩ elsewhere:
   1. ⟨i⟩ / _ V'   as in: *fià* /fja/ 'breath;' *ier* (but also *jer*) /jer/ 'yesterday'
   2. ⟨j⟩ / elsewhere   *baj* /baj/ 'yawn'

[l]   a voiced dental or alveolar lateral approximant, orthographically ⟨l⟩. Dentality is not marked in the phonological transcription. E.g.: *laver* /'laver/ 'lip;' *maleur* /ma'lør/ 'misfortune;' *gal* /gal/ 'rooster'

Final trill and lateral dropping

Word-final /r/ and /l/ are often dropped in most varieties, and often in the koine, too. Thus, *dil* 'finger' is most commonly /di/—and therefore homophonous with *di* 'day,' with *dij* as the combination of the Attributive preposition *ëd* (☞ 13.5.) and the Determiner Plural *ij* (☞ 8.2.3.), and with both the Infinitive and the Imperative Plural of the Verb 'to say.' Likewise, *mercol* /ˈmærkul/ 'Wednesday,' *sartor* /sarˈtur/ 'tailor,' *sotror* /sutˈrur/ 'gravedigger,' and the like are often /ˈmærku, sutˈru, sarˈtu/, etc. The process is apparently lexically determined; in particular, the word-final segment of most monosyllabic words, e.g., *sal* /sal/ 'salt' or *fior* /fjur/ 'flower' is rarely dropped (but cf. *dil* /di/ 'finger' above).

[i] a close front unrounded vowel, orthographically ⟨*i*⟩. E.g.: *bie* /ˈbi-e/ 'marbles.' In many cases written etymologically ⟨*ij*⟩, as in *fija* /fia/ 'girl, daughter'

[y] a close front rounded vowel, orthographically ⟨*u*⟩. E.g., *dur* /dyr/ 'hard.' It is instead [i] or close to [i] in the Monfrà and Langhe dialects of South Piedmont (yielding an interesting typological counterexample to the strong tendency for a close-mid front rounded vowel [ø] to imply a corresponding high [y]; ☞ 18.2.).

[e] a close-mid front unrounded vowel, its orthographic expression intermingles with that for /æ/. In particular, it is written ⟨*é*⟩ when stressed in word-final position and when stressed before a word-final syllable ending in a consonant; it is ⟨*e*⟩ elsewhere:
1. ⟨*é*⟩ /e/ /{ˈ_#, _r #, ˈ_CVC #}
                  as in: *maslé* /mazˈle/ 'butcher'
                            séler /ˈseler/ 'celery'
2. ⟨*e*⟩ / elsewhere   *let* /let/ 'bed'

[ø] a close-mid front (or in certain varieties open-mid front [œ]) rounded vowel, always written with the digraph ⟨*eu*⟩. It is found in stressed syllable only. E.g.: *beu* /bø/ 'ox'

[ə] a central unrounded vowel, written ⟨*ë*⟩; it never occurs word-finally. E.g.: *ël* /əl/ 'the' (DET), *për* /pər/ 'for' (BEN), *majëtta* /maˈjətta/ 't-shirt'

[æ] a raised low front (or in certain varieties open-mid front [ɛ]) unrounded vowel is written either ⟨*è*⟩ or ⟨*e*⟩, and in particular (with N standing for a nasal):
1. ⟨*e*⟩ /_ {N, r}   as in: *ten-e* /ˈtæŋe/ 'to hold,' *fer* /fær/ 'iron'
2. ⟨*è*⟩ / elsewhere   *rè* /ræ/ 'king'

The orthography of /e/ and /æ/ is subject to many inconsistencies and downright irregularities, on which more will be said below. In particular, only when stressed and in word-final position are [e] and the following [æ] consistently marked with an accent; this follows the rules of the Italian orthography, whereby word-final stressed vowels are marked with an accent mark.

[a] an open central unrounded vowel, generally open back unrounded [ɑ] when stressed. In the phonological transcription /a/ will be used throughout. Orthographically, it is generally written ⟨a⟩, as in *sangh* /saŋg/ 'blood;' sometimes it is written ⟨ë⟩ (Clivio 1992: 160fn.) and at least in the case of the Classifier *un* /aŋ/ 'a' (☞ 8.2.) as ⟨u⟩. The pronunciation as open back seems more common and the basic allophone; front [a] and back rounded [ɒ] allophones are found as a result of vowel harmony processes and/or as local variants.

Phonological back /a/ (/ɑ/, /ɒ/)
Stressed /a/ usually have a more backward pronunciation that unstressed ones: a word like *rata* 'she-mouse' may sound /ˈrata/ or /ˈrɑta/ or even /ˈrɒta/ depending on various factors, such as individual habits, rural-non rural environment and so on. In particular, as discussed by Berruto (1974), the back varieties seem typical of the Southern varieties. In some of these varieties, a phonological opposition between /a/ and /ɑ/ or /ɒ/ has arisen. When writing in these varieties, Piedmontese authors have introduced a supplementary grapheme ⟨ä⟩ that symbolizes both /ɑ/ or /ɒ/: *värda!* /ˈvɒrd-a/ 'take a look!' (Imperative form of the Verb *vardé*) vs *varda* /ˈvard-a/ 'green' (Singular Feminine). Other minimal pairs are /ɒt/ 'tall' (elsewhere *àut* /awt/) and /at/ 'act' (in the koine written *at*), or *pa'* /pɒ/ 'pole' (common Piedmontese *pal* /pal/) vs. *pa* /pa/ 'not (NEG.EMPH).'

[ɔ] an open-mid (or in certain varieties close-mid [o]) back rounded vowel. In the phonological transcription /o/ will be used. Orthographically it is expressed by ⟨ò⟩ and is almost always stressed. E.g.: *còl* /kol/ 'neck' (cf. below *col*). It is irregularly written ⟨o⟩ in the very common disjunctive conjunction ⟨o⟩ /o/ 'or;' /o/ is on the whole rare and /u/ stands for most neighboring languages' /o/s—a feature which gives Piedmontese a "dark" or back quality.

[u]   a close back rounded vowel; often near-close near-back rounded [ʊ] (Ricca 2016). Orthographically ⟨o⟩. E.g.: *col* /kul/ 'that, the one over there.' As /o/ is instead written ⟨ò⟩, the question remains how to mark a stressed /u/; the somewhat cumbersome solution (in dictionaries and grammars) is to use an acute accent (⟨ó⟩): *otóber* /uˈtubær/ 'October.'

Medio-palatal occlusive phonemes

In some Valsesian varieties both the voiceless /c/ and voiced medio-palatal occlusives /ɟ/ are attested, from Latin CL (*chjaf* /caf/ 'key;' *orëgghja* /uˈrəj:a/ 'ear') and CT (*lachj* /lac/ 'milk'); they are oftentimes expressed with ⟨chj⟩ and ⟨ghj⟩. This is clearly linked to the different distribution of palatal sounds in varieties from the Valsesia, where the affricate sounds /tʃ/ and /dʒ/ are often found in the same position they occupy in Italian: *cena* /ˈtʃena/ instead of *sin-a* /ˈsiŋa/ 'dinner,' *dòcc* /dɔtʃ/ instead of *doss* /dus/ 'sweet.'

The same phoneme can be found in a single variety of the South-Western valleys, i.e., Valàuria,[2] at the linguistic border between Piedmontese and Occitan dialects: *grichj* /gric/ instead of *gril* /gril/ 'cricket,' *pagghja* /ˈpaj:a/ instead of *paja* /ˈpaja/ 'straw,' *orëgghja* /uˈrəj:a/ instead of *orija* /uˈrija/ 'ear,' *figghja* /ˈfij:a/ instead of *fija* /ˈfia/ 'daughter, girl.'

Attention is drawn to the following phonological transcription conventions:

[t̪]   phonological transcription: /t/
[d̪]   phonological transcription: /d/
[n̪]   phonological transcription: /n/
[ɑ]   phonological transcription: /a/
[ɔ]   phonological transcription: /o/

2.2   Loan Phonemes, Borrowing and Adaptation

In heavily Italianized speech, the Italian palato-alveolar voiceless fricative /ʃ/ may be retained instead of being shifted to /s/. Different is the case of the palato-alveolar affricates /tʃ/ and /dʒ/, whose place in the phonemic inventory of Piedmontese has been extended by borrowing, especially in word-initial position. Dozens of couplets are nowadays established. In the following examples, the first is the native form, the second an Italianism:

---

2   Valàuria /vaˈlawrja/, Italian Valloriate /valloˈrjate/ (44°20′N 07°22′E).

sercc /ˈsærtʃ/ ~ *cercc* /ˈtʃærtʃ/ 'circle'
serv /ˈsærv/ ~ *cerv* /ˈtʃærv/ 'deer' (the first homophonous with *serv* 'servant')
sénter /ˈsenter/ ~ *cénter* /ˈtʃenter/ 'center'

Other alternations go back to a double borrowing, earlier from French and later from Italian:[3]

siman /siˈmaŋ/ ~ *ciman* /tʃiˈmaŋ/ ~ *cement* /tʃeˈmænt/ 'concrete'

The following correspondences generally hold true for the adaptation of recent borrowings from Italian:

1. Italian /u/ → /y/
   Italian *super* /ˈsuper/ → *super* /ˈsyper/ 'super'

2. Italian /o/ → /u/
   Italian *socialista* /sotʃaˈlista/ → *socialista* /sutʃaˈlista/ 'socialist'

   but a stressed /o/ is preserved as such:

   Italian /ˈo/ → /o/
   Italian *logico* /ˈlodʒiko/ → *lògich* /ˈlodʒik/ 'logical'

   With recent borrowings the most common behavior is to shift, regularly, all unstressed /o/ to /u/, but Italianization may result in an unstressed /o/ being preserved, especially in word-final position:

   Italian *sciopero* /ˈʃopero/ → *siòpero* /ˈsjoperu/, but also /ˈsjopero/ 'strike'
   (and also, with further Italianization, just unassimilated /ˈʃopero/).
   Italian *moto* /ˈmoto/ → *mòto* /ˈmotu/, but maybe more frequently /ˈmoto/ 'motorbike'

3. Italian /e/ (either [ɛ] or [e] in the Italian of Piedmont) shifts to either /e/ or to /æ/ except when followed by a geminate consonant, in which case it is changed to /ə/:

---

3 Heavy interference of Italian started probably in the early 19th century. Dictionaries of that period already note a few /s/ ~ /tʃ/ pairs (Clivio 1976: 98). In this case, the earlier loan is better accommodated into the phonology of Piedmontese (Clivio 1976: 97).

Italian *fermezza* /fer'mettsa/ → *fërmëssa* /fər'məssa/
'steadfastness'

A word-final /e/ is normally deleted:

Italian *insolazione* /insola'tsjone/ → *insolassion* /iŋsula'sjuŋ/
'sun-stroke'

4. other vowels (It. /a/ and /i/) do not undergo changes (see above *insolassion* 'sun-stroke')

Among consonants, apart from the optional retention of /ʃ/ and /tʃ/, /dʒ/, the following correspondences hold true:

5. Italian /n/ is velarized word-finally and before consonants (see above *insolassion* 'sun-stroke');

6. Italian /ʎ/ (palatal lateral) is a rare phoneme; examples of recently-borrowed Italian words containing it are difficult to find, but on the whole /ʎ/ seems to be either retained (in heavily-Italianized speech), or shifted to /j/ (as in the cognates of Italian /ʎ/ from Latin /l/ + palatal vowel; e.g.: Italian *paglia* /'paʎa/, Piedmontese *paja* /'paja/ 'straw' from Latin *palea*). On the other hand, dialectal remnants of /ʎ/ are attested locally (AIS map 1334) and may be phonological, with minimal or semi-minimal pairs attested.

7. the Italian affricate written ⟨z⟩—always a single phoneme realized as either voiced /dz/ or voiceless /ts/ according to context in the Northern accents of Italian—always loses its stop component and is shifted to /z/ word-initially and to /s/ word-internally:

Italian *zelante* /dze'lante/ → *zelant* /ze'lant/ 'zealous'
Italian *prenotazione* /prenota'tsjone/ → *prenotassion* /prenota'sjuŋ/
'reservation'

8. Italian orthographic ⟨s⟩ is a phoneme realized as voiceless /s/ word-initially and voiced /z/ word-internally in the Piedmontese accent of Italian; the same correspondence holds true for recent borrowings:

Italian *successo* /sut'tʃesso/ → *sucess* /sy'tʃes/ 'success'
Italian *casuale* /ka'zwale/ → *casual* /ka'zwal/ 'casual'

9. all Italian geminate consonants are reduced in Piedmontese, except for Feminine diminutives in *-etta*, to which correspond in Piedmontese *-ëssa* /-əssa/ and *-ëtta* /-ətta/ (☞ 2.7.2.6.).

2.3 Previous Accounts of the Phonology of Piedmontese

The first scientific accounts of the phonology of Piedmontese date back to the late 1940s. Soffietti's (1949) early description of Turinese (basically, the koine) includes 8 vowels and 18 consonants:

TABLE 4   The Piedmontese inventory of consonants according to Soffietti (1949: 17; adapted by Garvin 1951: 193)

Vowels	Grave	Bipolar acute-grave	Acute
Loud	a	ë	
Bipolar loudness	o	ö	e
Non-loud	u	ü	i

Consonants					Non-loud		Loud	
					Acute	Grave	Acute	Grave
Non-liquid	Non-nasal	Stop	Unvoiced	t	p	č	k
			Voiced	d	b	j	g
		Constrictive	Unvoiced	s	f		
			Voiced	z	v		
	Nasal			n	m	ñ	ŋ
Liquid	Non-intermittent		l				
	Intermittent		r				

Clivio's (1964: 3) first increased the number of vocalic phonemes to nine, and the number of consonantal phonemes to twenty, by including amongst the consonantal phonemes /j/, and also /stʃ/, graphically represented by ⟨s-ci⟩ (sic). /w/ was not considered an autonomous phoneme by Soffietti nor by Clivio. The difference between Soffietti's and Clivio's vowel descriptions lies in the phonemic status accorded by the latter to /æ/ vs /e/.

Berruto (1974: 17), on the other hand, sides with Clivio as to the number and quality of vocalic phonemes, but with Soffietti in relation to the number and type of consonantal phonemes; in the end, Berruto's inventory includes nine vowels and 18 consonants.

Telmon (1988: 476) maintains Soffietti's proposal, while Parry (1997: 239–240), Clivio (1988), Clivio (2002: 160–162), and Ronco (2016: xxxv) follow Berruto's. Clivio (2002: 162) also confirms 18 consonantal phonemes for the koine, but /j/ and /stʃ/ are not included among the consonantal repertoire any more.

Ricca (2016: 7) increases the number of consonantal phonemes to twenty, by adding /w/ and /j/.

To sum up, in all the recent accounts /æ/ and /e/ appear as distinct phonemes, albeit with a low phonemic load. The same holds for /ə/ vs. /æ/, by virtue of the existence of "at least two minimal pairs:" chërpo /(i=)'kərp-u/ '(I) crack up, snuff it' vs chèrpo /'kærpu/ 'hornbeam,' and tërsa /'tərsa/ 'braid' vs. tersa /'tærs-a/ 'third (Singular Feminine)' (Clivio 2002: 159).

Previous descriptions are not unanimous as regards the phonetic realization of the following phonemes: /ø/, /a/, /æ/ and /u/. This is partly due to the lack of reliable phonetic analyses of the koine.

/ø/ is said to be prevalently realized as [ø] by Berruto (1974), Telmon (1988), Parry (1997). Clivio (2002) and Ronco (2016) indicate that is rather pronounced as a mid-low [œ]. So do Grassi, Sobrero and Telmon (1997: 95–96). Ricca (2016: 6) gives /œ/ as a phoneme, realized by two allophones, [œ] and [ø], in a regime of free distribution. Clivio's (1964: 3) description of the phoneme reads: "a higher mid rounded front vowel."

As Parry (1997: 239), a.o., points out, stressed /a/ is realized as [ɑ] (and even [ɒ] in the Monfrà dialects). This realization of /a/ also emerges in the variety of Italian spoken in Piedmont (see Canepari 1980). According to Ricca (2016: 6), it happens only in some varieties, while the average realization is [a]. Clivio (1976: 110), on the contrary, indicates /ɑ/ as only low vocalic phoneme in koine Piedmontese, and assumes [ɑ] to be its most frequent allophone.

The most frequent realization of /æ/ is alternatively described as [ɛ] or [æ], but, as seen before, Soffietti (1949) and the scholars following his phonetic sketch do not give /æ/ a phonemic status.

Finally, according to Ricca (2016: 6) the most frequent realization of the high back rounded /u/ is [ʊ].

For what concerns consonants, let aside the recent acknowledgement of /j/ and /w/ as phonemes and not just allophones of /i/ and /u/, the only inconsistencies in previous accounts concern the realization of /r/. In this connection, only Clivio (2002: 161–162) notes that it (often) has a uvular point of articulation, just as [ʀ] *à la française*, even though some speakers pronounce a fully alveolar [r]. All other scholars consider the alveolar as the most common realization.

2.4 Phonetic Processes

The presentation of phonetic processes is couched in a broad Natural framework. Central to this approach is the distinction between rules and processes. The latter are fully automatic, exceptionless changes, which are inherent to the language and apply whenever their structural description is met. Rules, on the other hand, are changes which are either lexically or morphologically conditioned.

Under the heading of Phonological Processes (PPs) not only fully phonological changes—i.e., those which change the phonological status of a unit or a group of units—are listed, but also allophonic processes, which account for the realizations of phonemes different from the default ones stated in the preceding sections.

Notwithstanding this Natural approach, in the following sections PPs are formalized in a manner reminiscent of the phonological rules of generative phonology. Processes are numbered for ease of reference only, without any implication of extrinsic ordering—which is excluded by definition.

Purely allomorphic rules are instead excluded and are considered in the relevant sections in the grammar.

The following Phonetic Processes (PPs) will be discussed:

PP 1. CENTRALIZATION-1 (☞ 2.4.1.1.)
PP 2. CENTRALIZATION-2 (☞ 2.4.1.1.)
PP 3. EPENTHESIS (☞ 2.4.1.2.)
PP 4. DROPPING (☞ 2.4.1.3.)
PP 5. BACK RAISING (☞ 2.4.1.4.)
PP 6. CLOSING (☞ 2.4.1.5.)
PP 7. GLIDING (☞ 2.4.2.1.)
PP 8. DELETION (☞ 2.4.2.2.)
PP 9. DELATERALIZATION (☞ 2.4.2.3.)
PP 10. FINAL DEVOICING (☞ 2.4.3.)
PP 11. DEVELARIZATION (☞ 2.4.4.1.)
PP 12. CLUSTER REDUCTION (☞ 2.4.4.2.)

2.4.1 *Vowels*

The phonetic processes affecting vowels can be graphically represented as follows:

PHONETICS AND PHONOLOGY   71

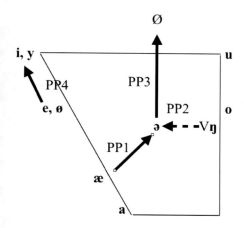

FIGURE 4
Phonetic processes affecting vowels

2.4.1.1   Centralization
Both /e/ and /æ/ have doubtlessly phonemic status, although exact minimal pairs are rare; the following three are common:

Chér /ker/	(a town name)	vs.	*cher*	/kær/	'cart, wagon'
pess /pes/	'piece'	vs.	*pèss*	/pæs/	'fish'
pet /pet/	'(male) breast'	vs.	*pèt*	/pæt/	'fart'
vera /ˈvera/	'wedding ring'	vs.	*vèra*	/ˈværa/	'true'

The vowel /ə/ (orthographic ⟨ë⟩) is centralized, and phonetically rather different from French *e muet* (although Piedmontese speakers pronounce the *e muet* as /ə/ when speaking French). Among Romance languages, its closest correspondent is possibly the phoneme written ⟨î⟩ in Romanian (cf. Villata 1995: 8). It is extremely common and certainly phonemic, although subject to a number of restrictions:
- it is never found in word-final position (except at the phonetic level after the operation of an optional process of vowel-centralization), nor
- adjacent to another vowel, nor
- as first vowel in CVCV words.

A /e/ vs. /ə/ quasi-minimal pair is:

pessa /ˈpesa/ 'roll of cloth'   vs.   *pëssa* /ˈpəssa/ 'white fir'

More commonly, /æ/ and /ə/ are in regular alternation: /ə/'s most common position is before a consonant cluster in its turn followed by a vowel and most instances of /ə/ occur when this condition arises out of various suffixation rules. In particular, whenever to a word ending in /æ/ followed by a consonant cluster (__æCC #) a further vowel is suffixed (and resyllabification ensues), /æ/ changes into /ə/:

PP 1. CENTRALIZATION-1: æ → ə / _CCV

A typical application of this process is found in the Feminine form of Adjectives:

verd /værd/ (and [vært]; s. below PP 8) vs. *vërda* /ˈvərd-a/ 'green'
(Masculine vs. Feminine Singular)

the same process is found in derivation:

vërdastr   /vərˈdastr/   'greenish'

The process is not found in all varieties: certain have a central vowel in all the forms of a lexeme, others have /æ/ and no vocalic alternation occurs. In a few cases lexical doublets are found with both /æ/ and /ə/ before CC:

senté = *sënté*   /sæŋˈte ~ səŋˈte/   'path'

As anticipated and as already shown by Clivio (1992: 159), /æ/ and /ə/ are nevertheless distinct phonemes:

C__CC: (*a*) *chërd* /(a=)kərd/ 'it believes' vs.
(*a*) *perd* /(a=)pærd/ 'it loses'

sëstin-a /səˈstiɲa/ 'small basket' vs.
sestin-a /sæˈstiɲa/ 'six-line stanza'

C_ˈ_C: *chërde* /ˈkərde/ 'to believe' vs.
perde /ˈpærde/ 'to lose'

C___C: *chërdù* /kərˈdy/ 'believed' vs.
perdù /pærˈdy/ 'lost'

The process applies also in the adaptation of Italian borrowings:

Italian *correttezza* /korretˈtettsa/ → *coretëssa* /kureˈtəssa/ 'correctness'

PHONETICS AND PHONOLOGY   73

Vowel centralization does not occur with other vowels followed by a consonant cluster:

ressia /ˈresja/ 'saw'

An unrelated decentralization process appears in word-initial position and affects a pretonic word-initial vowel followed by /ŋ/, which is optionally centralized to [ə] in fast speech:

PP 2. CENTRALIZATION-2: #VˈX → ə / _ŋˈX

ansari /aŋsaˈri/ → [əŋsaˈri] 'hoarse'

The process most commonly applies within phonological words, e.g., between a Grounder and a Noun:

un can /aŋ kaŋ/ → [əŋ kaŋ] 'a dog'

2.4.1.2   Epenthesis
An epenthetic /ə/ is inserted in order to avoid an inadmissible consonant cluster (☞ 2.7.2.), represented herebelow as *CC(C):

PP 3. EPENTHESIS: /ə/ / *CC(C)

The process has operated historically in a great number of words (one example among many is *pnansëmmo* /pnaŋˈsəmmu/ 'parsley' from PETROSEMOLUM; cf. Italian *prezzemolo* and French *persil*) and has phonological and even orthographic consequences. The clitic Determiner *ël* /əl/ and its Plural *ij* /i/ and the Indefinite *un* /aŋ/ (☞ 8.2.3.), as well as the Attributive preposition *ëd* /əd/ (☞ 13.5.), all have allomorphic forms *dë, jë, në, dë* with dropping of the initial vowel and insertion of a final /ə/, used before a word with initial consonant cluster:

ël cheur /əl=ˈkør/ 'the heart'   vs.   *lë stòmi* /lə=ˈstomi/ 'the stomach'

In obsolete spellings, words with an inadmissible consonant cluster were likewise written with an initial, often not-capitalized in the case of proper Nouns, prosthetic ⟨ë⟩,[4] as in *an ëSvissera* /aŋ=əˈzvisera/ for *an Svissera* /aŋ=ˈzvisera/ 'in Switzerland' (☞ 3.1.5.).

---
4   The same was true of older, pre-World War 2 spellings of Italian.

2.4.1.3   Dropping

A word-initial pretonic central vowel /ə/ is optionally deleted in fast speech both utterance-initially and after a vowel-final word:

PP 4. DROPPING: /ə/ → Ø / {#_X, _V#}

After a vowel-final word this process has been lexicalized in the context forms of the Masculine Singular article *ël* 'the' and the preposition *ëd* 'of'—where they are written *'l* and *'d*, respectively (unless the following word begins with a vowel—in which case *ël* and *ëd* are written *l'* and *d'*, respectively; ☞ 8.2.3.):

fé 'l pito   /fe l='pitu/   'to complain for nothing' [to do the turkey]
na bala 'd fum   /na='bala d=fym/   'a trifle' [a ball of smoke]

vs.

pien ëd fum   /pjæŋ əd=fym/ (*/pjæŋ d=fym/)   'haughty' [full of smoke]

Vowel-deletion applies to both phonological and phonetic [ə]s—i.e., derived from the application of the Vowel-Centralization process (PP1). E.g.:

ancalesse   /aŋka'le=se/ → [əŋ=ka'lese] → [ŋka'lese]   'to dare'

The vowel of the indeterminate article *un* /yŋ/ first undergoes centralization to [əŋ] (PP 2.) and is then dropped both utterance-finally and after a vowel-final word. Again, the result of the process finds its orthographical expression in the form *'n* (*n'* before a vowel):

fé 'n boro   /fe ŋ='bur u/   'to make an error'

Both vowel-centralization and vowel-dropping apply also to *an* /aŋ/ 'in,' reducing it to /ŋ/; in order to keep them orthographically separate, this is never written *'n*:

andé an campagna   /aŋ'de ŋ=kam'paɲa/   'to go to the countryside.'

2.4.1.4   Back Raising

As /o/ (phonetically an open-mid back rounded [ɔ]) only occurs in stressed position, any /o/ is raised to close back rounded /u/ under stress loss:

PP 5. BACK RAISING: /o/ → /u/ / _ ' v

còl /kol/ 'neck' → colet /kuˈlæt/ 'collar'

This process has particularly momentous consequences in verbal morphology:

pòrta /ˈport-a/ 'bring (s)!' vs. porté /purˈt-e/ 'to bring.'

2.4.1.5   Closing
This process is not really part of the phonology of the koine but is very typical of many varieties, especially in the South and East. The process applies to every word-final unstressed /e/ closing it to /i/:

PP 6. CLOSING: /e/ → /i/ / ' X _ #

| roe | /ˈru-e/ | → | [ˈrui] | 'wheels' |
| cheurb-te | /ˈkørb=te/ | → | [ˈkørbti] | 'cover (s) yourself!' |

2.4.2 *Approximants*
Contrary to previous analyses (cf. Berruto 1974: 14), glides—called here central approximants following Laver (1994: 148)—are given phonemic status on the basis of their phonotactic behavior. E.g., /j/ occurs next to /ə/, which is never found in the immediate proximity of another vowel; while a sequence /jə/ is possible, and actually found (see below), a sequence /iə/ or /əi/ is excluded:

majëtta   /maˈjətta/   't-shirt'

However, the phonological status of /w/ is not beyond doubt, given its overall rarity (most occurrences of phonetic [w] are the result of an optional process turning /v/ into [w] in certain positions; see below). Again, /w/ is found with a following /ə/, such as in:

aquëtta   /aˈkwətta/   'drizzle; (fig.) light wine.'

2.4.2.1   Gliding
An optional process changes a labiodental voiced fricative into a labiovelar central approximant in word-final and pre-consonant position:

PP 7. GLIDING: v ~ w /{_#, _C}

nav	/nav/ [naw]	'ship'
neuv	/nøv/ [nøw]	'nine; new'
gavte	/ˈgav=te/ [ˈgawte]	'get lost!' [put yourself away]

2.4.2.2 Deletion

Both approximants may undergo deletion, especially in fast speech: a palatal approximant is optionally but commonly deleted when occurring before a vowel after a close unrounded vowel /i/; a labiovelar approximant is optionally deleted when occurring before a vowel after a close rounded vowel (/u/ or /y/):

PP 8. DELETION: a. j → Ø / i _V; b. w → Ø / {u, y} _V

The process has been partially lexicalized, and accounts for many orthographic instances of ⟨ij⟩ corresponding to /i/ in pronunciation, as in:

fi(j)a	/ˈfija ~ ˈfia/	'girl'
ch'a ri(j)a	/(k=a=)ˈria/	'let him laugh'
pijé	/pj-e/	'to take'

With a labiovelar approximant the process is applied to the result of Gliding (PP 6.). Again, the process has been lexicalized in a few cases:

co(v)	/kuv/ ~ [kuw]	→ /ku/	'whetstone'
ruvé	/ryˈve/ ~ [ryˈwe]	→ [ryˈe]	'to arrive'

(the variant *rivé* /riˈve/ of course does not undergo any of these processes)

2.4.2.3 Delateralization

In many varieties—especially Southern—/l/ loses its laterality and is centralized to [ɹ] post-consonantally. In this case /l/ is also more alveolar than dental:

PP 9. DELATERALIZATION: /l/ → [ɹ] / C

cogg-lo	/ˈkudʒ=l-u/	→	[ˈkudʒɹu] 'lie it down!'
vard-la	/ˈvard=l-a/	→	[ˈvardɹa] 'look at her!'

2.4.3 Final Devoicing

As many other languages, Piedmontese may undergo Final Devoicing, i.e., all obstruents are realized as voiceless in word-final position, irrespective of

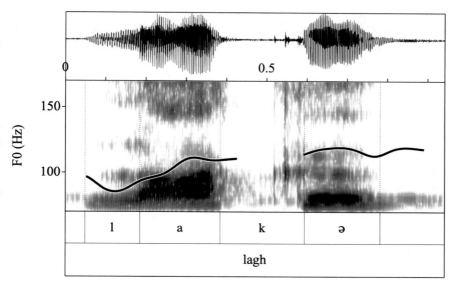

FIGURE 5　Final devoicing in *lagh* /*lag*/ 'lake' (male speaker born near Turin in 1947)

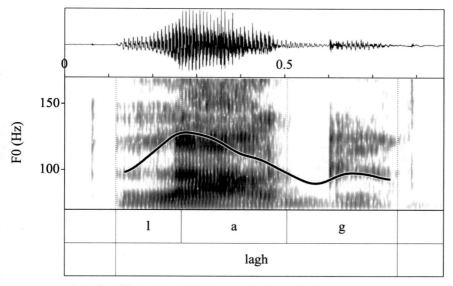

FIGURE 6　*lagh* /*lag*/ 'lake' with no final devoicing (male speaker born in Turin in 1956)

whether they are underlyingly voiced or voiceless. Final Devoicing is completely absent in some areas of Piedmont but in the Central-western varieties voiced consonants with the exception of /v/ (for which see 2.4.2) are devoiced word-finally:

PP 10. FINAL DEVOICING: {b, d, g, z, dʒ} → {p, t, k, s, tʃ} / _#

gheub	/gøb/	→	[gøp]	'hunchbacked' (Masculine)
verd	/værd/	→	[vært]	'green' (Masculine)
largh	/larg/	→	[lark]	'wide' (Masculine)
formagg	/fur'madʒ/	→	[fur'matʃ]	'cheese'
pes	/pez/	→	[pes]	'worse'

2.4.4 Nasals and the Status of /ŋ/

The velar nasal consonant /ŋ/ is subject to a number of positional restrictions:
– it is never found word-initially;
– word-internally is found in intervocalic position after a stressed vowel only:

lun-a /'lyŋa/ 'moon'

in this same position /n/ is very rarely found. A minimal pair is:

cana /'kana/ 'stick' vs. *can-a* /'kaŋa/ 'white hair' (rare)

both can be further opposed to

cagna /'kaɲa/ 'bitch'

yielding a triple /ŋ ~ n ~ ɲ/ opposition.

A process of nasal assimilation has yielded in certain dialects a few minimal pairs, in which the word-final palatal nasal goes back historically to a plural suffix *-i:

ann /an/ 'year' vs. /aɲ/ 'years' (< *ani* /'a.ni/, also attested)

In a few cases, probably reflecting different regional dialects, /ŋ/ and /n/ are in free variation:

cun-i /'kyŋi/ and *cuni* /'kyni/ 'wedge'

PHONETICS AND PHONOLOGY

– c. /ŋ/ is very common word-finally, where /n/ is very rare, but a few minimal pairs do exist:

an	/aŋ/	'in'	vs.	ann	/an/	'year'
ton	/tuŋ/	'tone'	vs.	tonn	/tun/	'tuna fish'
pan	/paŋ/	'bread'	vs.	pann	/pan/	'cloth'
(a) dan	/(a=)daŋ/	'they give'	vs.	dann	/dan/	'damage'

If one disregards these few examples (it could be further claimed that *tonn* /tun/ may well be considered a semi-nativized loan from Italian *tonno* /ˈtonno/) an allophonic realization rule could be proposed under which [ŋ] would be considered an allophone of /n/ in:
– word-final position
– intervocalically after stress
    E.g.:
    /n/ → [ŋ] / vˈ __ v

In certain dialects, many more minimal pairs are produced by the historical loss of many final unstressed /e/, as in:

/n/__#: (*a l'ha*) *pia-ne*   /(a=ˈla) ˈpj-a=ne/ →   /(a=ˈla) pjan/   'he caught us'

contrasting with:

/ŋ/__#:   *pian*   /pjaŋ/   'slow; smooth'

and with:

/m/__#:   *a pia-me*   /(a=ˈla) ˈpja=me/ →   /(a=ˈla) pja=m/   'he caught me'

If on the other hand one considers the—admittedly few—minimal pairs, and the productivity of the /n/ ~ /ŋ/ alternation, it is necessary to consider both /n/ and /ŋ/ as phonemic, although subject to positional restrictions. In particular, allophonic neutralization occurs in the following contexts, in which /ŋ/ only is found:
– before any other consonant—not only velar. It will be noted that before a bilabial consonant, where free alternation between [m] and [ŋ] occurs. In such cases, in the glosses we always transcribe /m/.

tenca	/ˈtæŋka/	'tench'
sens	/sæŋs/	'meaning'
sent	/sæŋt/	'hundred; hear!'
campé	/kamˈp-e/	'to throw'
ambajé	/ambaˈj-e/	'to leave ajar'

– in word-final position:

nen   /næŋ/   'not' (NEG)

The velar nasal is retained even if the following word begins with a vowel:

a l'han otnù   /(a=ˈlaŋ) utˈny/   'they obtained, got'

(the realization [ŋ] for /n/ pre-consonantally and word-finally is also true of the spoken Italian of Piedmont; Canepari 1979: 205).

Sin-a vs. sina
Although the development of a velar nasal in post-tonic intervocalic context is widespread in Piedmont, in some areas and especially in the South it keeps a diachronic marked status, whereby a sequence of velar and dental nasal is found: against *vèn-a* /ˈvæŋa/ 'vein,' *sin-a* /ˈsiŋa/, or *lun-a* /ˈlyŋa/ 'moon' of the koine, one thus finds *vèn-na* /ˈvæŋna/ 'vein,' *sin-na* /ˈsiŋna/, *lun-na* /ˈlyŋna/ 'moon.' Moreover, the velar nasal is not found in certain Western varieties in contact with Occitan, that preserved the etymological nasal dental: *vèna, sina, luna*.

2.4.4.1   Develarization
A velar nasal shifts to dental whenever word stress shifts to the nasal-initial syllable in affixation:

PP 11. DEVELARIZATION: /ŋ/ → /n/ / ˈ_

The contrary process (to have /n/ shift to /ŋ/ in *post-tonic* syllables) is disproved by the—admittedly very few and doubtful—examples of postonic /n/-initial syllables, such as *cana* /ˈkana/ 'stick.'

Vowel Centralization and Vowel Dropping centralize and optionally delete a pretonic vowel closed by /ŋ/—thus creating a word-initial syllabic /ŋ/; e.g.:

ancalésse /aŋkaˈle=se/ 'to dare'
↓
Vowel Centralization-2 (PP 2.) → [əŋkaˈlese]
↓
Vowel Dropping (PP 4.) → [ŋkaˈlese]

Examples of the application of the Develarization process are:

cun-a /ˈkyŋa/ 'crib' → *cun-é* /kyˈn-e/ 'to rock, lull'

Another example is provided by /ŋ/-final Adjectives: the affixation of the Feminine suffixes *-a* (Singular) and *-e* (Plural) preserves /ŋ/; instead, borrowing of the Italian superlative suffix *-issim* (< It. *-issimo*), which is stressed on its first vowel, results in /ŋ/ ~ /n/ alternation:

fin /fiŋ/ 'thin'
fin-a /ˈfiŋ-a/ 'thin (Feminine Singular)'
finissim /fiˈnisim/ 'very thin'

In verbal paradigms application of the Develarization process is triggered by the affixation of different subject suffixes:

i ten-o /(i=)ˈtæŋ-u/ 'I hold'
it ten-e /(it=)ˈtæŋ-e/ 'you (s) hold'
a ten /(a=)ˈtæŋ/ 'he/she holds'
i tnoma /(i=)ˈtn-uma/ (through *tenoma*; a local variant) 'we hold'

2.4.4.2 Cluster Reduction

A triple cluster N-C-N is optionally but generally reduced to N-N in rapid, casual speech. The process yields an otherwise impossible nasal cluster:

PP 12. CLUSTER REDUCTION: NCN → NN

pento /ˈpæntu/ [ˈpæŋtu] 'comb'

but:

pentné (also Southern *pëntné*) /pænˈtne, pənˈtne / → (opt.) [pænˈne, pənˈtne] 'to comb'
pentnòira (also Southern *pëntnòira*) /pænˈtnojra, pənˈtnojra, / → (opt.) [pænˈnojra, pənˈnojra] 'hair-dresser'

2.4.5 Sibilants

As stated above, /z/ is on the whole a rare phoneme; in a word-count, /z/ appeared 21 times out of 502 words (but in a token and items calculation, in only 12 items—considering only once different morphological forms of the same root), i.e., 4.18%.[5]

Word-initially /z/ is rare in native vocabulary; an example is:

zanzij /zanˈzij/   'lust, ardent wish'

and often alternates with /s/:

zabò ~ sabò /zaˈbo ~ saˈbo/   'sabot'

In this position it is mostly found in Italian loans (cf. I.1.2.1.), in which it replaces the Italian affricate /dz/ ~ / ts/:

Italian *zero* /ˈdzero/   →   *zero* /ˈzeru/   'zero'

/z/ is common as first member of consonant cluster whose second member is a voiced stop. Word-internally and finally it contrasts with its voiceless correspondent /s/:

| *bassé* | /baˈs-e/ | 'to lower' | vs. | *basé* | /baˈz-e/ | 'to kiss' |
| *bass* | /bas/ | 'low' | vs. | *bas* | /baz/ | 'kiss' |

2.5 Positional Restrictions on the Occurrence of Phonemes

2.5.1 Consonants
The following restrictions apply:
– word-initially:
  1. the velar nasal stop /ŋ/ does not occur;
  2. the voiced alveolar sibilant fricative /z/ is rare.
– word-finally:
  1. the voiced stops /b/, /d/, /g/ are rare (and they are often devoiced word-finally);

---

5 The text used is the one-page story *Mesaneuit (bate la lorda)* by Dario Pasé (Pich and Pasé 1996: 97).

PHONETICS AND PHONOLOGY

2. the voiceless labiodental fricative /f/ is rare;
3. the central unrounded vowel /ə/ does not occur.

2.5.2 Vowels

All vowels with the exception of /o/ may occur in word-initial position; /ə/ is very rare in this position (but occurs in the Masculine Singular Determiner; ☞ 8.2.):

/i/	istà	/isˈta/	'summer'
/y/	uss	/ys/	'(outside) door'
/e/	eva	/ˈeva/	'water'
/ø/	euj	/øj/	'eye'
/ə/	ël	/əl/	'the' (Determiner)
/æ/	erbo	/ˈærbu/	'tree'
/a/	aso	/ˈazu/	'donkey'
/u/	orìa	/uˈria/	'ear'

All vowels with the exception of /ə/ may occur in word-final position; /æ/ is rare in this position:

/i/	giari	/ˈdʒari/	'rat'
/y/	cru	/kry/	'raw'
/e/	brandé	/branˈde/	'firedog'
/ø/	feu	/fø/	'fire'
/æ/	rè	/ræ/	'king'
/a/	barba	/ˈbarba/	'uncle'
/o/	comò	/kuˈmo/	'chest of drawers'
/u/	caluso	/kaˈlyzu/	'soot'

2.6 Syllables

The canonical syllable has the shape:

(C)(C)(C)V(C)(C)

Null onsets are possible, and words beginning in a vowel (or even composed of a vowel only) are perfectly admissible. The following examples show the possible syllable types in monosyllabic words:

V	e	/e/	'and'
CV	pé	/pe/	'foot'
CCV	fré	/fre/	'blacksmith'
CCCV	stra	/stra/	'road'
VC	ann	/an/	'year'
VCC	arch	/ark/	'bow'
CVC	sal	/sal/	'salt'
CCVC	frel	/frel/	'brother'
CCCVC	strass	/stras/	'rag'
CVCC	sang	/saŋg/	'blood'
CCVCC	bronz	/bruŋz/	'bronze'
CCCVCC	strenz	/stræŋz/	'tighten, squeeze (Singular)!'

2.7 Clusters

2.7.1 Sequences of Vocoids

No phonological diphthongs and triphthongs need to be posited in Piedmontese; all sequences of vocoids can be treated as either sequences of a (vocoid) approximant plus vowel, or as ambisyllabic sequences of vowels. Approximant + vowel sequences are covered by the following formula:

(APPROX.) + VOWEL + (APPROX.)

in which either one or both approximants may be present.

The following sequences are found:

1. VOWEL + PALATAL APPROXIMANT

	Orthographic	Example	Phonological	Gloss
/ij/	ij	rij	/rij/	'laugh!'
/yj/	ui	suit	/syjt/	'dry'
/ej/	ej	vej	/vej/	'old'
/øj/	euj	ancheuj	/aŋˈkøj/	'today'
/əj/	NO EXAMPLES FOUND			

(cont.)

	Orthographic	Example	Phonological	Gloss
/æj/	ej, èj	sèj	/sæj/	'thirst'
/aj/	aj	rair	/rajr/	'rare'
/oj/	òi	pòis	/pojz/	'peas'
/uj/	oi	doi	/duj/	'two (Masculine)'

2. PALATAL APPROXIMANT + VOWEL

/ji/	ji	bují	/by'ji/	'boiled'
/jy/	ju	piuma	/'pjyma/	'feather; pen'
/je/	ié, ijé	pijé	/pje/	'to take'
/jø/	ieu	fieul	/fjøl/	'boy; son'
/jə/	ië, ijë	fi(j)ëtta	/'fjətta/	'little girl'
/jæ/	ie, iè	chiel	/kjæl/	'he'
/ja/	i(j)à	pijà	/pja/	'taken'
/jo/	iò	fiòca	/'fjok-a/	'snow'
/ju/	io	piovù	/pju'vy/	'rained'

3. VOWEL + LABIOVELAR APPROXIMANT

The only sequence found is /aw/ (always written ⟨au⟩—not *⟨ao⟩); other sequences arise out of the application of the gliding /v/ → /w/ process:

/iw/	iv	(a) scriv	/(a=)'skriw/	'(s)he writes'
/yw/	found only as a result of the optional gliding process:			
	uv	suva	/'syv-a/, opt. /'syw-a/	'dry! (Singular)'
/ew/	ev	frev	/frew/	'fever'
/øw/	euv	neuv	/nøw/	1. 'nine' 2. 'new'
/æw/	èu	rèuma	/'ræwma/	'rheumatism'
/aw/	au	sauté	/saw't-e/	'to jump'
	further as a result of the optional gliding process:			
	av	nav	/nav/, opt. /naw/	'ship'
/ow/	NO EXAMPLES FOUND			
/uw/	found only as a result of the optional gliding process			
	ov	nova	/'nuv-a/, opt. /'nuw-a/	'swim! (Singular)'

4. Labiovelar Approximant + Vowel

| /wa/ | ua | quand | /waŋd/ | 'where' |
| /we/ | ue | guera | /ˈgwæra/ | 'war' |

5. Palatal Approximant + Vowel + Palatal Approximant

/jij/	ij-i	pij-jë-je	/ˈpji=je/	'take (Singular) them from him!'
/jyj/	no examples found			
/jej/	ije-i	pijé-ji	/pjej/	'to take them'
/jøj/	ieuj	fieuj	/fjøj/	'sons, boys'
/jæj/	jèi	(i) pijèisse	/(i=)ˈpjejs-e/	'you (Plural) would take'
/jaj/	ijai	pijaj	/pjaj/	'taken them'
/joj/	jòi	sfojòira	/sfuˈjojr-a/	'in-love' (Feminine Singular)
/juj/	ioj	pioj	/pjuj/	'lice'

6. As for Palatal Approximant + Vowel + Labiovelar Approximant sequences, apart from /jaw/ (orthographic ⟨iau⟩) found, e.g., in *biauta* /ˈbjawta/ 'swing', other sequences can arise out of the application of the optional process leading to /w/ from /v/; e.g.:

| /jøw/ | ieuv | a pieuv | /(a=)ˈpjøv/, opt. /(a=)ˈpjøw/ 'it is raining' |

7. Ambisyllabic Vowel Sequences

Sequences of vowels are always ambisyllabic. A syllabic boundary is marked below with a dot between the relevant vowels:

/i.e/	fie	/ˈfi-e/ (~ /ˈfij-e/)	'daughters, girls'
/u.e/	doe	/ˈdue/	'two (Feminine)'
/u.æ/	foèt	/fuˈæt/	'whip'
/u.a/	(a) noa	/(a=)ˈnu-a/	's/he swims'
/i.e/	nijé	ni-ˈe/	'to drown'

PHONETICS AND PHONOLOGY

Vowel sequences can have stress on either the first or the second element; thereby minimal pairs are created:

| /'i.a/ | (a) nija | /(a=)'ni-a/ | 's/he drowns' |
| /i.'a/ | (a l'é) nijà | /(a='le) ni-'a/ | 's/he drowned' |

8. IDENTICAL VOWEL SEQUENCES

In many varieties of P, due to the operation of PP 4. all /Ve/ sequences of other varieties are shifted to /V.i/, giving rise to identical vowel sequences, eventually contrasting with vowel-approximant sequences:

/i.i/: /'fii/ 'daughters, girls' (koine *fie* /'fi-e/) vs. /ij/: *fij* /fij/ 'threads' (Plural form of *fil* /fil/; Telmon 2001: 71).

Cf. also the following example of V.V vs. V-Approximant opposition:

/u.i/: /'du.i/ 'two (F)' (standard *doe* /'du-e/) vs. /uj/ /uj/: *doi* /duj/ 'two (M)'

2.7.2 Consonant Clusters

Consonant clusters are admitted up to three elements word-initially and internally and up to two word-finally.

2.7.2.1 Word-Initial Clusters

The following restrictions apply:

1. the first member can be either an oral or a nasal stop, or a fricative; with an oral stop as first member, the second element is either a trill, an approximant (either central or lateral) or a nasal (always dental) stop; the labiovelar approximant /w/ is only found after a velar /k/, or, more rarely, /g/:
{p, t, k$_1$, b, d, g$_1$} + {r, y, w$_2$, l, n}

Examples:

/pr/	pruss	/prys/	'pear'
/pj/	pien	/pjæŋ/	'full'
/pl/	plissa	/'plisa/	'fur'
/pn/	pnel	/pnel/	'brush'

/tr/	trè	/træ/	'three'
/tj/	tian	/tjaŋ/	'pan' (rare; the only example)
/tl/	tlé	/tle/	'loom'
/tn/	tnì	/tni/	'to hold'

/kr/	crin	/kriŋ/	'pig'
/kj/	chiel	/kjæl/	'he'
/kw/	quaté	/kwaˈt-e/	'to cover'
/kl/	clementin-a	/klemeŋˈtiŋa/	'a variety of oranges'
/kn/	No examples found		

/br/	brajé	/braˈj-e/	'to cry, shout'
/bj/	bialera	/bjaˈlera/	'canal'
/bl/	blëssa	/ˈbləssa/	'beauty'
/bn/	bna	/bna/	'craziness'

NOTE: only three words are listed in Brero's (1982: 80) dictionary—all rare, and with alternative unclustered forms for two of them:

bnal/bënnal /bnal ~ bənˈnal/ 'straw-hut'
bnastre/banastre /ˈbnastre ~ baˈnastr-e/ 'junk'

/dr/	drapò	/draˈpo/	'flag'
/dj/	diav	/djav/	'devil'
/dl/	dlicà	/dliˈk-a/	'delicate'
/dn/	dné	/dne/	'money' (two cases only)

A few cases of /dm/ and /dz/ are reported:

| /dm/ | dmora | /ˈdmur-a/ | 'toy' |

(rare for *dësmura* /dəzˈmur-a/; /dm/ is found only in a few other derivates of the same root and in another word, always in alternative to a more common /dV-/ sequence)

/dz/ is always found in alternative to the more common /dəz-/ sequence:

| /dz/ | dzèmber | /ˈdzæmbær/ | 'December' |

| /gr/ | gròss | /gros/ | 'big, great' |
| /gj/ | ghiòm(o) | /gjom(u)/ | 'rabbet plane' (REP 755, s.v.; from French *guillaume*) |

/gw/	guera	/ˈgwæra/	'war'
/gl/	gliss	/glis/	'slippery'
/gn/	gh-nìa, ghënìa	/ˈgni-a (~ gəˈni-a)/	'trifle, little thing'

A nasal is allowed as first member of word-initial clusters only when followed by another nasal. The only word-initial nasal cluster is /mn/:

| /mn/ | mné | /mn-e/ | 'to lead' |

2. when the first member of a word-initial consonant cluster is a non-sibilant fricative, the second member may be either a trill or an approximant; with a sibilant fricative as first member, the second member may be again a trill or an approximant, but also a non-sibilant fricative or still a stop (oral or nasal) or an affricate—with the sibilant agreeing in voice with the second member. With a trill or an approximant as second member the voiceless sibilant only is found.

$\{f, v, s_1, z_2\} + \{r_1, j_1, l_1, p_1, t_1, k_1, tʃ_1, f_1, b_2, d_2, g_2, m_2, n_2, ɲ_2, dʒ_2, v_2\}$

Examples:

/fr/	frust	/fryst/	'worn-out'
/fj/	fiap	/fjap/	'withered, flabby'
/fl/	flecia	/ˈfletʃa/	'arrow'
/vr/	vrin	/vriŋ/	'gimlet'
/vj/	vié	/vj-e/	'to watch, guard'
/vl/	vlu	/vly/	'velvet'
/sj/	siass	/sjas/	'sieve'
/sw/	soasì	/swaˈzi/	'chosen'
/sp/	spatuss	/spaˈtys/	'display, ostentation'
/st/	stabi	/ˈstabi/	'stall'
/sk/	scu	/sky/	'shield'
/stʃ/	s-ciass	/stʃas/	'tight, thick'
/sf/	sfërvajé	/sfərvaˈj-e/	'to crumble'
/zb/	sbaruv	/zbaˈryw/	'fright'
/zd/	(a) sdòss	/(a=)ˈzdos/	'without saddle; (fig.) badly'

(only two examples in Brero's dictionary, both rare, plus a few others, such as *sdentà* /zdæŋˈt-a/ 'toothless')

/zl/	slòira	/ˈzlojra/	'plough'
/zg/	sgairé	/zgajˈr-e/	'to waste'
/zm/	smens	/zmæŋs/	'seed(s)'
/zn/	snicé	/zniˈtʃ-e/	'to dislodge'
/zɲ/	sgnaché	/zɲaˈk-e/	'to squash'
/zdʒ/	sgiaj	/zdʒaj/	'disgust, horror'
/zv/	svicc	/zvitʃ/	'lively'

TABLE 5   Word-initial two-consonants clusters

1 2	p	b	t	d	k	g	m	n	ɲ	ŋ	tʃ	dʒ	f	v	s	z	r	l	w	j
p																+				
b																+				
t																+		+		
d																+				
k																+				
g																+				
m				+												+				
n	+	+	+	+			+									+				
ɲ																+				
ŋ																				
tʃ															+					
dʒ																+				
f															+					
v																+				
s																	+			
z				+																
r	+	+	+	+	+	+					+	+			+					

PHONETICS AND PHONOLOGY

TABLE 5   Word-initial two-consonants clusters (*cont.*)

1	p	b	t	d	k	g	m	n	ɲ	ŋ	tʃ	dʒ	f	v	s	z	r	l	w	j
2																				
l	+	+	+	+	+	+							+	+		+				
w				+	+									+						
j	+	+	+	+	+								+	+	+					

2.7.2.2   Three-Consonant Clusters

The first member of a three-consonant cluster may only be a sibilant fricative, agreeing in voicing with a following oral stop or fricative; the third member is either a trill or an approximant. Not all possibilities are attested.

{s₁, z₂} + {p₁, t₁, k₁, f₁, b₂, d₂, g₂, v₂} + {r, j, l}

Examples:

/spr/	spron	/spruŋ/	'spur'
/spl/	splua	/ˈsplya/	'spark'
/spj/	spiatlé	/spjatˈl-e/	'to blab out'
/str/	strass	/stras/	'rag'
/stl/	stlëtta	/stlətta/	'whalebone'
/stj/	No examples		
/skr/	scracé	/skraˈtʃ-e/	'to spit'
/skl/	sclin	/skliŋ/	'clear'
/skj/	No examples		
/sfr/	sfrasé	/sfraˈz-e/	'to discarry' (of animals only)
/sfl/	No examples		
/sfj/	sfiochiné	/sfjukiˈn-e/	'to snow in a thin way'
/zbr/	sbrincé	/zbriŋˈtʃ-e/	'to squirt'
/zbl/	sbloché	/zbloˈk-e/	'to unblock'
/zbj/	sbiaji	/zbjaˈji/	'to fade'
/zgr/	sgrujé	/zgryˈj-e/	'to shell'
/zgl/	sgliss	/zglis/	'slippery'
/zvj/	svijarin	/zvjaˈriŋ/	'alarm-clock'

A single case of optional /zvn/ is found:

| /zvn/ | svnì | /zvni/ | 'to faint' (also *sven-e* /ˈzvæɲe/ and *svënì* /zvəˈni/) |

2.7.2.3 Word-Final Clusters

Word-finally, far fewer restrictions are found. The first element may be either a fricative, a trill or a nasal, and the second either a stop or a fricative.

{r, l, m, n} + {p, t, k, b, d, g, v, s, z}

A few examples are:

/rd/	chërd	/kərd/	'believe!' (Singular)
/rs/	chërss	/kərs/	'grow!' (Singular)
/ŋg/	fengh	/fæŋg/	'hay'
/ns/	sens	/sæns/	'meaning'

2.7.2.4 Word-Internal Clusters

Other two- and three-member clusters are found word-internally after the application of various cliticization rules. These cluster may not obey the constraints set above for word-initial clusters. In particular, both the first and the third member may be other than a sibilant and an approximant/trill, respectively. E.g.:

| /stl/ | rastlé? | /rastˈl-e/ | 'to rake' |

As remarked by Clivio (2002: 162), Piedmontese allows nasal clusters, in particular:

| /ŋn/ | an-namoresse | /aŋnamuˈre=se/ | 'to fall in love' |
| /ŋm/ | an-mochesse | /aŋmuˈke=se/ | 'to make fun of' (literary) |

2.7.2.5 Word-Internal Identical-Consonant Clusters

Due to the operation of various cliticization rules, a sequence of two identical consonants may result. These clusters are usually not pronounced as a single geminate consonant, but as a sequence of two heterosyllabic consonants:

$C_a = C_a \rightarrow [C_a . C_a]$

seta /'set-a/ 'seat! (Singular)' + *te* /te/ → *set-te* /'set=te/ ['sette,*'setːe]
'sit down! (Singular)'
[sit yourself]

Pending a detailed phonetic analysis of this phenomenon with an electroglottograph (EEG), it seems certain that the time of the occlusion is not an issue; a certain decrease in the amplitude of the last vowel[6] seems rather to point to an increased pulmonary pressure.[7]

Three-member clusters with identical $C_2 = C_3$ ($C_\alpha C_\beta C_\beta$) may likewise arise:

pent-te /'pænt=te/ ['pæntte] 'comb yourself! (Singular)'

2.7.2.6 Gemination

The only exception to the Clustering process occurs with the central vowel /ə/, after which a sequence of two identical consonants is pronounced as a single geminated one:

$C_a + C_a \rightarrow C_aː / ə\_$

Examples:

blëssa /'bləssa/ ['bləsːa] 'beauty'

/əC_aC_b/ is obviously possible; e.g.:

fiësca /'fjəska/ (also *fiusca* / 'fjyska /) 'slice, clove of garlic'

(a sibilant is always allocated to the same syllable of the following consonant)

As exemplified by *blëssa* /'bləssa/ above, geminated consonants are often created by the Feminine abstract suffix *-ëssa*; another source is the suffix of Fem-

---

6 It is noteworthy in this regard the spontaneous writing ⟨sett-e⟩ for *set-te* found on Facebook (https://m.facebook.com/groups/piemonteis/permalink/1813826912113451/?fs=2&focus _composer=0).
7 Antonio Romano, p.c., April 26, 2021.

inine diminutives (also found in formally diminutive words without a diminutive meaning), which are formed with the suffix *-tta*, before which the ending of Feminine Nouns *-a* shifts to /ə/:

| *fija* | /ˈfia/ | 'girl' | → | *fijëtta* | /ˈfjətta/ [ˈfjət:a] | 'little girl' |
| *cher* | /kær/ | 'cart, wagon' | → | *carëtta* | /kaˈrətta/ [kaˈrət:a] | 'hand-cart' |

As /ə/ is *always* followed by a sequence of two consonants, a case could be made for the suffix to be *-ët-* (further followed by the F ending *-a*), and gemination to be induced by the presence of /ə/; the corresponding M diminutive ending is *-èt* /æt/, in which no vowel centralization occurs, and after which no gemination occurs:

| *cher* | /kær/ | 'cart' | → | *carèt* | /kaˈræt/ | 'barrow' |
| *sitron* | /siˈtruŋ/ | 'cedar' | → | *sitronèt* | /sitruˈnæt/ | 'marigold' |

2.8 Length

Length is not distinctive in vowels, but is used as a correlate of stress and pitch for pragmatic purposes. A stressed vowel is phonetically longer than an unstressed one:

| *bass* | /bas/ | [baːs] | 'low' |
| *bassé* | /baˈs-e/ | [baˈse] | 'to lower' |

Only the vowel /ə/ seems to be consistently shorter than other vowels.
Consonants may be geminated as a result of suffixation (cf. 2.7.2.6 Gemination above).

2.9 Stress

Piedmontese is basically a syllable-timed language. All plurisyllabic words have one primary stress. Stress is regularly used to distinguish words, especially among different derivational or inflectional forms from the same stem. A few minimal pairs are:

PHONETICS AND PHONOLOGY

sara /ˈsara/ 'close! ((Singular)' vs. *sarà* /saˈr-a/ 'closed'
vache /ˈvak-e/ 'cows' vs. *vaché* /vaˈke/ 'cowherd'

In other cases, the words distinguished by stress are not derived from one and the same stem, such as in:

mosca /ˈmuska/ 'fly' vs. *moscà* /musˈka/ 'spotted (a kind of wine)'
àncora /ˈaŋkura/ 'anchor' vs. *ancora* /aŋˈkura/ 'still; again'

The usual position of stress is either on the last or the penultimate syllable. For simple (not derived) Nouns and Adjectives a general rule is that stress falls on the penultimate on most vowel-final words (such as most Feminine Nouns) and on the last syllable on most consonant-final words (such as most masculine Nouns):

amis /aˈmiz/ vs. *amisa* /aˈmiza/ 'friend' (Masculine vs. Feminine Singular)

Stress on the antepenultimate syllable is rare, and limited to a few verbal forms:

(a) *capita* /(a=)ˈkapit-a/ 'it happens' vs. *capità* /kapiˈt-a/ 'happened'

as well as to a few loans:

ancora /ˈaŋkura/ 'anchor'

and native words:

sòtola /ˈsotula/ 'top (toy)'

Stress may be shifted as a result of suffixation:

chërd /kərd/ 'believe! (Singular)' vs. *chërdù* /kərˈdy/ 'believed'

In many cases stress shift is accompanied by a process of vowel gliding or dropping:

pija /ˈpi-a/ 'take!' (Singular) vs. *pijà* /pj-a/ 'taken'

The main phonetic correlates of stress are intensity and height, the stressed syllable being realized with greater intensity and on a higher pitch than an unstressed syllable. Vowel length correlates with stress, and even more so with pitch.

There is no distinction between different levels of stress, but any syllable can be upgraded in stress for contrastive purposes.

2.10 Pitch and Intonation

Pitch is used to distinguish forms at utterance level only, and not to distinguish lexical items. In utterances of one phonological word pitch may distinguish different functions:

lait /**lajt**/ 'milk' (a statement, used, e.g., as an answer to 'what do you want?')

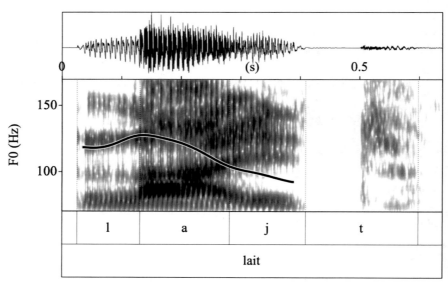

FIGURE 7   *lait /lajt/* 'milk,' declarative intonation

PHONETICS AND PHONOLOGY

lait /**lajt**/ 'milk?' (a question)

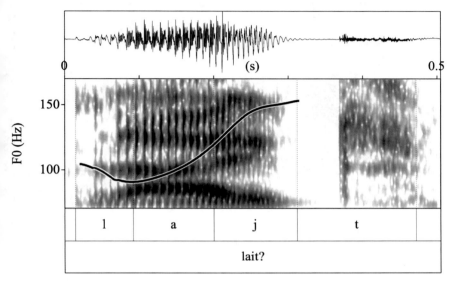

FIGURE 8   *lait* /***lajt***/ 'milk,' question

lait /**lajt**/ 'milk!' (a contrastive emphatic answer)
lait /**lajt**/ 'milk?!' (a rhetoric question implying surprise, disbelief, etc.)

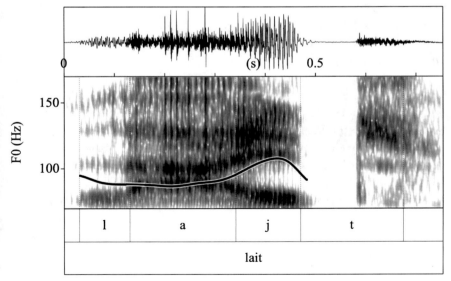

FIGURE 9   *lait* /***lajt***/ 'milk,' rhetoric question implying surprise, disbelief, etc. (male speaker born in Turin in 1956)

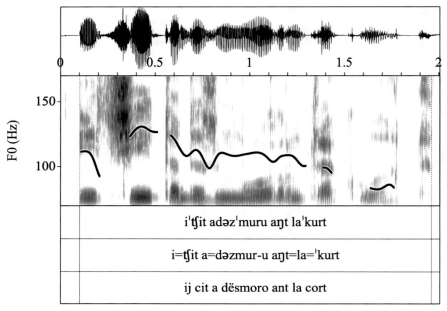

FIGURE 10   ij cit a dësmoro ant la cort /i=ˈtʃit a=ˈdəzmur-u ant=l-a=kurt/ 'the children are playing in the yard' (declarative, neutral statement) (male speaker born in Turin in 1956)

Pitch interacts with specific lexical and syntactic devices in this function. Stress is not affected phonologically by pitch. A statement is uttered with a lowering in pitch on its final part (the last word or phrase in the case of long utterances), and a question with a rising pitch.[8] In neutral (non-emphatic) statements the pitch rises until the main sentence stress and then drops, with an overall ascending-falling movement (see Figure 10):

In polar, yes-no questions (☞ 14.9.1.) the ascending movement is further followed by a rising pitch after the main sentence stress (see Figure 11):

Emphasis on an element (a phonological word or phrase) is signalled by an ascending pitch on that element (see Figures 12–14):

Non-polar, constituent questions (☞ 14.9.4.) are marked by a falling pitch on the question-word, followed by the same intonation pattern of neutral statements.

Tag-questions (in which the tag is most commonly lexically expressed by *neh* /næ/; ☞ 14.9.2.; 16.7.) take the same intonation pattern of neutral statements and the rising pitch typical of questions on the tag only—which is separated from the rest by an audible pause.

---

8   The same holds true for the Piedmontese accent of Italian; cf. Canepari (1979: 116; 1980: 98, 177).

PHONETICS AND PHONOLOGY

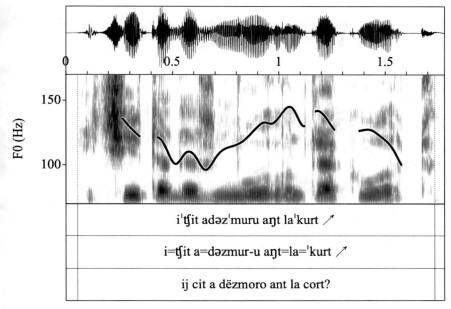

FIGURE 11   ij cit a dësmoro ant la cort? /i= ˈtʃit a=ˈdəzmur-u ant=l-a=kurt ↗/ 'are the children playing in the yard?' (male speaker born in Turin in 1956)

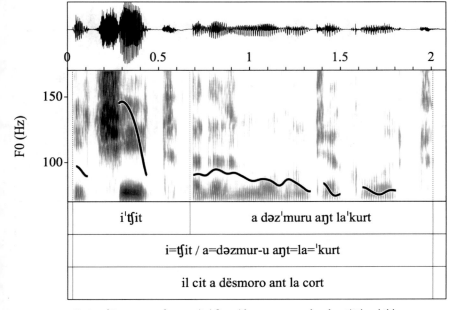

FIGURE 12   ij cit a dësmoro ant la cort /i= ˈtʃit a=ˈdəzmur-u ant=l-a=kurt/ *the children* are playing in the yard' (male speaker born in Turin in 1956)

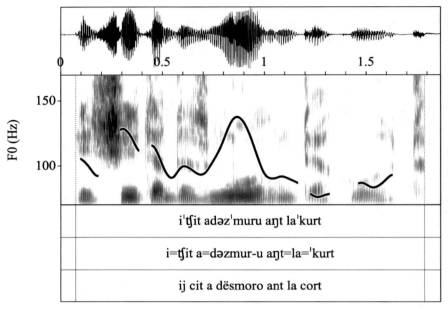

FIGURE 13   ij cit a dësmoro ant la cort /i= 'tʃit a= 'dəzmur-u ant=l-a=kurt/ 'the children *are playing* in the yard' (male speaker born in Turin in 1956)

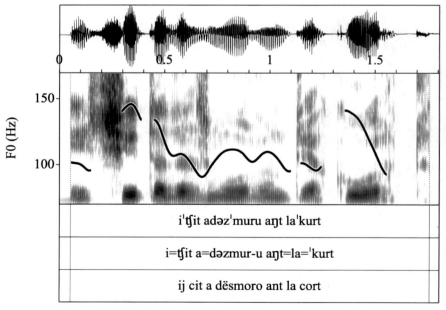

FIGURE 14   ij cit a dësmoro ant la cort /i= 'tʃit a= 'dəzmur-u ant=l-a=kurt/ 'the children are playing *in the yard*' (male speaker born in Turin in 1956)

CHAPTER 3

Writing System and Orthography

3.1 Overview

From a typological point of view, the Piedmontese writing system uses a phonographic segmental alphabetical script. Since its very first written attestations until today, Piedmontese script has been based on the Latin alphabet. Today's script contains 25 letters (Brero 1971: 15, Villata 1997: 14; see also Clivio 1964: 5):

(capital letters:) ⟨A B C D E Ë F G H I J L M N N- O Ò P Q R S T U V Z⟩
(small letters:) ⟨a b c d e ë f g h i j l m n n- o ò p q r s t u v z⟩[1]

In the remaining of the chapter, we will deal with the Piedmontese orthography from a theoretical point of view. Thus, following Sgall (1987), we will not speak of letters, but rather of graphemes. For the purposes of this chapter, we define a grapheme as a character that can occupy a single slot of the written string and that may be associated, even by laypeople, with a specific phonetic realization, or with the morphological origin of a word. Thus, ⟨n-⟩ will not be included amongst the graphemes of Piedmontese, since it is rather an allograph of ⟨n⟩ (☞ 3.1.3.).

3.1.1 Grapheme-Phoneme Correspondences

Grapheme-phoneme correspondences are shown in Table 6. In this table, and in the remaining of the chapter unless stated otherwise, all phonetic realizations correspond to the pronunciation of contemporary Turinese.

The Piedmontese standard orthography was codified during the 1930s on the basis of the pronunciation of the literary koine. Turinese pronunciation has slightly changed in the last 50 years or so, and these changes have not been reflected in the orthography.

More recently (see Clivio 1971 and Brero and Bertodatti 1988: 24), special graphemes were suggested in order to cope with the necessity to write down phonemes that were present in some dialect's inventory, but not in the Turinese

---

[1] In Piedmontese the distribution of capital and small letters is contextually determined (e.g., a capital letter is required after full stops). Therefore, they are treated here as allographs of a common grapheme. In what follows, exemplifications will contain only small letters.

TABLE 6   Grapheme-phoneme correspondence in the Piedmontese writing system

Grapheme	Phoneme(s)	Example(s)
⟨a⟩	/a/	*asil* /a'zil/ 'vinegar'
⟨b⟩	/b/, /p/	*babi* /'babi/ 'toad,' *gheub* /gøp/ 'hunchbacked'
⟨c⟩	/k/, /tʃ/	*mica* /'mika/ 'crumb,' *macé* /ma'tʃ-e/ 'to stain'
⟨d⟩	/d/, /t/	*mudande* /my'dande/ 'underpants,' *verd* /væːrt/ 'green'
⟨e⟩	/e/, /æ/	*pes* /pes/ 'worse,' *rusnent* /ryz'næŋt/ 'rusty'
⟨ë⟩	/ə/, /a/	*fërtà* /fər'ta/ 'rubbed', *për* /par/ 'for'
⟨f⟩	/f/	*stofi* /'stufi/ 'fed up'
⟨g⟩	/g/, /dʒ/	*magon* /ma'guŋ/ 'stomach knot,' *angagé* /aŋga'dʒ-e/ 'to enlist'
⟨h⟩	[Ø]	*hai* /aj/ '(I) have'
⟨i⟩	/i/, /j/	*cit* /tʃit/ 'little,' *peui* /pøj/ 'then'
⟨j⟩	/j/, [Ø]	*fojòt* /fu'jot/ 'pan, pie dish,' *fija* /'fia/ 'daughter, girl'
⟨l⟩	/l/	*fòl* /fol/ 'fool'
⟨m⟩	/m/	*mare* /'mare/ 'mother'
⟨n⟩	/n/, /ŋ/	*neuv* /nøw/ 'new,' *canton* /kaŋ'tuŋ/ 'corner'
⟨ò⟩	/o/	*lòsa* /'loza/ 'floe'
⟨o⟩	/u/, /o/, /w/	*coa* /'kua/ 'tail,' *fòto* /'foto/ 'photo,' *s-ciao* /stʃaw/ 'hi'
⟨p⟩	/p/	*cop* /kup/ 'tile'
⟨q⟩	/k/	*quaj* /kwaj/ 'bladder'
⟨r⟩	/r/	*baron* /ba'ruŋ/ 'bunch, pile'
⟨s⟩	/s/, /z/	*sol* /sul/ 'sun,' *basin* /ba'ziŋ/ 'little kiss'
⟨t⟩	/t/	*baròt* /ba'rot/ 'redneck'
⟨u⟩	/y/, /w/	*rusa* /'ryza/ 'quarrel,' *pàuta* /'pawta/ 'mud'
⟨v⟩	/v/, /w/	*volèj* /vo'læj/ 'to want,' *ciav* /tʃaw/ 'key'
⟨z⟩	/z/	*dabzògn* /dab'zoɲ/ 'need'

one. For some of these graphemes—scarcely used even in cultured publications—see below, Table 8.

In Table 6, ⟨ë⟩ and ⟨ò⟩ are the only 'complex' graphemes listed, i.e., the only graphemes containing diacritics such as a diaeresis or an accent. They have been treated as plain graphemes because they are somewhat 'flag-characters' of the Piedmontese writing system, since they mark a difference with neighbouring Italian orthographies—where ⟨ë⟩ is not used, and ⟨ò⟩ is a mere allograph of ⟨o⟩. Moreover, they occupy a single slot in the written string, as all other graphemes by our definition, but unlike ⟨n-⟩ (☞ 3.1.3.).

WRITING SYSTEM AND ORTHOGRAPHY 103

⟨h⟩ is never pronounced. When it is not part of a bigrapheme (☞ 3.1.2.), it signals, as the first character of some monosyllabic words, that they belong to the verb *avèj* /a'væj/ 'to have:' cf. (*a l'*)*ha* (SBJ.3=have\PRS.3S) '(he/she/it) has' vs *a* (ADE) 'to,' both pronounced /a/; (*it l'*)*has* (SBJ.2S=have\PRS.2S) '(you (S)) have' vs *as* (SBJ.3=REFL) both pronounced either /as/ or /az/. In this and other forms of 'to have' (from Latin HABERE) ⟨h⟩ is etymological.

⟨j⟩ is mute only when preceded by ⟨i⟩ and followed by a vowel grapheme. For all other pronunciation rules ☞ 2.

How to write unusual phonemes?

The writing system of Piedmontese was created with the aim to reproduce the phonological system of the koine. Nevertheless, the problem of reproducing more complex phonological systems has been faced when authors committed themselves in writing local varieties. In the last version of his grammar (Brero and Bertodatti 2000: 24), for instance, Camillo Brero, the codifier of Piedmontese *par excellence*, offered an interesting inventory of the "particular graphic signs" useful for writing some local varieties.

⟨ä⟩ was proposed for /ɑ/ or /ɒ/ that have the status of phoneme in some Southern varieties. In many dialects (and sometimes in the koine itself) /ɑ/ or /ɒ/ are simple allophones of /a/ in a stressed position and it may be useless to signal them (☞ the boxes under § 2.1);

⟨ł⟩ and ⟨ř⟩ can reproduce the same phoneme /ɹ/ that in some Southern varieties is the outcome of etymological L and R (☞ the boxes under § 2.1);

⟨ĝ⟩ writes /ʒ/ and is very common in the varieties of the Biela area: *leĝe* /'leʒe/ instead of *lese* /'leze/ 'to read,' *peĝ* for *pes* /pes/ 'worse.' All of these dialects display also the voiceless counterpart, i.e., the phoneme /ʃ/, equally unknown to koine, but it is easily reproduced by borrowing from Italian the diagraph/trigraph ⟨sc(i)⟩: *scerne* /'ʃærne/ for *serne* /'særne/ 'to choose,' *sciumia* /'ʃymja/ instead of *sumia* /'symja/ 'ape.'

These two phonemes are also widely attested but with a totally different distribution in some Southern varieties in contact with Ligurian or/and Occitan dialects: for istance Kje *ciamiĝa* /tʃa'miʒa/ instead of *camisa* /ka'miza/ 'shirt', *sciròt* /ʃi'ɹot/ for *assul* /a'syl/ 'ax.' Nevertheless, people writing in these Southern dialects often do not accept the grapheme ⟨ĝ⟩, and prefer to use symbols such as ⟨j⟩ (borrowed from French), ⟨ž⟩ (modeled on the writing systems of Slavic languages), ⟨x⟩ (traditionally used for Genoese), or digraphs/trigraphs such as ⟨zh⟩, ⟨sg(i)⟩, ⟨zg(i)⟩ and so on.

⟨ts⟩ reproduces the same IPA symbol /ts/ and is common in Biela and Langhe dialects, but also in some varieties spoken on the Alps to the south of ël Mondvì: Biela/Langhe *tsuca* /ˈtsyka/ instead of *cossa* /ˈkusa/ 'pumpkin.'

⟨n-n⟩ simply represents the sequence of a velar nasal /ŋ/ followed by /n/, that often corresponds to intervocalic ⟨n⟩ /ŋ/ in Langhe and Monfrà dialects: *lun-na* /ˈlyŋna/ for *lun-a* /ˈlyŋa/ 'moon'.

3.1.2 Bigraphemes

Bigraphemes, or digraphs, are sequences of two graphemes pronounced as a single phoneme. In Table 7 the bigraphemes of the Piedmontese orthography are contrasted with the phonemes of the traditional variety of Piedmontese spoken in Turin they stand for:

TABLE 7   Bigraphemes-phoneme correspondence in the Piedmontese writing system

Bigrapheme	Phoneme	Example(s)
⟨cc⟩	/tʃ/	*baricc* /baˈritʃ/ 'squint,' (*a*) *marcc-rà* /marˈtʃra/ 'it will walk, it will function'
⟨ch⟩	/k/	*cheuit* /køjt/ 'cooked'
⟨ci⟩	/tʃ/	*macia* /ˈmatʃa/ 'stain'
⟨eu⟩	/ø/	*scheur* /skør/ 'disgust'
⟨gg⟩	/tʃ/, /dʒ/	*formagg* /furˈmatʃ/ 'cheese,' *magg* /madʒ/ 'May', (*i*) *mangg-rai* /maŋdʒˈraj/ 'I will eat'
⟨gh⟩	/g/, /k/	*ghignon* /giˈɲuŋ/ 'dislike,' *lagh* /lak/ 'lake'
⟨gi⟩	/dʒ/	*agiut* /aˈdʒyt/ 'help'
⟨gn⟩	/ɲ/	*magna* /ˈmaɲa/ 'aunt'
⟨nn⟩	/n/	*pann* /pan/ 'cloth'
⟨ss⟩	/s/	*cossa* /ˈkusa/ 'pumpkin'

Only ⟨gn⟩ is a "pure" bigrapheme, i.e., a sequence of graphemes that may only represent a single phoneme, which in turn is not represented by any other grapheme or group of graphemes in the language.

⟨cc⟩, ⟨ch⟩, ⟨ci⟩, ⟨gg⟩, ⟨gh⟩, ⟨gi⟩, ⟨nn⟩ and ⟨ss⟩ stand for phonemes that may be spelt also in other ways (see Table 6 and Table 9). ⟨eu⟩, on the other hand, is 'exclusive' (i.e., /ø/ can only be spelled ⟨eu⟩ in Piedmontese), but it is not unambiguous, since the sequence ⟨eu⟩ can also be pronounced /ew/ such as in *Euròpa* /ewˈropa/ 'Europe,' *europèo* /ewruˈpeu/ 'European' and the like.

⟨cc⟩, ⟨gg⟩ may occur word-finally or at the end of a verbal lexical morpheme. ⟨nn⟩, on the other hand, only occurs word-finally. ⟨nn⟩, instead, only

WRITING SYSTEM AND ORTHOGRAPHY

occurs word-finally, and might thus be treated as an allograph of ⟨n⟩. However, here we consider ⟨nn⟩ as composed by two graphic symbols.

⟨ss⟩ cannot appear word-initially. ⟨gh⟩ may stand for /k/ only word-finally.

⟨ci⟩ and ⟨gi⟩ may also be read as two distinct graphemes, in words such as *cipress* /tʃi'pres/ 'cypress' and *agità* /adʒi'ta/ 'shaken,' respectively. The pronunciation /tʃi/ and /dʒi/ is found when ⟨ci⟩ and ⟨gi⟩ are not followed by a vowel or when they are followed by a vowel but the ⟨i⟩ in the string is stressed, cf. *farmacìa* /farma'tʃia/ 'drugstore,' and *magìa* /ma'dʒia/ 'magic.'

3.1.3   Allographs

Some graphemes have allographs, i.e., variants of the grapheme that occur in such contextual positions where the usual grapheme does not occur.

⟨a⟩, ⟨e⟩, ⟨i⟩, ⟨o⟩ and ⟨u⟩ have ⟨à⟩, ⟨è⟩ or ⟨é⟩, ⟨ì⟩, ⟨ó⟩, ⟨ù⟩, respectively, as allographs.

⟨è⟩ and ⟨é⟩ are allographs of /æ/ and /e/, respectively, used in the (rare) contrastive pairs (☞ 2.4.1.1.).

The vowel allographs occur:

(a) when the vowels that the graphemes represent are under prosodic stress at the end of a word:
sità /si'ta/ 'city'
bolè /bu'læ/ 'mushroom'
bolé /bu'le/ 'to stamp'
andurmì /aŋdyr'mi/ 'asleep'
ragó /ra'gu/ 'ragout';

(b) in some monosyllabic words, when a diacritic is needed to differentiate between two homographs:
dà /da/ '(he/she/it) gives' vs *da* (ABL) 'from'
sì /si/ 'here' vs *si* 'yes'
as well as—as grammarians such as Brero (1967: 20) Villata (1997: 8–9, 16–22) and Rubat Borel, Tosco and Bertolino (2006: 21–22) prescribe:

(c) when the graphemes represent the stressed, vocalic part of a descendent diphthong or of a triphthong:
càuda /'kawda/ 'hot (Singular Feminine)'
pèis /pæjz/ 'weight'

(d) when the graphemes stand for a stressed vowel occurring before the penultimate syllable of the word:
barìcole /ba'rikule/ 'eye-glasses'
régola /'regula/ 'rule'

(e) when the graphemes stand for a stressed vowel of a word that ends with a consonant and is not accented on the last syllable:

quàder /ˈkwader/ 'painting'
ùtil /ˈytil/ 'useful'

(f) when the graphemes stand for a stressed vowel of words accented on the second-to-last syllable and ending with a hiatus graphized as either ⟨ia⟩, ⟨ie⟩, ⟨ua⟩ or ⟨ue⟩:
andasìa /aŋdaˈzia/ '(I, /s/he) went'
finìe /fiˈni-e/ 'ended (Plural Feminine)'
batùa /baˈtya/ 'joke, gag'

⟨ò⟩ always stands for a stressed /o/.

Prescriptions (c)-(f) are at times neglected also in cultured or semi-cultured publications. For instance, the Piedmontese column of *torinosette*, a weekly insert of the popular Turinese newspaper *La Stampa*, is entitled ⟨An piemonteis⟩ /aŋ=pjemuŋˈtæjz/ 'in Piedmontese,'[2] albeit orthography rules would require ⟨An piemontèis⟩, with an accent on the third-to-last grapheme. Likewise, in the articles, short stories and poetry in Piedmontese published in the 1970s in the *Almanacco piemontese*, stressed ⟨è⟩ is sometimes not used in the word ⟨piemontèis⟩, and rule (d) is not consistently applied (e.g., ⟨politiche⟩ instead of ⟨polìtiche⟩ /puˈlitike/, see also, on this particular text, Berruto 1971).

Language activists and planners (see Tosco 2002, Miola 2015: 149) have long proposed the suppression of these prescriptions, with the intent to avoid excessive usage of diacritics. This volume follows these suggestions.

⟨s⟩ has an allograph, namely ⟨s-⟩. It is used when the grapheme is followed by a ⟨c⟩ standing for [tʃ], compare

masca /ˈmaska/ 'witch' and *mas-cc* /mastʃ/ 'male'
scòla /ˈskola/ 'school' and *s-ciopé* /stʃuˈp-e/ 'to burst, to explode'

Also ⟨n⟩ has an allograph: ⟨n-⟩. ⟨n-⟩ is used when the grapheme stands for [ŋ] and appears between vowels, such as in *person-a* /perˈsuŋa/ 'person' as opposed to *cana* /ˈkana/ 'cane,' *ann* /an/ 'year,' *pan* /paŋ/ 'bread,' *mandé* /maŋˈd-e/ 'to send,' and so on.

Table 8 (☞ the relevant box in 2.1) shows the set of graphemes and bigraphemes used to represent phonemes that are not in the Turinese inventory, but

---

2 This spelling appeared on paper, where the title is in capital letters, as well as on the online version of the insert. Online, the title is in small letters, except for the first, which is, as usual, capitalized.

WRITING SYSTEM AND ORTHOGRAPHY   107

TABLE 8   Grapheme-phoneme correspondences for phonemes in local dialects

Grapheme	Phoneme	Example(s)	Dialect[a]
⟨ä⟩	/ɑ/	mäta /ˈmɑta/ 'girl'	Ast dialect, Langhe, Monfrà
⟨ĝ⟩	/ʒ/	ĝenĝiva /ʒeŋˈʒiva/ 'gum'	Bielèis
⟨l̕⟩	/ɾ/	al̕a /ˈaɾa/ 'wing'	Ast dialect, Langhe, Monfrà
⟨ř⟩	/ɾ/	ařbi /ˈaɾbi/ 'vat'	Ast dialect, Langhe, Monfrà
⟨ó⟩	/ʊ/	fiór /fjʊr/ 'flower'	Bielèis, Canavzan[b]
⟨sc⟩	/ʃ/	scinch /ʃiŋk/ 'five'	Bielèis, Monregalèis
⟨ts⟩	/ts/	blëtsa /ˈblətsa/ 'beauty'	Bielèis
⟨w⟩	/w/	warir /waˈrir/ 'to cure, to heal'	Canavzan

a   Reference is made to the dialects listed in Table 1.2.
b   Note that ⟨ó⟩ is also an allograph in the standard orthography. Its phonetic realization is very similar in Turinese, Bielèis and Canavzan.

are part of some dialect's inventory. As said above, they are used, albeit scarcely, in local publication.

3.1.4   *Phoneme-Spelling Correspondence*
On the basis of Table 6 and 7, the relations Orth for Piedmontese are illustrated in Table 9. Relations Orth (Sgall 1987: 10-ff.) are formalizations of rules of orthography, i.e., rules of pronunciation/spelling. Any relation Orth SP /X/, ⟨Y, Z, Q, …⟩ on Table 9 can be read as follows: the phoneme /X/ can be spelt in the given language as ⟨Y⟩, ⟨Z⟩, ⟨Q⟩, etc.

As one can see, any Piedmontese phoneme can be spelt in no more than four different ways. On average, any phoneme has two possible spellings. Only in four cases there is a perfect and bi-unique correlation between sound and grapheme, namely (/m/, ⟨m⟩), (/f/, ⟨f⟩), (/r/, ⟨r⟩), (/l/, ⟨l⟩). Nonetheless, rules of orthography and/or pronunciation may specify the conditions for choosing one spelling/pronunciation or the others. For instance, the sequence /kw/ is always graphized ⟨qu⟩, i.e., /k/ is always represented by ⟨q⟩ when followed by a bilabial approximant /w/, and /w/ is represented by ⟨u⟩ any time it is preceded by an unvoiced velar plosive /k/. For other orthographic rules ☞ 2.

3.1.5   *Prosthetic ⟨ë⟩*
Traditional spelling enforced by modern grammars (Brero 1971: 21–22, Villata 1997: 9–10) renders as ⟨ë⟩ the prosthetic vowel occurring before any cluster [s]+consonant/[j] when the preceding word ends with a consonant (see Clivio

TABLE 9 Relations Orth for Piedmontese

SP /b/, ⟨b⟩
SP /p/, ⟨b, p⟩
SP /d/, ⟨d⟩
SP /t/, ⟨d, t⟩
SP /g/, ⟨g, gh⟩
SP /k/, ⟨c, ch, gh, q⟩
SP /m/, ⟨m⟩
SP /n/, ⟨n, nn⟩
SP /ŋ/, ⟨n, n-⟩
SP /dʒ/, ⟨g, gi⟩
SP /tʃ/, ⟨c, cc, ci, gg⟩
SP /v/, ⟨v⟩
SP /f/, ⟨f⟩
SP /z/, ⟨s, z⟩
SP /s/, ⟨s, s-, ss⟩
SP /r/, ⟨r⟩
SP /l/, ⟨l⟩
SP /j/, ⟨i, j⟩
SP /w/, ⟨o, u, v⟩
SP /i/, ⟨i, ì⟩
SP /y/, ⟨u, ù⟩
SP /u/, ⟨o, ó⟩
SP /e/, ⟨e, é⟩
SP /ø/, ⟨eu⟩
SP /o/, ⟨o, ò⟩
SP /ə/, ⟨ë⟩
SP /æ/, ⟨e, è⟩
SP /a/, ⟨a, à, ë⟩

1976: 125–136). ⟨ë⟩ can either appear juxtaposed to end of the first word of the syntagm, or to the beginning of the second word, e.g.: *specc* /spetʃ/ 'mirror,' but *në specc* /nə='spetʃ/ 'a mirror' and *set ëspecc* /set ə'spetʃ/ 'seven mirrors.' ⟨ë⟩ is written at the end of the first word if this word is an article or a form of the grammatical word *ëd*, which therefore in these cases is written ⟨dë⟩.

Note that, when the prosthetic ⟨ë⟩ is put at the beginning of the second word of the syntagm, this slightly modifies the written form of the lexical base of the

WRITING SYSTEM AND ORTHOGRAPHY   109

word, so that the identification of the lexical morpheme may be hindered or result less easy for the reader.

3.1.6   Other Graphic Symbols
As regards punctuation, full stops ⟨.⟩, commas ⟨,⟩, colons ⟨:⟩, semicolons ⟨;⟩, question marks ⟨?⟩ and exclamation marks ⟨!⟩ are used similarly to other European languages. For instance, commas separate individual parts in lists, isolated parts in sentences, such as parenthetical sentences or vocatives.

Angle brackets ⟨« ...»⟩ usually introduce reported speech, with the function of quotation marks.

Other than the aforementioned punctuation marks, two others graphic symbols are relevant in the Piedmontese writing system, namely ⟨'⟩ and ⟨—⟩.

The orthography of Piedmontese makes a generous use of hyphens. The hyphen occurs:
- as was seen above, in the digraphs ⟨n-⟩ for the velar nasal stop (/ŋ/) in intervocalic position, and
- in the digraphs ⟨s-c⟩ for the consonant cluster /stʃ/ (as opposed to ⟨sc⟩ = /sk/) and ⟨s-g⟩ for the consonant cluster /sdʒ/ (as opposed to ⟨sg⟩ = /sg/);
- in specific combinations of morphemes, such as, among the others:
  - ⟨a-i⟩ /a=j/ (SBJ.3=IND): *a-i é* /a=ˈje/ 'there is'
  - ⟨i-i⟩ /i=j/ (SBJ.1=OBJ\P): *i-i dissegnoma* /i=j=diseˈɲuma/ 'we draw them'
  - ⟨i-j⟩ /i=j/ (SBJ.1=IND): *i-j lo disoma* /i=j=lu diˈzuma/ 'we say it to him'
- in compound deictic forms, both pronominal and adjectival:
  - *chiel-sì* /kjælˈsi/ 'he (over here)'
  - *col-là* /kulˈla/ 'that (over there)'
  - *sa fomna-là* /s-a fumn-aˈla/ 'that woman' [that woman-there]
- in compound Nouns: *dòp-mesdì* /dop=mezˈdi/ 'afternoon,' *col-lì* /kulˈli/ 'that' (DIST=there);
- somehow irregularly, to separate verbal forms and their enclitics, when the former ends with a cluster of consonants and the latter begins with a consonant, such as in *vist-lo* /ˈvist=lu/ 'seen-him.' Also between Imperative forms ending in ⟨cc⟩ or ⟨gg⟩ and their object: *specc-te* /ˈspetʃ=te/ 'look at yourself in a mirror!'
- between a Pronoun beginning with the same consonant of the final consonant of an immediately preceding Infinitive verbal form, whose final vowel is dropped:
  - *avèj* /aˈvæj/ 'to have:' *avèj-je* /aˈve=je/ (with /e/ notwithstanding orthographic ⟨è⟩) 'to have them.'

- finally, hyphens (and more rarely em dashes ⟨—⟩) may also function as a quotation mark.[3]

⟨'⟩ stands for an elided vowel (or, rarely, consonant). ⟨'⟩ is used to signal allomorphs of articles, proclitics and of the preposition ⟨ëd⟩, which therefore appears in its allomorphic forms ⟨'d⟩ or ⟨d'⟩ (☞ 20.2.1). Nonetheless, a vowel may be deleted in writing—independently from the actual pronunciation—if it immediately precedes a word beginning with a vowel, or if it immediately follows a word ending with a vowel. The latter kind of elision usually involves the written form ⟨ël⟩, when preceded by a vowel-ending word. See for instance the following quote from Tesio (2016: 37; emphasis added), where the word ⟨'L⟩ precedes a vowel-ending word, but these two words are separated by a full stop, i.e. a major pause in reading and speech:

> *fisa e paròle gropà da na liassa fòrta e **drua**. **'L librèt** a l'é stàit cudì da Luciano Bertello*

> accordion and words tied together by a strong and fierce bond. The small book has been edited by Luciano Bertello

The elision takes place even though in speech the pronunciation of the relevant words would be /... e ˈdrya // əl=liˈbræt .../.

3.2   History

Romance languages tend to maintain the alphabet already used in writing by their mother language, Latin, because it was the only cultured, and the most written, language at least up to the 16th century (for Piedmont, see Clivio 1970b: 65, Ronco 2015: LV-LVI). Moreover, Latin was the language read and spoken by priests as well as by faithfuls in most religious rites. Therefore, Catholic Christianity enforced and strengthened the use and maintenance of the Latin alphabet—as it is known that religion is one of the most important criteria for choosing and using a script (Diringer 1968, in Coulmas 2003: 201).

As further evidence of the close link between religion and writing system, suffice it to cite that the only Piedmontese document written with a non-Latin script is the 16th-century *Glossario di Alba*, also called *Glossary A*. Its author is

---

3   Hyphens or dashes may at times introduce, and end, parenthetical sentences. This, however, happens much less frequently than in English.

Jacob ben Nathan de Olmo, of Jewish origin and religion, who used a Hebrew script for writing his Piedmontese dialect (Berenblut 1949, Terracini 1956).

3.2.1 First Attestations and Fluctuations in the Early Modern Period

The *terminus post quem* a full-fledged variety of Piedmontese is documented is 1321,[4] when the *Sarament* and the *Statut ëd la Companìa 'd San Giòrs* ('Oaths' and 'Statutes of the Company of St. George,' see Salvioni 1886: 345–355) were translated in Chér from Latin into the local vernacular (also ☞ 1.7.1).

Other texts of great philological interest document 14th- and 15th-century Piedmontese (Bollati and Manno 1878, Clivio 1970a, Gasca Queirazza 1965, 1966a, b; for an overview see Clivio 1970b and Gasca Queirazza 1971; for an anthology of texts, with a normalized orthography, see Brero and Gandolfo 1967, see also Clivio 2002b: 31–100). The scripts of these texts are highly consistent with the *scriptae* of other Northern Italian documents of the same time, borrowing graphemes and *usus scribendi* from the Latin, the Tuscan and, to a lesser extent, the French scriptorial traditions (Rossebastiano and Papa 2011: 64–65).

Fluctuations of grapheme-phoneme correspondence are large during the 16th and 17th century. By way of example, in Alion's 1521 masterpiece /s/ may be represented by ⟨s⟩ and ⟨ss⟩ in the middle of a word, while ⟨x⟩, ⟨z⟩ and ⟨s⟩ are used word-finally. /i/ can be graphized as ⟨i⟩, ⟨y⟩ or ⟨j⟩ depending on the context. ⟨eu⟩, ⟨o⟩, ⟨oe⟩, ⟨oeu⟩ and ⟨ou⟩ alternatively stand for /ø/, although ⟨ou⟩ and ⟨o⟩ may also stand for /u/, as it is in today's orthography, and /y/, along with ⟨u⟩. In most cases, the influence of French orthography is evident (see Bottasso 1953: XI-XVI; see also Clivio 1974 on 17th century's graphic conventions).

3.2.2 18th Century Stabilization

At the end of the Early modern period Piedmontese orthography begins to stabilize. Pipino (1783), the first to propose a graphic distinction between the grapheme for /o/, namely ⟨ö⟩/⟨ò⟩, and that for /u/, namely ⟨o⟩, utilized ⟨ë⟩, which is today used for /ə/, for /æ/ and ⟨ę⟩ for /ə/. In the same grammar, /w/ was alternately represented by ⟨o⟩ or ⟨u⟩. As for consonants, ⟨ñ⟩ stood for /ŋ/ while ⟨z⟩, today marginally used for /s/, is never attested. The bigrapheme

---

4 10th-/11th-century inscriptions of Vërsèj and Casal Monfrà, as well as 12th-/13th-century *Sermons Subalpins*, probably document a common Gallo-Romance vernacular rather than full-fledged Ancient Piedmontese: on these issues see, among others, Clivio (2002b: 17–20), Gasca Queirazza, Clivio and Pasero (2003: 13–16), Gasca Queirazza (1996) and Tressel (2004), and references therein (☞ also 1.8.1.).

⟨sc⟩ is found in lieu of today's trigrapheme ⟨s-c⟩. Pipino's script is adopted, at times with minor modifications, by all writers, vocabularists, and grammarians of 1800 and early 1900. The choice of ⟨o⟩ for [u], done by Pipino possibly under etymological or Italianizing reasons, was easily accepted because it gave the possibility of writing a great amount of lexical bases in a common way in Piedmontese, and in the two culture, written languages of that time, Latin and Italian. For instance, following Pipino's proposal 'warmth' might have been written ⟨calor⟩ in all the three aforementioned languages, despite the difference in pronunciation.

Different editions of Isler's poems (Pasero 2011) and other 18th- and 19th-century publications show the gradual adoption and stabilization of contemporary norms. ⟨ö⟩ for /o/ is abandoned, and ⟨o⟩, ⟨ò⟩, and ⟨ô⟩ remain the only graphemes used for that phoneme (the latter, also used for /u/ by other authors, later disappears due to typographic reasons). By the end of 1800 ⟨ę⟩ for /ə/ is abandoned and ⟨ë⟩ is consistently used for that phoneme. So are ⟨o⟩ for /u/, ⟨eu⟩ for /ø/, and ⟨u⟩ for /y/ (Perrini 2011). ⟨ñ⟩ was the usual grapheme for /ŋ/, but was subsequently abandoned in favour of ⟨n-⟩, again due to typographical reason.

3.2.3 *The* ortografia moderna

Today's standardized and normalized orthography is usually referred to either as *ortografia moderna*, /urtugra'fia mu'dærna/, 'modern orthography', *ortografia stòrica*, 'classic orthography', Pacotto-Viglongo, by the names of its codifiers, Giuseppe Pacotto e Andrea Viglongo, or "dij Brandé" (of the Brandé), a cultural association founded by the aforementioned Pacotto. The *ortografia moderna* has been definitely codified in the 1930s (Pacotto 1930). This codification, as it has been seen in the course of the present paragraph, is very consistent with the writing/transcription systems adopted for the language from mid-1700 first onward. Pacotto-Viglongo has since been consistently used in virtually all cultured, semi-official and official publications in Piedmontese, including the regional Wikipedia (https://pms.wikipedia.org) and some pages of the Piedmont Regional Council's official website[5] (Clivio 2002: 155, Miola 2013).

During the early-2000, following the process of dekoinization of Piedmontese (Regis 2012a; also ☞ 19.), local dialects have become more used as a means of literary expression and have been the object of amateur lexicographers' work, so that the use of dialect-only graphemes and bigraphemes, or downright deviant orthographies, has increased (Telmon 2006, Regis 2012b). In these

---

5 http://www.cr.piemonte.it/web/lingue-top/pie.

years, scholars and language activists Bruno Villata and Enrico Eandi proposed radical changes of the Pacotto-Viglongo. Villata and Eandi proposed to use ⟨o⟩ for /o/, ⟨u⟩ for /u/, ⟨ö⟩ for /ø/ and ⟨ü⟩ for /y/ in all their occurrences in the written language. These changes, for their proponent, mainly aimed at making the orthography of Piedmontese more similar to Italian and thus allegedly easier for Piedmontese speakers, since they all are literate in Italian (Villata 2001, 2010, Eandi 2008, but cf. Miola 2015, 2021). Despite being endorsed by other scholars (see Regis 2012a: 268) and some activists, their attempt at orthographic reform has until now been scarcely successful.

3.3 Evaluation

3.3.1 *Appropriateness*

Following, albeit with some modifications, Sgall's (1987) model for the "appropriateness" of an orthography, Piedmontese graphemes, allorgraphs and bigraphemes have been positioned on Table 10. The appropriateness of an orthography correlates with less deviation from a one-to-one correspondence between grapheme and phoneme. The more an orthography is deviant from such a correspondence, the more it is complicated.

Table 10 illustrates the degree of complication of an orthography, by taking into account two scales. Scale A, or the scale of complexness, concerns the complexity of the graphemic string that may stand for a phoneme in a given orthography. Since Piedmontese orthography is mainly phonemic (see above), its scale of complexness boils down to four possible levels (vs Sgall's seven), namely

1. a protographeme, i.e., a single grapheme, without any diacritic;
2. a grapheme with a diacritic whose pronunciation regularly correlates with a single sound;
3. a string of graphemes, i.e., a bigrapheme;
4. a string of graphemes whose pronunciation presents a difference between the number of graphemes and the number of phonemes.

On Scale B, i.e., the scale of univocality, graphemes, allographs and bigraphemes are positioned according to their consistency with a one-to-one correlation with a grapheme.

- level (a) is that of absolute bi-uniqueness of the correlation grapheme-phoneme;
- level (b) is that of relative bi-uniqueness;
- level (c) is that of regular deviations, i.e., when different graphemes are used for a single sound and the choice between graphemes is due to a general (orthographic or phonetic/phonemic) rule;

TABLE 10   Appropriateness of the Piedmontese orthography

Scale B		bi-uniq.	rel. biun.	regul. alt.	irreg. dev.
A		(a)	(b)	(c)	(d)
(1)	simple	f, l, m, r	a, b, d, e, j, p, t	c, g, n, u, v, z	i, o, q, s
(2)	diacr. reg.		à, é, è, ë, ì, (n-), ò, ó, (s-), ù		ël
(3)	string	cc, gn, eu, nn	gg, ss	ci, gi	
(4)	excessive phoneme	Has, cH, gH, ij			

- level (d) concerns irregular deviations that take place in the language orthography by a difference between lexemes, or idiosincratically, that is without any functional justification (Sgall's scale B for Czech had seven levels).

Scale A is generally considered less relevant than scale B for the appropriateness of an orthography, since the rules of pronunciation are more easily inferred by speakers of a given language, while the rules of spelling are more difficult to learn. In other words, reading a language one can speak is easier than writing it (Sgall 1987: 18).

Being a mainly phonemic orthography, that of Piedmontese seems highly appropriate for a language, as far as Sgall's model is taken into account. Piedmontese would be easily readable even by people who do not speak it, provided that they learn very few correspondences and orthographic rules concerning pronunciation. A strictly or mainly phonemic orthography—i.e., a shallow orthography (Klima 1972)—is common for those languages whose graphic standardization, like Piedmontese's, or Finnish's, is not very old.

Piedmontese's relations Orth are nonetheless much simpler than those holding in very popular languages' orthographies, such as English's. By way of comparison, there is no bi-unique one-to-one correspondence between grapheme and phoneme in the English orthography. The only relations Orth that holds a one-to-one correspondence between sound and symbol have to do with the bigrapheme ⟨th⟩, which can be used for both /θ/ and /ð/ (see various editions of the *Longman Dictionary of Contemporary English*, quoted in Robinson and Gardelii 2003: 22-ff). All others phonemes have several different spellings: e.g., the relation Orth for /ʃ/ in English is SP /ʃ/ ⟨ce, ch, ci, s, sc, sch, sh, ss, ti⟩ (cf. Iannàccaro 2005: 92). Nonetheless, orthographic tradition of the English language is well established, and no one would consider the English orthography as unappropriate for writing English, although it is uneasy to learn for non-native as well as native speaker.

3.3.2 Effectiveness

Orthographies for minor languages might also be evaluated by their effectiveness. Orthographic effectiveness, according to Cahill (2015), is higher when a script is linguistically sound, acceptable to all stakeholders, and usable (cf. also Smalley 1963). Amongst these three, the crucial factor is the acceptance of the orthography, especially by the speech community (see also Lane 2015).

Although from the strictly linguistic point of view the *ortografia moderna* appears to be appropriate as an orthography for Piedmontese (see previous paragraph), its usability might be questioned. Miola (2015) suggests that the *ortografia moderna* is easier to use than Villata-Eandi for printed and online material, since almost all *ortografia moderna*'s graphemes can be easily typed on an Italian keyboard, while Villata-Eandi's flag characters, i.e., ⟨ö⟩ and ⟨ü⟩, as well as ⟨ë⟩, cannot. Nonetheless, it must be acknowledged that ⟨ë⟩ is also part, and a possible flag character (see below), of the Pacotto-Viglongo script, as are several superfluous diacritics which are even more uneasy to type. The suppression of the latter might be one of the small orthographic changes (Clivio 2001) and other scholars and activists call for.

Furthermore, the speech community does not really seem to have been involved or taken into account in the process of orthography development. As was the case for virtually all European languages before the late-20th century, orthography development has been a top-down process, with intellectuals, activists and writers designing an orthography for an élite of few literates. This holds true for the development of both the Pacotto-Viglongo and the Villata-Eandi orthographies.

Spontaneous writings in Piedmontese reveal that a major difficulty for Italians, and possibly Europeans, in learning to write down Piedmontese with the *ortografia moderna* is the correspondence between /u/ and ⟨o⟩. This is doubtlessly due to the fact that in the Italian orthography ⟨o⟩ always stands for a mid-velar vowel (/o/ or /ɔ/), while ⟨u⟩ generally stands for /u/ and, since all Italians are literate in the Italian orthography, which is very shallow, they tend to use Italian orthographic rules for both languages. But Piedmontese speakers do not spontaneously align with Villata and Eandi's proposal: they tend to use ⟨u⟩ for both /u/ and /y/, and ⟨o⟩ for /o/ and, at times, /ø/ (Miola 2021).[6]

---

[6] The same considerations hold also for Piedmontese migrants in Argentina, who are literate in Spanish.

Another possible criticism to the *ortografia moderna* is that it turns out to be oblivious of the phonetic differences between Piedmontese and the more prestigious, dominant language spoken in Piedmont, i.e., Italian. As shown by Tosco (2008: 5–7), the presence of words with an identical spelling, despite having a different pronunciation, make Piedmontese look like "some kind of Italian," diminishing the visual distinctiveness a minor language's orthography, and its users, may need. So, the issue of visual distinctiveness remains unsolved in the *ortografia moderna* even though it displays at least two possible flag characters that may well differentiate the Piedmontese from the Italian script: ⟨ë⟩ and ⟨ò⟩.[7]

3.3.3 Conclusions

To sum up, today's Piedmontese orthography seems appropriate for the language, although it is generally unknown or plainly refused by Piedmontese speakers.

Given that it is still uncertain whether for a minor language's orthography it is better to look different from the other language(s) spoken in the territory or look like them (Cahill 2015: 13–15; Adams 2015: 232), a reasonable choice for Piedmontese might be an orthography not too far from the Italian one, that is, more similar to that the Piedmontese speech community not alphabetized in their language spontaneously uses (see above), and capable of encompassing variation, perhaps allowing different dialect standards or, better, via a multilectal or polynomic approach (Karan 2015: 117; Dell'Aquila and Iannàccaro 2008). It is worth noting that neither the *ortografia moderna* nor the Villata-Eandi perfectly fit such an ideal Piedmontese orthography. What is more, since Piedmontese is not actually an unwritten/newly written language, the role of its graphic tradition must be taken in due consideration, too.

---

7 On the importance of flag characters, visual distinctiveness, iconisation and branding for minor languages' orthographies, see among others Irvine and Gal (2000: 37), Dell'Aquila and Iannàccaro (2004: 76), Cahill (2015: 14–15), and Sebba (2015).

CHAPTER 4

Words, Word Constituents and Word Classes

As in other Romance varieties, different word classes may be established in Piedmontese on the basis of semantic, morphological and syntactic features. As will become apparent in the relevant chapter, Piedmontese is typologically a moderately fusional language (☞ 19.3.): it has a rich and far from regular morphology, especially (again, as expected) in the verbal domain.

4.1 Roots, Stems, Words, Affixes and Clitics

Words, stems, affixes and clitics must be taken into account in a treatment of the grammar of Piedmontese. Neither of them has a canonical form and all the general phonological rules on permissible clusters apply to them.

The following sections will attempt a definition of each.

4.1.1 Roots and Stems

The part of a word that is common to all its inflected and derived forms and which bears its main lexical meaning is defined here as its stem. Following Stump's (2001: 33) definition, a root is a lexeme's "ultimate default form, devoid of any overt inflectional marking and therefore potentially a bound expression," while a stem is defined as "any expression to which inflectional exponents may potentially be added." It will be noted that his definition makes crucial reference to inflectional (vs. derivational) morphology—a distinction which is well-known to be dubious or maybe fuzzy.

The Piedmontese inventory of roots is not completely disjoint from its inventory of words, and a word may be equivalent to a root or a stem (and a lexeme), as in the case of the written string *cor* and the phonological string /**kur**/:

(1) *cor!*
     kur
     run\IPV.2S
     'run!'

More commonly, morphological processes operate upon stems in order to form words, as in the case of the diminutive derivational affix /at/ frequently used with verbs. Note that derivational affixes are not glossed separately:

© MAURO TOSCO, EMANUELE MIOLA AND NICOLA DUBERTI, 2023 | DOI:10.1163/9789004544291_005

(2) *corata!*
 kuˈrat-a
 run_a_bit-IPV.2S
 'run around a bit!'

Correspondingly, their orthographic representation has the stems as always written together with preceding or following affixes.

4.1.2 *Words*

Lexemes are distinct from words in Piedmontese, because morphology may cause a lexeme to be realized as different words; in a very simple case, the lexeme ⟨REUSA⟩ is instantiated as either *reusa* /ˈrøza/ 'rose' in the Singular and *reuse* /ˈrøze/ 'roses' in the Plural. In the case of Verbs, several dozen words may instantiate a single lexeme.

At the same time, as is often the case in natural languages (Ramat 2016), it is not easy to define what constitutes a 'word' in Piedmontese. The matter is rather straightforward in writing: a word is in principle written isolated in a text—i.e., with a blank space on both its left and right sides—or with a preceding blank space and a following punctuation mark.

Phonologically, a word can be defined as the domain of a (major) stress. Given the internal composition (and complexity) of Nouns, the word stress may fall on the word stem or one of its affixes (but never on a clitic):

(3) *parlé*
 parˈl-e
 speak-INF
 'to speak'

(4) *parlejne*
 parˈl-e=j=ne
 speak-INF=IND=ATTR.PRO
 'to talk to him/her/them about it/them' [to speak to *x* about *y*]

Morphologically, a word can be equivalent to a stem or, more frequently, be made up by a stem enlarged with one or more affixes and clitics:[1]

---

1 In the recent typological literature the label 'index' is used for bound person forms of Verbs (such as *a* in (5) and *a-j na* in (6)), while 'flag' is used for case or adpositional marking (Haspelmath 2013). In this volume—except for Ch. 19 which is typologically-oriented—the

(5) a pieuv
    a='pjøv
    SBJ.3=rain\PRS.3S
    'it is raining'

(6) a-j na parla
    a=j=na='parl-a
    SBJ.3=IND=ATTR.PRO=speak-PRS.3S
    s/'he tells him/her/them about it/them' (or: *x* tells *y* about *z*)

Syntactically, a word can by itself make a predication:

(7) andoa?
    aŋ'dua ↗
    where Q
    'where?'

4.1.3 Affixes

Affixes are defined here as bound elements that bear grammatical meaning, or for which, in the case of derivational affixes, a central grammatical meaning can be identified. Affixes may either appear before (prefixes) or after (suffixes) a stem, but prefixes are reserved for derivational morphology. Non-concatenative morphology plays a great role, especially in Verbs.

As strings of affixes are common, affixes may also follow another affix. Moreover, certain affixes or allomorphs involve internal morphology only through stem modification.

Inflectional affixes are glossed in small caps and affix boundaries are marked by "-;" derivational affixes are unglossed. Internal, non-concatenative morphology is marked by "\:"

Inflectional suffix:

(8) paisan-a
    paj'zaŋ-a
    she_peasant-s
    'female peasant'

---

traditional labels 'affixes' and 'clitic' are also used at times, although their distinction in Romance languages is not problem-free from the theorical point of view (see Miller 1992 and Monachesi 1999).

Stem modification:

(9) *giornaj*
ʤurˈnaj
newspaper\P
'newspapers'

Unglossed derivational prefix:

(10) *independent*
aŋdipenˈdæŋt[2] (< aŋ-dipenˈdæŋt)
independent
'independent'

Stems and affixes are never graphically isolated nor hyphenated and are always joined to another affix or a stem.

4.1.4 Clitics

A phonological approach to clitics is followed here, and clitics are defined as elements identified on the basis of their prosodic behavior; different from words, clitics are never uttered in isolation, but different from affixes, they attach to full words rather than to stems. Moreover, clitics never bear accent and they make a single phonological word together with the word they precede (proclitics) or follow (enclitics).

While such a definition goes a long way towards separating clitics from affixes, it is still not sufficient to consistently separate them from words. The solution adopted here is totally empirical and based upon our own practices and intuitions as native speakers: we have consistently transcribed and glossed as clitics those elements which mostly combine phonologically with other (following) elements, such as the Prepositions (☞ 13.) and the Subordinator *che, ch'* /ke, k=/ (☞ 15.3.), but we have avoided to do so in the case of, e.g., most Possessives (☞ 8.4.) and certain conjunctions or connectives used in coordination (☞ 16.1.). This is certainly an area in need of future, in-depth analysis.

Clitics are glossed in small caps and clitic boundaries are marked by "=."

---

2 The prefix /aŋ-/ may be realised as /iŋ-/ or /əŋ-/ and appears in writing as either *in-* or *an-*, but the former is way more common. The same applies to its allomorph before a bilabial consonant /am-/, usually written *im-* (☞ 6.5.2.).

WORDS, WORD CONSTITUENTS AND WORD CLASSES 121

Orthographically, proclitics are as a rule written separately (just as words), while enclitics are separated from the preceding word by a hyphen or, still, joined graphically to a preceding word or another clitic. Examples (4) and (6), repeated herebelow, show different graphic realizations:

(4) *parlejne*
 par'l-e=j=ne
 speak-INF=IND=ATTR.PRO
 'to talk to him/her/them about it/them' [to speak to *x* about *y*]

(6) *a-j na parla*
 a=j=na='parl-a
 SBJ.3=IND=ATTR.PRO=speak-PRS.3S
 s/'he tells him/her/them about it/them' (or: '*x* tells *y* about *z*')

Leaving aside for the moment compound words, the preceding notes give rise to the following tabular representation of the graphical expression of the categories:

TABLE 11   Graphical representation of words, clitics, stems and affixes

	Words	Clitics	Stems	Affixes
Isolated	✓	✓	✗	✗
Hyphenated	✗	✓	✗	✗
Joined to stems	✗	✓	✗	✓
Joined to affixes	✗	✓	✓	✓

4.1.5 *Canonical Form of Words and Palindromes*

There is in principle no maximum or minimum number of phonemes per word, and therefore theoretically no restriction on the length (measured in terms of number of phonemes) of a word, with one being the minimal number of phonemes. The possible number of phonemes in a phonological word is greatly augmented by clitics.

TABLE 12   Word length and number of phonemes per word

No. of phonemes	Word	Meaning (and gloss)
1	é [e]	'yes'
2	mi [mi]	'I' ("IDP.1SG")
3	bel [bel]	'nice'
4	tron [truŋ]	'thunder'
5	lòsna [ˈlozna]	'lightning'
6	sotror [sutˈrur]	'gravedigger'
7	ninsòla [niŋˈsola]	'hazelnut'
8	travajòt [travaˈjot]	'small piece of work'
...		
12	i-j na parlëria [i=j=na=parləˈria]	'I would talk to him/her/them about it/them'
...		

Palindromic words are possible but very rare: an example is the Adjective *tut* /tyt/ 'all.' An orthographic (but not phonological) palindrome is the numeral *ses* /sez/ 'six'—in its turn homophonous with the 2nd Singular of the Main Present of the Verb 'to be.' A palindromic clause is *a-i nia* /a=j=ˈni-a/ ('SBJ.3=IND =drown-PRS-3S'), roughly 'it drowns there.'

On the other hand, the cumulative effect of various historical phonological rules upon the parent language (Latin) has led to the presence of a sizable number of homographes and an even larger number of homophones:

aut /awt/ 'high,' *autr* /awt(r)/ 'other'
mars /mars/   'March' / 'rotten'
neuv /nøw/   'nine' / 'new'
sent /sæɲt/   'hundred' / 'hear!'

4.2   Morphological Mechanisms

– Affixation is the main morphological mechanism and may take two forms: suffixation and prefixation. Suffixation only is used in inflectional morphology, while derivation uses both suffixation and, more rarely, prefixation.

WORDS, WORD CONSTITUENTS AND WORD CLASSES 123

– Stem modification is again only used in inflectional morphology and is very common.
– Reduplication does not play a role in morphology, is limited to phonological words and has expressive value. It is overall very rare, although it is possible in order to express the superlative of Adjectives or Adverbs (☞ 6.4.2.):

(11) *fa mach **bin bin** atension, për piasì*
      fa   mak biŋ biŋ atæŋˈsjuŋ / pərˈpjaˈzi
      do\IPV.2S only well well attention BEN=favor
      'just take very much care, please'

– Suprasegmental features play a role in the occasional use of stress in grammar. A case in point is, among First Class Verbs (☞ 10. 2.2.), the Imperative Singular and the 3rd Singular Main Present, which are homophonous and bear their word stress on the penultimate syllable, vs. the stress on the final syllable in the Participle:

(12) *sara!*
      ˈsar-a
      close-IPV.2S
      'close (s)!'

(13) *(a l'ha) sarà*
      (a=ˈla)   saˈr-a
      (SBJ.3=have\PRS.3S) close-PTCL
      's/he closed'

More often, stress alternation is accompanied by vowel change and/or other stem-internal processes:

(14) *gieug-a!*
      ˈdʒøg-a
      play-IPV.2S
      'play (s)!'

(15) *(a l'ha)*   *giug-à*
      (a=ˈla)   dʒyˈg-a
      (SBJ.3=have\PRS.3S) play-PTCL
      's/he played'

Taking into account intonation patterns, a rising intonation is used to express questions.

4.3 Suppletion

As the Verb is the major locus of morphological variation, it is also where phenomena of suppletion, syncretism, alternation, etc. are more extensively attested. A few examples only are presented here.

Features in the various parts of speech differ and they are treated separately; the Verb is again where the highest number of features interplay.

Suppletion is abundantly attested in verbal morphology, as (predictably in Romance) in the Verbs 'to be' and 'to go:'

TABLE 13 Suppletion in the Main Present of 'to be' and 'to go' (Subject clitics not included)

	'to be,' Main Present	'to go,' Main Present
1SG	*son*	*vad(o)*
2SG	*ses*	*vas*
3SG	*(l')é*	*va*
1PL	*soma*	*andoma*
2PL	*seve*	*andeve*
3PL	*son*	*van*

The different pronominal series may be conceived of as another instance of suppletion, as exemplified in the different forms of the First Singular:

TABLE 14 Suppletion in the First Singular Pronouns

	First Singular Pronouns
Independent	*mi* (IDP.1SG)
Subject Clitic	*i* (SBJ.1)
Object clitic	*m* (OBJ.1SG)
Possessive	*me* (POSS.1SG)

4.4 Syncretism

Syncretism (Maiden 2021) is rampant, especially again in verbal morphology. A common pattern is {1SG&3SG} vs. {2} vs. {1PL&3PL}, as in the Imperfect Main of the regular Verb *pijé* 'to take' (but found in other paradigms as well):

TABLE 15 Syncretism in the Verb: 'to take,' Main Present

	'to take,' Main Imperfect
1S	*pijava*
2S	*pijave*
3S	*pijava*
1P	*pijavo*
2P	*pijave*
3P	*pijavo*

Another pattern is found in the Subject clitics: {1&2PL} vs. {2SG} vs. {3}:

TABLE 16 Syncretism in the Subject clitics

	Subject clitic
1S	*i*
2S	*it*
3S	*a*
1P	*i*
2P	*i*
3P	*a*

4.5 Word Classes

Words in Piedmontese can be classified in a number of major word classes (not counting internal subclasses) on the basis of their morphology and their syntactic distribution.

- *Nouns* (☞ 5.) encompass semantically the category of non-relational entities, or things; they have inherent gender, they may inflect for number through affixes and for definiteness and countability through the grounders and the classifiers, although specific subclasses of Nouns, such as proper names, are a partial exception. Syntactically, Nouns can act as
  - heads of Noun phrases, whereby they command agreement in gender and number on several types of modifiers;
  - modifiers in attributive phrases
  - predicates in nominal clauses
  - subjects of clauses
  - objects of transitive clauses
  - complements of Prepositions

  Nouns are an open class. New members of the class are created through internal derivation (from other Nouns), trans-categorial derivation (from other word classes), or borrowing.
- *Adjectives* (☞ 6.) are a robust category in Piedmontese. They encompass semantically the subset of the members of the category of atemporal relations with a nominal trajector (Langacker 1987); they may inflect for gender and number, and may act syntactically as Noun modifiers or as predicates. When grounded, Adjectives may act as Nouns and cover the same syntactic roles of Nouns. Adjectives are in Piedmontese an open class and new members are derived from either Nouns, Verbs or other Adjectives.
- *Personal pronouns* (☞ 7.), maybe strictly speaking a subclass of Nouns, will be treated separately. They are a closed class of words and clitics sharing nominal features in both morphological and syntactic terms and adding features flagging the syntactic role of the referent, such as subject, direct or indirect object, etc.
- We posit a closed class of *grounders* (☞ 8.) on the basis of semantic roles only, i.e., the capacity to ground an element. The short list of members in this class is supplemented by elements from other classes via grammaticalization, a notable example being the Attributive Preposition *ëd* /əd/ (ATTR).
- Among the *quantifiers* (☞ 9.), the cardinal numbers are the only open word class made up of morphologically invariabile items (with the exception of the cardinals for 'one' and 'two'—as well as, in a few varieties, 'three'—which are gendered). New membership in the category is obtained through the recursive mechanism of counting. Syntactically, the quantifiers usually act as Noun modifiers.
- *Verbs* (☞ 10.) encompass semantically the category of temporal relations as defined in Cognitive Grammar; they encompass, with many exceptions, all four main categories (Van Valin and LaPolla 1997: 83) of Situations, Events,

Processes, and Actions. Morphologically, they may inflect for a high number of features, such as the number of the subject of the clause, the tense of the clause, etc. Verbs are an open word class: new members of the class are created through internal derivation (from other Verbs), trans-categorial derivation (from other word classes), or through borrowing.
– *Adverbs* (☞ 12.) are a large but closed class of invariable elements whose basic role is to act as second-degree modifiers (i.e., modifiers of Noun phrases), modifiers of predicates or of whole clauses.
– *Connectives* (☞ 13., 16.) are a closed set of invariable words used in linking Noun phrases and clauses. They are supplemented in their functions by Adverbs.
– *Prepositions* (☞ 13.) can be invariable words but are more often clitics that profile non-processual relationships and confer focal prominence on a landmark (Langacker 2008: 115–117). They are a closed class, while the prepositional phrases built via Prepositions may be nominal modifiers to Noun phrases, or arguments/adverbials in clauses.
– Piedmontese does not have a separate class of *ideophones* but has *onomatopoeias*, used in an expressive function, such as in exclamation and swearing, but without a syntactic role and usually intonationally separated. They will not systematically be dealt with. To the same expressive effect elements from different parts of speech (such as Nouns or Adjectives), Noun phrases and even full clauses may be used.

CHAPTER 5

Nouns

Although commanding agreement in gender and number when acting as syntactic heads, Piedmontese Nouns often flag both categories only covertly and their inflection is on the whole relatively simple and limited. Syntactic functions are expressed in prepositional phrases or through word order. Nominal derivational morphology is richer—but only partially productive.

5.1   Overview

Nouns encompass semantically the category of non-relational entities, or "things." The usual distinction between count and mass Nouns is marked only syntactically in Piedmontese, through the use of grounders (☞ 8.). Count Nouns are by definition not homogeneous: they are "objects," composed of parts or components which are not themselves the same entities of the whole: a countable Noun cannot be split without losing its identity. Count Nouns are also discrete or bounded, i.e., they are conceptualized as involving a boundary separating them from other instances of the same entity and from the outer (physical or mental) world.[1]

On the contrary, mass Nouns are "substances," which are rather made up of portions, and which are homogeneous (each part of them is still an instance of the same substance), divisible (they can be split without losing their identity), and are continuous and unbounded: they are not defined as necessarily involving a boundary or limit in the physical or mental world, and any quantity of them still counts as an instance of that substance.

Finally and most crucially for what involves the category of Number, count Nouns are replicable, while mass Nouns are not: a substance can be shrinked or expanded by taking or adding portions of it without losing its identity, while,

---

[1] A major distinction expounded by Rijkhoff (2000, 2002) splits the traditional category of count Nouns between sort Nouns—Nouns which do not imply any number of objects when used in their unmarked form—and singular object Nouns, which are "nouns that in their unmarked form denote a single object" (Rijkhoff 2000: 232). Sort and singular object Nouns are distinguished by the feature [± Shape], with sort Nouns going together with mass Nouns in being [– Shape] and singular object Nouns [+ Shape]. The distinction between sort and singular object Nouns does not seem to be instantiated in Piedmontese.

by "replicating" an object, an increased number of instances of the same object will be obtained, each of them *per se* identifiable and bounded (Langacker 1990: 69–74).

Much the same defining features of mass Nouns apply also to collective Nouns, which "designate a property of several discrete entities that are conceived as a unit" (Rijkhoff 2002: 53). Just like mass Nouns are composed of portions, collectives are made up of members, whose addition or subtraction does not lead to a change in the nature of the entity (as when a family or a people shrinks or enlarges without losing its status as an entity). In Rijkhoff's terms, both mass and collective Nouns are homogeneous. The members of a collective Noun are themselves discrete entities (e.g., members of the same species), while mass Nouns typically denote continuous substances: they are opposite in terms of their "state of Dividedness" in Talmy's (2000) terminology.[2]

The inflectional morphology of Piedmontese Nouns is relatively simple; in comparison to other Romance languages, few irregular forms are found (possibly as a consequence of the absence of morphological number marking on many Nouns). On the other hand, the derivational nominal morphology is very rich, both in frozen word formatives and in productive affixes.

Although no maximal number of phonemes is assigned to nouns, a good number of basic Nouns are monosyllabic and CVC in shape:

can   /kaŋ/   'dog/-s'
fior /fjur/ 'flower/-s'

Nouns may be primitive or derived on the basis of their morphology: primitive Nouns may be monomorphemic and appear in their stem form. Primitive Nouns may also be bimorphemic, i.e., composed of a stem and an inflectional affix or stem variation that marks number and to some extent makes gender overt. Derived Nouns are always composed with at least a derivational affix (☞ 5.4.2.).

– Primitive Nouns:
  – monomorphemic:
     cheur   /kør/   'heart/-s'

---

2   In Talmy's view, mass and collective Nouns are also opposed in terms of their "State of Boundedness," with collectives being bounded and mass Nouns unbounded. Rijkhoff uses to this effect the feature [± Shape], with mass Nouns being [– Shape] and collectives [+ Shape]: mass Nouns, being unbounded, cannot be counted, while collectives (which are bounded) can.

- bimorphemic:
  fije /fi-e/ 'girls, daughters' ('girl-P')
  giornaj /dʒurˈnaj/ 'newspapers' ('newspaper\P')
- Derived Nouns:
  omet /uˈmæt/ 'cairn' (from *òm* /om/ 'man' followed by the derivational diminutive affix *-et* /ˈæt/; lit.: 'tiny man')
  intrada /iŋˈtrada/ 'entrance' (from the verb *intré* /iŋˈtre/ 'to enter' followed by the derivational affix *-ada* /ˈada/)

The genders are M (Masculine) and F (Feminine). Numbers are S (Singular) and P (Plural).

Gender is lexically determined on primitive Nouns.

Number marking is covert for many Nouns and plurality may be recovered through agreement on the Classifiers Quantifiers or on the Verb. Singular is the default number.

Piedmontese Nouns may be divided into three inflectional classes on the basis of their behavior in number marking (☞ 5.3.); gender is shown in brackets and further discussed in 5.2.

Class 1 has no overt number marking; Class 2 has separate singular and plural affixes, and Class 3 changes the final segment of the stem:

TABLE 17   Inflectional classes of Nouns

Class	Ending	Gender	Pluralization strategy	Examples
1.	bare stem	M, F	no plural marking	*fior* /fjur/ 'flower' (F)
				odor /uˈdur/ 'smell' (M)
				badòla /baˈdola/ 'moron' (M)
				masnà /mazˈna/ 'child' (F)
2.	unstressed *-a*	F	substitutive: *-a* → *-e*	*facia* /ˈfatʃa/, *facie* /ˈfatʃe/ 'faces' (F)
3.	*-l*	M (F)	substitutive: *l#* → *j#*	*caval* /kaˈval/—*cavaj* /kaˈvaj/ 'horses' (M)
				pel /pel/—*pej*/pej/ 'skins' (F)

A couple of nouns not belonging clearly to any class are: *ann* /an/ 'year,' Pl. *ani* /ˈani/ or *agn* /aɲ/ and *òm* /om/ 'man, husband,' which along with the regular Plural *òm* /om/ may also exhibit irregular forms such as *òmini* /ˈomini/ (notably, this one is attested in Turin), *eumi* /ˈømi/, and (ancient or rural) *òimi* /ˈo(j)mi/.[3]

---

3 For 'man, husband' also *òmo* /ˈomu/, with an invariable Plural, may be used (see also below).

All inflectional morphology is exclusively suffixal. Derivational morphology is generally suffixal but may also be, although marginally, prefixal. Derivational morphology can be intra- and inter-categorial. Nouns can be derived from other Nouns, Adjectives and Verbs. Nouns can in their turn be the source of inter-categorial derivation and yield Adjectives and Verbs.

Definiteness is expressed through preposed Grounders agreeing in gender and number with their head Noun.

The different syntactic roles which may be played by Nouns are expressed through word order (☞ 18.1.). or the use of prepositions (☞ 13.).

5.2   Gender

Piedmontese Nouns are assigned to one of two noun classes, traditionally called genders and which oppose a Masculine (M) and a Feminine (F). Together with number (☞ 5.3.), gender in Piedmontese determines agreement on noun modifiers (☞ 10.2. for gender agreement in verbs).[4] Gender is inherent, is assigned to any Noun and is only minimally semantically based. The expression of biological sex on humans and other culturally-important animates is often based upon different stems (and the resulting Nouns are then assigned in general the semantically "correct" gender; ☞ 5.2.2.). Following Corbett (1991: 57) for French, we can express this state of affairs as follows:
– sex-differentiatiable Nouns denoting males are masculine.
– sex-differentiatiable Nouns denoting females are feminine.
Morphological assignment of gender is found in the compound Nouns: as in French and Italian, compound Nouns whose first element is a verb are in their great majority Masculine (☞ 5.4.4.).

Gender is only moderately an overt category in Piedmontese: for historical reasons, gender assignment is unpredictable in a sizable number of cases, and especially in consonant-ending primitive Nouns. Except for a few Masculine Nouns ending in /a/ (such as *poeta* /puˈeta/ 'poet'), *a*-ending Nouns are Feminine, thereby contrasting with the preference for a final consonant in Masculine (but also a sizable number of Feminine) Nouns:

---

4   Cf. Corbett (1991: 4) for agreement as the determining criterion for the linguistic category of gender.

(1) *na bela fija bionda*
 n-a=ˈbel-a   ˈfia   ˈbjuŋd-a
 INDEF-F=pretty-F girl-S blonde-F
 'a pretty blonde girl'

(2) *un bel fieul biond*
 aŋ=ˈbel   fjøl bjuŋd
 INDEF=pretty boy blonde
 'a pretty blonde boy'

Gender predictability is found in derived Nouns (☞ 5.4.); as a general rule, Nouns derived with consonant-ending affixes are Masculine, although an exception is provided by the highly productive nouns in *-assion* (-aˈsjuŋ/), that are Feminine.

5.2.1 Inherent Gender

As anticipated above, in their Singular form most Masculine and many Feminine Nouns are consonant-ending, while many Feminine and a few Masculine Nouns end in /a/. In the former group many Nouns are monosyllabic, in the latter at least bisyllabic.

Consonant-ending Masculine Nouns:

| *taj* | /taj/ | 'cut (noun)' |
| *vrin* | /vriŋ/ | 'gimlet' |

Consonant-ending Feminine Nouns:

| *sal* | /sal/ | 'salt' |
| *tor* | /tur/ | 'tower/-s' |

/a/-ending Feminine Nouns:

| *camisa* | /kaˈmiza/ | 'shirt' |
| *sòtola* | /ˈsotula/ | 'top' (the toy) |

/a/-ending Masculine Nouns:

NOUNS

barba   /ˈbarba/   'uncle'[5]
girola /dʒiˈrula/ 'wanderer'

Derivational morphemes (either frozen or productive) trigger gender assignment:[6]

arferiment /arferiˈmæɲt/ 'reference' (Masculine, as all *-ment*-derived nouns)
decision   /detʃiˈsjuŋ/ 'decision' (Feminine, as all *-s(s)ion*-derived nouns)
blëssa   /ˈbləssa/   'beauty' (Feminine, as all *-ëssa*-derived nouns)

5.2.2 Gender Inflection

Many Masculine Nouns referring to male entities may have a corresponding Feminine in *-a*. The rule is productive for Adjectives, scarcely so (being limited to cases of biological gender assignment) in Nouns:

gat /gat/ 'cat; tom-cat'   *gata* /ˈgata/ 'she-cat'
cit /tʃit/ 'small; he-baby; son'   *cita* /ˈtʃita/ 'small (Feminine); she-baby; daughter'

Excluded are those adjective-derived Nouns ending in *-a* in their Masculine form and which are therefore invariable for gender in the Singular:

fassista /faˈsista/ 'fascist' (but *fassiste* /faˈsiste/ 'fascist (women, Feminine Plural)')

Several cases of biological gender are expressed through different stems; the Feminine forms are further gender-marked by the gender marker *-a* /a/:

barba /ˈbarba/   'uncle'   vs. *magna*   /ˈmaɲa/   'aunt'
fieul /fjøl/   'son; boy'   vs. *fija*   /ˈfia/   'daughter; girl'
frel, fradel, fratel /frel, fraˈdel, fraˈtel/ 'brother'
                                                       vs. *sorela, seur(e)* /suˈrela, sør, ˈsøre/ 'sister'
gënner /ˈdʒənnær/   'brother-in-law' vs. *nòra*   /ˈnora/   'sister-in-law'
nòno   /ˈnonu/   'grandfather'   vs. *nòna*   /ˈnona/   'grandmother'

---

5 A homophonous *barba* /ˈbarba/ 'beard' is Feminine.
6 Only in this chapter, derivational morphemes are kept separated in transcription, but no glossing of the derivational affixes is provided.

òmo, òm	/ˈomu, om/	'man; husband'	vs.	*fomna, dòna*	/ˈfumna, ˈdona/	'woman; wife'
pare	/ˈpare/	'father'	vs.	*mare*	/ˈmare/	'mother'
monsù	/munˈsy/	'Mr'	vs.	*madama* *madamin*	/maˈdama/ /madaˈmiɲ/	'Ms, lady' 'Ms, lady' (eventually younger or, traditionally, unmarried)
bech	/bæk/	'ram'	vs.	*crava*	/ˈkrava/	'goat'
beu	/bø/	'ox'	vs.	*vaca*	/ˈvaka/	'cow'
crin	/kriŋ/	'pig'	vs.	*trua, treuja*	/ˈtrya, ˈtrøja/	'sow'
gal	/gal/	'rooster'	vs.	*galin-a*	/gaˈliɲa/	'chicken'
moton	/muˈtuŋ/	'mutton'	vs.	*fea, feja*	/ˈfæ(j)a/	'sheep'

The longer forms *fradel, fratel* 'brother' and *sorela* 'sister,' as well as *nòno, nòna*, and *dòna* 'woman' are long-established Italian loans. Both *òmo* /ˈomu/ and *òm* /om/ 'man; husband' are part of the native vocabulary.

As anticipated, many derivational morphemes are semantically and morphologically gendered:

artajor /artajˈur/ 'delicatessen owner' (Masculine)
artajòira /artajˈojra/ 'delicatessen owner' (Feminine)

Gender-sensitive affixes are nevertheless also found as productive affixes in nouns for inanimate and asexual entities:

assenseur /asæŋˈsør/ (also *assensor* /asæŋˈsur/) 'elevator, lift' (Masculine)

5.3 Number

As discussed in 5.1., number is not morphologically expressed on most Nouns, especially Masculine:

liber /ˈlibær/ 'book/books'

disambiguation is provided by agreement and the use of Determiners and Classifiers (☞ 10.):

NOUNS

ël liber   /əl=ˈlibær/   'the book'
ij liber   /i=ˈlibær/   'the books'
ëd liber   /əd=ˈlibær/   'books'

Zero-marking of number applies to both C-ending Nouns (a majority of all nouns) and vowel-ending Masculine Nouns:

poeta   /puˈeta/   'poet/-s' (Masculine)
saba   /ˈsaba/   'Saturday/-s' (Masculine)

Nouns with final-stress are invariable in the Plural even if Feminine. This applies a fortiori to monosyllabic nouns:

ca   /ka/   'house/-s'
ragnà   /raˈɲa/   'cobweb/s'

Nouns ending in *-l* (most of them M) change it to *-j* in the Plural:

caval	/kaˈval/	*cavaj*	/kaˈvaj/ ('horse\P')	'horse/-s'
giornal	/dʒurˈnal/	*giornaj*	/dʒurˈnaj/ ('newspaper\P')	'newspaper/-s'
fieul	/fjøl/	*fieuj*	/fjøj/ ('son\P')	'son/-s; boy/-s'
fil	/fil/	*fij*	/fij/ ('thread\P')	'thread/-s'
dil	/dil/	*dij*	/dij/ ('finger\P')	'finger/-s; toe/-s'

The very few primitive Feminine Nouns ending in *-l* optionally follow the same pattern, although zero-marking seems more common.

pel /pel/ *pel, pej* /pel, pej/ ('skin\P') 'skin/-s; hide/-s'

Most Feminine Nouns in *-l* are either synchronically or historically derived from Adjectives in *-al*. Different from Adjectives, where agreement patterns for adjectives in *-l* are subject to much variation (☞ 6.3.), the change of final *-l* to *-j* in plurals is quite regular in Nouns:

capital	/kapiˈtal/	*capitaj*	/kapiˈtaj/ ('capital\P')	'capital city/-ies'
nassional	/nasjuˈnal/	*nassionaj*	/nasjuˈnaj/ ('national\P')	'national team/-s'
vocal	/vuˈkal/	*vocaj*	/vuˈkaj/ ('vowel\P')	'vowel/-s'

vs., e.g.,

(3) ëd batibeuj a l'han s-ciopà ant le sità **capitale** dij doi pais
    əd=bati'bøj a='laŋ   stʃu'p-a   aŋt=l-e=si'ta
    ATTR=riot   SBJ.3=have\PRS.3P blow-PTCL   INE=DET-F.P=town
    kapi'tal-e   d=i='duj   pa'iz
    capital-F.P ATTR=DET\P=two\M country
    'riots erupted in the capital towns of the two countries' (Sandron 2004c: 20)

Feminine Nouns ending in -*a* change it to -*e* (/e/) in the Plural:

reusa /'røza/ ('rose-S')   *reuse* /'røze/ ('rose-P') 'rose/-s'

In those dialects which close final unstressed /e/ to /i/ (☞ 2.4.1.4., PP 5. Closing), the Feminine Plural affix is realized as [i].

The survival of metaphony

No trace of any ancient metaphony from final proto-Romance -*i* is preserved in the contemporary koine. Many local varieties show instead some traces of it, especially with words like *òm* /ɔm/ 'man'~ *eumi* /'ømi/ 'men,' *pciòt* /ptʃɔt/ 'child' ~ *pcieuti* /'ptʃøti/ 'children,' *matòt* /ma'tɔt/ 'boy' ~ *mateucc* /ma'tøtʃ/ 'boys,' *gat* /gat/ 'cat' ~ *ghèt* /gæt/ 'cats.' The phenomenon is widely attested in ancient texts even from the town of Turin (Berruto 1974; Tonso 2017).

5.4 Derivational Morphology of Nouns

Derivation may be frozen or productive, and many derivational affixes are shared with Adjectives. Zero-derivation and suffixes are used, as well as, to a limited extent, prefixes and compounding.

Many derived Nouns are borrowed rather than directly formed from Piedmontese primitive Nouns. The affixes used in productive derivation are a subset of the elements found in frozen derivation. No distinction will be drawn in the following sections between productive and frozen derivation and Noun formation.

5.4.1 *Zero-Derivation*

Any Piedmontese Adjective may act as a Noun without any further derivation. An Adjective used as a Noun may express the quality referred to by the Adjective or any instance of it, or, in other cases, an entity endowed of or dedicated to the quality:

fòl /**fol**/ 'fool' → 'a fool'

A few de-adjectival Nouns are Feminine, although the basic (Masculine) form of the Adjective is found in adjectival use:

caud /**kawd**/ 'warm; hot' *la caud* /**la=ˈkawd**/ 'the heat; the hot weather'
freid /**fræjd**/ 'cold' *la freid* /**la=ˈfræjd**/ 'the cold' (noun)

Occasionally, adverbs may also be lexicalized as Nouns, as is the case for *bin* 'well' > *la bin* 'prayer:'

(4) *mi 'm consumo ant la mia **bin** servaja*
    mi   m=kuŋˈsym-u   aɲt=l-a=ˈmi-a   biŋ   serˈvaj-a
    IDP.1S OBJ.1S=wear_out-PRS.1S   INE=DET-F=POSS.1S-F   prayer   wild-F
    'and I am consumed in my wild prayer' (Milo Bré, https://pms.wikisource .org/wiki/Milo_Br%C3%A9/An_mes_a_l%27erba)

Verb-to-Noun derivation may be expressed through the bare verbal stem. Different from what is the case with deadjectival derivation (☞ 6.5.), deverbal zero-derivation is not productive:[7]

balé /**baˈl-e**/ ('dance-INF')[8] 'to dance' → *bal* /**bal**/ 'dance' (Noun)
gatijé /**gaˈt(i)je**/ 'to tickle'→ *gatij* /**gaˈtij**/ 'tickle' (Noun)
tiré /**tiˈre**/ 'to pull; to shoot' → *tir* /**tir**/ 'shot'
volé /**vuˈle**/ 'to fly' → *vòl* /**vol**/ 'flight'

The same applies to verbs containing a productive or frozen prefix:

artorné /**artorˈne**/ 'to return' → *artorn* /**arˈturn**/ 'return' (Noun)

Zero-marked Verb-to-Noun derivation is mainly used for action Verbs (unsurprisingly, Verbs that may undergo this nominalization belong mostly to the First Class; ☞ 10.2.2.) and nominalizes the action itself, either in its generality or as a single instance of it.

In most such cases, zero-derivation is excluded (**poss, s-cianch* from *possé* /**puˈs-e**/ 'to push' and *s-cianché* / **stʃaŋˈk-e**/ 'to tear,' respectively).)

---

[7] Cf. Tosco (2012) on the rarity of Ø-derivation in Piedmontese and the derivational affixes used in its place in contemporary Piedmontese.
[8] Derivation is here conventionally shown as starting from the Infinitive form of the verb—itself an inflectionally derived category, of course.

A special kind of Verb-to-Noun derivation is found with the rare—and mainly expressive—use of a 3SG form of the Main mood of the Verb in order to describe a habitual doer of the action expressed by the Verb:

dësblé /dəz'bl-e/ ("take_apart-INF") 'to disassemble, take apart' → *dësbela* /dəz'bel-a/ ("take_apart-PRS.3S") 'rascal' (mainly used for a young boy)

Similar is the case of Feminine Verb-derived Nouns in -*a*:

dësmentié /dəzmæŋ'tje/ 'to forget' → *dësmentia* /dəz'mæŋtj-a/ ('forget-PRS.3S') 'forgetfulness'

Finally, a non-productive apparent prefix *ba- (from Latin BIS 'twice' ☞ 6.5.2. for the same prefix in Adjectives) is found in a few expressive nouns for which no unprefixed form is attested, such as *balengo* /ba'læŋgu/ 'moron,' or with little or no change in meaning in respect to the unprefixed form:

bòja, babòja /'boja, ba'boja/ 'larva; caterpillar;' *cicio, bacicio* /'tʃitʃu, ba'tʃitʃu/ 'fool; puppet.'

5.4.2 *Suffixal Derivation*
Nominalization of a verb through their assignment to the /a/-ending Feminine Nouns is common:

spussé /spy'se/ 'to stink' → *spussa* /'spysa/ 'stink'

In both zero-derivation and Feminine-marked derivation, the contrary derivation path may of course also be assumed:

fiòca /'fjoka/ 'snow' → *fioché* /fju'ke/ 'to snow'
bësbij /bəz'bij/ 'murmur' → *bësbijé* /bəzbi'je/ 'to whisper'

More commonly, a number of derivational affixes are used. They are often shared by denominal, deadjectival and deverbal derivation, and, as anticipated, they are also found as frozen elements in noun formation at large. Moreover, their semantic content is often ambiguous or the same value is shared by different affixes. Due to their limited productivity or their status as frozen noun formatives, derivational affixes are not glossed in the grammar.

A first group of affixes involves the use of a few adjectival diminutive and pejoratives affixes, but with nominal stems; or still the use of the Noun derived with such an affix is more common as a noun than as an adjective:

NOUNS

motor /mu'tur/ 'engine' → *motorin* /mutu'riŋ/ 'motor scooter'
madama /ma'dama/ 'Mistress, lady' → *madamin* /mada'miŋ/ 'Miss, young lady' (M)[9]

An indirect proof of the peculiar usage of diminutive affixes with Noun is shown by the existence of various idiosyncratic stem changes in the derived noun:

vej /vej/ 'old' → *veciòt* /ve'tʃot/ 'oldster' (M), *veciòta* /ve'tʃota/ (F)

Here, the regularly derived *vejòt, vejòta* /ve'jot/, /ve'jota/ are possibly more common as Adjectives.

giovo /'dʒu(v)u/ 'young' → *giovnòt* /dʒuv'not/ 'youngster' (M), *giovnòta* /dʒuv'nota/ (F) (**giovòt* and **giovòta* do not exist, either as Nouns or Adjectives).

Multiple derivation is possible; again, regular phonological changes may apply:

veciotin   /vetʃu'tiŋ/   'a little oldster'

Semantic specialization of Nouns derived with the diminutive affixes is of course common:

machina   /'makina/   'car; machine'
machinòta   /maki'nota/   'little or cheap car'
machinëtta   /maki'nətta/   'little machine' (mainly not a car, more a 'gizmo')
machinin-a   /maki'niɲa/   'toy car'

Diminutives and pejoratives are obviously widely used in expressive speech and in the formation of hypocorisms expressing endearment:

Gioann /dʒu'an/ 'John' → *Gioanin* /dʒua'niŋ/ 'Jim'

In this function, affixation may combine with other non-productive morphological means, such as syllable dropping:

---

9   The Feminine form *madamin-a* /mada'miɲa/ is also attested. However, when the affix *-in* is applied to a Noun the output is often Masculine even with a Feminine base.

Anna /ˈanna/ 'Anne' → *Neta* /ˈneta/ 'Annette'[10]

A few derivational affixes express a single instance of the action expressed by the verbal stem as well as the action in itself. Primary among them is

- *-on*[11] /uŋ/: as this affix is used in the derivation of augmentatives and pejoratives Adjectives (☞ 6.6.1.), there is a certain bleaching in meaning. All Nouns derived with *-on* are Masculine in gender, even those derived from a Feminine base:

pansa /ˈpaŋs-a/ 'belly (F)' → *panson* /paŋˈsuŋ/ 'potbelly (M)'
possé /puˈs-e/ 'to push' → *posson* /puˈsuŋ/ 'thrust, shove'
s-cianché /stʃaŋˈke/ 'to tear' → *s-ciancon* /stʃaŋˈkuŋ/ 'tear, rip'
sgiaflé /zdʒafˈle/ 'to slap' → *sgiaflon* /zdʒafˈluŋ/ 'hard slap, backhand' (implying a harder or augmentative version of *sgiaf* /zdʒaf/ 'slap')

Moreover, Nouns are often found with this affix as a frozen formative or simply with /ˈuŋ/ as the last part of what is synchronically their stem. E.g., *boton* /buˈtuŋ/ 'button' is from old French *bouton* (and ultimately from the same Germanic stem from which *but* /byt/ and its English translation 'bud' are derived); synchronically it is at the origin of the Verb *botoné* /butuˈn-e/ 'to button up.'

Still, *-on* is used in derivation, often to denote a male individual who behaves in such a way as is thought typical of the entity expressed by the underived Noun or, in deverbal derivation, who engages in the activity expressed by the Verb if the latter has a negative connotation:

pòrch /pork/ 'swine' → *porcon* /purˈkuŋ/ 'slob, filthy person; lecher'

The female counterpart is then regularly derived with the Feminine gender suffix *-a* found in Adjectives and many Pronouns and Grounders:

sgair-é /zgajˈre/ 'to waste' → *sgairon* /zgajˈruŋ/ 'squanderer, waster' (M),
　　　　　　　　　　　　　　　sgairon-a /zgajˈruŋa/ 'squanderer, waster' (F)

10　Official naming is in Italian only and most names in current use lack a native Piedmontese form. Regulation on name-change is cumbersome and there are no provisions for the nativization of Italian names.
11　The symbol for affix boundary ('-') is used here and below for disambiguation only and is disregarded in the glosses.

A larger and diversified group of formatives expresses the agent of an action (usually but not exclusively human). The history and alternating fortune of these elements has been carefully traced by Regis (2013), who points out the competing influence of Italian and French for, respectively, -*ator* and -*eur*, but also the role of Occitan in the case of -*aire*.

In their Masculine form these suffixes are:
- -*or* /'ur/ and its Feminine counterpart -*òira* /'ojra/
- -*eur* /'ør/
- -*ador* /ad'ur/ and -*ator* /at'ur/

as well as a non-productive
- -*aire* /'ajre/.

Of these, -*or* /'ur/ is probably the most common, and its Feminine counterpart -*òira* /'ojra/ a Piedmontese isogloss:

sartor /sar'tur/, *sartòira* /sar'tojra/ 'tailor'
tessior /tes'sjur/, *tessiòira* /te'sjojra/ 'weaver'
pentnòira /pæɲt'nojra/ 'hair-dresser' (from *pentné* /pæɲt'ne/ 'to comb,' itself from *pento* /'pæɲto/ 'comb')

-*or* is also fully productive:

controlé /kuɲtru'le/ 'to control' → *controlor* /kuɲtru'lur/ 'controller'

Words in -*eur* /'ør/ are old or re-established French loans in -*eur* /œʁ/:

assenseur /asæɲ'sør/ 'elevator, lift'
blaghé /bla'ge/ 'to boast' → *blagheur* / bla'gør/ 'boaster'
dissegn /di'sæɲ/ 'drawing' → *dissegneur*[12] / dise'ɲør/ 'illustrator, designer'
travaj /tra'vaj/ 'work' → *travajeur* /trava'jør/ 'worker'

This affix is productive in the contemporary language in the derivation of abstracts and of agent nouns on the pattern of French (Tosco 2008):

longh /luŋg/ 'long' → *longheur*[13] / luŋ'gør/ 'length'
lese /'leze/ 'to read' → *leseur* / le'zør/ 'reader'

---

12 Alongside *dissegnador*, *dissegnator* (/diseɲa'dor, /diseɲa'tur/) as well as *disegnador* and *disegnator* (/dizeɲa'dor, /dizeɲa'tur/), all from Italian *disegnatore* /dizeɲa'tore/ with different degrees of nativization.

13 *Longheur* is rare and calqued on French *longueur* / lɔ̃gœʁ/ in order to avoid the Italian-

Words in *-ador* /adˈur/ and *-ator* /atˈur/ are historically more recent loans from Italian agentive Nouns in *-atore*, with the former mediated through Northern dialects and languages as evidenced by the voicing of intervocalic /t/:

gieughe /ˈdʒøge/ 'to play' → *giogador* /dʒugaˈdur/ 'player'
letor /leˈtur/ 'reader' (in everyday speech, instead of the aforementioned *leseur* / leˈzør/)

-ator /atˈur/ has a Feminine counterpart *-tris* /ˈtriz/, equally from Italian (*-trice*):
letris /leˈtriz/ '(female) reader' (the contemporary language also has a scarcely used *lesòira* /leˈzojra/)

also:

ator /aˈtur/, *atris* /aˈtriz/ 'actor, actress'

- *-aire* /ˈajre/: as anticipated, it is not productive and is used in the derivation of Masculine Nouns of agent, especially with a derogatory meaning and nowadays mostly archaic (many examples can be found, e.g., in Canini's 2007 rhyming dictionary but not in repertoires of current usage):

badinaire /badiˈnajre/ 'joker'
ciacotaire /tʃakuˈtajre/ 'waspish'
mangiaire /maŋˈdʒajre/ 'glutton'
rusaire /ryˈzajre/ 'quarrelsome'

Other affixes are less specific in their meaning and range of uses. The following list has no pretension to exhaustiveness:

- *-à* /ˈa/: denotes a single instance of an action; all these Nouns are Feminine in gender:

baròt /baˈrot/ 'stick' → *barotà* /baruˈta/ 'a blow struck with a stick'
pugn /pyɲ/ 'fist' → *pugnà* /pyˈɲa/ 'handful'

Idiosyncratic semantic shifts are common:

---

looking, but common, *longhëssa* (cf. Italian *lunghezza* /lunˈgetstsa/). The same applies to other couplets, such as *grandëssa* /graŋˈdəssa/ and *grandeur* /graŋˈdør/ 'size; greatness.'

NOUNS

rama /ˈram-a/ '(tree) branch' → *ramà* /raˈma/ 'hard blow'

- *-ada* /ˈada/: similar in meaning to the preceding, and like it fully productive. The affix ends in /a/ and all Nouns thereby derived are Feminine. Again, many idiosyncratic semantic shifts are found:

gavé /gaˈv-e/ 'take off' → *gavada* /gaˈvad-a/ 'nonsense'

- *-agi* or *-age* /ˈadʒi, ˈadʒe/: all Nouns containing this, mostly frozen, affix are Masculine:

lenga /ˈlæŋg-a/ 'tongue; language'→ *lengagi* /læŋˈgadʒi/ 'language'
messagi /meˈsadʒi/ 'message'

- *-aja* /ˈaja/: not productive. Again, the affix ends in /a/ and all nouns thereby derived are Feminine:

bataja /baˈtaj-a/ 'battle'
gusaja /gyˈzaj-a/ 'riff-raff'

- *-am, im, -um* /ˈam, ˈim, ˈym/: not productive. Nouns containing this affix are Masculine:

liam /ljam/ 'manure'
mangé /maŋˈdʒ-e/ ("eat-INF") → *mangim* /maŋˈdʒim/ 'fodder'
vansé /vaŋˈs-e/ ("leave-INF") → *vansum* /vaŋˈsym/ 'leftovers'

- *-ament* /aˈmæŋt/: productive in deverbal derivation in order to express a single instance of the action. Here too, all Nouns containing this affix are Masculine:

lancé /laŋˈtʃ-e/ 'to launch' → *lanciament* /laŋtʃaˈmæŋt/ 'launch'
spantié /spaŋˈtj-e/ 'to spread' → *spantiament* /spaŋtjˈmæŋt/ 'spreading'

- *-an* /ˈaŋ/: a frequent but scarcely if at all productive affix; Nouns thereby derived are Masculine:

fagnan /faˈɲaŋ/ 'lazybones'
gadan /gaˈdaŋ/ 'buffoon'
pais /paˈiz/ 'country' → *paisan* /pajˈzaŋ/ 'farmer'

– -*anda*, -*enda* /ˈaŋda, ˈæŋda/. A not productive affix yielding Feminine Nouns:

cio(v)enda /tʃuˈ(v)eŋd-a/ 'fence'
mudanda /myˈdaŋd-a/ 'underpant'

– -*ansa*, -*ensa* /ˈaŋsa/, ˈæŋsa/, generally used to express a state but also an activity. Again, all nouns thereby derived are Feminine:

grev /grew/ 'heavy' → *grevansa* /greˈvaŋs-a/ 'weight' (mostly used metaphorically)
arziste /arˈzist-e/ 'to resist' → *arzistensa* /arziˈstæŋs-a/ 'resistance'

– -*ant*, -*ent* /ˈaŋt, ˈæŋt/. A Present Participle affix not productive in the verbal morphology (☞ 10.5.8.) but often used in the derivation of Masculine nouns:

comandé /kumaŋˈd-e/ 'to command' → *comandant* /kumaŋˈdaŋt/ 'commander'

– -*ard* /ˈard/. Not productive and used in the derivation of Masculine nouns:

busia /byˈzia/ 'lie' → *busiard* /byˈzjard/ 'liar'

– -*aria*, -*eria* /aˈria, eˈria/. A productive /a/-ending affix making derived Feminine Nouns:

busiard /byˈzjard/ 'liar' → *busiardaria* /byzjardaˈri-a/ 'falsehood'
përfum /pərˈfym/ 'perfume'[14] → *përfumeria* /pərfymeˈri-a/ 'perfumery'

– -*assion* /aˈsjuŋ/. Used in deverbal derivation mainly to express a single instance of an action but also an abstract. Even if this affix does not end in /a/, all Nouns thereby derived are Feminine:

consideré /kuŋsideˈr-e/ 'to consider' → *considerassion* /kuŋsideraˈsjuŋ/ 'consideration'

The same is also used as a frozen formative, but often with allomorphic irregular variation:

---

14   More commonly *profum* /pruˈfym/.

condission /kuŋdiˈsjuŋ/ 'condition'
pression /preˈsjuŋ/ 'pressure'

– *-era* /ˈera/. This affix is generally used to denote the place where the entity expressed by the underived noun is found. All the Nouns containing this /a/-ending affix are Feminine:

bialera /bjaˈler-a/ 'irrigation canal'
giassa /ˈdʒasa/ 'ice' → *giassera* /dʒaˈser-a/ 'icebox'

– *-ëss-a* /ˈəssa/. Again, all the Nouns containing this /a/-ending affix are Feminine:

longh /luŋg/ 'long' → *longhëssa* /luŋˈgəss-a/ 'length'

– *-ism, -esim* /ˈizm, ˈezim/. Used to denote abstracts, formally from adjectives (often in loans). Nouns thereby derived are Masculine:

comunism /kumyˈnizm/ 'communism'
umanesim /ymaˈnezim/ 'humanism'

– *-ita* /-ita/. An /a/-ending affix making Feminine nouns:

arnasse /arˈnas-e/ ("be_reborn-INF") 'to be born again' → *arnassita* /arˈnasit-a/ 'renaissance; rebirth'

– *-issia* /-ˈisja/. Again, all the Nouns containing this /a/-ending affix are Feminine:

gram /gram/ 'bad' → *gramissia* /graˈmisj-a/ 'meanness'

– *-(i)tà* /-(i)ˈta/. An affix used to derive abstract Feminine nouns:

strach /strak/ 'tired' → *strachità* /strakiˈta/ 'tiredness'

– *-ura* /-ˈyra/. All the Nouns containing this /a/-ending affix are Feminine:

ambotì / ambuˈt-i/ 'to stuff' → *ambotiura* /ambuˈtjyr-a/ 'filling'

5.4.3 Prefixation

Apart from the presence of prefixes in adjectives in their use as nouns, or in deadjectival nouns, as in *andipendensa* /aŋdipæŋˈdæŋs-a/ 'independence,' or *iregolarità* /**iregulariˈta**/ 'irregularity,' productive prefixation is mainly limited to the Piedmontese variants of international prefixes in learned vocabulary. An exception is provided by the partially productive use of *ar-* /**ar-**/ in order to express the repetition of an action, or the use of the same prefix *dës-* /**dəz-**/ found in verbs (☞ 10.7.) with a pejorative or negative meaning:

nassita /ˈ**nasit-a**/ 'birth' → *arnassita* /**ar**ˈ**nasit-a**/ 'rebirth'
gust /**gyst**/ 'taste; flavor' → *dësgust* /**dəz**ˈ**gyst**/ 'dislike'

In many international words prefixation is etymological only; e.g., against *interpretassion* /iŋterpretaˈsjuŋ/ 'interpretation,' neither Piedmontese **pretassion* nor English **pretation* exist.

A few examples among many others are:[15]

– *acro-*

acrolet /**akruˈlet**/   'acrolect'

– *anti-*

anti-fassism /**aŋtifaˈsizm**/   'anti-fascism'

– *inter-* (and its variants *anter-* and *antër-*):

interpretassion /**iŋterpretaˈsjuŋ**/   'interpretation'
anterussion /**aŋteryˈsjuŋ**/   'interruption'
antërsession /**aŋtərseˈsjuŋ**/   'intersection'

– *iper-*

ipersurfassa /**ipersyrˈfas-a**/   'hypersurface'

– *ipo-*

---

15   All examples from the Piedmontese Wikipedia (https://pms.wikipedia.org/wiki/Intrada).

ipotipòsi /iputiˈpozi/ 'hypotyposis'

– *macro-*

macro-lìvel /makruliˈvel/ 'macro-level'

– *micro-*

micro-clima /mikruˈklima/ 'microclimate'

– *sub-*

sub-afluent /sybaflyˈæŋt/ 'secondary tributary'

– *super-*

super-famija /sypærfaˈmi-a/ 'super-family; phylum'

5.4.4 Compound Nouns

Compound nouns are limited to two elements and may be formally identical to nominal, prepositional or verbal phrases. Their gender and number is determined by the noun in case of inter-categorial compounds, and by the first noun in Noun—Noun (N+N) compounds. While each element generally retains its accentual pattern, the compounding nature of these forms is evidenced syntactically by the impossibility of inserting any modifier between the elements.

cap-repart /kap=reˈpart/ ("head=unit")[16] 'foreman'
meistr da bòsch /mæjstr=da=bosk/ ("master=ABL=wood")[17] 'carpenter'
dòp-mesdì, dòp-disné /dop=mezˈdi/ ("after=noon"), /dop=dizˈne/ ("after=lunch") 'afternoon'

Another pattern is Noun—Adjective (N+Adj). The adjective may to all practical extents be limited in use to the compound, as in the following everyday words:

---

16   There is much variation about the writing of compound words, particularly in the use of the hyphen (cf. *ciapa-pover* vs. *pissasangh* below), as well as for what concerns stress placement and the resulting phonological changes, such as the Back Raising, whereby /o/ (always stressed; ☞ 3.5.1.3.) → /u/.
17   Locally also /mæjdaˈbosk/.

sin-a /ˈsiŋ-a/ 'dinner' → *sinòira* in: *merenda sinòira* /meˈr-æŋd-a=siˈnojr-a/ 'early dinner' [dinner-like snack]
volé /vuˈl-e/ 'to fly' → *volòira* in: *rata volòira, ratavolòira* /ˈrat-a=vuˈlojr-a/ 'bat' [flying rat]
cop /kup/ 'shingle' → *copera* in: *bissa copera* /ˈbis-a=kuˈper-a/ 'turtle' [tiled grass-snake]

Together with N+N, the pattern Verb—Noun (V+N) is quite productive in compounding, especially with generic verbs (such as *ciapé* /tʃaˈpe/ 'to catch, grab' and *porté* /purˈte/ 'to bring'). As anticipated (☞ 5.2.), compounds whose first element is a verb are always Masculine in gender:

ciapa-po(v)er /ˈtʃap-a=ˈpu(v)er/ ("take-PRS.3S=dust")[18] 'knick knack'
pissasangh /ˈpis-a=ˈsaŋg/ ("piss-PRS.3S=blood") 'hematuria, blood in urine'
pòrta-mantel /ˈport-a=maŋˈtel/ ("bring-PRS.3S=mantle") 'coat hanger'

The pattern is particularly productive in expressive vocabulary and nicknames:

ciaparat /ˈtʃap-a=ˈrat/ ("take-PRS.3S=rat") 'good-for-nothing'
fafioché /fa=fjuˈk-e/ ("do\PRS.3S=snow-INF") 'blabberer'
ficabech /ˈfik-a=ˈbæk/ ("stick-PRS.3S=beak") 'busybody'

as well as in modern—especially scientific and technical—vocabulary, and in particular with shortened forms of the first element and in parallel with adjectival formation (☞ 6.5.2.):

eletrostàtica /eˈletru=ˈstatika/ 'electrostatics'
fantassiensa /ˈfaŋta=ˈsjæŋsa/ 'science fiction'
sociolenghistica /ˈsutʃu=læŋˈgistika/ 'sociolinguistics'

---

18 Here and below, the verbal form is glossed as a Main Present 3rd Singular form on semantic grounds only.

CHAPTER 6

Adjectives

6.1 Overview

A separate open class of Adjectives may be identified on the basis of its morphology and its distributional behavior. Just as Nouns, Adjectives may be predicates, but different from Nouns they may also appear as modifiers of a Noun in attributive phrases without being preceded by a preposition and without yielding a compound Noun.

Moreover, and again different from Nouns, Adjectives have no inherent gender and assume the gender (and number) of the head Noun they modify in attributive phrases, and of the subject in predicate function.

Adjectives can be primitive or derived from Nouns, Verbs, or other Adjectives. Derivation from other word classes, such as the Numerals, is limited and not productive.

6.2 Semantics of Adjectives

Adjectives belong to several semantic classes and, in particular, all those considered basic by Dixon (2004):

a. Dimension

gròss	/**gros**/	'big, large'
cit	/**tʃit**/	'small, little'
largh	/**larg**/	'wide'
streit	/**strægjt**/	'narrow'
aut	/**awt**/	'tall'
curt	/**kyrt**/	'short'

b. Age

vej	/**vej**/	'old'
neuv	/**nøw**/	'new'
giovo	/**ˈdʒuwu**/	'young'

c. *Value*

bel	/**bel**/	'beautiful, nice'
brut	/**bryt**/	'awful'
bon	/**buŋ**/	'good'
gram	/**gram**/	'bad'

d. *Color*

In terms of Berlin and Kay's (1969) basic color theory and later modifications, Piedmontese has the following basic color terms (☞ 20.4):

bianch	/**bjaŋk**/	'white'
bleu	/**blø**/	'blue'
giaun	/**dʒawn**/[1]	'yellow'
gris	/**griz**/	'grey'
neir	/**næjr**/	'black'
ross	/**rus**/	'red'
verd	/**værd**/	'green'

The following color terms are derived from Nouns and are invariable:

| *reusa* | /ˈ**røza**/ | 'pink' (also: 'rose,' a plant of the Rosa genus) |
| *viòla* | /ˈ**vjola**/ | 'purple' (also: 'violet,' a plant of the Viola genus) |

Bleu /**blø**/ 'blue' is invariable for many speakers (while others have F *bleuva* /ˈ**bløva**/); *maròn* /maˈ**roŋ**/ 'brown' is invariable too, and has arguably been borrowed from French (REP s.v. *maron*).

Dixon's (2004) "peripheral classes" are likewise represented:

e. *Physical property*

| *caud* | /**kawd**/ | 'warm; hot' |
| *freid* | /**fræjd**/ | 'cold' |

---

1 Although written with final single *n*, the final nasal follows a glide and is apical, not velar (☞ 2.1.).

ADJECTIVES

dur   /dyr/   'hard'
mòl   /mol/   'soft'

also corporeal properties and states:

malavi   /maˈlavi/   'sick'
strach   /strak/   'tired'

f. Human propensity

svicio   /ˈzvitʃu/   'smart'
stupid   /ˈstypid/   'stupid'
anteligent /aɲteliˈdʒæŋt/   'clever'

g. Speed

lest   /lest/   'quick'
meusi   /ˈmøzi/   'slow; lazy'

As is typical of languages with large and open Adjective inventories, a number of other semantic classes might be identified; it is important on the other hand to note that Quantifiers, and among them cardinal numbers, belong to a different, separate word class (☞ 9).

Relative clauses may play the role of Adjectives or of ordinal numbers (☞ 9.1.2.): *che a fa des* /k(e)=aˈfa ˈdez/ ('SUB=SBJ.3=do\PRS.3S ten') 'tenth' (lit. 'which makes ten').

6.3 Morphology of Adjectives

The Piedmontese Adjectives show a fairly uniform morphological behavior, especially as regards Feminine endings. Six different subclasses of Adjectives might be identified; classes have no semantic basis.

TABLE 18   Subclasses of Adjectives

Class	M.S	M.P	F.S	F.P	example
I	Ø	Ø	-a	-e	gròss/gròss/gròssa/gròsse 'huge'
II	-u	-u	-a	-e	svicio/svicio/svicia/svicie 'smart'
III	-a	-a	-a	-e	balista/balista/balista/baliste 'deceitful, bullshitter'
IVa	-l	-j	-a	-e	bel/bej/bela/bele 'nice, beautiful'
IVb (recent neologisms and borrowings)	-l	-j	-l	-j	nòbil/nobij/nòbil/nòbij 'noble'
V (Italianisms)	-e	-i	-e	-i	velòce/velòci/velòce/velòci 'fast, rapid'
VI (Nouns acting as Adjectives)	Ø	Ø	Ø	Ø	reusa/reusa/reusa/reusa 'pink'

The class to which the majority of Adjectives belongs displays no ending for Masculines (both Singular and Plural), while Feminines are marked by a final -*a* in the S and -*e* in the P. Gender and number marking involve therefore only three possible endings: Ø (M {S & P}), -*a* (F.S) and -*e* (F.P):

M {S & P}	F.S	F.P	
carestios /kares'tjuz/	carestiosa /kares'tjuz-a/	carestiose /kares'tjuz-e/	'expensive'
creus /krøz/	creusa /'krøz-a/	creuse /'krøz-e/	'deep'
goregn /gu'ræɲ/	goregna /gu'ræɲ-a/	goregne /gu'ræɲ-e/	'fibrous, tough'
grotolù /grutu'ly/	grotolua /grutu'ly-a/	grotolue /grutu'ly-e/	'coarse'

A few Adjectives have a Masculine (both Singular and Plural) ending in -*o* /**u**/ but follow the general pattern insofar as they do not have number variation in the Masculine Plural:[2]

---

2   Dependng on dialects and registers, the Masculine Plural form for these Adjectives may add a final -*i* to the stem.

ADJECTIVES

M {S & P}	F.S	F.P	
dròlo /ˈdrolu/	dròla /ˈdrol-a/	dròle /ˈdrol-e/	'odd,' 'strange'
mòro /ˈmoru/	mòra /ˈmor-a/	mòre /ˈmor-e/	'dark-skinned'
svicio /ˈzvitʃu/	svicia /ˈzvitʃ-a/	svicie /ˈzvitʃ-e/	'smart'

In some cases, final -o is in free variation with Ø; choice between the two may be a matter of personal style or prosody but does not obey clear rules nor geographic patterns:

M {S & P}	F.S	F.P	
bòrgn(o) /ˈborɲ(u)/	bòrgna /ˈborɲ-a/	bòrgne /ˈborɲ-e/	'blind'
ciòrgn(o) /ˈtʃorɲ(u)/	ciòrgna /ˈtʃorɲ-a/	ciòrgne /ˈtʃorɲ-e/	'deaf'

Addition of or change to -a in the Feminine Singular is barred in Adjectives ending in -a in their basic (Masculine) form; these are apparently limited to those built with the derivative affix -ista /ˈista/. In these Adjectives final -a is changed into -e /e/ only in the Feminine Plural:

M {S & P}& F.S	F.P	
socialista /sutʃaˈlista/	socialista /sutʃaˈlist-e/	'socialist'

(1) anventomse le provinse *"federaliste"*
 aŋveŋˈt-um=se   l-e= pruˈviŋs-e   federaˈlist-e
 invent-PRS.1P=REFL DET-F.P=province-P federalist-F.P
 'let's make up the federalist provinces' (Garuss 2004a)

(2) *Teòlogi scolastich e* **casuista**
 teˈoludʒi   skuˈlastik e   kazyˈista
 Theologians scholastic and casuist
 'scholastic and casuist theologians' (Calvo 1845, Cant 2, Par. 99)

6.3.1 L-*ending Adjectives*

Just as Nouns (☞ 5.3.), Adjectives ending in -*l* in their basic form may be subject to the alternation of -*l* to -*j* in the Masculine Plural, yielding therefore a fourfold opposition:

M.S	M.P	F.S	F.P	
bel /bel/	*bej* /bej/	*bela* /ˈbel-a/	*bele* /ˈbel-e/	'nice, beautiful'
fòl /fol/	*fòj* /foj/	*fòla* /ˈfol-a/	*fòle* /ˈfol-e/	'fool'
mòl /mol/	*mòj* /moj/	*mòla* /ˈmol-a/	*mòle* /ˈmol-e/	'soft, tender'
sutil /syˈtil/	*sutij* /syˈtij/	*sutila* /syˈtil-a/	*sutile* /syˈtil-e/	'thin'

Adjectives in -*al* and in -*bil* which entered the Piedmontese lexicon via indirect tradition—through Italian and/or French—may align to other Adjectives in -*l* (especially in written and cultured varieties), or display -*l* for all genders' singular and -*j* for all genders' plural (Ricca 2006: 141 ff.). Such a paradigm resembles that of Italian cognate Adjectives (ending in -*ale* and -*bile*), although the phonetic realization of the respective cells is always different.

{M & F} S	{M & F} P	
general /dʒeneˈral/	*generaj* /dʒeneˈraj/	'general' (vs. *general, generaj, generala, generale*)
possibil /puˈsibil/	*possibij* /puˈsibij/	'possible' (vs. *possibil, possibij, possibila, possibile*)
ufissial /yfiˈsjal/	*ufissiaj* /yfiˈsjaj/	'official' (vs. *ufissial, ufissiaj, ufissiala, ufissiale*)

Absence of gender agreement is widespread in colloquial speech, as in

(3) *La lenga **ufissial** a l'é mach ël franseis*
l-a=ˈlæŋg-a yfiˈsjal a=ˈle mak əl=franˈsæjz
DET-F=language-S official SBJ.3=be\PRS.3S only DET=French
'French is the only official language' (Picardìa, https://pms.wikipedia.org/wiki/Picard%C3%ACa)

vs., with gender agreement:

ADJECTIVES 155

(4) La mastinarìa ch'a l'ha fame ancheuj a l'é nen **naturala** an chila
l-a=mastina'ri-a k=a=la='fa=me   aŋ'køj
DET-F=spite-S   SUB= SBJ.3=have\PRS.3S=do\PTCL=OBJ.1S today
a='le   næŋ naty'ral-a aŋ='kila
SBJ.3=be\PRS.3S   NEG natural-F   INE=IDP.3F
'The spite she made me today is not natural for her' (Anonymous 1969 [1800–1802], II, 3; quoted in Ricca 2006: 143)

vs., with gender agreement

(5) A mira ciair a na poesia **metaregionala**
a='mir-a   tʃajr a=n-a=pue'zi-a   metaredʒu'nal-a
SBJ.3=aim-PRS.3S clear ADE=INDEF-F=poetry-S   metaregional-F
'She aims directly at meta-regional poetry' (Gilardin 2017: 12)

Conscience of the Italian origin of the "zero-gender" tendency seems to be lost. To the contrary, use of the genuine Piedmontese pattern sounds local and rustic to many speakers, and use of this pattern has penetrated in writing and is widely found also in language-conscious or cultured texts.

Other Adjectives borrowed from Italian with singular endings -e, such as *capace, semplice, grave* etc., inflect according to the Italian rules: i.e., for both genders, to singular -e (Masculine and Feminine) corresponds plural -i: *le person-e pi semplici* (DET-F=person-F.P more simple-F.P) (Anonymous 1969 [1800–1802], II, 6, quoted in Ricca 2006: 143) 'the simplest people.'[3]

Finally, Nouns acting as Adjectives, as is for a number of color terms, such as *reusa* /'røza/ 'pink' and *viòla* /'vjola/ 'violet', lose both gender and number agreement.

6.3.2 Allomorphic Variation in the Stem
Other allomorphic variation follows from general word-formation rules:

– a stressed /æ/ is subject to closing and centralization to /ə/ upon suffixation; a following single consonant is geminated:

---

3 Scantly in the literature and almost never in the spoken variety Adjectives ending in *-ant/ent* may not inflect for gender in the Feminine Singular, e.g., *còsa interessant* 'interesting thing' (vs. *còsa interessanta*, quoted in Ricca 2006: 143fn).

M {S & P}	F.S	F.P	
sech /sæk/	*sëcca* /ˈsəkk-a/	*sëcche* /ˈsəkk-e/	'dry'
s-cet /stʃæt/	*s-cëtta* /ˈstʃətt-a/	*s-cëtte* /ˈstʃətt-e/	'frank,' 'sincere'
verd /værd/	*vërda* /ˈvərd-a/	*vërde* /ˈvərd-e/	'green'

Variation is rampant on this point, and local dialects may have /æ/ or /ə/ throughout.

- in the context /C_r/—i.e., after a consonant and before /r/—/æ/ is dropped upon suffixation; the rule actually involves the insertion of /æ/ between a final /Cr/ cluster in the basic form:

M {S & P}	F.S	F.P	
alegher /aˈlegær/	*alegra* /aˈlegr-a/	*alegre* /aˈlegr-e/	'cheerful'
pigher /ˈpigær/	*pigra* /ˈpigr-a/	*pigre* /ˈpigr-e/	'lazy'
pòver /ˈpovær/	*pòvra* /ˈpovr-a/	*pòvre* /ˈpovr-e/	'poor'

6.3.3 Prenominal Position and Syntactically-Governed Allomorphs

As detailed in the relevant sections (☞ 13.3.), Adjectives in attributive function may either precede or follow the Noun, but only the postonominal position is productive: as in other Romance languages, prenominal position is either reserved to frozen expressions and compounds or subject to the presence of other postnominal Adjectives. In prenominal position the Adjective forms a closer linkage with the Noun it qualifies, yielding sometimes a new meaning scarcely derivable from that of the Adjective and the following Noun. The Adjective may cliticize to the following Noun, as shown in (6) below, where final /ŋ/ of *bon* 'good' changes to /n/ in intervocalic position. As in the corresponding French word *bonhomme* /bɔˈnɔm/, cliticization may be orthographically expressed by writing the Adjective-Noun phrase as a single word:

(6) *un bon òm, un bonòm*
 aŋ=bun=ˈom
 INDEF=good=man
 'a simpleton'

ADJECTIVES

vs.

(7) *n'òm **bon***
    n=om   buŋ
    INDEF=man
    'a good guy'

In prenominal position, a few Adjectives show special allomorphic forms:

– the Adjective *grand* /graŋd/ 'great, big' has a special form *gran* /graŋ/ in prenominal position before a consonant. Agreement does not apply:

(8) *'t ses na **gran** testassa*
    t=ses   n-a=graŋ=testas-a
    SBJ.2S=be\PRS.2S   INDEF-F=big=bad_head-S
    'you're a blockhead' ["a big bad head"] (Garelli 1874b: 9, Act 1, Scene 1)

– the Adjective *pòver* /povær/ 'poor' becomes *pòr* /povr/ before a following Noun:

(9) *a l'era pròpi un **pòvr**'òm*
    a='lera   'propi aŋ='povr   om
    SBJ.3=be\IMPF.3S   really INDEF=poor man
    'he was really a poor guy'

Agreement is preserved:

(10) *a l'é mach na **pòvra** fija*
    a='le   mak   n-a='povr-a   'fi-a
    SBJ.3=be\PRS.3S   only INDEF-F=poor-F   girl-S
    'she is just a poor girl'

– the Adjective *sant* /saŋt/ 'holy' is subject to a great deal of variation before a personal name in the meaning 'Saint.' Usually capitalized and building a compound with the following name, it is reduced to *San* /saŋ/ before a consonant. The Feminine form *Santa* is instead reduced to *Sant'* /saŋt/ before a vowel:

San Stev /saŋ='stew/ 'Saint Stephen'
Sant'Ana /saŋt='ana/ 'Saint Anne'

vs.

Sant'Antoni /saŋt=aŋˈtoni/ 'Saint Anthony'
Santa Teresa /saŋt-a=teˈreza/ 'Saint Therese.'

6.4 Comparative Constructions

Analytical means are used for inequality as well as equality comparison, while no morphological change in the Adjectives' shape is involved. Residual morphological expression for constructions of relative superiority and inferiority is preserved in *mej* /mej/ 'better' and *pes* /pez/ 'worse,' respectively (see Brero 1971: 46, Villata 1997: 79; they may also be used as Adverbs ☞ 12.2.3).

For inequality comparison, the comparee (i.e., the entity being compared) is usually followed by the adverbs *pì* /pi/ 'more' or *men, meno* /mæŋ, ˈmenu/ 'less', which in turn precede the Adjective ((11)), but may also follow it, albeit rarely ((12)). The standard (i.e., the second term of comparison) may follow, always preceded by the standard marker *che* /ke/ (for the terminology, see Treis 2018):

(11) *a smija meno vej che mi*
 a=ˈsmi-a   ˈmenu vej ke mi
 SBJ.3=seems-PRS.3S less   old SUB IDP.1S
 'he looks less old than me'

(12) *bërnufie | Incostante pi che 'l mar*
 bərˈnyfj-e iŋkusˈtaŋt-e pi   ke   l=mar
 fool-P   fickle-F.P   more SUB DET=sea
 'fool girls more capricious than the sea' (Isler 2013 [1799], *Canson* 18, verse 11–12: 148)

Adjectives are preceded by the determiner (in agreement with the nominal head) for absolute comparison:

(13) *ël pì vej a l'era ëdcò ël pì gram*
 əl=ˈpi   vej a=ˈlera   ədˈko əl=ˈpi   gram
 DET=more old SBJ.3=be\IMPF.3S also   DET=more bad
 'the oldest was also the meanest one'

6.4.1 Equative and Similative Constructions

At an abstract level (see Haspelmath 2017), equative constructions are made of a comparee, a parameter marker, a parameter (i.e., the Adjective expressing the property that is compared by the construction), a standard marker, and a standard of comparison. In Piedmontese the parameter marker *tan(t)* /taŋ(t)/ is optional (and in fact in common speech usually avoided); no morphological change affects the parameter/Adjective; while the standard marker is *com* (*coma, come, 'me*) /kum/, /ˈkuma/, /ˈkume/, /me=/ 'as,' or similar expressions, chiefly *parej ëd* /paˈræj əd=/ and *parej che* /paˈræj ke=/:

(14) *Aldo a l'é (tan(t)) anteligent come lor*
ˈaldo a=ˈle (taŋ[t]) aŋteliˈdʒæɲt ˈkume lur
A. SBJ.3=be\PRS.3S as clever as IDP.3P
'Aldo is as clever as they are' (Villata 1997: 77)

Less frequently the parameter marker may be *ansì* /aŋˈsi/ and *csì* /(ə)kˈsi/ (Villata 1997: 77).

The (bookish) correlation *tan(t) ... quant* /taŋ(t) ... kwaɲt/ may also be used for equatives, in this case, however, the parameter marker is virtually mandatory.

(15) *a l'é tan bela quant Maria*
a=ˈlera taŋ ˈbel-a kwaɲt marˈia
SBJ.3=be\IMPF.3S as_much nice-F how_much M.
'she is as beautiful as Mary'

6.4.2 Superlative and Elative Constructions

Piedmontese has a superlative affix in the form *-issim* /ˈisim/, again with affixed gender and number markers in the Feminine. In the spoken language its use has probably increased under pressure from the corresponding Italian affix *-issimo*. This could be indirectly confirmed by the fact that the use of *-issim* still sounds definitely odd or simply impossible with many basic Adjectives, especially if the stem ends in a glide (?*vejissim* /veˈjisim/ 'very old,' *giovissim /dʒuˈvisim/ 'very young'—one would have to resort to the Italianism *giovanissim /dʒuvaˈnisim/; cf. Italian *giovanissimo* /dʒovaˈnissimo/).

In much contemporary writing this suffix is generally avoided, although it is certainly old and attested since an early period. The following is a literary example from 1877:

(16) *chiel a conossia tut; ant la musica, peui, a l'era **abilissim***
 kjæl a=kunu'sia tut // aŋt=l-a='myzik-a / peuj /
 IDP.3M SBJ.3=know\IMPF.3S all // INE=DET-F=music-S / then /
 a='lera abi'lisim
 SBJ.3=be\IMPF.3S very_skilled
 'he knew everything; in music, moreover, he was very skilled' (Pietracqua 1979 [1877]: 171)

More commonly, Adjectives are modified in order to show intensity, superiority, etc. by preposed degree and focalizer Adverbs and Adverbials (☞ 12.3.), such as *motobin* /mutu'biŋ/ 'much,' *franch* /fraŋk/ or *pro* /pru/ 'indeed,' *pròpi* /propi/ or *vreman* /vre'maŋ/ 'really,' etc.:

(17) *a l'é **motobin** onest për esse un politich*
 a='le mutu'biŋ u'nest pər='ese aŋ=pu'litik
 SBJ.3=be\PRS.3S much honest BEN=be\INF INDEF=political
 'as politicians go, he is quite honest'

Also the the quantifier *tut* /tyt/ 'all' can be used to intensify Adjectives, in full agreement with the Noun modified by the Adjective:

(18) *i son **tuta** afessionà a chila*
 i='suŋ 'tyt-a afesju'n-a a='kila
 SBJ.1=be\PRS.1S all-F be_fond_of-PTCL ADE= IDP.3FS
 'I am very fond of her' (Bersezio 1980 [1863]; Act 3, Scene 7)

Iconically, intensification may also be obtained through the complete reduplication of the Adjective:

(19) *Ma a la fin a l'é rivà 'nt un pais **lontan, lontan** ch'a smijava ch'a fussa 'l pais dij rat.*
 ma a=l-a='fiŋ a='le ri'v-a aŋt=aŋ=paiz
 but ADE=DET-F=end SBJ.3=be\PRS.3S come-PTCL INE=DET=country
 luŋ'taŋ / luŋ'taŋ / k=a=zmi'j-ava
 far far SUB=SBJ.3=look_like-IMPF.3S
 k=a='fysa əl=pa'iz d=i='rat
 SUB=SBJ.3=be\SUBJ.IMPF.3S DET=country ATTR=DET\P=rat
 'But in the end he arrived in a land far, (so) far that it looked like it was the rats' land' (Autelli 1985 [1931]: 37)

Or with dedicated comparisons following the pattern 'X as NP.'

(20) *fòl com na mica*
 fol   kum na=ˈmik-a
 fool   as   INDEF=loaf-s
 'dumb as a donkey' [fool as a loaf] (Aly-Belfàdel 1933: 307)

Aly-Belfàdel 1933: 298 ff. reports one hundred of these formulaic expressions under the label "popular Piedmontese comparisons." Some of these 'X as NP' constructions enjoy a moderate grade of grammaticalization, since they may apply to more than one single Adjective:

(21) *cioch/pien/spòrch parej 'd/com un crin*
 tʃuk/pjæŋ/spork paˈræj d=/kum aŋ=ˈkriŋ
 drunk/full/dirty as   INDEF=pig
 'very drunk/satiated/dirty' [drunk/full/dirty as a pig] (cf. Bonavero 2020: 33, Artuffo 1960)

Whereas the semantics of *cioch* and *spòrch* is somewhat derogative, the pejorative sense is nuanced with irony—or completely absent, at least in the native-like perception of the Authors—from the construction containing *pien*.

Moreover, the formula *X com tut*, literally 'X as everything,' is completely grammaticalized as a superlative strategy for Adjectives and can be applied to every Adjective (cf. Cerruti 2009: 108 ff.):

(22) *a l'é freid com tut*
 a=ˈle   fraejd kum tyt
 SBJ.3=be\PRS.3S   cold   as   all
 'it's very cold'

Also frozen phrasal expressions may be used as elatives:

(23) *a l'é gram ch'a sagna*
 a=ˈle   gram k=a=ˈsaɲ-a
 SBJ.3=be\PRS.3S   bad   SUB=SBJ.3=bleed-PRS
 'he is awfully bad' [(so) bad that he bleeds]

For other expressive elatives ☞ 13.5.10.

6.5 Adjectives as Nouns

Adjectives may be nominalized and be grounded or used as head of NPs.

They may therefore be used metaphorically and enter into fixed configurations, such as:

(24) *deje ël bleu*
ˈde=je əl=ˈblø
give\INF=IND DET=blue
'to quit (tr.); to fire, sack' [to give someone the blue]

6.6 Derivational Morphology of Adjectives

As in the case of other categories, derivation may be frozen or productive, and many derivational affixes are shared with Nouns. Both prefixes and suffixes are used.

6.6.1 *Derivational Suffixes*

A first group of derivational affixes is intracategorial and enables the creation of evaluatives (i.e., diminutives, pejoratives, and the like):

- *-ass* /ˈas/: productive mainly in expressive speech to express a negative attitude to the quality expressed by the Adjective:

neir /**næjr**/ 'black' → *nejrass* /**næjˈras**/ 'awfully black'

- *-astr, -estr* /ˈastr, ˈestr/: productive in expressive speech to express an approximation to the quality expressed by the Adjective:

verd /**værd**/ 'green' → *vërdastr* /**vərˈdastr**/ 'greenish'

- *-et* /ˈæt/: productive in order to express a limited degree or an approximation to the quality expressed by the Adjective:

giaun /**dʒawn**/ 'yellow' → *giaunet* /**dʒawˈnæt**/ 'yellowish'

- *-in* /ˈiŋ/: less productive than the former with the same meaning:

car /**kar**/ 'dear' → *carin* /**kaˈriŋ**/ 'pretty'

ADJECTIVES 163

- *-on* /'uŋ/: productive mainly in expressive speech to express a great degree of the quality expressed by the Adjective:

grass /**gras**/ 'fat' → *grasson* /**gra'suŋ**/ 'very fat'

- *-òt* /'ot/: productive mainly in expressive speech to express a limited degree or a positive attitude to the quality expressed by the Adjective:

alegher /a'legær/ 'cheerful' → *alegròt* /ale'grot/ 'rather cheerful'

- *-ucio* /'ytʃu/: productive mainly in expressive speech in order to imply a limited degree:

palid /'palid/ 'pale' → *paliducio* /pali'dytʃu/ 'a bit pale'

A second group of derivational affixes is intercategorial, and yields Adjectives from Nouns or Verbs. Many forms are borrowed rather than directly formed from Piedmontese bases:

- *-abil, -ibil* /'abil, 'ibil/:

sacòcia /sa'kotʃa/ 'pocket' → *sacociabil* /saku'tʃabil/ 'pocket-like' (as in *liber sacociabil* /'libær saku'tʃabil/ 'pocket book')
ripetibil /ripe'tibil/ 'repeatable' (from Italian *ripetibile*; 'to repeat' is *arpete* /ar'pete/)

- *-al, -il* /'al, 'il/ (the latter not productive):

përson-a /pər'suŋa/ 'person' → *përsonal* /pərsu'nal/ 'personal'
sivil /si'vil/ 'civil'

- *-an* /'aŋ/ (widely used, but not only, in derivation from place names):

republica /re'publika/ 'republic' → *republican* /republi'kaŋ/ 'republican'
Venessia /ve'nesja/ 'Venice' → *venessian* /vene'sjaŋ/ 'Venetian'

- *-ar* /'ar/ (not productive):

volgar /vul'gar/ 'vulgar'

- *-ari* /ˈari/:

reassion /reaˈsjuŋ/ 'reaction' → *reassionari* /reasjuˈnari/ 'reactionary'

- *-ard* /ˈard/ (scarcely productive, mainly used in derivations with a negative connotation):

busia /byˈzia/ 'lie' → *busiard* /byˈzjard/ 'lying' (and, as a Noun, 'liar')

- *-asch, -esch* /ˈask, ˈesk/:

sumia /symia/ 'ape' → *sumiesch* /syˈmjesk/ 'ape-like'

- *-efich, -ifich* /ˈefik, ˈifik/ (not productive):

benefich /beˈnefik/ 'beneficial'

- *-eis* /ˈæjz/ (widely used in derivation from place names):

Fransa /ˈfraŋsa/ 'France' → *franseis* /fraŋˈsæjz/ 'French'

- *-engh* /ˈæŋg/ (not productive):

fiamengh /fjaˈmæŋg/ 'gorgeous'

- *-evol* /ˈevul/:

pieghé /pjeˈge/ 'to fold' → *pieghevol* /pjeˈgevul/ 'foldable'

- *-ich* /ik/:

stòria /ˈstorja/ 'history' → *stòrich* /ˈstorik/ 'historical'

- *-in* /ˈiŋ/ (used in derivation, mainly but not only from place names):

mar /mar/ 'sea' → *marin* /maˈriŋ/ 'marine'

- *-istich* /ˈistik/:

art /art/ 'art' → *artistich* /arˈtistik/ 'artistic'

ADJECTIVES

- *-itan, -etan* /i'taŋ, e'taŋ/ (not productive; used in derivation from place names):

Napoli /'napuli/ 'Neaples' → *napolitan* /napuli'taŋ/ 'Neapolitan'

- *-iv* /'iw/ (not productive):

passiv /pa'siw/ 'passive'

- *-òri* /'ori/ (not or scarcely productive):

ilusion /ily'zjuŋ/ 'delusion' → *ilusòri* /ily'zori/ 'deceptive'

- *-os* /'uz/ (not or scarcely productive):

colin-a /ku'liŋa/ 'hill' → *colinos* /kuli'nuz/ 'hilly'

The productive Past Participle and the residual lexicalized forms of Present Participle (☞ 10.5.8.), are also used in attributive phrases. The participial affixes are also used in Noun-to-Adjective derivation or frozen formations:

- *-ant/-ent* /'aŋt, æŋt/:

anteresse /aŋte'rese/ 'interest' → *anteressant* /aŋtere'saŋt/ 'interesting'
divertent /divertæŋt/ 'amusing'

- *-ù* /'y/:

barba /'barb-a/ 'beard' → *barbù* /bar'by/ 'bearded'

6.6.2 Prefixation

Historically, prefixation played a bigger role than nowadays, as may be seen in pairs such as *ross* /rus/ 'red' → *baross* /ba'rus/ 'reddish;' *cioch* /tʃuk/ 'drunk' → *bacioch* /ba'tʃuk/ 'stunned, numb' (where the origin and value of a possible prefix *ba- remains completely opaque); but also *content* /kuŋ'tæŋt/ 'satisfied' → *malcontent* /malkuŋ'tæŋt/ 'dissatisfied,' and a few others, where the origin of the prefix is apparent (cf. in the example the Adverb *mal* /mal/ 'badly').

Contemporary, productive prefixation is mainly limited to the Piedmontese variants of international prefixes in learned vocabulary and to antonymic Adjectives in *in-/im-* (and related allomorphs).

Although usually written with *in-*, and apart from the present spreading of the spelling *an-* (maybe as a result of Ausbauization; ☞ cf. 19.2.2.), the pronunciation with /aŋ/ is dominating.

The same prefix has a reduced allomorph in *i-* where an historical geminate has been dropped:

– *-in/-an, -im* (before a bilabial), *-iC:*

impossibil (rare: *ampossibil*) /impuˈsibil, ampuˈsibil/   'impossible'
indipendent, andipendent /iŋdipæŋˈdæŋt, aŋdipæŋˈdæŋt/   'independent'
iregolar /ireguˈlar/   'irregular'

(25) *Dal 1991 Kijv a l'é vnùita capital dl'Ucrain-a **andipendenta***
      da=l=ˈ1991   K.   a=ˈle   ˈvnyjt-a   kapiˈtal
      ABL=DET=1991 K. SBJ.3=be\PRS.3S come\PTCL-F capital
      d=l=ykraˈiŋ-a   aŋdipæŋˈdæŋt-a
      ATTR=DET(-F)=Ukraine-S independent-F
      'Since 1991 Kijv has been the capital of independent Ucraine' ("Kijv;" https://pms.wikipedia.org/wiki/Kijv)

A selection of learned prefixes found in modern scientific literature includes, among others:

– *anti-*

anti-ossidant /aŋtiusiˈdaŋt/   'antioxidant'

– *extra-*

extra-europengh /ekstraewruˈpæŋg/   'extra-European'

– *inter-, anter, antër-:*

internassional /iŋternasjuˈnal/   'international'

– *meso-*

mesoamerican /mezuameriˈkaŋ/   'Mesoamerican'

– *pseudo-*

pseudo-metrich /**psæudu'metrik**/ 'pseudo-metric'

– *sub-*

subatòmich /**syba'tomik**/ 'sub-atomic'

Finally, Adjectives may be compounded by sheer juxtaposition:

(26) *a l'é nen limità a j'aspet lògich-formaj*
a='le næŋ limi't-a a=j=as'pet 'loʤik=fur'maj
SBJ.3=be\PRS.3S NEG limit-PTCL ADE=DET\P=aspect logical-formal\P
'it is not limited to the logical/formal aspects' ("Gottfried Leibniz;" https://pms.wikipedia.org/wiki/Gottfried_Leibniz)

Shortened forms of Adjectives denoting places and ethnic or language groups may be found in adjectival compounds:

franco-provensal /**fraŋku=pruvæŋ'sal**/ 'Franco-Provençal'
italo-franseis /**italu=fraŋ'sæjz**/ 'Italo-French.'

CHAPTER 7

Personal Pronouns

7.1 Overview

The following account is limited to the expression of personal Pronouns as independent words or as items traditionally called clitics; it does not deal with the pronominal expression of the subject of the clause through indexes to the verbal forms (to be dealt with in Ch. 10). Also the Possessives, which are person-sensitive but fulfil a completely different syntactic role (and which are dealt with in 8.4.), will be left aside here.

The personal Pronouns operate on the basis of the common three-persons opposition, and no need to identify a "fourth person" is found. Among the persons, the usual semantic, syntactic and morphological differences oppose the 3rd person to the participants (1st and 2nd persons).

Identifying the personal Pronouns and defining them as a *bona fide* grammatical category poses several problems, mainly connected, in Piedmontese as elsewhere, with the status of the 3rd person Pronouns: for example, 3rd person Pronouns do not constitute strictly speaking a closed class, and can, although marginally, take modifiers (☞ 7.1.3.). As in many languages, the personal Pronouns come in several paradigms identifiable on the basis of their syntactic roles. Paradigms are person-sensitive: while a few have forms for all persons, others are limited to the participants or to the third persons.

The number of different exponents also varies, with certain paradigms displaying a good amount of syncretism.

Personal Pronouns are either words or clitics. Clitics are often strung together in a clitic complex. Clitics are often strung together in a clitic complex, and often appear in two slightly different forms on the basis of their pre- or postverbal position. Phonologically, all bound personal Pronouns are monosyllabic and minimally consist of one segment.

The following semantic categories find their expression in personal Pronouns:

– person: 1 vs. 2 vs. 3 (the opposition is partially overcome in the Subject series);
– number: S vs. P (again, the opposition is overcome in many series);
– gender (with limitation to the 3S person and the Exclusive forms of 1P, 2P and sometimes 3P): M vs. F;
– marginally, exclusiveness (with limitation to the 1P).

Syntactically, the following categories are expressed:
- syntactic unboundedness (which also covers the pragmatic roles of topic and focus, as well as the syntactic role of prepositional object);
- subject of the clause, further distinguished, although marginally, according to the clause type, between declarative vs. interrogative;
- object, with limitation to the 3rd person and further distinguished between direct and indirect;
- attribution to another Noun or Noun phrase, with limitation to a 3rd person;
- location or movement, with limitation again to a 3rd person

The following series of personal Pronouns may be distinguished on the basis of their phonological behavior, their morphological make up and their syntactic role:
- Independent (IDP);
- Subject (SBJ);
- Object;
- Indirect Object, with a separate form for 3rd persons only, phonetically identical to the locative (☞ 7.4.—3rd persons' Indirect Objects and locatives are consistently glossed IND in this volume)
- Reflexive, with a separate form for the 3rd persons and 1P only, here glossed REFL;
- Attributive (ATTR.PRO; with a separate form for 3rd persons only)
- Subject Interrogative (INT)

Clitic personal Pronouns may form very complex clusters. These Pronouns form a single phonetic word with the Verb (which usually follows them; ☞ 7.9.), and play a crucial role in making Piedmontese a rather strong head-marking language as far as clauses are concerned, since many arguments, even when represented also by full NPs, are indexed on the Verb form.

Table 19. provides an overview of the personal Pronouns. Both the orthographic hyphen found in certain forms and the marking of the clitic boundary in the glosses are left aside: the former for its variability, and the latter because the direction of cliticization is variable and depends on a number of phonological and morphological conditions.

TABLE 19 An overview of the Personal Pronouns

	Independent (IDP)	Subject (SBJ)		Object (OBJ)				Indirect Object (IND)				Reflexive (REFL)				Interrogative (INT)	
		Preverbal		Preverbal		Postverbal		Preverbal		Postverbal		Preverbal		Postverbal		Postverbal	
1S	*mi*	*i*	i	*m*	m	*me*	me	(OBJ)				(OBJ)				*ne*	ne
2S	*ti*	*it*	it	*t*	t	*te*	te									*to, tu*	tu, ty
3S	*chiel* (M), *chila* (F)	*a*	a	*lo* (M), *la* (F) *l'*		lu, la, l (_V)		*j, i, jë*	j, jə	*je*	je	*s*	s, z	*s(s)e*	se	*lo* (-M), *la* (-F)	l-u, l-a
1P	*noi, nojautri/-e* (EXCL-M/F)	*i*	i	*n*	n	*ne*	ne	(OBJ)				*s*	s, z	*s(s)e*	se	*ne*	ne
2P	*voi, vojautr-i/-e* (EXCL-M/F)	*i*	i	*v*	v	*ve*	ve	(OBJ)				(OBJ)				*ve*	ve
3P	*lor, lu'r-awtri/-e* (EXCL-.M/F)	*a*	a	*j*	j	*je*	je	*j, i, jë*	j, jə	*je*	je	*s*	s, z	*s(s)e*	se	*ne*	ne

Attributive (ATTR.PRO)			
Preverbal		Postverbal	
na, n'	na, n (_V)	*ne*	ne

7.2 Independent Personal Pronouns

7.2.1 *Independent Status*

The Independent personal Pronouns are independent both phonologically and morphosyntactically.

Phonologically, they may take primary stress. They may also be used alone constituting a whole utterance, as typically in the reply ((2)) to a question ((1)):

(1) *chi ch'a l'ha vist-lo?*
ki   k=a=ˈla   ˈvist=l-u   ↗
who SUB=SBJ.3=have\PRS.3S see\PTCL=OBJ.3-M Q
'who saw him?'

(2) *mi*
mi
IDP.1S
'I did'

They constitute full words, as shown by the ability to be involved in coordination:

(3) *i-i soma mach pì mi e ti*
i=j=ˈsuma   mak pi   mi   e   ti
SBJ.1=IND=be\PRS.1P only more IDP.1S and IDP.2S
'now it is just me and you'

7.2.2 *The Exclusive Pronouns*

The 1S and 2S forms show considerable consistency across the Piedmontese *Sprachraum* (and in most Gallo-Romance languages). By contrast, the 1P and 2P forms have been enlarged through the plural of the adjective *autr* /awtr/ (but see below) 'other.'[1] The extension, as elsewhere in Romance, originally had an exclusive meaning, although the use of the unextended forms has been considerably reduced, and most speakers judge them incorrect or awkward in most contexts, in particular in topical position or as subjects:

---

1 According to Rohlfs (1968: 134), Turinese prefers the non-augmented forms.

(4) *nojautri i-i la foma pì nen*
nuˈjawtr-i   i=j=l-a=ˈfuma   pi   næŋ
IDP.1P.EXCL-M SBJ.1=IND=OBJ.3-F=do\PRS.1P more NEG
'we can't stand it anymore'

(4′) ?*noi i-i la foma pì nen*

The unextended 1P form is instead normal, and actually preferred, in prepositional phrases, where the use of the extended forms has retained more of its exclusive meaning:

(5) *për **noi** a va bin parej*
pər=ˈnuj   a=ˈva   biŋ paˈræj
BEN=IDP.1P SBJ.3=go\PRS.3S well so
'as for us it is ok like that'

(5′) *për **nojautri** a va bin parej*
pər=nuˈjawtr-i   a=ˈva   biŋ paˈræj
BEN= IDP.1P.EXCL-M SBJ.3=go\PRS.3S well so
'as for us it is ok like that'

The same tendency is not found with the 2P, where the use of the long forms is preferred in all syntactic contexts. The long forms of 3P, *lorautri/-e*, are rare.

The short forms are possibly more common in literary texts:

(6) *Iv arcòrdo, frej, la bela notissia ch'i l'hai nonsiave, che **voi** i l'eve arseivù*
i=v=arˈkord-u /   frej /   l-a=ˈbel-a   nuˈtisj-a
SBJ.1=OBJ.2P=remind-PRS.1S / brother\P / DEF-F=beautiful-F news-S
k=i=ˈlaj   nunˈsj-a=ve /   ke=vuj
SUB=SBJ.1=have\PRS.1S announce-PTCL=OBJ.2P/ SUB=IDP.2P
i=ˈleve   arsæjˈvy
SBJ.2P=have\PRS.2P receive\PTCL
'Brethren, I declare unto you the gospel which I preached unto you, which also ye have received …' (1Corinthians 15.1, https://pms.wikipedia.org/wiki/Cristian%C3%A9sim)[2]

---

[2] Interestingly, neither the Piedmontese Bible online nor the "Valdese Gospels" (cf. e.g., *L'Evangeli secound Matteo* 1861 [1834]) contain the Independent Pronoun *voi*.

Dialectal Exclusive 1P and 2P

The Exclusive forms display a good amount of variation, with allegro speech and many local dialects involving among other changes the dropping of the final syllable, as in the following examples 1P /nuˈjajt, njætʃ/, 2P /vuˈjajt, vjætʃ/, etc.

These changes go back to the dialectal allomorphy of the adjective *autr*, which involves dropping of final /r/ when in isolation or before a consonant.

Varieties that drop the final syllable in the extended personal Pronouns may have generalized the pre-pausal forms to all contexts. Still other varieties extend the pattern of Exclusive 1P and 2P to 3P *lorautri/-e* 'they.'

7.2.3 Third Persons and Deictic Extensions

Third person Pronouns *chiel* (/kjæl/) 'he' e *chila* (/ˈkila/) 'she' result from the grammaticalization of the Latin deictic elements ĒCCU ĪLLE, ĒCCU ĪLLA, whose closest relatives in the contemporary language are the deictics *col* /kul/ 'that' (M), *cola* /ˈkula/ 'that' (F), *coj* and *cole* /kuj/ (M.P), 'kule/ 'those' (F.P; ☞ 8.3.4.).

They are used mainly for humans, although expressive usage may involve animals and objects. On the contrary, deictic Pronouns are mainly used for non-human referents; among them, the proximal deictic *sòn* /soŋ/ 'this' (also used as a cataphoric Pronoun), and the distal deictic *lòn* /loŋ/ 'that' (also used as an anaphoric Pronoun). Still, these elements are mainly deictic:

(7) *Lòn a m'avansa la pruca a Marianin*
 ˈloŋ a=m=aˈvaŋs-a l-a=ˈpryk-a a=marjaˈniŋ
 DIST.PRO SBJ.3=OBJ.1S=spare-PRS.3S DEF-F=wig-S ADE=M.
 'this saves me [saves me the wig] from reproaching Marianin' (Bersezio 1980 [1863], Act 3, Scene 4)

More often, the deictics are enlarged with the adverbials *sì* /=si/ and *lì* /=li/ or *là* /=la/ (☞ 8. for details).
 A few such forms are:

sossì /suˈsi/ 'this one' (locally also *so-lì* /suˈli/ 'that one'), *lo-lì* /luˈli/ 'that one'
cost-sì /kustˈsi/, but mainly /kusˈsi/ or /kustʃˈsi/ 'this one' (M); F: *costa-sì* /kust-aˈsi/
ës-sì /əsˈsi/, also *ës-cì* /əsˈtʃi/ 'this one' (M); F: *sta-sì* /st-aˈsi/
col-là /kulˈla/ 'that one' (M); F: *cola-là* /kul-aˈla/

The 3rd person Pronouns can also be enlarged through the same deictics *sì* /si/ 'here' and *lì, là* /la/ 'there', resulting in pronominal expressions with a clear deictic meaning:

chiel-sì /kjæl='si/ 'the one nearby' (M); F: *chila-sì* /kila='si/
chiel-lì, chiel-là /kjæl='li, ='la/ 'the one over there' (M); F: *chila-lì, chila-là* / kila='li, ='la/
lor-sì /lur='si/ 'the ones nearby,' *lor-lì, lor-là* /lur='li, ='la/ 'the ones over there:'

(8) ... *a smijëria mostré che lor-sì a chërdìo për da bon a lòn ch'a contavo.*
    a=smij-ə'ria   mus'tr-e ke=lur='si
    SBJ.3=seem-COND.3S show-INF SUB=IDP.3P=here
    a=kər'diu   pər=da='buŋ   a='loŋ
    SBJ.3 believe\IMPF.3P BEN=ABL=good ADE=DIST.PRO
    k=a=kuŋ't-avu
    SUB=SBJ.3=count-IMPF.3P
    '... it would seem to show that they really believed what they were saying' ("Cristianésim;" https://pms.wikipedia.org/wiki/Cristian%C3%A9sim)

Chiel-sì is often found with a mildly derogatory meaning:

(9) *varda mach chiel-sì!*
    'vard-a   mak kjæl='si
    look-IPV.2S only IDP.3M=here
    'just look at this guy!' (e.g., in a context where the person is doing something unusual or wrong)

7.2.4 *Use of the Independent Pronouns*

Use of the Independent Pronouns in the subject role is always optional, being mainly used for emphasis or in order to disambiguate. It is obligatory when used contrastively:

(10) *mia fomna a l'é surtia; mi i son stait a ca*
    'mi-a   'fumn-a a='le   syr'ti-a //   mi
    POSS.1S.F woman-S SBJ.3=be\PRS.3S go_out\PTCL-F IDP.1S
    i='suŋ   stajt   a='ka
    SBJ.1=be\PRS.1S be\PTCL ADE=house
    'my wife went out; I stayed home'

PERSONAL PRONOUNS 175

Without an Independent Pronoun the sentence is possible with a consequential reading:

(10′) *mia fomna a l'é surtia; i son stait a ca*
    'mi-a   'fumn-a   a='le   syr'ti-a //   i='suŋ
    POSS.1S.F woman-S SBJ.3=be\PRS.3S go_out\PTCL-F SBJ.1=be\PRS.1S
    stajt   a='ka
    be\PTCL ADE=house
    'my wife went out; (therefore,) I stayed home'

while an adversative reading is excluded, as also shown by the impossibility of the presence of an Adverb:

(10″) **mia fomna a l'é surtia; anvece i son stait a ca*

In principle, Independent Pronouns can be used in whichever syntactic position. They are also the only admissible forms in prepositional phrases (☞ 13., and especially 13.2.). Different from nominals, which occur postverbally as object in neutral statements, the postverbal positioning of Independent Pronouns is reserved for contrast but is always preceded by the bound enclitic Object Pronoun:

(11) *mi i l'hai vist na fomna*
    mi   i='laj   vist   n-a='fumn-a
    IDP.1SG SBJ.1=have\PRS.1S see\PTCL INDEF-F=woman-S
    'I saw a woman'

(12) *na fomna a l'ha vistme mi*
    n-a='fumn-a   a='la   vist=me   mi
    INDEF-F=woman-S SBJ.3=have\PRS.3S see\PTCL=OBJ.1S IDP.1SG
    'a woman saw *me*'

The default position of the Independent personal Pronouns is pre-verbal (i.e., before the bound Pronouns):

(13) (*chiel*) *a va*
    (kjæl)   a='va
    (IDP.3M) SBJ.3=go\PRS.3S
    'he is going'

Use of the Independent Pronouns in preverbal position in interrogative sentences (as a more common alternative to the use of the Interrogative Subject clitics; ☞ 7.5.) implies question on the Verb; question on the entity referred to is marked by its left- or right-dislocation sentence-finally (☞ 17.1.):

(14) *ti it vas?*
 ti   it='vaz   ↗
 IDP.2S SBJ.2S go\PRS.2SG Q
 'are you (S) going?'

(15) *ti, it vas?*
 ti /   it='vaz   ↗
 IDP.2S SBJ.2S go\PRS.2SG Q
 'you, are you (S) going?'

(16) *it vas, ti?*
 it='vaz /   ti   ↗
 SBJ.2S=go\PRS.2S IDP.2G Q
 'are *you* going?'

⚘ *Chiel, cel, le, lu*

Local dialects may exhibit different forms for Third person Pronouns. The most common variation concerns the plurals: instead of *lor*, some varieties have *chièj* /kjæj/ for masculine and *chile* /ˈkile/ for feminine, in perfect symmetry with the singular scheme *chiel/chila*.

In some other varieties (most notably in Bielèis, see Di Stefano 2017: 57), The 3S Pronouns show palatalized forms such as *cel, cël* /tʃel, tʃəl/ instead of *chiel, cëlla* /ˈtʃəlla/ instead of *chila*, and so on.

A few local dialects have completely different forms of third person's Pronouns, such as *lu* /lu/, *le* /le/.

7.2.5 *Use of the Independent Pronouns as Politeness Markers*

While the use of the 2P form as a polite addressing is attested in the literature ((17)), in the modern language the Singular forms of 3rd person Independent Pronouns are used as polite forms in addressing persons. The 3M Pronoun is used with male individuals and the 3F with females (see (18) and (19), respectively). Much rarely, 3P is used in addressing several people. Agreement is determined by the Subject clitic and is at the 3rd person. In this use, the Independent Pronouns are sometimes capitalized:

(17) *Cosa ch'i feve lì **voi**?*
 ˈkoza k=i=ˈfeve   li   vuj   ↗
 what SUB=SBJ.2P=do-PRS.2P there IDP.2P Q
 [seeing Brigida] 'What are you doing, Madam?' (Bersezio 1980 [1863], Act 1, Scene 7)

(18) ***Chiel** a rij mentre mi im sento a meuire*
 kjæl   a=ˈrij   ˈmæntre mi   i=m=ˈsænt-u
 IDP.3M SBJ.3=laugh\PRS.3S while   IDP.1S SBJ.1S=RFX.1S=feel-PRS.1S
 a=ˈmøjre
 ADE=die\INF
 'You laugh, while I feel like I'm dying' (Mania Reida 1995: 29)

(19) *cò ch'a na pensa, **Chila**?*
 ko   k=a=na=ˈpæŋs-a /   ˈkila   ↗
 what SUB=SBJ.3=ATTR=think-PRS.3S IDP.3F Q
 'what do you think about it, Madam?'

7.3 Subject Clitic Personal Pronouns

Piedmontese has both subject and non-subject clitic Pronouns.

The declarative Subject personal Pronouns (SBJ) display a high degree of syncretism and can be regrouped as follows:

SBJ.2S   *it*
SBJ.1 & SBJ.2P   *i*
SBJ.3   *a*

In Feature Geometry terms (cf. Harley and Ritter 2002 for a general theoretical presentation and Tosco 2007 for a comparative analysis of Romance and Cushitic subject clitics), the doubly marked 2P only is specified against the two unmarked forms for Participant (1 and 2 persons) and Individuation (: 3 person), where RE (Referring Expression) is not branched (☞ Figure 15).

Subject clitic Pronouns precede a following verbal form. There are mandatory in the written language (except perhaps in poetry for prosodic reasons) and in many varieties in main clauses ((20)) and tensed dependent clauses ((21)):[3,4]

---

3 1st person Subject clitics in particular may be absent locally and are often omitted in allegro

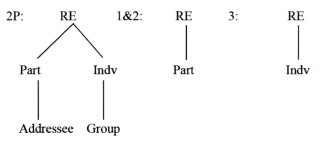
FIGURE 15 A feature-geometric representation of the Subject clitics

(20) *i chërdo*
i=ˈkərd-u
SBJ.1=believe-PRS.1S
'I believe'

(21) *i chërdo che a vada bin parej*
i=ˈkərd-u   k=a=ˈvad-a   biŋ paˈræj
SBJ.1=believe-PRS.1S SUB=SBJ.3=go-SBJV.PRS.3S well so
'I this it is ok this way'

(21′) is not acceptable in the koine but it is common in many varieties:

(21′) **ke=vada*
ke=ˈvad-a
SUB=go-SBJV.PRS.3S

With vowel-initial Verbs the presence of the Subject clitic may induce dropping of the initial vowel of vowel-initial Verbs:

---

speech (Bonato 2004). Different systems (in both the number and shape of the Subject clitics) are found in local dialects. Cf. Heap (2000) for a geographical overview in the Romance domain and many useful maps, Renzi and Vanelli (1983) for some generalizations on the different Subject clitic systems and Poletto and Tortora (2016) for a more recent account taking into consideration the Romance subject clitics in general.

(22) *i andoma*
   i=aŋˈduma → [i=ŋduma]
   SBJ.1=go\PRS.1P
   'we go, are going'

while the form without Subject clitic would instead be used in exhortative contexts (☞ 15.7.):

(22′) *andoma*
   aŋˈduma
   go\PRS.1P
   'let's go!'

With a 3rd person Subject clitic the dropping of the following vowel results in a form phonetically undistinguishable from a bare verbal form without Subject clitic:[4]

(23) *a andasia*
   a=aŋdaˈzia → [a=ŋdaˈzia]
   SBJ.3=go\IMPF.3S
   's/he used to go'

The 2S clitic Pronoun *it* /it/ is subject to loss of its initial vowel and changes to *ti* /ti/ when followed by a consonant cluster—therefore becoming homophonous with the Independent Pronoun:

(24) *it lo vëdde*
   it=l-u=ˈvədde
   SBJ.2=OBJ.3-M=see\PRS.2S
   'you (S) see it'

vs.

(24′) *ti-j lo das*
   ti=j=l-u=ˈdas
   SBJ.2=IND=OBJ.3-M=give\PRS.2S
   'you (S) give it to him/her/them'

---

4 One may suspect that many claims about the absence of Subject clitics in local varieties and in casual speech are the result not only of sloppy transcriptions, but also of a general disregard for these assimilatory phenomena.

3rd singular Subject clitics are also used with zero-valent Verbs such as *pieuve* 'to rain,' *tëmpësté* 'to hail' (e.g., *a pieuv* 'it rains/it's raining'), and generally with Verbs whose subject is a Completive sentence.[5]

Variation in Subject clitics

The clitic subjects system of the koine does not differentiate any person for gender but subject clitics show a great deal of variation, as everywhere in Romance. Many varieties have a clitic subject specialized for the Masculine (*al* or *o*) and another one specialized for Feminine (*la* or *a*, more rarely *i*). A few dialects may distinguish also a Masculine (*i*) and a Feminine (*e*) Third Plural forms, instead of the common 3rd person *a* of the koine. This implies a sometimes very different distribution of the forms in the whole system. Defective systems with just three or two subject clitics (most commonly the Second and the Third Singular) are also found. Some South-Western varieties around Coni show no clitics at all—even less than the Occitan dialects they are in contact with.

7.4 Non-subject Personal Pronouns: Object and Indirect Object

The 3s Pronouns have different forms for the direct (OBJ) and indirect (IND) roles; moreover, the Direct Object forms are gender-sensitive. The Indirect Object Pronoun shows no gender nor number variation, and is identical to the Direct Object 3P Pronoun *j, je* /**j, je**/.

3s direct Object forms are sensible in some varieties to PP 8. (Delateralization; ☞ 2.4.2.3.), whereby, e.g., *lo* /l-u/ becomes [ju].

(25) *i-j pijo mi*
   i=j=ˈpi-u   mi
   SBJ.1=OBJ.3P=take-PRS.1S IDP.1S
   'I take them'

(26) *i-j conòsso bin*
   i=j=kuˈnosu   biŋ
   SBJ.1=OBJ.3P=know\PRS.1S well
   'I know them well'

---

5 In those dialects where SBJ.3SM is different from SBJ.3SF the Masculine form is usually used.

PERSONAL PRONOUNS

When followed by a consonant cluster, the 3P preverbal form *j* (as in (25) and (26)) is pronounced /jə/ and spelled *jë* (as in (27)):

(27) *it jë s-ciaire?*
   it=jə=ˈstʃajr-e ↗
   SBJ.2S=OBJ.3P=glimpse-PRS.2S Q
   'do you (s) manage to see them?'

The following examples show the use of the Direct Object and Indirect Object Pronouns of 3rd person.
Direct Object forms:

(28) *it lo conòsse?*
   it=l-u=kuˈnose ↗
   SBJ.2S=OBJ.3-M=know\PRS.2S Q
   'do you (s) know him?'

(29) *i la vëddo sovens*
   i=l-a=ˈvəddu su'æŋs
   SBJ.1S=OBJ.3-F=see\PRS.1S often
   'I often see her'

(30) *s'it je vëdde daje sossì*
   s=it=je=ˈvədde ˈda=je su=ˈsi[6]
   if=SBJ.2S=OBJ.3P=see\PRS.2S give\IPV.2S=IND PROX.PRO=here
   'if you see them, give them this'

Indirect Object:

(31) *a-j dà   sossì*
   a=j=ˈda su=ˈsi
   SBJ.3=IND=give\PRS.3S PROX.PRO=here
   's/he gives this to her/him' (Pivron; Manzini and Savoia 2005b: 262)

Direct + Indirect Object:

---

[6] An alternative form with PP 5. /e/-Closing (☞ 2.4.1.4.) and reduction of *je* to *j* is /se ti-j ˈvəddi da=j su=ˈsi/.

(32) *a-j lo dà*
 a=j=l-u=ˈda[7]
 SBJ.3=IND=OBJ.3-M=give\PRS.1S
 's/he gives it to her/him' (Massran; Manzini and Savoia 2005b: 262)

No Direct vs. Indirect Object distinction is found for the participants (1st and 2nd persons):

(33) *quand che **am** ved **am** da sempe queicòs*
 kwaŋd k=a=m=ˈvæd   a=m=ˈda
 when SUB=SBJ.3=OBJ.1S=see\PRS.3S SBJ.3=OBJ.1S=give\PRS.3S
 ˈsæmpe kwæjˈkoz
 always something
 'when he sees me, he always gives me something'

Moreover, the non-subject clitics occur in two different series according to the position in which they appear, either preverbally or postverbally. Their use depends on the verbal form: tensed paradigms require the use of the preverbal forms; with untensed verbal forms the postverbal forms are found. The Main Past is a compound verbal form made up of an auxiliary and a Past Participle (PTCL; ☞ 10.2.6, 10.6.); the non-subject clitics attach postverbally to the Participle (as in other untensed forms). Examples (34)–(36) show the use of the Object clitics with a tensed verbal form ((34), a Present), an untensed one ((35), an Imperative Singular), and a compound verbal form ((36), a Past). Both preverbally (as shown among others in (32) above) and postverbally ((37)) the non-subject clitics co-occur in the order Indirect Object—Direct Object.

The postverbal position of the object clitics in the Past is very possibly the most important isogloss separating Piedmontese from all other Romance languages and will be covered in more detail in Ch. 18:

(34) *e peui am fa ...*
    e   pøj a=m=ˈfa
    and then SBJ.3=OBJ.1S=do\PRS.3S
    'and then s/he tells [does] me ...'

---

7 A coalesced form /a=ʎu=ˈda/ is also attested in Pivron /piˈvruŋ/ (Italian Piverone /piveˈrone/; 45°27′N 08°00′E) and Massran /maˈsraŋ/ (Italian Masserano /masseˈrano/; 45°58′N 08°21′E).

(35) *fame un piasì*
 'fa=me aŋ=pja'zi/
 do\IPV.2S=OBJ.1S INDEF=favor
 'make me a favor'

(36) *a l'ha fame un piasì*
 a=la   'fa=me   aŋ=pja'zi/
 SBJ.3=have\PRS.3S do\PTCL=OBJ.1S INDEF=favor
 's/he made me a favor'

(37) *i l'hai sempe dijlo*
 i='laj   'sæmpe 'di=j=l-u
 SBJ.1=have\PRS.1S always say\PTCL=IND=OBJ.3-M
 'I always told him/her/them so' ("I always said it to him/her/them")

The Indirect object clitic for 3rd persons has merged with the reflex of the Late Latin locative adverbial HĪCE (from HĪC) 'here,' preserved in other Romance languages (cf. French *y* [i], Italian *ci* [tʃi]). Although treated separately in normative and pedagogic grammars, it shares the same allomorphs of the Indirect and is best treated as a locative reading of the Indirect object clitic, with which it cannot co-occur. With the Indirect it also shares the writing *jë* when preverbal after a consonant and /jə/ when postverbal, while a peculiar writing ⟨i⟩ is used after a vowel (i.e., after a Subject clitic):

(38) *i-i vado ëdcò mi*
 i=j='vadu   əd'ko mi
 SBJ.1=IND=go\PRS.1S also IDP.1S
 'me, too I am going [there]'

(39) *a l'avio parlame d'ës post e i son andaje*
 a=la'viu   par'l-a=me   d=əs='post   e
 SBJ.3=have\IMPF.3P speak-PTCL=OBJ.1S ATTR=DEICT=place and
 i='suŋ   an'da=je
 SBJ.1=be\PRS.1S go\PTCL=IND
 'they told me about this place and I went there'

The Indirect *qua* locative enters into a limited number of configurations; namely, it is restricted in use to intransitive Verbs and cannot therefore occur with either Object nor Indirect Pronouns. Its use with an Imperative (as in French *vas-y* 'go on!' or Italian *vacci* 'go there!') is possible for many speakers but ungrammatical or doubtful for others:

(40) ?*va-je sùbit*
 'va=je   'sybit
 go\IPV.2S=IND at_once
 'go (S) there immediately!'

Its most common occurrence is with the Verb 'to be,' either in the Present or in other tenses (☞ 10.2.4.4. for the allomorphy of 'to be' with the Indirect object Pronoun with a locative value):

(41) *a-i é*
 a='j=e
 SBJ.3=IND=be\PRS.1S
 'there is'

Its use with other Verbs (especially but not only of location, such as *vive* /'vive/ 'to live,' *sté* /ste/ 'to stay') is also common:

(42) *a-i viv tanta gent*
 a=j='viv   'taŋt-a dʒæŋt
 SBJ.3=IND=live\PRS.3S much-F people
 'a lot of people live there'

(43) *a-i travajavo fieuj e fije*
 a=j=trava'jav-u   fjøj e 'fi-e
 SBJ.3=IND=work-IMPF.3P boy\P and girl-P
 'boys and girls worked there'

Just as this reading is excluded with Object clitics and a further, pronominal copy of the Indirect Pronouns, its use is also limited with the Reflexive (☞ 7.6.) but is attested in literature:

(44) *adòss as-jë precipita*
 a'dos a=s=jə=pre'tʃipit-a
 upon SBJ.3=REFL=IND=plummet-PRS.3S
 'it rushes upon it' (Peyron 1830: 62)

and is well possible for many speakers and in different varieties:

(45) *ambelessì as-jë sta bin*
    ambele'si a=s=jə='sta biŋ
    here   SBJ.3=REFL=IND=stay\PRS.3S well
    'one lives well here'

but doubtful or downright ungrammatical for others, who prefer to drop the Indirect *qua* Locative here (these speakers likewise exclude it after an Imperative):

(45') *ambelessì a së sta bin*
    ambele'si a=s='sta biŋ
    here   SBJ.3=REFL=stay\PRS.3S well

7.5 Interrogative Subject Clitics

As seen in 7.3., in current usage the Subject clitics are used in both main positive and interrogative sentences. Special postverbal Interrogative Subject clitics are used in literature and locally, but are obsolete for most speakers.

(28), repeated herebelow, can be replaced by (46):

(28) *it lo conòsse?*
    it=l-u=ku'nose ↗
    SBJ.2S=OBJ.3-M=know\PRS.2S Q
    'do you (s) know him?'

(46) *(it) lo conòsses=**to**?*
    (it=)l-u=ku'noses=tu ↗
    (SBJ.2S)= OBJ.3-M=know\PRS.2S=INT.2S Q
    'do you (s) know him?'

As shown in (46) and as further exemplified below, the use of the Interrogative Subject clitics does not exclude the presence of the (declarative) Subject Pronouns. Three configurations are therefore possible:
– (declarative) Subject clitics
– Interrogative Subject clitics
– (declarative) Subject clitics + Interrogative Subject clitics
These possibilities are shown in (47), (47'), and (47''). It is noteworthy that the absence of the (declarative) Subject clitics (as in (47')) involves the absence of the Subordinator *che* /ke/ (☞ 14.3.):

(47) cò ch'it fas sì?
　　 ko　 k=it='fas　　　　　　　si　 ↗
　　 what SUB=SBJ.2S=do\PRS.2S here Q
　　 'what are you (s) doing here?'

(47') cò fas-to sì?
　　 ko　 'fas=tu　　　　　si　 ↗
　　 what do\PRS.2S=INT.2S here Q
　　 'what are you (s) doing here?'

(47″) cò ch'it fas-to sì?
　　 ko　 k=it='fas=tu　　　　　　　si　 ↗
　　 what SUB=SBJ.2S=do\PRS.2S=INT.2S here Q
　　 'what are you (s) doing here?'

Which configuration will be chosen is first and foremost a matter of dialect (presence or absence of the Interrogative Subject clitics in the spoken inventory) and, furthermore, of stylistic and prosodic choices.

In compound verbal forms, the Interrogative clitic follows the Auxiliary, while other clitics follow the Participle. (48) shows the use of the Interrogative and two other clitics in the Past:

(48) has-to dajlo?
　　 'as=tu　　　　　　　 'da=j=l-u　　　　　　　　↗
　　 have\PRS.2S=INT.2S give\PTCL=IND=OBJ.3-M Q
　　 'did you give it to him/her/them?'

These Pronouns may also be used in exhortative function after an Imperative or Subjunctive verbal form, and also for speakers who do not normally use them in other clause types:

(49) andom-ne!
　　 aŋ'dum=ne
　　 go\PRS.INT.1P=INT.1P
　　 'let's go!'

7.6 Reflexive, Reciprocal and Impersonal Personal Pronouns

A special object Reflexive Pronoun (REFL) is used for the 3 and the 1P persons only, with the allomorphs -s /s, z/ (preverbal) and -s(s)e /se/ (postverbal; the orthographic variant -sse is used after a vowel-ending form). For all other persons, the Object Pronouns are used. The Reflexive has either a, reciprocal or reflexive reading:

im diso	/i=m='diz-u/ ("SBJ.1=OBJ.1S=say-PRS.1S")	'I say to myself'
t'ët dise	/t=ət='diz-e/ ("SBJ.2S=OBJ.2S=say-PRS.2S")	'you say to yourself'
as dis	/a=s=diz/ ("SBJ.3=REFL=say\PRS.3S")	'he/she says to him-/herself'
is disoma	/i=s=di'z-uma/ ("SBJ.1=REFL=say-PRS.1P")	'we say to ourselves'
iv dize	/i=v='diz-e/ ("SBJ.2=OBJ.2P=say-PRS.2P")	'you say to yourselves'
as diso	/a=s='diz-u/ ("SBJ.3=REFL=say-PRS.3P")	'they say to themselves'

or, postverbally:

i son dime	/i='suŋ 'di=me/ ("SBJ.1=BE\PRS.1S say\PTCL=OBJ.1S")	'I said to myself'
a l'é disse	/a='le 'di=se/ ("SBJ.3=be\PRS.3M= say\PRTC=REFL")	'he/she told himself/herself'

Reflexive Pronouns may be followed by a further Object or Indirect pronoun:

(50) *im lo diso sovens*
 i=m=l-u='diz-u su'æŋs
 SBJ.1=OBJ.1S=OBJ.3-M=say-PRS.1S often
 'I often tell myself'

(51) *a l'é nen chila ma as jë smija*
 a='le næŋ 'kila ma a=s=jə='zmi-a
 SBJ.3=be\PRS.3S NEG IDP.3F but SBJ.3=REFL=IND=look_alike-PRS.3S
 'it is not her but she looks alike'

(52) *la volp a l'ha vist soa tan-a e a l'é andàita a stërmessje andrinta*
 l-a='vulp a='la vist 'su-a 'taŋ-a e
 DET-F=fox SBJ.3=have\prs.3s see\PTCL POSS.3-F lair-S and
 a='le aŋ'dajt-a a=stər'm-e=s=je aŋ'driŋta
 SBJ.3=be\PRS.3S go\PTCL-F ADE=hide-INF=REFL=IND inside
 'the fox saw its lair and went into hiding inside'

The Reflexive Pronoun is also used as an Impersonal (cf. Parry 1998 for a diachronic development of this usage), together with the 3rd person Subject clitic and agreement on the Verb:

(53) *as dis che a sia mòrt*
 a=s='diz ke a='sia mort
 SBJ.3=REFL=say-PRS.3S SUB SBJ.3=be\SBJV.3S dead
 'they say he is dead'

The same meaning may be expressed with a 3P verbal form and no Reflexive clitic:

(53') *a diso che a sia mòrt*
 a='dizu ke a='sia mort
 SBJ.3=say-PRS.3P SUB SBJ.3=be\SBJV.3S dead

Double clitics

In the past, Piedmontese Object and Indirect clitics were usually appeared both before and after the verbal form: that is, instead of contemporary *a l'ha dime* 's/he told to me,' forms like *a m'ha dime* were more common. This is still possible in some lateral areas, especially in the Southern dialects between Piedmont and Ligury.

Clitic doubling in contemporary koine is still acceptable with Reflexive clitics. In fact, *as peul fesse* 'it can be done' is actually more common than *a peul fesse*.

7.7 Attributive Pronoun

The 3rd person Pronoun *na* (preverbal; *n'* /n/ before a vowel) / *ne* (postverbal) is used in the same wide array of uses of the Attributive Preposition *ëd* (☞ 13.5.) and the same label will be used for the Pronoun.

(54) *còs ch'it na dise?*
 koz k=it=na='dize
 what SUB=SBJ.2S=ATTR.PRO=say\PRS.2S
 'what do you say about it?'

(55) *a l'ha parlamne*
 a='la   par'l-a=m=ne (← par'l-a=me=ne)
 SBJ.3=have\PRS.3S speak-PTCL=OBJ.1S=ATTR.PRO
 's/he told me about it'

(56) *a l'avìa tre fije e a l'ha mariane doe*
 a=la'via   træ 'fi-e e a='la
 SBJ.3=have\IMPF.3S three girl-P and SBJ.3=have\PRS.3S
 ma'rj-a=ne   'due
 marry-PTCL=ATTR.PRO two\F
 's/he had three daughters and gave two of them in marriage'

There is no Attributive Pronoun for the other persons, and a prepositional phrase will be used; thus, corresponding to (55) above, one would have for a 2S person:

(57) *a l'ha parlame ëd ti*
 a='la   par'l-a=me   əd='ti
 SBJ.3=have\PRS.3S speak-PTCL=OBJ.1S ATTR=IDP.2S
 's/he told me about you (s)'

7.8 Lexicalized Verb-Clitic Constructions

As is often the case in languages that are predominantly spoken, Piedmontese has a number of lexicalized Verb-clitic constructions (Masini 2015), i.e., expressions made of a Verb and one or more pronominal clitics, conveying a specialized or idiomatic meaning.

Many of these constructions are formed juxtaposing to the Verb the 3F Object Clitic *la*. As in other Romance languages (Russi 2008), the use of the Pronoun expresses a higher degree of affectedness of the subject:

(58) *chit-la!*[8]
 'kit=l-a
 stop\IPV.2S=OBJ.3-F
 'stop it!' or 'give it a break!' (e.g., to someone doing something annoying)

---

8 Also, and perhaps more frequently, *chit-la lì* 'give it a break!' lit. 'stop\IPV.2S=OBJ.3F there', with the deictic Adverb adding a sense of carelessness towards the activity performed by the addressee (see Strik Lievers and Miola 2019).

La may also appear attached to Verbs that are part of multiword expressions:

(59) *paghela cara e salà*⁹
pa'g-e=l-a   'kar-a e   sa'l-a
pay-INF=OBJ.3-F dear-F and salt-PTCL
'to pay dearly' (Gentile 1911: 82)

(60) *savejla longa*
sa'væj=l-a   'lung-a
know\INF=OBJ.3-F long-F
'to know a lot'

Sometimes *la* appears in combination with other clitics, such as Indirect Objects or a Reflexive Pronoun.

In (61) the Verb *fejla vëdde*, literally 'to make see it to her/him/them,' must display the Indirect Object and *la* in order to acquire the meaning of 'to beat her/him/them off, make her/him/them succumb;' compare *fe(la) vëdde* 'to show (her/it).'

(61) *A finirà nen parej, 'v la faroma vëdde noi!*
a=finira   næŋ pa'ræj v=l-a=fa'ruma   'vədde
SBJ3=end\DUB.3S NEG so   OBJ.2P=OBJ3-F=do\1DUB.1P see\INF
nuj
IDP.1P
'it won't end like this, we will show you up' (Oddoero, No Date; https://www.ateatro.info/copioni/na-portiera-ficapocio/)

Another example is *fessla bin* /'fe=s=l-a biŋ/ ("do\INF=REFL=OBJ.3-F well") or *passesla bin* / pa's-e=s=l-a biŋ/ ("pass-INF=REFL=OBJ.3-F well") 'to have a good life, to enjoy life:'

(62) *butesse ansema për fessla bin*
bu't-e=se   ansema pər='fe=s=l-a   biŋ
put-INF=REFL together BEN=do\INF=REFL=OBJ.3-F well
'spend the time together and have fun' (Villata 2013: 1)

---

9 One can also find *paghela cara* and *paghela* alone with the same meaning.

When a Reflexive Pronoun is used, as in (62) and in *ciapessla* /tʃaˈp-e=s=l-a/ ("catch-INF=REFL=OBJ.3-F") 'to take offence', *gavessla* /gaˈv-e=s=l-a/ ("take_off-INF=REFL=OBJ.3-F") 'to survive, to manage,' it generally marks the affectedness of the Subject, as in (63), and following the same pattern of the "Transitive Middle Constructions" (Masini 2012 for Italian), as in (64) (☞ 11.3. for the ethcal datives and the Middle):

(63) *a venta nen pijessla*
    a=ˈvænt-a   næŋ ˈpj-e=s=l-a
    SBJ3=need-PRS.3S NEG take-INF=REFL=OBJ.3-F
    'you must not take offence' (Soldati 2010: 247)

(64) *im beivo un cafè*
    i=m=ˈbæjv-u   aŋ=kaˈfæ
    SBJ.1S=OBJ.1S=drink-PRS.1S INDEF=coffee
    'I am having a coffee'

Although, as anticipated, mainly used in spoken registers, the use of these lexicalized constructions often creeps in more formal domains, as in the following recurring sentence from the Piedmontese Wikipedia:

(65) *tute cole pàgine che a-j giuto a la gent a gavessla*
    ˈtyt-e ˈkul-e   ˈpadʒin-e ke=a=j=ˈdʒyt-u
    all-F.P DIST.F.P page-P   SUB=SBJ.3=IND=help-PRS.3P
    a=l-a=ˈdʒæŋt   a=gaˈv-e=s=l-a
    ADE=DET-F=people ADE=remove-INF=REFL=OBJ.3-F
    'all those pages that help people to get by' (Piedmontese Wikipedia, disambiguation page)

Reflexive Pronouns may also be used in Verb-clitic constructions, alone (in the so-called ethical dative expressions) or in combination with *na*. In both cases the affectedness of the Subject or, for ethical datives (☞ 11.3.), of the Indirect Object is stressed:

(66) *i vado*
    i=ˈvadu
    SBJ.1S=go\PRS.1S
    'I'm leaving'

(67) *im na vado*
 i=m=na=ˈvadu
 SBJ.1S=OBJ.1S=ATTR.PRO=go\PRS.1S
 'I'm definitely leaving'

In a few cases the whole construction is fully lexicalized, as for *anfessne* /anˈfe=s=ne/ ("do\INF=IND=ATTR") 'not to give a damn, not to care.'

In a few other cases the construction is available for a single verbal form. Only the Imperative Singular is used in the case of the expression *dajla* /da=j=l-a/ ("give\IPV.2S=IND=OBJ.3-F"), often preceded by the conjunction *e* 'and' and used for an emphatic affirmation or reiteration, as in the following, from a fictive debate about the identity of someone:

(68) *e dajla ch'a l'é chiel!*
 e   ˈda=j=l-a   k=a=ˈle   kjæl
 and give\IPV.2S=IND=OBJ.3-F   SUB=SBJ.3=BE\PRS.3S   IDP.3M
 'sure it is him!'

Reflexive and reciprocal *se* is also found in these idioms, as in *contessla* /kuŋˈt-e=s=l-a/ ("tell-INF=REFL=OBJ.3-F") 'to chat (with).'

This Verb may of course take different meanings when modified by different clitics, as shown by a comparison of the previous construction with the followings, all involving *conté* 'to tell, to count:' *contela* /kuŋˈt-e=l-a/ ("tell-INF=OBJ.3-F") 'to tell tall tales, to speechify,' *contela giusta* /kuŋˈt-e=l-a ˈdʒyst-a/ ("tell-INF=OBJ.3-F right-F") 'to tell the truth.'

Perhaps less frequently, other clitics may form a Verb-clitic lexicalized construction, such as:
– Indirect object clitic with a locative reading *je*, as found in constructions where some emphasis on or actualization of a state or activity is intended:
  – *andeje* /anˈde=je/ ("go\INF=IND") 'to fit; to be needed,' as in

(69) *sì a-j va la ciav dël tërdes*
 si   a=j=ˈva   l-a=ˈtʃaw   d=əl=ˈtərdæz
 here SBJ.3=IND=go-PRS.3S   DET-F=key   ATTR=DET-F=thirteen
 'a 13" wrench is needed here'

  – *voleje* /vuˈle=je/ ("want\INF=IND") 'to be needed,'
  – *deje (andrinta)* /ˈde=je (anˈdriŋta)/ ('give\INF=IND (inside)') 'to get it on, to come on,'

- *essje* /ˈes=je/ ("be\INF=IND"), lit. 'to be there,' partially lexicalized and typically used in expressions such as *i-j soma* /i=j=ˈsuma/ ('SBJ.3=IND=be\PRS.1P') 'here we go; that's it!'
- Attributive *ne*: *savejne* /ˈsavæj=ne/ ("know\INF=ATTR") 'to be skilled, savvy'
- Object clitics other than 3F, such as Masculine Singular: *andesslo a pijé ant la giaca* /aŋˈd-e=s=l-u a=ˈpje aŋt=l-a=ˈdʒak-a/ ("go-INF=REFL=OBJ.3-M ADE=take-INF INE=DET-F= jacket-S") 'to be screwed' [to go and get it in the jaket], or Plural: *pijeje* /ˈpj-e=je/ ("take-INF=OBJ.3P") 'to be beaten off,' *deje* /ˈde=je/ ("give\INF=OBJ.3P") 'to beat off,' *tireje vërde* /tiˈr-e=je ˈvərd-e/ ("pull-INF=OBJ.3P green-F.P") 'to live in hardship,' *feje bon-e* /ˈfe=je boŋ-e/ ("do\INF=OBJ.3P good-F.P") 'to endear.'

7.9 Post-Tonic Vowel Dropping

As many examples have shown, the Postverbal forms of the clitics lose their final vowel before another clitic, e.g., in (55), repeated herebelow, the object clitic of 1S *me* is reduced to *m* /m/ in both writing and pronunciation before the following Attributive Pronoun *ne* /ne/, and the sequence /parˈl-a=me=ne/ ("speak-PTCL=OBJ.1S=ATTR.PRO") is reduced to /parˈl-a=m=ne/:

(55) *a l'ha parlamne*
a=la=parˈl-a=m=ne (← parˈl-a=me=ne)
SBJ.3=have\PRS.3S speak-PTCL=OBJ.1S=ATTR.PRO
's/he told me about it'

Similarly, untensed verbal forms followed by clitics are subject to final vowel dropping; e.g., the sequence /aŋˈduma=ne/ ("go\PRS.INT.1P=INT.1P") is reduced to /aŋˈdum=ne/:

(70) *andom-ne!*
aŋˈdum=ne (← aŋˈduma=ne)
go\PRS.INT.1P=INT.1P
'let's go!'

All these and other examples show the application of a single rule of vowel dropping which operates across clitic boundaries on the post-tonic syllable of a CV́CVCV sequence, reducing it to CV́CCV:

Post-Tonic Vowel Dropping: CV́CV=CV → CV́C=CV

7.10 Sequences of Clitics

As abundantly shown in the examples above, sequences of clitics are allowed, and they follow the general templates:
- with tensed verbal forms: SBJ + IND + REFL + {OBJ, ATTR.PRO} + V + INT
- with untensed verbal forms: V + {IND, REFL} + {OBJ, ATTR.PRO}
- with compound verbal forms: SBJ + AUX + PTCL + {IND, REFL} + {OBJ, ATTR.PRO} + INT

The templates can be worded out as:
- Subject clitics may occur only with tensed verbal forms;
- they always come at the edge of a tensed verbal form, either first or, in the case of the Interrogative Subject clitics, last;
- in tensed configurations, the Indirect object clitic follows the Subject clitic and precedes the direct Object clitic (with the Subject clitic being particularly prone to dropping before an Indirect object clitic);
- Indirect and Reflexive, as well as Object and Attributive Pronouns, can co-occur in this order;
- with an untensed verbal form, the Indirect (or Reflexive) and the Object (or an Attributive Pronoun) clitic follow the Verb in the same order.

With the exception of the Interrogative Subject Clitics, the following sentences exemplify all possible combinations of zero, one, two, and three clitics (for the compound verbal forms and their use ☞ 10.6.).

- No clitic constructions:

(71) *gieuga!*
ˈdʒøg-a
play-IPV.2S
'play!'

- One clitic constructions:

  - Subject:

(72) *a gieuga*
a=ˈdʒøg-a
SBJ.3=play-PRS.3S
's/he plays'

  - Direct object:

(73) *falo an pressa*
 'fa=l-u   aŋ='pres-a
 do\IPV.2S=OBJ.3-M INE=hurry-S
 'do it quickly!'

- Indirect object:

(74) *faje vëdde*
 'fa=je   'vədde
 do\IPV.2S=IND see-INF
 'let him/her/them see!'

- IND *qua* Locative:

(75) *camp-je l'amnis*
 'kamp=je   l=am'niz
 throw=IND DET=garbage
 'throw the garbage in it!'

- Reflexive:

(76) *as lavo le man*
 a='s=lav-u   l-e='maŋ
 SBJ.3=REFL=wash-PRS.3P DET-F.P=hand
 'they wash their hands'

- Attributive:

(77) *fane quaidun*
 'fa=ne   kwaj'dyŋ
 do\IPV.2S=ATTR.PRO some
 'make a few of them!'

- Two clitics constructions:

  - Subject + Indirect:

(78) *a-j dis*
 a=j='diz
 SBJ.3=IND=say\PRS.3S
 's/he says to him/her/them'

- Subject + Reflexive:

(79) *a së stërma*
 a=sə=ˈstərm-a
 SBJ.3=REFL=hide-PRS.3S
 's/he hides her/himself'

- Subject + Object:

(80) *i lo cuso*
 i=l-u=ˈkyzu
 SBJ.1=OBJ.3-M=sew-PRS.1S
 'I sew it'

- Subject + Attributive:

(81) *i na sërno doi*
 i=na=ˈsərn-u   **duj**
 SBJ.1=ATTR.PRO=choose-PRS.1S two
 'I choose two of them'

- Indirect + Object:

(82) *fajlo*
 ˈfa=j=l-u
 do\IPV.2S=IND=OBJ.3-M
 'do it to him/her/them!'

- Reflexive + Object:

(83) *a l'é fasslo*
 a=ˈle   **ˈfa=s=l-u**
 SUB3=be\PRS.3S do\PTCL=REFL=OBJ.3-M
 'he did it for himself!'

- Reflexive + Attributive:

(84) *a l'é fassne tre*
 a=ˈle   **ˈfa=s=ne**   **tre**
 SUB3=be\PRS.3S do\PTCL=REFL=ATTR.PRO three
 'he did three (of them) for himself!'

PERSONAL PRONOUNS 197

- Three clitics constructions:
  - Subject + Indirect + Object:

(85) *a-j je dis*
 a=j=je=ˈdiz
 SBJ.3=IND=OBJ.3P=do\PRS.3S
 's/he says those (things) to him/her/them'

  - Subject + Reflexive + Object:

(86) *as la conta*
 a=s=l-a=ˈkuɲt-a
 SBJ.3=REFL=OBJ.3-F=count-PRS.3S
 's/he deceives him/herself' [s/he narrates it to him/herself]

  - Subject + Indirect + Attributive:

(87) *i-j na parlo doman*
 i=j=na=ˈparl-u   duˈmaŋ
 SBJ.1=IND=ATTR.PRO=speak-PRS.1S tomorrow
 'I'll tell him/her/them about it tomorrow'

  - Subject + Reflexive + Indirect:

(88) *as j'avzin-a*
 a=s=j=awˈziŋ-a
 SBJ.3=REFL=IND=come_near-PRS.3S
 's/he comes close to him/her/them'

  - Subject + Reflexive + Attributive:

(89) *as n'ancala nen*
 a=s=n=aŋˈkal-a   næŋ
 SBJ.3=REFL=ATTR.PRO=dare-PRS.3S NEG
 's/he dare not' [dare not him/herself about it]

CHAPTER 8

Grounding and Deixis

8.1 Overview

Nouns and Noun Phrases cannot be grounded by themselves in Piedmontese: they cannot appear in their bare form and need a grounding element (in Cognitive Grammar's terms; cf. Langacker 1987), i.e., a temporal, physical or textual anchorage to some reference point. An exception is provided by proper names, which are the only type of Nouns that always appear without Grounders. Ungrounded nouns are only possible when non referential, as when used in citations, in predicate use, or in fixed expressions in which nouns get incorporated (e.g., *sensa eva* 'without water' in example (3) below):

(1) *com as dis **ambossor** an anglèis?*
 kum a=s=ˈdiz ambuˈsur an=aŋgˈlæjz ↗
 how SBJ.3=REFL=say\PRS.3S funnel INE=English Q
 'how do you say *ambossor* in English?'

(2) *sòn a l'é **eva**, nen vin*
 soŋ a=ˈl=e ˈev-a / næŋ viŋ
 PROX.PRO SBJ.3=be\PRS.3S water-S / NEG wine
 'this is water—not wine'

(3) *sensa eva a-i é nen vita*
 ˈsæŋsa ˈev-a a=ˈj=e næŋ ˈvit-a
 without water-S SBJ.3=IND=be\PRS.3S NEG life-S
 'without water there is no life'

In the last example the use of a Determiner is possible with no change in meaning:

(3′) *sensa **l'eva** a-i é nen vita*
 ˈsæŋsa l=ˈev-a a=ˈj=e næŋ ˈvit-a
 without DET=water-S SBJ.3=IND=be\PRS.3S NEG life-S
 'without water there is no life'

In other words, nouns in Piedmontese are not referential without a grounder, and cannot therefore be used alone:

(4) *a-i é ëd gent che a-j chërd*
a=ˈj=e ǝd=ˈdʒæɲt k=a=j=ˈkǝrd
SBJ.3=IND=be\PRS.3S ATTR=people SUB=SBJ.3=IND=believe\PRS.3S
'there are people who believe it'

In (4), *gent* must be preceded by the Grounder *ëd*, or the sentence will be judged agrammatical by most speakers.

(4′) **a-i é gent che a-j chërd*

As Herslund (2008: 31) puts it writing about the definite article, such an element "'points outwards' to the surrounding text or discourse and anchors the noun phrase in that environment." In our view, this is a true of all the grounders, under which term we encompass different categories of traditional grammar:

– the determiners (traditionally, "definite" or "determinate articles"):

la fomna /l-a=ˈfumn-a/ 'the woman'

– the Classifier ("indefinite" or "indeterminate articles"):

na masnà /n-a=mazˈna/ 'a child'

– the deictics:

ës fieul /ǝs=ˈfjøl/ 'this boy'

– the possessives:

soa ca /ˈsu-a ka/ 'his/her house'

– the quantifiers (among which, but not exclusively, the numerals):

doi amis /ˈduj aˈmiz/ 'two friends (M)'

As these examples show, with the exception of possessive and quantifiers, the grounders may cliticize to a following NP.

Apart from grounding, each of these elements adds further semantic content to the whole NP, and this is true also of those items traditionally called articles: they are the grounders *par excellence*, whose syntactic role in grounding clearly overshadows any other possible semantic content. Moreover, given the absence of overt number marking on most nouns (☞ 5.), the presence of a grounder is often the only element showing the gender and number of an NP. This is actually the basic role of the "articles" in Piedmontese according to Parry (1997: 241).

Apart from the quantifiers, treated separately (☞ 9.), this chapter deals with the "articles," the Deictics, and the Possessives.

The element following the Grounder may be a Noun, an Adjective, a Quantifier, or a Possessive. It is therefore apparent that two grounding elements may co-occur. In certain varieties, a Determiner may also precede a Possessive or follow the Classifier *ëd* with the Determiners (☞ 8.3. below):

- *na masnà*   /n-a='maz'na/   'a child'
- *un bel cit*   /aŋ='bel tʃit/   'a beautiful baby'
- *ij doj amis*   /i='duj a'miz/   'the two friends'

Locally:

- *la soa ca*   /l-a='sua ka/   'her/his house' (*soa ca* /'sua ka/ in most varieties)
- *dj'amis*   /d=j=a'miz/   'some friends' (alongside *d'amis* / d=a'miz/)

As remarked by Villata (1997: 21–22), the Piedmontese "articles" (here divided between Determiners and Classifiers) show quite a substantial number of allomorphs when compared to neighbouring Romance languages. In writing, the situation is even more complicated; nonetheless, all the allomorphs are phonologically motivated and their distribution is easily described.

8.2 Determiners and Classifiers

8.2.1 *Semantics of the Determiners*

Determiners (glossed DET) have traditionally been described as articles and the alternation between definite and indefinite articles analyzed in terms of definiteness. Definiteness in Piedmontese can be characterized in the usual terms of familiarity, identifiability, and anaphora (Lyons 1999).

For instance:

(5) *pass-me ël tornavis*
ˈpas=me¹   əl=turnaˈviz
pass-IPV.2S=OBJ.1S DET=screwdriver
'hand me the screwdriver!'

can be uttered without pointing on the part of the speaker to any particular item: the hearer assumes that the speaker has a particular screwdriver in mind and sets out to find it.

Familiarity is included in the wider concept of identifiability, as is shown in:

(6) *la lun-a a l'é nen na steila*
l-a=ˈlyŋ-a   a=ˈle   næŋ n-a=ˈstæjl-a
DET-F=moon-S SBJ.3=be\PRS.3S NEG INDEF-F=star-S
'the Moon is not a star'

(7) *ël cusiné a l'é mè amis*
əl=kyziˈne a=ˈle   me   aˈmiz
DET=cook SBJ.3=be\PRS.3S POSS.1S friend
'the cook is a friend of mine'

In (6), familiarity with the moon may easily be assumed for any adult human being, while in (7) either the situation or the discourse may provide identification (e.g., the participants may be discussing where to go dine, or may physically be in a restaurant).

Definiteness through anticipatory anaphora (i.e., cataphora) is instead involved in

(8) *ël sindich a l'é col che a smija na sumia*
əl=ˈsiŋdik   a=ˈle   kul k=a=ˈzmi-a
DET=mayor SBJ.3=be\PRS.3S DIST SUB=SBJ.3=look_like-PRS.3S
n-a=ˈsymj-a
INDEF-F=ape-S
'the mayor is the one who looks like an ape'

As pointed out by Lyons (1999) there are cases where identifiability gives way to uniqueness. (9) below translates one of Lyons' (1999: 7) examples:

---

1 ˈpas=me ← ˈpas-a=me through Post-tonic Vowel Dropping (☞ 7.9.).

(9) *i son pen-a stait a un mariagi. **La sposa** a l'era an bleu*
 i=ˈsuŋ   ˈpæŋa stajt   a=aŋ=maˈrjagi //
 SBJ.1S=be.PRS.1S just   be\PTCL ADE=INDEF=marriage //
 l-a=ˈspuz-a   a=ˈlera   aŋ=ˈblø
 DET-F=bride-S SBJ.3S=be.IMPF.3S INE=blue
 'I've just been to a wedding. The bride wore blue' [was in blue]

The hearer understands the sentence because s/he knows marriages usually involve brides, even though s/he cannot really "identify" who the bride is in this instance.

Moreover, example (9) shows that it is not completely correct to assume, with Parry (1997: 241), that the "articles" are basically just gender and number markers, while other determinative values would be carried by the Deictic *ës* (☞ 8.3.5.). In (9) the Determiner *la* cannot be replaced with the same meaning by its Deictic counterpart *sa* 'DEICT-F:'

(9') ?*i son pen-a stait a un mariagi. Sa sposa a l'era an bleu*

Different from (9), the bride in (9') is definitely identifiable, and, if anything, (9') could mean 'this bride wore blue' and be uttered in order to contrast another bride in another marriage ('this bride was .... that one was ...') or if the bride had been mentioned before.

The use of a Deictic seems instead excluded under all circumstances in textual anaphora:

(10) *i l'hai catà un bass a ses còrde. **Le còrde** a l'ero fruste*
 i=ˈlaj   kaˈt-a   aŋ=ˈbas   a=sez   ˈkord-e //
 SBJ.1S=have\PRS.1S buy-PTCL INDEF=bass ADE=six chord-P //
 l-e=ˈkord-e   a=ˈleru   ˈfryst-e
 DET-F.P= chord-P SBJ.3S=be\IMPF.3P worn_out-P
 'I bought a six-string bass. The chords were worn out'

(10') **I l'hai catà un bass a ses còrde. Se còrde a l'ero fruste*

Contrarywise, the use of a Determiner seems excluded where psychological proximity and affectedness are implied:

(11) *it l'has sentù **ës** bordel?*
 it=ˈlas   sæŋˈt-y   əs=burˈdel   ↗
 SBJ.1S=have\PRS.2S hear-PTCL DEICT=noise Q
 'did you (S) hear the noise?'

(11′) *it l'has sentù ël bordel?

With plural referents, the use of the determiners implies inclusiveness, with reference being made in this case "to the totality of objects or the mass in the context which satisfy the description" (Lyons 1999: 11). E.g., in (12) the implication is that any newspaper is untrustworthy (and can be used as an ideal introduction to (4) above):

(12) *ij giornaj a conto mach ëd bale*
  i=dʒurˈnaj   a=ˈkuɲt-u   mak əd=ˈbal-e
  DET\P=newspaper\P SBJ.3=count-PRS.3P only ATTR=ball-P
  'newspapers just tell bullshit' [balls]

8.2.2 Semantics of the Classifiers

According to Herslund (2008: 34), the indeterminate article "'points inwards' to the semantic/referential value of a noun." In his view nothing puts together determinate and indeterminate articles, while in our analysis such a commonality is provided by grounding. We follow instead Herslund's suggestion of interpreting the indeterminate articles in terms of Classifiers.

Yet, the Classifiers of Piedmontese classify nouns only indirectly, through non-dedicated markers—after all, both Classifiers, as we are going to see, can combine with any noun.

As in many other languages, Piedmontese nouns are not lexically (nor morphologically) marked for homogeneity. Homogeneity, e.g., has no bearing on either plural or gender marking, and both countable (or heterogeneous, or, still, inhomogeneous) and mass (homogeneous) nouns may be determined.

Obviously, nouns still get a default countable or mass reading; but this default reading can be reversed during the process of grounding, with countable nouns getting a mass reading and mass nouns being used as countable.

It is here that homogeneity affects grounding: heterogeneous entities only can be counted and individualized, and to this effect an Indefinite (INDEF) grounder is used. While a heterogeneous reading is the default reading of a heterogeneous noun, in the case of a mass noun a reading as a countable, heterogeneous entity is forced upon it by the use of the Indefinite:

(13) *a l'avio fin-a un caval*
  a=laˈviu   ˈfiŋa aŋ=kaˈval
  SBJ.1=have\IMPF.3P even INDEF=horse
  'they even had a horse'

(14) *i pijo n'eva*
 i=ˈpi-u   ˈn=ev-a
 SBJ.1=take-PRS.1S INDEF=water-S
 'I'll have a (bottle of) water'

In order to ground a homogeneous noun and force a homogeneous reading of a heterogeneous noun, the Attributive *ëd* /əd=/ (ATTR) is used. Syntactically, a prepositional phrase with *ëd*, as with any preposition, modifies (in cognitive terms, profiles) a preceding head.

The basic function of *ëd* is to profile a relationship between two things, and attribute the thing profiled by the preposition to another. It will therefore simply be glossed ATTR (for Attribution) here. The relationship may be intrinsic, as in the case of a part of a whole or of alienable or inalienable possession, or express the substance (i.e., a mass) out of which a thing is made, or still the instantiation of one of the elements in a list. In Pennacchietti's (2015, and other articles) view, such prepositions (called "retroapplicative") "have the function of decomposing, separating or simply distinguishing the 'first correlate' from the 'second correlate.'" Through them, the flow of attention is channeled away from the 'second correlate' or LANDMARK [...] towards the 'first correlate' or TRAJECTOR (Pennacchietti 2015: 123).

These prepositions are therefore a typical target of a metonymical process whereby, as argued by Langacker (2008: 343), the profiled element may be reversed, as typically happens in quantifications. Thus, in English *a flock of geese* (to repeat one of Langacker's examples) may (and actually most often does) profile the *geese* rather than the *flock* (☞ 13.5.7. for the use of Attributive *ëd* in Quantification).

This metonymical process has been grammaticalized in many Romance languages, so that the head can be simply omitted and the preposition becomes a "partitive article," as in Italian (*del, della*, etc.) and French (*du, des* …). As described by Miola (2017a; also ☞ 19.), Piedmontese has gone one step further along this grammaticalization cline and, in the 19th century (Cerruti and Regis 2020: 662), eliminated the Determiner altogether, leaving the bare preposition alone before the noun (cf. (12) above).

The Attributive may operate on either a countable or mass ungrounded noun, and either singular or plural. Thus, *eva* /ˈeva/ 'water' is by default a mass noun and can be determined as such:

(15) *l'eva am pias nen*
 ˈl=ev-a   a=m=ˈpjaz   næŋ
 DET=water-S F SBJ.3=OBJ.1S=like\PRS.3S NEG
 'I do not like water'

But the same mass noun can also be grounded without being determined through the Applicative:

(16) *I l'avia d'eva da bejve pen-a për eut di*
 i=la'via 'd=ev-a da='bæjv-e 'peŋa pər='øt di
 SBJ.1=have\PRS.3P ATTR=water-S ABL=drink-INF just BEN=eight day
 'I had enough drinking water for just eight days' (Saint-Exupéry 2005: 11)

A hypothetical alternative sentence without grounder is unacceptable (even in Italianized speech and contrary to Italian, which allows bare grounding):

(16') **I l'avia eva da bejve pen-a për eut di*
 i=la'via 'ev-a da='bæjv-e 'peŋa pər='øt di
 SBJ.1=have\PRS.3P water-S ABL=drink-INF just BEN=eight day
 (cf. Italian 'avevo acqua da bere per appena otto giorni,' Saint-Exupéry 2016: 15)

Conversely, *caval* /ka'val/ 'horse' is by default a countable noun, and may be determined and grounded as in (17), but also get a mass reading through the Attributive in (18):

(17) *ël caval a l'é l'animal pi bel*
 əl=ka'val a='le l=ani'mal pi bel
 DET=horse SBJ.3=be\PRS.3S DET=animal more beautiful
 '[the] Horse is the most beautiful animal'

(18) *a-i é ëd caval an sa burnia*
 a=i='e əd=ca'val aŋ=s-a=byr'ni-a
 SBJ.3=IND=be\PRS.3S ATTR=horse INE=DEICT-F=jar-S
 'there is horse (meat) in this jar'

The mass/countable opposition is neutralized in the plural, where every noun becomes mass-like or homogeneous (Herslund 2008, 2012), in the sense that it is by definition made up of a multiplicity of members of the same entity. If you "cut up" a group of horses you still get horses—just as, with a mass noun, you can scoop some salt from a mass of salt or gulp some water from running water. In grounding, the Attributive can apply to plural nouns, yielding to both countable ((19)) and mass ((20)) nouns a partitive reading:

(19) *a s'invento 'd còse tute fausse*
    a=s=iŋˈvæɲt-u   əd=ˈkoz-e   ˈtyt-e ˈfaws-e
    SBJ.3=REFL=invent-PRS.3P ATTR=thing-P all-F.P false-F.P
    'they come up with completely false things' (Pipino 1783b: 100)

(20) *a-i é ëd bire bin carestiose*
    a=j=ˈe   əd=ˈbir-e   biŋ karesˈtjuz-e
    SBJ.3=IND-be\PRS.3S ATTR=beer-P well expensive-F.P
    'there are very expensive beers'

Corresponding sentences without Attributive is still acceptable in local varieties (Berizzi and Zanini 2011) and in Italianized speech:

(19′) *a s'invento còse tute fausse*
    a=s=iŋˈvæɲt-u   ˈkoz-e   ˈtyt-e ˈfaws-e
    SBJ.3=REFL=invent-PRS.3P ATTR=thing-P all-F.P false-F.P

Furthermore, that the Determiners are indifferent to the homogeneity value of the noun is shown by the possible extension of the invariable Homogeneous Classifier *ëd* with the relevant Determiners, as shown below in 8.2.3.

8.2.3 *Morphonology of the Determiners and the Classifiers*
The Determiners show variation according to gender in both the Singular and Plural:

TABLE 20   Allomorphs of the Determiners

		S		P
M	*ël*	/əl=/	*ij*	/i=/
M	*lë* / _CC	/lə=/	*jë*	/jə=/
M	*l'* / _V	/l=/	*j'*	/j=/
F	*la*	/l-a=/	*le*	/l-e=/
F	*l'* / _V	/l=/	*le*	/l-e=/

It seems evident that *l-* is the real morpheme expressing determination. As in nouns, the Masculine is not overtly marked (and the initial *ë* /ə/ is epenthetic), while, as in the vast majority of Feminine Adjectives and Nouns, the Feminine Singular is marked by *-a* and the feminine Plural by *-e*. As to the Masculine Plu-

GROUNDING AND DEIXIS 207

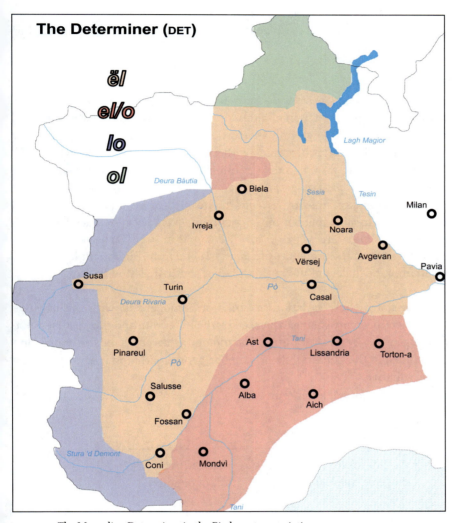

MAP 9   The Masculine Determiner in the Piedmontese varieties
Note: Map 8.1. covers the whole area of Piedmont: to the West, *lo* is Occitan and, to the Northeast, *ol* is a general Lombard form.
COURTESY OF LORENZO FERRAROTTI

ral, *ij* /i/ is easily interpreted as deriving from *li* (widely found in Romance). This is further borne out by the dropping of initial *ë* in the Masculine Singular and of the final vowel in the Feminine whenever the following noun begins with a vowel (see below).

An example of gender and number variation in the Determiners is provided by:

- DET: *ël luv* /əl=ˈlyw/; DET\P: *ij luv* /i=ˈlyw/ 'the wolf/wolves'
- DET-F: *la cio(v)enda* /l-a=tʃuˈæŋd-a/; DET-F.P: *le cio(v)ende* /l-e=tʃuˈæŋd-e/ 'the fence/-s'

🐺 *Ël pan* vs *o sol*

In some local dialects, besides the normal alternation *ël/lë/l'*, there is another interesting phenomenon of alternation between two different forms of Singular Masculine determinative article: it may sound *ël* (or *ëř* /əɹ/) before Masculine nouns beginning with a non-coronal consonant, while it displays the *o* /u/ form before Masculine nouns beginning with a coronal consonant: *ëř gat* /əɹ=ˈgat/ 'the cat' vs *o giari* /u=ˈdʒari/ 'the mouse', *ëř matòt* /əɹ=maˈtot/ 'the boy' vs *o nas* /u=ˈnɑz/ 'the nose,' and so on. This feature was probably much more spread in the past, because it is widely attested in Alion's farces (1521). Now it is found in some Southern rural dialects between the provinces of Lissandria and Coni. The examples are given from the dialect of Viola[2] (in the Alps, south of ël Mondvì).

The Classifiers show variation in terms of homogeneity, with the negative value (heterogeneity) being expressed by the Indefinite and the positive value (homogeneity) by the Attributive. The Indefinite has gendered forms only and is excluded in the Plural, while no number/gender variation is expressed with the Attributive.

The most frequent allomorphs are:

TABLE 21   Allomorphs of the Classifiers

	Indefinite (heterogeneous)			Attributive (homogeneous)	
	S			S & P	
INDEF	*un*	/aŋ=/			
	n' / _V	/n=/			
	në / _CC	/nə=/		*ëd*	/əd=/
			ATTR	*d'* / _V	/d=/
				dë / _CC	/də=/

---

2 Viola /ˈvjula/, Italian Viola /ˈvjola/ (44°17′N 07°58′E).

TABLE 21   Allomorphs of the Classifiers (*cont.*)

	Indefinite (heterogeneous)		**Attributive** (homogeneous)
	S		S & P
INDEF-F	*na* *n'* / _V	/n-a=/ /n=/	

In many varieties and in Italianized speech, but not in the koine (Bonato 2003–2004; Ricca 2006), Attributive *ëd* is optionally enlarged with no change in meaning with the Determiners, yielding a fourfold distinction according to the gender and number of the noun:

TABLE 22   Local enlargement of the Attributive with the Determiners

Attributive (homogeneous)

	S		P	
M	*dël*	/d=əl=/	*dij*	/d=i=/
F	*dla*	/d=l-a=/	*dle*	/d=l-e=/

Thus, parallel to (4) above (repeated herebelow), (4″) is also possible locally:

(4)   *a-i é **ëd gent** che a-j chërd*
      a=j=ˈe   əd=ˈdʒæŋt   k=a=j=ˈkərd
      SBJ.3=IND=be\PRS.3S ATTR=people SUB=SBJ.3=IND=believe\PRS.3S
      'there are people who believe it'

(4″) *a-i é **dla gent** che a-j chërd*
      a=j=ˈe   d=l-a=ˈdʒæŋt
      SBJ.3=IND=be\PRS.3S ATTR=DET-F=people
      k=a=j=ˈkərd
      SUB=SBJ.3=IND=believe\PRS.3S

Although the Classifier *un* ("INDEF") is orthographically (as well as, of course, etymologically) identical to the counting and Masculine form of the numeral 'one' (from whose grammaticalization it is derived), the two are phonologically distinguished: Indefinite /aŋ=/ vs. Numeral /yŋ/. In its turn, the Indefinite is instead pronounced just as the Inessive preposition *an* /aŋ=/:

/yŋ/	*un*	'one'
/aŋ=/	*un*	INDEF
/aŋ=/	*an*	INE

Na /n-a/ ("INDEF-F") has a variant identical to the Feminine form of the numeral *un-a* /ˈyŋ-a/ (☞ 9.1.1.), used as a grounder in many varieties.

Determiners and Classifiers are also best treated together from the point of view of their morphonological variation, which is basically the same. Upon cliticization to a following nominal, a number of allomorphic processes occur. Basically, the clitic Classifiers are sensitive to the first element of the following word as per the following two rules:
1. if vowel-ending, they lose their final vowel before another vowel (_V);
2. if consonant-ending:
    – they insert an epenthetic central vowel /ə/ before a cluster—in most cases, only if beginning with a fricative (_SC);
    – they drop their initial vowel after a vowel-ending word (V_); this rule is only optionally represented in the orthography.

As the Feminine Classifiers are vowel-ending, rule 2. does not apply; on the other hand, they are subject to a good deal of local variation.

Finally, /i/ (orthographically *ij*) is glided into /j/ (orthographically *j'*) before a vowel.

8.2.3.1 Allomorphy of the Determiners
For the Determiners, the following allomorphs are found:

– DET:

  – *'l* /l/ / V__C (after a V-ending word and before a C-initial word)

fé 'l pito   /fe l=ˈpitu/   'to complain over nothing' ['to do the turkey']

The orthography *'l* is found in prescriptive grammars as a possible—and closer to phonetic reality—alternative to the allomorph *ël*. The latter only is found in many writings and will be used here (except in quotations).

GROUNDING AND DEIXIS

– *l'* /l=/ / __ V (before a V-initial word)

l'euj   /l=øj/   'the eye'

The same allomorph is also used after a V-ending word (thus pre-empting the possible cliticization to a preceding vowel-ending word and the writing *'l*):

pijé l'andi   /pje l=ˈaŋdi/   'to take a run-up'

  – *lë* /lə=/ / __ CC (before a consonant cluster)

lë vlu   /lə=ˈvly/   'the velvet'

  – *ël* /əl=/ (elsewhere)

ël brichet   /əl=briˈkæt/   'the match'

– DET\P:

  – *j'* /j=/ / __ V (before V-initial word)

j'amis   /j=aˈmiz/   'the friends'

  – *jë* /jə=/ / __ CC (before a consonant cluster)

jë mlon   /jə=ˈmluŋ/   'the melons'

  – *ij* /i=/ (elsewhere)

ij cotej   /i=kuˈtej/   'the knives'

– DET-F:

  – *l'* /l=/ / __ V (before V-initial word)

l'orija   /l=uˈri(j)-a/   'the ear'

  – *la* /l-a=/ (elsewhere)

la ca   /l-a=ˈka/   'the house'

- DET-F.P:

- a. *j'* /j=/ / ___ V (before V-initial word)

j'amise   /j=a'miz-e/   'the girlfriends'

- *le* /l-e=/ (elsewhere)

le cese   /l-e=ˈtʃez-e/   'the churches'

🌿 *Le fomne/ël fomne/ij fomne/ ij fomni*
The Plural Feminine Determiner is *le* in the koine but in many local varieties, even very close to the koine, it displays the form *ël* homophonous with the Singular Masculine: *ël fomne* instead of *le fomne* 'the women.' In still other varieties the Plural Feminine Determiner is identical to the Masculine Plural Determiner, yielding, i.e., *ij fomne* (see Di Stefano 2017: 56 for the area of Biela; Zörner 1998: 57 for the Canavzan dialects). This is also the case of those varieties where all final unstressed /e/ become /i/: *ij fomni* (Ferrarotti 2022: 135). This is apparently an Eastern feature, even if it is not attested in most Eastern varieties where instead sometimes the final ending of Feminine nouns is simply dropped, like in Lombard dialects.

8.2.3.2 Allomorphy of the Classifiers

As to the Classifier, final /ŋ/ of the Indefinite shifts to /n/ before a vowel (the /ŋ/-beginning syllable is always unstressed):

- INDEF:

- *'n* /ŋ=/ / V__C (after V-ending word and before a C-initial word)

mangé 'n bocon /maŋˈdʒe ŋ=buˈkuŋ/ 'to have a quick bite' [to eat a mouthful]

As it was the case for *'l*, the orthography *'n* is mainly found in prescriptive grammars as a possible—and closer to phonetic reality—alternative to the allomorph *un*. The latter only is found in much writing and will be used here (except in quotations).

GROUNDING AND DEIXIS 213

- *n'* /n/ / ___ V (before V-initial word)

n'osel /n=u'zel/   'a bird'

- *në* /nə/ / ___ SC (before a consonant cluster whose first element is a fricative)

në strass /nə='stras/   'a rag'

- *un* /aŋ/ (elsewhere)

un babi /aŋ='babi/   'a toad'

- INDEF-F:

- *n'* /n=/ / ___ V (before V-initial word, as was the case for *ël* e *un*)

n'ongia /'n=uŋdʒ-a/   'a nail'

- *na* /n-a=/ (elsewhere)

na fija /n-a='fi-a/   'a girl'

- *ëd* (ATTR):

- *'d* /d=/ / V ___ C (after V-ending word and before a C-initial word)

fé 'd ciadel /fe d=tʃa'del/   'to make noise'

As in the case of *'l* and *'n*, the writing *'d* is mainly found in prescriptive grammars as a possible—and closer to phonetic reality—alternative to *ëd*. The latter only is found in many writings and will be used here (except in quotations).

- *d'* /d=/ / ___ V (before V-initial word)

d'aso /'d=azu/   'donkeys'

- *dë* /də=/ / __ SC (before a consonant cluster whose first element is a fricative)

dë sbòss /də='zbos/   'drafts'

- *ëd* /əd=/ (elsewhere)

ëd crin /əd='kriŋ/   'pigs'

8.3   Deixis

8.3.1   *Spatial Frame of Reference*

In Piedmontese like in other languages of Europe the default frame of reference (Levinson 2003) is relative. Apart from toponyms and other words which can intrinsically mark a location in space, various deictic words express the position of entities in the physical or psychological (e.g., but not only, textual) environment. No data is available on the acquisition of the relative frame of reference by native Piedmontese-speaking children.

A spatial relative frame of reference implies that the viewpoint of the perceiver is the origin of the virtual coordinates that determine the position of objects in space; *dëdnans* /dəd'naŋs/ 'in front' and *daré* /da're/, *drita* /'drita/ 'right' e *snistra* /'znistra/[3] 'left' are therefore interpreted with reference to the speaker. As they are adverbs, they can be used absolutely without a relatum:

(21) *Ch'a pija contrà Prinsi Amedeo, a l'é la prima a **drita***
k=a='pi-a   kuŋ'tra 'priŋsi ame'deu / a='le
SUB=SBJ.3=take-SUBJ.3S quarter prince A.   SBJ.3=be\PRS.3S
l-a='prim-a   a='drita
DET-F=first-F ADE=right
'take contrà Prince Amedeo, it is the first on the right' (Rubat Borel, Tosco and Bertolino 2006: 156)

When followed by a relatum, they are often supplemented by the prepositions *ëd* /əd / 'ATTR' or *a* /a/ ADE, without any difference in meaning:

---

3 A loanword from Italian, *snistra* is nowadays the most common form; *gaucia* /'gawtʃa/ and *mancin-a* /maŋ'tʃiŋa/ are still locally used.

(22) *Daré l'autar magior a-i é na statua ëd San Veran*
 da're   l-aw'tar   ma'dʒur   a='j=e   n-a='statu-a
 behind   DET=altar   main   SBJ.3=IND=be\PRS.3S   INDEF-F=statue-F
 əd='saŋ=ve'raŋ[4]
 ATTR=Saint_Veran
 'behind the main altar there is a statue of Saint Veran' ("Cesa ëd San Veran (Utelle);" https://pms.wikipedia.org/wiki/Cesa_%C3%ABd_San_Veran_ (Utelle))

(23) *a-i passava ij bërgé con ij cavaj e 'l leson tacà **daré** dij cavaj*
 a=i=pa'sa-v-a   i=bər'dʒe   kuŋ=i=ka'vaj
 SBJ.3=IND=pass_by-IMPF.3S   DET\P=shepherd   COM=DET\P=horse\P
 e=l=le'zuŋ   ta'k-a   da're   d=i=ka'vaj
 and=DET=snowplow   attach-PTCL   behind   ATTR=DET\P= horse\P
 'the shepherds used to pass with the horses and the snowplow attached behind the horses' (Bonato 2003–2004: 77)

8.3.2   The Deictics: An Overview

Deictics are linguistic items that refer to the context of the utterance, i.e., to the persons, time, place of the conversation, and relations between the participants involved in the conversation. In this Section, however, we will not deal with person and social deixis, usually encoded by pronouns (for which ☞ 7.2.5.), temporal adverbial deictics, such as those referring to English 'now,' 'yesterday' and the like (see ☞ 12.4.1.), deictic verbs, such as 'come' and 'go' (see Ricca 1993), and deictic adjectives whose interpretation may change in relation to the context of their utterance, such as 'distant,' 'neighboring' and the like. Here, we will take into account spatial adverbial deictics, and pronominal and adnominal deictics.

The system of Piedmontese positional adverbs exhibits three terms that designate the location in space with reference to the place in which the dyad of conversation (i.e., the speaker, the hearer, and the space between them) is located, namely *sì* /si/ 'here,' *lì* /li/ 'there (but closer to the addressee than to the speaker),' and *là* /la/ 'over there' (glossed 'yonder' for simplicity).

In pronominal and adnominal deictics, three deictic exponents may be used. *Cost* /kust/, with its phonetically-reduced form *st* /st/, approximatively meaning 'this,' will be glossed PROX (for Proximal); *col* /kul/ 'that,' will be glossed DIST (for Distal); and *ës* /(ə)s/, which is regarded as spatially unmarked and

---

4 This is the common Piedmontese pronunciation of French /verã/.

encodes psychological proximity (Ledgeway 2016: 84 and references therein; *ës* will be simply glossed DEICT for '(unmarked) Deictic'). These deictics may be reinforced by one of the positional adverbs mentioned *sì*, *lì* o *là*: if the positional adverb strengthens a pronominal deictic, it is juxtaposed to it; if on the other hand the adverb is added to an adnominal deictic, it immediately follows the noun of the NP.

8.3.3 *Spatial Deixis*

Spatial deixis may be expressed by means of adverbs that have mainly exophoric use, i.e. that are able to designate the location of human beings, animals and objects in the space surrounding the position of the dyad of conversation (see Jungbluth 2003). These adverbs' system is based on a three-term opposition.

Sì /si/ is used to refer to those entities that are close to the speaker/hearer(s) dyad and roughly corresponds to English 'here;' *lì* /li/ is used for those entities that are closer to the hearer than they are to the speaker or that are not close to the dyad of conversation, but within their reference area (see 1); *là* /la/ is used for those entities that are further away from the speaker and the hearer(s). These adverbs may be translated with 'there' or 'over there,' respectively. The latter is especially used to locate referents that are outside of the reference area of the conversational dyad and may be separated by an interposed barrier;

(24) *A l'é lì, tacà a soa fija. I lo vëdde 'dcò vojàutri? A l'é sì, davzin a noi, ch'an sorid.*
a=ˈle   li /   taˈk-a   a=sˈu-a   ˈfi-a /
SBJ.3S=be\PRES.3S there attach-PTCL ADE=POSS.3-F girl-S
i=l-u=ˈvədde   dko vujˈawtr-i   ↗ a=ˈle
SBJ.2P=OBJ.3-M=see\PRS.2P also IDP.2P.EXCL-M Q SBJ.3S=be\PRS.3S
si   dauˈziŋ a=ˈnuj /   k=a=ŋ=suˈrid
here near   ADE=IDP.1PL SUB=SBJ.3=OBJ.1P=smile\PRS.3S
'He is there, close to his daughter. Do you see him too? He is here, near to us, smiling at us' (Donna 2015)

(25) *andé là*
anˈdæ   ˈla
go\IPV.2P yonder
'go there!' (stimulus: *andate là!, geht dort hinüber!, allez là!*) (AIS, map 1610; informant from Turin)

When used as exophoric deictics, spatial adverbs may be accompanied by a pointing gesture of the finger or of the hand. They may also be followed by other spatial adverbs (☞ 12.4.1.) referring to the position of the referent in relation to the up-down axis and/or the left-right axis. The meaning of these constructions is usually compositional, with the exception of the construction *là giù*, literally 'yonder down,' that indicates a location even further away from the dyad of communication.

(26) *Là giù, là giù, ch'a guarda, sota a col pinacol*
    la='dʒy   la='dʒy /   k=a='gwarda /   'suta
    yonder=down yonder=down SUB=SBJ.3S=look\SUBJ.3S under
    a='kul   pi'nakul
    ADE=DIST pinnacle
    'Over there, over there, look, under that pinnacle' (Garelli 1874a: 62; Act 2, scene 7)

Sì does not necessarily refer to the precise location of the speaker, but may also indicate a larger location near or surrounding them. *Là* is less precise than *lì*, insofar as it may refer to less clearly defined points in space and time. All three spatial exponents take on the prefix *ambele* /am'bele/ or *bele* /'bele/: this prefixation sometimes indicates that the location referred to is more precise than with the simple adverb. However, there are cases where *ambelessì* /ambele'si/, *ambelelì* /ambele'li/, and *ambelelà* /ambele'la/ do not refer to a precise location either:

(27) *Ambelessì as parla 'cò piemontèis*
    ambele'si a=s='parla   ko   pjemoŋ'tæjz
    right_here SBJ.3S=REFL=speak\PRS.3P also Piedmontese
    'Piedmontese, too spoken here' (sticker on the front door of shops in Turin)

Obviously, the sign does not mean that Piedmontese can be spoken by costumers and assistants only right on the threshold of the shop or near the entrance, but rather that one of the languages that costumers and assistants may speak *in the whole shop* is Piedmontese.

Another spatial adverb, *sa* /sa/ 'this way, in this direction' (more generic than *sì*) is nowadays almost exclusively used in combination with prepositions such as *ëd* ATTR and, most of all, *an* INE with the meaning 'on this side, towards here, on the side of/towards the dyad of conversation' (for the prepositions ☞ 13.). It is therefore never a modifier and will be glossed "DEICT.ADV:"[5]

(28) *ven an sa*
 'væŋ aŋ='sa
 come\IPV.2S INE= DEICT.ADV
 'come (s) (towards) here' (Griva 2007: 99)

Another specific item, *dëdlà* 'beyond' (but from **ëd + da + là* "ATTR=ABL= yonder") is used to locate the position of referents separated from the dyad of conversation by interposed barriers. Usually, *dëdlà* refers to places out of sight:

(29) *Mi adess i vado **dëdlà** a telefoneje a Pierin*
 mi a'des i='vadu də=d='la a=telefu'ne=je
 IDP.1S now SBJ.1S=go\PRS.1S ATTR=ABL=yonder ADE=call\INF=IND
 a=pjæ'riŋ
 ADE=P.
 'I am going in the other room and call Pierin' (Luigi Oddoero 2012: 7; Act 1; http://www.piccolovarieta.com/copioni/NATOTASFARAGIA.pdf)

When the speaker contrasts the location of two referents (one of them being, for instance, their position or something on their side), the contrasting pairs are *da sì / dassì* versus *da là / dalà*, or *dëdsì / dëdsà* versus *dëdlà*. *Dalì* and *dëdlì* are not used in these contexts, and are overall rare.

(30) *rivà 'n certo ponto deuv distendme përchè l'hai mal **da sì**, l'hai mal **da là***
 ri'v-a ŋ='tʃærtu 'punto døv dis'tænd=me pər'kæ
 come-PTCL a=certain point must\PRS.1S relax\INF=OBJ.1S because
 laj mal da='si / laj mal da='la
 have\PRS.1S pain ABL=here / have\PRS.1S pain ABL=yonder
 'at some point I need to lay down because it hurts me here and there' (Bonato 2003–2004: 215)

Such and similar expressions often undergo routinization and lose their deictic components, but keep their content component. Sentences like (30) may "express that a situation applies to a whole spectrum of different, non-

---

5 *sa* is also used as a discourse marker (☞ 16.3.).

specific reference points, thus expressing both quantification and vagueness" (Koenig 2018).

Sì, *lì*, and *là* may also be used endophorically, i.e., in order to refer to an item in the co-text and not in the context:

(31) *a l'era nassù a Turin ant ël 1861 e lì a l'é mòrt ant ël 1935*
    a=ˈlera   a=ˈlera   a=tyˈriŋ
    SBJ.3S=be\IMPF.3S be_born\PTCL ADE=Turin
    a ŋ t=əl=milaøtsæntsesanˈtyŋ e   li   a=ˈle   mort
    INE=DET =1861   and there SBJ.3S=PRS.3S die\PTCL
    a ŋ t=əl=milanøvsænttranteˈsiŋk
    INE=DET=1935
    'he was born in Turin in 1861 and he died there in 1935' ("Leone Fino;" https://pms.wikipedia.org/wiki/Leone_Fino)

8.3.4 *The Demonstrative System: Deixis in Grounding*

Piedmontese exhibits adnominal and pronominal demonstrative grounders, i.e., elements whose basic function is "to orient the hearer [...] in the surrounding situation [and] to organize the information flow in the ongoing discourse" (Diessel 1999: 2) and/or in the discourse. All these demonstratives are both exophoric and endophoric.

The pronominal and the adnominal system are three-term, two-distance systems (Miola 2015b, 2017) including

- *cost* /kust/ and its reduced form *sto* /stu/ indicate referents that are spatially or psychologically near to the dyad of conversation;
- *ës* /əs/ indicates referents that are spatially or, more often, psychologically near to the dyad of conversation;
- *col* /kul/ indicates referents that are spatially or psychologically far from the dyad of conversation.

These exponents inflect for gender and also for number (see Tables 23 and 24 below) and might be reinforced by the postnominal spatial adverbs *sì* /si/ 'here,' *lì* /li/ 'there (near the addressee)' or *là* /la/ 'yonder,' therefore giving rise to a strict ternary system (Ledgeway 2016: 84; see also Lombardi Vallauri 1995: 219).

8.3.5 *Adnominal Demonstratives*

As all other adjectives (☞ 6.), adnominal demonstratives inflect for gender, but they also (different from the main class of adjectives) inflect for number, and both for Masculine and Feminine heads.

TABLE 23 The adnominal demonstratives and their gendered and numbered allomorphs[a]

	Proximal		Distal		Deictic	
	S	P	S	P	S	P
M	cost, stu /kust=/, /stu=/	(co)sti, /(ku)sti=/	col /kul=/	coj /kuj=/	ës /əs=/	si /s-i=/
F	(co)sta /(ku)st-a=/	(co)ste /(ku)st-e=/	cola /kul-a=/	cole /kul-e=/	sa /s-a=/	se /s-e/

a Before vowel, ës and sa become s' /s=/.

These elements precede the head noun and cliticize to it. Proximal *cost* usually loses its final /t/ upon cliticization:

- *cost can* /kus='kaŋ/   'this dog (near us)'
  ës can /əs='kaŋ/   'this dog (near us)', 'this dog (that we hear barking)'
  col can /kul='kaŋ/   'that dog (far from the speaker/addressee)'
- *(co)sta fija* /(ku)st-a='fi-a/   'this girl (near us)'
  se fije /s-e='fi-e/   'these girls (near us)'
  coj can /kuj='kaŋ/   'those dogs (far from the speaker/addressee)'

All adnominal demonstratives may be—and very often are—reinforced postponing to the noun that is modified by the deictic one of the spatial adverbs: *sì*, *lì* or *là*. A strong preference is observed for the posposition of *sì* with proximal adnominals, and *lì* and *là* with the distals (☞ 8.3.6. for some qualifications), albeit every adverb may apparently combine with any spatial adverb (Berruto 1974: 21, Parry 1997: 241).

(32) *sto feuj-là*
  stu=føj='la
  PROX=sheet=yonder
  'that sheet [there]' (Berruto 1974: 21)

For exophoric proximals, the predominance of *ës* in spoken Piedmontese is evident. Note in the following two examples the absence of the spatial adverbs:

(33) *sa spala am fa mal*
  s-a=s'pal-a   a=m='fa   mal
  DEICT-F=shoulder-S   SBJ3S=OBJ.1S=do\PRS.3S   pain
  'my shoulder hurts' (Parry 2005: 151)

GROUNDING AND DEIXIS 221

Cost, on the other hand, is or is perceived as bookish, as can be seen from (34), a scientific article about physics (Carlo Demichelis, *Ël conteur Geiger— Müller*):

(34) *Sfrutand coste interassion ant la giusta manera as peul arlevé la presensa 'd coste partìcole e 'l conteur Geiger—Müller a l'é giusta n'ëstrument ideal për sòn.*
sfry't-and   'kust-e   intera'sjuŋ   an=l-a='dʒyst-a   ma'ner-a
exploit-GER PROX-F.P interaction INE=DET-F=right-F way-S
a=s='pøl   arle'v-e   l-a=pre'zæŋs-a   d='kust-e
SBJ3=REFL=can\PRS.3S observe-INF DET-F=presence-S ATTR=PROX-F.P
par'tikul-e e   l=kuŋ'tør   gajger='myl:er a='le   'dʒysta
particle-P and DET=counter G.-M.   SBJ3=be\PRS.3S precisely
n=əstry'mæŋt   ide'al pər='soŋ
INDEF=instrument ideal BEN=PROX.PRO
'Using these interactions in the right way one can observe the presence of these particles and the Geiger counter is precisely an ideal instrument for this' (https://digilander.libero.it/dotor43/sientifich/conteurg.pdf)

8.3.6 *Pronominal Demonstratives*

The deictics may act as grounders without a nominal head, i.e., pronominally. In this case they are generally followed directly by the spatial adverbs that we have seen often accompany the head noun when used as modifiers of an NP: *cust* and *sto* 'PROX' are most usually followed by the spatial adverb *sì* 'here,' yielding *cost-sì* (generally pronounced /kus='si/) as a proximal deictic pronominal element; Distal *col* /kul/ 'DIST' is usually reinforced by either *lì* /li/ or *là* /la/ according to the same rules seen for the use of the deictics as modifiers.

As to the neutral *ës* 'DEICT,' it cannot be used alone as a pronominal but must be reinforced by *sì* (because *ës* implies psychological proximity; cf. 8.3.2.); only marginally (and especially in the South), the gendered and numbered allomorphs *sa*, *si*, and *se* are used pronominally with a following *sì*. Otherwise, only *ës-sì* / əs='si / is used.

It has to be noted, however, the fact that when referring to human beings these pronouns are used at best marginally and usually with an attitudinal orientation. With human beings the Third person pronoun *chiel / chila + sì, lì* or *là* is preferred (for pronouns, ☞ 7.2.3.).

TABLE 24   The pronominal demonstratives with a spatial adverb

	Proximal		Distal		Deictic	
	S	P	S	P	S	P
M	cost-sì /kus(t)='si/	costi-sì /kusti='si/	col(-lì/-là) /kul(='li/la)/	coj(-lì/-là) /kuj(='li/la)/	ës-sì /əs='si/	(si-sì /s-i='si/)
F	costa-sì /kust-a='si/	coste-sì /kust-e='si/	//kul-a(='li/la)/	cole(-lì/-là) /kul-e(='li/la)/	(sa-sì /s-a='si/)	(se-sì /s-e='si/)

(35) *i veuj nen cost-sì, i veuj col-là!*
 i='vøj   næŋ kus='si /   i='vøj   kul='la
 SBJ.1=want\PRS.1S NEG PROX=here / SBJ=want\PRS.1S DIST=yonder
 'I do not want this one, I want that one!'

(36) [*A torna butesse a còl ël faudal, as gropa ij cavèj ant ël folar, a arpija soa ramassa e a la mostra coma un sìmbol.*]
 PETRONILLA:—*A l'é cost-sì mè spasimant!* ...
 a='le   kust='si   me   spazi'maɲt
 SBJ3=be\PRS.3S PROX=here POSS.1S suitor
 '[She puts her apron back on, ties her hair with the scarf, picks up on her broom again and shows it as a badge of honor.]
 Petronilla:—This is my suitor!' (Bonavero 2018: 7; https://pms.wikisource .org/wiki/Michel_dij_Bonavé/Stòrie_d%27ordinaria_portierìa/Pàgina_7)

In this example one may note the ostensive move of Petronilla showing the broom in her hand to the addressee as if it were his suitor while using the proximal pronoun *cost-sì*.

While all the aforementioned items can refer alternatively to animate and inanimate referents (for some qualifications, see below), *sòn* /soŋ/ and *lòn* /loŋ/ must refer to inanimates, when used exophorically. Moreover, *sòn* is a proximal, *lòn* a distal; they will be glossed 'PROX.PRO' and 'DIST.PRO,' respectively. When used endophorically, *sòn* and *lòn* may be either anaphoric or cataphoric and refer to the whole proposition or assertion.

As usual, also these can be extended via the suffixation of a spatial adverb; however, their suffixed counterparts, *sossì* /su'si/, *lolì* /lu'li/ and *lolà* /lu'la/, are pronounced as a single word and are univerbated in writing.

(37) *Ël govern fransèis a l'ha nen fait d'autr che legalisé l'intoleransa religiosa, con la scusa dla laicità 'd lë Stat. Pericolos 'dcò sòn.*
əl=gu'væɾŋ   fɾaŋ'sæiz a='la   næŋ fajt
DET=government French   SBJ=have\PRS.3S NEG do\PTCL
d=awtr   ke=legal'iz-e   l=intule'raŋs-a   reli'dʒuz-a
ATTR=other SUB=legalize-INF DET(-F)=intolerance-S religious-F
kuŋ=l-a='skyza   d=l-a=lajtʃi'ta   d=lə='stat //   periku'luz
COM=DET-F=excuse   ATTR=DET-F=laicity   ATTR=DET=state dangerous
əd'ko soŋ
also PROX.PRO
'French Government did nothing but legalize religious intolerance with the excuse of the laicity of the State. This is also dangerous' (Chessa 2006: 6)

(38) *për noi che vivoma dzora coste colin-e 'l Piemontèis a l'é mach sòn: la lenga dël cheur.*
pər='nuj   ke=vi'v-uma   'dzura 'kust-e   ku'liŋ-e
BEN=IDP.1P   SUB=live\PRS.1P   above   PROX-F.P   hill-P
l=pjemoŋ'tæjz   a='le   mak   'soŋ /
DET=Piedmontese SBJ.3=be\PRS.3S only PROX.PRO /
l-a='læŋg-a   d-əl='kør
DET-F=language-S   ATTR=DET=heart
'for us living over these hills Piedmontese is just this: the tongue of our heart' (Giovannini 2017; http://anviagi.it/26/piemonteis)

Col, without the strengthening spatial adverbs, and *lòn* have specialized for the nominal head of a restrictive relative clause, human and non-human respectively (for the relative clauses ☞ 14.5.).

(39) *Dal 1884, për convension, ël meridian d'arferiment a l'é col ch'a passa për Greenwich*
da=l=milaøtsæŋtutaŋte'quatr /   pər=kuŋvæn'sjuŋ / əl=meri'djaŋ
ABL=DET=1884 /   BEN=convention /   DET=meridian
d=arferi'mæŋt   a='le   kul   k=a='pas-a   pər=G.
ATTR=reference   SBJ.3=be\PRS.3S DIST SUB=SBJ.3=pass-PRS.3S BEN=G.
'Since 1884 the reference meridian is conventionally the one passing through Greenwich'
(Coordinà geogràfiche; https://pms.wikipedia.org/wiki/Coordin%C3%A o_geogr%C3%Aofiche)

(40) *i v'òfro tut lòn ch'i l'hai*
 i=v='ofru   tyt loŋ   k=i='laj
 SBJ.1S=OBJ.2P=offer\PRS.1S all DIST.PRO SUB= SBJ.1S=have\PRS.1S
 'I am giving you all I have' (Terracini 1925: 13)

8.3.7 Intersubjective Use and Other Uses of the Demonstratives

In discourse, demonstratives may also codify the different stances and attitudes that the components of the dyad of communication, i.e., the speaker and the hearer(s), have towards each other and towards the topic of the discourse. It has been noted that "a connection holds between demonstratives and heightened emotional states" (Zanchi 2018: 99, and see also references therein). The vast range of intersubjective and non-deictic use of demonstratives in Piedmontese still lacks a throughout description.

However, in general, pronominal *cost-sì* and *ës-sì* and *sto-sì*, especially when used to refer to human beings, convey a derogative or a strong negative attitude of the speaker towards the referent(s), which is always in the reference area of the dyad of communication. *Sto-sì* does not take on this nuance when used with non-humans. Note however that *cost-sì* may exhibit a positive attitude towards the referent(s), e.g., when used with small children and the like:

(41) *cost-sì a l'é Mario, cost-sì a l'é Nico*
 kus='si   a='le   'marju / kust='si   a='le   'niku
 PROX=here SBJ.3=be\PRS.3S M. / PROX=here SBJ.3=be\PRS.3S N.
 'this is Mario, this is Nico'

Col-lì (as well as *chiel-lì* and *chila-lì*) may also convey a derogative or a strong negative attitude towards the referent, which is usually human. As for adjectives, *sto* seems to convey a similar derogative and negative sense, as well as *ës* (and *sto*) reinforced with the spatial adverb *lì*:

(42) *col-lì a l'é na carògna gënita*
 kul='li   a='le   n-a=ka'roɲ-a   gə'nit-a
 DIST=there SBJ.3=be\PRS.3S INDEF-F=carrion-S authentic-F
 'he's a real son of a bitch'

Demostratives in local varieties

Local dialects have reduced the demonstrative system down to only one demonstrative adjective, e.g., (*ë*)*s/s*(*ë*) in Cairo (Parry 1991; 2005: 150–156),

Biela (Vv.Aa 2000), and Ast (Musso 2003: 68–69), *ca* in Pinareul and Viana (Calosso 1973: 142–149). Different degrees of (psychological or spatial) distance from the speaker are expressed via the postposition of a deictic adverb.

8.4 Possessives

Except for the absence of Determiners with kinship terms,[6] no distinction is made between alienable and inalienable possession.

The Possessives (POSS) show reduced agreement with the possessor and the possessee:
- there is no agreement in either gender or number to a 3rd person possessor, with a single *sò* /so/ form;
- agreement with the possessee is more widespread but is subject to a good deal of free (and local) variation. In particular:
    - just as for the nouns and the adjectives (☞ 5.3., 6.3.), there is no number agreement for Masculine possessees in the case of a Singular possessor (and apart from the local, but still used and attested in literature, Plural Masculine forms *mèi, tòi, sòi*);
    - full agreement in gender and number of the possessee is instead found with a Plural possessor (with the exclusion of a 3rd person Plural possessor, where the unmarked form *sò* will be used);
    - in the forms for a Plural possessor (*nòstr, vòstr*, etc.), the presence of a final *r* /r/ is subject as usual to much variation.

TABLE 25   The Possessives

	M.S	M.P	F.S	F.P
POSS.1S	*mè* /me/	*mè, mèi* /me, mej/	*mia* /ˈmia/	*mie* /ˈmie/
POSS.2S	*tò* /to/	*tò, tòi* /to, toj/	*toa* /ˈtua/	*toe* /ˈtue/
POSS.3	*sò* /so/	*sò, sòi* /so, soj/	*soa* /ˈsua/	*soa* /ˈsue/
POSS.1P	*nòst(r)* /nost(r)/	*nòst(r)i* /ˈnost(r)i/	*nòst(r)a* /ˈnost(r)a/	*nòst(r)e* /ˈnost(r)e/
POSS.2P	*vòst(r)* /vost(r)/	*vòst(r)i* /ˈvost(r)i/	*vòst(r)a* /ˈvost(r)a/	*vòst(r)a* /ˈvost(r)e/

---

6   The absence of a Determiner is almost obligatory when adnominal Possessives are used with kinship terms, such as *mare* /ˈmare/ 'mother,' *pare* /ˈpare/ 'father,' *frel* /frel/ 'brother,' *sorela* /suˈrela/ and *seur(e)* /ˈsør(e)/ 'sister,' *òm* /om/ 'husband,' and *fomna* /ˈfumna/ 'wife.'

When used as noun modifiers, the Possessives, like the other grounders, precede and often cliticize to a following noun. The Determiner generally precedes the Possessive with a Masculine Plural possessee but is always excluded in the Singular.

(43) *a l'é mè amis*
    a=ˈle   me   aˈmiz
    SBJ.3=be\PRS.3S POSS.1S friend
    'he is my friend'

(44) *a son ij mè amis*
    a=ˈsuŋ   i=ˈme   aˈmiz
    SBJ.3=be\PRS.3P DET\P=POSS.1S friend
    'they are my friends'

Possessives in local varieties

In the koine the possessives never co-occur with the determinative article, with the exception of the plural masculine forms *ij mè, ij tò, ij sò* that must be determined in order to be distinguished from the Singular ones. Alternative koine forms *mèi, tòi, sòi* on the other hand require no article, since they are already formally distinct from the Singular *mè, tò, sò*.

Not all the local varieties behave in this way: in many of them Possessives may be used with or without a Determiner, with some speakers judging any construction without a Determiner ungrammatical except for kinship nouns while others admit the Determiner even with kinship nouns. All these possibilities, in fact, are not unknown to the koine and may be found in its wide literary corpus.

Another Possessive system, widespread in Piedmont but very rare in the koine (and of course also found well beyond the Piedmontese-speaking area), has a full neutralization of gender and number agreement with the possessee: this is what happens in the Possessive Singular forms of Eastern varieties. The result is in the Singular a simple system *mè, tò, sò*: *ël mè amis* 'my boyfriend,' *la mè amisa* 'my girlfriend,' *ij mè amis* 'my boyfriends,' *le mè amise* 'my girlfriends;' *ël sò gal* 'his/her rooster,' *la sò galin-a* 'his/her hen,' *ij sò gaj* 'his/her roosters,' *le sò galin-e* 'his/her hens.' Corresponding to (45) in the koine one finds therefore (45'):

(45) *a l'é mia amisa*
    a=ˈle   ˈmia   aˈmiz-a
    SBJ.3=be\PRS.3S POSS.1F girlfriend-S
    'she is my friend'

(45′) *a l'é mè amisa*
 a='le   me   a'miz-a
 SBJ.3=be\PRS.3S POSS.1S girlfriend-S

In such a system the usage of the Determiner is much more widespread, except again for kinship nouns (*mè pare* 'my father,' *mè mare* 'my mother,' *tò frel* 'my brother,' *tò seure* 'my sister'). On the issue, cf. also Grassi and Telmon (1990).

As anticipated, with a Plural possessor the Possessives show gender and number agreement with the possessee:

(46) *nòst padron a l'é gram*
 nost=pa'druŋ   a='le   gram
 POSS.1MP=employer   SBJ.3=be\PRS.3S bad
 'our employer is bad' (AIS, map 1602; informant from Turin)

(47) *nòsta cusin-a l'é tròp streita*
 'nost-a   ky'siŋ-a   'le   trop 'strӕjt-a
 POSS.1P-F   kitchen-S   be\PRS.3S   too   narrow-F
 'our kitchen is too narrow' (AIS, map 942; first informant from Turin)

This interesting neutralization pattern of gender and number opposition for a 3rd person Masculine Possessor is shown in (48) and (49). In (48), the possessor is a woman, but the Possessive exhibits inflection since it agrees with the possessees, which are Masculine (Plural), Feminine Plural, and Masculine (Singular) respectively. In (48), *basin* exhibits the same morphology of (49) although there is one possessor only, while in (49) more than one possessor are involved (all of them grammatically Masculines: *doi fòj* 'two fools'—the two referents of *fòj* are a girl and a boy, but in such cases Piedmontese uses the so-called "overextended Masculine" for grammatical agreement):

(48) *Chila a l'ha bin sërcà 'd scaudela con ij sò basin, soe lacrime, sò fià*
 'kila   a='la   biŋ   sər'k-a   d=skaw'd-e=l-a
 IND.3FS   SBJ.3= have\PRS.3S   well try-PTCL   ATTR=warm-INF=OBJ.3-F
 kuŋ=i=so=ba'siŋ /   'su-e   'lakrim-e / so='fja
 COM=DET\P=POSS.3=little.kiss   POSS.3F.P tear-P /   POSS.3=breath
 'She really tried to warm her up with her little kisses, her tears, her breath' (Invernizio 1976 [1890]: 46)

(49) [*Che gust vedde doi fòj a basotesse!* |] *na siola, un mes toscana e un bon grapin,* | *i-j preferisso a tuti ij sò basin*
n-a='sjul-a / aŋ='mez tus'kana e=aŋ='buŋ gra'piŋ/
INDEF-F=onion-S INDEF=half cigar and=INDEF=good grappa /
i=j=prefe'ris-o a='tyt-i i=so=ba'siŋ
SBJ.1=OBJ.3P=prefer-PRS.1S ADE=all-P DET\P=POSS.3=little_kiss
'[What a pleasure to see two crazy people kissing!] I prefer an onion, half a cigar and a good grappa to all their little kisses' (Solferini 1923: 56)

With a Feminine possessee gendered and numbered forms *soa* and *soe* (see (50)) are used:

(50) *Clarin a l'ha contaje **soa** vita*
kla'riŋ a='la kuŋ't-a=je 'sua 'vit-a
C. SBJ.3= have\PRS.3S tell-PTCL=IND POSS.3F life-S
'Clarin told her about her life' (Invernizio 1976 [1890]: 72)

As anticipated, the use of the Determiner is common with Masculine Plural possessees but by no means exceptionless. In (51) the Determiner is even preceded by the Attributive *ëd*, giving rise to a construction that otherwise will be judged not genuinely Piedmontese (see 8.2.3). A phrase without determiner (*la mèj formassion punk ëd **nòstri** di*) is equally possible.

(51) *la mèj formassion punk dij **nòstri** di*
l-a='mæj furma'sjuŋ puŋk d-i='nostr-i di
DET-F=best formation punk ATTR=DET\P=POSS.1P-P day
'the best punk group of nowadays' (Green Day, https://pms.wikipedia.org/wiki/Green_Day)

The following examples show the irregular presence of the Determiner with Possessives of gender and number other than Masculine Plurals. The grammaticality of such constructions is due to dialectal (and possibly register) variation:

(52) *Ij diao a son **le mie** doe madòne*
i=djau a='suŋ l-e='mi-e 'du-e
DET\P=devil SBJ3= be\PRS.3S DET-F.P=POSS1S-F.P two-F
ma'don-e
mother-in-law-P
'the demons are my two mothers in law' (Mania Reida 1995 [1902]: 28)

(53) *Con na grimassa 'n sël sò brut moro*
 kuŋ=n-a=gri'mas-a   ŋ=s=əl='so   bryt 'muru
 COM=INDEF-F=grimace-S INE=SUP=DET=POSS.3 ugly snout
 'with a grimace on her ugly face' (Sapino 2021: 14)

The Possessives may act as heads of NPs (i.e., as pronominal Possessives). In this case they need to be grounded by a Determiner both in the Singular and Plural:

(54) *son montà 'nsima la mia*
 suŋ   muŋ't-a   nsima=la='mi-a
 be\PRS.1S get_on-PTCL on_top_of=DET-F=POSS.1S-F
 'I got upon mine [car]' (Bonato 2003–2004: 195)

CHAPTER 9

Quantifiers

We define Quantifiers as any modifying expression which may be used to express quantity. In this sense, numerals are a subset of Quantifiers. Most Quantifiers may act both as heads or modifiers. On the other hand, when compared with other modifiers, they often display a special morphosyntactic behavior. For the most part, they are invariables.

9.1 Numerals

9.1.1 Cardinals

The cardinals are an open class created by the recursive mechanisms of counting. Cardinals are positioned before the Noun they count; the counted Noun is in the plural (if morphologically expressed) for numerals after one. The numeral may be preceded by a Grounder:

(1) *le tre fije*
 l-e='træ   'fi-e
 DET-F.P=three girl-P
 'the three girls'

The numerals display a good number of morphological irregularities.

With the exception of 'one' and 'two' (but see below), numerals are invariable for gender.

'One' and 'two' have different gendered forms in the koine and most varieties. In counting, the Masculine form only is used; as adjectival modifiers, 'one' and 'two' agree with their nominal head. The same applies to all higher numerals where the unit is 'one' or 'two' (such as 'twenty-one,' 'twenty-two,' etc.).

(2) *i l'hai mach vistne un*
 i='laj   mak   'vist=ne   yŋ
 SBJ.1=have\PRS.1S   only see\PTCL=ATTR.PRO   one
 'I only saw one of them'

(3) *i l'hai doe fije; chiel a n'ha **un-a***
    i=ˈlaj   'due 'fi-e //   kjæl
    SBJ.1=have\PRS.1S two\F daughter-P // IDP.3M
    a=n=ˈa   'yŋ-a
    SBJ.3=ATTR.PRO= have\PRS.3M one-F
    'I have two daughters; he has one'

In teens, the order is unit-ten in numerals from 'eleven' to 'sixteen,' and ten-unit from 'seventeen' to 'nineteen.'

The conjunction *e* 'and' is used after tens ending in consonant and before units which start with a consonant (i.e., all of them except 'one' and 'eight'). If the ten ends in a consonant and the unit start with a vowel, the final vowel of the ten is dropped. The last element bears the main accent:

vintedoi /**viŋteˈduj**/ (= *vint e doi* 'twenty and one') 'twenty-two'
sentequatr /**sæŋteˈkwat**/ (= *sent e quatr* 'hundred and four') 'one hundred and four'

but:

novantatrè /**nuvaŋtaˈtræ**/ 'ninety-three'
vintun /**viŋtˈyŋ**/ 'twenty-one'
vinteut /**viŋtˈøt**/ 'twenty-eight'
novantun /**nuvaŋˈtyŋ**/ 'ninety-one'

The following list shows the numerals from 'one' to 'twenty' and a few higher ones that exemplify their morphological patterning:

un (M), *un-a* (F)	/yŋ, ˈyŋa/	'one'
doi (M), *doe* (F)	/duj, ˈdue/	'two'
tre	/træ/	'three'
quatr	/kwat; kwatr/__V	'four'
sinch	/siŋk ~ siŋg/	'five'
ses	/sez/	'six'
set	/sæt/	'seven'
eut	/øt/	'eight'
neuv	/nøw/	'nine'
des	/dez/	'ten'
ondes	/ˈuŋdæz/	'eleven'
dodes	/ˈdudæz/	'twelve'

tërdes	/ˈtərdæz/	'thirteen'
quatòrdes	/kwaˈtordæz/	'fourteen'
quindes	/ˈkwiŋdæz/	'fifteen'
sëddes	/ˈsəddæz/	'sixteen'
disset	/diˈsæt/	'seventeen'
disdeut	/dizˈdøt/	'eighteen'
disneuv	/dizˈnøw/	'nineteen'
vint	/viŋt/	'twenty'
vintun(M), *vintun-a* (F)	/viŋˈtyŋ, vintˈtyŋa/	'twenty-one'
vintedoi (M), *vintedoe* (F)	/viŋteˈduj, viŋteˈdue/	'twenty-two'
vintetre	/viŋteˈtræ/	'twenty-three'
tranta	/ˈtraŋta/	'thirty'
trantun	/traŋˈtyŋ/	'thirty-one'
trantedoi (M), *trantedoe* (F)	/traŋteˈduj, traŋteˈdue/	'thirty-two'
quaranta	/kwaˈraŋta/	'fourty'
sinquanta	/siŋˈkwaŋta/	'fifty'
sessanta	/seˈsaŋta/	'sixty'
stanta	/ˈstaŋta/	'seventy'
otanta	/uˈtaŋta/	'eighty'
novanta	/nuˈvaŋta/	'ninety'
sent	/sæŋt/	'one hundred'
sent e un	/sæŋt=e=yŋ/	'one hundred and one'
dosent	/duˈzæŋt/	'two hundred'
tërsent	/tərˈzæŋt/	'three hundred'
quatsent	/kwatˈsæŋt/	'four hundred'
singhsent	/siŋ[g]ˈsæŋt/	'five hundred'
mila	/ˈmila/	'one thousand'
doimila	/dujˈmila/	'two thousand'
un milion	/aŋ=miˈljuŋ/	'one million'
un miliard	/aŋ=miˈljard/	'one billion'

🦋 Old and new numerals

Numerals from 'eleven' to 'sixteen' are relatively recent innovations: in the new forms, the etymological suffix -DECIM is clearly recognizable. These forms are clearly not autochtonous, because no other proparoxyton Latin word has such an irregular outcome. The genuine Piedmontese forms were totally different:

onze	/ˈuŋze/	'eleven'
dose	/ˈduze/	'twelve'

tërze	/ˈtərze/	'thirteen'
catòrse	/kaˈtorze/	'fourteen'
chinse	/ˈkiŋze/	'fifteen'
sëzze	/ˈsəz:e/	'sixteen'

Such forms are very similar to the correspondent words in Occitan and Old French. Found in the oldest Piedmontese texts, they are still attested in the popular Turinese of the 18th century and are not unknown to contemporary local dialects, especially the peripherical ones in contact with Occitan (Miola 2013a for Kje) or Western Ligurian varieties. Sometimes the labiovelar sounds have been reintroduced in both the forms *quatòrze* /kwaˈtorze/ 'fourteen' and *quinze* /ˈkwiŋze/ 'fifteen,' while the other ones keep their original forms.

Some scholars (e.g., Clivio 1975) have suggested that the substitution of the numerals is linked to the strong influence of the variant of Lombard spoken in Milan that probably also led to the replacement of some autochthonous outcomes with the corresponding Lombard ones (as in *carea* becoming *cadrega* /kaˈdrega/ 'chair').

Final /r/ in *quatr* 'four' is preserved only before a vowel-initial word, while it is dropped in isolation (as in counting) and before a consonant:

(4) *is vedoma a **quatr** ore*
 i=s=veˈduma   a=ˈkwatr   ˈur-e
 SBJ.1=REFL=see\PRS.1P ADE=four hour-P
 'we'll meet at four' (☞ 13.6. for time telling)

(5) *i n'hai **quatr***
 i=n=ˈaj   kwat (*kwatr)
 SBJ.1=ATTR.PRO=have\PRS.1S four
 'I have four (of it)'

A gendered 'three'

A few local varieties have separate gendered forms also for 'three.' One of them is the dialect of Viola (southwestern Piedmont), where at least older speakers oppose forms such as *trè òmi* [tɹɛ ˈomi] 'three men' and *trě frome* [tɹe ˈfɹume] 'three women.' Another is the dialect of Seraval Scrivia[1]

---

1 Seraval Scrivia /seraˈval ˈskrivja/, Italian Serravalle Scrivia /serraˈvalle ˈskrivja/ (44°44′N 08°51′E).

in the extreme Southeast and actually a transitional dialect with Ligurian, where 'three' is *tre* for Masculine Nouns and *traj* for Feminine Nouns (Dal Negro 2013).

9.1.2 Ordinals

Dedicated ordinal forms different from the cardinals are limited to the lowest numbers. They are Adjectives from both a morphological and syntactic point of view:

prim /**prim**/ 'first'
scond /**skuŋd**/ 'second'
ters /**tærs**/ 'third'
quart /**kwart**/ 'fourth'
quint /**kwiŋt**/ 'fifth'
sest /**sest**/ 'sixth'
setim /ˈ**setim**/ 'seventh'
otav /uˈ**taw**/ 'eighth'

(6) *Stoma al **quart** pian*
 ˈstuma a=l=ˈkwart ˈpiaŋ
 stay\PRS.1P ADE=DET=fourth floor
 'We live at the fourth floor' (Pietracqua 1859b: 83)

There is no "synthetic" ordinal for 'ninth' and 'tenth.' These and all other numerals are built with the relative clause *che a* (usually spelled *ch'a*) *fa* /k=a=ˈfa/ ("SUB=SBJ.3=do\PRS.3S") followed by the corresponding cardinal number.

Metà /meˈta/ 'half' is a dedicated form for fractions and morphologically a Feminine Noun:

(7) *da la **metà** dël secol ch'a fa XIX*
 da=l-a=meˈta d=əl=ˈsekul k=a=ˈfa dizˈnøw
 ABL=DET-F=half ATTR=DET=century SUB=SBJ.3S=do\PRS.3S nineteen
 'from the mid-19th century' ("Seattle;" https://pms.wikipedia.org/wiki/Seattle)

The corresponding Adjective is *mes* /**mez**/. Starting from *ters* /**tærs**/ 'third,' the ordinals are used for fractions:

(8) ël teritòri dël Canavèis a l'é për **doi ters** montagnin
 əl=teri'tori d=əl=kana'væjz a='le për='duj tærs
 DET=territory ATTR=DET=Canaveis SBJ.3S=be\PRS.3S BEN=two third
 muŋta'ɲiŋ
 mountainous
 'the Canaveis territory is for two thirds mountainous' ("Canavèis;" https://pms.wikipedia.org/wiki/Canav%C3%A8is)

9.1.3   Numerals-Derived Nouns

The suffix -*en-a* /'-æŋa/ creates derived Quantificational Nouns (☞ 9.5.) implying an approximate number of items:

(9) Lassé beuje, mitonand, për na **vinten-a** 'd minute
 la's-e 'bøje / mitu'n-aɳd / pər=n-a=viŋ'tæŋ-a
 let-IPV.2P boil\INF / simmer-GER / BEN=INDET-F=about_twenty-S
 d=mi'nyt-e
 ATTR=minut-P
 'let it boil, cooking over low heat, for about twenty minutes' (Brero 1978: 23)

Also, *dosen-a* /du'zæŋ-a/ 'dozen' is built with the same suffix (and is arguably the most common of these Nouns) but it can also denote (most notably with *euv* /øw/ 'egg') a set containing exactly twelve elements of an item. This derivational suffix is not productive.

9.1.4   A Note on Finger-Counting

Figure-counting is usually only done in face-to-face interaction and may be accompanied by the oral expression of the number.

For 'one' the thumb is raised, and from 'two' to 'five' the other fingers, starting from the index, are raised. 'Five' is expressed by the hand with all five fingers raised.

The system is repeated with the other hand for the numbers from 'six' to 'ten,' and usually the counting does not go any further.

9.2   Generic Quantifiers

- *minca* /'miŋka/ 'any, every, each' is a distributive modifier; its compound form *mincadun* /miŋka'dyŋ/ is a nominal head and is used for both animate ('anybody, everybody') and inanimate entities ('anything, everything').

As other *bona fide* Adjectives, *mincadun* has the gendered forms *mincaduna* /miŋkaˈdyŋ-a/ for referring to a Feminine Singular entity and *mincadun-e* /miŋkaˈdyŋ-e/ for the Feminine Plural:

(10) *ëd durmì **minca** neuit con Vossurìa*
 əd=dyrˈm-i ˈmiŋka nøjt kuŋ=vusyˈria
 ATTR=sleep-INF every night COM=your_lordship
 'of sleeping every night with you, Sir' (Tana 1784: 8; Act 1, Scene 1)

(11) *Sota **mincadun-a** dle paròle ch'a la compon-o*
 ˈsuta miŋkaˈdyŋ-a d=le=paˈrol-e
 under everybody-F ATTR=DET-F.P=word-P
 k=a=la=kumˈpuŋ-u
 SUB=SBJ.3=OBJ.3F=compose-PRS.3P
 'under each of the words that compose it' (Girardin 2020: 11)

In the modern spoken language *ògni* /ˈoɲi/ 'every' (an Italian loan) is in general use as a distributive an takes often the place of *minca*, except in *mincadun* /miŋkaˈdyŋ/ 'anybody, everybody,' in frozen expressions such as *mincatant* /miŋkaˈtaŋt/ 'sometimes,' and the like:

(12) *Ant un sachèt ëd caramele: **ògni** gust ël sò color*
 aŋt=yŋ=saˈkæt əd=karaˈmel-e ˈoɲi ˈgyst əl=so=kuˈlur
 INE=INDET=bag ATTR=candy-P each taste DET=POSS.3.M=color
 'in a bag of sweets: each taste its colour' (Baron 2021: 15)

– also *quaich* /kwajk/ (also *cheich* /kæjk/ and locally /kæj/) 'some' is a modifier with no agreement with its head. It has different head forms when used as a head according to animateness: *quaidun* /kwajˈdyŋ/ (also *cheidun* /kæjˈdyŋ/) 'somebody,' and *quaicòs, quaicòsa* /kwajˈkoz(a)/ (also *cheicòs, cheicòsa* /kajˈkoz(a), kæjˈkoz(a)/) 'something.'

Quaich and *quaidun/quaicòs* are in complementary distribution: while the former may only be a modifier, *quaidun* and *quaicòs(a)* generally act as a NP head. The head Noun following *quaich* is always in its Singular form. This is not always the case in local varieties: in the area of ël Mondvì there is full gender and number agreement, yielding forms such as *chèich òm* /kæjk om/ or *chèichi eumi* /ˈkæjk-i ˈøm-i/ 'a few men,' and *chèica fomna* /ˈkæjk-a ˈfumna/ and *chèiche fomne* /ˈkæjk-e ˈfumn-e/ 'a few women.'

(13) *Tant për capisse mej i faso **quàich** esempi*
'taŋt pər=ka'p-i=se   mej   i='fazu   'kwajk
just ben=understand-INF=REFL better SBJ.1=make\PRS.1S some
e'zæɲpi
exemple
'just to understand better I provide a few examples' (Barba Sergin 2021a: 5)

Quaidun behaves as a Noun and occasionally as a modifier and has different gendered forms:

quaidun /k(w)aj'dyŋ/ 'some' (Masculine, either Singular or Plural)
quaiduna /k(w)aj'dyŋ-a/ 'some-F'
quaidun-e /k(w)aj'dyŋ-e/ 'some-F.P'

(14) *a l'era coma dì constrenzi **cheidun** a gavesse da 'nt ij càuss*
a='lera   'kuma di   kuŋ'strænzi kæi'dyŋ
SBJ.3=be\IMPF.3S like   say\INF   force\INF   somebody
a=ga'v-e=se   da=ŋt=i='kaws
ADE=take_off-INF=REFL ABL=INE=DET\P=kick
'it was, let's say [as saying], like forcing somebody to get out of the way' (Cosio 1975: 116)

In the case of *quaicòs, quaicòsa* both forms are in free variation:

(15) *Bin da soens **quaicòs** a riva a vasté la serenità 'd col moment*
biŋ   da=su'æŋz kwaj'koz   a='riv-a   a=vas't-e
well ABL=often something SBJ.3=arrive-PRS.3S ADE=spoil-INF
l-a=sereni'ta   d=kul   mu'mæŋt
DET-F=serenity ATTR=DIST moment
'very often something comes to spoil the serenity of that moment' (Vaira 2021: 9)

(16) *a manca nen ch'it diventi **quaicòsa** 'd gròss*
a='maŋka næŋ   k=it=di'væŋti   kwaj'koza
SBJ.3=miss.PRS3S NEG SUBJ=SBJ.2S=become.PRS.2S something
əd='gros
ATTR=big
'there is no lack of possibility that you will become something great' (Garelli 1874b: 9)

- *dontrè* /duŋˈtræ/ 'a few' (made of *doi* 'two' and *tre* 'three') is of rarer use. Different from the other Quantifiers, it is an invariable modifier whose head is in the Plural:

(17) *dòp **dontrè** di 'l Teit ëd Matìa a l'era diventà 'l punto 'd riunion ëd tuti ij fieuj e 'd tute le fije*
 dop duŋˈtræ di   l=ˈtæjt   əd=maˈtia a=ˈlera
 after a_few   day DET=roof   ATTR=M.   SBJ.3=be\IMPF.3S
 divæŋˈt-a   l=ˈpuŋtu   d=riyˈnjuŋ   əd=ˈtyt-i   i=ˈfjøj
 become-PTCL DET=point   ATTR=meeting ATTR=all-P DET\P=boy\P
 e   d=ˈtyt-e   l-e=ˈfi-e
 and ATTR=all-F.P DET-F.P=girl-P
 'after a few days Matthew's cottage has become the meeting point of all the boys and all the girls' (Leoni 1986: 75)

- the most complex of the generic Quantifiers is certainly *vaire* /ˈvajre/ 'several.' *Vaire* can be used as a head Noun with the meaning 'enough' or 'much:'

(18) *a na capiss pa **vaire***
 a=na=kaˈpis   pa   ˈvajre
 SBJ.3=ATTR.PRO=understand\PRS.3S NEG.EMPH several
 's/he does not understand too much'

As a head, *vaire* can be followed by a Classifier:

(19) *an **vaire** dle veje colònie dla Fransa ant l'Africa*
 aŋ=ˈvajre   d=l-e=ˈvej-e   kuˈlonj-e   d=l-a=ˈfraŋsa
 INE=several ATTR=DET-F.P=old-F.P   colony-P   ATTR=DET-F=France
 aŋt=l=ˈafrika
 INE=DET=Africa
 'in several of the fromer French colonies in Africa' ("Lenga franseìsa;" https://pms.wikipedia.org/wiki/Lenga_frans%C3%A8isa)

In the following everyday question, *vaire* is better understood as the modifier of an implicit Noun (such as *di* 'day'):

(20) ***Vaire** che i n'oma?*
 ˈvajre   k=i=n=ˈuma   ↗
 several   SUB=SBJ.1=ATTR.PRO=have\PRS.1PL Q
 'What is the date today?' [How many do we have of them today?]

QUANTIFIERS 239

Vaire can also be an Adjective or an Adverb; in this case it always precedes the attributive Noun or Adjective, respectively:

(21) *Sëgnor, **vaire** vòlte, se mè fratel a m'ofend, é-lo ch'i son obligà dë përdonelo?*
     sə'ɲur 'vajre 'volt-e se me=fra'tel   a=m=u'fæŋd
     Lord   several time-P if POSS.1S=brother SBJ.3=OBJ.1S=offend\PRS.3S
     'e=lu   k=i='suŋ   ubli'ga
     be\PRS3S=SBJ.3 SUB=SBJ.1=be\PRS.1S oblige\PTCL
     də=pərdu'n-e-lu   ↗
     ATTR=forgive-INF=OBJ.3M Q
     'Oh Lord, how many times, if my brother offends me, [is it that] I am obliged to forgive him?' (*Il vangelo* 1861 [1834], Matthew 18:21)

– *tut* /tyt/ 'all' is a total Quantifier; as the other Quantifiers, it can be used as a head or as a modifier. When used as a modifier, it always precedes the head Noun It also has a full set of gendered and numbered forms:

tut /**tyt**/ 'all'
tuta /**tyt-a**/ 'all-F'
tuti /**tyt-i**/ 'all-M.P'
tute /**tyt-e**/ 'all-F.P'

The Masculine Plural form *tuti* has subject to much local variation, usually involving internal modification: *tui* / **tyj**/, *tuit* /**tyjt**/ e *tucc* /**tytʃ**/ are the most common local forms.

(22) ***Tut** ël trop d'animaj a s'é precipitasse ënt ël mar*
     tyt əl='trup   d=ani'maj
     all DET=herd ATTR=animal\P
     a=s=e=pretʃipi'ta=se   əŋt=əl='mar
     SBJ.3=REFL=be\PRS.3S=precipitate\PTCL=REFL.3 INE=DET=sea
     'The whole herd of animals rushed into the sea' (*Il vangelo* 1861 [1834], Matthew 8:32)

(23) *A son capì da **tuti** coj ch'a fan part ëd la koinè coltural piemontèisa*
a=ˈsuŋ   kaˈpi   da=ˈtyt-i   ˈkuj
SBJ.3=be\PRS.3P understand\PTCL ABL=all-M.P   DIST\M.P
k=a=ˈfaŋ   ˈpart əd=l-a=kujˈne   kultyˈral
SUB=SBJ.3=make\PRS.3P part ATTR=DET-F=koine cultural
pjemuŋˈtæjz-a
Piedmontese-F
'They are understood by all those who belong to [make part of] the Piedmontese cultural koine' (Donna 2021: 10)

Alone among the quantifiers, *tut* can float:

(24) *ël pais pì grand dont ël teritòri a resta **tut** an Euròpa.*
əl=paˈiz   pi   graŋd duŋt   əl=teriˈtori   a=ˈresta
DET=country   more big ATTR.SUB DET=territory SBJ.3=stay-PRS.3P
tyt aŋ=ewˈrop-a
all INE=Europe-S
'the biggest country whose territory is totally within Europe' ("Ucrain-a;" https://pms.wikipedia.org/wiki/Ucrain-a)

– *tant* /taŋt/ 'much,' *tròp* /trop/ 'too much' and *pòch* /pok/ 'few; too little' are similar in morphosyntactic behavior. Just as *tut* 'all,' they have a full set of gendered and numbered forms, a Masculine Plural included. As modifiers they are directly followed by the head without an intervening Determiner:

(25) *a veul dì che a conten-o **tròpa** eva e **pòch** sùcher*
a=ˈvøl   di   k=a=kuŋˈtæŋu   ˈtrop-a
SBJ.3=want\PRS.3S say\INF SUB=SBJ.3=contain\PRS.3P too_much-F
ˈev-a   e   pok ˈsykær
water-S and few sugar
'it means they contain too much water and a low quantity of sugar' ("Rape 'd San Martin;" https://pms.wikipedia.org/wiki/Rape_%27d_San_Martin)

(26) *Pòver diao, ch'j'heu avù **pòchi** piasì*
ˈpover ˈdjaw k=ˈj=ø   aˈvy   ˈpoki pjaˈzi
poor   devil SUB=SBJ\1=have\PRS.1S have\PTCL few\P pleasure
'poor devil, that I had few pleasures' (Ferrua-Clerico 1871: 45)

9.3 Negative Quantifiers

Negative Quantifiers negate a clause without the need of a modifier. They are:

- *gnun* /ˈɲæŋte/ 'nobody'
- *gnente* /ɲyŋ/ 'nothing'

Characteristics of the negative Quantifiers is the possibility to negate a clause without the presence of another negator (see also chapter 17):

(27) *a l'ha dime **gnente***
a=ˈla   ˈdi=me   ˈɲæŋte
SBJ.3=have\PRS.3S say\PTCL=OBL.1S nothing
's/he didn't tell me anything'

The presence of a negator is on the other hand not excluded (☞ 17., and especially 17.5.):

(28) *i l'hai nen vist **gnun***
i=ˈlaj   næŋ vist   ɲyŋ
SBJ.1=have\PRS.1S NEG see\PTCL nobody
'nobody ever told me anything'

As the other Quantifiers, the negative Quantifiers can be reinforced by an Adverb:

(29) *i l'hai vist **gnente** d'autut*
i=ˈlaj   vist   ˈɲæŋte   dayˈtyt
SBJ.1=have\PRS.1S see\PTCL nothing at_all
'I did not see anything at all'

Gnun can also be used as a modifier and has separate gendered forms for the Feminine: Singular *gnun-a* /ˈɲyɲa/ and Plural *gnun-e* /ˈɲyŋe/.

(30) *Lor ch'a l'han **gnun** dné vorrio fé debit*
ˈlur   k=a=ˈlaŋ   ˈɲyŋ   dne   vurˈriu
IDP.3P SUB=SBJ.3=have\PRS.3P nobody money want\PRS.COND.3.P
ˈfe   ˈdebit
make\INF debt
'they who have no money would like to make debts' (Tana 1784: 37; Act 2, Scene 4)

(31) *La Fransa a arconòss **gnun-e** lenghe ò dialet regionaj ch'a sio.*
    la=ˈfraŋs-a   a=arkuˈnos   ˈɲyŋ-e   ˈlæŋg-e   o
    DET.F=France-S SBJ.3=recognize\PRS.3S nobody-F.P language-P or
    diaˈlæt redʒuˈnaj k=a=ˈsiu
    dialect regional\P SUB=SBJ.3=be\SBJ.3P
    'France does not recognize any regional language or dialect whatsoever'
    ("Loren-a;" https://pms.wikipedia.org/wiki/Loren-a)

Gnun is used predicatively with a human subject in the idiom *esse gnun* /ˈese ɲyŋ/ 'to be (a) nobody.' Moreover, *gnun* is used in the meaning of *gnente*, i.e., as a negative Quantifier for inanimate entities, in the formulaic expression *vagné quatr a gnun* /vaˈɲe kwat a=ˈɲyŋ/ 'to win hands down' [to win four to zero]. For the syntactic behaviour of *gnun* and gnente ☞ 17.4.

9.4 Interrogative Quantifiers

Interrogative Quantifiers are used in both direct and indirect speech (☞ 15.9.4.) in order to inquire about a quantity. They are:

- *quant*   /kwaŋt/ 'how many/much'
- *che ëd*   /ke=[ə]d=/ 'how (much/many) of'

Quant has both gendered and numbered forms, yielding *quant-i* /ˈkwaŋt-i/ (Masculine Plural), *quant-a* /ˈkwaŋt-a/ (Feminine Singular) and *quant-e* /ˈkwaŋt-e/ (Feminine Plural). It is sometimes perceived as an Italianizing form, for which a more native correspondent is *vaire*:

(32) ***Quante** vòlte i devo dite che ij tiroj as duerto nen?*
    ˈkwaŋt-e   ˈvolt-e i=ˈdevu   ˈdi=te
    how many-F.P time-P SBJ.1=must\PRS.1S say\INF=OBJ.2S
    ke=i=tiˈruj   a=z=dyˈærtu   ˈnæŋ
    SUB=DET\P=drawer\P SBJ.3=REFL=open\PRS.3P NEG
    'How many times do I have to tell you that the drawers don't open?'
    (Tuberga and Antonel 2022: 9)

QUANTIFIERS 243

(33) ël còdice l'é stàit 'd **quanti** nodar / ch'son lassasslo l'un l'àutr an sucession!
ǝl='koditʃe le='stajt   d='kwaɲt-i   nu'dar
DET=code be\PRS.3.S=be\PTCL ATTR=how_many-P notary
k= 'suŋ   la's-a=s=lu   l=yŋ   l='awt
SUB=be\PRS.3P leave-PTCL=REFL=OBJ.3M DET=one DET=other
aŋ=sytʃe'sjuŋ
INE=succession
'the code was of how many notaries, who left it to each other in succession' (Ferrua-Clerico 1871: 47)

The Subordinator *che* (☞ 14.3.) can be used as a generic Quantifier in exclamative clauses:

(34) **che** ëd ghigne!
ke=d='giɲ-e
SUB=ATTR=laughter-F.P
'what a laugh!'

Correlation is expressed by *quant ... quant* or *tant ... quant* and discussed in 16.1.4.

9.5 Quantificational Nouns

Mid-way between Classifiers and Quantifiers, a few Nouns have an inherent quantificational meaning. Apart from their use as fully-fledged Nouns, in which they retain their lexical meaning, they are also grammaticalized in order to denote different quantities for, typically, different kinds of objects; e.g., *stissa* /'stisa/ 'drop' will be used for small quantities of liquids. *Frisa* /'friza/ or *brisa* /'briza/ 'scrap, morsel' is found instead for a tiny quantity of solid substances or abstract entities, while *baron* /ba'ruŋ/ 'heap' is used for a big quantity; *cobia* /'kubja/ 'couple' and *paira* /'pajra/ 'pair' are found, respectively, for sets composed of two entities (and both for both animate and inanimate entities), but also, as in (35), with an approximative value.
    The aforementioned (☞ 9.2.) *pòch* /pok/ 'few; bit' and *tant* /taŋt/ 'much' are the most generic of them.
    In this use they are usually preceded by the Attributive *ëd* /ǝd/ and form with it an Attributive phrase (☞ 13.5.7 for a detailed analysis). A few of the resulting collocations and a limited sample of examples are:
– *un baron ëd* / aŋ=ba'ruŋ ǝd=/ 'a big amount of, a whole lot of'
– *na cobia ëd* /n-a='kubja ǝd=/ 'a couple of'

- *na brisa* or *na frisa ëd* /n-a=ˈfriza əd=/ 'a scrap of'
- *un paira ëd* /aŋ=ˈpajra əd=/ 'a pair of'
- *un pòch ëd* /aŋ=ˈpok əd=/ 'a bit of'
- *na stissa ëd* /n-a=ˈstisa əd=/ 'a drop of'
- *na brancà ëd* /n-a=ˈbraŋka əd=/ 'a habdful of'
- *un baron ëd* /aŋ=baˈruŋ əd=/ 'a lot of'

(35) *Cit avnì,* **na stissa** *d'agn: amor, famija, sòld, rivolussion*
ˈtʃit avˈni n-a=ˈstis-a dˈaɲ / aˈmur / faˈmi-a /
little future INDET-F=drop-S ATTR=year\P / love / family-S /
ˈsold / rivulyˈsjuŋ
money / revolution
'a small future, a handful of years: love, family, money, revolution' (Barba Tòni [Antonio Bodrero], *Ël grand dij grand*, quoted in Diego Anghilante, *Introduzione*, in Bodrero 2011: 150)

(36) *mi j'era andàit a tò pais për vende* **na cobia** *'d beu*
mi j=ˈera aŋˈdajt a=to=paˈiz pər=ˈvæɲde
IDP.1S SBJ.1=be\IMPF.1S go\PTCL ADE=POSS.2S=country BEN=sell\INF
n-a=ˈkubj-a d=ˈbø
INDEF-F=couple-S ATTR=ox
'I had gone to your country to sell a pair of oxen' (Malerba 1979, Act 3, Scene 2)

(37) *a-i son tre* **paira** *ëd caussèt*
a=j=ˈsuŋ ˈtre ˈpajr-a (ə)d=kawˈsæt
SBJ.3=IND=be\PRS.3P three pair-S ATTR=sock
'there are three pairs of socks' (Ferrero, Lupo and Lupo 2006: 56)

(38) *Viaman che nieiti gnero i crëssio e in butavo* **na brisa** *'d carn dantorn a j'òss ësporzent*
vjaˈmaŋ ke=ˈnjæjti ˈɲæru i=krəˈsiu e
as_long_as SUB=IDP.1P brat SBJ.1=grow\IMPF.1P and
i=n=byˈt-avu n-a=ˈbriz-a tˈkarn daŋˈturn
SBJ.1=OBJ.1P=put-IMPF.1P INDEF-F=crumb-S ATTR=meat around
a=j=os əspurˈzæŋt
ADE=DET\P=bone protruding
'as we brats grew up and put a shred of meat around the protruding bones' (Còsio 1975: 55)

CHAPTER 10

Verbs

Verbs are the richest (in terms of different morphological forms) and most complex (in terms of semantic values and morphological intricacy) part of speech of Piedmontese. The Verb agrees and varies with a wider number of categories than any other part of speech, and displays likewise the highest number of morphological irregularities. This applies both to the literary variety described here and across the local dialects.

10.1 Semantic Overview

Verbs in Piedmontese encompass elements belonging to all four prototypical verbal states of affairs (Vendler 1957; Van Valin and LaPolla 1997: 83; whence the following quotations):

– *Situations* are "static, non-dynamic state of affairs" involving "the location of a participant […], the state or condition of a participant […], or an internal experience of a participant." Situations lack an inherent terminal point and are often expressed in Piedmontese with Verbs but more frequently by Adjectives (☞ 6):

savèj /saˈvæj/ 'to know'
(*esse*) *frust* /(ˈese) fryst/ '(to be) worn-out'

– *Events* are "states of affairs which seem to happen instantly." They have an inherent terminal point and may be equated to Timberlake's (2007: 284-ff.) "liminal states." They are thoroughly expressed in Piedmontese by Verbs:

meuire /ˈmøjre/ 'to die'
droché /druˈke/ 'to fall, collapse'

– *Processes* are "states of affairs which involve change and take place over time." Processes are prototypical states of affairs expressed in Piedmontese by Verbs:

chërse /ˈkərse/ 'to grow'
stenze /ˈstæŋze/ 'to fade, lose its color'

– *Actions* are defined as "dynamic state of affairs in which a participant does something." Actions have no inherent terminal point and are expressed by Verbs:

bèive /ˈbæjve/ 'to drink'
sgnaché /zɲaˈke/ 'to crush, press'

10.1.1   Labiles and Inherent Reflexives

Labile Verbs are not prominent in Piedmontese although they do occur. A few of them are *bogé* /buˈdʒe/ 'to move,' *brusé* /bryˈze/ 'to burn,' *giré* /dʒiˈre/ (and its alternative form *viré* /viˈre/) 'to turn,' *pasturé* /pastyˈre/ 'to graze.'

(1) *Aqua, padre, che 'l convent **a brusa**!*
ˈakw-a   ˈpadre ke=l=ˈkuŋˈvæɲt   a=ˈbryz-a
water-s Father SUB=DET=convent SBJ.3=burn-PRS.3S
'Water, Father, the convent is burning!' (Garelli 1874, Act 1, Scene 1, p. 11)

(2) *un gran feu a **brusa** gran part ëd Roma midema*
aŋ=ˈgraŋ   fø   a=ˈbryz-a   graŋ part əd=ˈruma miˈdem-a
INDEF=big fire SBJ.3=burn-PRS.3S big   part ATTR=R.   self-F
'a great fire burns down a big part of Rome itself' ("Dinastìa Flavia;" https://pms.wikipedia.org/wiki/Dinast%C3%ACa_Flavia)

(3) *I **bogio** pi nen!*
i=ˈbudʒ-u   pi   næŋ
SBJ.1=move-PRS.1S more NEG
'I will not move any more!' (Bersezio 1980 [1863], Act 3, Scene 9)

(4) *a **bogia** na partissela d'un méter*
a=ˈbudʒ-a   n-a=partiˈsel-a   d=aŋ=ˈmeter
SBJ.3=move-PRS.3S INDEF-F=particle-S   ATTR=INDEF=meter
'it moves a particle for one meter' ("Joule;" https://pms.wikipedia.org/wiki/Joule)

Possibly under the influence of Italian, *bogé* is often used as a transitive, non-labile Verb, and is made intransitive with the Reflexive pronoun:

(5) *la fior as **bogia** tuta e a smija ch'a tërmola*
l-a=ˈfjur   a=s=ˈbudʒ-a   ˈtyt-a e   a=zˈmij-a
DET-F=flower SBJ.3=move-PRS.3S all-F   and SBJ.3=look_like-PRS.3S

k=a=tər'mul-a
SUB=SBJ.3=shiver-PRS.3S
'the flower moves, like it were trembling' ("Pulsatilla alpina;" https://pms.wikipedia.org/wiki/Pulsatilla_alpina)

(6) *ël mond a **gira***
ǝl='muŋd a='dʒir-a
DET=world SBJ.3=turn-PRS.3S
'the world is turning'

(7) ***giroma** pàgina*
dʒi'r-uma 'padʒin-a
turn-PRS.1P page-S
'let's turn the page'

(8) *a taca a **viré** la neuva dla mòrt ëd tanti ufissiaj*
a='tak-a a=vi'r-e l-a='nøv-a d-l-a='mort
SBJ.3=begin-PRS.3S ADE=turn-INF DET-F=news-S ATTR=DET-A=death
ǝd='tant-i yfi'sjaj
ATTR=many-M.P officer\P
'the news of the death of many officers starts spreading' ("Cont ëd San Bastian;" https://pms.wikipedia.org/wiki/Cont_%C3%ABd_San_Bastian)

(9) *ambelessì a-i é mach ëd bestie ch'a **pasturo***
ambele'si a='j=e mak ǝd='bestj-e
here SBJ.3=IND=be\PRS.3S only ATTR=beast-P
k=a=pas'tyr-u
SUB=SBJ.3=graze-PRS.
'here it is just animals grazing'

(10) *da cit a **pasturava** le vache, adess a l'é diretor ëd banca*
da='tʃit a=pasty'r-ava l-e='vak-e / a'des
ABL=child SBJ.3=graze-IMPF.3S DET-F.P=cow-P / now
a='le dire'tur ǝd='baŋk-a
SBJ.3=be\PRS.3S director ATTR=bank-S
'as a child he grazed the cows, now he is a bank director'

Piedmontese also displays a few inherent reflexives, such as:

ancalesse /aŋka'le=se/ 'to dare'
dës-ciolesse /dəstʃu'le=se/ 'to hurry up'
pentse /'pæŋt=se/ 'to repent'
vërgognesse /vərgu'ɲe=se/ 'to be ashamed.'

10.2 Morphological Overview

Piedmontese has eight verbal moods. Five of them are subject-variable (i.e., finite), namely
- Main (untagged; ☞ 10.5.1.)
- Subjunctive (SUBJ; ☞ 10.5.2.)
- Dubitative (DUB; ☞ 10.5.3.)
- Conditional (COND; ☞ 10.5.4.)
- Imperative (IPV; ☞ 10.5.5.)

Three other moods are subject-invariable (i.e., indefinite):
- Infinitive (INF; ☞ 10.5.6.)
- Gerund (GER; ☞ 10.5.7.)
- Participle (PTCL; ☞ 10.5.8.)

Piedmontese is a tense-prominent language (Bhat 1999): each mood has at least one tense, i.e., a paradigmatic set of forms used to express the time of occurrence of the state of affairs in reference to the moment in time. In fact, as pointed by Bertinetto and Squartini (2016: 939) the term "Tense" implies not only temporary localization of the event but also different aspectual viewpoints on the described state of affairs, by presenting it as a bounded whole or as an open situation in which the endpoint is left undetermined. In other terms, temporal and aspectual connotations may interact.

The Main and Subjunctive moods have four tenses:
- Present (PRS)
- Past
- Imperfect (IMPF)
- Pluperfect

The Past and the Pluperfect are compound forms built with an auxiliary (☞ 10.2.6., 10.6.). The Dubtitative, Conditional, Participle, Gerund, and Infinitive have two tenses: the Present (untagged) and the Past (PST). Again, the latter is a compound form. The Imperative has only one (the Present, untagged).

The Piedmontese Verb is made up of a stem, which mainly encodes lexical values and is either obligatorily or optionally extended by affixes and/or clitics. Many affixes are accompanied by stem changes, resulting in a great deal of "irregular Verbs" and partially non-concatenative morphology (marked in the transcription by "\").

In addition, there are compound forms built with an auxiliary and also functioning as a lexical Verb, either 'to be' or 'to have' (for their selection ☞ 10.6.) and carrying most morphological information. Considering that the auxiliary that translates 'to be' is also used in order to turn transitive Verbs into passive and reflexives (☞ 10.6.2.–3.), the auxiliary may appear twice in a verbal form (as a marker of tense and as a marker of passive or reflexive). Auxiliaries are found between the preverbal clitics and the verbal stem:

(11) *i mando*
　　 i='maŋd-u
　　 SBJ.1=send-PRS.1S
　　 'I send'

(12) *a l'ha mandà*
　　 a='la　　　　　　 maŋ'd-a
　　 SBJ.3=have\PRS.3S send-PTCL
　　 'he/she sent'

(13) *it ses stait mandà*
　　 it='sez　　　　　 stajt　　　 maŋ'd-a
　　 SBJ.2S=be\PRS.2S be\PTCL send-PTCL
　　 'you were sent'

(11)–(13) are all instances of the affirmative conjugation paradigm of *mandé* 'to send.' The Main Present form in (11) is made up of a preverbal index (the Subject Clitic, ☞ 7.3.) which in many varieties is not obligatory in the 1st person singular, a lexical stem (*mand-*), and a second index, the obligatory verbal ending agreeing with the subject in person and number. The compound form in (12) above exemplifies the Main Past, and displays a preverbal index, a perfective auxiliary Verb which exhibits agreement in person and number with the subject, and the Participle form of the lexical Verb. (13) is a compound form and encodes the Main Present Passive. It is made up of the preverbal index, followed by a passive auxiliary Verb agreeing in person and number with the subject, by a Participle of the auxiliary Verb (agreeing in gender and number with the subject) and finally by the Participle of the lexical Verb.

Agreement is mandatory with the subject through indexes (suffixes and/or clitics); it is also obligatory for indirect objects through clitics (☞ 14.3.); with direct objects the presence of a pronominal clitic is also very common in dislocations (☞ 17.1.).

The subject agrees with the person of the subject along a threefold opposition between 1st person (the Speaker) vs. 2nd (the Adressee) vs. 3rd (the Absentee); it further agrees in number along a simple Singular vs. Plural opposition. The gender of the subject plays a role instead only in the Past of intransitive Verbs (☞ 10.2.6.; 10.6.1.) and in the passive and reflexive (☞ 10.6.2.–3.). There, the nominal opposition Masculine vs. Feminine is encoded in the Participle.

Gender-varying conjugation in Ormea[1]

The dialect of Ormea displays a very interesting phenomenon: the conjugation of the Verb *avèa* 'to have' (koine: *avèj*) has, for the Third Singular of Main Present, different forms depending on the grammatical gender of the subject. We may compare *me fijo* (*o*) *l'ha ina bela famija* [me 'fiu (u)=l=a 'ina 'bɛla fa'mia] 'my son has a beautiful family' with *me fija* (*a*) *ř'hò ina bela famija* [me 'fia (a)=ɹ=ɔ 'ina 'bɛla fa'mia] 'my daughter has a beautiful family' (for an account of this phenomenon in Gallo-Italic and beyond, see Loporcaro and Vigolo 2002–2003).

The phono-syntactic change in the verbal paradigm is actually much more complex, as it takes place also when a Direct Object Clitic is displayed before the verb; compare two sentences such as *i n'tl'han däcio* [i=ŋ=tl='aŋ 'datʃ-u] ("SBJ.3P=NEG=OBJ.2S=OBJ.3=have\3P give\PTCL-M") 'yet they did not give him to you' and *i n'tř'hòn däcia* [i=ŋ=t=ɹ='ɔŋ 'datʃ-a] ("SBJ.3P=NEG=OBJ.2S=OBJ.3=have\3P give\PTCL-F") 'yet they did not give her to you'.

When a non-dislocated non-circumstantial argument of the Verb is expressed postverbally, in any syntactic role except for the direct object, it must be coreferenced on the Verb by the clitic *jë/j'/i* /jə/, /j/, /i/.

Negation is not morphologically expressed through dedicated paradigms but syntactically encoded by independent morphemes (☞ 17.)

Besides affirmative conjugation, Piedmontese has dedicated interrogative paradigms, which are scarcely productive nowadays in the spoken language (☞ 7.5.).

---

1 Ormea /ur'mea/, Italian Ormea /or'mea/ (44°09′N 07°55′E).

10.2.1 Morphological Classes: Previous Studies

While writing a grammar of Piedmontese, all grammarians since Ponza (1838) transposed the model drawn up for the teaching of the Italian Verbs in schools, as has been repeatedly pointed out by Gasca Queirazza (2002; 2003; 2005). The verbal system of Piedmontese has therefore always been expounded along three Classes. The model set by Italian grammarians has been followed also in the 20th century by Aly-Belfàdel (1933: 177–233), Brero (1967; 1971; 1975; 2008), Brero and Bertodatti (2000), Griva (1980), Villata (1997; 2009), Grosso (2000; 2002), and Capello et al. (2001). While Aly-Belfàdel shows many instances of an autonomous treatment of this topic, Brero, on the other hand, has adopted in an uncritical way the school model established for Italian. Since Brero's works soon acquired a high degree of authoritativeness, his choice of the Italian model has never been questioned, Gasca Queirazza's studies being a notable exception.

In the traditional perspective, therefore, Piedmontese exhibits three Classes, as Italian does:

- "1st conjugation", whose Infinitive ends in -é /'e/, corresponds to Latin -ĀRE and contains the largest number of Verbs e.g. *parlé* 'to speak,' *mangé* 'to eat,' *balé* 'to dance,' *sghijé* 'to slip,' etc.;
- "2nd conjugation", whose Infinitive ends in -e /e/, corresponds to both Latin conjugations in -ĒRE and -ĔRE, to the French Verbs in -re and to second Italian mixed conjugation in -ere. Second conjugation Verbs are, a.o., *scrive* 'to write,' *nasse* 'to be born,' *meuire* 'to die,' *rije* 'to laugh,' *sente* 'to hear, to feel,' *serne* 'to choose,' *vëdde* 'to see,' *vende* 'to sell,' *vive* 'to live;'
- "3rd conjugation", whose Infinitive ends in -ì /'i/, is the heir of the Latin fourth conjugation ending in -ĪRE that has given origin to French Verbs in -ir and Italian Verbs in -ire. Many Piedmontese Verbs belong to this Class, e.g. *finì* 'to end,' *capì* 'to understand,' *s-ciarì* 'to sight.'

Reality, as always, is much more complex than the previous simple scheme may suggest—as it is easy to understand from even a cursory glance at Brero (2008): the three conjugations leave many Verbs behind, because many (even very common) Verbs cannot be categorized into the second nor into the third conjugation, but seem in fact to belong to both of them. Grammarians call them *Verb fosonant* ('superabundant Verbs'). All these Verbs follow the second conjugation in some moods and tenses, and the third conjugation in others. The distribution of the forms, nevertheless, varies from Verb to Verb, and it is far from easy to find a regular pattern. Therefore, Piedmontese grammars have very long lists of Verbs that lie astride the second and third conjugations and one is left wondering whether to trace a clear-cut line between the two is really feasible.

Furthermore, the second conjugation contains Verbs from the second as well as the third Latin conjugations. It is also not true that the Latin Verbs in -ēRE simply became Piedmontese Verbs in -*e*: for instance some very common Verbs exhibit an -*ej* ending: *avèj* 'to have,' *dovèj* 'must; to have to' *piasèj* 'to like,' *podèj* 'can, to be able to', *savèj* 'to know,' *valèj* 'to be worth,' *vorèj* 'to want.' Grammarians often set them in the second conjugations but without any evident reason: it seems that what really matters in such classifications is that these Verbs belong to this conjugation in Italian.

As said, Gasca Queirazza (2005) proposed a completely different viewpoint for Piedmontese, namely a four-class system that follows more closely the Latin one. According to this view, "second conjugation" is the Class of Verbs in -*èj*, even if they are very few in number: Gasca Queirazza (2005: 161) maintains, however, that their small number should not be a reason for denying their specific status and refusing to consider them as a peculiar group. Much the same has recently been proposed by Ricca (2017: 280): in Ricca's view, the seven Piedmontese Verbs whose Infinitive ends in -*èj* must be treated as a fourth distinct inflectional class, with strong paradigmatic allomorphs (at least for five of them).

However, on the basis of purely synchronic morphological inflection, a reduction to only two Classes might be proposed: such a subdivision has been put forward for some peripheral varieties (e.g., Cairese, Parry 2005: 183, and Kje, Miola 2013: 143–148).[2] Since the latter description also fits the koine variety described in this volume, we will adopt it in the followings.

Parlé vs. *parlar* vs. *parlà*

As shown in Map 10, the Latin infinitive ending -ARE became -*é* (or, in some places, -*è*) in the greatest part of Piedmont. Nevertheless, there are many areas in which a more conservative ending -*ar* is preserved for all the First Class' Infinitives: *parlar, cantar, andar* are the normal Canavzan forms for *parlé* 'to speak,' *canté* 'to sing,' *andé* 'to go' (Tonso 2017), and many Eastern and Western varieties have forms like *parlà, cantà, andà*, sometimes pronounced with a stressed final [ɑ] that tends to become [ɔ]: *parlò, cantò, andò* (Sobrero, Grassi and Telmon 1997: 137).

---

2 Taking into consideration other Romance languages, this also applies to Italian (Dressler et al. 2003: 407; Thornton 2005: 131 and fn. 11).

VERBS 253

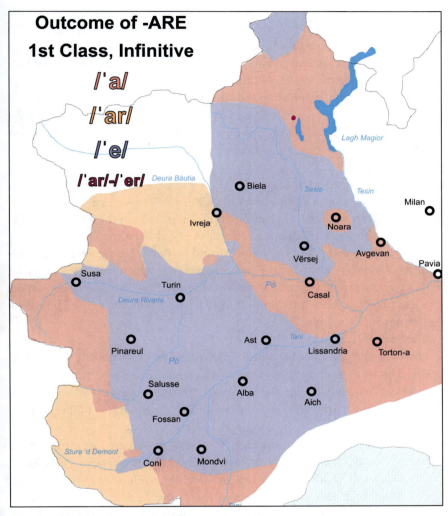

MAP 10   Outcomes of Latin Infinitive -ARE in the Piedmontese varieties
COURTESY OF LORENZO FERRAROTTI

10.2.2 *The First Verbal Class*
The First Class is a fully productive conjugation, and as such it is nowadays used whenever a new Verb is introduced. To this Class—precisely corresponding to the traditional First Conjugation (with the Infinitive ending in *-é*, from Latin -ĀRE)—belong Verbs such as *andé* /aŋˈde/ 'to go;' *buté* /byˈte/ 'to put;' *ciamé* /tʃaˈme/ 'to call, to ask;' *dovré* /duvˈre/ 'to use;' *fé* /fe/ 'to do, to make;' *gavé* /gaˈve/ 'to take off;' *intré* /iŋtˈre/ 'go in;' *lavé* /laˈve/ 'to wash;' *massé* /maˈse/ 'to kill;' *nijé* /nje/ 'to drown;' *océ* /uˈtʃe/ 'to spot;' *pioré* /pjuˈre/ 'to cry;' *quaté* /kwaˈte/ 'to cover;' *rangé* /raŋˈdʒe/ 'to fix, to arrange;' *toché* /tuˈke/ 'to touch;' *uché* /yˈke/

'to howl;' *vacé* /va'tʃe/ 'to watch;' *zonzoné* /zuŋzu'ne/ 'to buzz;' it is fully productive and is the Class of all modern loan Verbs and neologisms: *automatisé* /awtumati'ze/ 'to automatize.'

The First Class inflexional scheme pattern is characterized by the residual presence of a thematic vowel /a/ (but cf. Ricca 2017: 263): it shows up in the 3S of the Main Present (*a parla*), in the whole Imperfect Indicative (*i parlava, it parlave, a parlava, i parlavo, i parlave, a parlavo*), in the 1S and 3S of the Subjunctive Present (*che mi i parla; che chiel a parla*), in the 2S of the Imperative (*parla!*) and in the Gerund (*an parland*).

10.2.3 *The Second Verbal Class*

In Piedmontese, the 3S ending is identical for the Verbs classified in the traditionally-called Second Conjugation and for the Verbs in the Third Conjugation. As will be seen in Table 10.2., most other verbal indexes (actually, all of them with the exception of the Infinitive and Participle) are shared by the two traditionally-called Second and Third conjugations, which can thus be seen as parts of a single macro-class that we label Second Class. Second Class Participles are inflected for gender and number in the Feminine, while First Class Participles are invariable.

The Second Class thus includes four sub-classes:

– Class 2.a: the seven Verbs whose Infinitive ends in *-èj* (mostly from Latin Verbs in -ĒRE), such as: *avèj* /a'væj/ 'to have,' *dovej* /du'væj/ 'must,' 'to have to,' *piasèj* /pja'zæj/ 'to like,' *podèj* /pu'dæj/ 'can,' *savèj* /sa'væj/ 'to know,' *valèj* /va'læj/ 'to be worth,' *vorèj* /vu'ræj/ 'to want' (corresponding to Ricca's 2017: 280 "fourth" Class);

– Class 2.b: the Verbs whose Infinitive ends in unstressed *-e* (mostly from Latin Verbs in -ĔRE), such as: *ancòrze* /aŋ'korze/ 'to realize,' *bèive* /'bæjve/ 'to drink,' *core* /'kure/ 'to run,' *decide* /de'tʃide/ 'to decide,' *flete* /'flete/ 'to bend, to inflect,' *gòde* /'gode/ 'to enjoy,' *lese* /'leze/ 'to read,' *monze* /'muŋze/ 'to milk,' *nasse* /'nase/ 'to be born,' *onze* /'uŋze/ 'to oil,' *perde* /'pærde/ 'to lose,' *rende* /'rænde/ 'to yield,' *stende* /'stænde/ 'to spread out, lay out, hang clothes,' *tenze* /'tæŋze/ 'to dye,' *vëdde* /'vəd:e/ 'to see;'

– Class 2.c: the Verbs whose Infinitive ends in *-i* (mostly from Latin Verbs in -ĪRE) without the originally inchoative suffix *-iss-* in the conjugation; they often show a tendency to follow the scheme of Class 2.b in some tenses and moods, while in other forms appear more strictly related to the Class 2.d below. In the koine (but not in all Piedmontese varieties) they normally have two Infinitive forms, in *-e*[3] or in *-i*, without any difference in use nor

---

3 In many peripheral varieties, the final vowel in the paroxytone form is often *-i* instead of *-e* (*deurvi, meuiri, parti* and so on). See also Parry (2005: 185).

meaning. A few examples include: *asseurbe* /aˈsørbe/ or *assurbì* /asyrˈbi/ 'to absorb,' *averte* /aˈværte/ or *avertì* /averˈti/ 'to warn; to feel' *beuje* /ˈbøje/ or *bujì* /byˈji/ 'to boil,' *cheuje* /ˈkøje/ or *cujì* /kyˈji/ 'to pick up,' *cheurve* /ˈkørve/ or *curvì* /kyrˈvi/ 'to cover,' *cuse* /ˈkyze/ or *cusì* /kyˈzi/ 'to sew, stitch,' *deurme* /ˈdørme/ or *durmì* /dyrˈmi/ 'to sleep,' *deurve* /ˈdørve/ or *durvì* /dyrˈvi/ 'to open,' *empe* /ˈæmpe/ / *ëmpì* /əmˈpi/, 'to fill,' *eufre* /ˈøfre/ or *ufrì* /yfˈri/ 'to offer,' *meuire* /ˈmøjre/ or *murì* /myˈri/ 'to die,' *muse* /ˈmyze/ or *musì* /myˈzi/ 'to moo,' *parte* /ˈparte/ or *partì* /parˈti/ 'to leave,' *riesse* /ˈrjese/ or *riussì* /rjyˈsi/ 'to succeed,' *sente* /ˈsæɲte/ or *sentì* /seɲˈti/ 'to feel, to hear,' *serve* /ˈsærve/ or *sërvì* /sərˈvi/ 'to serve,' *seufre* /ˈsøfre/ or / *sufrì* /syˈfri/ 'to suffer,' *seurte* /ˈsørte/ / *surtì* /syrˈti/ 'to go out,' *ten-e* /ˈtæɲe/ or / *tnì* /tni/ 'to hold, to keep' (with its compounds such as *manten-e* /maɲˈtæɲe/ or *mantnì* /maɲtni/ 'to maintain,' *sosten-e* /susˈtæɲe/ or *sostnì* /susˈtni/ 'to sustain'; *ven-e* /ˈvæɲe/ or *vnì* /vni/ 'to come' (with many compounds such as *conven-e* /kuɲˈvæɲe/ or *convnì* /kuɲˈvni/ 'to be convenient,' 'to be apt,' *proven-e* /pruˈvæɲe/ or *provnì* /pruˈvni/ 'to come from,' *sven-e* /ˈzvæɲe/ / *svnì* /zvni/ 'to pass out'); *veste* /ˈveste/ or *vëstì* /vəsˈti/ 'to dress;'

- Class 2.d: the Verbs whose Infinitive ends in *-ì* (from Latin Verbs in -ĪRE) with a frozen inchoative suffix *-iss-* /is/ (from Latin -ISC-) in many forms, notably in the Main Present (except for the First person Plural) and in the Dubitative Present. Examples include: *anciorgnì* /aɲtʃurˈɲi/ 'to deafen,' *agradì* /agraˈdi/ 'to appreciate,' *arfiajì* /arfjaˈji/ 'to breathe again,' *argiojì* /ardʒuˈji/ 'to exult,' *brunì* /bryˈni/ or *burnì* /byrˈni/ 'to polish, tan,' *ciumì* /tʃyˈmi/ 'to smolder,' *ciupì* /tʃyˈpi/ 'to half-close,' *clochì* /kluˈki/ 'to cluck,' *dësternì* /dəsterˈni/ 'to remove the pavement,' *fiajì* /fjaˈji/ 'to breathe,' *fiapì* /fjaˈpi/ 'to wither,' *finì* /fiˈni/ 'to finish,' *fortì* /furˈti/ 'to assert,' *mufì* /myˈfi/ 'to become mouldy,' *nutrì* /nyˈtri/ 'to nourish,' *mentì* /meɲˈti/ 'to lie,' *rairì* /rajˈri/ 'to rarefy,' *rustì* /rysˈti/ 'to roast,' *sarzì* /sarˈzi/ 'to mend,' *sbiajì* /zbjaˈji/ 'to fade,' *sbianchì* /zbjaɲˈki/ 'to bleach,' *sbujì* /zbyˈji/ 'to scare,' *sburdì* /zbyrˈdi/ 'to scare,' *s-ciarì* /stʃajˈri/ 'to make clearer, see,' *scrussì* /skryˈsi/ 'to crack,' *sgiajì* /zdʒaˈji/ 'to be horrified,' *sgrandì* /zgraɲˈdi/ or *agrandì* /agraɲˈdi/ 'to enlarge,' *smasì* /zmaˈzi/ 'to dilute,' *sorzì* /surˈzi/ 'to spring,' *tërnì* /tərˈni/ 'to darken, to dim.'

10.2.4 *Irregular Verbs*

The auxiliaries *esse* /ˈese/ 'to be' and *avèj* /avˈæj/ 'to have' (☞ 10.2.4.3, 10.6), and a few other Verbs behave as truly irregular Verbs.

10.2.4.1 First Class Irregular Verbs

Four Verbs of the First Class are commonly labeled irregular since their conjugation stem appears unpredictable following the general paradigm. They are *dé* /de/ 'to give,' *sté* /ste/ 'to stay,' *fé* /fe/ 'to do, to make,' and *andé* /aŋˈde/ 'to go.'

Dé and *sté* show the same irregularities and share a similar flexional stem: a voiced velar stop appears in 1Sg of the Main Present (*i dago, i stago*) and in every person of the Present Subjunctive (*ch'i daga, ch'it daghe(s)* and so on); it creates a specific stem that is constantly different from the monosyllabic base predictable from the Infinitive form.

The monosyllabic base forms the other persons of the Main Present (*it das/it stas, a da/a sta, i doma/i stoma, i deve/i steve, a dan/a stan*), the Dubitative (*i darai/i starai*), the Conditional (*i darìa/i starìa*) and the Imperfective Subjunctive (*ch'i dèissa/ch'i stèissa*).

Main Imperfect displays a third stem, composed with a fricative (/z/) borrowed from the stem of *fé*: *i dasìa/i stasìa* by analogy with *i fasìa* (see below). The same holds for Gerunds *dasend, stasend* by analogy with *fasend*. Moreover, the Past Participle is also modeled on *fé*: *dàit, stàit*, exactly like *fàit*.

Fé too has two different stems: the first one is /faz-/, that forms 1s of the Main Present (*i faso*) as well as the entire paradigm of the Subjunctive (*ch'i fasa, ch'it fase(s)*, and so on; *ch'i fasèissa, ch'it fasèisse(s)* and so on), the Main Imperfect (*i fasìa, it fasìe(s)* and so on), and the Gerund (*fasend*). All the other forms show the monosyllabic stem /f-/: *it fas, a fà, i farìa, it faras* and so on. Past participle is *fàit*, etymologically from FACTU(M)>*fàitu > fàit*, that has become the model for many other Participles such as *dàit, stàit, andàit*, where it has no etymologic motivation.

As in many other Romance languages, the Verb *andé* has a highly irregular paradigm in which two different verbal bases have merged: in Piedmontese the base /and-/ alternates with the base /v-/, that shows two different specialized morphemes /v-/ and /vad-/: the latter forms 1s of the Main Present (*i vado*) and the whole Present Subjunctive (*ch'i vada, ch'it vade(s)* and so on), while the /v/ stem is found in 2s and 3s of the Main Present (*it vas, a va*) as well as in 3P (*a van*; Ricca 2017). All other forms come from the base /and-/, with a specialized stem /andaz-/ modeled on /faz-/ for the Main Imperfect (*i andasìa, it andasìe(s)* and so on) and for the Gerund (*andasend*). Past participle is also modeled on the Verb *fé*: *andàit*.

The four Verbs *andé, dé, fé* and *sté* have many different variants in the peripheral varieties even in written standard Piedmontese: 1s of Main Present, e.g. may be *i vad, i dagh, i fass, i stagh* without the *-o* ending, or may display forms like *i von* /i=ˈvuŋ/, *i don* /i=ˈduŋ/, *i ston* /i=ˈstuŋ/, *i fon* /i=ˈfuŋ/ modeled on *esse* 'to be' (*i son* /i=ˈsuŋ/ 'I am'). 2S of the Main Present may be spelled *it vade* /it=ˈvade/, *it fase* /it=ˈfaze/, instead of *it vas* /it=ˈvaz/, *it fas* /it=ˈfaz/. In many varieties and sometimes in koine Piedmontese too, the *faz-* stem of the Verb *fé* may take a lightly different form with a voiceless alveolar fricative, i.e., /fas-/, while Imperfect Subjunctive is very often formed on the base /f-/: *i fèissa, it fèisse(s)* and so on, instead of *fasèissa*.

10.2.4.2 Second Class Irregular Verbs

10.2.4.2.1 Class 2.a

This subgroup includes seven Verbs only, all but *piasèj* /pjaˈzæj/ 'to like' showing a high degree of irregularity. The auxiliary Verb *avèj* /aˈvæj/ 'to have' is treated separately in 10.2.4.3.

Dovèj /duˈvæj/ has at least two different stems, but its conjugation stem undergoes many variations not only in the local dialects but also in the written standard. The first stem is /**duv-**/ and forms the Infinitive (*dovèj*), the Past Participal (*dovù*), the Gerund (*dovend/dovand*), 1P of the Main Present (*dovoma*), the Main Imperfect (*dovìa, dovìe(s)* and so on), the Dubitative (*dovrai, dovras*, and so on), the Conditional (*dovrìa, dovrìe(s)*, and so on), the Subjunctive Imperfect (*dovèissa, dovèisse(s)* and so on).

The stem /**duv-**/ may have an alternative form /**dyv-**/: so, it is possible to find *i duvìa, i duvrìa, i duvrai* instead of *i dovìa, i dovrìa, i dovrai*.

The second stem is /**dev-**/: most forms of Main Present (*i devo, it deve(s), a dev, i deve, a devo*) are formed on this base, that is found also in Present Subjunctive (*i deva, it deve(s), a deva, i devo, i deve, a devo*). There is also an alternative form /**døv-**/: *i deuvo, it deuve(s)* and so on. Present Subjunctive is sometimes formed on a third base /**døbj-**/: *i deubia, it deubie(s)*, etc., following the same partition of *avèj*.

Podèj /puˈdæj/ 'can, to be able to' shows a large number of different stems and undergoes a high degree of variability not only in local dialects but in the koine itself.

In modern standard Piedmontese, nevertheless, it seems to have undertaken a path toward a sort of regularization: the most productive stems are now /**pud**/ and /**pød-**/.

A number of forms are formed on the base /**pud-**/: the Infinitive *podèj*, the Past Participle *podù*, the Gerund *podend/podand*, 1P of the Main Present *podoma*, the Main Imperfect *podìa, podìe(s)* etc, the Dubitative *podrai, podras* and so on, the Conditional *podrìa, podrìe(s)*, the Subjunctive Imperfect *podèissa, podèisse(s)* and so on. The base /**pud**/ has an alternative form /**pyd-**/, which is sometimes used in the same occurrences: *pudoma, pudìa, pudrai, pudrìa, pudèissa*.

The other base /pød-/ is used in order to form the other forms of Main Present (*i peudo, it peude(s), a peud, i peude, a peudo*) as well as the Present Subjunctive (*i peuda, it peude(s)* etc).

Another base /pøs-/ is also found in 1S person of the Main Present *i peuss* (without the *-o* ending) and in the entire conjugation of Present Subjunctive (*i peussa, it peusse(s)* and so on). The Singular forms of the Main Present may have another different stem /pøl-/: *i peulo, it peule(s), a peul*, and the same base is used for 3P, too: *a peulo*.

In some varieties very close to the koine it is possible to find a a paradigm of the Main present modeled on the scheme of *vorèj*: *i peuj, it peus, a peul*, but only for the singular persons.

Savèj /sa'væj/ 'to know' has most moods and tenses regularly formed with the base /sav-/, while Main Present seems to have been modeled upon the paradigm of *avèj*: *i sai, it sas, a sà, i soma, i seve, i san*. There is also a base /sap-/ which appears in the Present Subjunctive: *i sapia, it sapie(s), a sapia, i sapio, i sapie, a sapio*. Further variants may be found in some local dialects.

Valej /va'læj/ 'to be worth' is regular, except for the Past Participle that may be *valù, vajù* or *valsù*.

Vorèj /vu'ræj/ 'to want' has a base /vur-/, sometimes /vul-/, and on its basis all the Moods and Tenses are formed except for the Main Present, the Present Subjunctive and the Past Participle.

The Main Present is formed upon the base /vøl-/, except for 1P, that displays the base /vur-/ or an alternative base /vyr-/: *i veulo, it veule(s), a veul, i voroma/i vuroma, i veule, a veulo*. 1S (*i veuj*) may also been formed on a third base /vøj-/ on which all the Present Subjunctive is made up: *veuja, veuje(s), veuja* and so on. There is an alternative base /vøbj-/ for the Present Subjunctive: *veubia, veubie(s), veubia*.

Finally, the Past Participle has a specialized base /vurs-/: *vorsù* is much more common than the regular form *vorù*, which may sometimes also be replaced by *vojù*.

10.2.4.2.2 *Class 2.b*
A few Verbs have two forms of Past Participle, one regular and the other irregular. Sometimes they have the same use and meaning, while in others the regular one is used as a verbal voice in compound tenses and the irregular has become

VERBS   259

an Adjective. So, from *onze* /'uŋze/ 'to oil' we may find *onzù* /uŋ'zy/ 'oiled' and *ont* /uŋt/ 'oily,' from *perde* /'pærde/ 'to lose' *perdù* /per'dy/ and *pers* /pærs/ 'lost,' from *stenze* /'stæŋze/ 'to suffocate' *stenzù* /steŋ'zy/ 'suffocated' and *stent* /stæŋt/ 'choked,' from *stende* /'stæŋde/ 'to spread out, to hang clothes' *stendù* /steŋ'dy/ and *stèis* /stæjz/ (for more details ☞ 10.5.8.).

10.2.4.2.3   Class 2.c
All the 2.c Verbs show a high degree of instability, since they have at least two forms of Infinitive but in many cases also two forms of Participle (*ufrì* /yf'ri/ e *ufert* /y'fært/ 'offered;' *riessù* /rje'sy/ and *riussì* /rjy'si/ 'succeeded;' *sentù* /seŋ'ty/ and *sentì* /seŋ'ti/ 'heard;' *servù* /ser'vy/ and *servì* /ser'vi/ 'served;' *sufrì* /sy'fri/ and *sufert* /sy'fært/ 'suffered;' *tossù* /tu'sy/ and *tossì* /tu'si/ 'coughed'); sometimes with a different meaning: *curvì* /kyr'vi/ or *cuvrì* /kry'vi/ 'covered' and *cuvert* /ky'vært/ 'covered' but also 'roof;' *durvì* /dyr'vi/ 'opened' and *duvert* /dy'vært/ 'open' (more on this in 10.5.8.).

Verbs with roots in /ø/ have usually two different stems, and both of them may form the Infinitive form: for instance *asseurbe* /a'sørbe/ or *assurbì* /asyr'bi/, *beuje* /'bøje/ or *bujì* /by'ji/, *cheurve* /'kørve/ or *curvì* /kyr'vi/ 'to cover,' *deurme* /'dørme/ or *durmì* /dyr'mi/ 'to sleep,' and so on. The stem with /y/ forms the 1st plural person of the Main Present *bujoma* 'we boil,' *curvioma* 'we cover,' *surtoma* or *surtioma* 'we go out,' as well as the Main Imperfect *i surtìa*, the Dubitative *i surtirai*, the Conditional *i surtirìa* or *i surtrìa*, the Gerund *surtiend* or (more often) *surtiand*. All other Moods and Tenses normally show the stem with /ø/.

10.2.4.2.4   Class 2.d
The only irregular Verb of this subclass is *dì* 'to say' with its compounds *benedì* 'to bless' and *maledì* 'to curse.' This Verb has two forms /diz-/ and /di(j)-/ in free alternation: *i diso/i dijo, it dise/it dije* and so on. The compound forms are formed upon a third basis /dis-/ that appears in all the persons but 1P; e.g., from the verb *maledì* /male'di/ 'to curse,' 1S *i maledisso* /i=male'disu/, 2S *it maledisse* /it=male'dise/, and so on, but 1P *i maledioma* /i=male'djuma/.

10.2.4.3   Auxiliaries
The auxiliary Verbs 'to have' and 'to be' are highly irregular; they further show a special allomorphy in tensed, vowel-beginning forms.

Avèj /a'væj/ is both a lexical Verb and an auxiliary for compound active tenses. The stem /av-/ is used to form the Infinitive (*avèj* /a'væj/), Past article (*avù* /a'vy/), Gerund (*avend/avand* /a'væŋd / a'vaŋd/), Main Imperfect (*avìa, avìe(s)*

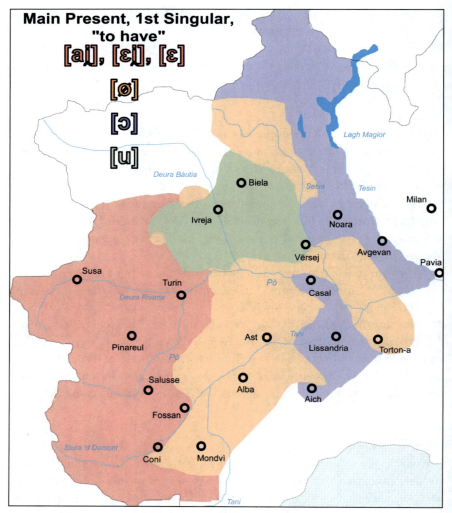

MAP 11   First Singular Main Present of 'to have' in the Piedmontese varieties
COURTESY OF LORENZO FERRAROTTI

/a'via, a'vie(z)/, and so on), Dubitative (*avrai, avras* /av'raj, av'raz/, and so on), Conditional (*avria, avrie(s)* /av'ria, av'rie(z)/, and so on), Subjunctive Imperfect (*avèissa, avèisse(s)* /av'æjsa, av'æjse(z)/, and so on).

A base /**ab**-/, closer to the etymological Latin root HAB-, is used only to form the Present Subjunctive (*abia, abie(s)* /'**abja**, '**abje(z)**/, and so on).

The conjugation of the Main Present remains unpredictable even if a third base /**a**-/ is taken into account, and it runs: *i l'hai* (or *i l'heu* or other forms; see Map 11), *it l'has, a l'ha, i l'oma, i l'eve, a l'han*. The ⟨h⟩ has no phonological status and it is a mere graphical device to distinguish certain verbal forms from the homophonous Preposition (or Prepositions plus Determiner) *ai, a, an*. This draws its inspiration from the orthography of Italian (☞ 3.), while other Romance languages (French, Occitan) have no trace of ⟨h⟩ and still others (Catalan, Spanish) keep it in the entire conjugation of the Main Present. The same etymological ⟨h⟩ is sometimes written in irregular forms of the Imperfective Subjunctive, such as *hèissa, hèisse(s)*, and so on.

The Verb 'to be' (also used as an auxiliary in the Past and the passive) is, as in many languages, highly irregular, with different stems used in separate paradigms and also within the same paradigm. Also many of the usual affixes are shunned and certain forms are best treated as synchronically unanalyzable portmanteau forms.

This is the case of the 3S of the Main Present *é* /e/ (*a=l'é* /a='le/), the Participle *stait* /stajt/ or *sta* /sta/ and the Infinitive *esse* /'ese/.

Other forms of the Main Present are built upon /s-/, combined with either the usual affixes (as in 1P *i=soma* /i='suma/, 2S *i seve* /i='seve/) or with special ones, as in 1S and 3P (1S *i son* /i='suŋ/, 3P *a son* /a='suŋ/).

The same base is found in the Subjunctive Present (*i sia* /i='sia/, *it sie(s)* /it='sie(z)/, etc.), the Dubitative (*i sarai* /i=sa'raj/, *it sara(s)* /it=sa'ra(z)/, etc.) and the Conditional (*i saria* /i=sa'ria/, *it sarie(s)* /it=sa'rie(s)/, etc.).

The Main Imperfect is built upon a base /er-/ with the usual affixes of this tense, yielding 1S *i l'era* /i='lera/, 2S *it l'ere(s)* /it='lere(s)/, etc.

The Subjunctive Imperfect is built upon a base /fy-/ (orthographic *fu-*) to which again the usual affixes of this paradigm are added (1S *i fussa*, 2S *it fusse(s)* /i='fysa, it='fyse(z)/, etc.).

10.2.4.4   The Prefixal Element in the Vowel-Beginning Tensed Forms of the Auxiliaries

In the koine and many varieties the forms of 'to have' beginning with a vowel show in tensed paradigms an initial element /l/ bearing synchronically no semantic value. This happens in all the forms of the tensed paradigms of 'to have:' Main Present and Imperfect, Subjunctive Present and Imperfect, Dubitative, Conditional.

In the Verb 'to be' /l/ is restricted to the 3S of the Main Present *é* /e/ and of the Main Imperfect *era* /'era/. The other forms of the Main Present begin with a consonant, while in the forms of the Main Imperfect other than the 3S an element /j/ is used.

Forms without *l* or *j* such as *i hai for 'I have' or *i ero for 'I was' are ungrammatical in the koine and most varieties.

TABLE 26   Main Present (above) and Main Imperfect (below) of 'to be' and 'to have'

1S	*i son* /i=ˈsuŋ/	*i l'hai* /i=ˈlaj/	
2S	*it ses* /it=ˈse[z]/	*it l'has* /it=ˈla[z]/	
3S	*a l'é* /a=ˈle/	*a l'ha* /a=ˈla/	
1P	*i soma* /i=ˈsuma/	*i l'oma* /i=ˈluma/	
2P	*i seve* /i=ˈseve/	*i l'eve* /i=ˈleve/	
3P	*a son* /a=ˈsuŋ/	*a l'han* /a=ˈlaŋ/	
1S	*i j'era* /i=ˈjera/	*i l'avìa* /i=laˈvia/	
2S	*it j'ere(s)* /it=ˈjere[z]/	*it l'avie(s)* /it=laˈvie[z]/	
3S	*a l'era* /a=ˈlera/	*a l'avìa* /a=laˈvia/	
1P	*i j'ero* /i=ˈjeru/	*i l'avìo* /i=laˈviu/	
2P	*i j'ere* /i=ˈjere/	*i l'avìe* /i=laˈvie/	
3P	*a j'ero* /a=ˈjeru/	*a l'avìo* /a=laˈviu/	

Synchronically, these elements are allomorphs of the verbal stem(s); thus, *a l'é* 'he, she, it is' is transcribed /a=ˈle/ and glossed "SBJ.3=be\PRS.3S."

The Main Present and Imperfect of both auxiliaries is reproduced in Table 26 with the Subject Clitics.

When it comes to clitic hosting, things get even more complicated: while the /l/ and /j/ elements have no synchronic value, they still get (synchronically) replaced by either the Indirect object clitic *i* (☞ 7.4.) or the Attributive Pronominal clitic *ne* (☞ 7.7.), as in the very common phonological words *a i-é* /a=ˈj=e/ (SBJ.3=IND=be\PRS.3S) 'there is' or, in the Main Imperfect, *a i-era* /a=ˈj=era/ (SBJ.3=IND=be\IMPF.3S) 'there was,' but also, e.g., *a n'avia* /a=n=aˈvia/ (SBJ.3= ATTR.PRO=have\IMPF.3S), lit. 'he had of it,' etc.

The origin of these elements is far from clear. In Tosco (2002a) the problem is discussed with limitation to the Verb 'to have' and the koine. One can in principle assume that /l/ is

- simply a euphonic element introduced in order to break up a vocalic sequence (Burzio 1986: 172, fn. 47). E.g., *a l'ha* /a=ˈla/ would derive from *a ha /a=ˈa/. But why is such a euphonic element never found with other Verbs?
- the last trace of a Subject Pronoun of 3rd person *al which was preserved only in front of the auxiliary Verbs, or even, as proposed by Parry (1997: 241), a special allomorph of the Subject clitic of 3rd person *a*: *al*, or rather *Vl*, is rather common all over Northern Italy as a Subject Pronoun (often restricted

to Masculine subjects and supplemented by a Feminine form with final /a/). Under this analysis, *a l'ha* /a='la/ would either be derived from or even synchronically analyzable as /a'l=a/ "SBJ.3=have\PRS.3S." Neither the saliency of the auxiliaries nor phonological reasons provide convincing explanations.
- the Object Pronominal clitic of 3rd person, which got stranded when pronominal objects got attached to the Participle in compound tenses (☞ 10.2.6, 10.6); i.e., *a l'ha* "SBJ.3=have\PRS.3S" would derive from "SBJ.3=OBJ.3=have\PRS.3S." This, together with the historically contemporaneous (late 18th and early 19th century) extension of the Subject clitics to all persons and syntactic roles in declarative clauses, is the hypothesis favored in Tosco (2002a). Under this analysis, a preverbal Object Pronoun in compound tenses would have first been replaced in its role by a post-participial Object pronoun (as in present-day Piedmontese) and later, once desemanticized, extended by analogy to the other persons of the paradigm:

i hai pijà 'I took' > *i lo hai pijà* > *i l'hai pijà* > 'I took it' > *i l'hai pijalo* 'I took it.'

10.2.5 *The Paradigms*
The classification into two verbal Classes (plus irregular Verbs) outlined above fits well the morphological data of the Piedmontese verbal system.

This classification will be used in Tables 27. to 30.: it fits the koine verbal system, even if it leaves some problems unsolved for the Southern peripheral varieties in which the First Plural ending *-oma* works only for the First Class and for the first two subgroups of the second one (Grassi, Sobrero and Telmon 1997: 146–149).

The Tables do not include the compound paradigms (☞ 10.2.6; 10.6.) and are limited to the paradigms used in the koine, with the exclusion of exclusively local forms. The Subject clitics are likewise not reported, as well as the division into stems, formants and affixes.

The transcription in the Tables does not provide morphological boundaries. All through the grammar, instead, the verbal indexes of the First Class Verbs are taken as a whole (without consideration of tense/mood and person indexes); in both transcriptions and glosses they are separated from the stem by a hyphen. Due to the high amount of irregular and non-concatenative morphological phenomena found in their conjugation, verbs of the Second Class and irregular Verbs are instead left undivided in the transcription, while affixes and stem are separated by "\" in glosses.

TABLE 27 The two regular Classes of Piedmontese Verbs

Verbal paradigms

Mood / Tense	First Class 'to speak'	Subgroup a. 'to like'	Second Class Subgroup b. 'to write'	Subgroup c. 'to go out'	Subgroup d. 'to finish'
Infinitive (INF)	*parlé* par'l-e	*piasèj* pjaz'æj	*scrive* 'skrive	*surtì* syr'ti	*finì* fi'ni
Main (—)					
Present (PRS)					
1S	*parlo* 'parl-u	*piaso* 'pjazu	*scrivo* 'skrivu	*seurto* 'sɔrtu	*finisso* fi'nisu
2S	*parle(s)* 'parl-e[z]	*piase(s)* 'pjaze[z]	*scrive(s)* 'skrive[z]	*seurte(s)* 'sɔrte[z]	*finisse(s)* fi'nise[z]
3S	*parla* 'parl-a	*pias* 'pjaz	*scriv* 'skriv	*seurt* sɔrt	*finiss* fi'nis
1P	*parloma* par'l-uma	*piasoma* pja'zuma	*scrivoma* skri'vuma	*surt(i)oma* syr't(j)uma	*fin-ioma* fi'njuma
2P	*parle* 'parl-e	*piase* 'pjaze	*scrive* 'skrive	*seurte* 'sɔrte	*fin-isse* fi'nise
3P	*parlo* 'parl-u	*piaso* 'pjazu	*scrivo* 'skrivu	*seurto* 'sɔrtu	*fin-isso* fi'nisu
Imperfect (IMPF)					
1S	*parlava* par'l-ava	*pias-i-a* pja'zia	*scrivia* skri'via	*surtia* syr'tia	*finia* fi'nia
2S	*parlave(s)* par'l-ave[z]	*pias-i-e(s)* pja'zie[z]	*scrivie(s)* skri'vie[z]	*surtie(s)* syr'tie[z]	*finie(s)* fi'nie[z]
3S	*parlava* par'l-ava	*pias-i-a* pja'zia	*scrivia* skri'via	*surtia* syr'tia	*finia* fi'nia
1P	*parlavo* par'l-avu	*pias-i-o* pja'ziu	*scrivio* skri'viu	*surtio* syr'tiu	*finio* fi'niu
2P	*parlave* par'l-ave	*pias-i-e* pja'zie	*scrivie* skri'vie	*surtie* syr'tie	*finie* fi'nie
3P	*parlavo* par'l-avu	*piasio* pja'ziu	*scrivio* skri'viu	*surtio* syr'tiu	*finio* fi'niu

VERBS 265

TABLE 27 The two regular Classes of Piedmontese Verbs (*cont.*)

Verbal paradigms

Mood / Tense	'to speak'	'to like'	'to write'	'to go out'	'to finish'
	First Class		Second Class		
		Subgroup a.	Subgroup b.	Subgroup c.	Subgroup d.
Subjunctive (SUBJ)					
Present (—)					
1S	*parla* par'l-æjsa	*piasa* 'pjaza	*scriva* 'skriva	*seurta* 'sɔrta	*finissa* fi'nisa
2S	*parle(s)* par'l-æjse[z]	*piase(s)* 'pjaze[z]	*scrive(s)* 'skrive[z]	*seurte(s)* 'sɔrte[z]	*finisse(s)* fi'nise[z]
3S	*parla* par'l-æjsa	*piasa* 'pjaza	*scriva* 'skriva	*seurta* 'sɔrta	*finissa* fi'nisa
1P	*parlo* par'l-æjsu	*piaso* 'pjazu	*scrivo* 'skrivu	*seurto* 'sɔrtu	*finisso* fi'nisu
2P	*parle* par'l-æjse	*piase* 'pjaze	*scrive* 'skrive	*seurte* 'sɔrte	*finisse* fi'nise
3P	*parlo* par'l-æjsu	*piaso* 'pjazu	*scrivo* 'skrivu	*seurto* 'sɔrtu	*finisso* fi'nisu
Imperfect (IMPF)					
1S	*parlèissa* par'l-æjsa	*piasèissa* pja'zæjsa	*scrivèissa* skri'væjsa	*surtièissa* syr't(j)æjsa	*finèissa* fi'n(j)æjsa
2S	*parlèisse(s)* par'l-æjse[z]	*piasèisse(s)* pja'zæjse[z]	*scrivèisse(s)* skri'væjse[z]	*surtièisse(s)* syr't(j)æjse[z]	*finèisse(s)* fi'n(j)æjse[z]
3S	*parlèissa* par'l-æjsa	*piasèissa* pja'zæjsa	*scrivèissa* skri'væjsa	*surtièissa* syr't(j)æjsa	*finèissa* fi'n(j)æjsa
1P	*parlèisso* par'l-æjsu	*piasèisso* pja'zæjsu	*scrivèisso* skri'væjsu	*surtièisso* syr't(j)æjsu	*finèisso* fi'n(j)æjsu
2P	*parlèisse* par'l-æjse	*piasèisse* pja'zæjse	*scrivèisse* skri'væjse	*surtièisse* syr't(j)æjse	*finèisse* fi'n(j)æjse
3P	*parlèisso* par'l-æjsu	*piasèisso* pja'zæjsu	*scrivèisso* skri'væjsu	*surtièisso* syr't(j)æjsu	*finèisso* fi'n(j)æjsu

TABLE 27   The two regular Classes of Piedmontese Verbs (*cont.*)

Verbal paradigms

	First Class	Subgroup a.	Subgroup b.	Subgroup c.	Subgroup d.
Mood / Tense	'to speak'	'to like'	'to write'	'to go out'	'to finish'
			Second Class		

Dubitative (DUB)

1S	*parlërai* parl-ə'raj	*piasrai* pjaz'raj	*scrivrai* skriv'raj	*surtirai* syrti'raj	*finirai* fini'raj
2S	*parlëras* parl-ə'raz	*piasras* pjaz'raz	*scrivras* skriv'raz	*surtiras* syrti'raz	*finiras* fini'raz
3S	*parlërà* parl-ə'ra	*piasrà* pjaz'ra	*scrivrà* skriv'ra	*surtirà* syrti'ra	*finirà* fini'ra
1P	*parlëroma* parl-ə'ruma	*piasroma* pjaz'ruma	*scrivroma* skriv'ruma	*surtiroma* syrti'ruma	*finiroma* fini'ruma
2P	*parlëreve* parl-ə'reve	*piasreve* pjaz'reve	*scrivreve* skriv'reve	*surtireve* syrti'reve	*finireve* fini'reve
3P	*parlëran* parl-ə'raŋ	*piasran* pjaz'raŋ	*scrivran* skriv'raŋ	*surt-i-r-an* syr'tiraŋ	*finiran* fi'niraŋ

Conditional (COND)

1S	*parlëria* parl-ə'ria	*piasria* pjaz'ria	*scrivria* skriv'ria	*surtiria* syrti'ria	*finiria* fini'ria
2S	*parlërie(s)* parl-ə'rie[z]	*piasrie(s)* pjaz'rie[z]	*scrivrie(s)* skriv'rie[z]	*surtirie(s)* syrti'rie[z]	*finirie(s)* fini'rie[z]
3S	*parlëria* parl-ə'ria	*piasria* pjaz'ria	*scrivria* skriv'ria	*surtiria* syrti'ria	*finiria* fini'ria
1P	*parlërio* parl-ə'riu	*piasrio* pjaz'riu	*scrivrio* skriv'riu	*surtirio* syrti'riu	*finirio* fini'riu
2P	*parlërie* parl-ə'rie	*piasrie* pjaz'rie	*scrivrie* skriv'rie	*surtirie* syrti'rie	*finirie* fini'rie
3P	*parlërio* parl-ə'riu	*piasrio* pjaz'riu	*scrivrio* skriv'riu	*surtirio* syrti'riu	*finirio* fini'riu

Imperative (IPV)

| 2S | *parla* parl-a | — | *scriv* skriv | *seurt* sørt | *fin-iss* fi'nis |
| 2P | *parlé* parl-e | — | *scriv-é* skri've | *surti* syr'ti | *fini* fi'ni |

TABLE 27 The two regular Classes of Piedmontese Verbs (*cont.*)

Verbal paradigms

Mood / Tense	First Class		Second Class			
	'to speak'	'to like'	'to write'	'to go out'	'to finish'	
		Subgroup a.	Subgroup b.	Subgroup c.	Subgroup d.	
Participle (PTCL)	*parlà* **par'l-a**	*piasù/-a/-e* **pja'zy/-a/-e**	*scrivù/-a/-e* **skri'vy/-a/-e**	*surtì/-a/-e* **syr'ti/-a/-e**	*finì/-a/-e* **fi'ni/-a/-e**	
Gerund (GER)	*parland* **par'l-aɲd**	*piaz-end* **pja'zæɲd**	*scrivend* **skri'væɲd**	*surtiend* **syr'tjæɲd**	*finiend* **fi'njæɲd**	

TABLE 28   First Class irregular Verbs

	'to go'	'to give'	'to do, make'	'to stay'
Infinitive (INF)	*andé* aŋ'de	*dé* de	*fé* fe	*sté* ste
Main (—)				
Present (PRS)				
1S	*vado* 'vadu	*dago* 'dagu	*faso* 'fazu	*stago* 'stagu
2S	*vas* vaz	*das* daz	*fa* faz	*stas* staz
3S	*va* va	*da* da	*fa* fa	*sta* sta
1P	*andoma* aŋ'duma	*doma* 'duma	*foma* 'fuma	*stoma* 'stuma
2P	*andeve* aŋ'deve	*deve* 'deve	*feve* 'feve	*steve* 'steve
3P	*van* vaŋ	*dan* daŋ	*fan* faŋ	*stan* staŋ
Imperfect (IMPF)				
1S	*andasìa* aŋda'zia	*dasìa* da'zia	*fasìa* fa'zia	*stasìa* sta'zia
2S	*andasìe(s)* aŋda'zie(z)	*dasìe(s)* da'zie(z)	*fasìe(s)* fa'zie(z)	*stasìe(s)* sta'zie(z)
3S	*andasìa* aŋda'zia	*dasìa* da'zia	*fasìa* fa'zia	*stasìa* sta'zia
1P	*andasìo* aŋda'ziu	*dasìo* da'ziu	*fasìo* fa'ziu	*stasìo* sta'ziu
2P	*andasìe* aŋda'zie	*dasìe* da'zie	*fasìe* fa'zie	*stasìe* sta'zie
3P	*andasìo* aŋda'ziu	*dasìo* da'ziu	*fasìo* fa'ziu	*stasìo* sta'ziu
Subjunctive (SUBJ)				
Present (—)				
1S	*vada* 'vada	*daga* 'daga	*fasa* 'faza	*staga* 'staga
2S	*vade(s)* 'vade(z)	*daghe(s)* 'dage(z)	*fase(s)* 'faze(z)	*staghe(s)* 'stage(z)
3S	*vada* 'vada	*daga* 'daga	*fasa* 'faza	*staga* 'staga
1P	*vado* 'vadu	*dago* 'dagu	*faso* 'fazu	*stago* 'stagu
2P	*vade* 'vade	*daghe* 'dage	*fase* 'faze	*stag-e* 'stage
3P	*vado* 'vadu	*dago* 'dagu	*faso* 'fazu	*stago* 'stagu
Imperfect (IMPF)				
1S	*andèissa* aŋ'dæjsa	*dèissa* 'dæjsa	*fèissa* 'fæjsa	*stèissa* 'stæjsa
2S	*andèisse(s)* aŋ'dæjse(z)	*dèisse(s)* 'dæjse(z)	*fèisse(s)* 'fæjse(z)	*stèisse(s)* 'stæjse(z)
3S	*andèissa* aŋ'dæjsa	*dèissa* 'dæjsa	*fèissa* 'fæjsa	*stèissa* 'stæjsa
1P	*andèisso* aŋ'dæjsu	*dèisso* 'dæjsu	*fèisso* 'fæjsu	*stèisso* 'stæjsu
2P	*andèisse* aŋ'dæjse	*dèisse* 'dæjse	*fèisse* 'fæjse	*stèisse* 'stæjse
3P	*andèisso* aŋ'dæjsu	*dèis-o* 'dæjsu	*fèisso* 'fæjsu	*stèisso* 'stæjsu
Dubitative (DUB)				
1S	*andarai* aŋda'raj	*darai* da'raj	*farai* fa'raj	*starai* sta'raj
2S	*andaras* aŋda'raz	*daras* da'raz	*faras* fa'raz	*staras* sta'raz
3S	*andarà* aŋda'ra	*darà* da'ra	*farà* fa'ra	*starà* sta'ra
1P	*andaroma* aŋda'ruma	*daroma* da'ruma	*faroma* fa'ruma	*staroma* sta'ruma
2P	*andareve* aŋda'reve	*dareve* da'reve	*fareve* fa'reve	*sta-eve* sta'reve
3P	*andaran* aŋda'raŋ	*daran* da'raŋ	*faran* fa'raŋ	*staran* sta'raŋ
Conditional (COND)				
1S	*andarìa* aŋda'ria	*darìa* da'ria	*farìa* fa'ria	*starìa* sta'ria
2S	*andarìe(s)* aŋda'rie(z)	*darìe(s)* da'rie(z)	*farìe(s)* fa'rie(z)	*starìe(s)* sta'rie(z)
3S	*andarìa* aŋda'ria	*darìa* da'ria	*farìa* fa'ria	*starìa* sta'ria
1P	*andarìo* aŋda'riu	*darìo* da'riu	*farìo* fa'riu	*starìo* sta'riu

VERBS

TABLE 28 First Class irregular Verbs (*cont.*)

	'to go'	'to give'	'to do, make'	'to stay'
	andarìe aŋdaˈrie *andarìo* aŋdaˈriu	*darìe* daˈrie *darìo* daˈriu	*farìe* faˈrie *farìo* faˈriu	*starìe* staˈrie *starìo* staˈriu
Imperative (IPV)	*va* va *andé* aŋˈde	*da* da *dé* de	*fa* fa *fé* fe	*sta* sta *sté* ste
Participle (PTCL)	*andàit/-a/-e* aŋˈdajt/-a/-e	*dàit/-a/-e* dajt/-a/-e	*fàit/-a/-e* fajt/-a/-e	*stàit/-a/-e* stajt/-a/-e
Gerund (GER)	*andasend* aŋdaˈzæŋd	*dasend* daˈzæŋd	*fasend* faˈzæŋd	*stasend* staˈzæŋd

TABLE 29 Second Class irregular Verbs

Infinitive (INF)	'must' *dovèj* du'væj	'can, to be possible' *podèj* pu'dæj		'to know' *savèj* sa'væj	'to want' *volèj* vu'læj	*vorèj* vu'ræj	'to say' *di* di
Main (—) Present (PRS)							
1S	*devo* 'devu	*deuvo* 'dovu	*peulo* 'polu	*peuss* pos	*peudo* 'podu	*sai* saj	*veulo* 'volu	*veuj* voj	*diso* 'dizu	*dijo* 'diju
2S	*deve(s)* 'deve(z)	*deuve(s)* 'dove(z)	*peule(s)* 'pole(z)	*peus* poz	*peude(s)* 'pode(z)	*sas* saz	*veule(s)* 'vole(z)	*veus* voz	*dise(s)* 'dize(z)	*dije(s)* 'dije(z)
3S	*dev* dev	*deuv* dov	*peul* pol	—	*peud* pod	*sà* sa	*veul* vol	—	*dis* diz	—
1P	*dovoma* du'vuma	*duvoma* dy'vuma	—	*podoma* pu'duma	*pudoma* py'duma	*soma* 'suma	*voloma* vu'luma	*vuroma* vy'ruma	*disoma* di'zuma	*dijoma* d(i)'juma
2P	*deve* 'deve	*deave* 'dove	*peule* 'pole	—	*peude* 'pode	*seve* 'seve	*veule* 'vole	—	*dise* 'dize	*dije* 'dije
3P	*devo* 'devu	*deuvo* 'dovu	*peulo* 'polu	—	*peudo* 'podu	*san* saŋ	*veulo* 'volu	—	*diso* 'dizu	*dijo* 'diju
Imperfect (IMPF)								
1S	*dovia* du'via	*duvia* dy'via	—	*pudia* py'dia	*pudia* py'dia	*savia* sa'via	*volia* vu'lia	*voria* vu'ria	*disia* di'zia	—
2S	*dovie(s)* du'vie(z)	*duvie(s)* dy'vie(z)	—	*pudie(s)* py'die(z)	*pudie(s)* py'die(z)	*savie(s)* sa'vie(z)	*volie(s)* vu'lie(z)	*vorie(s)* vu'rie(z)	*disie(s)* di'zie(z)	—
3S	*dovia* du'via	*duvia* dy'via	—	*pudia* py'dia	*pudia* py'dia	*savia* sa'via	*volia* vu'lia	*voria* vu'ria	*disia* di'zia	—
1P	*dovio* du'viu	*duvio* dy'viu	—	*pudio* py'diu	*pudio* py'diu	*savio* sa'viu	*volio* vu'liu	*vorio* vu'riu	*disio* di'ziu	—

TABLE 29 Second Class irregular Verbs (*cont.*)

	'must'		'can, to be possible'		'to know'		'to want'		'to say'	
2P	*dovie* du'vie	*davie* dy'vie	—	*pudie* py'die	*savie* sa'vie	*volie* vu'lie	*vorie* vu'rie	*disie* di'zie	—	
3P	*dovio* du'viu	*davio* dy'viu	—	*pudio* py'diu	*savio* sa'viu	*volio* vu'liu	*vorio* vu'riu	*disio* di'ziu	—	

Subjunctive (SUBJ)
Present (—)

1S	*deva* 'deva	*deubia* 'dobja	*peussa* 'posa	*peuda* 'poda	*sapia* 'sapja	*veubia* 'vobja	*veuja* 'voja	*disa* 'diza	*dija* 'dija
2S	*deve(s)* 'deve(z)	*deubie(s)* 'dobje(z)	*peusse(s)* 'pose(z)	*peude(s)* 'pode(z)	*sapie(s)* 'sapje(z)	*veubie(s)* 'vobje(z)	*veuj-e(s)* 'voje(z)	*dis-e(s)* 'dize(z)	*dije(s)* 'dije(z)
3S	*deva* 'deva	*deubia* 'dobja	*peussa* 'posa	*peuda* 'poda	*sapia* 'sapja	*veubia* 'vobja	*veuja* 'voja	*disa* 'diza	*dija* 'dija
1P	*devo* 'devu	*deubio* 'dobju	*peusso* 'posu	*peudo* 'podu	*sapio* 'sapju	*veubio* 'vobju	*veujo* 'voju	*diso* 'dizu	*dijo* 'diju
2P	*deve* 'deve	*deubie* 'dobje	*peusse* 'pose	*peude* 'pode	*sapie* 'sapje	*veubie* 'vobje	*veuje* 'voje	*dise* 'dize	*dije* 'dije
3P	*devo* 'devu	*deubio* 'dobju	*peusso* 'posu	*peudo* 'podu	*sapio* 'sapju	*veubio* 'vobju	*veujo* 'voju	*diso* 'dizu	*dijo* 'diju

Imperfect (IMPF)

1S	*dovèissa* du'væjsa	*duvèissa* dy'væjsa	*podèissa* pu'dæjsa	*pudèissa* py'dæjsa	*savèissa* sa'væjsa	*volèissa* vu'læjsa	*vorèissa* vu'ræjsa	*disèissa* di'zæjsa	*dijèissa* di'jæjsa
2S	*dovèisse(s)* du'væjse(z)	*duvèisse(s)* dy'væjse(z)	*podèisse(s)* pu'dæjse(z)	*pudèisse(s)* py'dæjse(z)	*savèisse(s)* sa'væjse(z)	*volèisse(s)* vu'læjse(z)	*vorèisse(s)* vu'ræjse(z)	*disèisse(s)* di'zæjse(z)	*dijèisse(s)* di'jæjse(z)
3S	*dovèissa* du'væjsa	*duvèissa* dy'væjsa	*podèissa* pu'dæjsa	*pudèissa* py'dæjsa	*savèissa* sa'væjsa	*volèissa* vu'læjsa	*vorèissa* vu'ræjsa	*disèissa* di'zæjsa	*dijèissa* di'jæjsa

TABLE 29   Second Class irregular Verbs (*cont.*)

	'must'		'can, to be possible'		'to know'		'to want'		'to say'	
1P	*dovèisso* du'væjsa	*davèisso* dyv'væjsu	*podèisso* pu'dæjsu	*pudèisso* py'dæjsu	*savèisso* sa'væjsu	*disèisso* di'zæjsu	*volèisso* vu'læjsu	*vorèisso* vu'ræjsu	*dijèisso* di'jæjsu
2P	*dovèisse* du'væjsu	*davèisse* dyv'væjse	*podèisse* pu'dæjse	*pudèisse* py'dæjse	*savèisse* sa'væjse	*disèisse* di'zæjse	*volèisse* vu'læjse	*vorèisse* vu'ræjse	*i dijèisse* di'jæjse
3P	*dovèisso* du'væjsu	*davèisso* dyv'væjsu	*podèisso* pu'dæjsu	*pudèisso* py'dæjsu	*savèisso* sa'væjsu	*disèisso* di'zæjsu	*volèisso* vu'læjsu	*vorèisso* vu'ræjsu	*dijèisso* di'jæjsu

Dubitative (DUB)

1S	*dovrai* duv'raj	*davrai* dyv'raj	*podrai* pud'raj	*pudrai* pyd'raj	*savrai* sav'raj	—	—	*vorërai* vurë'raj	*dirai* di'raj
2S	*voras* duv'raz	*davras* dyv'raz	*podras* pud'raz	*pudras* pyd'raz	*savras* sav'raz	—	—	*vorëras* vurë'raz	*diras* di'raz
3S	*dovrà* duv'ra	*davrà* dyv'ra	*podrà* pud'ra	*pudrà* pyd'ra	*savrà* sav'ra	—	—	*vorërà* vurë'ra	*dirà* di'ra
1P	*dovroma* duv'ruma	*davroma* dyv'ruma	*podroma* pud'ruma	*pudroma* pyd'ruma	*savroma* sav'ruma	—	—	*vorëroma* vurë'ruma	*diroma* di'ruma
2P	*dovreve* duv'reve	*davreve* dyv'reve	*podreve* pud'reve	*pudreve* pyd'reve	*savreve* sav'reve	—	—	*vorëreve* vurë'reve	*direve* di'reve
3P	*dovran* duv'raj	*davran* dyv'raj	*podran* pud'raj	*pudran* pyd'raj	*savran* sav'raj	—	—	*vorëran* vurë'raj	*diran* di'raj

Conditional (COND)

1S	*dovria* duv'ria	*davria* dyv'ria	*podria* pud'ria	*pudria* pyd'ria	*savria* sav'ria	—	*voria* vu'ria	*vorëria* vurë'ria	*diria* di'ria
2S	*vorie(s)* duv'rie(z)	*davrie(s)* dyv'rie(z)	*podrie(s)* pud'rie(z)	*pudrie(s)* pyd'rie(z)	*savrie(s)* sav'rie(z)	—	*vorie(s)* vu'rie(z)	*vorërie(s)* vurë'rie(z)	*dirie(s)* di'rie(z)

VERBS

TABLE 29 Second Class irregular Verbs (cont.)

	'must'	'can, to be possible'	'to know'	'to want'	'to say'
3S	*dovrìa* **duv'ria**	*podrà* **pud'ria**	*savrìa* **sav'ria**	*vorrìa* **vu'ria**	*Dirìa* **di'ria**
	—	—	—	—	—
1P	*dovriu* **duv'riu**	*podroma* **pud'riu**	*savrio* **sav'riu**	*vorërio* **vura'riu**	*dirìo* **di'riu**
	—	—	—	—	—
2P	*dovrie* **duv'rie**	*podreve* **pud'rie**	*savrie* **sav'rie**	*vorëria* **vura'rie**	*dirìe* **di'rie**
	—	—	—	—	—
3P	*dovrio* **duv'riu**	*podran* **pud'riu**	*savrio* **sav'riu**	*vorërio* **vura'riu**	*dirìo* **di'riu**
	—	—	—	—	—
Imperative (IPV)					
2S	—	—	*sapie* **'sapje**	*veuje* **'voje**	*dis* **diz**
2P	—	—	*sav-éj* **sa'væj**	*vorèj* **vu'ræj**	*dì* **di**
Participle (PTCL)	*dovù/-a/-e* **du'vy/-a/-e**	*podù/-a/-e* **pu'dy/-a/-e**	*savù/-a/-e* **sa'vy/-a/-e**	*volù/-a/-e* **vu'ly/-a/-e**	*dit/-a/-e* **dit/-a/-e**
Gerund (GER)	*dovend* **du'vænd**	*podend* **pu'dænd**	*savend* **sa'vænd**	*volend* **vu'lænd**	*disend* **di'zænd**

TABLE 30   Auxiliary Verbs

	'to be'	'to have'
Infinitive (INF)	*esse* ˈese	*avèj* aˈvæj

Main (—)
Present (PRS)

1S	*son* suŋ	*l'hai* laj
2S	*ses* sez	*l'has* laz
3S	*l'é* le	*l'ha* la
1P	*soma* ˈsuma	*l'oma* ˈluma
2P	*seve* ˈseve	*l'eve* ˈleve
3P	*son* suŋ	*l'han* laŋ

Imperfect (IMPF)

1S	*j'era* ˈjera	*l'avìa* laˈvia
2S	*j'ere(s)* ˈjere(z)	*l'avìe(s)* laˈvie(z)
3S	*l'era* ˈlera	*l'avìa* laˈvia
1P	*j'ero* ˈjeru	*l'avìo* laˈviu
2P	*j'ere* ˈjere	*l'avìe* laˈvie
3P	*j'ero* ˈjeru	*l'avìo* laˈviu

Subjunctive (SUBJ)
Present (—)

1S	*sia* ˈsia	*l'àbia* ˈlabja
2S	*sie(s)* ˈsie(z)	*l'àbie(s)* ˈlabje(z)
3S	*sia* ˈsia	*l'àbia* ˈlabja
1P	*sio* ˈsiu	*l'àbio* ˈlabju
2P	*sie* ˈsie	*l'àbie* ˈlabje
3P	*sio* ˈsiu	*l'àbio* ˈlabju

Imperfect (IMPF)

1S	*fussa* ˈfysa	*l'avèissa* laˈvæjsa
2S	*fusse(s)* ˈfyse(z)	*l'avèisse(s)* laˈvæjse(z)
3S	*fussa* ˈfysa	*l'avèissa* laˈvæjsa
1P	*fusso* ˈfysu	*l'avèisso* laˈvæjsu
2P	*fusse* ˈfyse	*l'av-èiss-e* laˈvæjse
3P	*fusso* ˈfysu	*l'avèisso* laˈvæjsu

VERBS 275

TABLE 30 Auxiliary Verbs (*cont.*)

	'to be'	'to have'
Dubitative (DUB)		
1S	*sarai* sa'raj	*l'avrai* lav'raj
2S	*saras* sa'raz	*l'avras* lav'raz
3S	*sarà* sa'ra	*l'avrà* lav'ra
1P	*saroma* sa'ruma	*l'avroma* lav'ruma
2P	*sareve* sa'reve	*l'avreve* lav'reve
3P	*saran* sa'raŋ	*l'avran* lav'raŋ
Conditional (COND)		
1S	*sarìa* sa'ria	*l'avrìa* lav'ria
2S	*sarìe(s)* sa'rie(z)	*l'avrìe(s)* lav'rie(z)
3S	*sarìa* sa'ria	*l'avrìa* lav'ria
1P	*sa-r-ì-o* sa'riu	*l'avrìo* lav'riu
2P	*sarìe* sa'rie	*l'avrìe* lav'rie
3P	*sarìo* sa'riu	*l'avrìo* lav'riu
Imperative (IPV)		
2S	*sie / esse* 'sie /'ese	*àbie* 'abje
2P	*sie / esse* 'sie /'ese	*àbie* 'abje
Participle (PTCL)	*stàit/-a/-e*	*avù/-a/-e*
	stajt/-a/-e	a'vy/-a/-e
Gerund (GER)	*essend* e'sæŋd	*avend* a'væŋd

10.2.6 *Compound Paradigms: An Overview*

As anticipated above and further discussed in 10.6., additional paradigms are built with an auxiliary—either *avèj* /a'væj/ 'to have' or *esse* /'ese/ 'to be' for different types of Verbs (basically, intransitive/unergative vs. unaccusative)—plus the Participle of a lexical Verb. A compound form shifts in the past the value of the auxiliary form. Therefore, the use of the Participle after the Present (of whatever Mood) of the auxiliary yields a Past, while with the Imperfect of the Main and Subjunctive Moods yields a Pluperfect. The Imperative and the Participle itself do not have compound forms.

Additional uses of the auxiliary *esse* /'ese/ 'to be' involve the formation of reflexive and passive forms (☞ 10.6.) and do not involve a temporal shift.

TABLE 31   Simple and Compound paradigms of the Verb *rusé* /ry'ze/ 'to scold'

Mood		Simple			Compound	
Main	Present	*i ruso*	i='ryzu	Past	*i l'hai rusà*	i='laj ry'za
	Imperfect	*i rusava*	i=ry'zava	Pluperfect	*i l'avia rusà*	i=la'via ry'za
Subjunctive	Present	*i rusa*	i='ryza	Past	*i l'abia rusà*	i='labja ry'za
	Imperfect	*i ruseissa*	i=ry'zæjsa	Pluperfect	*i l'aveissa rusà*	i=la'væjsa ry':
Dubitative	Present	*i rusrai*	i=ryz'raj	Past	*i l'avrai rusà*	i=lav'raj ry'za
Conditional	Present	*i rusrìa*	i=ryz'ria	Past	*i l'avrìa rusà*	i=lav'ria ry'za
Gerund	Present	*rusand*	ry'zaŋd	Past	*avend rusà*	av'æŋd ry'za
Infinitive	Present	*rusé*	ry'ze	Past	*avèj rusà*	av'æj ry'za

From the transitive regular Verb of the 1st Class *rusé* /**ry'z-e**/ 'to scold; to quarrel' the following Simple and Compound paradigms are obtained (the 1st Singular only is listed in Table 31 for finite paradigms and morpheme boundaries are not shown).

10.3   Affixes, Allomorphy and Syncretism

A great deal of allomorphy and syncretism is found in the conjugation of Verbs First, certain moods and tenses are analyzed as containing a (historical) formative between the stem and the actual affix, as follows:

TABLE 32   Mood and tense formatives

Ø	Ø	MAIN;
		SUBJ.PRS;
		IPV;
		INF;
		GER;
		PTCL
av	'av-	IMPF (CLASS 1.)
eiss	'æjs-	SUBJ.IMPF
i	'i-	IMPF (CLASS 2.)
(ë)r	(ə)r-	DUB;
		COND

VERBS 277

TABLE 33 Formatives and affixes: person affixes

∅	∅	PRS.3S (CLASS 2.)
		IPV.S (CLASS 2.)
a	a	1S (IMPF; SUBJ(.PRS); SUBJ.IMPF; COND)
		3S (PRS, CLASS 1.; IMPF; SUBJ(.PRS); SUBJ.IMPF; COND)
		IPV.S (CLASS 1.)
à	'(X)a	PTCL (CLASS 1.)
ai	'(X)aj	1S (DUB)
an	'(X)aŋ	3P (DUB)
and	'(X)aŋd	GER (CLASS 1.)
as	'(X)az	DUB.2S
e	e	2P (PRS; IMPF; SUBJ(.PRS); SUBJ.IMPF; COND)
		INF (CLASS 2.B)
e(s)	e(z)	PRS.2S (PRS; IMPF; SUBJ(.PRS); SUBJ.IMPF; COND)
é	'(X)e	INF (CLASS 1);
		IPV.P (CLASS 1., 2.A/B)
ej	'(V)æj	INF (2a. CLASS 2.A)
end	'(X)eŋd	GER (2 CLASS 2.)
eve	'eve	2P (DUB)
ì	'(X)i	INF (CLASS 2.C/D)
		2P (IPV, CLASS 2.C/D)
o	u	1S (PRS)
		1P (IMPF; SUBJ; COND)
		3P (PRS; IMPF; SUBJ; COND)
oma	'(X)uma	1P (PRS; DUB)
ù	'(X)y	PTCL (CLASS 2.A)

No further mention of these formatives will be made and the glosses used throughout in the grammar will distinguish the stem and an affix only. Taking the formatives into account, one may notice that out of a possible maximal theoretical number of 41 affixes,[4] only 17 affixes are actually in use, ∅ included.

As a matter of fact, and leaving aside the irregular Verbs, no category uses a single exponent exclusively, and minimally two markers are found in any

---

4 Main Present (6) + Main Imperfect (6) + Subjunctive Present (6) + Subjunctive Imperfect (6) + Dubitative (6) + Conditional (6) + Imperative (2) + Infinitive (1) + Gerund (1) + Participle (1).

paradigm (as in the Gerund, the Infinitive and the Participle, who oppose one First Class and one—or more—Second Class markers).

On the other hand, no category exhibits more than three allomorphs:

- 1S is marked by either -*a* /a/, -*aj* /aj/, or -*o* /u/ (but in many varieties the 1st Singular Main Present is Ø rather than -*o* /u/);
- 2S has a single ending, namely -*e*(*s*) /e(z)/ in all the paradigms with the exception of Dubitative -*as* /a(z)/; final /s/ is absent in most varieties, which leaves -*e* /e/ and -*a* /a/ (in the Dubitative) as markers;
- 3S has the ending -*a* /a/ everywhere except in the Present of Class 2 Verbs, where it is Ø-marked;
- 1P has the ending -*oma* /ˈuma/ in the Main Present and in the Dubitative, while in all other cases it displays -*o* /u/;
- 2P, with a uniform ending -*e* /e/ everywhere except in the Dubitative (-*eve* /ˈeve/);
- 3P has the ending -*o* /u/ everywhere except for Dubitative -*an* /ˈaŋ/.

10.4 Historical and Comparative Notes

The person and number markers of the Piedmontese verbal system may be summed up in four inflectional sets (see Table 34). The Main Present uses sets A. and B. according to the verbal Class, set C. is used for the Dubitative, and set D. is used for a wide number of paradigms. Again, one may note that the four sets mostly share the same endings.

In general, the inflectional system is greatly simplified compared to many local Piedmontese varieties. The analogical levelling had deeply reduced the morphological markers, and in the contemporary koine no person of regular Verbs is represented by more than three endings at the most. One could even say that only the First person Singular has three different morphological marks (-*o*, -*ai*, -*a*), because the three endings shown by the Third person Singular could be reduced to two, namely -*a*/-*à* by one side and Ø by the other. In some peripheral varieties Ø has disappeared, substituted by a generalized ending -*a*. Also the Second person Singular has two forms, -*e*(*s*) and -*as*, and the same is true for the Plural persons: the first (-*oma*, -*o*), the second (-*e*, -*eve*) and the third (-*o*, -*an*).

All the verbal endings are unstressed, except for -*oma* and for the future (DUB) markers, that correspond to the Present Indicative of the Verb *avèj*, like in many other Romance languages (Bertinetto and Squartini 2016: 951).

VERBS

TABLE 34 The person affixes at a glance

	1S	2S	3S	1P	2P	3P
Main Present (PRS), Class 1.	-o /u/	-e(s) /e(z)/	-a /a/	-oma /uma/	-e /e/	-o /u/
Main Present (PRS), Class 2.	-o /u/	-e(s) /e(z)/	Ø	-oma /uma/	-e /e/	-o /u/
Dubitative Present (DUB)	-ai /aj/	-as /az/	-à /'a/	-oma /uma/	-eve /eve/	-an /aŋ/
Main Imperfect (IMPF), Subjunctive Present (SUBJ(.PRS)), Subjunctive Imperfect (SUBJ.IMPF), Conditional Present (COND)	-a /a/	-e(s) /e(z)/	-a /a/	-o /u/	-e /e/	-o /u/

10.4.1 First Person Singular

In the Main Present, the Piedmontese koine maintains (or, more probably, has restored) the First Singular ending -o /u/ that is instead dropped in all the Langhe and Monfrà varieties (Parry 2005: 186) but is attested in Turin at least since the 17th Century (Clivio 1974). This situation is shown in Map 12. This feature links the Piedmontese koine to the Occitan linguistic space, where (at least in the varieties spoken in Italy) this ending is always preserved (Miola 2013: 149).

I parlo vs. i parl

A large part of the Piedmontese-speaking area shows a zero ending in the 1S of polysyllabic Verbs: *i parl* instead of *i parlo* 'I speak,' *i vad* instead of *i vado* 'I go,' *i stagh* instead of *i stago* 'I stay.' Some of these forms can be found in the koine too, especially for irregular Verbs.

10.4.2 Second Person Singular

The Second person Singular normally ends in *-e*; in some varieties—often very close to the koine—it keeps the sigmatic morpheme *-es*, that is of everyday usage not only in rural areas but also in towns like Salusse and Lans[5] (Telmon 2001: 70). This phenomenon, too, seems strictly related to the Occitan area. In the 20th Century koine (as in many peripheral varieties) the *-(e)s* ending concerns only the monosyllabic irregular Verbs (*ti it sas* 'you know'; *ti it ses* 'you are'; *ti it fas* 'you do'; *ti it vas* 'you go', *ti it l'has* 'you have') while in all the polysyllabic forms it is reduced to *-e*. Nevertheless, this

---

5 Lans /laŋs/, Italian Lanzo /ˈlantso/ (45°16′N 07°29′E).

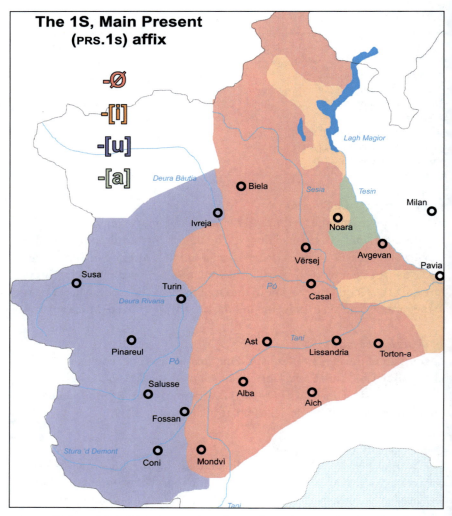

MAP 12   Ending of the 1s Main Present, First Class in the Piedmontese varieties
COURTESY OF LORENZO FERRAROTTI

ending cannot be considered foreign to the koine: there are many ideological reasons for paying attention to it, as has been suggested by Brero (2008: 68):

> We think [...] that we are still in time to save that beautiful verbal treasure that is the Second person Singular of Present and Imperfect of all moods ending in *-es*. It is still alive in the district of Salusse and in the town of Salusse itself. E.g.: *se ti it ven-es con noi, it manges, it bèives e it*

paghes gnente (If you come with us, you eat, you drink and you don't pay anything). Instead of disdaining people who use it, we should try to adopt it. It is a delicacy!"[6]

In our Tables we therefore always signal the possible presence of final *-s*, which is widely attested diachronically and in many diatopic varieties, and at the same time is "ideologically" suitable in an Ausbauization perspective (Tosco 2011)—as it is highly different from the corresponding Italian ending for the Second person Singular *-i*. This Italian ending, in fact, is not completely unknown to Piedmontese, as it is attested in peripheral varieties (such as Langhe, Monregalèis, Monfrà varieties); but in the Ausbauization perspective, promoted *ante litteram* by Brero himself, this is another reason for restoring the sigmatic ending which seems the genuine Piedmontese form.

It sei, it canti

In the koine the Second person Singular ending *-s* has been preserved for a very long time and still is in some varieties (e.g. Lans and Salusse). Nowadays the koine has almost lost its interrogative conjugation—where *-es* had been preserved—and, as discussed above, the *-s*-ending appears only in monosyllabic Verbs such as *it ses, it l'has, it vas, it sas, it das*, and so on, and in the Dubitative (*it l'avras, it diras*, and so on).

Some varieties (often very close to the koine) show a *-i* ending in polysyllabic Verbs: *it canti* /it='kaŋti/ 'you sing,' *it peuli* /it='pøli/ 'you can/you may,' *it disi* /it='dizi/ 'you say,' *it finissi* /it=fi'nisi/ 'you finish.' A few dialects extend the *-i* ending also to monosyllabic Verbs: *it sei* /it='sæi/ 'you are,' *it hai* /it='aj/ 'you have,' *it vai* /it='vaj/ 'you go,' *it sai* /it='saj/ 'you know,' and so forth; sometimes the presence of *-i* triggers other phonological changes that may lead to forms like *it é* /it='e/, *it hè* /it='æ/, *it vè* /it='væ/, *it sè* /it='sæ/. Some other varieties drop the final segment, like *it se* /it='se/, *it ha* /it='a/, *it va* /it='va/, *it sa* /it='sa/: sometimes it is hard to understand if they come from the dropping of *-i* or *-s* in final position.

It must be pointed out that those varieties in which the Second person Singular ends in *-i* have forms in *-eu* instead of *-ai* for the First person Sin-

---

6 Original: *I pensoma /.../ che i soma ancora an temp a salvé cola bela richëssa verbal che a l'é la seconda përson-a singolar dël present e dl'impërfet ëd tuti ij meud che a finiss an «es» e che a l'é ancora bin viva ant j'anviron ëd Salusse e a Salusse sità. Esempi: se ti it ven-es con noi, it manges, it bèives e it paghes gnente (Se vieni con noi, mangi, bevi e non paghi nulla). Anvece 'd dëspresié coj che a la dòvro, sercoma d'adotela anche noi! A l'é na galuparìa!*

gular of some monosyllabic Verbs: *i seu* /i='sø/ 'I know' instead of *i sai, i l'heu* /i='lø/ 'I have' instead of *i l'hai*.

Finally, in some peripheral areas other Second person Singular endings are attested, such as *-t* or zero.

10.4.3 Third Person Singular

The Third person Singular has two endings: *-a*, for Verbs belonging to the First Class scheme, and zero for all the other Verbs. The opposition between the *-a* form and the zero form clearly distinguishes two macro-classes in the koine. In other peripheral dialects, such as varieties from ël Mondvì and Neuve,[7] the distinction has been cancelled by the generalisation of the *-a* form as the only Third person ending.

10.4.4 First Person Plural

The First person Plural ending *-oma* /uma/ is often considered a distinguishing feature of Piedmontese. Its origin is a vexed question to which many studies in historical dialectology have been devoted. The first scholar showing an interest in this ending was probably Biondelli (1853): he stressed how the First person Plural of Piedmontese ends in *-óma* (original spelling; at that time the pronunciation was still /oma/) while several peripheral varieties have different endings (Biondelli 1853: 483–484), namely *-én* (Cheuri,[8] Vaudié,[9] Vinàj,[10] Assèj,[11] Castelmagn[12]) or *-án* (Limon[13]). Even the much bigger town of ël Mondvì still in the mid-19th century showed a different verbal ending: the stressed form *-má* that has now totally disappeared in the urban varieties (for an overview of 1P endings, see Sobrero, Grassi and Telmon 1997: 145–146).

On the other hand, Biondelli, although deeply interested in mapping the diffusion of this feature, never tried to explain its origin nor to trace the steps of its development. Rohlfs (1968: § 530) accepted the traditional common view according to which the ending *-oma* comes from the Latin form SUMUS, i.e. the

---

7   Neuve /'nøve/, Italian Novi Ligure /'novi 'ligure/ (44°45'42"N 08°47'26"E).
8   Piedmontese Cheuri /'køri/, Italian Corio /'korjo/, Franco-Provençal Koeri (45°19'N 07°32'E).
9   Piedmontese Vaudié /vau'dje/, Italian Valdieri /val'djeri/, Occitan Vaudier (44°17'N 07°24'E).
10 Piedmontese Vinàj /vi'naj/, Italian Vinadio /vi'nadjo/, Occitan Vinai (44°18'N 07°10'E).
11 Piedmontese Assèj /a'sæj/, Italian Acceglio /atʃ'tʃeʎo/, Occitan Acelh (44°29'N 06°59'E).
12 Piedmontese Castelmagn /kastel'maɲ/, Italian Castelmagno /kastel'maɲo/, Occitan Chastelmanh (44°25'N 07°13'E).
13 Piedmontese Limon /li'muŋ/, Italian Limone Piemonte /li'mone pje'monte/, Occitan Limon (44°12'N 07°34'E).

First person Plural of the Main Present of the Verb ESSE 'to be.' The same phenomenon seems to be attested in French and, as pointed out by Rohlfs, it has a wider geographical extension than normally thought: from Western Liguria to Ossola valley, and concerns many other Italian regions such as Emilia, Eastern Lombardy, Trentino as well as the Swiss Tessin. Interestingly, this feature is found even in the so-called Gallo-Italic (possibly Southern Piedmontese) colonies of Sicily: they have for the First person Plural of Verbs forms like /'woma/ (Piazza Armerina), or just /'uma/ (Aidone). The *-oma* ending, then, should be a very ancient feature; still, the Middle Age texts written in Piedmontese show no trace of it. A brief historical survey of the explanations that have been proposed all along the 20th century can easily be found in Telmon (1988: 473; 477–478). Zörner (1996) proposed another hypothesis, according to which *-oma* is just the generalization of an originally exhortative form. Indeed, in the Canavzan varieties the Main ending is an unstressed /aŋ/ while the Imperative has *-oma* exactly as in koine Piedmontese. Its historical origin should go back not to *somo* /'sumu/, 'we are', but to *omo* /'umu/ 'we have', the other auxiliary form of Piedmontese. In fact, *omo* /'umu/ is commonly used instead of *oma* /'uma/ in some varieties very closely related to the koine (e.g. in Teston-a, a village within the municipality of Moncalé[14]). On the other hand, it is possible for the ending *-oma* to have an extra-Turinese origin (Regis 2012): there is no *-oma* ending in the 17th century texts from Turin collected by Clivio (1974).

10.4.5 Second Person Plural

For the Second person Plural two morphological markers deserve some attention. The first one, *-e*, seems to be identical to the correspondent Second person Singular without *-s*—and this is why many scholars have thought it was just an extension of the Second person Singular to the Plural. In some varieties the two forms are distinguished only by the preceding clitic pronoun: e.g., in the contemporary ël Mondvì variety *it canti* 'you (S) sing' is opposed to *i canti* 'you (P) sing' only through the clitic pronoun; and the same seems to happen in the koine too, were we find (*ti*) *it cante* vs. (*vojàutri*) *i cante*. But, as we have seen before, some varieties of Piedmontese very close to the koine oppose a form like *it cantes* to a plural form like *i canti*. This shows that the hypothesis of a simple extension of the Second person Singular does not fit a

---

14 Piedmontese Moncalé /muŋkaˈle/, Italian Moncalieri /monkaˈljeri/ (45°00'N 07°41'E). Teston-a is Testona in Italian.

more complex state of affairs. Certainly, the original Second person Plural form was *-é, vojàutri canté*, to which the brief pronominal form *-ve* has been affixed through the interrogative form: *vojàutri canté* was the form used in the affirmative, *canteve vojàutri?* the interrogative form. So, *-eve* rapidly became a morphological ending, still used for the Dubitative. Later, the new form in *-e*, maybe derived from the Second person Singular, took the place of *-eve* and was established as the standard Second person Plural morphological marker.

10.4.6 Third Person Plural

Very scarce attention has been paid to the morphological marking of the Third person Plural. As a matter of fact, its form is shared by almost all the peripheral varieties (but not by Canavzan dialects) and has been adopted (in forms such as *-oma*) by many bordering Ligurian or Occitan dialects, sometimes in variants such as /ɔ/ (Ormea), /ɔŋ/ (Viola), /uŋ/ (Susa valley). It is probably the result of a generalization to all Verbs of the second Class ending (from Latin third conjugation -UNT)—apart from some irregular Verbs such as *andé* (*lor a van* /lur a=ˈvaŋ/ 'they go'), *avèj* (*lor a l'han* /lur a=ˈlaŋ/ 'they have'), *dé* (*lor a dan* /lur a=ˈdaŋ/ 'they give'), *fé* (*lor a fan* /lur a=ˈfaŋ/ 'they do'), *savèj* (*lor a san* /lur a=ˈsaŋ/ 'they know'), *sté* (*lor a stan* /lur a=ˈstaŋ/ 'they stay'), in which the same *-an* ending featured in the Dubitative of the regular Verbs appears.

10.4.7 Beyond Piedmontese

This section and Tables 35–49. offer some generalizations about the partition of verbal paradigms in the Piedmontese koine. The verbal forms of each paradigm may be seen as slots, with some of them sharing phonemes not present in others and making a partition of the paradigm, or Base (Thornton 2005: 121; 125).

In Italian, for example, a Verb such as *udire* has a Base *od-* which appears in the Main and Subjunctive Present in the three persons of the Singular as well as in the Third Plural (*od-o; od-i; od-e; od-ono*) while the First and Second person Plural are formed on another Base, *ud-*, the same we find in the Infinitive form. This verb has therefore two Bases, whose distribution is not casual (Thornton 2005: 123): in Italian many Verbs show a distribution with a Base 2, upon which the Singular forms plus the Third Plural forms are formed, and a Base 1 upon which the First and Second persons of Plural plus the Infinitive are built. This is the case of Italian Verbs such as *sedere* 'to sit down,' where we find a Base 1 *sed-* (in the Infinitive, but also in the 1P and 2P of the Main Present: *sed-iamo, sed-ete*) opposed to a Base 2 *sied-* that fills the cells of the Singular persons of Present Indicative plus the Third Plural (*sied-o, sied-i, sied-e, sied-ono*). This opposition naturally seems to be explainable by virtue of historical phonology:

TABLE 35   N distribution: the (literary) Italian Verb *udire* 'to hear'[a]

	Main Present	Subjunctive Present
1S	**odo** /ˈɔdo/	**oda** /ˈɔda/
2S	**odi** /ˈɔdi/	**oda** /ˈɔda/
3S	**ode** /ˈɔde/	**oda** /ˈɔda/
1P	*udiamo* /uˈdjamo/	*udiamo* /uˈdjamo/
2P	*udite* /uˈdite/	*udiate* /uˈdjate/
3P	**odono** /ˈɔdono/	**odano** /ˈɔdano/

a   The close-mid vs. open-mid distinction in vowels only applies to literary Italian and a few spoken vareties; it is of course absent in the regional Italian of Piedmont. The verb itself is rarely if ever used in spoken Italian.

Italian phonological system knows the so-called "mobile diphthong" (Serianni 1989: 22–23). But the historical explanation does not fill the contemporary synchronic situation, because there is no rule universally valid for predicting the presence or absence of the "mobile diphthong" in an Italian Verb conjugation.

This is the reason why Maiden (2009) proposes that in the Romance domain in general the partition of verbal stems, or morphomes (Aronoff 1994), plays a very important role in the morphological system. The partition of a Verb such as Italian *udire*, for example, is a typical case of "N distribution" (Maiden 2009: 51–53) widespread in Romance.

Here and in Tables 35 to 49, in order to make forms in Base 1 and 2 maximally distinctive, both data and transcriptions of Base 1 forms will be bold, while Base 2 (and, occasionally, Base 3) data will be in italics (and their transcription bold italics).

Beside the "N distribution," Romance languages show a "L distribution" in which only 1S of Main Present has a final consonant that appears in all the Subjunctive Present inflection. In this distribution scheme, Base 2 works for 1S of the Main Present and for the entire Subjunctive Present, while Base 1 (the Base of the Infinitive) forms all the rest of the Main Present. This is the case of Portuguese *dizer* /diˈzɛr/ 'to say,' in which the voiced alveolar fricative /z/ of Base 1 is opposed to the voiced velar stop /g/ of Base 2.

This situation is the same in some peripheral Piedmontese varieties, such as the High Monregalese language of Viola (Mongia Valley), were in the same Verb a Base 1 /diʒ/ alternates with a Base 2 /dig/, but unlike Portuguese the Infinitive has a Base 3 reduced to a simple /d/.

TABLE 36   L distribution: the Portuguese Verb *dizer* 'to say'

	Main Present	Subjunctive Present
1S	digo /ˈdigu/	diga /ˈdigə/
2S	*dizes* /ˈdizəʃ/	digas /ˈdigəʃ/
3S	*diz* /diʒ/	diga /ˈdigə/
1P	*dizemos* /diˈzemuʃ/	digamos /diˈgamuʃ/
2P	*dizeis* /diˈzɛjʃ/	digais /diˈgajʃ/
3P	*dizem* /ˈdizẽ/	digam /ˈdigɐ̃/

TABLE 37   L distribution: the Verb *dì* 'to say' in the Piedmontese variety of Viola

	Main Present	Subjunctive Present
1S	e digh /e=ˈdig/	ch'e diga /k=e=ˈdiga/
2S	ti dis(i) /ti=ˈdiʒ(i)/	ch'ti dighi /k=ti=ˈdigi/
3S	o/a dis /o/a=ˈdiʒ/	ch'o/a diga /k=o/a=ˈdiga/
1P	e disòma /e=diˈʒɔma/	ch'e dígmon /k=e=ˈdigmoŋ/
2P	e disi /e=ˈdiʒi/	ch'e dighi /k=e=ˈdigi/
3P	i/e díson /i/e=ˈdiʒoŋ/	ch'i/e dígon /k=i/e=ˈdigoŋ/

In some other Romance Verbs the distribution of a distinctive consonant (e.g., /g/ in Tables 36 and 37) occupies not only the cells of Present Subjunctive and of 1S, but also 3P of the Main Present. These are examples of another partition system, called by Maiden (2009: 47) "U pattern." It seems to be a simple variant of the "L distribution" pattern and it is very widespread in Italian: it suffices to consider Verbs like *crescere* 'grow up,' where the Base 1 /kreʃː/ opposes Base 2 /kresk/ (see Table 38).

The U pattern has undergone a further evolution, because all the Romance territories (except Iberia and Sardinia) tend to cancel the difference between U and N pattern in the First and Second person Plural of Present Subjunctive.

In this perspective, it is possible to find many examples of verbal partition in Piedmontese. First of all, it appears clear that in Piedmontese paradigms the forms stressed on the verbal root are more in number than in Italian, in Occitan or in French: indeed, the whole Main Present and Subjunctive Present (but

VERBS

TABLE 38   U distribution: the Italian Verb *crescere* 'to grow'

	Main Present	Subjunctive Present
1S	cresco /ˈkresko/	cresca /ˈkreska/
2S	*cresci* /**ˈkreʃi**/	cresca /ˈkreska/
3S	*cresce* /**ˈkreʃe**/	cresca /ˈkreska/
1P	*cresciamo* /kreˈʃamo/	cresciamo /kreˈʃamo/
2P	*crescete* /kreˈʃete/	cresciate /kreˈʃate/
3P	crescono /ˈkreskono/	crescano /ˈkreskano/

for the First person Plural) show a form in which the stress lies on the verbal root itself, not on the morphological ending. This clearly means that in order to find the partitions strictly connected to the stress position we have to assume a different point of view: even the "N pattern" will have a shape that does not correspond to the one we can find in other Romance languages. Nevertheless, partitions are without doubt very relevant in the Piedmontese paradigms system. Tables 39–43 show a series of possible oppositions between Base 1 (unstressed on the verbal root) and Base 2 (with stress on the verbal root):[15]

TABLE 39   U distribution: the Piedmontese Verbs *soné* 'to play music' (Base 1 son /sun/, Base 2 *son-*/suŋ/) and *porté* 'to bring, carry' (*Base 1* port /purt/, Base 2 pòrt /pɔrt/)

Main Present	Subjunctive Present	Main Present	Subjunctive Present
son-o /ˈsuŋu/	son-a /ˈsuŋa/	pòrto /ˈpɔrtu/	pòrta /ˈpɔrta/
son-e(s) /ˈsuŋe(z)/	son-e(s) /ˈsuŋe(z)/	pòrte(s) /ˈpɔrte(z)/	pòrte(s) /ˈpɔrte(z)/
son-a /ˈsuŋa/	son-a /ˈsuŋa/	pòrta /ˈpɔrta/	pòrta /ˈpɔrta/
sonoma /suˈnuma/	son-o /ˈsuŋu/	*portoma* /purˈtuma/	pòrto /ˈpɔrtu/
son-e /ˈsuŋe/	son-e /ˈsuŋe/	pòrte /ˈpɔrte/	pòrte /ˈpɔrte/
son-o /ˈsuŋu/	son-o /ˈsuŋu/	pòrto /ˈpɔrtu/	pòrto /ˈpɔrtu/

---

15   Verbal forms of Piedmontese koine are reported without any subject clitic unless otherwise stated.

TABLE 40   U distribution: the Piedmontese Verbs *prové* 'to prove' (Base 1 prov /pruv/, Base 2 *preuv* /prøv/ and *durmì* 'to sleep' (Base 1 *durm* /dyrm/, Base 2 *deurm* /dørm/)

	Main Present	Subjunctive Present	Main Present	Subjunctive Present
1S	preuvo /ˈprøvu/	preuva /ˈprøva/	deurmo /ˈdørmu/	deurma /ˈdørma/
2S	preuve(s) /ˈprøve(z)/	preuve(s) /ˈprøve(z)/	deurme(s) /ˈdørme(z)/	deurme(s) /ˈdørme(z)/
3S	preuva /ˈprøva/	preuva /ˈprøva/	deurm /dørm/	deurma /ˈdørma/
1P	*provoma* /pruˈvuma/	*preuvo* /ˈprøvu/	*durmoma* /dyrˈmuma/	deurmo /ˈdørmu/
2P	preuve /ˈprøve/	preuve /ˈprøve/	deurme /ˈdørme/	deurme /ˈdørme/
3P	preuvo /ˈprøvu/	preuvo /ˈprøvu/	deurmo /ˈdørmu/	deurmo /ˈdørmu/

TABLE 41   U distribution: the Piedmontese Verbs *plé* 'to peel' (Base 1 *pl* /pl/, Base 2 *pel* /pel/) and *pentné* 'to comb' (Base 1 *pentn* /peŋtn/, Base 2 *pentèn-* /peŋˈtæŋ/)

	Main Present	Subjunctive Present	Main Present	Subjunctive Present
1S	pelo /ˈpelu/	pela /ˈpela/	pentèn-o /peŋˈtæŋu/	pentèn-a /peŋˈtæŋa/
2S	pele(s) /ˈpele(z)/	pele(s) /ˈpele(z)/	pentèn-e(s) /peŋˈtæŋe(z)/	pentèn-e(s) /peŋˈtæŋe(z)/
3S	pela /ˈpela/	pela /ˈpela/	pentèn-a /peŋˈtæŋa/	pentèn-a /peŋˈtæŋa/
1P	*ploma* /ˈpluma/	pelo /ˈpelu/	*pentnoma* /peŋtˈnuma/	pentèn-o /peŋˈtæŋu/
2P	pele /ˈpele/	pele /ˈpele/	pentèn-e /peŋˈtæŋe/	pentèn-e /peŋˈtæŋe/
3P	pelo /ˈpelu/	pelo /ˈpelu/	pentèn-o /peŋˈtæŋu/	pentèn-o /peŋˈtæŋu/

TABLE 42   U distribution: the Piedmontese Verb *sëmné* 'to sow' (Base 1 *sëmn* /səmn/, Base 2 *smèn-* /smæŋ/)

	Main Present	Subjunctive Present
1S	smèn-o /ˈsmæŋu/	smèn-a /ˈsmæŋa/
2S	smèn-e(s) /ˈsmæŋe(z)/	smèn-e(s) /ˈsmæŋe(z)/
3S	smèn-a /ˈsmæŋa/	smèn-a /ˈsmæŋa/
1P	*sëmnoma* /səmˈnuma/	smèn-o /ˈsmæŋu/
2P	smèn-e /ˈsmæŋe/	smèn-e /ˈsmæŋe/
3P	smèn-o /ˈsmæŋu/	smèn-o /ˈsmæŋu/

All these examples come from Ricca (2007, 2017), who stresses how the last two may be seen as the union of the preceeding ones. The oppositions under *soné* 'to play music' and *porté* 'to bring, carry' does not seem a true case of paradigmatic partition, because the alternation between the two different Bases is connected to some phonological rules that are still active at a general level:

TABLE 43 U distribution: the Piedmontese Verb *peisé* 'to weigh' (Base 1 *pes* /**pez**/, Base 2 *pèis* /**pæjz**/)

	Main Present	Subjunctive Present
1S	pèiso /ˈpæjzu/	pèisa /ˈpæjza/
2S	pèise(s) /ˈpæjze(z)/	pèise(s) /ˈpæjze(z)/
3S	pèisa /ˈpæjza/	pèisa /ˈpæjza/
1P	pesoma /peˈzuma/	pèiso /ˈpæjzu/
2P	pèise /ˈpæjze/	pèise /ˈpæjze/
3P	pèiso /ˈpæjzu/	pèiso /ˈpæjzu/

in accordance with these rules, in pretonic position every /ŋ/ → /n/ (*spin-a* /ˈspiŋa/ 'thorn' → *spinos* /spiˈnuz/ 'thorny') and every /ɔ/ → /u/ (*pòrta* /ˈpɔrta/ 'door' → *porton* /purˈtuŋ/ 'gate'). The examples *prové* 'to prove' and *durmì* 'to sleep,' on the contrary, may be considered true cases of a paradigmatic partition of the "N pattern," since the reduction of /ø/ in pretonic position is still obligatory in the paradigm, but it is not predictable—according to any phonological rule—if the final result will manifest itself as /ø/ → /u/ or as /ø/ → /y/. The alternation in *plé* 'to peel,' which Ricca (2007) considers as a sure instance of paradigmatic partition, may also be connected to the phonological rules that establish the reduction to a zero degree of each pretonic /e/ like in *pel* /**pel**/ 'skin' → *plassa* /ˈplasa/ 'bad skin,' or *vel* /**vel**/ 'fleece' → *vlù* /**vly**/ 'velvet,' and these forms are in a situation quite similar to Verbs like *soné* 'to play music' and *porté* 'to bring, carry.' This was surely the situation in old Piedmontese, and it is still so in many peripheral varieties. Today, in koine Piedmontese the presence of /e/ before the phonological stress in words such as *p(e)nel* /p(e)ˈnæl/ 'brush' and *tenent* /teˈnæŋt/ 'lieutenant' (and more in general in all the Italian borrowings) is widely considered grammatical, and that is the reason why it is possible to say—as argued by Ricca (2007)—that by now such a partition is not connected any longer to phonological rules universally operating in all the contexts. It has then acquired a purely morphologically relevant value.

As seen above, the situation appears totally different in those peripheral varieties that maintain the same scheme that probably characterized Piedmontese in the past centuries. For instance, again in the dialect of Viola, where the reduction rules /ɔ, o/ → /u, ø/ → /y/ (but also /ø/ → /u/, /ɑ/ → /a/, /a/ → /ə/, /æ/ → Ø) are universally operating, there is no distinction at all between these various groups of Verbs.

TABLE 44 The Main Present in the Piedmontese variety of Viola: Verbs *caté* /kaˈte/ 'to buy,' *pard* /pard/ 'to lose,' and *bzé* /bdze/ 'to weigh' (Subject clitics added)

1S e cät /e=ˈkɑt/	e pard /e=ˈpard/	e pès /e=ˈpæz/
2S ti cät(i) /ti=ˈkɑt(i)/	ti pardi /ti=ˈpard(i)	ti pès(i) /ti=ˈpæz(i)/
3S o/a cäta /u/a=ˈkɑta/	o/a pard /u/a=pard/	o/a pèsa /u/a=ˈpæza/
1P *e catòma* /e=kaˈtɔma/	*e përdòma* /e=pərˈdɔma/	*e bdzòma* /e=ˈbdzɔma/
2P *e catévi* /e=kaˈtevi/	*e përdévi* /e=pərˈdevi/	*e bdzévi* /e=ˈbdzevi/
3P i/e cäton /i/e=ˈkɑtoŋ/	i/e pàrdon /i/e=ˈpardoŋ/	i/e pèson /i/e=ˈpæzoŋ/

Table 44 shows the partitions exhibited by some Verbs in the Viola variety of Piedmontese.

In this peripheral variety forms such as /peˈnel/ are impossible, and from /ˈpɛna/ 'pain' is derived the First Class Verb /pne/ 'to suffer.' The partition in *bzé* /bdze/ 'to weigh' above is attested in the koine too, as in the Verb *peisé* 'to weigh,' but it manifests itself as an opposition between Base 1 *pes* /pez/ and Base 2 *pèis* /pæjz/ (cf. Table 43).

In the Viola variety there is another alternation, namely /y/ vs. /w/, which seems totally unknown to the present day koine Piedmontese:

TABLE 45 The Main Present in the Piedmontese variety of Viola: Verb *dzoé* /dzwe/ 'to play games' (Subject clitics added)

	Main Present
1S	e dzùj /e=ˈdzyj/
2S	ti dzùj /ti=ˈdzyj/
3S	o/a dzùa /u/a=ˈdzya/
1P	*e dzoòma* /e=ˈdzwɔma/
2P	*e dzoévi* /e=ˈdzwevi/
3P	i/e dzùon /i/e=ˈdzyoŋ/

Other dialectal varieties of Piedmontese, although being closer to the koine in both phonology and vocabulary, show a very divergent behaviour under a morphological point of view. It is the case of the modern town variety of ël Mondvì, in which all the oppositions between the verbal Bases seem to be almost completely effaced.

VERBS 291

TABLE 46 The Main Present in the town variety of ël Mondvì: Verb *porté* /por'te/ 'to bring, carry,' *seurte* /'sørte/ 'to go out' and *vèghe* /'væge/ 'to see' (Subject clitics added)

	porté /por'te/ 'to bring, carry'	*seurte* /'sørte/ 'to go out'	*vèghe* /'væge/ 'to see'
1S	i port /i='port/	i seurt /i='sørt/	i vègh /i='væg/
2S	it pòrti /it 'porti/	it seurte /it='sørti/	it vèghi /it='vægi/
3S	o/a pòrta /u/a='porta/	o/a seurta /u/a='sørta/	o/a vèga /u/a='væga/
1P	*i portoma* /i=pɔr'tuma/	*i sortoma* /i=sur'tuma/	*i vegoma* /i=væ'guma/
2P	i pòrti /i='porti/	i seurti /i='sørti/	i vèghi /i='vægi/
3P	i pòrto /i='portu/	i seurto /i='sørtu/	i vègo /i='vægu/

In all these Verbs the "N pattern" distribution has been dropped and only one base (the original Base 1) is used for all the Present Indicative and Subjunctive.

As for the "L pattern" partition, in the koine it is widely attested in the irregular monosyllabic Verbs of the First Class (☞ 10.2.4.1.). In the fourth of these, *andé* 'to go,' the alternation appears strictly interlaced with an original "N pattern" that has been someway kept thanks to a kind of suppletive alternation (Ricca 2007, 2017):

TABLE 47 L distribution: the Piedmontese Verbs *dé* /de/ 'to give' (Base 1 *d* /d/, Base 2 *dag* /dag/) and *fé* /fe/ 'to do, make' (Base 1 *f* /f/, Base 2 *fas* /faz/)

	Main Present	Subjunctive Present	Main Present	Subjunctive Present
1S	dago /'dagu/	daga /'daga/	faso /'fazu/	fasa /'faza/
2S	das /daz/	daghe(s) /'dage(z)/	fas /faz/	fase(s) /'faze(z)/
3S	da /da/	daga /'daga/	fa /fa/	fasa /'faza/
1P	doma /'duma/	dago /'dagu/	foma /'fuma/	faso /'fazu/
2P	deve /'deve/	daghe /'dage/	feve /'feve/	fase /'faze/
3P	dan /daŋ/	dago /'dagu/	fan /faŋ/	faso /'fazu/

As far as the Second Class of Verbs is concerned, one finds some other examples of a sort of hybridation between the L and the N pattern, where the Second person Plural has not preserved its original stem; the latter has been modeled on the Second Singular and often merged with it. Table 49 illustrates this pattern.

TABLE 48   L distribution: the Piedmontese Verbs *sté* /*ste*/ 'to stay' (Base 1 *st* /*st*/, Base 2 *stag* /*stag*/) and *andé* 'to go' (Base 1 *and* /*and*/, Base 2 *v* /*v*/, Base 3 *vad* /*vad*/; Bases 2 and 3 graphically conflated)

	Main Present	Subjunctive Present	Main Present	Subjunctive Present
1S	stago /ˈstagu/	staga /ˈstaga/	vado /ˈvadu/	vada /ˈvada/
2S	stas /staz/	staghe(s) /ˈstage(z)/	vas /vaz/	vade(s) /ˈvade(z)/
3S	sta /sta/	staga /ˈstaga/	va /va/	vada /ˈvada/
1P	stoma /ˈstuma/	stago /ˈstagu/	andoma /əŋˈduma/	vado /ˈvadu/
2P	steve /ˈsteve/	staghe /ˈstage/	andeve /əŋˈdeve/	vade /ˈvade/
3P	stan /staŋ/	stago /ˈstagu/	van /vaŋ/	vado /ˈvadu/

TABLE 49   L distribution: the Piedmontese Verbs *podèj* /*puˈdæj*/ 'can' (Base 1 *pod* /*pud*/, Base 2 *peul* /*pøl*/, Base 3 **peuss** /*pøs*/) and *vorèj* /*vuˈræj*/ 'to want' (Base 1 *vor* /*vur*/, Base 2 *veul* /*vøl*/, Base 3 *veuj* /*vøj*/; Bases 2 and 3 graphically conflated)

	Main Present	Subjunctive Present	Main Present	Subjunctive Present
1S	peuss /pøs/	peussa /ˈpøsa/	veuj /vøj/	veuja /ˈvøja/
2S	peule(s) /ˈpøle(z)/	peusse(s) /ˈpøse(z)/	veule(s) /ˈvøle(z)/	veuje(s) /ˈvøje(z)/
3S	peul /pøl/	peussa /ˈpøsa/	veul /vøl/	veuja /ˈvøja/
1P	podoma /puˈduma/	peusso /ˈpøsu/	voroma /vuˈruma/	veujo /ˈvøju/
2P	peule /ˈpøle/	peusse /ˈpøse/	veule /ˈvøle/	veuje /ˈvøje/
3P	peulo /ˈpølu/	peusso /ˈpøsu/	veulo /ˈvølu/	veujo /ˈvøju/

As shown by Ricca (2007, 2017), Piedmontese offers many interesting examples of a new partition totally unknown to Italian and to many other Romance varieties and characterized by the insertion of a non-etymological voiced fricative in the Main Imperfect of a wide series of Verbs built on monosyllabical roots.

The trigger of this new partition is indeed the Verb *fé* /fe/ 'to do, make' whose Base for the Main Imperfect is *fas* /faz/, on which the Gerund too is formed: *fasìa* /faˈzia/, *fasend* /faˈzæŋd/.

By attraction, this partition has been extended to the other irregular Verbs belonging to the First Class: we have therefore *dé* /de/: *dasìa* /daˈzia/, *dasend* /daˈzæŋd/; *sté* /ste/: *stasìa* /staˈzia/, *stasend* /staˈzæŋd/; *andé* /aŋˈde/: *andasìa* /aŋdaˈzia/, *andasend* /aŋdaˈzæŋd/.

VERBS 293

An analogical process takes place for the Verb *dì* /di/ 'to say', whose model *disìa* /di'zia/, *disend* /di'zæŋd/ exerts its attractive force on *ven-e* /'veɲe/ or *vnì* /vni/ (*vnisìa* /vni'zia/, *vnisend* /vni'zæŋd/), as well as on *ten-e* /'teɲe/ or *tnì* /tni/ (*tnisìa* /tni'zia/, *tnisend* /tni'zæŋd/): in both of these forms, obviously, the presence of /z/ has no etymological justification.

10.5 Moods and Tenses

10.5.1 *Main*

The Main mood basically expresses reality. It is therefore no surprise that it has, together with the Subjunctive, the greatest number of tense distinctions and it is also the most widely-used mood in everyday speech. The Main is as such left untagged in glosses, the Tense only being glossed. The Main has one tense dedicated to states of affairs which are thought of as occurring at the time of utterance, i.e. Present (PRS). The other three tenses are used to refer to states of affairs which are thought of, at different levels, as happened or started before the time of utterance (Imperfect, Past, Pluperfect). This distinction is merely based on the tense category. In fact, Piedmontese verbal system expresses through tense variation two other categories, namely aspect and action.

10.5.1.1 Main Present

Main Present (PRS) basically expresses proximity between event and utterance. In this sense, it is a deictic tense and can be associated with Adverbs or adverbials such as *adess* /a'dæs/ or *àora* /'awra/ 'now,' *ant ës moment-sì* /aŋt=əs=mumæŋt='si/ 'at this very moment,' *sùbit* /'sybit/ 'at once.' With *sùbit* a durative Verb is normally barred and when used with a durative Verb, the Verb takes on an inchoative sense:

(14)   *sùbit i tribulo
       'sybit   i=tri'byl-u
       at_once   SBJ.1=suffer-PRS.1S
       'at first I have troubles'

(15)   *sùbit i tribulo a capilo*
       'sybit   i=tri'byl-u   a=ka'pi=l-u
       at_once   SBJ.1=suffer-PRS.1S   ADE=understand\INF=OBJ.3-M
       'at first I have troubles understanding him'

Adverbs like *adess* and *àora* associated with the Main Present may refer to a wider extension of time. They are then equivalent to other adverbials like *st'ann* /st=an/ 'this year' or *al di d'ancheuj* /a=l=di d=aŋ'køj/ 'nowadays.'

(16) *ël sol a l'é na stèila*
    əl=ˈsul   a=ˈle   n-a=ˈstæjl-a
    DET=sun SBJ.3=be\PRS.3S INDEF-F=star-S
    'sun is a star'

In these cases there is no direct relation between the utterance time and the propositional content, since the latter refers to a scientific truth. In this function, the Main Present normally occurs with stative Verbs, except for gnomic uses:

(17) *la cativa lavandera a treuva mai la bon-a pera*
    l-a=kaˈtiv-a   lavaŋˈder-a   a=ˈtrøv-a   maj   l-a=ˈbuŋ-a
    DET-F=mean-F washerwoman-S SBJ.3=find-PRS.3 never DET-F =good-F
    ˈper-a
    stone-S
    'the bad washerwoman never finds the good stone'

Sometimes, the Main Present is used to express an event that clearly precedes the utterance moment, especially for narrative or dramatic purposes. It can co-occur with the Imperfect, Past and Pluperfect.

(18) *lor a l'ero già tuti intrà an ca, mi i son ancora nen rivà dal cancel e sùbit am ven ancontra un can talment gròss ch'a së smijava 'n vitel*
    lur   a=ˈleru   dʒa   ˈtyt-i iŋˈtr-a   aŋ=ˈka /   mi
    IDP.3P SBJ.3=be\IMPF3P already all-P enter-PTCL INE=house / IDP.1S
    i=ˈsuŋ   aŋˈkura næŋ riˈv-a   da=l=kaŋˈtʃel e   ˈsybit
    SBJ.1=be\PRS.1S still   NEG arrive-PTCL ABL=DEF=gate and at_once
    a=m=ˈvæŋ   aŋˈkuŋtra aŋ=ˈkaŋ   talˈmæɲt gros
    SBJ.3=OBJ.1S=come\PRS.3S in_face   INDEF=dog so   big
    k=a=sə=smi-ˈava   ŋ=viˈtel
    SUB=SBJ.3=REFL=look_like-IMPF.3S INDEF=veal
    'everybody else had already gone in the house; I have not yet reached the gate and suddenly a dog comes toward me, so big that it looked like a calf'
    (overheard conversation in Crava,[16] Jan. 20, 2017)

---

16   Piedmontese and Italian Crava /ˈkrava/; a separate village within the municipality of La Ròca /la=ˈroka/ (Italian Rocca de' Baldi /rokka=de=ˈbaldi/; 44°26′N 07°45′E).

On the contrary, the Main Present is very often used to express events that will take place in a time that follows the moment of utterance (so-called *Praesens pro Futuro* 'Present in the place of Future'). It is the default construction for expressing future in Piedmontese, especially when it is preceded or followed by Adverbs and adverbials such as *dòp* /dop/ 'afterwards,' *peui* /pøj/ 'afterwards,' *pì tard* /pi='tard/ 'later,' *da sì 'n pòch* /da='si ŋ='pok/ 'in a few time,' *da sì doe ore* /da='si du-e='ur-e/ 'in a two hours time,' *doman* /du'maŋ/ 'tomorrow,' or more specifically an imminent future:

(19) *doman a diso ch'a pieuv*
    du'maŋ   a='dizu   k=a='pjøv
    tomorrow SBJ.3=say\PRS.3P SUB=SBJ.3=rain\PRS.3S
    'they say that tomorrow it will rain'

(20) *da sì 'n mèis a-i riva ij mè parent american*
    da='si   ŋ='mæjz   a=j='riv-a   i='me
    ABL=here INDEF=month   SBJ.3=IND=arrive-PRS.3S   DET\P=POSS.1S
    pa'ræŋt   ameri'kaŋ
    relative American
    'in a month my American relatives will arrive'

As far as verbal aspect is concerned, Main Present displays both imperfective and perfective senses, but imperfective ones are much more common. In many imperfective uses it can be substituted by the Progressive periphrasis (☞ 11.5.) *esse an camin che/esse an camin che*:

(21) *a fiòca*
    a='fjok-a
    SBJ.3=snow-PRS.3S
    'it is snowing'

(21') *a l'é an camin ch'a fiòca*
    a='le   aŋ=kamiŋ k=a='fjok-a
    SBJ.3=be\PRS.3S   INE=way   SUB=SBJ.3=snow-PRS.3S
    'it is snowing'

(22) *Lorens adess a fà sin-a*
    lu'ræŋs a'des a='fa   'siŋ-a
    L.   now   SBJ.3=do\PRS.3S dinner-s
    'Lorens is having dinner now'

(22′) *Lorens adess a l'é an camin ch'a fà sin-a*
    lu'ræŋs a'des a='le   aŋ=ka'miŋ k=a='fa
    L.   now SBJ.3=be\PRS.3S INE=way SUB=SBJ.3=do\PRS.3S
    'siŋ-a
    dinner-S
    'Lorens is having dinner now'

On the other hand, the Main Present takes on a perfective reading when the imminent conclusion of a process is intended, as in

(23) *i son sùbit da chiel, monsù*
    i='suŋ   'sybit   da='kjæl /   muŋ'sy
    SBJ.1=be\PRS.1S at_once ABL=IDP.3M / Mister
    'I will be at your service immediately, Sir'

10.5.1.2 Main Imperfect

As a tense, the Main Imperfect (IMPF) basically expresses simultaneousness in the past:

(24) *ier mentre ch'a **piuvìa** i lesìa 'd poesie*
    jer   'mæŋtre k=a=pjy'via   i=le'zia
    yesterday while   SUB=SBJ.3=rain\IMPF.3S SBJ.1=read\IMPF.1S
    d=pue'zi-e
    ATTR=poetry-P
    'yesterday while it was raining I read some poems'

Imperfect can be regarded as "the present in the past:"

(25) *Pòl ier a l'ha dime: "Adess i son pròpi strach"*
    pol jer   a='la   di=me   a'des
    P. yesterday SBJ.3=have\PRS.3S say\PTCL=OBJ.1S now
    i='suŋ   'propi strak
    SBJ.1=BE\PRS.1S really tired
    'Pòl yesterday told me: "Now I am really tired."'

(26) *Pòl ier a l'ha dime che an col moment-là a **l'era** pròpi strach*
    pol jer   a='la   di=me   ke aŋ='kul
    P. yesterday SBJ.3=have\PRS.3S say\PTCL=OBJ.1S SUB INE=DIST
    mu'mæŋt=la   a='lera   'propi strak
    moment=there SBJ.3=be\IMPF.3S really tired
    'Pòl yesterday told me that he was very tired in that moment'

(25) contains direct speech with Main Present. When transforming it into an indirect speech, a Main Imperfect form is required ((26)).

Imperfect may also express the habitual aspect of an action, normally with Adverbs or adverbials such as *sempre* /ˈsæmp(r)e/ 'always,' *tuti ij di* /tyt-i iˈdi/ 'everyday,' *ògni sman-a* /ˈoɲi zˈmaŋ-a/ 'every week,' and so on.

(27) *tuti j'istà ij fieuj a **andasio** an colònia*
ˈtyt-i   j=isˈta   i=ˈfjøj   a=aŋdaˈziu
all-M.P DET\P=summer DET\P=boy\P SBJ.3=go\IMPF.3P
aŋ=kuˈlonj-a
INE=summer_camp-S
'each summer the kids used to go to the summer camp'

In all these cases, the Main Imperfect refers to events or states of affairs that have taken place prior to the utterance moment. The distance between the two moments may be very long:

(28) *j'antich abitant dël Piemont a **l'ero** ij Gaj e ij Ligurian*
j=aŋˈtik   abiˈtaŋt   d=əl=pieˈmuŋt   a=ˈlero
DET\P=ancient inhabitant ATTR=DET=Piedmont SBJ.3=be\IMPF.3P
i=ˈgaj   e   i=ligyˈrjaŋ
DET\P=Gaul\P and DET\P=Ligurian
'the ancient inhabitants of Piedmont were the Gauls and the Ligurians'

The Main Imperfect may be also used to express the future in the past. Examples (29) and (30) may be classified as instances of prospective Imperfect.

(29) *ier chila a l'ha dime che sò òm a **vnisìa** ancheuj*
jer   ˈkila   a=ˈla   di=me   ke
yesterday IDP.3F SBJ.3=have\PRS.3S say\PTCL=OBJ.1S SUB
so=ˈom   a=vniˈzia   aŋˈkøj
POSS.3=man SBJ.3=come\IMPF3S today
'yesterday she told me that her husband would come today'

When part of a conditional clause the Main Imperfect may have a futural value:

(30) *se ij murador a **finìo** 'l travaj sta sman-a i **pudìo** già cangé ca dumìnica*
se i=myraˈdur   a=fiˈniu   l=traˈvaj   sta=ˈzmaŋ-a
if DET\P=bricklayer SBJ.3=finish\IMPF.3P DET=work PROX-F=week-S

>   i=pu'diu   dʒa   kaŋ'dʒ-e   ka   dy'minik-a
>   SBJ.1=can/IMPF.1P already change-INF house Sunday-S
>   'if the bricklayers finished their work this week, we could have moved next Sunday'

The Main Imperfect also displays some modal values, which do not depend on tense or aspect parameters. For instance, it is normally used for expressing imminence ((31)), hypothetical statements and also an instance of what Bertinetto (2001: 82) has called an "epistemic Imperfect" ((32)) or a mild request ((33)):

(31) *mi i vnisìa da ti, cand it l'has soname 'l ciochin*
     mi   i=vni'zia   da='ti   kaŋd it='laz
     IDP.1S SBJ.1=come\IMPF.1S ABL=IDP.2S when SBJ.2S=have\PRS.2S
     su'n-a=me   l=tʃu'kiŋ
     play-PTCL=OBJ.1S DET=bell
     'I was going to visit you, when you rang the bell of my house'

(32) *le masnà a **dovìo** già esse sì, ma a l'é rivaje gnun*
     l-e=maz'na   a=du'viu   dʒa   'ese   si / ma
     DET-F.P=child SBJ.3=must\IMPF.3P already be\INF here / but
     a='le   ri'v-a=je   ɲyŋ
     SBJ.3=be\PRS.3S come-PTCL=IND nobody
     'the children should be here by now, but nobody arrived'

(33) *mi i **volìa** doi chilo 'd pan*
     mi   i=vu'lia   duj 'kilu d='paŋ
     IDP.1S SBJ.1=want\IMPF.1S two kilo ATTR=bread
     'I want two kilos bread'

The aspectual value of the Main Imperfect is basically connected to its imperfective nature. This fact implies that the states of affairs expressed by the tense are normally characterized by indeterminatedness and sometimes by mere virtuality. It may have a perfective value when used as a prospective Imperfect.

Another type of Main Imperfect

In the formation of the Main Imperfect the koine displays an opposition between the Verbs belonging to First Class and all the other Verbs. While First Class Verbs form their Main Imperfect with the suffix *-av-* (*i cant-av-a, it cant-av-e, a cant-av-a* and so on), the other inflectional groups display a different suffix, i.e. *-ì-* (*i sav-ì-a, it sav-ì-e, a sav-ì-a* from *savèj* 'to know;' *i les-ì-a, it les-ì-e, a les-ì-a* from *lese* 'to read;' *i fin-ì-a, it fin-ì-e, a fin-ì-a* from *finì* 'to finish'). Such an opposition can be found almost everywhere in Piedmont, but there are a few varieties (such as the dialect of ël Mondvì, of Neuve and the Canavzan dialects) that tend to uniform the system by extending the usage of the suffix *-(a)v-* to all the inflectional schemes: *i les-av-a, it les-av-i, o/a les-av-a* from *lese* 'to read;' *i fin-iv-a, it fin-iv-i, o/a fin-iv-a* from *finì* 'to finish.' These examples are from the ël Mondvì dialect, in which this trend reaches its widest extension and even the Main Imperfect of *esse* 'to be' sounds *i é-v-a, it é-v-i, o/a ř̃é-v-a*, and so on.

10.5.1.3   Main Past

The Main Past (PST) is a compound form made up of an Auxiliary (in its Present tense) and a Participle. As for the Auxiliary, Intransitive Verbs are divided in two classes: unergative Verbs require *avèj* /a'væj/ 'to have' like transitive active Verbs, because their sole argument is treated as an external argument, i.e a subject; unaccusative Verbs require *esse* /'ese/ 'to be' like transitive passive Verbs, because their sole argument is treated as an internal argument, i.e. as an object (the issue is further discussed under 10.6. and 12.6.1.).

The Main Past normally expresses a state of affairs prior to the moment of utterance, like the Imperfect. The difference from Imperfect is basically aspectual: unlike Imperfect, Past has a resultative and perfective value (see Harris 1982):

(34) *ier mè frel a lesìa tò liber*
   jer   me='frel   a=le'zia   to='libær
   yesterday POSS.2S=brother SBJ.3=read\IMPF.3S POSS.2S=book
   'yesterday my brother was reading your book'

(35) *ier mè frel a l'ha lesù tò liber*
   jer   me='frel   a='la   le'z-y
   yesterday POSS.2S=brother SBJ.3=have\PRS.3S read-PTCL
   to='libær
   POSS.2S=book
   'yesterday my brother read your book'

In (34) the utterance does not make any reference to the end of the process: the listener cannot understand if my brother did or not finish the reading, while in (35) it is clearly expressed. There is no difference in the temporal dimension: the difference lays only in the aspect.

In a subordinate clause it may simply express priority with respect to the state of affairs of the regent clause in (36)

(36) *stassèira i devo andé via, doman i-j diso al professor ch'i l'hai nen studià*
  sta'sæjra i='devu   aŋ'de via / du'maŋ
  tonight SBJ.1=must\PRS.1S go\INF away / tomorrow
  i=j='dizu   a=l=prufe'sur k=i='laj   næŋ
  SBJ.1=IND=say\PRS.1S ADE=DET=professor SUB=SBJ.1=have\PRS.1S NEG
  sty'dj-a
  study-PTCL
  'tonight I have to go out, tomorrow I will tell the teacher that I did not study'

In this sentence, all the states of affairs are located in a time that follows the moment of utterance. Nevertheless, the tense does not lose its perfective value; it is simply prior to the reference's moment, not to the utterance's.

The Main Past may take also the value of a future when it is used with Adverbs or adverbials such as *doman* /du'maŋ/ 'tomorrow,' *da sì quajch di* /da_si=kwaj='di/ 'in a few days,' and so on. The Adverbs and adverbials specify the reference moment which the Past is prior to.

(37) *che bel, doman i l'hai finì j'esam*
  ke=bel / du'maŋ i='laj   fi'n-i   j=e'zam
  SUB=nice / tomorrow SBJ.1=have\PRS.1S finish-PTCL DET\P=exam
  'how nice, tomorrow I will have finished my examinations!'

Sometimes, however, it does not express any priority to the reference moment but it simply conveys that an event has already happened at least one time in the past: it is the "experiential Past" in which no temporal anchorage is concerned:

(38) *mi a Paris i son già staje*
  mi a=pa'riz i='suŋ   dʒa 'sta=je
  IDP.1S ADE=Paris SBJ.1=be\PRS.1S already stay\PTCL=IND
  'I have already been to Paris'

10.5.1.4 Main Pluperfect

Like the Main Past, the Main Imperfect is a compound form. The auxiliary selection follows the same rules of the Past, but the auxiliary displays Imperfect tense:

(39) *sta sman-a i **l'hai ciapà** l'influensa e i **son pijame** na patela 'd meisin-e për femla passé*
    sta='zmaŋ-a   i='laj   tʃa'p-a   l=iŋfly'æŋs-a e
    PROX-F=week-S SBJ.1=have\PRS.1S catch-PTCL DET=flu-S and
    i='suŋ   'pja=me   n-a=pa'tel-a   d=mæj'ziŋ-e
    SBJ.1=be\PRS.1S take-PTCL=OBJ.1S INDEF-F=blow-S ATTR=drug-P
    pər='fe=m=l-a   pa's-e
    BEN=make\INF=OBJ.1S=OBJ.3-F pass-INF
    'this week I caught the flu and I took a lot of medicines to get over it'

(40) *sman-a passà i **l'avìa ciapà** l'influensa e i **j'era pijame** na patela 'd meisin-e për femla passé*
    'zmaŋ-a pa's-a   i=la'via   tʃa'p-a   l=iŋfly'æŋs-a e
    week-S pass-PTCL SBJ.1=have\IMPF.1S catch-PTCL DET=flu-S and
    i='jera   'pja=me   n-a=pa'tel-a   d=mæj'ziŋ-e
    SBJ.1=be\IMPF.1S take-PTCL=OBJ.1S INDEF-F=blow-S ATTR=drug-P
    pər='fe=m=l-a   pa's-e
    BEN=make\INF=OBJ.1S=OBJ.3-F pass-INF
    'last week I caught the flu and I took a lot of medicines to get over it'

The Pluperfect implies a reference moment located in the past, between the event and the utterance's moment. That is why it is widely used in temporal clauses ((41)) and in causal clauses ((42)), but also in relative clauses ((43)) and completive clauses ((44)):

(41) *dòp ch'a **l'avìa telefoname** a mi a l'ha 'dcò ciamà mia fomna*
    dop k=a=la'via   telefu'n-a=me   a='mi
    after SUB=SBJ.3=have\IMPF.3S phone-PTCL=OBJ.1S ADE=OBJ.1S
    a='la   d'ko tʃa'm-a   'mi-a   'fumn-a
    SBJ.3=have\PRS.3S also call-PTCL POSS.1S-F woman-S
    'after he [had] phoned me he called my wife too'

(42) *sicome ch'a **l'avìo mai tastà** la bagna càuda, ij matòt scossèis a j'ero un pòch genà*
    si'kume k=a=la'viu   maj tas't-a   l-a='baɲ-a
    since   SUB=SBJ.3=have\IMPF.3P never taste-PTCL DET-F=sauce-S
    'kawd-a / i=ma'tot   sku'sæjz a='jeru   aŋ='pok
    hot-F   DET\P=lad Scottish SBJ.3=be\IMPF.3P INDEF=bit
    dʒe'n-a
    be_shy-PTCL

'since they had never tasted the *bagna cauda*,[17] the Scottish lads were a little bewildered' (overheard conversation in ël Mondvì, Feb. 11, 2017)

(43) *it l'has torna trovaje j'ociaj ch'it l'avìe përdù?*
    it='laz   'turna tru'v-a=je   j=u'tʃaj
    SBJ.2S=have\PRS.2S again find-PTCL=OBJ.3P DET\P=glass\P
    k=it=la'vie   pər'd-y ↗
    SUB=SBJ.2S=have\IMPF.2S lose-PTCL Q
    'did you find [again] the glasses you had lost?'

(44) *it lo savìe già che gnun ëd nojàutri a l'avìa mai vistlo prima*
    it=l-u=sa'vie   dʒa ke ɲyŋ əd=nu'jawtri
    SBJ.2S=OBJ.3-M=know/IMPF.2S already SUB nobody ATTR=IDP.1P
    a=la'via   maj 'vist-l-u   'prima
    SBJ.3=have\IMPF.3S never seen\PTCL=OBJ.3-M before
    'you already knew that none of us had ever seen him before'

The Pluperfect is often used in independent clauses in order to create a psychological distance between the event moment and the utterance's moment. Therefore, it may take the function to attenuate the utterance, diminishing the hearer's expectations and the social involvement of the speaker:

(45) *i j'era mach vnù a vëdde se i l'avìi finì ël travaj*
    i='jera   mak v'ny   a='vədde   se
    SBJ.1=be\IMPFV.1S only come\PTCL ade=see\INF if
    i=la'vij   fi'ni   l=tra'vaj
    SBJ.2=have\IMPF.2P finish\PTCL DET=work
    'I just came to see if you finished the work' (overheard conversation in Moross,[18] Feb. 7, 2017)

Actually, (45) displays a prototypical modal use, that is shared by Imperfect too. In Piedmontese, unlike other Romance languages, this modal use is very common.

Another modal use of the Pluperfect is found in the apodosis of the conditional clause, like in (46)

---

17 A typical Piedmontese hot dish made from garlic and anchovies.
18 Moross /mu'rus/, Italian Morozzo /mo'rottso/ is a village in South-Western Piedmont (44°25'N 07°43'E).

(46) *se chiel at lassava fé a ti, a st'ora sì it l'avìe già bele che finì tut*
  se 'kjæl   a=t=la's-ava   fe   a='ti /
  if IDP.3M   SBJ.3=OBJ.2S=leave-IMPF.3S   make\INF   ADE=IDP.2S /
  a=st-ur-a='si   it=la'vie   dʒa   'bele ke
  ADE=PROX=hour-S=here   SBJ.2S=have\IMPF.2S   already   even   SUB
  fi'n-i   tyt
  finish-PTCL   all
  'if he only had let you do by yourself, at this time you would have had everything done already'

10.5.2 *The Subjunctive*

The Subjunctive mood has two time-defined paradigms, the Present and the Imperfect. The former is left untagged in the glosses (and "SUBJ" only is used). Two further compound tenses built on the model of the Main Past (i.e., auxiliary in the Subjunctive Present or Imperfect and Participle of the lexical Verb) are in use: a Subjunctive Present Perfect and a Subjunctive Past Perfect.

The Subjunctive is mainly used in subordinate clauses, while in independent clauses its presence is very rare. Basically, there are two possible independent subjunctives, namely optative (as in (47) and (48)) and dubitative ((49)):

(47) *s'it l'avèisse scotame...!*
  s=it=la'væjse   sko't-a=me
  if=SBJ.2S=have\SUBJ.IMPF.2S   listen-PTCL=OBJ.1S
  'if you had just listened to me ...!'

(48) *(le nìvole) podèisso slonghene un cavijon / a salvene mentre is përdoma*
  (l-e='nivul-e)   pu'dæjsu   zluŋ'g-e=ne
  (DET-F.P=cloud-P)   can\SUBJ.IMPF.3P   lengthen=INF=ATTR.PRO
  aŋ=ka'vjuŋ /   a=sal'v-e=ne   'mæntre   is=pər'duma
  INDEF=end /   ADE=save-INF=OBJ.1P   while   SBJ.1=REFL=lose\PRS.1P
  'if just (the clouds) could hand us an end (of the rope) / to save us if we get lost' (Bertolino 2006: 31)

(49) *ch'a sia già rivaje la postin-a?*
  k=a='sia   dʒa   ri'v-a=je   l-a=pust'iŋ-a
  SUB=SBJ.3=be\SUBJ.3S   already   come-PTCL=IND   DET-F=mail_woman-S
  ↗
  Q
  'maybe has the mailwoman already arrived?'

In (49) the use of the Subjunctive is an alternative option for the much more frequent Dubitative, as in (50)

(50) *a sarà già rivaje la postin-a?*
    a=sa'ra   dʒa   ri'v-a=je   l-a=pust'iŋ-a   ↗
    SBJ.3=be\DUB.3S already come-PTCL=IND DET-F=mail_woman-S Q
    'maybe has the mailwoman already arrived?' (overheard conversation in Salusse, Dec. 2016)

Subjunctive is commonly found in subordinate clauses, where it displays a close syntactic relation between the two clauses. This is why, unlike the Main mood, it follows strictly the so-called *consecutio temporum* (☞ 15.2.2.). Compare (51) and (51'), and (52) and (52'):

(51) *i savìa pa ch'it j'ere malavi*
    i=sa'via   pa   k=it='jere   malavi
    SBJ1=know\IMPF.1S NEG.EMPH SUB=SBJ.2S=be\IMPF.2S ill
    'I did not know you were ill'

(51') *i savìa pa ch'it ses malavi*
    i=sa'via   pa   k=it='sez   malavi
    SBJ1=know\IMPF.1S NEG.EMPH SUB=SBJ.2S=be\PRS.2S ill
    'I did not know you are ill'

(52) *i savìa pa ch'it fusse malavi*
    i=sa'via   pa   k=it='fyse   malavi
    SBJ1=know\IMPF.1S NEG.EMPH SUB=SBJ.2S=be\SUBJ.IMPF.2S ill
    'I did not know you were ill'

vs. ungrammatical:

(52') **i savìa pa ch'it sies malavi*
    i=sa'via   pa   k=it='sies   malavi
    SBJ1=know\IMPF.1S NEG.EMPH SUB=SBJ.2S=be\SUBJ.2S ill

While (51') is grammatical, (52') is not. When the main clause displays an Imperfect, a Past or a Pluperfect, in fact, Subjunctive Present is strictly avoided in the subordinate clause. Present is used to express simultaneousness when main clause displays a Main Present, while simultaneousness to the historical tenses (Imperfect, Past and Pluperfect) is granted by Subjunctive Imperfect. Compound tenses express priority both to Present (Subjunctive Past) and to historical tenses (Subjunctive Pluperfect).

The uses of Subjunctive in dependent clauses may be gathered in three categories:
1. volitional Subjunctive;
2. dubitative Subjunctive;
3. evaluative Subjunctive.

1. The Volitional Subjunctive is found in argument clauses ((53), (54), (55)), final clauses ((56)) and relative clauses ((57)). As for argument clauses, matrix sentences have some semantic restrictions: they must encode a Verb or a Noun expressing willing, desire, expectations, fear such as *vorèj* /vuˈræj/ 'to want,' *veuja* /ˈvøja/ 'will, wish,' *comandé* /kumaŋˈde/ 'to order,' *comand* /kuˈmaŋd/ 'order,' *damanca* /daˈmaŋka/ e *dabzògn* /dabˈzoɲ/ 'need,' *pàu* /paw/ 'fear,' and so on.

(53) *i veuj nen ch'am parlo, sa gent lì!*
    i=ˈvøj   næŋ k=a=m=ˈparl-u /
    SBJ.1=want\PRS.1S NEG SUB=SBJ.3=OBJ.1S=speak-SBJ.3P /
    s-a=dʒæɲt=ˈli
    DEICT-F=people=there
    'I do not want these people to talk to me!'

(54) *a vantava bin che i-j lo dijèisso a sò pare*
    a=vaŋˈtava   biŋ
    SBJ.3= be_necessary-IMPF.3S well
    ke=i=j=l-u=ˈdjæjsu   a =so=ˈpare
    SUB=SBJ.1=IND=OBJ.3-M=say\SUBJ.IMPF.1P ADE=POSS.3M=father
    'we really had to tell [it to] his father'

(55) *i l'avìa pàu che chila a rivèissa mai*
    i=laˈvia   paw ke   ˈkila   a=riˈvæjsa
    SBJ.1=have\IMPF.1S fear IDP.3F IDP.3F SBJ3=come\SUBJ.IMPF.3S
    maj
    never
    'I was afraid that she would never come'

(56) *ciama mach l'oberge përtant ch'an ten-o na stansia*
    ˈtʃam-a   mak l=uˈbærdʒe pərˈtaŋt k=a=n=ˈtæŋ-u
    call-IPV.2S only DET=hotel so_that SUB=SBJ.3=OBJ.1P=keep-SUBJ.3P

n-a=ˈstaŋsj-a
INDEF-F=room-S
'just call the hotel so that they keep a room booked for us'

(57) *i l'heu catame doi plòt che as **cobièisso** con mi*
i=ˈlø ka'ta=me duj plot
SBJ.1=have\PRS.1S buy\PTCL=OBJ.1S two rag
ke=a=s=kuˈbj-æjsu kuŋ=ˈmi
SUB=SBJ.3=REFL=couple-SUBJ.IMPF.3P COM=OBJ.1S
'I bought myself a couple of clothes that would fit for me' (overheard conversation in Viola, Sep. 2010)

2. **The Dubitative Subjunctive** is mostly found in argument clauses depending upon Verbs, Nouns or Adjectives (often in grammaticalized configurations, as in (61)) expressing doubt, opinion, assumption such as *chërde* /ˈkərde/ 'to believe,' *nen esse sigur* /næŋ ˈese siˈgyr/ 'not to be sure,' *nen savèj* /næŋ saˈvæj/ 'do not know,' *pënsé* /pəŋˈse/ 'to think,' *smijé* /zmiˈje/ 'to seem,' *(pa) possibil* /pa puˈsibil/ '(im)possible,' *dubi* /ˈdybi/ 'doubt.'

(58) *chërdes-to ch' a sia già rivà la magistra?*
ˈkərdes=tu k=a=ˈsia dʒa riˈv-a
think\INT.2S=INT.2S SUB=SBJ.3=be\SUBJ.3S already come-PTCL
l-a=maˈdʒistr-a ↗
DET-F=teacher-S Q
'do you think the teacher has already arrived?'

(59) *i j'era nen sigur ch'a **fussa** chila dabon*
i=ˈjera næŋ siˈgyr k=a=ˈfysa ˈkila
SBJ1=be\IMPF.1S NEG sure SUB=SBJ.3=be\SUBJ.IMPF.3S IDP.3F
daˈbuŋ
really
'I was not sure it was really her'

(60) *a l'era smijame ch'a-i **manchèissa** la sal*
a=ˈlera smiˈj-a=me
SBJ3=be\IMPF.3S seem-PTCL=OBJ.1S
k=a=j=maŋˈk-æjsa la=ˈsal
SUB=SBJ.3=IND=lack-SUBJ.IMPF.3S DET-F=salt
'I thought [it seemed to me] that there were no more salt'

(61) *gnun dubi ch'i l'avèissa rason mi*
    ɲyŋ   'dybi   k=i=la'væjsa   ra'zuŋ mi
    nobody doubt SUB=SBJ.1=have\SUBJ.IMPF.1S reason IDP.1S
    'no doubt that I was right'

The Dubitative subjunctive appears as well in some extra-nuclear sentences, for instance in temporal ((62)–(63)), causal ((64)), conditional ((65)), hypothetical comparative ((66)), and relative clauses (e.g., when they refer to a specific referent; (67) to (70)).

(62) *la mare a l'ha ciapà 'l cit prima ch'a **tombèissa** da la scala*
    la='mare   a='la   tʃa'p-a   l='tʃit   prima
    DET-F=mother SBJ.3=have\PRS.3S catch-PTCL DET=baby before
    k=a=tum'b-æjsa   da=l-a='skal-a
    SUB=SBJ.3=fall-SUBJ.IMPF.3S ABL=DET-F=stairs-S
    'the mother caught the kid before he (could) tumble down the stairs'

(63) *anans che le prime a fusso / j'ero lus dnans a la lus*
    a'naŋs ke l-e='prim-e   a='fysu /
    in_front SUB DET-F.P=spring-P SBJ.3=be\SUBJ.IMPF.3P
    i='eru   lyz dnaŋs a=l-a='lyz
    (SBJ1)=be\IMPF.1P light in_front ADE=DET-F=light
    'before there were springtimes, we were light in front of the light' (Dorato 1990: 49)

(64) *i l'heu sërnù ës can-lì nen përchè ch'a **fussa** bel, ma përché ch'am fasìa pì gòj a vëddlo*
    i='lø   sər'ny   əs=kaŋ='li   næŋ pər'kæ
    SBJ1=be\PRS.1S choose\PTCL DET =dog=there NEG because
    k=a='fysa   bel / ma pər'kæ
    SUB=SBJ.3=be\SUBJ.IMPF.3S nice / but because
    k=a=m=fa'zia   pi goj a='vədd-l-u
    SUB=SBJ.3=OBJ.1S=do\IMPF.3S more joy ADE=see\INF=OBJ.3-M
    'I chose this dog not because he was cute, but because seeing him gave me more good feelings' (overheard conversation in Carù,[19] Feb. 14, 2017)

---

19   Carù /ka'ry/, Italian Carrù /**kar'ru**/ (44°29′N 07°53′E).

(65) *s'a **vnèissa** a troveme me frel, am farìa piasì*
     s=a='vnæjsa   a=tru'v-e=me   me='frel
     if=SBJ.3=come\SUBJ.IMPF.3S ADE=find-INF=OBJ.1S POSS.1S=brother
     a=m=fa'ria   pja'zi
     SBJ.3=OBJ.1S=make\COND.IMPF.3S pleasure
     'it would be a pleasure for me if my brother comes'

(66) *ëd dolor i muirërai e i tardrai pa vàire ché mè fieul a l'é pendù com s'a fussa 'n làder!*
     əd=du'lur i=myjrə'raj   e   i=tard-'raj   pa
     ATTR=pain SBJ.1=die\DUB.1S and SBJ.1=be_late-DUB.1S NEG_EMPH
     'vajre ke me='fjøl   a='le   pæŋ'd-y kum
     several SUB POSS.1S=son SBJ.3=be\PRS.3S hang-PTCL as
     s=a='fysa   ŋ='ladær
     if=SBJ.3=be\SUBJ.IMPF.3S INDEF=thief
     'I will not delay in dying from sorrow, because my son is getting hanged as if he was a thief' (https://wikisource.org/wiki/Complenta_%C3%ABd_Turin)

(67) *conòsses-to chejdun ch'a **veuja** vagnesse doi sòld?*
     ku'noses=tu   kæj'dyŋ   k=a='vøja
     know\PRS.2SG=INT.2S someone SUB=SBJ.3=want\SUBJ.3S
     va'ɲe=se   duj sold ↗
     earn-INF=REFL two money Q
     'do you know anyone who wants to earn some money?'

(68) *i vëddo gnun-e màchine ch'am **piaso***
     i='vəddu   'ɲyŋ-e   'makin-e k=a=m='pjazu
     SBJ.1=see\PRS.1S nobody-F.P machine-P SUB=SBJ.3=OBJ.1S=like\SUBJ.3P
     'I do not see any car I like'

In this sentence the presence of a Subjunctive (rather than the homophonous Main Present) is made evident by the corresponding sentence with a singular subject:

(68') *i vëddo gnun-a màchina ch'am **piasa***
     i='vəddu   'ɲyŋ-a   'makin-a k=a=m='pjaza
     SBJ.1=see\PRS.1S nobody-F machine-S SUB=SBJ.3=OBJ.1S=like\SUBJ.3S
     'I do not see any car I like'

and the ungrammaticality of the Main:

(68″) *i vëddo gnun-a màchina ch'am pias
    i=ˈvəddu   ˈɲyŋ-a   ˈmakin-a   k=a=m=ˈpjaz
    SBJ.1=see\PRS.1S nobody-F machine-S SUB=SBJ.3=OBJ.1S=like\PRS.3S

(69) *a l'é l'òm pi furb ch'i conòssa*
    a=ˈle   l=om   pi   fyrb   k=i=kuˈnos-a
    SBJ.3=be/PRS.3S DET=man more smart SUB=SBJ.1S=know-SUBJ.PRS.1S
    'he is the smartest guy I know'

The following is also an example of Subjunctive Past:

(70) *l'unich amis ch'a l'abia giutame a l'é Luis*
    l=ˈynik   aˈmiz   k=a=ˈlabja   dʒyˈt-a=me
    DET=unique friend SUB=SBJ.3=have\SUBJ.3S help-PTCL=OBJ.1S
    a=ˈle   luˈiz
    SBJ.3=be/PRS.3S Luis
    'Luis is the only friend who helped me'

In all these cases, a dubitative Subjunctive expresses uncertainty or hypothetical statement, except for (63), where the fact that springs do exist cannot be called into question. In the relative clauses, like in (67) and (68), Subjunctive is used when the antecedent is denied or its existence is given as a mere probability. In (69) the antecedent is an Adjective in superlative degree, while in (70) the antecedent is an Adjective such as *unich* /ˈynik/ 'unique,' *sol* /sul/ 'only,' *prim* /prim/ 'first,' *ultim* /ˈyltim/ 'last.'

3. *The Thematic Subjunctive*, unlike the volitional and dubitative Subjunctives, expresses states of affairs that are not just desired nor called in question, but presupposed as real things. It is found in argument clauses depending on Verbs, Nouns and Adjectives that express an evaluation of the statement encoded in the depending sentence. The evaluation may be both ideological and affective like in *dëslaudé* /dəzlawˈde/ 'to blame,' *dzaprové* /dzapruˈve/ 'to disapprove,' *lamenté* /lamæŋˈte/ 'to lament,' *maravijesse* /maraˈvjese/ 'to wonder,' *stupisse* /styˈpise/ 'to be surprised,' *sagrinesse* /sagriˈnese/ 'to grieve,' *argioji* /ardʒuˈi/ 'to rejoice,' *argiojisse* /ardʒuˈise/ 'to be glad,' *arlegresse* /arleˈgrese/ 'to cheer up,' *scusesse* /skyˈzese/ 'to apologize,' *anrabiesse* /aŋraˈbjese/ 'to get angry,' *dësmontesse* /dəzmuŋˈtese/ 'to become annoyed,' *ringreté* /riŋgreˈte/ or *regreté* / regreˈte/ 'to regret,' *seufre* /ˈsøfre/ 'to suffer,' *content* /kuŋˈtæŋt/ 'happy,' *bel*

/bæl/ 'nice,' *lògich* /ˈlodʒik/ 'logical,' *natural* /natyˈral/ 'natural,' *gòj* /gɔj/ 'joy,' *fàit* /fajt/ 'fact,' *afé* /aˈfe/ 'matter,' *piasì* /pjaˈzi/ 'pleasure,' *dëspiasì* /dəspjaˈzi/ 'displeasure,' and so on.

(71) *am fa dëspiasì che chila a ven-a nen*
 a=m=ˈfa dəspjaˈzi ke ˈkila a=ˈvæŋ-a
 SBJ.3=OBJ.1S=do\PRS.3S displeasure SUB IDP.3F SBJ.3=come\SUBJ.3S
 næŋ
 NEG
 'the fact that she does not come gives me sorrow'

(72) *a l'é bel che ij tò fieuj a-i sio tuti!*
 a=ˈle bel ke i=to=ˈfjøj
 SBJ.3=be\PRS.3S nice SUB DET\P=POSS.2S=boy\P
 a=j=ˈsiu ˈtyt-i
 SBJ.3=IND=be\SUBJ.3P all-P
 'it is good that all of your sons are there'

(73) *a l'era lògich che coj dël pais a fasèisso visa ëd nen savejne gnente dël tut*
 a=ˈlera ˈlodʒik ke kuj d=əl=paˈiz
 SBJ.3=be\IMPF.3S logical SUB DIST\M ATTR=DET=country
 a=faˈzæjso ˈviz-a əd=næŋ saˈvæj=ne
 SBJ.3=do\SUBJ.IMPF.3P feint-F ATTR=NEG know\INF=ATTR.PRO
 ˈɲæŋte d=əl=ˈtyt
 nothing ATTR=DET=all
 'it was obvious that the villagers acted as if they knew nothing at all'

Unlike other Romance languages (Salvi and Vanelli 2004: 258–259) Piedmontese makes a scarce use of thematic Subjunctive in extra-nuclear clauses: concessive subordinate sentences are normally introduced by a complementizer such as *anche se* /ˈaŋke se/ 'even if' that requires the Main mood in the encoded clause.

Nevertheless, it is possible to find the thematic Subjunctive used in some concessive constructions. These constructions may have both factual and conditional values (Cerruti 2009: 214–216). Example (74) shows a factual sense, while (75) is a borderline constructions in which it seems not easy to understand whether a thematic or a dubitative Subjunctive is actually concerned; finally, (76) is straightforwardly dubitative:

(74) *bele che **a sia** già un mèis che a pieuv nen, Ele d'eva a n'ha ancor*
 bele ke a=ˈsia dʒa aŋ=ˈmæjz
 even SUB SBJ.3=be\SUBJ.3S already INDEF=month
 ke=a=ˈpjøv næŋ / ˈæle d=ˈev-a
 SUB=SBJ.3=rain\PRS.3S NEG / E. ATTR=water-S
 a=n=ˈa aŋˈkur
 SBJ.3=ATTR.PRO=have\PRS.3S still
 'even though it has not been raining for a month, the Ele river still has some water' (overheard conversation in ël Mondvì, Feb. 18, 2017)

(75) *bele che a **pieuva**, i ven-o 'dcò mi*
 bele k=a=ˈpjøv-a / i=ˈvæŋ-u dko mi
 even SUB=SBJ.3=rain-SUBJ.3S / SBJ.1=come\PRS.1S also IDP.1S
 'even if it is raining, I will come too'

(76) *i dovèissa ben vnì a pé, i mancrai nen*
 i=duˈvæjsa bæŋ vˈni a=ˈpe /
 SBJ.1= must\SUBJ.IMPF.1S well come.INF ADE=foot /
 i=maŋˈk-raj næŋ
 SBJ.1=miss-DUB.1S NEG
 'should I even go on foot, I won't be missing'

10.5.3 *The Dubitative*

Cordin (1997: 87) says that generally speaking in the minority languages of Italy as well as in the dialects of Italian the so-called future tense form "expresses not future time but rather an epistemic value," while the real future time is expressed by the present tense form associated with Adverbs or adverbials.

This applies to Piedmontese too, as was seen previously (cf. also Berruto 1984: 133). The so-called "future" (Aly-Belfàdel 1933: 185; Brero and Bertodatti 1988: 88) has mainly a modal value, and it is more correct to consider it not a tense but rather a mood on its own. We therefore use the label "Dubitative."

Just as the Conditional (with which the Dubitative shares the same formative, but with different affixes; ☞10.5.4.), the Dubitative is a mood with two tenses: a Present and a Past (the latter a compound form with the auxiliary in the Dubitative followed by the Participle of the lexical Verb). In glosses, the Mood only will be glossed ("DUB").

The main value of the Dubitative mood strictly adheres to its name:

(77) *j'andran-le bin a mia fija se fàude?*
   j=aŋˈdraŋ=le   biŋ   a=ˈmi-a   ˈfi-a
   IND=go\DUB.3P=SBJ.INT.3 well ADE=POSS.1S-F daughter-S
   s-e=ˈfawd-e   ↗
   DEICT-F.P=skirt-P Q
   '(do you think that) these skirts fit my daughter?'

Another common use of the Dubitative is concessive: the speaker admits a statement, but denies that it can have any impact on another statement that immediately follows:

(78) *Ghitin a sarà fòla, ma a l'é na bela fomna*
   giˈtiŋ a=saˈra   ˈfol-a / ma a=ˈle
   G.   SBJ.3=be\DUB.3S fool-F / but SBJ3=be\PRS.3S
   n-a=ˈbel-a   ˈfumn-a
   INDEF-F=beautiful-F woman-S
   'Ghitin may be stupid, but she is a beautiful woman'

With Verbs expressing assertion, confession, acknowledgment and so on, the Dubitative often displays a mitigation of the declarative illocutionary force (Van Valin and La Polla 1997):

(79) *për adess it **dirai** ch'i son sentume bin soagnà*
   pər=aˈdes i=t=diˈraj   k=i=ˈsuŋ
   BEN=now SBJ.1=OBJ.2S=say\DUB.1S SUB=SBJ.1=be\PRS.1S
   sæŋˈt-y=me   biŋ suaˈɲ-a
   hear\PTCL=OBJ.1S well treat-PTCL
   'for now I can tell you that I felt well taken care of'

Another very common use of Dubitative is epistemic: in this strictly modal value, Dubitative expresses a subjective assumption of the speaker, concerning the present state of affairs of a given situation. It is generally possible with both stative and non-stative Verbs, but with non-stative Verbs it normally requires an explicit determination of time:

(80) *mah, a **saran** tre bòt ...*
   ma /   a=saˈraŋ   træ bot
   who_knows SBJ.3=be\DUB.3P three toll
   'who knows, it is probably three o'clock'

(81) *ant ës moment sì, mia fomna a **farà** già da mangé*
 aŋt=əs=muˈmæŋt=si   ˈmi-a   ˈfumn-a a=faˈra
 INE=DEICT=moment=here POSS.1S-F woman-S SBJ.3=do\DUB.3S
 dʒa   da=maŋˈdʒ-e
 already ABL=eat-INF
 'by now, my wife will probably be cooking already'

In an interrogative sentence, a Dubitative may be changed into a Subjunctive:

(82) *a pico a la pòrta: **sarà-lo** tò fieul?*
 a=ˈpiku   a=la=ˈport-a /   saˈra=lu   to
 SBJ.3=bump-PRS.3P ADE=DET-F= door-S be\DUB.3S=SBJ.INT.3 POSS.2
 ˈfjøl ↗
 son Q
 'someone is knocking on the door: could it be your son?'

(82') *a pico a la pòrta: ch'a sia tò fieul?*
 a=ˈpiku   a=la=ˈport-a /   k=a=ˈsia
 SBJ.3=bump-PRS.3P ADE=DET-F= door-S SUB=SBJ.3=be\SUBJ.PRS.3S
 to=ˈfjøl   ↗
 POSS.2S=son Q

A last value, rare and found almost exclusively in literary texts (and most probably due to influence from neighboring Romance literary languages, such as French and Italian) is with a future temporal meaning:

(83) *un di **marcc-rai** da sol*
 aŋ=ˈdi   martʃˈraj   da=ˈsul
 INDEF=day walk\DUB.1S   ABL=alone
 'one day I'll walk alone' (Clivio 1972)

In still other cases, also found in the spoken language, Dubitative does have an apparent temporal value as well:

(84) *lassme perde, i lo **farai** doman*
 ˈlas=me   ˈpærde / i=l-u=faˈraj   duˈmaŋ
 leave(-IPV)=OBJ.1S lose\INF SBJ.1=OBJ.3-M=do\DUB.1S tomorrow
 'give me a break [let me get lost], I will do it tomorrow'

However, in such cases a difference from the same sentence in the Main Present is given again by a stress on uncertainty, doubt or lack of confidence, when using the Dubitative:

(85) *sossì i lo faso doman*
su'si   i=l-u='fazu   du'maŋ
DEICT_here SBJ.1=OBJ.3-M=do\PRS.1S tomorrow
'I am going to do it tomorrow'

Instead of (19) above, one could also have (86):

(86) *doman a **diran** ch'a pieuv*
du'maŋ   a=di'raŋ   k=a='pjøv
tomorrow SBJ.3=say\DUB.3P SUB=SBJ.3=rain\PRS.3S
'tomorrow they will say that it is going to rain'

A similar opposition is mentioned by Parry (1997: 242) who speaks of the Dubitative (which she calls future) as implying "temporally unspecified intentions," vs. the Main Present expressing "definite future commitments."

10.5.4 *The Conditional*

Morphologically, the Conditional shares the same formative with the Dubitative. Moreover, like the Dubitative, the Conditional has two tenses: a Present and a Past (the latter a compound form with the auxiliary in the Conditional followed by the Participle of the lexical Verb). In glosses, the mood only will be glossed ("COND").

As for the Dubitative, in the grammatical tradition of a few Romance languages (e.g., Catalan) it is classified among Main tenses and not treated as a Mood on its own. But in fact it is, as it expresses a state of affairs the speaker does not believe probable, even less probable than the Dubitative. Its default usage is in the consequence of a conditional clause (the subsequent, or apodosis), with the Subjunctive in the clause expressing the condition (the antecedent, or protasis):

(87) *se a feisso nen un pò pen-a, a sarìa na vera gòj*
se a='fæjsu   næŋ aŋ='po   pæŋ-a
if SBJ.3=make\SUBJ.IMPF.3P NEG INDEF=bit pity-S
a=sa'ria   n-a='ver-a   goj
SBJ.3=be\COND.3 INDEF-F=true-F joy
'if they would not move to pity, it would be a real joy' (Frusta 1969: 25)

The hypothetical statement in Subjunctive mood may lack and Conditional may be used all alone. In this case, it can express an eventuality that never took place (as in (88)), if it is used in the Past tense, or an eventuality that should actually take place according to the speaker's point of view:

(88) *a l'avrìa nen dovù pijé chiel-lì!*
    a=lav'ria   næŋ du'vy   pj-e   kjæl='li
    SBJ.3=have\COND.3S NEG must\PTCL take-INF IDP.3M=there
    'she should never have married [taken] him'

(89) *it farìe mej a tnì ël cit a ca*
    it-fa'rie   mej a='tni   əl='tʃit   a='ka
    SBJ.2S=make\COND.2S better ADE=hold-INF DET=little ADE=house
    'you would better keep (your) child at home'

(90) *mi i andarìa via sùbit*
    mi   i=aŋda'ria   'via 'sybit
    IDP.1S SBJ.1=go\COND.1S away at_once
    'I would go away immediately'

The Conditional is also widely used when expressing a request, to mitigate the illocutionary force of the statement:

(91) *mi i pijrìa un café*
    mi   i=pij'ria   aŋ=ka'fæ
    IDP.1S SBJ.1=take-COND.1S INDEF=coffee
    'I would take a coffee'

The following is instead a mild shopping order:

(92) *i l'avrìa damanca ëd chèich ciò*
    i=lav'ria   da='maŋka əd='kæjk   tʃo
    SBJ.1=have\COND.1S ABL=need ATTR=some nail
    'I need some nails'

While (93) is an instance of reported speech:

(93) *Tàcit a dis ch'a sarìa stàit ël nòm ëd na tribù sola*
    'tatʃit a='diz   k=a=sa'ria   stajt   əl='nom
    Tacitus SBJ.3=say\PRS.3S SUB=SBJ.3=be\COND.3S be\PTCL DET=name

əd=n-a=tri'by   'sul-a
ATTR=INDEF-F=tribe alone-F
'Tacitus thought it was [would have been] the name of a single tribe' ("Tribù germàniche;" https://pms.wikipedia.org/wiki/Trib%C3%B9_ger m%C3%Aoniche)

Other Conditional affixes

Most Piedmontese varieties have the same Conditional system as the koine with the suffix -*ì*-: *i savr-ì-a* 'I would know', *it savr-ì-e* 'you (S) would know,' and so on.

Some dialects (in the Monfrà area, but also much more to the West around ël Mondvì or on the hills near Turin) have a different form with the suffix -*è(i)v*-: *i savr-èiv-a* 'I would know,' *it savr-èiv-i* 'you (S) would know,' and so on.

A third system has the suffix -*iss*-: *i savr-iss-a* 'I would know,' *it savr-iss-i* 'you would know,' and so forth. It covers a very large area, from the South-Western dialects in contact with Ligurian varieties to Northern and Eastern areas directly connected to the Lombard-speaking territories (including the Canavzan dialects).

10.5.5   *The Imperative*

Imperative forms (IPV) are limited to the addressee(s): Second Singular, that always formally corresponds to the Third Singular of Main Present, and Second Plural, that formally corresponds to the Infinitive in most cases:

(94) *canta n'autra canson!*
      'kaŋt-a   'n=awtr-a   kaŋ'suŋ
      sing-IPV.S INDEF=other-F   song
      'sing (S) another song!'

(95) *canté d'autre canson!*
      kaŋ't-e   'd=awtr-e   kaŋ'suŋ
      sing-IPV.P ATTR=other-F.P   song
      'sing (P) other songs!'

For a First Plural the Main Present (without Subject Clitics) may be used with an exhortative or imperative meaning (☞ 14.6.):

(96) *i son strach,* **andoma** *a ca!*
    i=ˈsuŋ   strak / aŋˈduma a=ˈka
    SBJ.1=be\PRS.1S tired   go\PRS.1P ADE=house
    'I am tired, let's go home!'

An imperative and exhortative meaning is likewise expressed for all persons by the use of a Subjunctive Verb form preceded by the Subordinator *che* (☞ 14.7.).

In many Western and Southern varieties a Second Plural Main Present may be used instead of the corresponding Imperative:

(97) *a fa freid,* **sere** *mach sa pòrta!*
    a=ˈfa   fræjd / ˈsær-e   mak s-a=ˈport-a
    SBJ.3=make\PRS.3S cold /   close-PRS.2P only DEICT-F=door-S
    'it is cold, just close this door!' (overheard conversation in Pinareul,[20] Mar. 28, 2017)

In the following examples, the Main Present forms in (98) and (99) are opposed to the Imperative forms in (100) and (101). Forms in (98) and (99) end in -*i* not in -*e* because the text is written in a Piedmontese variety, still very close to the koine, in which all Second Plural Main forms display -*i* instead of -*e* as their own ending (*i canti* for *i cante*):

(98) **tiri** *via ste manasse da lì*
    ˈtir-i   ˈvia st-e=maˈnas-e   da=ˈli
    pull-PRS.2P away PROX-F.P=bad_hand-P ABL=there
    'pull away your bad hands from there!' (Cosio 1980: 4)

(99) **isti** *pòch ciuto un moment!*
    ˈisti   pok ˈtʃytu aŋ=moˈmæŋt
    stay\PRS.2P bit   quiet INDEF=moment
    'be quiet for a moment!' (Cosio 1980: 40)

(100) **lassé sté** *mè moros!*
       laˈs-e   ste   me=muˈruz
       let-IPV.P let-IPV.P stay-INF POSS.1S=sweetheart
       'keep your hands off my sweetheart!' (Cosio 1980: 25)

---

20   Pinareul /pinaˈrøl/, Italian Pinerolo /pineˈrolo/ (44°53′N 07°20′E).

(101) *pijé chëlla*²¹ *pòrta gròssa là giù*
 pj-e   ˈkəll-a   ˈport-a   ˈgros-a   la=ˈdʒy
 take-IPV.2P DIST-F   door-S   big-F   there=down
 'take that big door over there' (Cosio 1980: 72)

From an illocutive point of view, the use of the Main Present conveys a milder illocutionary force than the corresponding Imperative.

10.5.6 The Infinitive

Infinitive has no person and number variation. It may be Present (*parlé, vorèj, lese, sentì*) or Past (*avèj parlà, avèj lesù, avèj sentù*) and it is scarcely used in independent clauses, essentially only in an exclamatory context or as a verbal Noun:

(102) *savèjlo, lòn ch'it pense!*
 saˈvæj=l-u /   loŋ   k=it=ˈpæŋs-e
 know\INF=OBJ.3-M /   DIST.PRO   SUB=SBJ.2S=think-PRS.2S
 'if I could just know what you think!' [to know, what you think!]

(103) *figuresse chiel, che veuja ...!*
 figyˈr-e=se   kjæl /   ke   ˈvøja
 imagine-INF=RIFL   IDP.3M   SUB   will
 'just fancy, what a will he could have!'

Infinitive, on the other hand, is widely current in dependent clauses (☞ 14.2.) and it may be both introduced by a Preposition acting as a complementizer (*ëd, për, a*) or under the direct control of the main Verb.

10.5.7 The Gerund

The Gerund mood (GER) has two forms: a simple form (*parland* /parˈlaŋd/ 'speaking,' *scrivend* /skriˈvæŋd/ 'writing,' *finiend* /fiˈnjæŋd/ 'finishing') and a compound form (*avend parlà* /aˈvæŋd parˈla/, *avend scrivù* /aˈvæŋd skriˈvy/, *avend finì* /aˈvæŋd fiˈni/ 'having spoken/written/finished'). Local forms of the Gerund in *-anda* /-aŋda/, *-enda* /-æŋda/ are also widely attested. The compound tense is very rare and also the simple Gerund is less used than in many other Romance languages.

Basically, the Gerund can express three different values: instrumental or hypothetical, modal, and temporal.

---

21   A local variant of *cola* /kul-a/, the Feminine form of the Distal (DIST) deictic *col* /kul/.

(104) *as peul osservesse la difrassion ëd la lus **an beicand** na sorgiss luminosa leugna*
a=s=ˈpøl user'v-e=se l-a=difraˈsjuŋ
SBJ.3=REFL=be_able/PRS.3 observe-INF=REFL DEF-F=diffraction
əd=l-a=ˈlyz aŋ=bejˈk-aŋd n-a=surˈdʑis lymiˈnuz-a
ATTR=DET-F=light INE=glance-GER INDEF-F=source luminous-F
ˈløɲ-a
far-F
'you can observe the light diffranction by looking at a light source far away' ("Difrassion;" https://pms.wikipedia.org/wiki/Difrassion)

(105) *Pàul, **an beicand** ij mèmber dël Sinedri, a l'ha dit: "Mè frej!"*
pawl aŋ=bejˈk-aŋd i=ˈmæmbær dəl=siˈnedri
P. INE=glance-GER DET\M=member ATTR=DET=S.
a=ˈla dit / me frej
SBJ.3=have\PRS.3S say\PTCL / POSS.1S brother\P
'Paul, looking straight at the [members of the] Sanhedrin, said: "My brothers!"' (Acts 23; https://wikisource.org/wiki/La_Bibia_piemont%C3%A8isa/Testament_Neuv/At/At_23)

(106) *Gancil a l'ha butà la ramin-a pien-a d'eva sël feu për fé la mnestra e, **an spetand** ch'a bujèissa, tuti doi a son setasse sla banca a scaudesse.*
gaŋˈtʃil a=ˈla byˈt-a l-a=raˈmiɲ-a ˈpjæŋ-a
G. SBJ.3=have/PRS.3 put-PTCL DET-F=pot-S full-F
d=ˈev-a səl=ˈfø pərˈfe l-a=ˈmnestr-a e
ATTR-water-S SUP=DET=fire BEN=do/INF DET-F=soup-S and
aŋ=speˈtaŋd k=a=byˈj-æjsa ˈtyt-i duj
INE=wait-GER SUB=SBJ.3=boil-SUBJ.IMPF.3S all-M.P two
a=suŋ seˈta=se s=la=ˈbaŋk-a
SBJ.3=be/PRS.3P sit-PTCL=REFL SUP=DET-F=bench-S
a=skawˈd-e=se
ADE=warm_up-INF=REFL
'Gancil put the pot full of water on the fire to make a soup and, waiting for it to boil, both of them sat on the bench to warm themselves' (Buzzati 2000) (http://giannidavico.it/gopiedmont/files/2014/01/San-Gancil.pdf)

As these examples clearly show, a Gerund form is often preceded by the Inessive Preposition *an* /aŋ/, yielding what we can call a gerundive construction. The conditions, if any, governing the choice between the two remain to be properly understood, and certainly much variation is present. If anything, it seems that *an* can be absent, and it normally is when the Gerund expresses a wider span of time and not strictly simultaneous events. In (107) the bare Gerund denotes a general circumstance of time (the speaker's coming back home) in which the event of doing something is situated, but it does not signal that the two events take place in the very same time:

(107) *i lo faso peui **tornand** a ca*
       i=lo=ˈfazu   pøj turˈn-aŋd   a=ˈka
       SBJ.1=OBJ.3M=do\PRS.1S then come_back-GER ADE=house
       'I'll do it later on my way back home'

Both the simple Gerund and the gerundive construction may have a concessive value, when introduced by complementizers such as *ëdcò* /ədˈko/ 'also,' *bele* /ˈbele/ 'even,' *pur* /pyr/ or *pura* /ˈpyra/ 'even though,' and so on:

(108) *ëdcò **fasend** pian, i l'hai dësvijà ël cit*
       ədˈko faˈzæŋd pjaŋ i=ˈlaj   dəzviˈj-a   əl=ˈtʃit
       also do/GER slow SBJ.1=have/PRS.1S wake-PTCL DET=small
       'even if I kept quiet, I woke up the baby'

(109) *bele (che) an **travajand**, a l'ha finì ij sò studi*
       ˈbæle (ke) aŋ=travaˈj-aŋd a=la   fiˈni
       even (SUB) INE=work-GER SBJ.3=have/PRS.3 finish\PTCL
       i=ˈso ˈstydi
       DET\P=POSS.3 study
       'even if he kept working, he managed to finish school'

As shown in (109), *bele* can be followed by the Subordinator *che* /ke/.

The rare occurrence of the Gerund (normally not in the gerundive construction) with causal value is probably due to contact: it is very usual in Italian and its introduction in the Piedmontese system can be regarded as an instance of Italianization (Brero 1994: 73):

(110) ***essend** già scur a l'é pì nen partì*
       eˈsæŋd dʒa   skyr a=ˈle   pi næŋ parˈti
       be\GER already dark SBJ.3=be/PRS.3S more NEG leave\PTCL
       'as it was already dark he did not leave anymore' (Brero 1994: 73)

Nevertheless, some samples of Gerund (and of the gerundive construction, as in (109)) can be found in literature, even among authors who usually avoid Italianisms both in lexicon and in morphosyntax:

(111) *Pietrin [...] a la fin-a dla torna a l'avìa giò*[22] *dame në s-ciancon d'un bel trabuch, ën essend che, lòn che mi i l'avìo pì 'd fià chiel a l'avìa pì'd gambe.*
pjet'riŋ a la='fiŋa   dla='turn-a   a=la'via
P.   ADE=DET-F=end ATTR=DET-F=round-S SBJ.3=have\IMPF.3S
dʒo   'da=me   nə=stʃaŋ'kuŋ d=aŋ='bæl
already give\PTCL=OBJ.1S INDEF=jerk ATTR=INDEF=nice
tra'byk / ən=e'sænd   ke   loŋ   ke   mi
T. /   INE=be\GER   SUB DIST.PRO SUB IDP.1S
i=la'viu   pi   d=fja   kjæl   a=la'via
SBJ.1=have\IMPF.1S More ATTR=breath   IDP.3M   SBJ.1=have\IMPF.3S
pi   d='gamb-e
more ATTR=leg-P
'Pietrin [...] at the end of the round was already more than a *trabuch*[23] ahead of me [had already given me a jerk of a good *trabuch*], because what I had more in breath he had more in (his) legs' (Cosio 1980: 90)

Another use of the Gerund alone (but never of the gerundive construction)—possibly induced by contact with Italian—is the co-ordinated Gerund. In this construction a Gerund is always placed at the right periphery of the embedding clause and can be paraphrased by a co-ordinate sentence:

(112) *tuti a son ambaronasse d'antorn al bërgé importunandlo con sinquanta mila domande.*
'tyt-i a=suŋ   ambaru'n-a=se   d=aŋ'turn
all-P   SBJ.3=be\PRS.3P gather-PTCL=REFL   ATTR=around
a=l=bər'dʒe   əmpurty'n-aŋd=l-u   kuŋ=siŋkwaŋta'mila
ADE=DET=shepherd bother-GER=OBJ.3-M   COM=fifty_thousand
du'maŋd-e
question-P

---

22 The text is written in the Vilafalèt dialect (where the author was born; ☞ 1.8.4.); slightly different from the koine, in this excerpt one has *giò* /dʒo/ for *già* /dʒa/ 'already' and, as in many Southwestern dialects, a First person Singular identical to the Third Plural in Verbs: therefore *i l'avio* /i=la'viu/ for *i l'avia* /i=la'via/ 'I had.'
23 The *trabuch* /tra'byk/ is an old Piedmontese unit of measurement and is equivalent to 3.086 meters.

'everybody huddled around the shepherd, bothering him with 50,000 questions' (Leoni 1986: 126)

10.5.8 *The Participle*

The Participle (PTCL) has only the past form (the Latin Present Participle has been lost, although lexicalized Present Participles survive as Nouns or Adjectives). It ends in *-à* for Verbs belonging to the First Class, such as *catà* /ka'ta/ 'bought' from *caté* /ka'te/ 'to buy,' *trovà* /tru'va/ 'found' from *trové* /tru've/ 'to find,' *mangià* /maɲ'dʒa/ 'eaten' from *mangé* /maɲ'dʒe/ 'to eat,' and so on. The Verbs of the Second Class displays different endings, but most of them have *-ù* or *-ì*. The Verbs derived from the second or third Latin conjugations normally end in *-ù*, such as *savù* /sa'vy/ 'known' from *savèj* /sa'væj/ 'to know' or *beivù* /bæj'vy/ 'drunk' from *bèive* /'bæjve/ 'to drink,' while the Verbs derived from the fourth Latin conjugations tend to have *-ì*, e.g. *durmì* /dyr'mi/ 'slept' from *durmì* /dyr'mi/ or *deurme* /'dørme/ 'to sleep.' But there are many exceptions that make hardly predictable which Participle ending a second group Verb will really have. Some Verbs may have both forms with the same meaning: *sentì* /sæŋ'ti/ or *sente* /'sæŋte/ 'to hear' has both *sent-ù* /sæŋ'ty/ and *sentì* /sæŋ'ti/; *servì* /ser'vi/ or *serve* /'særve/ 'to hear' has both *servù* /ser'vy/, and *servì* /ser'v i/, and so on. Second Class Participles add *-a* if they are Feminine Singulars, and *-e* if they are Feminine Plural. First Class Participles are invariable.

On the other hand, many Verbs have two (or more) different forms of Participle with two different morphosyntactic values: one form can be used only as an Adjective, while the other one has strictly verbal usage (Aly-Belfàdel 1933: 222–223; Brero and Bertodatti 1988: 115). This is the case of Verbs like *cheurve* /'kørve/ 'to cover,' *cheuse* /'køze/ 'to cook,' *confonde* /kuɲ'fuɲde/ 'to confuse,' *decide* /de'tʃide/ 'to decide,' *deurve* /'dørve/ 'to open,' *difende* /di'fæɲde/ 'to defend,' *dispon-e* /dis'puɲe/ 'to dispose,' *divide* /di'vide/ 'to divide,' *espon-e* /es'puɲe/ 'to expose,' *eufre* /'øfre/ 'to offer,' *finge* /'fiɲdʒe/ 'to feign,' *gionze* /'dʒuɲze/ 'to join,' *meuire* /'møjre/ 'to die,' *nasse* /'nase/ 'to be born,' *onze* /'uɲze/ 'to grease,' *perde* /'pærde/ 'to lose,' *rompe* /'rumpe/ 'to break,' *scrive* /'skrive/ 'to write,' *seufre* /'søfre/ 'to suffer,' *stòrze* /'storze/ 'to twist,' *strenze* /'stræɲze/ 'to clasp,' *vëdde* /'vədde/ 'to see,' *vince* /'viɲtʃe/ 'to win.' All of them have at least a regular Participle that is normally used in verbal compound forms, and an irregular one that is mainly (or only) used as an Adjective.

Murì and *nassù* are actually rare and in their place the irregular Participles are commonly used both in verbal compounds and as an Adjective. *Streit*, the irregular Participle of *strenze* 'to tighten,' is also simply 'narrow.'

The Participle as a verbal form is not only found in compounds. It may have a verbal value on its own, e.g., in relative clauses, although not as frequently as in Italian or French (Brero 1994: 67):

VERBS

TABLE 50 A list of regular and irregular Participles

Infinitive	Regular Participle (verbal)	Irregular Participle (mainly adjectival)
cheurve /'kørve/ 'to cover'	*curvì* /kyr'vi/	*cuvert* /ky'vært/
cheuse /'køze/ 'to cook'	(*cusì* /ky'zi/) *cusù* /ky'zy/	*cheuit* /køjt/
confonde /kuŋ'fuŋde/ 'to confound'	*confondù* /kuŋfuŋ'dy/	*confus* /kuŋ'fyz/
decide /de'tʃide/ 'to decide'	*decidù* /detʃi'dy/	*decis* /de'tʃiz/
deurve /'dørve/ 'to open'	*durvì* /dyr'vi/	*duvert* /dy'vært/
difende /di'fæŋde/ 'to defend'	*difendù* /difæŋ'dy/	*difèis* /di'fæjz/
dispon-e /dis'puɲe/ 'to arrange'	*disponù* /dispu'ny/	*dispòst* /dis'post/
divide /di'vide/ 'to divide'	*dividù* /divi'dy/	*divis* /di'viz/
espon-e /es'puɲe/ 'to display'	*esponù* /espu'ny/	*espòst* /es'post/
eufre /'øfre/ 'to offer'	*ufrì* /yf'ri/	*ofert* /u'fært/
finge /'fiŋdʒe/ 'to feign'	*fingiù* /fiŋ'dʒy/	*fint* /fiŋt/
gionze /'dʒuŋze/ 'to join'	*gionzù* /dʒuŋ'zy/	*giont* /dʒuŋt/
meuire /'møjre/ 'to die'	(*murì* /my'ri/)	*mòrt* /mort/
nasse /'nase/ 'to be born'	(*nassù* /na'sy/)	*nà* /na/
(*v*)*onze* /'(v)uŋze/ 'to anoint'	(*v*)*onzù* /'(v)uŋ'zy/	(*v*)*ont* /(v)uŋt/
perde /'pærde/ 'to lose'	*perdù* /per'dy/	*pers* /pærs/
rompe /'rumpe/ 'to break'	*rompù* /rum'py/	*rot* /rut/
scrive /'skrive/ 'to write'	*scrivù* /skri'vy/	*scrit* /skrit/
seufre /'søfre/ 'to suffer'	*sufrì* /syf'ri/	*sufert* /su'fært/
stòrze /'storze/ 'to twist'	*storzù* /stur'zy/	*stòrt* /stort/
strenze /'stræŋze/ 'to tighten'	*strenzù* /stræŋ'zy/	*strèit* /stræjt/
vëdde /'vəd:e/ 'to see'	*vëddù* /və'd:y/	*vist* /vist/
vince /'viŋtʃe/ 'to win'	*vinciù* /viŋ'tʃy/	*vint* /viŋt/

(113) *ij cit **rivà** stamatin i l'oma faje buté le tende ant ël pra*
       i='tʃit   ri'v-a   st-a=ma'tiŋ   i='luma
       DET\P=little arrive-PTCL PROX-F=morning SBJ.1=have\PRS.1P
       'fa=je   by't-e   l-e='tæŋd-e   aŋt=əl='pra
       do-PTCL=IND put-INF DET.F.P=tent-P INE=DET=meadow
       '(as to) the children who arrived this morning, we had them put up their tents in the meadow.'

This construction is possible only with transitive Verbs (and then it has a passive meaning, like in (114)) or with unaccusative Verbs (and then it has an active meaning, as in the sentence above). It is ungrammatical with unergative Verbs:

(114) *mach ij cit sbaruvà dai bram a son scapà*
mak i=ˈtʃit zbaryˈv-a da=i=ˈbram a=ˈsuŋ
only DET\P=little scare-PTCL ABL=DET\M=moo SBJ.3=be/PRS.3P
skaˈp-a
run_away-PTCL
'just the kids scared by the mooing ran away'

(115) **ij cit parlà ai sò amis a j'ero ij pì content*
*'the kids spoken to their friends were the happiest ones'

Participle may also display the role of a circumstantial clause, with causal ((116)), temporal ((117)) and conditional meaning ((118)):

(116) *sburdì da la notissia, a l'é partì*
zbyrˈd-i da-l-a=nuˈtisj-a a=ˈle parˈt-i
stun-PTCL ABL=DET-F=news-S SBJ.3=be\PRS.3 leave-PTCL
'stunned by the news he left' (Brero 1994: 73)

(117) *na vòlta rivà a ca, i l'hai gavame la maja*
n-a=ˈvolta riˈv-a a=ˈka / i=ˈlaj
INDEF-F=time arrive-PTCL ADE=house SBJ.1=have\PRS.1S
gaˈv-a=me l-a=ˈmaj-a
take_off=PTCL=OBL.1S DET-F=sweater-S
'when I got home I took off my sweater'

(118) *pijà për temp, la gripa a l'é bon curé*
pj-a pər=ˈtæmp l-a=ˈgrip-a a=ˈle buŋ kyˈr-e
take-PTCL BEN=time DET-F=flu-S SBJ.3=be\PRS.3 good cure-INF
'when treated early flu is easily cured'

When it displays a temporal meaning, the Participle is often introduced by a Complementizer such as *na vòlta* /n-a=ˈvolta/ 'once,' *dòp* /dop/ 'after,' *pen-a* /ˈpæŋa/ 'as soon as.' If it is built with a transitive Verb, the Participle may show both an active ((119)) and a passive form with gender agreement ((119')) without changing the meaning of the clause (Brero 1994: 70):

(119) *na vòlta fait la valis i partoma*
  na=ˈvolta   fajt   l-a=vaˈliz   i=parˈt-uma
  INDEF-F=time do\PTCL DET-F=suitcase SBJ.1=leave-PRS.1P
  'when we are done packing we leave'

(119′) *na vòlta faita la valis i partoma*
  na=ˈvolta   fajt-a   l-a=vaˈliz   i=parˈt-uma
  INDEF-F=time do\PTCL-F DET-F=suitcase SBJ.1=leave-PRS.1P

Sometimes the Participle of transitive Verbs (with passive interpretation) may take on a concessive meaning (☞ 15.2.10.). With this value it is often introduced by *bele* (*che*) /ˈbæle ke/ 'even if' and the like:

(120) *bele che ferì, a l'ha nen chità 'd batse*
  ˈbæle ke   feˈri   a=ˈla   næŋ   kiˈt-a
  even SUB wound\PTCL SBJ.3=have\PRS.3S NEG   stop-PTCL
  d=ˈbat=se
  ATTR=fight-(INF)=REFL
  'even wounded he did not stop fighting'

The construction in (120) it is not possible when the Participle as an active value, i.e., with intransitive Verbs, either unergative or unaccusative.

10.6 Use of the Auxiliaries

As anticipated (☞ 10.2.6.), both Verbs *esse* /ˈese/ 'to be' and *avèj* /aˈvæj/ 'to have' are used as auxiliaries to form compound tenses. Rarely, other verbs, such as *vnì* /vni/ 'to come' and *andé* /aŋˈde/ 'to go,' are also used as auxiliaries.

There is a deep difference between Active and Reflexive diatheses, on the one hand, and Passive, on the other: while in Active and Reflexive conjugations auxiliaries can only form past tenses, for Passive diathesis they play a role in the whole conjugation. In other terms, there is no Passive voice without auxiliary, except for the Participle.

We will then deal with two different settings of auxiliarization: the first one concerning Past, for Active and Reflexive diatheses, and the second one concerning the whole Passive diathesis on its own.

10.6.1 Past: Active

The Past tense of Main, Subjunctive, Dubitative and Conditional, and the Pluperfect of Main and Subjunctive of the transitive Verbs are formed by *avèj* followed by the Participle of the lexical Verb (e.g.: *catà* /kaˈt-a/ 'bought'). Presents of *avèj* followed by the Participle builds up the corresponding Past: *i l'hai catà* /i=ˈlaj kaˈt-a/ is the Main Past, *i l'abia catà* /i=ˈlabja kaˈt-a/ the Subjunctive Past, *i l'avrai catà* /i=lavˈraj kaˈt-a/ the Dubitative Past, *i l'avrìa catà* /i=lavˈria kaˈt-a/ the Conditional Past. The Pluperfect is built in the same way, when *avèj* displays its Imperfect forms. There is no exception to this rule, and all compound forms of transitive active Verbs are formed with the auxiliary *avèj*.

As regards intransitive compound forms, Piedmontese exhibits split intransitivity (Burzio 1986, Bentley 2016). In other terms, it uses more than one auxiliary in the compound forms of Intransitive Verbs.

The auxiliary *esse* is used to form the compound tenses of core unaccusatives intransitive Verbs (e.g., Verbs belonging to the class of Verbs indicating definite and indefinite change of state and location, such as *murì/meure* 'to die,' *rivé* 'to arrive,' *partì/parte* 'to leave;' continuation of a pre-existing state, such as *rësté* 'to remain;' and existence of a state, e.g., *esiste* 'to exist' and *esse* itself). *Avej*, on the other hand, is used as a perfective auxiliary for intransitives that are usually called unergatives, i.e., those Verbs that describe controlled processes (e.g., *telefoné* 'to make a phone call,' *travajé* 'to work'). The Verb class of intransitives indicating uncontrolled processes (e.g., *pieuve* 'to rain') may use alternatively *avej* and *esse*, without any variation in meaning. The same conditions are observed in contemporary Italian, while in other languages of Europe and Italy, as well as in some Piedmontese varieties, the auxiliary corresponding to 'to have' has replaced 'to be' in all Verb classes, to the extent that split intransitivity, at least in relation to perfective auxiliaries, has disappeared or is about to do so, such as in Spanish, or in some varieties of Napoletano-Calabrese (see Sorace 2000, Cennamo 2001), and in the Piedmontese dialect of Valansengh,[24] near Biela, and Sijé,[25] in the province of Coni (see Cerrone and Miola 2011, Miola 2017).[26] Table 10.26. shows the different choices of different varieties in relation to perfective auxiliary selection (French, another split-intransitivity language, is added for comparison).

---

24   Valansengh /valaŋˈsæŋg/, Italian Vallanzengo /vallanˈzengo/ (45°36′N 08°03′E).
25   Sijé /siˈje/, Italian Cigliè /tʃiˈʎe/ (44°26′N 07°56′E).
26   Other dialects in Southwest Piedmont and elsewhere, have eliminated split intransitivity the other way round, overextending *esse* instead of *avèj* as their only perfective auxiliary in the active conjugation (see Miola 2017: 149–153 and references therein).

VERBS 327

TABLE 51 Perfective auxiliary selection in some varieties spoken in Europe (H: 'to have;' E: 'to be')

Variety / Verb class	Reflexives	Definite change of location/ state	Indefinite change of location	Continuation of a pre-existing state	Existence of a state	Uncontrolled process	Controlled process
French	E	E	E/H	H	H	H	H
Italian	E	E	E	E	E	E/H	H
Nap.-Calabr.	H	H	H	H	H	H	H
Piedmontese	E	E	E	E	E	E/H	H
Alanzenghese	H	H	H	H	H	H	H
Spanish	H	H	H	H	H	H	H

Therefore, unergative Verbs behave as transitive active Verbs and take the auxiliary *avèj* ((120)), while unaccusative Verbs behave as transitive passive Verbs and take the auxiliary *esse* ((121)):

(121) *i l'hai parlà al teléfono con toa seure*
i='laj   par'l-a   a=l=te'lefunu   kuŋ='tua
SBJ.1=have\PRS.1S speak-PTCL ADE=DET=phone COM=POSS.2SG.F
'søre
sister
'I spoke on the phone with your sister'

(122) *ël pan fresch a l'é rivà mach adess*
əl='paŋ   fræsk   a='le   ri'v-a   mak   a'des
DET=bread   fresh   SBJ.3=be\PRS.3S   arrive-PTCL   only   now
'fresh bread has come in right now'

When the subject is postverbal, unaccusative Verbs may exhibit either *esse* or *avèj*:

(123) *a l'é rivame ëd pan fresch*
a='le   ri'v-a=me   əd='paŋ   fræsk
SBJ.3=be\PRS.3S   arrive-PTCL=OBJ.1S   ATTR=bread   fresh
'I got fresh bread'

(123') *a l'ha rivame ëd pan fresch*
a='la   ri'v-a=me   əd='paŋ   fræsk
SBJ.3=have\PRS.3S   arrive-PTCL=OBJ.1S   ATTR=bread   fresh
'I got fresh bread'

In unmarked sentences, the Piedmontese koine is almost exactly matching with Italian. This is not the case of its local dialects, that highly differ in assigning the auxiliary to intransitive active Verbs.

10.6.2 Past: Reflexive

Reflexives denote coreference between Agent and Object or between the Agent and the Recipient/Beneficiary of a trivalent Verb. Like all Romance languages, Piedmontese signals this diathesis by a formative derived from Latin SE 'self' (Cennamo 2016: 967).

Grammarians, from Pipino (1783: 80) to Villata (1997: 168–169), have paid very little attention to perfect auxiliary selection for reflexive diathesis. All have implicitly stated that Piedmontese works as Italian, selecting only *esse* for reflexive and pronominal conjugation. Villata (1997: 168) states this explicitly: '*esse* is used in order to form the compound tenses [...] of all the Verbs in the reflexive form.'[27]

But this is only partially true: *esse*, 'to be,' is the auxiliary Verb commonly selected for reflexive compound tenses in koine, but even fluent speakers tend to select *avèj* 'to have' in alternative to *esse*. There are very few written examples of this, because when writing Piedmontese poets and prose writers tend to uniforme themselves to contemporary Italian in a specific feature that nobody has even outlined.

Nevertheless, the web can offer some examples of both auxiliary selections even in the same text:

(124) *ëd soldà a l'han fasse na coron-a 'd spin-e*
əd=sul'da   a='laŋ   'fa=se   n-a=ku'ruɲa
ATTR=soldier SBJ.3=have\PRS.3P do/PTCL=REFL INDEF-F=crown
d='spiŋ-e
ATTR=thorn-P
'a few some soldiers twisted a crown of thorns' (John 19.2) (https://wikisource.org/wiki/La_Bibia_piemont%C3%A8isa/Testament_Neuv/Gioann/Gioann_19)

(125) *ij soldà ch'a l'avìo butà an cros Gesù a son pijasse soa tunica*
i=sul'da   k=a=la'viu   by't-a   aŋ='kruz dʒe'zy
DET\P=soldier SUB=SBJ.3=have\IMPF.3P put-PTCL INE=cross Jesus

---

27   Original: esse *si usa per formare i tempi composti [...] di tutti i verbi di forma riflessiva.*

a='suŋ   'pj-a=se   'sua   'tynik-a
SBJ.3=be\PRS.3P take-PTCL=REFL POSS.3F tunic-S
'the soldiers who had crucified Jesus took his tunic' (John 19.23) (https:
//wikisource.org/wiki/La_Bibia_piemont%C3%A8isa/Testament_Neu
v/Gioann/Gioann_19)

The selection of the auxiliary does not depend on the syntactic usage of the reflexive form, that is the same in both context: both reflexives have an object and in both cases the reflexive clitic has a dative-benefactive value. Besides, there is no lexical reason to choose *avèj* instead of *esse*, nor the opposite. The same Verb *pijé* can be found with the other auxiliary in other contexts:

(126)   *a l'han pijasse ben varda fin-a lor*
        a='laŋ   'pj-a=se   bæŋ 'varda 'fiŋa lur
        SBJ.3=have\PRS.3P take-PTCL=REFL well care   even IDP.3P
        'even them, they took extra care' (http://www.gioventurapiemonteisa
        .net/tavo-burat-la-storia-del-gran-fume-a-larame/)

In local varieties, even if not very distant from koine, the selection of *avèj* instead of *esse* as an auxiliary is widespread. (127) and (128) come from South-Western Piedmont:

(127)   *j'han pijasse la bice*[28]
        'j=aŋ   'pj-a=se   l-a='bitʃe
        SBJ.3=have\PRS.3P take-PTCL=REFL DET-F=bike
        'they took the bike' (https://vimeo.com/42639684)

(128)   *cole pòche fomne inacidìe j'han tacasse sùbit a sparlé*
        'kul-e   'pok-e   'fumn-e inatʃi'di-e   jaŋ
        DIST-F.P few-F.P woman-P get_sour\PTCL-F.P have\PRS.3P
        ta'ka=se   'sybit   a=spar'l-e
        attach-PTCL=REFL at_once ADE=X-INF
        'those few embittered women started gosspiping at once' (https://www
        .youtube.com/watch?v=CnhuKyxf134)

The Piedmontese situation fits the conditions laid down by Loporcaro (2007: 200) for the hypothesis of "triple auxiliation:" "while unaccusatives take 'be'

---

28   Corresponding in the koine to *a l'han pijasse la bici*.

and transitives/unergatives take 'have,' just like in Italian, all reflexive display person-related alternation and/or free variation of aux E/H in some or all persons of the paradigm."

10.6.3 *Passive*

Passive voice of Verbs, unlike active and reflexive, has only compound forms. The only simple form is the Participle: *cant-à* /kaŋˈta/ 'sung,' *beiv-ù* /bejvˈy/ 'drunk,' *fin-ì* /fiˈni/ 'finished.' All the other are compounds with the Past Participle always preceded by a form of *esse* 'to be.' The tense of the auxiliary is the tense of the whole compound: so, a form like *a l'é mangià* /a=ˈle maŋˈdʒa/ '(it) is eaten,' in which the auxiliary displays a present tense, is present.

In fact, Piedmontese follow the mainstream strategy of Romance languages, that canonically form a passive voice by ESSE 'be' + past participle (Cennamo 2016: 974).

Like in the whole Romance domain, in Piedmontese the passive voice is typical of formal registers. It is normally reserved to transitive Verbs denoting accomplishment or achievement. It is usually avoided when an agent is overtly expressed. Therefore, (129) sounds rather artificial and its meaning is rather expressed in everyday speech by a form with left-dislocation ((130)):

(129)   *cola ca-lì a l'é staita fàita da n'albanèis*
        kul-a   ka=ˈli   a=ˈle   ˈstajt-a   ˈfajt-a
        DIST-F house=there SBJ.3=be\PRS.3S be\PTCL-F   do\PTCL-F
        da=n=albaˈnæjz
        ABL=INDEF=Albanian
        'that house has been built by an Albanian'

(130)   *cola ca lì a l'ha fala n'albanèis*
        kul-a   ka=ˈli   a=ˈla   ˈfa=l-a
        DIST-F house=there SBJ.3=have\PRS.3S do\PTCL=OBJ.3-F
        n=albaˈnæjz
        INDEF=Albanian
        'that house, an Albanian built it'

Nevertheless, there are many examples of passive voice patterns in religious, political or bureaucratic prose, although all these usages seem rather unnatural to a Piedmontese speaker:

(131) *lòn ch'a l'é stàit concepì an chila a l'é da lë Spirit Sant*
   loŋ   k=a=ˈle   stajt   kuŋtʃeˈpi
   DIST.PRO SUB=SBJ.3=be/PRS.3S be\PTCL conceive\PTCL
   aŋ=ˈkila a=ˈle   da=lə=ˈspirit saŋt
   INE=IDP.3F SBJ.3=be\PRS.3S ABL=DET=spirit holy
   'what has been conceived in her comes from the Holy Spirit' (https://
   www.youtube.com/watch?v=9J7Wwnxus9E)

(132) *la problemàtica /…/ a l'é stàita superà*
   l-a=prubleˈmatik-a /…/ a=ˈle   ˈstajt-a sypeˈr-a
   DET-F=problem-S /…/ SBJ.3=be\PRS.3S be\PTCL-F overcome-PTCL
   'the issue has been overcome' (http://www.gioventurapiemonteisa.net
   /litalia-ladra-a-massa-piemonteis-ancheuj/)

On the other hand, passive forms are very common with a resultative value with core telic Verbs, such as *bate* /ˈbate/ 'to hit; to thresh:'

(133) *le machine sl'èira / s'arpòso ant la sèira / che 'l gran l'é batù*
   l-e=ˈmakin-e s=l=ˈæjr-a /   s=arˈpoz-u
   DET-F.P=machine-P SUP=DET=barnyard-S / REFL=rest-PRS.3P
   aŋt=l-a=ˈsæjr-a / ke=l=ˈgraŋ le baˈt-y
   INE=DET-F=evening-S / SUB=DET=wheat be\PRS.3S hit-PTCL
   'the engines on the barnyard / they rest in the evening / as wheat has been threshed' (Costa 2014: 186)

In this case the action of *being threshed* has a passive voice indeed, but it is seen in its perfective aspect. The present tense, here, gets a highly resultative value and it is very close to its Latin counterpart.

 When the passive forms are built with the auxiliary *ven-e* /ˈvæŋe/ 'to come' instead of *esse* /ˈese/ 'to be' they cannot have a resultative or perfective nuance. The action is clearly in progress, as in (134):

(134) *coste lavorassion a vnisìo fàite dël tut a man*
   ˈkust-e lavuraˈsjuŋ a=vniˈziu   ˈfajt-e
   PROX-F.P production SBJ.3=come/IMPF.3P do/PTCL-F.P
   d=əl=ˈtyt a=ˈmaŋ
   ATTR=DET=all ADE=hand
   'these productions were completely hand-made' (http://www.mepiem
   ont.net/doi-punt/pagine/dicembre_10.pdf)

Finally, certain periphrastic constructions, such as *andé* /aŋˈde/ 'to go' followed by a Participle, may have a passive meaning with a deontic value (☞ 11.4.).

10.7 Verbal Derivation

Internal verbal derivation is rather restricted in Piedmontese.

Many inherited prefixes do not have a clear semantic import, as seen in verbs such as *conven-e* /kuŋˈvæŋe/ or *convnì* /kuŋˈvni/ 'to be convenient; to be apt,' *proven-e* /pruˈvæŋe/ or *provnì* /pruˈvni/ 'to come from,' *sven-e* /ˈzvæŋe/ or *svnì* /zvni/ 'to pass out,' all etymologically connected with *ven-e* /ˈvæŋe/ or *vnì* /vni/ 'to come' (☞ 10.2.3.).

A frozen prefix that conveys an intensive but also, conversely, an approximative meaning is *bër-* /bər/, as seen respectively in:

lëcché /ləkˈke/ 'to lick' vs. *bërliché* /bərliˈke/ 'to lick' (originally 'many times'?)
luse /ˈluze/ 'to glow' vs. *bërluse* /bərˈluze/ 'to shimmer'

Still, *lëcché* /ləkˈke/ 'to lick' is overall rare and *bërliché* /bərliˈke/ is mainly used.
Bër- is definitely intensive in:

sgnaché /zɲaˈke/ 'to press' vs. *bërgnaché* /bərɲaˈke/ 'to crush, squash'

with the latter possibly from **bërsgnaché* /bərzɲaˈke/, but usually provided with a further intensive prefix *s-* /z/ (see below) in *sbërgnaché* /sbərɲaˈke/ 'to crush, squash.'

The same prefix often accompanies unexpected semantic changes, as in:

ghigné /giˈɲe/ 'to smile; to laugh' vs. *bërghigné* /bərgiˈɲe/ 'to feign, to act cunningly'

Another scarcely productive prefix is *dë(s)-* /də(s)/ (and sometimes with *s-* /s, z/), which yields antonymic Verbs:

stopé /stuˈpe/ 'to cork' → *dëstupé* /dəstuˈpe/ 'to uncork'
quaté /kwaˈte/ 'to cover' → *dësquaté* /dəskwaˈte/ 'to uncover'

On the other hand, many *dës-*derived Verbs may also bear no semantic relation to their base:

ciolé /tʃuˈle/ 'to have sex' → *dësciolesse* /dəstʃuˈle=se/ 'to hurry up' (an inherent reflexive; ☞ 10.1.1.)

s- may also have an intensive meaning (as noted above for *sbërgnaché*):

tire /tiˈre/ 'to pull' → *stiré* /stiˈre/ 'to stretch out; to iron'

and, again, it may also involve no semantic change at all:

fërté /fərˈte/ 'to rub' → *sfërté* /sfərˈte/ 'to rub'

While prefixal derivation is therefore on the whole mainly etymological, there are instead a few productive derivational verbal suffixes.

With *-at-* /at/ or *-ot-* /ut/ one may derive diminutive Verbs; the Verb containing this suffix implies a less-than-usual amount of accomplishment of the action, and is therefore akin to a verbal modality (☞ 11.). These derived Verbs always belong to the First Class, whatever the class of the underived Verb:

gieughe /ˈdʒøge/ 'to play' → *giugaté* /dʒugaˈte/ 'to play a bit'
mangé /maŋˈdʒe/ 'to eat' → *mangioté* /maŋdʒuˈte/ 'to eat a bit or slowly'
marcé /marˈtʃe/ 'to walk' → *marcioté* /martʃuˈte/ 'to walk slowly'

The affix *-ass-* /as/ makes Verbs with a pejorative meaning; the affix is often supplemented by the prefix *s-* /s, z/ and yields Verbs of the First Class:

beive /ˈbæjve/ 'to drink' → *sbeivassé* /zbæjvaˈse/ 'to gulp down, drink a lot of different beverages'

The same pejorative meaning is provided by the unproductive suffix *-ostr-* /uˈstr/, yielding again Verbs of the First Class:

mangé /maŋˈdʒe/ 'to eat' → *mangiostré* /maŋdʒuˈstre/ 'to eat here and there or in an irregular way'

Noun-to-Verb and Adjective-to-Verb derivation may non-productively be realized through zero-derivation or conversion:

pastiss /pasˈtis/ 'botch, hodgepodge' → *pastissé* /pastiˈse/ 'to mess up'
sal /sal/ 'salt' → *salé* /sale/ 'to salt'
strach /strak/ 'tired' → *straché* /straˈke/ 'to tire, wear out'

Adjective-to-Verb derivation is realized, again non-productively, through the same prefix *s-* /s, z/ which builds antonymic Verbs. The derived Verbs may have either (or both) inchoative or causative meaning and belong either to the First or the Second Class:

bòrgn /**borɲ**/ 'blind' → *sborgnì* /**zbur'ɲi**/ 'to blind'
ciòrgn /**tʃorɲ**/ 'deaf' → *sciorgnì* /**stʃur'ɲi**/ 'to deafen'
giaun /**dʒawn**/ 'yellow' → *sgiaunì* /**zdʒaw'ni**/ 'to become yellow; to paint yellow'
curt /**kyrt**/ 'short' → *scursé* /**skyr'se**/ 'to shorten'
longh /**luŋg**/ 'long' → *slonghé* /**zluŋ'ge**/ 'to lengthen; to pass on'

Many derived Verbs are borrowed from Italian with the affix *-is* /iz/ and the formation of First Class Verbs (corresponding to Italian Verbs in *-izzare* /-**iddzare**/):

stabil /'**stabil**/ 'stable' → *stabilisé* /**stabili'ze**/ 'to stabilize'

On the other hand, this affix is also occasionally attested in old literary works, sometimes yielding what are today largely obsolete words:

cabala /'**kabala**/ 'Kabbalah; scam' → *cabalisé* /**kabali'ze**/ 'to ponder; to brainstorm'

CHAPTER 11

Verbal Periphrases and Modalities

Simple and compound verbal forms (☞ 10.) do not exhaust the range of verbal constructions: various modalities are expressed by periphrastic constructions or through dedicated Verbs. Verbal periphrases are defined here as constructions expressing modality that are fully grammaticalized or that display at least some degree of grammaticalization of their elements. More common is the use of dedicated Verbs preceding a tensed or untensed verbal phrase. In the case of the Verbs traditionally called modals, dedicated Verbs, and impersonal constructions precede a Verb in the Infinitive in order to express the epistemic or deontic modality and volition.

As an example, the Piedmontese progressive (☞ 11.5.) with *esse an camin a* + INF /*che* 'to be in path to' certainly satisfies the grammaticalization condition for being a periphrasis. On the contrary, an inchoative construction with *ancaminé a* /aŋkami'ne a=/ 'to begin, start to' hardly does, as the same Verb may be followed by either the Adessive preposition a nominal or a verbal phrase without much difference in its basic meaning:

(1) *i l'hai ancaminà a travajé*
i='laj   aŋkami'n-a   a=trava'j-e
SBJ.1=have\PRS.1S start-PTCL   ADE=work-INF
'I started working'

(2) *i l'hai ancaminà ël travaj*
i='laj   aŋkami'n-a   əl=tra'vaj
SBJ.1=have\PRS.1S start-PTCL   DET=work
'I started to work' [the work]

The modalities expressed in Piedmontese correspond to those of other European languages and of Romance in particular (Squartini 1998). Paramount among them are deontic and epistemic modality, and progressivity. There are no dedicated periphrases (nor specific Verbs) expressing the number of times a state of affairs holds true. Neither there are specific semelfactive (implying that an action or state takes place only once), or frequentative modalities (which also includes habitual meaning and "additionally specifies that a state of affairs is frequent during that period of time;" Bybee, Perkins and Pagliuca 1994: 127). These may find their expression only through different adverbs or adverbialized noun phrases, like *soens* 'often,' *mincatant* 'sometimes,' *na vira* 'once,' etc. Still, the Imperfect tense (☞ 10.5.1.2.) is used to express habituality in the past and therefore some degree of frequentativity.

Equally missing are periphrases expressing the number of agents or patients in the action (the number of both being always clearly flagged by verbal agreement and, often, in the noun phrases).

A more-than-usual or less-than-usual amount of accomplishment of the action may be expressed in verbal derivation through affixes (and sometimes prefixes), and usually with evaluative nuances (☞ 10.7.).

The same affixes, but also Adverbs or Noun phrases may be used with an evaluative meaning, a value for which verbal periphrases or dedicated affixes are again lacking. A weak degree of confidence finds its expression at least partially in the Dubitative mood (☞ 10.5.3.). On the other hand, valency-increasing operations (so-called Causative and Middle) belong here syntactically.

11.1 Valency-Increasing Operation, 1: Causative

Labile Verbs (☞ 10.1.1.) and lexical Causatives are limited in number, and the expression of Causative has recourse to syntactic rather than lexical or morphological means (Duberti 2014). Just as with Modal Verbs, the Causative is expressed with a light Verb with little semantic content of its own and followed by a Verb in the Infinitive.

As a *bona fide* valency-increasing operation, the Piedmontese Causative construction makes transitive out of intransitive Verbs and reassigns the syntactic roles of transitive Verbs. The light Verb is *fé* /fe/ 'to do, to make' and the causer is the subject. With transitive Verbs, the causee—if different from the causer—is expressed as an indirect object; a noun phrase is always copied as an indirect object after the Verb *fé*; if the two subjects are one and the same a reflexive pronoun is affixed to the light Verb (with a change in the Auxiliary; ☞ 10.6.2.)

(3) *l'ha fait soné a baodëtta le campane*
 la fajt su'n-e a=bawdət't-a l-e=kam'pan-e
 have\PRS.3S do\PTCL ring-INF ADE=celebration-S DET-F.P=bell-P
 'it made the bells ring in celebration' (Còsta 1982a: 48)

(4) *a s'é fasse campé giù ij longh barbis*
    a='s=e   'fa=se   kam'p-e   dʒy   i='luŋg
    SBJ.3=REFL=be\PRS.3S do\PTCL=REFL throw-INF down DET\P=long
    bar'biz
    mustache
    'he had his long mustache cut' (Mania Reida 1995: 62)

With intransitive, compound Verb forms take *avej* as an Auxiliary, regardless of the Auxiliary usually selected by the lexical Verb (☞ 10.4.2.3.):

(5) *Maria a l'ha fait meuire le reuse*
    ma'ria   a='la   fajt   'møjre   l-e='røz-e
    M.   SBJ3=have\PRS.3S   do\PTCL   die\INF   DET-F.P=rose-P
    'Maria let the roses die'

With the Causative the causer retains full control of the action. Nevertheless, some speakers find a semantic difference (Duberti 2014: 136–164) between the two forms in (6) and (6') in terms of affectedness of the causee, therefore matching the French constructions with *faire par* and *faire à* (Kayne 1975). When the causee is presented as a full-fledged agent with the Ablative preposition *da* (☞ 13.4.2.3.) her or his affectedness is higher than when the causee is introduced with Adessive *a* (☞ 13.4.2.1.):

(6) *i fareu vèghe ël bocin **dal** veterinari*
    i=fa'rø   'væge   əl=bu'tʃiŋ   da=l=veteri'nari
    SBJ.1=do\DUB.1S   see\INF   DET=calf   ABL=DET=veterinary
    'I'll let the vet have a look at the calf' (Duberti 2014: 156)

(6') *i fareu vèghe ël bocin **al** veterinari*
    i=fa'rø   'væge   əl=bu'tʃiŋ   a=l=veteri'nari
    SBJ.1=do\DUB.1S   see\INF   DET=calf   ADE=DET=veterinary
    'I'll let the vet have a look at the calf' (Duberti 2014: 156)

As anticipated, intransitive Verbs are made transitive with the Causative construction:

(7) *lassé cheuse për mesora bondosa*
    la's-e   'køz-e   pər=me's=ur-a   boŋdos-a
    leave-IPV.2P   cook-INF   BEN=half=hour-S   abundant-F
    'leave it cook for a good half hour' (http://www.arcancel.eu/arsete.pdf)

(8) *ant la bagna del prim peilin fé cheuse, con na feuja 'd laur, ëd siole a fëtte*
    aŋt=l-a=ˈbaɲ-a   d=əl=ˈprim   pæjˈliŋ   fe   ˈkøze /
    INE=DET-F= sauce-S ATTR-DET=first frying_pan do\IPV.2P cook\INF
    kuŋ=n-a=ˈføj-a   d=ˈlawr /   əd=ˈsjul-e   a=ˈfətt-e
    COM=INDEF-F=leaf-S ATTR=laurel ATTR=onion-P ADE=slice-P
    'in the sauce of the first pan cook sliced onions with laurel' (Brero 1978: 47)

For some speakers (9), where the same Verb is labile (☞ 10.1.1), is acceptable, while others consider it ungrammatical (and it could actually be calqued upon the corresponding Italian labile Verb *cuocere* /ˈkwotʃere/, see also AIS, map 952, points 155, Turin, and 153, Giaveno,[1] and compare, e.g., 146, Montanaro,[2] and 163, Pancalieri):[3]

(9) *pì che i lo cheuse e pì che vòstr crèn av resta dlicà.*
    pi   ke=i=l-u=ˈkøze   e   pi   ke=ˈvostr
    more SUB=SBJ.2S=OBJ.3-M=cook\PRS.2P and more SUB=POSS.2P
    kræŋ   a=v=ˈrest-a   dliˈka
    crèn   SBJ.3=OBJ.2P=remain-PRS.3S delicate
    'the more you cook it and the more your *crèn* will be [remain] delicate' ("Cren a la piemontèisa;" https://pms.wikipedia.org/wiki/Cr%C3%A8n_a _la_piemont%C3%A8isa)

11.2 Valency-Increasing Operation, 2: Permissive

Very similar to the Causative, the Permissive construction makes transitive out of intransitive Verbs and reassigns the syntactic roles of transitive Verbs. The light Verb in this construction is not *fé* /fe/ but *lassé* /laˈs-e/ 'to let' and the causer is the subject as well, but, unlike in the Causative, the causer (or "permitter") does not have full control of the action.

As s for the Causative, with the transitive Verbs, the causee—if different from the causer—is expressed as an indirect object; a noun phrase is always copied as an indirect object after the Verb *fé*; if the two subjects refers to the same referent, a Reflexive pronoun is affixed to the light Verb:

---

1 Piedmontese Giaven /dʒaˈvæŋ/ (45°02′N 07°21′E).
2 Piedmontese Montanar /muɲtaˈnar/ (45°14′N 07°51′E).
3 Piedmontese Pancalé /paŋkaˈle/ (44°50′N 07°35′E).

(10) *lassje nen fé tròp bordel a le masnà*
 'las=je   næŋ   fe   trop   bur'del   a=l-e=mas'na
 let(-IPV.2S)=IND NEG do\INF too   mess   ADE=DET-F.P=child
 'do not let (S) the children mess around too much' (Duberti 2014: 124)

Unlike the Causative construction, in some contexts the Permissive may be replaced by a subordinate clause introduced by the Subordinator *che*:

(11) *lassé nen che le masnà a fasso tròp bordel*
 la's-e   næŋ   ke   l-e=mas'na   a='fasu   trop   bur'del
 let-IPV.2P NEG SUB DET-F.P=child SBJ.3=do\SUBJ.3P too   mess
 'do not let (P) the children mess around too much' (Duberti 2014: 124)

11.3   Valency-Increasing Operation, 3: Middle

The typical European "ethical-dative" construction (Haspelmath 1998) is robustly attested in Piedmontese. In this construction a transitive Verb acquires a reflexive Indirect Object; as a consequence, the auxiliary used in compound verbal forms will be 'to be.' The resulting meaning implies a certain degree of personal affectedness and is often benefactive or, more rarely, malefactive.

As in French (Haspelmath 1998), there is a preference for the construction to be used with the Verb 'to do,' but in principle any Verb can be made into a middle. As in other languages, the construction has a familiar flavor and tends to be avoided in writing:

(12) *dòp-mesdì i son fame na bela spassëgiada*
 dop=mez'di   i=s'uŋ   'fa=me   n-a='bel-a
 afternoon   SBJ.1=be\PRS.1S do(\PTCL)=OBJ.1S INDEF-F=nice-F
 spasə'dʒad-a
 walk-S
 'in the afternoon I took a nice walk'

(12') *dòp-mesdì i l'hai fait na bela spassëgiada*
 dop=mez'di   i='laj   fajt   n-a='bel-a   spasə'dʒad-a
 afternoon   SBJ.1=have\PRS.1S do\PTCL INDEF-F=nice-F walk-S

(13) *a-j pias pijesse un cichèt dòp sin-a*
 a=j='pjaz   'pj-e=se   aŋ=tʃi'kæt   dop   'siŋ-a
 SBJ.3=IND=like\PRS.1S take-INF=REFL INDEF =shot after dinner-S

(13′) *a-j pias pijé un cichèt dòp sin-a*
    a=j=ˈpjaz   ˈpj-e   aŋ=tʃiˈkæt   dop ˈsiŋ-a
    SBJ.3=IND=like\PRS.1S take-INF INDEF =shot after dinner-S
    's/he likes to take a shot after dinner'

The Middle construction is the source of many idioms, such as *pijess-la* /pje=s=l-a/ ("take-INF=REFL=OBJ3-F") 'to take offence,' lit. 'to take it to oneself' (☞ 7.8.).

Choosing the auxiliary

As shown in (14) below, standard Piedmontese assigns the auxiliary *esse* 'to be' to the compound reflexive forms of the verbal conjugation.
In a few areas of Piedmont, especially in the areas around Biela (in northern Piedmont; Di Stefano 2017: 81–82) and ël Mondvì (in Southern Piedmont), the auxiliary *avèj* 'to have' is selected for reflexive forms with a Direct Object, yielding

(14) *i l'oma catasse sinch crajon neuv*
    i=ˈluma   kaˈt-a=se   siŋg kraˈjuŋ nøw
    SBJ.1=have\PRS.1P buy-PTCL=REFL five pencil new
    'we bought ourselves five new pencils'

instead of or alongside

(14′) *i soma catasse sinch crajon neuv*
    i=ˈsuma   kaˈt-a=se   siŋg kraˈjuŋ nøw
    SBJ.1= be\PRS.1P buy-PTCL=REFL five pencil new

This may happen—but less frequently—even with a true reflexive, and

(15) *i son vestime*
    i=ˈsuŋ   vesˈti=me
    SBJ.1=be\PRS.1S dress\PTCL=OBJ.1S
    'I got dressed'

may appear also in the form

(15′) *i l'hai vestime*
    i=ˈlaj   vesˈti=me
    SBJ.1=have\PRS.1S dress\PTCL=OBJ.1S

11.4 Modal Verbs

We reserve the label "Modal" to those Verbs which express the modality of a following Verb in its Infinitive form. The presence of an intervening prepositions or a tensed clause with the Subordinator *che* is excluded.

Deontic and partially epistemic modality is expressed through the use of the irregular Verbs (☞ 10.2.4.) *podèj* /puˈdæj/ 'can, to be able to,' and *dovèj* /duˈvæj/ 'must' (to which a certain number of impersonal constructions may be added), and *volèj* /vuˈlæj/ 'to want.'

The possibility (deontic modality) and likelihood (epistemic modality) for a state of affairs to be or become true is expressed through the irregular Verb *podèj* /puˈdæj/.

Deontic possibility:

(16) *San Pero a lassa [...] la lista 'd chi ch'a peul intré col di-lì 'n Paradis*
saŋ=ˈperu a=ˈlas-a   l-a=ˈlist-a   əd=ˈki
Saint=P. SBJ.3=leave-PRS.3S DET-F=list-S ATTR=who
k=a=ˈpøl   iŋˈtr-e   kul=di=ˈli   ŋ=paraˈdis
SUB=SBJ.3=can\PRS.3S enter-INF DIST=day=there INE=Paradise
'Saint Peter leaves the list of those who are allowed to enter Heaven that day' (Sapino 2021: 13)

Epistemic possibility:

(17) *i l'hai nen podù resiste pi 'd sinch minute*
i=ˈlaj   næŋ puˈdy   reˈsiste   pi   əd=ˈsiŋk
SBJ.1S=have\PRS.1S NEG can\PTCL resist\INF more ATTR=five
miˈnyt-e
minute-P
'I couldn't hang on more than five minutes' (Invernizio 1976 [1890]: 57)

Dovèj /duˈvæj/ is the principal means to express necessity and obligation, again either in a deontic or epistemic modality.

Deontic obligation:

(18) *e peuj an soa cà 'l padron a dev esse chiel*
e   pøj aŋ=ˈsu-a   ka əl=padrˈuŋ a=ˈdev   ˈese
and then INE=POSS.3-F house DET=master SBJ.3=must\PRS.3S be\INF
kjæl
IND.3M

'and moreover in his own house he must be the master' (Bersezio 1863, Act 4, Scene 2)

Epistemic obligation:

(19) [*Gnun a rispond. La porta però a l'era duverta,*] *e quajdun **a-i dev** essje*
e   kwajˈdyŋ   a=j=ˈdev   ˈes=je
and   someone   SBJ.3=IND=must\PRS.3S   be\INF=IND
'[Nobody answers. But the door was open,] and someone must be there' (Bersezio 1863, Act 1, Scene 1)

Volition is basically expressed with the Verb *volèj* /vuˈlæj/ 'to want' (and its variant *vorèj* /vuˈræj/). Different from *podèj* and *dovèj*, *volèj* may be followed by a tensed clause introduced by the Subordinator *che* when two different subjects are involved. In this sense, *volèj* is only partially a modal Verb in Piedmontese:

(20) *a **veul torné** ai valor american, e a **veul liesse** an na manera neuva con soa sossietà.*
a=ˈvøl   turˈn-e   a=i=vaˈlur   ameriˈkaŋ /
SBJ.3=want\PRS.3S   return-INF   ADE=DET-P=value   American /
e=a=ˈvøl   liˈ-e=se   aŋ=n-a=maˈner-a   ˈnøv-a
and=SBJ.3=want\PRS.3S   link-INF=REFL   INE=INDET-F=manner-S   new-F
kuŋ=ˈso-a   susjeˈta
COM=POSS.3F   society
'he wants to go back to the American values and wants to connect in a new way with his society' ("Frank Lloyd Wright;" https://pms.wikipedia.org/wiki/Frank_Lloyd_Wright)

(21) *mia mama **a veul ch'i fila** al lun-es*
ˈmi-a   ˈmam-a   a=ˈvøl   k=i=ˈfil-a
POSS.1S-F   mom-S   SBJ.3=want\PRS.3S   SUB=SBJ.1=spin-SBJ.1S
a=l=ˈlyŋæz
ADE=DET=Monday
'my mom wants me to spin wool on Mondays' (traditional folk song)

Semantically akin is the meaning 'to claim, pretend' ((22)), while, followed by the Verb *dì* 'to say' the Verb *volèj* stands for 'to mean' (also metaphorically 'to imply', see (23)):

(22) *veus-to che i lo sapia nen?!*
 'vøs=tu k=i=l-u='sapja nen ↗
 want\PRS.2S=INT.2S SUB=SBJ.1S=OBJ.3S-M=know\SBJV.1S NEG Q
 'do you really think I don't know it?' [are you pretending that I do not know it?]

(23) *Son 'dcò mi giovo, e i lo sai lòn ch'a veul dì*
 suŋ   əd'ko mi   'dʒuvu / e=i=l-u='saj
 be\PRS.1S also IND.1S young and=SBJ.1S=OBJ.3S-M=know\PRS.1S
 loŋ   k=a='vøl   di
 what SUB=SBJ.3=want\PRS.3S say\INF
 'I am young too, and I know what it means' (Pietracqua 1871, Act 1 Scene 2)

With an inanimate subject the Verb *volèj* may express epistemic modality:

(24) *a veul pieuve*
 a='vøl   'pjøve
 SBJ.3=want\PRS.3S rain\INF
 'it will probably rain'

Alternative ways to express deontic possibility are with the impersonal *a venta* /a='væŋt-a/ (or locally *a vanta* / a='vaŋt-a/, from the defective scarcely used Verb *venté* /væŋ't-e/ 'to be necessary'), *a toca* /a='tuk-a/ from the Verb *toché* /tu'k-e/ 'to touch' (whose semantic shift is exemplified below), or still *a bzògna* /a='bzoɲa/ 'it is necessary.'

With *a venta* and *a bzògna* the subject of the Verb involved in the volition act is introduced with an object verbal clause introduced by the Subordinator *che*:

(25) *Roma a l'ha dije ch'a venta ch'i sio tuti italian*
 'ruma a='la   'di=je   k=a='væŋta
 R.   SBJ.3=have\PRS.3S say\PTCL=IND SUB=SBJ.3=must\PRS.3S
 k=i='siu   'tyt-i ita'ljaŋ
 SUB=SBJ.1P=must\SBJV.1P all-P Italian
 'Rome told them that we must all be Italians' (Sandrone 2006a)

(26) *cole còse lì a bsògna vëddje da davsin, për podej-je giudiché*
 'kul-e   koz-e='li   a='bzoɲ-a   'vədd=je
 DIST-F.P thing-P=there SBJ.3=be_necessary-PRS.3S see\INF=OBJ.3P

da=d=av'ziŋ   pər=pu'de=je   dʒydi'k-e
ABL=ATTR=near BEN=can\INF= OBJ.3P go-INF
'one must see such things closely to be able to judge them' (Bersezio 1863, Act 1 Scene 9)

Bzògna, although looking and often felt like a loan from Italian, actually finds its first attestation in Piedmontese in the early 16th century in the following excerpt by Alion (☞ 1.7.1.) written in an old variety of the Ast dialect of Piedmontese: *o ne bisògna / dir che d'onor ni de vergògna / nessun me pòssa reproger* 'we need to say that nobody can reproach me for honor or for shame' (Farsa de Zoan Zavattino, Scene1 I, 29–31; in Clivio 2003a: 142).

As for *toché*, its original meaning 'to touch' is still alive in Piedmontese, along with the more grammaticalized meaning 'to be necessary.' Berizzi (2012: 203) sketches the grammaticalization cline of this Verb as follows:
- Stage 1: *toché* is used as a transitive verb with its full lexical meaning ('to touch');
- Stage 2: *toché* co-occurs with an experiencer flagged as an Indirect Object; at this stage, *toché* takes on a modal/deontic nuance ('someone has to/must do something, although he would have preferred not to;' 'someone is obliged to do something;' 'it's someone's turn');
- Stage 3: raising constructions with *toché*;
- Stage 4: 3rd Person Singular form of *toché*+INF; at this stage; the meaning of *toché* is that of a straightforward modal Verb (i.e., 'it is necessary');
- Stage 5: *toché* co-occurs with a preverbal negative marker; this stage completes the grammaticalization cline of *toché* as a deontic modality Verb.

While—as far as we know—raising constructions with *toché* are not attested in Piedmontese, there are evidence for all other stages of grammaticalization, albeit some qualifications are in order for Stage 5 constructions. Stage 1, 2, and 4 are exemplified below:

(27) *Via **tocheme** ampò la man.*
'via /   tu'k-e=me   am'po l-a='maŋ
away / touch-IPV.2P=OBJ.1S a_bit DET-F=hand
'come on, touch my hand a little' (Tana 1966 [1784] Act 1, Scene 12)

(28) *Di' pur, mia fija, | stavòta **a toca** a ti.*
di   pyr /   'mi-a   'fi-a / st-a='vot-a   a='tuk-a
say\IPV.2S even / POSS1S-F girl-s PROX-F=time-s SBJ.3=touch-PRS.3S

a='ti
ADE=IND.2S
'speak up your mind, my daughter, this time it's your turn' (Tana 1966 [1784] Act 2, Scene 4)

(29) *A toca sie-j(e) ij pra*
a='tuk-a   'sj-e=jᵉ   i='pra
SBJ.3=touch-PRS.3S cut-INF=IND DET\P=lawn
'his/her/their lawns must be cut' (AIS 1391–1392, p. 163 informant from Pancalieri)[4]

As regards Stage 5, Piedmontese shows today only post-verbal Negators with Finite Moods (☞ 17.), and *toché*, as a deontic Verb, is defective and lacks any Infinitive, Gerund/Gerundive and Participial forms. However, until the 18th century Negation was still marked discontinuously before and after the Finite Verb form, and *toché* was actually found with a clitic preverbal Negator *n*:

(30) *An toca nen a mi | ma a tocrà a la fija | 'd dormì minca neuit con Vossurìa*
a=ŋ='tuk-a   næŋ a='mi   ma=a=tok-'ra
SBJ.3=NEG=touch-PRS.3S NEG ADE=IND.1S BUT= SBJ.3=touch-DUB.3S
a=l-a='fi-a   əd=dur'm-i   'miŋka nøjt kuŋ=vussy'ria
ADE=DET-F=girl-S ATTR=sleep-INF every night COM=Your_Lordship
'I shan't, but the girl shall sleep every night with Your Lordship' (Tana 1966 [1784] Act 1, Scene 1)

This shows that the grammaticalization cline of this Piedmontese Verb reached Stage 5. Note also that *toché* may be complemented by a bare INF ((29)) or, especially in ancient and peripheral varieties, by *ëd* + an INF Clause ((30)).

Locally, this Verb is often provided with a prefix (possibly grammaticalized from IND.1S -*m* or PART -*n*) and takes the form *antoca* /aŋtuk-a/:

(31) *a-j antoca fé tut chiel*
a=j=aŋ'tuk-a   fe   tyt kjæl
SBJ.3=IND=be_necesssary-PRS.3S do-INF all IDP.3M
'he has to get everything done himself'

---

4 The sentence may also be interpreted as -*j(e)* as an Object pronoun of 3P (OBJ.3P; ☞ 7.4.). In this case, the sentence would present a right dislocation of the Object (☞ 18.1.) and would roughly mean 'it is necessary to cut the lawns.'

Finally, also the Verb *andé* /aŋˈde/ 'to go' can express deontic modality (on these issues, see also Giacalone Ramat 1995), when followed by the Past Participle of the lexical Verb:

(32) *a va fait parej e pro!*
    a=ˈva   fajt   paˈræj e   pru
    SBJ.3= go\PRS.3S do-PTCL so   and enough
    'it must be done this way, and that's it!'

11.5 Progressive and Continuous

A typical Piedmontese construction is the Progressive/Continuous construction built around the grammaticalized prepositional phrase *an camin* /aŋ=kaˈmiŋ/, lit. 'in path' ("INE=path"), preceded by a form of the Verb 'to be' and followed by either an untensed or tensed verbal clause. In the former case *an camin* will be followed by the Adessive preposition *a* and an Infinitive verbal form, and in the latter by a clause introduced by the Subordinator *che*:

Progressive: *esse* 'to be' + *an camin a* + INF / *che* + Main

(33) *Antant ch'a l'era an camin a petnesse a l'é passà da lì 'n bel òm*
    aŋˈtaŋt k=a=ˈlera   aŋ=kaˈmiŋ a=pætˈn-e=se
    while   SUB=SBJ.3=be\IMPF.3S INE=path   ADE=comb-INF=REFL
    a=ˈle   paˈs-a   da=ˈli   n=bel=ˈom
    SBJ.3=be\PRS.3S pass-PTCL ABL=there INDEF=nice=man
    'while she was combing her hair, a handsome man passed by' (Bré and Barba Guido 2011: 117)

(34) *a l'era già an camin ch'a andasìa an ruin-a dël 1355*
    a=ˈlera   dʒa   aŋ=kaˈmiŋ k=a=aŋdaˈsia
    SBJ.3=be\IMPF.3S already INE=path SUB=SBJ.3=go\IMPF.3S
    aŋ=ryˈiŋ-a d=əl=1355
    INE=ruin-S ATTR=DET=1355
    'it was already decaying in 1355' ("Ospissi ëd Véres;" https://pms.wikipedia.org/wiki/Ospissi_%C3%ABd_V%C3%A9res)

Partially similar to the construction with *esse an camin che* is *esse daré a* /ˈese daˈre a/ ("be\INF behind ADE="), lit. 'to be behind to,' followed by an Infinitive or a clause introduced by the Subordinator *che* and with the meaning 'to be busy doing' (as a result of a semantic shift from 'to be behind' or, with the Verb

VERBAL PERIPHRASES AND MODALITIES   347

andé 'to go,' 'to follow,' through 'to manage; to be responsible for'). *Daré* may appear also as *dré* /dre/ e the variants *dapress* /dap'res/ or still *apress* /ap'res/ are also found:

(35) *L'era sempre daré a fé su e giù*
 'l=era   'sempre da're   a='fe   sy e   dʒy
 SBJ.3S=be\IMPF.3S always   behind ADE=do\INF up and down
 's/he was always going up and down' (Cerruti 2012: 606)

Still another Progressive periphrastic construction is *esse sì/lì* ('to be here/there') followed by a tensed verbal phrase introduced by the Subordinator *che* (cf. also Cerruti 2007):

(36) *ël partisan, | a l'é lì, sol ant la neuit, a confidene| che chiel a l'ha lesù | andrinta ai nòstri cheur*
 əl=parti'zaŋ   a='le   li   sul aŋt=l-a='nøjt
 DET=partisan   SBJ.3=be\PRS.3P   there   alone INE=DET-F=night
 a=confi'd-e=ne   ke   kjæl   a l='a   le'zy
 ADE=confide-INF=OBJ.1P   SUB   IDP.3M   SBJ.3=have\PRS.3S   read-PTCL
 aŋ'driŋta   a=i='nostr-i   kør
 inside   ADE=DET\P=POSS.1P-P   heart
 'the partisan / is there, alone in the night, confiding to us / that he read / inside our hearts' (Ronco 1968)

(37) *son lì ch'i l'ardriss*
 suŋ   li   k=i=l=ar'dris
 be\ PRS.1S   there   SUB= SBJ.1=OBJ.3(-M)=straighten\PRS.1S
 'I'm fixing it' (Cerruti 2011: 73)

All the periphrases discussed above are not compatible with stative Verbs. Moreover, *esse an camin a/che, esse sì a/che* and *esse lì che* cannot be followed by perfective Verb forms. Note however that perfectives are compatible with *esse lì a*+INF and *esse daré a*+INF. Telic Verbs cannot be modified by *esse an camin a/che*, with very few exceptions. In these rare cases the periphrasis has an imminential, rather than progressive, meaning. The perphrases with *esse dare* and *esse sì/lì*, on the other hand, can be used with telic Verbs, take on an imminential nuance and, even if used with perfective morphology, modify the Aktionsart of the lexical Verb to non-telic (Cerruti 2011).

At least in Luigi Pietracqua's novels (second half of the 19th century; ☞ 1.7.4.), the progressive construction *trovesse/esse an tren a/ëd* + INF (lit. 'to find oneself/be in train to/of') is found, albeit rarely:

(38) *trovesse an tren a balé*
 truˈv-e=se aŋ=ˈtreŋ a=baˈl-e
 find-INF=REFL INE=train ADE=dance-INF
 'to be dancing' (Pietracqua 1971 [1877]: 55)

(39) *A l'é pròpe an tren ëd beive*
 a=ˈle ˈprope aŋ=ˈtreŋ d=ˈbejve
 SBJ.3=be\PRS.3P really INE=train ATTR=drink\INF
 's/he is actually drinking' (Pietracqua 1971 [1877]: 55)

Finally, also the Italian progressive construction with the Verb *stare* 'to stay' and the Gerund is sometimes found in more Italianized spoken and even written varieties of Piedmontese:

(40) *Ant j'ùltime sman-e i ston dedicand pì temp a un proget*
 aŋt=j=ˈyltim-e ˈsman-e i=ˈstuŋ dediˈk-aŋd pi tæmp
 INE=DET\P=last-F.P week-P SBJ.1=stay\PRS.1S offer-GER more time
 a=aŋ=proˈdʒet
 ADE=INDET=project
 'in the past weeks I have been spending more time on a project' (Davico 2016)

11.6 Imminential

The imminential construction involves the Verb *esse* with the Adverb *lì* 'there' (sometimes doubled: *lì lì*) and the Preposition *për*. The lexical Verb is in Infinitive mood.

(41) *quand che i son stait lì për paghé*
 kwaŋd k=i=ˈsuŋ stajt li pər=paˈg-e
 when SUB=SBJ.1S=be\PRS.1S be-PTCL there BEN=pay-INF
 'When I was about to pay'

11.7 Inchoative

An inchoative meaning is expressed through the use of the Verb *taché* 'to start' or *butesse* 'to set oneself to,' the latter often followed by the adverb *lì* 'there.' Both are followed by an untensed verbal form introduced with the Adessive preposition *a*. Apparently, the synonyms *anandié* and *cominsé* (and its Italianizing variant *ancominsé* /aŋkumiŋˈse/) 'to begin' are more rarely used in an inchoative meaning with a following Verb:

(42) *Nosgnor a s'è 'nrabiasse e a l'ha tacà a sbrajassé*
  nuzˈɲur   a=ˈs=e   ŋraˈbj-a=se   e
  God   SBJ.3=REFL=be\PRS.3S get_angry-PTCL=REFL and
  a=ˈla   taˈk-a   a=zbrajaˈs-e
  SBJ.3=have\PRS.3S start-PTCL ADE=scream-INF
  'God got angry and started to scream' (*La predica 'd don Cocala*, vaudeville number, 1950s)

(43) *Chiel a s'é butasse a rije*
  kjæl   a=ˈs=e   byˈt-a=se   a=ˈri-e
  IND.3MS SBJ.3=REFL=be\PRS.3S put-PTCL=REFL ADE=laugh-INF
  'He started laughing' (Invernizio 1976 [1890]: 42)

The primary meaning of *taché* is 'to attach, paste' and its inchoative meaning historically derived (a third meaning is 'to attack,' and all three meanings are also found in Italian, although the value 'to start, begin' is in Italian definitely secondary).[5]

11.8 Durative

A durative meaning can be expressed by a Verb meaning 'to continue, persist, keep on doing,' such as *seguité* or *continué*, or still *andé anans* /aŋˈde aˈnaŋs/ 'to go on, ahead:'

---

5 The participle *tacà* is often used adverbially (and generally followed by Adessive *a*) with the meaning 'close to'—obviously as a result of a semantic shift from the 'to attach, paste' meaning:
  *a stavo **tacà** a na dòira ciamà Vindilicus*
  a=ˈstavu   taˈk-a   a=n-a=ˈdojr-a   tʃaˈm-a   viŋdiˈlikus
  SBJ.3=stay\IMPF.3P attach-PTCL ADE=INDET-F=stream-s call-PTCL V.
  'they lived close to a creek called Vindilicus' ("Longobard;" https://pms.wikipedia.org/wiki/Longobard)

(44) *basta ch'a **continuo** a regolesse ben*
    'bast-a   k=a=kuɲti'nw-u   a=regu'l-e=se
    suffice-PRS.3S SUB= SBJ.3=continue-SBJV.3P ADE=regolate-INF=REFL
    beŋ
    well
    'they just have to keep behaving' (Bersezio 1863, Act 2, Scene 3)

(45) *a l'han **seguità** a ten-e e mné 'l baston*
    a='laŋ   segwi't-a   a='tæɲe   e   mn-e
    SBJ.3=have\PRS.3P persist-PTCL ADE=keep\INF and beat-INF
    l=bas'tuŋ
    DET=stick
    'they kept holding and beating with the stick' (Bré and Barba Guido 2011: 21)

With *andé* 'to go', also the periphrasis with a postponed Gerund is attested. Its durative meaning is usually plurifocalized:

(46) *J'é 'd certun ch'a **van disend** | Tuti j'agn as gionta 'd ca*
    j=e   d=tʃært'uŋ   k=a='vaŋ   di'z-æŋd / 'tyt-i
    IND=be\PRS.3S ATTR=someone SUB= SBJ.3=go\PRS.3P say-GER / all-P
    j=aɲ   a=s='dʒuɲt-a   d=ka
    DET\P=year\P SBJ.3=REFL=add-PRS.3S ATTR=house
    'Someone keeps saying that every year one pays a higher rent' (Pansoya 1827: 43)

11.9 Terminative

A terminative meaning can be imparted through the use of the Verbs *chité* or *molé* 'to stop, quit.' They may be followed by the adverbial *lì* 'there,' which is cliticized to the preceding verbal form and attracts the main accent:

(47) *a l'ha fait bin a **chité** 'd fé 'l pruché*
    a='la   fajt   biŋ a=ki't-e   'd=fe
    SBJ.3=have\PRS.3S do\PTCL well ADE=stop-INF ATTR=do\INF
    l=pru'ke
    DEF=hairdresser
    'he was right to stop being a hairdresser' (Pietracqua 1859b, Act 2 Scene 3)

The same Verbs are also frequently followed by a 3rd feminine Object pronoun with a generic reading (☞ 7.8.):

(48) *chit-la lì dë sgonfié!*
    kit=l-a=ˈli   də=zguŋˈfj-e
    quit-IPV.2S=OBJ.3-F=there ATTR=deflate-INF
    'stop annoying!'

Still another Verb used in order to express the terminative, and most commonly followed in this role by the adverb *lì*, is *pianté lì* /**pjaŋt-e=ˈli**/, lit. 'to plant there:'

(49) *j'uman a peulo mai **pianté lì** d'amparé*
    i=yˈmaŋ   a=ˈpølo   maj   pjaŋt-e=ˈli
    DET\P=human SBJ.3=can\PRS.3P never plant-INF=there
    d=ampaˈr-e
    ATTR=learn-INF
    'humans can never stop learning' ("Confucianism;" https://pms.wikipedia.org/wiki/Confucianism)

11.10 Immediative

A typical Piedmontese construction[6] has the Subordinator *che* (SUB) preceding the Infinitive:

(50) *foma che andé!*
    ˈfoma   ke   aŋˈde
    do\PRS.1P SUB go\INF
    'let's go!' [let's do that to go]

For many speakers also the use with a tensed verbal form is possible with the same meaning:

(50′) *foma ch'i andoma!*
    ˈfoma   k=i=aŋˈduma
    do\PRS.1P SUB=SBJ.1=go\PRS.1P
    'let's go!' [let's do that we go]

---

6 The construction has entered the colloquial Italian of Piedmont, where (50) would be 'facciamo che andare.'

Both are more or less equivalent to a simple exhortative clause made with the Main Present without Subject clitic:

(51) *andoma!*
    aŋˈduma
    go\PRS.1P
    'let's go!'

As noted by Ricca (2001), the construction involves a completely desemanticized use of 'to do' and is possible in any tense and mood, except with a progressive construction (such as *esse an camin a/che*; ☞ 11.4.), and with both telic and atelic Verbs.[7] Ricca further suggests a preference for use with a 1st person subject, but actually any person and any subject, provided it is human, seems possible as an agent in this construction. Either an aspectual or modal analysis has been put forward, in terms of immediacy and as a "correction" or counter-expectation to a previously proposed or planned course of action. As to the origin of the construction, Ricca points to a negative construction *nen fé che* 'not to do (anything else) than'—well attested in literature—followed by the loss of the negative during the shift to postverbal negation.

It seems that the central function of the construction is to set the stage for the further development of the state of affairs and it certainly has a pragmatic function alongside a modality value. We propose to call this modality Immediative:

(52) *finì ëd mangé a l'ha fait che parte*
    fiˈni   əd=manˈdʒ-e   a=ˈla   fajt   ke   ˈparte
    finish\PTCL ATTR=eat-INF SBJ.3=have\PRS.3S do\PTCL SUB leave\INF
    '(just as s/he) finished eating s/he left'

(53) *foma ch'is vedoma vënner?*
    ˈfoma   k=i=s=veˈdoma   ˈvənnær ↗
    do\PRS.1P SUB=SBJ.1=REFL= see\PRS.1P Friday   Q
    'should we meet on Friday?' [do we do that we see each other Friday?]

identical in meaning to:

---

7 Ricca (2001: 359) maintains that many speakers are uncertain on the possibility of using this construction with atelic verbs, but, at least for Piedmontese (rather than Italian), this does not seem to be the case.

VERBAL PERIPHRASES AND MODALITIES

(54) *foma che vëddse vënner?*
  'foma ke='vəd=se   'vənnær ↗
  do\PRS.1P SUB=see(\INF)=REFL Friday Q
  'should we meet on Friday?' [do we do that to see each other Friday?]

It must be noted that, when used as a first clause and asyndetically linked (☞ 15.1.) to a following one, the structure becomes a normal object clause and gets a concessive meaning (☞ 15.2.10.):

(55) *foma ch'is vedoma vënner: lòn ch'i foma peui?*
  'foma k=i=s=ve'doma   'vənnær / loŋ
  do\PRS.1P SUB=SBJ.1=REFL= see\PRS.1P Friday / DIST.PRO
  k=i='fuma   pøj ↗
  SUB=SBJ.1S=do\PRS.1P then Q
  'let's say we meet on Friday: what do we do then?'

The preceding may be extended with a concessive adverbial such as *pura* /'pyra/ 'even:'

(55') *foma pura ch'is vedoma vënner: lòn ch'i foma peui?*
  'foma pyra k=i=s=ve'doma   'vənnær // loŋ
  do\PRS.1P even SUB=SBJ.1=REFL= see\PRS.1P Friday // DIST.PRO
  k=i='fuma   pøj ↗
  SUB=SBJ.1S=do\PRS.1P then Q
  'let's even say [do] we meet on Friday: what do we do then?'

Furthermore, in this construction the Verb 'to do' may be replaced by the Verb *buté* /by'te/ 'to put:'

(56) *butoma ch'is vedoma vënner*
  'bytoma k=i=s=ve'doma   'vənnær
  put-PRS.1P SUB=SBJ.1=REFL= see\PRS.1P Friday
  'let's say we meet on Friday'

11.11 Iterative

Although only residually attested in contemporary peripheral varieties, Piedmontese had a dedicated periphrasis expressing iterativity, i.e., describing an event that is repeated on (a) particular occasion(s). The periphrasis at issue is *tnì* /tni/ 'to hold' + PTCL, and it is attested in the language since the first documents written in the *volgare*:[8]

(57) *E chiel me teniva aggrezà*
 e   kjæl   me=te'niva   aggre'z-a
 and IDP.3M OBJ.1S=keep\IPFV3S   annoy-PTCL
 'and he kept annoying me' (Alion 1953 [1521]: 135, v. 282)

(58) *I euvr j'orie, e ten scotà*
 j=øvr   j=u'ri-e   e   tæŋ   sku't-a
 SBJ.1S=open\PRS.1S DET=ear-P and keep\PRS.1S   listen-PTCL
 'I open my ears and keep listening' (Tana 1784 Act 1, Scene 3, verse 190)

This periphrasis seems to be peculiar to the minority languages of Northern Italy, but contemporary usage is restricted to Piedmontese, Ligurian and Venetan (Ricca 1998), since Lombard last attestations apparently date back to the end of 1700s (Salvioni 1919: 537). (59) attests the usage of *tnì* + PTCL, especially in interrogatives, in the conservative dialect spoken in la Prea (Rocafòrt):[9]

(59) *Cos ten-lo grignà?*
 kuz   'tæŋ=l-u   gri'ɲ-a   ↗
 what keep\PRS.3S=INT.3-M   laugh-PTCL   Q
 'why does he keep making noise?' (Priale 1973: 125)

---

8 Elsewhere in Romance the construction originating from Latin *tenere* + PTCL has given rise to a periphrasis expressing resultative meaning (i.e., in Portuguese and in languages of Southern Italy, see Vincent 2016: 42).
9 Piedmontese Rocafòrt /ruka'fort/, talian Roccaforte Mondovì /rokka'forte mondo'vi/ (44°19′N 07°45′E).

CHAPTER 12

Adverbs

12.1 Overview

Piedmontese Adverbs constitute a separate word class and fit Ramat and Ricca's (1998: 187–189) cross-linguistic definition: "formally, adverbs are invariable and syntactically dispensable lexemes," while "[f]unctionally, [they] are modifiers of predicates, other modifiers or higher syntactic units" ((1)–(3)) or of "the content of the sentence in which they occur" ((4)):

(1) *Lë stil manerista [...] a l'é spantiasse **lest** ant le Venessie e a Milan*
lə='stil   mane'rista a='le   spaŋ'tj-a=se   lest
DET=style mannerist SBJ.3=be\PRS.3S spread-PTCL=REFL quickly
aŋt=l-e=ve'nesj-e   e   a=mi'laŋ
INE=DET-F.P=Venice-P and ADE=Milan
'The mannerist style quickly spread in the Venetian dominions and [in] Milan' ("Architetura manerista;" https://pms.wikipedia.org/wiki/Architetura_manerista)

(2) *i soma rivà a d'arsultà **motobin** màire*
i='suma   ri'v-a   a=d=arzyl'ta   mutu'biŋ 'majr-e
SBJ.1=be\PRS.1P arrive-PTCL ADE=ATTR=result very   thin-F.P
'we obtained very poor results' (Chessa 2005: 5)

(3) *A son **giust** gate morban-e | Ch'anganrio l'Anticrist*
a='suŋ   dʒyst 'gat-e   mur'baŋ-e /   k=aŋgaŋ-'riu
SBJ.3=be\PRS.3P right cat-F.P simpering-F.P / SUB=swindle-COND.3P
l=aŋti'krist
DET=Antichrist
'They are just flirters, who would swindle the Antichrist' (Isler 2013 [1799], *Canson* 18, verses 15–16: 148)

(4) ***ultimament** a l'é chiel che a cusin-a, ahahah!*
yltima'mæŋt a='le   kjæl   ke=a=ky'ziŋ-a /
lately   SBJ.3=be\PRS.3S IDP-3M SUB=SBJ.3=cook-PRS.3S /
[laughter]
[laughter]

© MAURO TOSCO, EMANUELE MIOLA AND NICOLA DUBERTI, 2023 | DOI:10.1163/9789004544291_013

'*he* is the one who cooks lately, ahahah!' (https://www.facebook.com/groups/99619783845/?fref=nf; normalized orthography and punctuation)

Functionally, Adverbs can be divided into five groups:[1]
- predicate Adverbs,
- degree Adverbs (or intensifiers),
- focalizers,
- sentence Adverbs,
- text Adverbs (or conjuncts).

Adverbs belonging to the first group modify Verbs or Verb phrases. Predicate Adverbs include many sub-groups, notably manner Adverbs ((5)) and phasal and aspectual Adverbs. Intensifiers, also called degree Adverbs, modify a modifier (i.e., an adverb(ial)[2] or an Adjective, such as *ponciùe* in (6) and *probabilment* in (7), which are modified by *bin* and *ben* 'very', respectively), while focalizers modify Noun phrases (such as *ëd ponte 'd ròch* in (6), modified by *mach* 'just').

Sentence Adverbs refer to the event denoted by the sentence, to its illocutionary content, or to the specific domain for which the sentence has to be regarded as valid. They may also express the speaker's feelings or evaluations about the sentence or their commitment to the truth value of the sentence ((7)). Setting Adverbs of time and space and directional adverb(ial)s are included in this group.

Adverbs belonging to the last sub-group operate on the textual level, and connect the clause they appear in, or a part of it, to another clause ((8)). Given their nature, they may also be regarded as connectives, and indeed they are used as such—frequently followed by *che* (☞12.5 and 16.).

(5) *Ognidun a peul imparé* | [...] *Ch' l'òm dev sempre operé* | ***Dritament***
uɲiˈdyŋ a=ˈpøl imp aˈre / k=l=ˈom dew
everyone SBJ.3=can\PRS.3S learn-INF / SUB=DET=man must\PRS.3S
ˈsæmpe upeˈr-e / dritaˈmæɲt
always operate-INF righteously
'everyone can learn that man must always do right' (Anonymous 1969 [1800–1802]: 3)

---

[1] Our subdivision mainly follows Ramat and Ricca (1994, 1998). Other subdivisions of Adverbs are present in the literature, notably Jackendoff (1972), Quirk et al. (1985), Biber et al. (1999), Lonzi (1991), Lenker (2010: 35-ff.).
[2] See next paragraph for terminology and definitions.

(6) *Ma a l'avia vist **mach** ëd ponte 'd ròch **bin** ponciùe*
    ma a=la'via   vist   mak əd='puɲt-e   d='rok
    but SBJ.3=have\IMPF.3S see\PTCL only ATTR=point-P ATTR=rock
    biŋ   puŋ'ʧy-e
    very sharp-F.P
    'but he had seen just peaks of rock as sharp as needles' (Saint-Exupéry 2005: 63)

(7) *a mostré ossitan a-i sarà **ben**[3] probabilment un che a sà nen l'ossitan*
    a=mus'tr-e   usi'taŋ   a=j=sa'ra   beŋ prubabil'mæŋt
    ADE=teach-INF Occitan SBJ.3=IND=be\DUB.3S very probably
    yɲ   k=a='sa   næŋ l=usi'taŋ
    one SUB=SBJ.3=know\PRS.3S NEG DET =Occitan
    'very probably, the teacher of Occitan will be someone who does not know Occitan' (Garuss 2004b: 4)

(8) *Ma finiomla ch'a l'é temp. **Pura** veuj nen dësmentié na còsa.*
    ma fi'njum=l-a   k=a='le   tæmp // 'pyra
    but stop\PRS.1P=OBJ.3-F SUB=SBJ3=be\PRS.3S time // however
    'vøj   næŋ dəzmæŋ'tj-e   n-a='koz-a
    want\PRS.1SG NEG forget-INF   INDEF-F=thing-S
    'but it's time to stop. However, there's one thing I do not want to forget' (Frusta 1969: 15)

From a morphological point of view Adverbs can be
– completely opaque lexical forms, and their formation rules are now, if ever, non-productive, such as *ancheuj* /aŋ'køj/ 'today' (etymologically from Latin HANC HODIE 'this today');
– homonymous with the singular masculine forms of Adjectives, e.g., *giust* /dʒyst/ 'correctly, exactly, really' from *giust* /dʒyst/ 'right, correct;'
– formed with the suffix -*a*, e.g., *fin-a* /'fiɲa/ 'even' (from *fin* /fiŋ/ 'until' +*a*); *comensa* /ku'mæŋsa/ 'initially, for a start' (from *comensé* /kumæŋ's-e/ 'to start' +*a*);
– formed via the suffixation of an adjectival form with -*ment*, e.g., *normalment* /nurmal'mæŋt/ 'usually' (from *normal* /nur'mal/ 'normal' +*ment*); *ultimament* /yltima'mæŋt/ 'lately' (from *ultima* /'yltim-a/ 'last-F.S' +ment).

---

3 A local variant of *bin* 'well, very.'

For a deeper investigation and discussion of functional and morphological types of Adverbs ☞ 12.2–5. and 12.6., respectively. As will be further discussed in 12.6, monolexical Adverbs do not seem to be an open class in contemporary Piedmontese.

12.1.1 Terminology and Prototypicality

Cross-linguistically, the difference between Adverbs and Adjectives is not always clear-cut. However, Adverbs and Adjectives are considered two different word classes because the latter modify Nouns, whereas the former typically modify other word classes.[4]

In relation to the difference between Adverbs and adverbials, from a functional viewpoint both categories modify or further specify Verbs, Adjectives, other Adverbs, Prepositions, a whole sentence, or, in some cases, Nouns. Still, they are usually distinguished formally, since Adverbs are monolexical units, while adverbials consist of group of words and constructions.

However, for less standardized languages such as Piedmontese the boundary between Adverbs and adverbial appears to be even fuzzier than it is for major, standardized languages: issues surrounding the concept of (orthographic) word play a major role here. Indeed, only some "happy fews" were able in the past and can nowadays write Piedmontese (☞ 3., 20.), a condition enabling high conservatorism in graphic choices. Therefore, a number of adverbial periphrases one finds in Piedmontese would probably be regarded as univerbated Adverbs. Let us consider for instance *ëd vòte* and two of its counterparts in the languages of Europe, namely English *sometimes* and Italian *talvolta*.[5] *Sometimes* and *talvolta* would be without doubt classified as single monolexical units (i.e., words), therefore "Adverbs," although diachronically they come from the periphrases *some times* and *tal volta*, lit. 'such time,' respectively. Piedmontese *ëd vote* /əd='vot-e/ ("ATTR=time-P"), on the other hand, would be classified as an adverbial only because it is, graphically, composed by two words, notwithstanding that it is a single phonological word composed with the Attributive clitic preposition *ëd* /əd/, and it is phonetically often realized as ['**dvote**] and even written *dvòte* (and ⟨dvote⟩ in spontaneous or non-standard writing). Likewise, expressions that are, or originally were, a Prepositional Phrase (or another type of phrase), e.g. *për maleur* /pər=ma'lør/ ("BEN=bad_luck") 'unfortunately,' might not *stricto sensu* be treated as Adverbs even though they are pronounced as a unique tonal unit and a single phonetic word; on the contrary, *dëltut*

---

4 Nonetheless, specifier Adverbs can also modify Nouns.
5 Piedmontese *ëd vòte* can also mean 'perhaps', 'by chance.'

/d=əl=ˈtyt/ ("ATTR=DET=all") or *dautut* 'completely,' lit. 'of the whole,' might be considered as an Adverb since the first grammar of Piedmontese (Pipino 1783) already attests it under a univerbated form, although non-univerbated *dël tut* can be found, even in cultured publications.

For the sake of clarity, in this chapter we will consider Adverbs those monolexical units and expression of two (graphic) words between which one cannot insert linguistic material (or at least no "full" words) without giving way to a construction that native or fluent speakers would judge odd, creatively expressive, or completely ungrammatical. In this sense, *për maleur* will be regarded, alongside *dvòte* and *dëltut/dautut*, as an Adverb, since speakers would hardly utter ?*për gran maleur* and the like. Other constructions will be labelled "adverbials."

As for prototypicality, the features characterizing a prototypical Adverb, according to Ramat and Ricca (1994, 1998), are:
- invariability,
- optionality,
- possibility to be modified by other Adverbs,
- capability to modify word categories other than Nouns.

Linguists usually identify the prototypical Adverbs with those displaying a high degree of morphological opacity (Ramat and Ricca 1998). Accordingly, the most typical Adverbs in Piedmontese would be *sì* /si/ 'here,' *mal* /mal/ 'badly,' *doman* /duˈmaŋ/ 'tomorrow,' and the like. As a matter of fact, speakers are no longer able to identify the words and the rules behind the formation of these Adverbs, namely reinforcement of a pre-existing Adverb (Latin ECCUM HIC > *sì*), suffixation with -E (Latin MAL-US > MAL-E > *mal*), or the lexicalization of a Prepositional phrase (Latin DE MANE 'of morning' > *doman*). Nonetheless, "at least for a modern western language speaker, the most typical adverb is the one that can be defined as characterized by high diagrammaticity, i.e., a clear and systematic relation between formal segments and semantic correlates and, consequently, by morphological transparency and productivity" (Cuzzolin, Putzu and Ramat 2006: 6). Furthermore, speakers identify as Adverbs those formed by the suffix -*ment*, such as the aforementioned *ultimament* /yltimaˈmæŋt/ 'lately' or *finalment* /finalˈmæŋt/ 'finally.'

In any of these views, multiword adverbials are to be considered non-prototypical Adverbs.

12.2 Predicate Adverbs

Predicate Adverbs are bound to and modify a Verb or a Verb phrase. This group includes manner and phasal Adverbs, as well as other sub-groups, such as Adverbs characterizing the predicate with respect to aspect or to intensity.

In the following subsections each sub-group will be briefly dealt with.

12.2.1 Manner Adverbs

Manner adverb(ial)s indicate the way in which the event predicated by the Verb happens.

If they are monolexical Adverbs their meaning is roughly paraphrasable with 'in an X way,' where X is the base of the Adverb. In Piedmontese such a base is an Adjective. They can be homonymous with the singular masculine form of the Adjective X ((9)), or can be formed postponing the suffix *-ment* /-'**mæŋt**/ to the feminine form of the Adjective X ((10)). Of course, several morphologically opaque items fall within this group, such as *bin* /**biŋ**/ 'well,' *volenté* or *volonté* /**vulæŋ**'te, vuluŋ'te/, or still *volentera* /**vulæŋ**'tera/ 'gladly, with pleasure' and *mal* /**mal**/ 'badly.'

(9) *se it veuj amprendi a scrive **giust** an Piemontèis ...*
 se it='vøj amp'ræŋdi a='skrive ʤyst
 if SBJ.2S=want/PRS.2S learn\INF ADE=write\INF correct
 aŋ=pjemuŋ'tæjz ...
 INE=Piedmontese
 'if you want to learn to correctly write Piedmontese' (https://www.face book.com/groups/99619783845/?fref=nf)

(10) ***visibilment** sodisfait da costa marca 'd confidensa*
 vizibil'mæŋt sudis'fajt da='kust-a 'mark-a d=kuɲfi'dæŋs-a
 visibly satisfy-PTCL ABL=PROX-F sign-S ATTR=confiance-S
 'visibly satisfied by this sign of closeness' (Pietracqua 1979 [1877]: 77)

(11) *andoma a fess-la **bin**!*
 aŋ'duma a='fe=s=l-a   biŋ
 go\PRS.1P ADE=do\INF=REFL=OBJ.3-F well
 'let's go party!'

A few adverbial constructions that are fairly routinized in Piedmontese to express manner are

- [*an* + *manera* + Adjective] 'in a X manner': the Adjective agrees in gender and number with its Singular Feminine Nominal Head *manera* /**maner-a**/ ((12));
- [*a* +(*la*) + *moda* + Adjective] 'the X way', lit. 'to the X fashion' ((13)), and
- [*a* + *la* + *mòda* + *ëd* + Noun], 'the X's way,' lit. 'to the fashion of (the) X' ((14)).

(12) *as peul nen vëddse **an manera ciàira***
  a=s='pøl   næŋ 'vəd=se   aŋ=ma'ner-a 'tʃajr-a
  SBJ.3=REFL=can\PRS.3S NEG see\INF=REFL INE=way-S   clear-F
  'it can't be clearly seen' (http://piemonteis.xoom.it/litre.php?leggo=3)

(13) *Memoria* [...] | *l'ha mës-cià, **a mòda veja**, gena e ben*
  me'morj-a [...] la   məs'tʃ-a /   a='mod-a   'vej-a /
  memory-S   have\PRS.3S mix-PTCL / ADE=fashion-S old-F /
  'dʒen-a   e   beŋ
  shyness-S and goodness
  'Memory mixed shyness and love the old-fashion way' (Goria 2000, *Serman I*, verse 10)

(14) *a pòrta anans con passion e convinsion, **a la mòda dij piemontèis***
  a='port-a   a'naŋs kuŋ=pa'sjuŋ e   kuŋviŋ'sjuŋ /
  SBJ.3=carry-PRS.3S forward COM=passion and determination /
  a=l-a='mod-a   d=i=pjemuŋ'tæjz
  ADE=DET-F=fashion-S ATTR=DET\P=Piedmontese
  'it pursues with passion and determination, the Piedmonteses' way' (Malerba 2015: 23)

Other Prepositional phrases that have been lexicalized or are in the process of lexicalizing as manner Adverbs include *al vòl* /a=l='vol/ ("ADE=DET=flight") 'immediately,' lit. 'to the flight;' *an pressa* /aŋ='presa/ ("INE=hurry") 'quickly,' *ëd pianta* /əd='pjaŋta/ ("ATTR=plant") 'completely,' lit. 'of plant,' and, among many others, a number of Prepositional phrases containing a Noun ending with *-on* whose meaning outside the phrase itself is largely or even completely opaque to the speaker: *an rablon* /aŋ=rab'luŋ/ 'dragging,' *dë squacion* /də=skwa'tʃuŋ/ 'furtively,' *an pendion* /aŋ=peŋ'djuŋ/ 'dangling, hanging,' *an ginojon* /aŋ=dʒinuj'uŋ/ 'on the knees,' *ëd nascondion* /əd=naskuŋ'djuŋ/ 'furtively,' etc.

12.2.2 *Phasal and Aspectual Adverbs*

Phasal Adverbs or adverbials "express that a state does or does not continue or that it has or has not come into existence" (van der Auwera 1998b: 25). The four primary Piedmontese phasals are the following:

– *ancor(a)* /aŋˈkur(a)/ indicates that a state does continue and roughly translates English 'still:'

(15) *për adess it ses **ancora** 'n pòch mia*
     pər=aˈdes it=ˈsez   aŋˈkura ŋ=pok   ˈmi-a
     BEN=now SBJ.2S=be\PRS.2S still   INDEF=little POSS.1S-F
     'for the time being, you are still mine' (Invernizio 1976 [1890]: 74)

When followed by *nen* /næŋ/ 'not (NEG),' *ancora* takes on the meaning of 'not yet,' and expresses a state that has not yet come into existence. The same meaning is displayed by *pancor* /paŋˈkur/ (crasis of *pa* and *ancor*):

(16) *i soma **ancora** nen a sa mira*
     i=ˈsuma   aŋˈkur næŋ a=s-a=mir-a
     SBJ.1=be\PRS.1P still   NEG ADE=DEICT-F=point-S
     'we are not yet at this point' (Pacòt 1967: 362)

(17) *Pipì a l'é **pancor** sautà fora*
     piˈpi a=ˈle   paŋˈkur sawˈt-a   ˈfora
     P.   SBJ.3=be\PRS.3S not_yet jump-PTCL outside
     'Pipì still hasn't been found' (Chiapetto and Hajek 2012: 7 [unnumbered], Ch. 5)

– *pi* /pi/ 'more' indicates that a state of affairs does not continue any longer. Especially, but not only, when it is not in the sentence-final position, *pi* is usually reinforced with the negative marker *nen* or the presuppositional negative marker *pa* (see van der Auwera 1998b: 60; while *nen* must be postponed to *pi*, *pa* must precede it):

(18) *a-i é **pi** nen temp!*
     a=ˈj=e   pi   næŋ tæmp
     SBJ.3=IND=be\PRS.3S more NEG time
     'time is over!' (flyer distributed in Turin, Apr. 2015)

(19) *a-i é pa pi* temp!
    a='j=e   pa   pi   tæmp
    SBJ.3=IND=be\PRS.3S NEG.EMPH more time
    'time is over!' (flyer distributed in Turin, Apr. 2015)

(20) *a-i é pi* temp!
    a='j=e   pi   tæmp
    SBJ.3=IND=be\PRS.3S more time
    1. 'time is over!;' 2. 'there is more time!'

(21) *a-i é pi ëd* temp!
    a='j=e   pi   əd='tæmp
    SBJ.3=IND=be\PRS.3S more ATTR=time
    'there is more time!'

(18) and (19) have roughly the same meaning. While (20) would be judged odd and ambiguous but probably understood in everyday speech, (21) is only possible with the meaning 'there is more time!' (22) exhibits similar issues of grammaticality if, as in (22'), *nen* is not present:

(22) *i l'hai pi nen* ciapalo
    i='laj   pi   næŋ   tʃa'p-a=l-u
    SBJ.1=have\PRS.1S more NEG catch-PTCL=OBJ.3-M
    'I could not catch it anymore'

(22') *i l'hai pi* ciapalo
    i='laj   pi   næŋ   tʃa'p-a=l-u
    SBJ.1=have\PRS.1S more NEG catch-PTCL=OBJ.3-M
    'I could not catch it anymore'

(23) *i l'hai pa pi* ciapalo
    i='laj   pa   pi   tʃa'p-a=l-u
    SBJ.1=have\PRS.1S NEG.EMPH more catch-PTCL=OBJ.3-M
    'I could not catch it anymore'

On the other hand, (24) and (25) are perfectly acceptable:

(24) *i lo vëddo pi (nen)*
    i=l-u='vədd-u   pi   (næŋ)
    SBJ.1=OBJ.3-M=see\PRS.1S more (NEG)
    'I can't see him/it anymore'

(25) *i lo vëddo **pa pi***
 i=l-u=ˈvədd-u   pa   pi
 SBJ.1=OBJ.3-M=see\PRS.1S NEG.EMPH more
 'I can't see him/it anymore' (contrary to what it was/the speaker expected)

- *già* /dʒa/ means 'already'. In other words, it indicates that a state of affairs has come into existence (prior and/or contrary to what one expected):[6]

(26) *a la guèra a-j toca **già** 'ndé*
 a=l-a=ˈgwær-a   a=j=ˈtuk-a   dʒa   [a]ŋˈde
 ADE=DET-F=war-S SBJ-3=IND-touch-PRS.3S already go\INF
 '(he) already has to go to [the] war' (La Lionetta 2010; https://www.youtube.com/watch?v=leTHdhbQ1kw)

A similar meaning, i.e., that a state of affairs has come into existence prior to what it was expected, is also displayed by the quasi-synonyms *bele* (*che*) /ˈ**bele** (**ke**)/ and *giumai* /dʒyˈmaj/. *Bele* (*che*) and *giumaj* may also entail that the state of affairs at hand is frustrating for the speaker or for the participants to the speech act and can be roughly translated with 'by now:'

(27) *Con tre plissasse armise, Ch'a son **giumai** an frise*
 kuŋ=ˈtræ   pliˈsas-e   arˈmiz-e /   k=a=ˈsuŋ   dʒyˈmaj
 COM=three fur_coat-P refurbished-F.P / SUB=SBJ.3=be/PRS.3P by_now
 aŋ=ˈfriz-e
 INE=crumb-P
 'with three refurbished fur coats, that are by now reduced to pieces' (Isler 2013 [1799], *Canson* 14, verses 45–46: 119)

where *giumaj* may be changed into *bele che*:

(27') *Con tre plissasse armise, Ch' a son **bele che** an frise*
 kuŋ=ˈtræ   pliˈsas-e   arˈmiz-e /   k=a=ˈsuŋ   ˈbele
 COM=three fur_coat-P refurbished-F.P / SUB=SBJ.3=be/PRS.3P even
 ke   aŋ=ˈfriz-e
 SUB INE=crumb-P

- *torna* /ˈturna/ 'again' expresses repetition. Its grammaticalization process has been studied by Parry (2009: 159–170):

---

6 For the use of *già* as an *Erinnerungsfragepartikel* ☞ 18.3.

(28) *Torna, 'l pòrte 'd Palass as deurvo*
 'turna l=ˈport-e d=paˈlas a=s=ˈdørvu
 again DET-F.P=door-P ATTR=palace SBJ.3=REFL=open\PRS.3P
 'The Palace gates open again' (*La slòira* 2002: 5; ex. 23 in Parry 2009: 165)

As in other languages, but in this case under the influence of Italian, *ancora* may sometimes also mean 'again:'

(29) *a sud con la Lombardìa* [...], *a est **ancora** con la Lombardia*
 a=ˈsyd kuŋ=l-a=lumbarˈdi-a a=ˈæst aŋˈkura
 ADE=South COM=DET-F=Lombardy-S ADE=East still
 kuŋ=l-a=lumbarˈdi-a
 COM=DET-F=Lombardy-S
 '(it borders) south with Lombardy, east with Lombardy again' ("Provincia ëd Noara;" https://pms.wikipedia.org/wiki/Provincia_%C3%ABd_Noara)

Piedmontese aspectual Adverbs include, among others, *comensa* /kuˈmæŋsa/ 'at first, for a start,' *pen-a* /ˈpæŋa/ 'just,' *maraman* or *manaman* /maraˈmaŋ, manaˈmaŋ/ 'immediately' (bookish), *subit* /ˈsybit/ 'at once,' *s-quasi* /ˈskwazi/ 'almost.'

12.2.3 Intensity Adverbs

Intensity Adverbs express the degree, the quantity or the intensity with which the action of the predicate takes place. A good number of intensity Adverbs may also be used as degree Adverbs[7] and focalizers (albeit with possible difference in meaning and shape), the main difference between them being that the former only modify verb phrases, while the latter modify adjectival/adverbial phrases.

Piedmontese intensity Adverbs include *bastansa* /basˈtaŋsa/ 'more or less, so and so,' *tant* /taŋt/ 'a lot, very much,' *gnent(e)* /ˈɲæŋt(e)/ 'not at all,' *vaire* /ˈvajre/ 'a lot, very much,' *dabon* /daˈbuŋ/ 'really, very much,' *tròp* /trop/ 'too much, very much,' and many others.

One can add to this category the Adverbs of comparison *mej* /mej/ 'better' and *pes* /pez/ 'worse.'

---

7 And can therefore be used in comparative and superlative constructions (☞ 6.4.1.–2.).

12.3 Degree Adverbs and Focalizers

Other than modifying verb phrases ((30)), degree Adverbs and focalizers can also modify an Adjectival phrase ((31)) or an Adverbial phrase ((32), (33)). The latter, moreover, can also modify a Noun phrase ((34)):

(30) *a l'ha mangià assé*
 a=ˈla maɲˈdʒ-a aˈse
 SBJ.3=HAVE\PRS.3S eat-PTCL enough
 's/he ate enough'

(31) *Costi wafer a son ëd doss assé antich*
 ˈkust-i ˈvafer a=ˈsuŋ əd=ˈdus aˈse aŋˈtik
 PROX-P wafer SBJ.3=be\PRS.3P ATTR=sweet enough ancient
 'These wafer cookies are very old-fashioned sweets' (dij Bonavé 2022)

(32) *a l'ha mangià tant/*tanto*
 a=ˈla maɲˈdʒ-a taŋt
 SBJ.3=have\PRS.3S eat-PTCL a_lot
 's/he ate a lot'

(33) *Ma s'it vas tanto bin*
 ma s=it=ˈvaz ˈtaŋtu biŋ
 but if=SBJ2=go\PRS.2S a_lot well
 'But you look pretty good' (Pietracqua 1871: Act 3, Scene 14)

(34) *I vad 'dcò mi*
 i=ˈvad dko mi
 SBJ1=go\PRS.1S also IDP.1S
 'I am leaving, too' (Pietracqua 1871: Act 3, Scene 14)

As is evident from the examples, the sense of degree Adverbs may vary according to whether they modify a Verb phrase or an Adjectival/Adverbial phrase. Moreover, some of these Adverbs may only be used as modifiers of Adverbial/Adjectival phrases and not as Verb phrase modifiers, like *tanto* /taˈŋtu/ (*ma s'it vas tant bin*, on the other hand, is an acceptable variant for (33)).

Degree Adverbs are placed before the word they modify, except if it is a Verb, which they follow. Focalizers are generally placed before the word they modify, and before the lexical Verb, if it is in a compound form. They follow the Verb (if the latter is not in a compound form).

ADVERBS

The following are some other degree Adverbs and adverbials, and frequently used focalizers:
- Degree adverb(ial)s: *assé* or *assè* /aˈse, aˈsæ/ 'enough,' *bastansa* /basˈtaŋsa/ 'quite, enough,' *pro* /pru/ 'enough,' *motobin* /mutuˈbiŋ/ 'very,' *vàire* /ˈvajre/ 'several,' *un pò* or *ampò* /aŋ=ˈpo/ 'a bit,' *un pochet* /aŋ=puˈkæt/ 'a little,' *tròp* /trop/ 'too (much),' *s-quasi* /ˈskwazi/ and *apopré* /apuˈpre/ 'almost,' *meno* /ˈmenu/ 'less,' *vraman* /vraˈmaŋ/ 'really, very,' *franch* /fraŋk/ 'really,' *dabon* /daˈbuŋ/ 'really,'[8] *na frisa* /na=ˈfriza/ and *na brisa* /na=ˈbriza/ 'a little bit,' *na frisin-a* /na=friˈziŋa/ 'a tiny little bit,' etc.
- Focalizers: *fin-a* /ˈfiŋa/, *bele* /ˈbele/ and *adritura* /adriˈtyra/ 'even,' *mach* /mak/ 'only,' *giusta* /ˈdʒysta/ 'just, really,'[9] *pròpe* or *pròpi* /ˈprope/i/ 'just, really,' *anca* /ˈaŋka/ 'also, too,' *gnanca* /ˈɲaŋka/ 'not even,' etc.

12.4 Sentence Adverbs

Under the category of sentence Adverbs we include setting and directional Adverbs and adverbials, and sentence Adverbs in the narrow sense.

12.4.1 *Setting and Directional Adverbials*
Setting and directional adverb(ial)s locate in space and time the state of affairs at hand, or specify the direction intended in the predicate of the sentence. Normally, these Adverbs are placed immediately after the Verb they modify, but, when they are pragmatically salient, they can also occur dislocated at the beginning or the end of a sentence, or between its constituents, if they are pragmatically salient.

(35) *Un alogèt alegher e còmod parej 'd cost i lo treuvi pa **doman***
aŋ=aluˈdʒæt aˈleger e ˈkomud paˈræj d=ˈkust
INDEF=flat happy and comfortable like ATTR=PROX
i=l-u=ˈtrøv-i pa duˈmaŋ
SBJ.2P=OBJ.3-M=find-PRS.2P NEG.EMPH tomorrow
'You (P) will not find a happy and comfortable house like this tomorrow'
(Garelli 1874a: Act 1, Scene 5)

---

[8] Contrary to other degree Adverbs, *dabon* is generally placed immediatly after the word it modifies.

[9] *Giust* /ˈdʒyst/, homonymous to the masculine Adjective, is nowadays less used in the sense of 'just, really.'

(35′) *Doman, un alogèt alegher e còmod parej 'd cost i lo treuvi pa*

(35″) *Un alogèt alegher e còmod parej 'd cost doman i lo treuvi pa*

(35‴) ?*un aloget alegher e còmod, doman, parej 'd cost i lo treuvi pa*

A few common space, time and direction adverb(ial)s follow:
- space Adverbs (also ☞ 8.3.3.): *sì* /si/ '(right) here,' *lì* /li/ 'there,' *là* /la/ 'yonder,' *(am)belessì* /ambeleˈsi/ '(right) here,' *antëcà* /aɲtəˈka/ 'at home;'
- time Adverbs (also ☞ 14.4.): *adess* /aˈdes/ '(right) now,' *dun-a* /ˈdyŋa/ 'right now,' *ancheuj* /aɲˈkøj/ 'today,' *ier* /jer/ 'yesterday,' *doman* /duˈmaŋ/ 'tomorrow,' *tòst* /tost/ 'soon,' *peuj* /pøj/ 'then, after that,' *l'autr dì* /l=awtərˈdi/ 'the day before yesterday (also: 'a few days ago'),' *dòp-doman* /dopduˈmaŋ/ or *passadoman* /pasaduˈmaŋ/ 'the day after tomorrow' and others. Amongst these Adverbs are also *semp(r)e* /ˈsæmp(r)e/ 'always,' *mincatant* /miɲkaˈtaɲt/ 'sometimes,' *da rair* /da=ˈrajr/ 'rarely,' *so(v)ens* /suˈ(v)æŋs/ 'often,' and the like, which express the frequency of occurrence of the state of affairs;
- direction Adverbs (also ☞ 8.3.3.): *sota* /ˈsuta/ 'downwards', *dzora* /ˈdzura/ 'upwards,' *a snist(r)a* /a=ˈznist(r)a/ or *a mancin-a* /a=ˈmaɲtʃiŋa/ 'leftwards,' *a drita* /a=ˈdrita/ 'rightwards,' *giù* /dʒy/ 'down(wards),' *su* /sy/ 'up(wards),' etc.

12.4.2 Other Sentence Adverbs

Sentence Adverbs share the characteristic of having scope over the whole sentence rather than a single constituent.

Sentence Adverbs may refer to the event denoted by the utterance in an objective way. Amongst these are adverb(ial)s expressing modality such as (*ëd*) *sigur* /əd=siˈgyr/ 'surely,' *sigura* /siˈgyra/ 'surely,' *për fòrsa* /par=ˈforsa/ 'necessarily, obligatorily,' *ëd sòlit* /əd=ˈsolit/ 'usually,' *normalment* /nurmalˈmæŋt/ 'usually.' More often, however, sentence Adverbs express the speaker's evaluation of the state of affairs or the speaker's commitment towards the truth value of the utterance.

The speaker's evaluation of the state of affairs may invove the event (such as is for *naturalment* /natyralˈmæŋt/ 'obviously,' *as capiss* /a=s=kaˈpis/ 'obviously,' *për maleur* /pər=maˈlør/ 'unfortunately,' *për boneur* /pərbuˈnør/ 'luckily,' *maleureusman* /malørøzˈmaŋ/ 'unfortunately,' *boneur che* /buˈnør ke/ 'luckily,' *belavans* /belaˈvaŋs/ 'unfortunately,' *purtròp* /pyrˈtrop/ 'unfortunately,' *dërmage* /dərˈmadʒe/ 'too bad, unfortunately'), or may be oriented towards one of the participants to the speech act (such as *saviament* /saviaˈmæŋt/ 'wisely'), or the illocutionary content of the speech act (such as *francament* /fraɲkaˈmæŋt/

'frankly,' *seriament* /seriaˈmæŋt/ 'seriously,' *probabil (che)* /pruˈbabil (ke)/ 'probably,' *possibilment* /pusibilˈmæŋt/ 'if possible,' *praticament* /pratikaˈmæŋt/ 'basically'). Adverbs of the latter two sub-classes are unfrequently used in contemporary casual speech, and arguably are adapted loans from surrounding languages, such as Italian or French.

Commitment towards the truth value of the utterance may be expressed in Piedmontese with adverb(ial)s, such as *miraco* /miˈraku/ 'maybe,' *peud esse (che)* /pød=ˈese (ke)/ 'maybe, perhaps,' *fòrsi* /ˈforsi/ 'maybe, perhaps,' *magara* /maˈgara/ 'maybe, perhaps, hopefully,' *sigura (che)* /siˈgyra (ke)/ 'certainly,' *maraman/manaman* /maraˈmaŋ/, /manaˈmaŋ/ 'perhaps' (bookish), *salacad* /salaˈkad/ 'perhaps' (obsolete), *certament che* /tʃertaˈmæŋt (ke)/ 'certainly.'

Lastly, some sentence Adverbs are often called domain Adverbs (Bellert 1977): they indicate the domain regarding which the utterance has to be considered true, and limited. In Piedmontese, Adverbs such as *lenghisticament* /leŋgistikaˈmæŋt/ 'linguistically, linguistically speaking' and the like may occur, but some speakers may consider these Adverbs unnatural. For domain Adverbs, especially in formal language, the construction [*da+la/na+mira+* Adjective] 'from the/a X viewpoint' is used: *da la mira teòrica* /da=l-a=ˈmir-a teˈorik-a/ 'thoerically,' *da na mira literal* /da=n-a=ˈmir-a liteˈral/ 'literally, literally speaking.'

(36) *La Repùblica franseisa a l'é dividùa, da la mira aministrativa, an 18 region.*
l-a=repˈyublik-a fraŋˈsæjz-a a=ˈle diviˈdy-a /
DET-F=republic-S French-F SBJ.3=be/PRS.3S divide\PTCL-F /
da=l-a=ˈmir-a aministraˈtiv-a/ aŋ=dizˈdøt reˈdʒuŋ
ABL=DET-F=point-S administrative-F INE=eighteen region
'the French Republic is administratively divided into 18 Regions' ("Region franseise;" https://pms.wikipedia.org/wiki/Region_frans%C3%A8ise)

These Adverbs are usually used parenthetically and generally placed at the beginning or at the end of the sentence. By way of example, consider (37) (an excerpt from a 17th-century text published in the 18th) and (38) (contemporary):

(37) *s'manaman Col camré roman 'm fa caich spamparà*
s[e]=manaˈmaŋ kul kamˈre ruˈmaŋ [a]=m=ˈfa kajk
if=perhaps DIST valet Roman [SBJ.3]=OBJ.1S=do\PRS.3S some
spampaˈra
trick
'if perhaps that Roman valet plays nasty tricks on me ...' (Tana 1966 [1784]; Act 2, Scene 8, verses 423–427)

(38) *Francament, Francesca ... se i l'aveissa scotala un pò ëd pì ...*
fraŋkaˈmæŋt / fraŋˈtʃeska / se i=laˈvæjsa
frankly /   F. /   if   SBJ.1S=have\SBJV.IMPF.1S
skuˈt-a=l-a   aŋ=ˈpo   əd=ˈpi
listen-PTCL=OBJ.3-F   INDEF=bit ATTR=more
'Honestly, Francesca, if only I had listened to her a little bit more ...'
(https://www.facebook.com/groups/99619783845/?fref=nf, retrieved on Jan. 27, 2015)

As one can see from some of the above examples, Piedmontese exhibits a number of sentence Adverbs that are always followed by the Subordinator *che*, such as *probabil* /pruˈbabil/ 'probably,' *sigura* /siˈgyra/ 'certainly' (from *ëd sigura*), *boneur* /buˈnør/ 'luckily' (from *për boneur*), *as capiss* /a=s=kaˈpis/ ("SBJ.3=REFL=understand\PRS.3S") 'obviously,' etc.:

(39) *Tute ròbe che, as capiss, a resto ëd qualità pì grama*
ˈtyt-e ˈrob-e ke /   a=s=kaˈpis /
all-F.P thing-P SUB / SBJ.3=REFL=understand\PRS.3S /
a=ˈrest-u   əd=kwaliˈta pi   ˈgram-a
SBJ.3=remain-PRS.3P ATTR=quality more bad-F
'All things that, obviously, are of a lower quality' ("Apartheid;" https://pms.wikipedia.org/wiki/Apartheid)

12.5 Linking Adverbs

Linking Adverbs connect two sentences or two parts of the same sentence. These Adverbs frequently come to be used as conjuctions and discourse markers (☞ 16., 18.).

Piedmontese linking Adverbs include *tutun* /tyˈtyŋ/ 'however,' *comunque* /kuˈmyŋkwe/ 'any way, however,' *l'istess* /l=isˈtes/ 'any way, all the same,' *pura* /ˈpyra/ 'however,' *e pura* /e=ˈpyra/ 'and also, however,' *dël rest* /d=əl=ˈrest/ 'also, furthermore,' *anfati* /aŋˈfati/ and *difati* /diˈfati/ 'indeed,' *d'ògni mòdo* /d=oɲi ˈmodo/ 'anyway, so, then,' *anvece* /aŋˈvetʃe/ 'on the other hand,' *parej* /paˈræj/ 'so,' and many others.

12.6 Adverb Formation Rules and Productivity

As said before, besides completely opaque forms, whose etyma or formation rules the naïve speakers cannot account for anymore, monolexical Piedmontese Adverbs may be formed using three different strategies.

Some Adverbs are homophonous with the singular masculine forms of Adjectives, as is normal for a wide range of Romance languages. This conversion/formation rule does not appear to be productive nowadays, even though a great number of Adverbs formed in this way are still used in the language:

(40) *Basme s-ciass, bela tòta*
ˈbaz=me   ˈstʃas / ˈbel-a ˈtot-a
kiss(-IPV.2S)=OBJ.1S thick / nice-F miss-S
'kiss me hard, pretty baby' (https://www.facebook.com/groups/piemonteis/?fref=ts, retrieved on Feb. 20, 2017)

A good number of (non-manner) Adverbs exhibits the adverbial suffix *-a*, which is fairly common in minor languages of Italy (Rohlfs 1966–1969: § 889; Ledgeway 2009: 717–728 on Neapolitan, and many others). Some of these Adverbs directly derive from Latin where the suffix -A (< -AD, ablative feminine singular for Nouns of the first declension) was already used to form Adverbs. However, as also Parry (2009) shows, this suffix is not limited to Latin inherited word, but it has been quite productive until early/mid-1900s, when *anca* /ˈaŋka/ 'also, too' must have entered Piedmontese lexicon as an adapted borrowing from Italian *anche* /ˈaŋke/ (see AIS 1549, points 132, 149, 158). A small selection of this large group of Adverbs is given by Parry (2009: 170). Nowadays, nonetheless, the adverbial suffix *-a* (not etymologically justified in this position; ☞ 10.5.7. on Gerunds) does not seem to be productive anymore for Adverbs, but might be overextended, in cultured and language-consciuos publications, as a marker for circumstantials of time and space, e.g., on Gerunds (also ☞ 10.5.7.):

(41) *Am ciapa la malinconìa contanda sti arcòrd-si*
a=m=ˈtʃap-a   l-a=maliŋkuˈni-a kuŋˈt-aŋda
SBJ3=OBJ.1S=take-PRS.3S DET-F=grief-S   count-GER
st-i=arkord=ˈsi
PROX-P=memory=here
'I get melancholy in laying down these memories' (Saint-Exupéry 2005: 20).

Lastly, the only Adverb-formation rule that seems today slightly productive in Piedmontese is the suffixation of the feminine form of an Adjective with -*ment*: *atenta* /a'tæŋt-a/ 'careful-F' → *atentament* /atæŋta'mæŋt/ 'carefully.' If the adjectival base is a recent borrowing from Italian and ends with -*l* or -*r*, the feminine suffix of the Adjective -*a* is dropped: e.g., *regolara* /regu'lar-a/ 'regular-F' → *regolarment* /**regular'mæŋt**/ 'regularly.'

This suffix comes from Latin MENTE, literally 'with the/a mind, with the/an attitude,' the Ablative Singular of the Noun MENS 'mind.' This Adverb-formation rule is present in all Romance languages (among many others: Ledgeway 2012: 18; Ramat 2011: 507–508). However, in Piedmontese recent neoformations attested with -*ment* seem to involve sentence Adverbs and not, or not so much, manner Adverbs, as is instead in other Romance languages.[10]

Most of all, it is possible that neologisms like these are coined (and/or perceived by speakers as natural) only when the Piedmontese adjectival base is similar to another language available to the speaker (notably, Italian). For instance, Ricca (2006: 134–135) argues that **dësdeuitament* ('clumsily,' from *dësdeuit* /dəz'døit/ 'clumsy' and -*ment*) would be unnatural to speakers since *dësdeuit* is rather different from any of its possible Italian counterparts (such as *goffo* /'goffo/). On the contrary, *ciairament* /tʃajra'mæŋt/ 'in an evident way' is attested in contemporary Piedmontese,[11] since its adjectival base, *ciàira* /'tʃajra/, is slightly similar to its Italian counterpart, *chiara* /'kjara/.[12]

Some of these judgments might be not totally agreed upon by all speakers; nevertheless, since these newly-coined Adverbs could still be regarded as plain adapted borrowings (e.g., from Italian), it seems correct to consider monolexical Adverbs not a fully open class in Piedmontese.

---

10   -*ment* is also used as a formant of *o purament* (☞ 16.1.2.).
11   Cf., e.g., https://pms.wikipedia.org/wiki/Inocybe_asterospora.
12   For 'clearly' Piedmontese also has the word *ciàir* /tʃajr/ 'clear,' as in *vëdde ciàir* /'vədde tʃajr/ 'to see clearly.' The adverb *ciàir* is homophonous with the Masculine Singular form of the Adjective meaning 'bright, clear.'

CHAPTER 13

Prepositions and Prepositional Phrases

This chapter deals with Prepositions, their morphology and semantics, and with phrases headed by Prepositions, or by Adverbs (☞ 12.) in their prepositional use.

The syntax of the noun phrases in general will be dealt with in Ch. 14.

13.1 The Expression of Location and Movement in Verbs

Piedmontese can be reasonably considered a verb-framed language (Fagard et al 2013) as far as the expression of movement and location is concerned. Thus, as is often the case in Romance, Motion and Path are usually conflated in the Verb, while Manner, Cause and Route, if expressed in the same sentence, are found in a phrase or a separate adverbial clause:

(1) *a l'é andait da Turin a Coni a pé an passand për Salusse*
    a=ˈle   aŋˈdajt   da=tyˈriŋ   a=ˈkuni   a=ˈpe   aŋ=paˈs-aɲd
    SBJ.3=be\PRS.3S go\PTCL   ABL=T.   ADE=C.   ADE=foot   INE=pass-GER
    për=saˈlyse
    BEN=S.
    'he went from Turin to Coni on foot passing through Salusse'

In the expression of the direction of motion along the vertical axis movement up and down is lexicalized by the Verbs *calé* /kaˈle/ 'to go down' and *monté* /muŋˈte/ 'to climb, go up,' while movement along the horizontal plain is conceptualized as the default option and is not specifically lexicalized. The Verbs *calé* /kaˈle/ and *monté* /muŋˈte/ may be supplemented by an Adverb (such as *giù* /dʒy/ 'down,' *su* /sy/ 'up;' ☞ 13.3.1.) or replaced by a default Verb of movement and the direction may be expressed by the Adverb alone (*andé giù/su* /aŋˈde dʒy, sy/ 'to go down, up').

Different and more basic manner of motion are expressed lexically in a number of cases, as in *core* /ˈkure/ 'to run,' *rabasté* /rabasˈte/ 'to trail,' *rampié* /ramˈpje/ 'to climb,' *sauté* /sawˈte/ 'to jump,' *sghijé* /zgiˈje/ 'to slip,' etc.

While Adverbs of location (☞ 8.3.) are used phrasally in the expression of location or movement (but neither for source nor path), Nouns—including toponyms—require a Preposition when used in the expression of location or direction.

13.2 Basic Prepositions

The prepositional system involves a morphosyntactic (and partially semantic) opposition between basic Prepositions, two non-basic Prepositions and the prepositional usage of Adverbs. The non-basic Prepositions and Adverbs are often followed by a basic Preposition that comes immediately before the Figure, defined as "a moving or conceptually movable entity whose site, path, or orientation is conceived as variable, the particular value of which is the salient issue" (Talmy 2000: 312).

It will be assumed that space relations are arranged around four intersected domains of location, direction, source and path. Both basic and non-basic prepositions are involved in the expression of location and movement.

Following the loss in Late Latin of the nominal case system and of the distinction between location and direction, Piedmontese lacks a separate coding for the two; i.e. {location = direction} ≠ source (Luraghi 2014: 104–105).

This section will leave aside the Attributive preposition *ëd* /əd/ (ATTR), actually the most general and abstract preposition. Attributive phrases will be discussed in a separate section (☞ 13.5.).

Phonologically, Prepositions are clitics to any following element of the prepositional phrase.

Morphologically, basic prepositions are followed directly by a Noun phrase, while in the prepositional usage of Adverbs the Adverb is usually followed by the Attributive preposition *ëd* or by the basic Prepositions *a* and *da*. Semantically, Prepositions are crucial in the expression of location and path, in the relationship between Nouns and Noun phrases and in a few other cases.

In cliticization to a following Determiner, a few basic and non-basic Prepositions undergo assimilation (both phonological and orthographic):

TABLE 52   The basic prepositions in combination with the Determiners

	ël DET	*l'* DET {M&F}	*ij* DET\P	*j'* DET\P	*la* DET-F	*le* DET-F.P
a a ADE	*al* a=l=	*a l'* a=l=	*ai* a=i=	*aj'* a=i=	*a la* a=l-a=	*a le* a=l-e=
ëd əd ATTR	*dël* d=ël=	*dl'* d=l=	*dij* d=i=	*dj'* d=j=	*dla* d=l-a=	*dle* d=l-e=
da da ABL	*dal* d=al=	*da l'* da=l=	*dai* da=i=	*da j'* da=i=	*da la* da=l-a=	*da le* da=l-e=
su sy SUP	*sël* s=əl=	*sl'* s=l=	*sij* s=i=	*sj'* s=i=	*sla* s=l-a=	*sle* s=l-e=

13.2.1 Adessive *a*

The preposition *a* /a/ encodes location, the goal of movement and also the beneficiary. Notwithstanding its manifold uses and idiosyncratic meanings, it will consistently be glossed 'ADE' (for "Adessive") in accordance with its etymological central meaning. With Adessive *a* the Figure is point-like or conceptualized as unstructured:

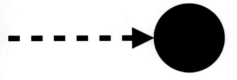

FIGURE 16
Pictorial representation of Adessive *a* (the arrow is dashed because either location or movement may be expressed)

(2) andé/sté *a* Turin
   aŋˈde / ste   a=tyˈriŋ
   go\INF / stay\INF ADE=T.
   'to go to/stay in Turin'

The use for beneficiaries may be understood on the basis of the metaphor BENEFICIARIES ARE DESTINATIONS:

(3) sossì dajlo *a* Tòjo
   suˈsi   ˈda=j=lu   a=ˈtoju
   DEICT_here   give\IPV.S=IND=OBJ.3M   ADE=T.
   'give this to Tòjo'

A further metaphorical step involves no movement at all, not even metaphorical; rather, the goal is the limitation of the Ground to a specific subset of entities represented by the Figure, which is conceptualized as unstructured and ungrounded. This is the case of many lexicalized expressions involving pain, since many nearby languages have the location of pain grounded (such as French *mal à la tête*, Italian *male alla testa*) or nominalized with an Attributive phrase (such as French *mal de tête*, Italian *mal di testa*)—the latter also possible in Piedmontese:

(4) mal *a/dë* stòmi
   mal   a/də=ˈstomi
   ache ADE/ATTR=stomach
   'stomach ache'

The same use of the Adessive in order to limit the possible field of application of the entity or state of affairs described in the Ground is visible in many other verbal and nominal configurations:

(5) *gieughe a balon*
 ˈdʒøge   a=baˈluŋ
 play\INF ADE=football
 'to play [at] football'

(6) *andé a ramengh*
 aŋˈde   a=raˈmæŋg
 go\INF ADE=ruin
 'to go to ruin'

(7) *màchina a vapor*
 ˈmakin-a   a=vaˈpur
 machine-S ADE=vapor
 'steam engine'

13.2.2 *Inessive* an

Also *an* /aŋ/ encodes both the goal of movement and location, but typically within or into a structured Figure. It will consistently be glossed 'INE' (for "Inessive"):

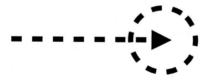

FIGURE 17
Pictorial representation of Inessive *an* (the arrow is dashed because either location or movement may be expressed)

(8) *andé/sté an Fransa*
 aŋˈde / ste   aŋ=ˈfraŋsa
 go\INF / stay\INF INE=F.
 'to work/live in France'

While with a more point-like Figure Adessive *a* will be used instead:

PREPOSITIONS AND PREPOSITIONAL PHRASES 377

(9) *travajé/vive a Paris*
 trava'j-e / 'vive   a=pa'riz
 work-INF / live\INF INE=P.
 'to work/live in Paris'

An takes the form *ant* /aŋt/ (from Latin INTUS 'within') before a Determiner:

(10) *s'a j'é 'd feste 'nt le borgià*
 s=a=j='e   d='fest-e   ŋt=l-e=bur'dʒa
 if=SBJ.3=IND=be\PRS.3S ATTR=feast-P INE=DET-F.P=township
 'if there are parties in the townships' (Costa 1982b [1938]: 18)

Ant is followed by an ungrounded Noun in the Adverb *antëcà* /aŋtə'ka/ 'at home,' lexicalized from *ant* plus *ca* 'house, home.'

The Inessive implies location or movement inside or within the Figure, while with the use of Adessive *a* the general location is expressed:

(11) *esse a ca*
 'ese   a='ka
 be\INF ADE=house
 'to be home'

The opposition may be further exemplified by the opposition in preposition between

(12) *mandé a scòla*
 maŋ'd-e a='skol-a
 send-INF ADE=school-S
 'to send to school'

and

(13) *mandé an galera*
 maŋ'd-e aŋ=ga'ler-a
 send-INF INE=jail-S
 'to send to prison'

Still, the following is expressed with the Adessive, but always grounded (and therefore more structured):

(14) *mandé a l'ospidal*
 maŋ'd-e a=l=uspi'dal
 send-INF ADE=DET=hospital
 'to hospitalize'

Other uses involve again metaphorical readings involving the expression of an instrument:

(15) *andé an bici*
 aŋ'd-e aŋ='bitʃi
 go\INF INE=bycicle
 'to ride the bycicle'

Or, still, of material:

(16) *un vej pont an bòsch*
 aŋ='vej   puŋt aŋ='bosk
 INDET=old bridge INE=wood
 'an old woodbridge'

Configurations are again common, as in:

(17) *esse an doi*
 'ese   aŋ='duj
 be\INF INE=two
 'to be two'

(18) *esse ant la bagna*
 'ese   aŋt=l-a='baɲ-a
 be\INF INE=DET-F=sauce-S
 'to be in trouble' [in the sauce]

(19) *pijé an ghignon*
 pj-e   aŋ=gi'ɲuŋ
 take-INF INE=dislike
 'to take a dislike'

13.2.3 *Ablative* da

The source of movement, either unstructured (or point-like) or structured, is encoded by the Ablative preposition *da* /da/ 'ABL.'

PREPOSITIONS AND PREPOSITIONAL PHRASES

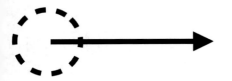

FIGURE 18
Pictorial representation of Ablative *da* (the circle is dashed because it can be conceptualized as either structured or unstructured)

(20) *a ven **da** Genoa / **dal** Portogal*
 a='væŋ   da='dʒenua / da=l=purtu'gal
 SBJ.3=come\PRS.3S   ABL=G. / ABL=DET=P.
 's/he comes from Genoa /from Portugal'

In the expression of movement, *da* is also found as a perlative in the expression of route:

(21) *ch'a passa sì **da** mi tra 'n meisòt*
 k=a='pas-a   'si   da='mi
 SUB=SBJ.3=pass-PRS.3S here ABL=IDP.1S
 tra=ŋ=mæj'zot
 INTER=INDEF=around_month
 'please come to me in about a month' (Tuberga and Antonel 2022: 9)

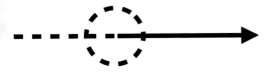

FIGURE 19 Pictorial representation of Ablative *da* in the expression of path (the circle is dashed because it can be conceptualized as either structured or unstructured; the path leading to the source is required by the semantics of the Verb but is immaterial to the conceptualization of *da*)

Consonant with the Ablative origin of *da*, its use for route implies movement within (as well as possibly stopping at) the Figure. Such an implication seems absent with the perlative use of the Benefactive *për* (☞ 13.2.4.).

The Ablative is further used to express temporal or logical origin:

(22) *Da pare 'n fieul*
 da=ˈpare ŋ=ˈfjøl
 ABL=father INE=son
 'from father to son' (head of the Coni section newspaper of the National Alpine Association https://www.anacuneo.org/da-pare--n-fieul.html)

(23) *As peul arzighé che 'l nòm Soris a sia na derivassion dal termo Or [...] e Usium*
 a=s=ˈpøl   arziˈg-e ke=l=ˈnom   suˈriz
 SBJ.3=REFL=can\PRS.3S risk-INF SUB=DET=name S.
 a=ˈsia   n-a=derivaˈsjuŋ   da=l=ˈtærmu   or e ˈusjum
 SBJ.3=be\SUBJ.3S INDET-F=derivation ABL=DET=term O. and U.
 'one may venture to say [risk] that the name Soris is a derivation from the terms Or [...] and Usium' (Lachello 2021b)

Temporal meaning of *da* often does not imply origin:

(24) *da cit am piasìa nen andé a scòla*
 da=ˈtʃit a=m=pjaˈzia   næŋ anˈde a=ˈskol-a
 ABL=child SBJ.3=OBJ.1S=like\IMPF.3S NEG go\INF ADE=school-S
 'as a child I did not like [to go to] school'

Da expresses also location and direction with humans as landmark. This is typically found with names of profession (where the actual landmark is the human workplace or the like) or with proper names (where the actual landmark is most typically the human's house or premises):[1]

(25) *andé dal dotor*
 aŋˈde   da=l=duˈtur
 go\INF ABL=DET=doctor
 'to go to the doctor'

(26) *sté da Gioanin*
 ste   da=dʒuaˈniŋ
 stay\INF ABL=G.
 'to stay at Gioanin's'

---

1 Obviously, coincidence in space with a human landmark is impossible, and the human is implied to be within or in close proximity to the actual landmark (Luraghi 2011: 214).

Still, the use of the motion Verbs is sensitive to the speaker's perspective (Ricca 1993, on Italian) and in the following examples the meaning of *da* is rather ventive and it implies that the speaker is him/herself at the doctor's:

(27) *ch'a ven-a pura da mi*
k=a='væŋa   'pyra da='mi
SUB=SBJ.3=come\SUBJ.3S even ABL=IDP.1SG
'just come by'

(28) *vnì dal dotor*
vni   da=l=du'tur
come\INF ABL=DET=doctor
'to come to the doctor'

The use of *da* in the expression of agents is the most prominent among its non-spatial uses and is consonant with the metaphor AGENTS ARE SOURCES. In this meaning it is most commonly found in passive sentences (☞ 10.6.3.):

(29) *adess i lassoma cure 'l ferì dal dotor*
ad'es i=la's-uma   ky'r-e   l=fe'ri   da=l=du'tur
now SBJ.1=let-PRS.1P cure-INF DET=wound\PTCL ABL=DET=doctor
'now we let the doctor treat the wounded' (Duberti 2014: 162)

Agent may easily lead to instrument (a non-human agent), and this in turn to both cause and goal (a frequent polisemy; Luraghi 2014: 128). Many lexicalizations (most of them possibly calques from Italian) involve *da* in the expression of goal; randomly selected among countless others: *machina da cuse* /'makina da='kyze/ ("machine ABL=sew\INF") 'sewing machine,' *machina da corsa* /'makina da='kursa/ ("machine ABL=running") 'race car,' *stansia da let* /'staŋsja da=let/ ("room ABL=bed") 'sleeping room,' *camisa da neuit* /ka'miza da='nøjt/ ("shirt ABL=night") 'nightdress.' Cf. also

(30) *studié da avocat*
sty'dj-e   da=avu'kat
study-INF ABL=lawyer
'to study in order to become a laywer'

which can be contrasted with the positional meaning of *da* with a grounded Noun:

(31) *studié **da** n'avocat*
 sty'dj-e   da=n=avu'kat
 study-INF ABL=INDEF=lawyer
 'to study at a laywer's'

Equally derived from *da* in the expression of agentivity is the modal meaning found in other lexicalized expressions:

(32) *sté **da** can*
 ste   da='kaŋ
 stay\INF ABL=dog
 'to lead a dog's life'

(33) *vive **da** sol*
 'vive   da='sul
 live\INF ABL=alone
 'to live alone'

(34) *dé **da** ment*
 de   da='mæŋt
 give\INF ABL=mind
 'to pay attention, listen closely'

(35) *vnì/essje **da** manca*
 vni / 'es=je   da='maŋk-a
 come\INF / be\INF=IND ABL=necessity-S
 'to become a necessity /to be necessary'

or the lexicalization *da s-ciopé* /da=stʃu'p-e/ "ABL=burst-INF," often used to imply an exaggerated quantity or degree, especially of heat:

(36) *st'istà a l'hai fait na caud **da** s-ciopé*
 st=is'ta   a='la   fajt   n-a='kawd
 PROX=summer SBJ.3=have\PRS.3S do\PTCL INDEF-F=hot
 da=stʃu'p-e
 ABL=burst-INF
 'last summer it was damn hot' [it did a hot to burst]

but also with the Verb *meuire* /'møjre/ 'to die' in the expression 'to die for:'

(37) a l'era bela **da** meuire
 a='lera 'bel-a da='møjre
 SBJ.3=be\IMPF.3S nice-F ABL=die\INF
 'she was beautiful to die for'

13.2.4 Benefactive **për**

In the case of *për* /pər/ the use as a Preposition of location and motion is still at the origin of a grammaticalization chain but definitely no longer the most common one. As a Preposition of motion, *për* has (as its very form and etymology suggest) a perlative meaning and expresses the route. *Për* is more commonly used in order to express the goal of motion, the cause or reason of an action or state or still its goal or beneficiary. *Për* will be glossed "BEN" (for 'Benefactive').

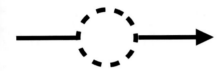

FIGURE 20 Pictorial representation of Benefactive and Goal *për* as a perlative (the circle is dashed because it can be conceptualized as either structured or unstructured; the arrow is solid because the expression of location is excluded and does not reach the figure; cf. Fig. 4 for the use of Ablative *da* for path)

(38) La stra roman-a pì amportanta ch'a passava **për** Ast
 l-a='stra ru'maŋ-a pi ampur'taŋt-a k=a=pa's-ava
 DET-F=road Roman-F more important-F SUB=SBJ.3=pass-IMPF.3S
 pər='ast
 BEN=A.
 'the most important Roman road that went through Ast' ("Hasta;" https://pms.wikipedia.org/wiki/Hasta)

(39) stra [...] **për** ël borgh vej
 stra pər=əl='burg vej
 road BEN=DET=village Old
 'road to the old village' ("Castel ëd Bard;" https://pms.wikipedia.org/wiki/Castel_%C3%ABd_Bard)

The common shift to the expression of beneficiary is evident in

(40) *a l'é n'ann decisiv për Farassin*
a='le   n=an   detʃi'ziw pər=fara'siŋ
SBJ.3=be\PRS.2S INDEF=year decisive   BEN=F.
'It is a decisive year for Farassin' ("Gipo Farassino;" https://pms.wikipedia.org/wiki/Gipo_Farassino)

The use of a preposition marking a beneficiary for the expression of a goal is just another instance of the common metaphorical transfer from human to non-human entities (Luraghi 2014: 124 ff.):

(41) *a possavo për la creassion ëd na lenga artifissial antërnassional*
a=pu's-avu   pər=l-a=krea'sjuŋ   əd=n-a='læŋg-a
SBJ.3=push-IMPF.3P   BEN=DET-F=creation   ATTR=INDEF-F=language-S
artifi'sjal aŋtərnasju'nal
artificial international
'they were pushing for an artificial, international language' ("Giuseppe Peano;" https://pms.wikipedia.org/wiki/Giuseppe_Peano)

(42) *esse vej për la guèra*
'ese   vej pər=l-a='gwær-a
be\INF old BEN=DET-F=war-S
'to be (too) old for war' ("Cavalier;" https://pms.wikipedia.org/wiki/Cavalier)

Less expected but common (Luraghi 2014: 128) is the shift of a goal marker to the expression of cause, as found for Ablative *da* (☞ 13.2.3.) and as witnessed again by *për*:

(43) *conossù për la produssion del fàuss frut dla fròla*
kunu'sy   pər=l-a=prudy'sjuŋ   d=əl='faws   fryt
know\PTCL   BEN=DET-F=production   ATTR=DET=false fruit
d=l-a='frol-a
ATTR=DET-F=strawberry-S
'known for the production of the fake strawberry [fruit]' ("Morej;" https://pms.wikipedia.org/wiki/Morej)

13.2.5 *Comitative* con

We leave the domain of the expression of location and motion in the case of *con* /kuŋ/ 'COM' (for "Comitative"), a Preposition which expresses company and co-agentivity with human Noun Phrases (NPs) and instrument with non-human NPs (on the basis of the metaphor AN INSTRUMENT IS A COMPANION; Luraghi 2014: 124):

(44) *i son coruje dapress **con** Gioanin*
    i='suŋ   ku'ry=je   da'pres kuŋ=dʒua'niŋ
    SBJ.1=be\PRS.1S run\PTCL=IND   behind   COM= G.
    'I ran behind him with Gioanin'

In the expression of co-agentivity *con* is often replaced by the adverbial *ansema* /aŋ'sema/ 'together' and Adessive *a*:

(44′) *i son coruje dapress **ansema a** Gioanin*
    i='suŋ   ku'ry=je   da'pres aŋ'sema a=dʒua'niŋ
    SBJ.1=be\PRS.\1S run\PTCL=IND behind   together ADE= G.
    'I ran behind him [together] with Gioanin'

as well as, obviously, by the two subjects in coordination (☞ 16.1):

(44″) *mi e Gioanin i soma coruje dapress*
    mi   e   dʒua'niŋ i='suma   ku'ry=je   da'pres
    IDP.1S and G.   SBJ.1=be\PRS.1P   run\PTCL=IND   behind
    'Gioanin and me ran behind him'

In a reciprocal action the Comitative may assume an antagonistic meaning ('against') more specifically assured by the Adverb *contra* /'kuŋtra/:

(45) *combate **con** ij Fransèis*
    kum'bate   kuŋ=i=fraŋ'sæjz
    fight\INF   COM=DET\P=French
    1. 'to fight against the French'
    2. 'to fight with the French (against a third party)'

(45′) *combate **contra** ij Fransèis*
    kum'bate   'kuŋtra   i=fraŋ'sæjz
    fight\INF   against   DET\P=French
    'to fight against the French'

or, simply, by the transitive use of the Verb:

(45″) *combate ij Fransèis*
    kumˈbate i=franˈsæjz
    fight\INF DET\P=French
    'to fight the French'

The use for an instrument (either physical or not) is at least as common:

(46) *ël partì che a l'ha atacà la neuva lèj fondamentala toscan-a* **con** *pì ëd violensa*
    əl=parˈti **k=a=ˈla**   **ataˈk-a**   **l-a=ˈneuv-a** **læj**
    DET=party SUB=SBJ.3=have\PRS.3S attack-PTCL DET-F=new-F law
    fuŋdamæŋˈtal-a tusˈkaŋ-a   **kuŋ=ˈpi**   **əd=vjuˈlæŋs-a**
    fundamental-F Tuscanian-F COM=more ATTR=violence-S
    'the party that attacked the new Fundamental Law of Tuscany with most violence' (Sandrone 2004b: 7)

Both instrument and company are often interpreted metaphorically:

(47) *con na pinta a l'é content*
    kuŋ=n-a=ˈpiɲt-a   **a=ˈle**   **kuŋˈtæɲt**
    COM=INDET-F=pint-S SBJ.3=be\PRS.3S happy
    'with a pint he is happy' (Costa 1982b [1938]: 17)

(48) *con sò deuit un pòch dësbela e soa lenga bin molà*
    kuŋ=so=ˈdøjt   **aŋ=ˈpok**   **dəzˈbela e=ˈsu-a**   **ˈlæŋg-a**
    COM=POSS3=manners INDET=few villain and=POSS.3-F tongue-S
    ˈbiŋ muˈl-a
    well grind-PTCL
    'with his somewhat rude way of treating people and his well-ground tongue' (Costa 1982b [1938]: 18)

Furthermore, NPs preceded by *con* enter into a great variety of idioms, such as

(49) *tajà con ël piolèt*
    taˈj-a   **kuŋ=əl=pjuˈlæt**
    cut-PTCL COM=DET=hatchet
    'coarse, surly' (but also 'straightforward, frank') [cut with the hatchet]

and may be the source of various lexicalizations, such as the concessive conjunction *contut* 'even if' (lit. 'with all;' ☞ 16.2.9.).

13.2.6 Combinations of Prepositions

Combinations of Prepositions are not uncommon. Apart from the combinations involving Superessive *su*, such as *an s(u)* (INE=SUP) and *da s(u)* (ABL=SUP), *da* and *an* join in *d'an(t)* (ABL=INE), especially with a following Adverb:

(50) *a vnisia **d'an** sa*
 a=vniˈzia   d=aŋ=ˈsa
 SBJ.3=come\IMPF.3S ABL=INE=DEICT.ADV
 's/he was coming this way'

Another combination is *da për*, completely lexicalized in *daspërlì, dampërlì* (ABL=BEN=there) 'about there,' and, with an independent Pronoun: *daspërmi* (ABL=BEN=IND.1S) 'me alone,' *daspërti, daspërchiel*, etc., as well as *daspërtut* or *dampërtut* (ABL=BEN=all) 'everywhere.'

(51) *Angelo a l'avìa'dcò madurà **daspërchiel** na coltura artìstica bin ancreusa*
 ˈaŋdʒelu a=laˈvia   dˈko madyˈr-a   das=pərˈkjæl
 A.   SBJ.3=have\IMPF.3S also mature-PTCL ABL=BEN=IND.3MS
 n-a=kulˈtyr-a   arˈtistik-a biŋ   aŋˈkrøz-a
 INDET-F=culture-S   artistic-F   well deep-F
 'A. had also developed a very deep artistic culture on his own' (Rabia 2022)

(52) *a cheui d'omagi **daspërtut** ch'a passa*
 a=ˈkøj   d=uˈmadʒi   das=pərˈtyt
 SBJ.3=collect\PRS.3S ATTR=homage   ABL=BEN=all
 k=a=ˈpas-a
 SUB=SBJ.3=pass-PRS.3S
 'he collects homages everywhere he goes by' (Costa 1982a [1928]: 31)

13.3 Non-basic Prepositions

The neat opposition between Prepositions and the prepositional usage of Adverbs breaks down somewhat with the following two Prepositions, which are often or even mostly used together with a preceding basic Preposition or are composed of a basic Preposition.

13.3.1 *Superessive* su

su /sy/ 'up' is both an Adverb and a Preposition; it expresses location and movement on something, either with contact or without. Still, as a Preposition it is always a clitic and has a special allomorphy: it loses its vowel before a determiner and is often (but not always: cfr. 54) preceded by Inessive *an*, resulting graphically in *ans*. This seems enough to warrant its treatment as a separate unit, which will be labelled SUP (for "Superessive"). The use without a preceding Inessive is probably more common in the written than in the oral style, and is fed by calqued configurations, such as /sy=pruˈposta/ 'upon proposal,' calqued upon Italian *su proposta* /su=proˈposta/.

With a following determiner the group /aŋ=s=/ is written separately and /s=/ is usually joined to the determiner ((53)), although alternative spellings occur:

(53) *baodëtta 'd Pasqua **sla** tera fiorìa*
    bawˈdətt-a d=ˈpaskw-a s=l-a=ˈtær-a fjuˈri-a
    chime-s ATTR=Easter-s SUP=DET-F=land-s flourish-PTCL-F
    'concert of Easter bells on the flowery land' (Costa 1982b [1938]: 27)

(54) *mace 'd sangh **su la** piassa stamatin, **an sle** pere grise*
    ˈmatʃ-e d=ˈsaŋg sy=l-a=ˈpjas-a stamaˈtiŋ
    stain-P ATTR=blood SUP=DET-F=square-s this_morning
    aŋ=s=l-e=ˈper-e ˈgriz-e
    INE=SUP=DET-F.P=stone-P grey-F.P
    'bloodstains on the square this morning, on the gray stones' (Regis 1960)

(55) *im treuvo an ritard **an sla** tabela 'd marcia*
    i=m=ˈtrøv-u aŋ=riˈtard aŋ=s=l-a=taˈbel-a
    SBJ.1=OBJ.1S=find-PRS.1S INE=delay INE=SUP=DET-F=table-s
    d=ˈmartʃ-a
    ATTR=march-s
    'I am behind schedule' (Ellena 2022)

Argument is the second main use of *su*:

(56) *a travaja dzortut **an sij** marcà dle telecomunicassion*
    a=traˈvaj-a dzurˈtyt aŋ=s=i=marˈka
    SBJ.3=work-PRS.3S above_all INE=SUP=DET\P=market

```
d=l-e=telekumynika'sjuŋ
ATTR=DET-F.P=telecommunication
```
'it operates mostly in the telecommunications markets' ("NTT Data;" https
://pms.wikipedia.org/wiki/NTT_Data)

Note in the following example the spelling *ans ij* rather than *an sij*:

(57) *a l'ha travajà **ans ij** process ëd radioatività*
```
a='la           trava'j-a       aŋ=s=i=pru'tʃes
SBJ.3=have\PRS.3S work-PTCL INE=SUP=DET\P=process
əd=radjuativi'ta
ATTR=radioactivity
```
'she worked on radioactive processes' ("Lise Meitner;" https://pms.wikipe
dia.org/wiki/Lise_Meitner)

13.3.2   *Interessive* (an)tra

(An)tra /('aŋ)tra/ expresses a location or movement between at least two entities; it will be glossed 'INTER' (for "Interessive"). Its use is not very frequent:

(58) *l'intersession **antra** la surfassa dla tèra e n'ipotétich pian*
```
l=iŋterse'sjuŋ        'aŋtra  l-a=syr'fas-a         d=l-a='tær-a        e
DET=intersection INTER DET-F=surface-S ATTR=DET-F=Earth-S and
ŋ=ipu'tetik          pjaŋ
INDEF=hypothetical  plane
```
'the intersection between the Earth surface and a hypothetical plane'
("Coordinà geogràfiche;" https://pms.wikipedia.org/wiki/Coordin%C3%
A0_geogr%C3%A0fiche)

In the Prepositional Phrase *antra lor*, *antra* is often followed by Attributive *ëd*:

(59) *tuti j'àngoj drit a son uguaj **antra** 'd lor*
```
'tyt-i      'j=aŋguj        drit   a='suŋ         yg'waj  aŋtra
all-M\P DET\P=angle\P right SBJ.3=be\PRS.3P equal INTER
d='lur
ATTR=IDP.3P
```
'all right angles are equal to one another' ("Postulà d'Euclid;" https://pms
.wikipedia.org/wiki/Postul%C3%A0_d%27Euclid)

13.4 Prepositional Use of Adverbs

Adverbs may often enter into prepositional usages, usually preceded or followed by a basic Preposition, most commonly Adessive *a*. What follows is a very partial list:

- *anans ëd/a* /aˈnaŋs əd=/a=/ and *dëdnans ëd/a* /dədˈnaŋs əd=/a=/ 'in front of/before'
- *andrinta a/ëd* /aŋˈdriŋta a/əd =/ 'within'
- *ansema a* /aŋˈsema a=/ 'together with'
- *ansima a* /aŋˈsima a=/ 'on top of'
- *anvers* /aŋˈværs/ 'toward'
- *a randa ëd* /a=ˈraŋda əd=/ 'beside; to the side of'
- *a travers* /a=traˈværs; locally also traˈvæs/ 'across'
- *an mes a* /aŋ=ˈmez a=/ 'in the middle of'
- *d(a)ré ëd/a* /d(a)ˈre əd=/a=/ 'behind'
- *dzora (ëd/a)* /ˈdzura (əd=/a=)/ 'upon'
- *sota (a)* /ˈsuta (a=)/ 'under, below'

Tipo /ˈtipu/ 'type, kind' is a loan from Italian *tipo* /ˈtipo/ and has been grammaticalized as a conjunction and Preposition. The history and grammaticalization of Italian *tipo* has been described by Voghera (2013). Apart from being used as a Noun, Piedmontese *tipo* has a prepositional value of approximate identification ('similar to') but also simply as 'like.' Just as its Italian counterpart (Voghera 2013: 306) *tipo*, without being marked as informal, it is more typical of the spoken registers but nevertheless attested in writing:

(60) *a l'ha vàire arcorense e feste ch'as s'ambaron-o **tipo** la Pasca o l'Aniversari dla Liberassion*
 a=ˈla ˈvajre arkuˈræŋs-e e=ˈfest-e
 SBJ.3=have\PRS.3S many recurrency-P and=feast-P
 k=a=s ambaˈruŋ-u / ˈtipu l-a=ˈpask-a
 SUB=SBJ.3=REFL=heap-PRS.3P/ like DET-F=Easter-S
 o=l=aniverˈsari d=l-a=liberaˈsjuŋ
 or=DET=anniversary ATTR=DET-F=liberation
 'it has various anniversaries and feasts that pile up, like Easter or the Anniversary of the Liberation' (Barba Sergin 2022)

More specific locations and movements may be obtained with full attributive phrases: *an sël fond ëd* /aŋ=s=əl=ˈfuŋd əd=/ or *al fond ëd* /a=l=ˈfuŋd əd=/ 'on the bottom of,' *con ël but ëd* /kuŋ=əl=ˈbyt əd=/ 'with the purpose of,' and many others:

(61) *na pi gran aotonomìa d'assion,* **con ël but ëd** *diminuì j'ostàcoj burocràtich*
　　 n-a=pi　　　　graŋ awtunu'mi-a d=a'sjuŋ /　　kuŋ=əl='byt
　　 INDET-F=more big　autonomy -S ATTR=action / COM=DET=goal
　　 əd=diminy'i　　　j=us'takuj　　　　byru'kratik
　　 ATTR=decrease\INF DET\P=obstacle\P bureaucratic
　　 'a greater autonomy of action, with the purpose of cutting down bureaucratic hurdles' ("Academia dle Siense ëd Turin;" https://pms.wikipedia.org/wiki/Academia_dle_Siense_%C3%ABd_Turin)

(62) and (63) are examples of the prepositional use of Adverbs:

(62) *ël marin a stërmava l'orisont* **andrinta** *a soa foschìa*
　　 əl=ma'riŋ　　　a=stər'm-ava　　　l=uri'zuŋt　　aŋ'driŋta
　　 DET=sea_wind SBJ.3=hide-IMPF.3S DET=horizon within
　　 a='su-a　　　　fus'ki-a
　　 ADE=POSS3-F mist-S
　　 'the southern wind hid the horizon in its mist' (Brero 1972: 3)

(63) *e serco* **'ndrinta'd** *mi 'l²* *paròle giuste*
　　 e　 'særk-u　　ŋ'driŋta d=mi　　l=pa'rol-e　　 'dʒyst-e
　　 and search-PRS.1S within ATTR=IND.1S DET=word-P right-F.P
　　 'I search within myself for the right words' (Tesio 2017: 223)

The opposition between the adverbial and prepositional usages may be exemplified with *dzora*:

(64) *fé sté cito coj aso dla malora përchè a disturbo coj ch'a son sì* **dzora**
　　 fe　　　　ste　　　'tʃitu kuj　　'azu　　d=l-a=ma'lur-a
　　 make\IPV.2P stay\INF quiet DIST\M donkey ATTR=DET-F=ruin-S
　　 pər'kæ　a=dis'tyrb-u　　　　kuj　　　k=a='suŋ　　　　　si
　　 because SBJ.3=disturb-PRS.3P DIST\M SUB=SBJ.3=be\PRS.3P here
　　 'dzura
　　 upon
　　 'silence those damn donkeys because they disturb those who are above' (Coccio 1966: 89)

---

2 Dialectal variant of *le*.

(65) *na malòca legera ch'a rotolava **dzora** a 'n tapiss ëd feuje sëcche*
n-a=maˈlok-a leˈdʒer-a k=a=rutuˈl-av-a ˈdzura
INDET-F=snowball-s light-F SUB=SBJ.3=roll-IMPF.3S upon
a=ŋ=taˈpis əd=ˈføj-e ˈsəkk-e
ADE=INDET=carpet ATTR=leaf-P dry-F.P
'a light snowball rolling over a carpet of dry leaves' (Vaira 2020)

13.5 Attributive Phrases and Binominal Constructions

Although technically a preposition, Attributive *ëd* /əd/ 'ATTR' is dealt separarately due to the wide range of semantic values it covers. Following Langacker (1992: 343), the Attributive may be conceptualized as ascribing an intrinsic relationship between a trajector and a landmark (or a Figure and a Ground). This is the role served by Genitive in languages with nominal cases.

Like with other prepositions, in an attributive phrase the Figure profiles the Ground.

The relationship covers a wide variety of functions that will be treated in turn. The list of functions of *ëd* is loosely based with many changes and additions upon Masini's (2016) account of Italian *di*.

13.5.1 *The Attributive in the Expression of Origin*

The origin of the Attributive is the same Latin preposition DE from which Ablative *da* (DE+AB) is derived (☞ 13.2.3.), although the expression of source is just one of the many uses of *ëd*. Source or origin may refer to a physical location, a period of time or the agent or creator of the trajector:

(66) *na fija ëd Milan*
n-a=ˈfi-a əd=miˈlaŋ
INDEF-F=girl-S ATTR=M.
'a girl from Milan'

(67) *a l'é n'euvra dël sécol ch'a fa XVIII ëd G.B. Vaccarini*
a=ˈle ˈn=øvr-a d=əl=ˈsekul
SBJ.3=be/PRS.3S INDEF(-F)=work-S ATTR=DET=century
k=a=ˈfa dizˈdøt əd=dʒi-bi=vakkaˈrini
SUB=SBJ.3=do/PRS.3S eighteen ATTR=G.=B.=V.
'it is a work from the 18th century by G. B. Vaccarini' ("Catania;" https://pms.wikipedia.org/wiki/Catania)

(68) *angign ëd Turing*
 aŋˈdʒiɲ əd=ˈturiŋg
 instrument ATTR=T.
 'Turing machine' ("Alan Turing;" https://pms.wikipedia.org/wiki/Alan_Turing)

13.5.2 The Attributive in Temporal Expressions

Derived from the use in the expression of origin, it is typical of Piedmontese the use of the Attributive in temporal expressions, as with numerals and inherently-temporal Nouns:

(69) *mi i l'hai ancaminà a travajé dël '63*
 mi i=ˈlaj aŋkamiˈn-a a=travaj-e
 IDP.1S SBJ.3=be\PRS.3S start-PTCL ADE=work-INF
 d=əl=sesaŋtaˈtræ
 ATTR=DET=sixtythree
 'I started working in 1963' (corpus ParlaTO, PTB026; starting at 9′35″)

(70) *a dasio ël BOT[3] al 20 %, dlë '78, d'interessi*
 a=daˈziu əl=ˈbɔt a=l=ˈviɲt pərˈsæŋt /
 SBJ.3=give\IMPF.3P DET=BOT ADE=DET=twenty BEN=hundred
 d=lə=staŋˈtøt / d=inteˈresi
 ATTR=DET=78 / ATTR=interest
 'they gave (you) 20% interest (rate) on Ordinary Treasury Bonds, in 1978' (corpus ParlaTO, PTB026; starting at 11′10′)

(71) *ëd neuit am ven sempe fam*
 əd=ˈnøjt a=m=ˈvæŋ ˈsæmpe fam
 ATTR=night SBJ.3=OBJ.1S=come\PRS.3S always hunger
 'I always get hungry at night'

The Attributive acts as a grounder here (☞ 13.5.8.), as can be seen by the ungrammaticality of its omission

(71′) **neuit am ven sempe fam*

but the possibility (with Nouns) of grounding through the Determiner:

---

3 BOT stands for Italian *Buono Ordinario del Tesoro*, Ordinary Treasury Bond.

(71″) *la neuit am ven sempe fam*
    l-a=ˈnøjt   a=m=ˈvæŋ   ˈsæmpe fam
    DET-F=night SBJ.3=OBJ.1S=come\PRS.3S always hunger
    'I always get hungry at night'

13.5.3 *The Attributive as a Marker of Possession*

In keeping with the metaphor POSSESSORS ARE SOURCES, possession is maybe the prototypical value of the Attributive and one of the most common. Again, the "semantic head" of the construction is the syntactic head of the Noun phrase:

(72) *la ca ëd Pinin*
    l-a=ˈka   əd=piˈniŋ
    DET-F=house ATTR=P.
    'Pinin's house'

13.5.4 *The Attributive of Inherent Relationship*

Among the prototypical uses of the Attributive is the expression of an inherent relationship between two items:

(73) *ël fieul dël sindich*
    əl=ˈfjøl   d=əl=ˈsiŋdik
    DET=boy ATTR=DET=mayor
    'the Mayor's son'

(74) *la sità ëd Coni*
    l-a=siˈta   əd=ˈkuni
    DET-F=town ATTR=C.
    'the town of Coni'

The frequent use in the expression of a part-whole relationship may be subsumed here:

(75) *ël coercc dla peila*
    əl=kuˈærtʃ d=l-a=ˈpæjl-a
    DET=lid   ATTR=DET-F=pan-S
    'the pot lid'

13.5.5 The Attributive in the Expression of Material

In her analysis of Italian *di*, Masini (2016) subsumes the use of the Attributive in the expression of the material and origin under "Modification." Both are certainly basic functions of the Attributive:

(76) *n'anel d'òr*
 n=a'nel d=or
 INDEF=ring ATTR=gold
 'a golden ring'

13.5.6 The Attributive in Nominalizations

Ëd expresses the agent or patient of a nominalization:

(77) *l'erussion dël vulcan*
 l=ery'sjuŋ d=əl=vyl'kaŋ
 DET=eruption ATTR=DET=volcano
 'the volcano eruption'

(78) *l'arcòrd dij bigat am torna an ment*
 l=ar'kord d=i=bi'gat a=m='turn-a
 DET=memory ATTR=DET\P=silkworm SBJ.3=OBJ.1S=return-PRS.3S
 aŋ='mæŋt
 INE=mind
 'the memory of silkworms comes back to me' (Cosio 1975: 47)

(79) *la dëscoerta d'important giassiment petrolifer*
 l-a=dəsku'ært-a d=impur'taŋt dʒasi'mæŋt petru'lifær
 DET-F=discovery-S ATTR=important deposit oil
 'the discovery of important oil fields' ("Càucas;" https://pms.wikipedia.org/wiki/C%C3%Aoucas)

13.5.7 The Attributive in Quantification

In other types of Attributive phrases the Ground is the profiler of the Figure, as the result of a general metonymical process. It is the case of the use of the Attributive in quantification with mass Nouns (countable entities being more commonly quantified through counting or a quantifier). Thus, in

(80) *un mucc ëd gent*
 aŋ='mytʃ əd='dʒæŋt
 INDET=pile ATTR=people
 'a lot of people'

people are profiled, not a pile, and this is in principle true of other "light Nouns" used in quantification (☞ 9.5. for quantificational Nouns).

The concrete meaning of light words may fade away, as in *baron* /baˈruŋ/, originally 'haystack' and then simply 'heap,' is now simply 'a great deal of' anything, even abstract entities like time or power:

(81) *cheiche përson-e a peulo passé un **baron** ëd sò temp për fé costi acòrd*
 ˈkæjk-e pərˈsuŋ-e a=ˈpølu paˈs-e aŋ=baˈruŋ
 SOME-F.P person-P SBJ.3=can\PRS.3P spend-INF INDEF=heap
 əd=ˈso tæmp pərˈfe ˈkust-i aˈkord
 ATTR=POSS.3 time BEN=do\INF PROX-P agreement
 'certain people may spend a lot of time in order to reach these agreements'
 ("Polìtica;" https://pms.wikipedia.org/wiki/Pol%C3%ACtica)

(82) *ël President a l'é elegiù e a l'ha un **baron** ëd podèj.*
 əl=preziˈdæŋt a=ˈle eleˈdʒy e a=ˈla
 DET=president SBJ.3=be\PRS.3S elect-PTCL and SBJ.3=have\PRS.3S
 aŋ=baˈruŋ əd=puˈdæj
 INDEF=heap ATTR=can\INF
 'the President is elected and has a lot of power.' ("Repùblica;" https://pms.wikipedia.org/wiki/Rep%C3%B9blica)

As remarked by Langacker (1992: 344), in the end '[a]ll that remains of their unit sense is the function of delimiting a mass in quantitative terms.'

The "semantic head" of the construction is therefore a Noun in the Attributive phrase. Alongside the many other light Nouns used in quantifications, such as *caterva* /kaˈtærva/ 'multitude,' *patela* /paˈtela/ 'slap,' *pugnà* /pyˈɲa/ 'fistful,' *sach* /sak/ 'sack,' *stissa* /ˈstisa/ 'drop,' etc., one can mention:

(83) *na frisa ëd sal*
 n-a=ˈfriz-a d=sal
 INDEF-F=scrap-S ATTR=salt
 'a bit of salt'

found again also metaphorically:

(84) *na frisa d'ironìa*
 n-a=ˈfriz-a d=iruˈni-a
 INDEF-F=scrap-S ATTR=irony-S
 'a bit of irony' ("Leonhard Euler;" https://pms.wikipedia.org/wiki/Leonhard_Euler)

The use with units of measurement also belongs here. The controller of agreement is on the quantifier in the following example:

(85) *doe giornà⁴ ëd tera am basto*
 'due dʒur'na əd='tær-a a=m='bast-u
 two\F daytime ATTR=land-S SBJ.3=OBJ.1S=be_enough-PRS.3P
 'two "days" of land are enough for me'

but cf. the following (☞ 11.3. for Middle constructions), where both agreement patterns seem possible (but agreement with the light Noun sounds awkward):

(86) *i son catame **un chilo ëd** cerese e i son mangiamje tute*
 i='suŋ ka't-a=me aŋ='kilu əd=tʃer'ez-e e
 SBJ.1=be\PPRS.1S buy-PTCL=OBJ.1S INDEF=kilo ATTR=cherry-P and
 i='suŋ maŋ'dʒ-a=m=je 'tyt-e
 SBJ.1=be\PRS.1S eat-PTCL=OBJ.1S=OBJ.3P all-F.P
 'I bought myself a kilo of cherries and slurped them all' (☞ 11.3. for ethical datives and the Middle construction)

(86') *? ... e i son mangiamlo tut*
 e i='suŋ maŋ'dʒ-a=m=l-u tyt
 and SBJ.1=be\PRS.1S eat-PTCL=OBJ.1S= OBJ.3-M all
 'I bought myself a kilo of cherries and slurped it all'

13.5.8 The Attributive as a Grounder

The use of the Attributive as a Grounder (☞ 8.2.) may be thought of as derived from its use in quantification and it involves *ëd* as a Grounder of uncountable, mass Nouns or of countable Nouns which are turned into grounded mass Nouns. The Attributive grounds an entity and thereby creates a Figure:

(87) *i veuj ëd sùcher*
 i='vøj əd='sykær
 SBJ.1=want\PRS.1S ATTR=sugar
 'I want sugar'

---

4 Traditional unit of land area, equivalent to 3,810 square meters (0.94 acres).

(88) *a sa 'd vaca*
 a='sa   d='vak-a
 SBJ.3=know\PRS.3S ATTR=cow-S
 'it tastes like beef'

13.5.9 The Attributive in the Expression of Categorization

Masini (2016) lists among others two separate functions: subcategorization and approximation for Italian *di*. The former is found with a limited number of taxonomic Nouns and is used in order "to split the whole extension of N2 into parts and to identify a subcategory, or a hyponymic class, of N2," while approximation "is used to identify a marginal and/or unstable element with respect to the category N2" (Masini 2016: 102). Actually, only the range of meanings of the trajector distinguishes the two, so that it is possible to subsume both under a single category of categorization.

While in the examples below *na class d'animaj* 'a class of animals' is certainly an instance of subcategorization, approximation is exemplified by *sòrta d'abilitassion* 'kind of habilitation.' As to *rassa*, it has both a categorizing meaning, as in *na rassa 'd vache* 'a variety of cows,' and an approximative meaning, as in *che rassa ëd na vita* 'what kind of life:'

(89) *na class d'animaj vërtebrà*
 n-a='klas   d=ani'maj   vərte'bra
 INDEF-F=class DET=animal\P vertebrate
 'a class of vertebrate animals' ("Osej;" https://pms.wikipedia.org/wiki/Osej)

(90) *sòrta d'abilitassion për l'ansegnament*
 'sort-a d=abilita'sjuŋ   pər=l=aŋseɲa'mænt
 kind-S ATTR=habilitation BEN=DET=teaching
 'kind of habilitation to teaching' ("Giuseppe Peano;" https://pms.wikipedia.org/wiki/Giuseppe_Peano)

(91) *për capì che rassa ëd na vita che a podèissa mai avèj fait la gent*
 pər=ka'pi   ke   'ras-a əd=n-a='vit-a
 BEN=understand\INF SUB race-S ATTR=INDEF-F=life-S
 k=a=pu'dæjsa   maj a'væj   fajt   l-a='dʒæɲt
 SUB=SBJ.3\can\SUBJ-IMPF.3S ever have\INF do\PTCL DET-F=people
 'in order to understand what kind of life people could ever had [done]' ("Età dla pera;" https://pms.wikipedia.org/wiki/Et%C3%A0_dla_pera)

Not surprisingly, the agreement pattern is often variable:

(92) *na rassa 'd vache ch'a s'anlevo an Piemont*
    n-a='ras-a   d='vak-e   k=a=s=aŋ'lev-u
    INDEF-F=race-S ATTR=COW-P SUB=SBJ.3=REFL=breed-PRS.3P
    aŋ=pie'muŋt
    INE=P.
    'a variety of cows [that are] bred in Piedmont' ("Rassa piemontèisa;" https://pms.wikipedia.org/wiki/Rassa_piemont%C3%A8isa)

but also, with the controller of agreement on the subcategorizing Noun:

(92') *na rassa 'd vache ch'a s'anleva an Piemont*
    n-a='ras-a   d='vak-e   k=a=s=aŋ'lev-a
    INDEF-F=race-S ATTR=COW-P SUB=SBJ.3=REFL=breed-PRS.3S
    aŋ=pie'muŋt
    INE=P.
    'a variety of cows [that is] bred in Piedmont'

13.5.10 The Attributive in the Expressive Elative

The Attributive enters in a peculiar expressive elative construction made up of a trajector followed by an Attributive phrase with an indefinite copy of the trajector as the landmark:

(93) *fòl d'un fòl*
    fòl   d=aŋ='fol
    fool ATTR=INDEF=fool
    'such a fool' [fool of a fool]

An apparently similar pattern is found in such evaluative constructions with a "light Noun" as in Italian *un amore di ragazza* or French *un amour de fille* 'a lovely girl' (*lit.* "a love of (a) girl") and other European languages (Masini 2016: 103). The Piedmontese expressive elative is different both syntactically and semantically, being restricted to exact copies of trajector and landmark (the latter being always indefinite, while the former is only grounded by the following Attributive phrase), and being semantically productive but restricted to insults and any word or expression with a highly derogatory meaning. In the following sentence a pig cannot be referenced, only a person who is considered to display a (culturally defined) pig's behavior:

(94) *crin d'un crin*
   kriŋ d=aŋ='kriŋ
   pig   ATTR=INDEF=pig
   'real animal' [pig of a pig]

The following shows that complex NPs may enter the construction as well and not being referential at all (*giuda fàuss* /ˈdʒyda faws/ *lit.* "false Judas" being a common swear word):

(95) *giuda fàuss d'un giuda fàuss*
   ˈdʒyda faws d=aŋ=ˈdʒyda   faws
   Judas false ATTR=INDEF=Judas   false

13.5.11 Sequences of Attributive Phrases

Given the wide range of meanings of the Attributive, sequences of Attributive phrases are not altogether uncommon:

(96) *n'esempi particolar dël prinsipi ëd conservassion ëd l'energìa*
   n=eˈzæmpi   partikuˈlar   d=əl=prinˈsipi   əd=kuŋsærvaˈsjuŋ
   INDEF=example   particular   ATTR=DET=principle   ATTR=conservation
   əd=l=enerˈdʒi-a
   ATTR=DET=energy-S
   'a particular example of the Law of Conservation of Energy' ("Lej ëd Lenz;" https://pms.wikipedia.org/wiki/Lej_%C3%ABd_Lenz)

13.5.12 Syntactic Properties of Binominal Constructions

As was seen above, agreement and quantification operate rather straightforwardly on the basis of semantic headedness: the head of the Noun phrase (N1) controls agreement in number but only if it is also the semantic head; agreement in gender is less easy to ascertain, given the limitation of gender flagging, although it is still visible on certain Adjectives and on the Participle of intransitive Verbs. The following shows agreement in both gender and number with N1:

(97) *le machine ëd na vira a saran staite pì bele, ma cole d'ancheuj a son pì sicure*
   l-e=ˈmakin-e   əd=n-a=vir-a   a=saˈraŋ
   DET-F.P=machine-P   ATTR=INDEF-F=time-S   SBJ.3=be\DUB.3P
   stajt-e   pi   ˈbel-e   ma ˈkul-e   d=aŋˈkøj   a=ˈsuŋ
   be\PTCL-F.P   more   nice-F.P   but DIST-F.P   ATTR=today   SBJ.3=be\PRS.3P
   pi   siˈkyr-e
   more   safe-F.P
   'past-time cars may have been more beautiful, but today's ones are safer'

PREPOSITIONS AND PREPOSITIONAL PHRASES 401

In quantification (☞ 13.5.7.) and categorization (☞ 13.5.9.) the "weight" of the head Noun determines its ability of being the controller of agreement; e.g., in the following examples agreement is on the Feminine word *gent* 'people,' not on Masculine *mucc* 'lot,' and the same patterns apply with 'letters' and 'heap:'

(98) *un **mucc** ëd gent a l'é già andaita via*
aŋ=ˈmytʃ əd=ˈdʒæɲt a=ˈle dʒa aŋˈdajt-a ˈvia
INDEF=pile ATTR=people SBJ.3=be\PRS.3S already go\PTCL-F away
'a lot of people already left'

(99) *un **baron** ëd litre scrivùe da stanteut corëspondent diferent*
aŋ=baˈruŋ əd=ˈlitr-e skriˈvy-e da=staŋˈtøt
INDEF=heap ATTR=letter-P write\PTCL-F.P ABL=seventy-eight
kurəspuŋˈdæɲt difeˈræŋt
correspondent different
'a great number of letters written by 78 different correspondents' ("Marin Mersenne;" https://pms.wikipedia.org/wiki/Marin_Mersenne)

(99′) ?/*... *scrivù da stanteut corëspondent diferent*
skriˈvy da=staŋˈtøt kurəspuŋˈdæɲt difeˈræŋt
write\PTCL ABL=seventy-eight correspondent different
'... written by 78 different correspondents'

Possibly reflecting more "weight" and a lesser degree of desemanticization of the light Noun, agreement is instead on N1 in the following:

(100) *As dis "omèt" [...] un **baron** ëd pere che a l'abia adoss nen natural*
a=s=ˈdiz uˈmæt aŋ=baˈruŋ əd=ˈper-e
SBJ.3=REFL=say\PRS.3S omèt INDEF=heap ATTR=stone-P
k=a=ˈlabja aˈdus næŋ natyˈral
SUB=SBJ.3=have\SUBJ.3S source NEG natural
'it is called *omèt* [...] a group of stones that does not have a natural origin' ("Omèt;" https://pms.wikipedia.org/wiki/Om%C3%A8t)

Agreement on N2 would logically imply that the stones do not have a natural origin:

(100′) *... che a l'abio adoss nen natural*
k=a=ˈlabju aˈdus næŋ natyˈral
SUB=SBJ.3=have\SUBJ.3P source NEG natural
'... that do not have a natural origin'

Other tests for headedness give similar results. Again, quantificational and categorizing Attributive phrases cannot be replaced by a Pronoun and cannot be dislocated, while both tests give positive results for other types:

(101) *i l'hai provà la maja ëd lan-a e cola ëd coton*
      i=ˈlaj   pruˈv-a   l-a=ˈmaj-a   əd=ˈlaŋ-a   e
      SBJ.1=have\PRS.1S try-PTCL DET-F=sweater-S ATTR=wool-S and
      ˈkul-a   əd=kuˈtuŋ
      DIST-F ATTR=cotton
      'I tried the wool sweater and the cotton one'

(102) **a i-era na patela ëd fieuj e un-a ëd fije*
      a=j=ˈera   n-a=paˈtel-a   əd=ˈfjøj   e   ˈyŋ-a
      SBJ.3=IND=be\IMPF.3S INDEF-F=fistful-S ATTR=boy\P and one-F
      əd=ˈfi-e
      ATTR=girl-P
      'there were a lot of boys and one of girls'

(103) *a l'é ëd Gioanin la ca ch'i l'hai vist*
      a=ˈle   əd=dʒuaˈniŋ   l-a=ˈka   k=i=ˈlaj
      SBJ.3=be\PRS.3S ATTR=G. DET-F=house SUB=SBJ.1=have\PRS.1S
      vist
      see\PTCL
      'the house I saw is Gioanin's'

(104) **a l'é ëd pess na rassa ch'a l'han trovà*
      a=ˈle   əd=ˈpæs   n-a=ˈras-a   k=a=ˈlaŋ
      SBJ.3=be\PRS.3S ATTR=fish INDEF-F=race-S SUB=SBJ.3=have\PRS.3P
      truˈv-a
      find-PTCL
      'it is of fish a kind they found'

cf.

(104') *a l'han trovà na rassa ëd pess*
      a=ˈlaŋ   truˈv-a   n-a=ˈras-a   əd=ˈpæs
      SBJ.3=have\PRS.3P find-PTCL INDEF-F=race-S ATTR=fish
      'they found a kind of fish'

CHAPTER 14

Phrases

This chapter deals with the syntax of phrases in general and with adjectival phrases (14.3) and time expressions (14.4.).

Possessive phrases are dealt with among the grounders (☞ 8.4.), and numeral and quantifying phrases in Ch. 9. The semantics of prepositions and prepositional phrases has been treated in Ch. 13. Modal, final, etc. phrases are instead discussed in Ch. 15., together with their clausal expression.

14.1 The Structure of the Noun Phrase

Noun phrases are by definition elements headed by a Noun or a Noun-like element. In either case the head must be grounded (☞ 8.).[1]

The following elements may act as heads in Noun phrases:
- Nouns
- Adjectives
- Deictics
- Possessives

Elements acting as modifiers in Noun phrases include:
- Adjectives
- Deictics
- Possessives
- Quantifiers
- prepositional phrases (☞ 13.)
- relative clauses (☞ 15.5.)

14.2 Grounding and Ordering of Phrases

Adjectives and Possessives may act as heads provided that they are grounded. Grounding may be done with a Determiner or a Deictic:

---

[1] However, proper names, as remarked in 8.1., are never grounded.

(1) *am pias ël ross*
 a=m=ˈpjaz   əl=ˈrus
 SBJ.3=OBJ.1S=like\PRS.3S DET=red
 'I like the color red'

In (1) the order of constituents is VS. *Ël ross am pias*, with SV order, would rather be uttered for contrast or in answering a request to choose between two or more options.

(2) *col ross am pias ëd pì*
 kul rus a=m=ˈpjaz   əd=ˈpi
 DIST red SBJ.3=OBJ.1S=like\PRS.3S ATTR=more
 'I like the red one more'

Grounded Adjectives may be subject to lexicalization and are often used as nominal heads:

(3) *ij Gheub i-j sopòrto nen*
 i=ˈgøb   i=j=suˈport-u   næŋ
 DET\M.P=hunchback SBJ.1=OBJ.3P=bear-PRS.1S NEG
 'I cannot stand the Hunchbacks' (a derogatory nickname of the Juventus Football Club and its supporters)

Apart from the use of the Determiner in order to disambiguate the number of Masculine Possessives (☞ 8.4.), Possessives must be grounded in order to act as heads:

(4) *ël mè a l'é pì bel*
 əl=ˈme   a=ˈle   pi   bel
 DET=POSS.1S SBJ.3=be\PRS.3S more nice
 'mine is more beautiful'

Deictics can by themselves act as heads:

(5) *col-lì a capiss pòch*
 kul=ˈli   a=kaˈpis   pok
 DIST=there SBJ.3=understand\PRS.3S few
 'that (guy) [there] does not understand much'

TABLE 53 Order of elements in the Noun Phrase

| | Determiner, Classifier, Deictic, | Possessive, Quantifier | Adjective | head | Adjective | prep. phrase | relative clause |

As shown in Table 53 and consonant with the basic VO order in clauses, modifiers by and large follow their head, but a few types of modifiers always appear before the head, while Adjectives, though basically post-head, may also be found in pre-head position.

Determiners, Classifiers and Deictics are always, if present, the first element of a NP, and therefore precede the Noun. The same applies to Possessives and Quantifiers, unless a Determiner or Classifier is present (in which case Possessives and Numerals follow and are sandwitched between the Determiner or Classifier and the Noun). An exception is the Quantifier *tut* /tyt/ 'all,' which always precede the Determiner.

Prepositional and attributive phrases (☞ 13.) and relative clauses (☞ 15.5.) always follow the Noun (although they may be, albeit very rarely, found in prenominal position, e.g., in poetry).

The positioning of Adjectives (☞ 14.3.) is more complex and will be discussed separately.

14.3 Adjectival Phrases

At first glance, Adjectives may appear either before or after the head, or even, when more than one Adjective are present, both before and after:

(6) *cola gròssa ca rossa*
    'kul-a 'gros-a ka 'rus-a
    DIST-F big-F house red-F
    'that big red house'

Actually, Adjectives overwhelmingly come after their head; the ratio behind the prenominal position are not easy to pinpoint (and are further subject to much personal and stylistic—but not geographic—variation).

A special, easy case is provided by adjectival Quantifiers (☞ 9.), which, *qua* Quantifiers, always precede the head:

(7) a l'ha **gnun** deuit
 a='la   ɲyŋ   døjt
 SBJ.3=have\PRS.3 nobody manners
 'he has no manners'

(8) ës motor a fa sempe **tant** ciadel
 əs=mu'tur   a='fa   'sæmpe taŋt tʃa'del
 DEICT=engine SBJ.3=do\PRS.3S always much noise
 'this engine always does a lot of noise'

The prenominal position of Adjectives is said to be triggered in French, *inter alia*, by factors of "subjective emphasis" (i.e., a strong orientation toward the speaker), quantification and weakness (i.e, a strong requirement of adjacency, like in incorporation; Laenzlinger 2000: 77 ff.). The problem with these requirements is the vagueness of the whole concept of "subjective emphasis" and the uncertainty of weakness in Piedmontese. Weakness is certainly shown by the Adjective *autr* 'other,' which is /awt/ rather than /awtr/ for most speakers but which always preserves its final /r/ in the lexicalized collocation:

(9) *l'autr dì*
 l=awt[ər]='di
 DET=other=day
 'the day before yesterday; a few days ago' [lit.: the other day]

Other instances of collocations without phonological evidence of weakness may be

(10) avèj **bel** deuit
 a'væj   bel døjt
 have\INF nice manners
 'to have good manners'

(11) avèj **bon** temp
 a'væj   buŋ tæmp
 have\INF good time
 'to waste one's time; to be a fun-lover' (Gribaudo 1996: 873)

Note that in collocations like these the Noun phrases may lack Grounders.
 In general, the default postnominal position is taken by Adjectives with a delimiting value, i.e., that restrict the subset of possible items described by the

head to those exhibiting the quality expressed by the Adjective; conversely, the prenominal position is reserved to Adjectives which add some inherent quality to the head.

Such inherent quality leads itself easily to lexicalization (and in case even to phonological and graphical incorporation with the head). An example well attested in Piedmontese as elsewhere in Romance is the case of the basic Adjective *bon* /buŋ/ 'good' followed by the equally generic Noun *òm* /om/ 'man; person;' *bon òm*, lit. 'good man' has been lexicalized into *bonòm* /buˈnom/ 'good fellow' or 'guy' (cf. French *bonhomme*). Phonologically, lexicalization is shown by the alveolar pronunciation of the nasal instead of the etymological /ŋ/ (*bon òm* /buŋ om/ > *bonòm* /buˈnom/):

(12) col **bonòm** ëd Celestin a l'ha trovalo mòrt ant la gabia
 kul buˈnom əd=tʃelesˈtiŋ a=ˈla truˈv-a=l-u
 that good_fellow ATTR=C. SBJ.3=have\PRS.3S find-PTCL=OBJ.3-M
 mort aɲt=l-a=ˈgabj-a
 dead INE=DET-F=cage-S
 'Poor Celestin found him dead in the cage' (Arnolfo 2021)

Leaving aside this and similar lexicalizations, the prenominal position of Adjectives is mainly reserved to monosyllabic and semantically basic, antonymic Adjectives expressing moral or physical quality, such as
- *bon* /buŋ/ 'good' and *gram* /gram/ 'bad'
- *bel* /bel/ 'nice, beautiful' and *brut* /bryt/ 'ugly'
- *gròss* /gros/ or *gran(d)* /graŋd/ 'big, large' and *cit* /tʃit/ 'small, little'
- *aut* /awt/ 'high' and *bass* /bas/ 'low'
- *vej* /vej/ 'old' and *neuv* /nøw/ 'new'

(13) për serché 'd perde col **brut** vissi
 pər=særˈk-e ˈd=pærde kul bryt ˈvisi
 BEN=search-INF ATTR=lose\INF that ugly vice
 'to try to lose that bad habit' (Barba Sergin 2021b)

(14) na s-cioendra 'd **veje** ca
 n-a=stʃuˈæŋdra ˈd=vej-e ka
 IND-F=fence ATTR=old-F.P house
 'a fence of old houses' (Duberti 1996: 19)

The prenominal position is not limited to these few Adjectives. In case of ambiguity the prenominal position is linked to an epistemic or moral reading, while a more literal reading of the Adjective is forced by its postonominal position:

(15) *na pòvra fomna*
   n-a=ˈpovr-a   ˈfumn-a
   INDEF-F=poor-F woman-S
   'a poor woman' (i.e., 'a woman to pity')

(16) *na fomna pòvra*
   n-a=ˈfumn-a   ˈpovr-a
   INDEF-F=woman-S poor-F
   'a poor woman' (i.e., 'a woman who is not rich')

Instead, the closest antonym of *pòvr*, *sgnor* /sɲur/ 'rich,' has no epistemic reading and can only occur postnominally:

(17) *na madamin sgnora*
   n-a=madaˈmiŋ   ˈsɲur-a
   INDEF-F=young_woman rich-F
   'a rich young woman'

In the absence of other modifiers the prenominal position seems impossible with other Adjectives:

(18) *na màchina nèira*
   n-a=ˈmakin-a   ˈnæjr-a
   INDEF-F machine-S black-F
   'a black car'

(18′) **na nèira màchina*

When both a prenominal and a postnominal Adjective co-occur, the first reading is with the pre-nominal Adjective having scope over the postnominal:

(19) *na bela màchina giaponèisa*
   n-a=ˈbel-a   ˈmakin-a   dʒapuˈnæjz-a
   INDEF-F=nice-F machine-S Japanese-F
   'a beautiful [Japanese car]'

However, the opposite reading 'a nice car that is Japanese' is not in principle excluded.

The same applies to Attributive phrases (☞ 13.5.), when an Adjective occurs prenominally and has scope over the whole phrase:

(20) *un **pressios** anel d'òr*
    aŋ=pre'sjuz   a'nel d=or
    INDEF=precious ring ATTR=gold
    'a precious golden ring'

On the contrary, a postnominal position seems odd before and after the attributive phrase (where the Adjective is more easily interpreted as modifying the Noun in the attributive phrase):

(20') ?*n'anel pressios d'òr*

(20") ?*n'anel d'òr pressios*
    (preferred reading: 'a ring made of precious gold')

(21) *un cancel ëd fer **batù***
    aŋ=kaŋ'tʃel əd='fær   ba'ty
    INDEF=gate ATTR=iron beat\PTCL
    'a wrought-iron gate'

Especially in fixed configurations two coordinated Adjectives may appear in prenominal position:

(22) *fé 'l **bel** e 'l **brut** temp*
    'fe   l=bel   e   l=bryt   tæmp
    do\INF DET=nice and DET=ugly time
    'to do whatever one likes ['to do the good and bad time']'

Asyndetic coordination is preferred between Adjectives in postnominal position:

(23) *a l'é catasse na màchina **neuva neira***
    a='le   ka't-a=se   n-a='makin-a   'nøv-a 'næjr-a
    SBJ.3=be\PRS.3S buy-PTCL=REFL INDEF-F=machine-S new-F black-F
    'he got [bought] himself a new black car'

Again, prenominal position is possible with the basic Adjectives identified above:

(24) *a l'é catasse na bela màchina neuva neira*
    a=ˈle   **kaˈt-a=se**   **n-a=ˈbel-a**   ˈmakin-a   ˈnøv-a
    SBJ.3=be\PRS.3S buy-PTCL=REFL INDEF-F=nice-F machine-S new-F
    ˈnæjr-a
    black-F
    'he got [bought] himself a nice new black car'

Prenominal position is generally excluded for quasi-synonyms to the basic prenominal Adjectives when occurring alone, but is allowed when the head Noun is further modified postnominally:

(25) ?*a l'é catasse na fiamenga màchina*
    a=ˈle   **kaˈt-a=se**   **n-a=fjaˈmæŋg-a**   ˈmakin-a
    SBJ.3=be\PRS.3S buy-PTCL=REFL INDEF-F=wonderful-F machine-S
    'he got [bought] himself a wonderful car'

(25') *a l'é catasse na fiamenga màchina neuva*
    a=ˈle   **kaˈt-a=se**   **n-a=fjaˈmæŋg-a**   ˈmakin-a
    SBJ.3=be\PRS.3S buy-PTCL=REFL INDEF-F=wonderful-F machine-S
    ˈnøv-a
    new-F
    'he got [bought] himself a wonderful new car'

A basic Adjective is also shifted prenominally when preceding an attributive phrase:

(26) *la nassion con la pi auta densità ëd popolassion*
    l-a=naˈsjuŋ   **kuŋ=l-a=pi**   ˈawt-a dæŋsiˈta əd=pupulaˈsjuŋ
    DET-F=nation COM=DET-F=more high-F density ATTR=population
    'the country with the highest population density' ("Densità ëd popolassion;" https://pms.wikipedia.org/wiki/Densit%C3%A0_%C3%ABd_po polassion)

The only other possibility being

(26') *la nassion con la densità ëd popolassion pi auta*

while the Adjective is dispreferred between the Noun and the prepositional phrase:

(26″) ?*La nassion con la densità pi **auta** ëd popolassion*

Long attributive phrases and relative clauses cannot in any case be followed by Adjectives modifying the head:

(27) *na bela fija ch'i conossia*
 n-a='bel-a   'fi-a   k=i=kunu'sia
 INDEF-F=nice-F girl-s SUB=SBJ.1=know\IMPF.1S
 'a nice girl I used to know'

(27′) **na fija ch'i conossia bela*

Apart again the basic Adjectives, the ordering pattern of Adjectives has the attributive Adjective(s) following any lexicalization, as *fonsionari pùblich* 'public servant, government official' and *arzigh sìsmich* 'seismic risk' below (the latter calqued upon Italian *rischio sismico*):

(28) *un fonsionari **pùblich** patanù*
 aŋ=fuŋsju'nari 'pyblik pata'ny
 INDEF=official public   naked
 'a naked government official'

vs. the unacceptable:

(28′) ** un fonsionari patanù pùblich*

(28″) ** un patanù fonsionari pùblich*

but, with a more basic Adjective:

(29) *na zòna a fòrt arzigh **sìsmich***
 n-a='zon-a   a='fort   ar'zig 'sizmik
 INDEF-F=zone-s   ADE=strong   risk   seismic
 'an area with high seismic risk' ("Messin-a;" https://pms.wikipedia.org/wiki/Messin-a)

Further Adjectives follow the same pattern:

(30) *un fonsionari **pùblich fransèis patanù***
aŋ=fuŋsjuˈnari ˈpyblik fraŋˈsæjz pataˈny
INDEF=official public French naked
'a naked French government official'

14.4 Temporal Phrases and Telling the Time

Lexicalized temporal expressions are not introduced by any prepositions. Very often, temporal expressions are expressed by temporal Adverbs (☞ 12.4.1.). In all other cases a preposition must precede the temporal word or phrase. Temporal phrases tend to be placed clause-initially but may take clause-final position when under focus.

(31) ***st'istà*** *a l'hai fait gnente bel*
st=isˈta aˈla fajt ˈɲæŋte bel
PROX=summer SBJ.3=be/PRS.3S do-PTCL nothing nice
'last summer weather was not nice at all'

(32) *a l'é mariasse **l'ann passà***
aˈle maˈrj-a=se l=an paˈs-a
SBJ.3=be/PRS.3S marry-PTCL=REFL DET=year pass-PTCL
's/he got married last year'

Staneuit /st-a=ˈnøjt/ ("PROX-F=night") 'tonight' is ambiguous between the readings 'last night' and 'tonight,' with the tense of the Verb or *ier neuit* 'yesterday night' being used for disambiguation:

(33) ***staneuit*** *a l'é andait sota zero*
sta=ˈnøjt aˈle aŋˈdajt ˈsuta ˈzeru
PROX-F=night SBJ.3=be\PRS.3S go\PTCL under zero
'last night the temperature dropped below zero'[2]

(34) *speroma mach ëd podej deurme **staneuit***
speˈr-uma mak əd=puˈdæj ˈdørme st-a=ˈnøjt
hope-PRS.1P only ATTR=can\INF sleep\INF PROX-F=night
'let's just hope we manage to sleep tonight'

---

2 Celsius degrees.

(35) *ier neuit a l'é vnume la bòja*
 jer nøjt a='le 'vny=me l-a='boj-a
 yesterday night SBJ.3=be\PRS.3S come\PTCL=OBJ.1S DET-F=bug-s
 'yesterday night I got belly ache' [the bug came to me]

With non-inherently temporal words and phrases the Inessive space preposition *an* /aŋ/ is often used in competition with an Attributive phrase (☞ 13.5.2.):

(36) *a l'é constituisse a Alpëtte ai 21 ëd luj dël 1974, ant ël di prinsipal dla Festa dël Piemont*
 a='le kuŋstity'i=se a=al'pətte
 SBJ.3=be/PRS.3S constitute\PTCL=REFL ADE=A.
 a=i=viŋ'tyŋ əd='lyj 1974 / aŋt=əl='di prinsi'pal
 ADE=DET\P=twenty-one DET=July 1974 / INE=DET=day principal
 d=l-a='fest-a d=əl=pje'muŋt
 ATTR=DET-F=holiday-S ATTR=DET=Piedmont
 'it was formed in Alpëtte[3] on July 21, 1974, in the main day of the Piedmont Holiday' ("Union ëd j'associassion piemontèise and ël mond;" https://pms.wikipedia.org/wiki/Union_%C3%ABd_j%27associassion_piemont%C3%A8ise_ant_%C3%ABl_mond)

(37) *ma 'nt la stagion dle feste e dl'abondansa*
 ma ŋt=l-a=sta'dʒuŋ d=l-e='fest-e e
 but INE=DET-F=season ATTR=DET-F.P=feast-P and
 d=l=abuŋ'daŋs-a
 ATTR=DET=plenty-S
 'but in the season of feasts and plenty' (Costa 1982a [1928]: 26)

In time telling the basic units are *ora* /'ur-a/, Pl. *ore* /'or-e/ 'hour,' *minuta* /mi'nyt-a/, Pl. *minute* /mi'nyt-e/ 'minute,' and *second* /se'kuŋd/ 'second.'
 Telling the time involves in the spoken registers the division of day between a.m. and p.m. (expressions such as *ëd matin* /əd=ma'tiŋ/ 'ATTR=morning,' *ëd dòp-disné* /əd=dopdiz'ne/ 'ATTR=afternoon,' *ëd seira* / əd='sæjra/ 'ATTR=evening' or *ëd neuit* /əd='nøjt/ 'ATTR=night' may be added for disambiguation). From 0 to 3 a.m./p.m. the number expressing the hour is followed by *bòt* /bot/ 'bang, chime' (but restricted in use to time-telling); for '1' the Grounder *un* /aŋ/ is used rather than the numeral *un* /yŋ/:

---

3 Alpëtte /al'pətte/, Italian Alpette /al'pette/ (45°25′N 07°35′E).

un bòt /aŋ=ˈbot/ '1 a.m./p.m.'
tre bòt /træ bot/ '3 a.m./p.m.'

Mes bòt /mez bot/ means 'half past midday/midnight.'
    The use of *bòt* with 4 a.m./p.m. seems restricted but possible:[4]

(38) *A quatr **bòt** dòp disné Roberto Gremmo a farà 'na ciaciarada [...]'*
    a=kwat   bot   dop dizˈne ruˈbærtu ˈgremmu a=faˈra
    ADE=four chime after lunch R.   G.   SBJ.3=do\DUB.3S
    n-a=tʃatʃaˈrad-a
    INDEF-F=chat-S
    'At four p.m. Roberto Gremmo will give a talk [...]' (https://centrostudidia
    logo.com/2018/09/13/incontro-a-borriana-con-roberto-gremmo-sabato-
    29-settembre-2018/)

After 3 or 4 a.m./p.m. and up to 11, hours are expressed with numbers that are not grounded by the Determiner but followed by *ore* /ˈur-e/ 'hours.' 'Midday' and 'midnight' are lexicalized as *mesdì* /mezˈdi/ and *mesaneuit* /mezaˈnøjt/ respectively.

Minutes are added after the hour preceded by *e* /e/ 'and' (and, from 4 to 11, without *ore*). From, usually, 40′ of each hour, reference is made to the next hour, either with the minutes preceding the hour and the latter as a Prepositional phrase headed by Adessive *a*, or with the hour first and the minutes preceded by *meno* /ˈmenu/ 'less.' With *mesdì* and *mesaneuit* the minutes may precede the hour (optionally followed by *minute* / miˈnyte / 'minutes') and by *dòp* /dop/ 'after.'

---

4 Pipino (1783b: 183) writes in his dictionary: *"Bòt*: this word is used here in order to count the French hours, from half an hour to two and a half, either after midday or after midnight. Therefore, we say: *"mes-bòt", "un-bòt", "un-bòt-e-mès", "doi-bòt", "doi-bòt-e-mès"*. The Provincials say *"mès-ora", "unˈora", "unˈora-e-mèsa"*; and some who want to use "bòt" say, for example, *"eut-bòt", "neuv-bòt", "dès-bòt", "ondès-bòt"*. From this alone the Provincials are different from the Turinese, who from "three" up to "eleven" always say *"ore"*. Almost nobody says *"dodes-ore"*, but rather *"mesdì", "mesaneuit"*. It is also used for "strike".' Original: BÒT. *Questa voce da noi si usa per contare le ore di Francia, dalla mezz'ora sino alle due e mezzo, sì dopo mezzogiorno, che dopo mezzanotte; onde diciamo "mes-bòt", "un-bòt", "un-bòt-e-mès", "doi-bòt", "doi-bòt-e-mès". I Provinciali, dicono "mès-ora", "un'ora", "un'ora-e-mèsa"; e taluni, che vogliono usare "bòt", dicono, per esempio, "eut-bòt", "neuv-bòt", "dès-bòt", "ondès-bòt". Da questo solo si distinguono i Provinciali dai Torinesi, che da "trè" fino a "ondès", dicono sempre "ore". Non usasi pressoché da veruno il dire "dodès-ore", ma bensì "mesdì", "mesaneuit". Si prende anche per "Colpo"*. The Provincials's speech is one of the dialects identified by Pipino (☞ 1.5.).

Quart /kwart/ and *mesa* /mez-a/ are 'quarter' and 'half,' respectively (the latter in its Feminine form—*ora* 'hour' being implied). With *bòt* the Masculine form *mes* /mez/ is used.

un quart a un bòt /aŋ=ˈkwart a=aŋ=ˈbot/ 'a quarter to 1 a.m./p.m.'
doi bòt e un quart /duj ˈbot e aŋ=ˈkwart/ 'a quarter past 2 a.m./p.m.'
doi bòt e mes /duj bot e mez/ '2:30 a.m./p.m.'
singh ore /siŋg ˈur-e/ '5 a.m./p.m.'
ses e vint /sez e viŋt/ '6:20 a.m./p.m.'
mesdì e des /mezˈdi e dez/ '10 past midday'
des (minute) dòp mesaneuit /dez (miˈnyte) dop mezaˈnøjt/ '10 past midnight'

When used predicatively no nominal subject is specified and the Verb takes 3S agreement:

(39) *a l'é des ore*
    a=ˈle   dez ˈur-e
    SBJ.3=be\PRS.3S ten hour-P
    'it is 10 a.m./p.m.'

Expressions of time-telling are preceded by Adessive *a* and/or Ablative *da* in prepositional phrases:

(40) *i travajo da doi bòt a neuv ore*
    i=traˈvaj-u   da=ˈduj bot a=ˈnøw   ˈur-e
    SBJ.1=work-PRS.1S ABL=two bang ADE=nine hour-P
    'I work from 2 to 9'

Weekdays and names of months follow the same rules:

(41) *a magg a ventrìa ch'a pissèisso gnanca ij rat*
    a=ˈmadʒ   a=væŋˈtria   k=a=piˈs-æjsu
    ADE=May SBJ.3=must.COND.3S SUB=SBJ.3=piss-SUBJ.IMPF.3P
    ˈɲanka   i=ˈrat
    not_even DET\P=rat
    'In May not even rats should piss'

Being full Nouns, they can also act as heads of phrases or subject of clauses:

(42) *a pòrta **Giugn** rame 'd ciresa an man*
 a=ˈport-a   dʒyɲ   ˈram-e   d=tʃiˈrez-a   aŋ=ˈmaŋ
 SBJ.3=bring-3S June   branch-P ATTR=cherry_tree-S   INE=hand
 'June carries cherry tree branches' (Donna 2022: 162)

CHAPTER 15

Clauses

The basic sentential word order is SVO, but variations in constituent's order are very common, especially in conversation, and are due to pragmatic or stylistic factors (☞ 18.).

Predication is centered around a Verb, but non-verbal predication is likewise possible.

15.1   Non-verbal Predication

15.1.1   *Bare (Elliptical) Non-verbal Predication*

In speech, any constituent, and actually any string may function as a predication (see Izre'el 2018), as in the following exchange:

(1)   a. *it lo sente?*
      it=l-u=ˈsæŋt-e   ↗
      SBJ.2S=OBJ.3-M=hear\PRS.2S Q
      'do you hear it?'

   b. *mh*
      mm
      'uh' (declarative intonation: 'yeah, I do')

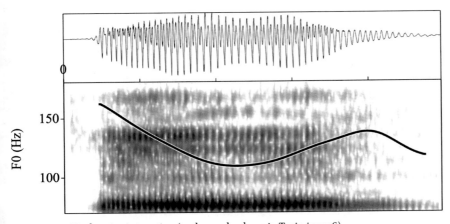

FIGURE 21   Declarative intonation (male speaker born in Turin in 1956)

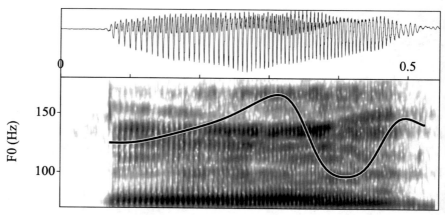

FIGURE 22   Interrogative intonation (male speaker born in Turin in 1956)

 b'. *mh?*
  mm ↗
  'mmh?' (rising, interrogative intonation: 'what did you say?')

Apart from these maybe extreme examples (but well possible and common in Piedmontese and perhaps in any language), any word belonging to a major class may function as predication. Affixes are excluded. A one-word predication may but does not need to involve the repetition of a word from a previous utterance:

(2) a. *lait ò sucher?*
   lajt o 'syker ↗
   milk or sugar Q
   'milk or sugar?'

  b. *sucher*
   'syker
   sugar
   'sugar'

(3) a. *it la vëdde cola ca?*
   it=l-a='vədde   **'kul-a ka** ↗
   SBJ.2S=OBJ.3-F=see\PRS.2S DIST-F house Q
   'do you see that house?'

b. *bela!*
   'bel-a
   nice-F
   'nice!'

(4) a. *com a l'é?*
    kum a='le   ↗
    how SBJ.3S=be\PRS.3S Q
    'how are you?'

   b. *bastansa*
      bas'taŋsa
      enough
      'not too bad'

   b'. *pa vaire*
       pa   'vajre
       NEG.EMPH several
       'not so well'

(5) a. *e cost-sì, vaire ch'a costa?*
       e   kust='si / 'vajre k=a='kust-a   ↗
       and PROX=here / several SUB=SBJ.3=cost-PRS.3S Q
       'and this one here, how much does it cost?'

   b. *quatòrdes*
      kwa'tordez
      fourteen
      'fourteen (Euros)'

The reply with non-verbal predication to a question involving a prepositional phrase generally involves the expression of the Preposition:

(6) a. *anté ch'it vas?*
       aŋ'te k=it='vaz   ↗
       where SUB=SBJ.2S=go\PRS.2S Q
       'where are you going?'

b. *a Turin*
   a=ty'riŋ
   ADE=T.
   'to Turin'

b'. *Turin*
   ty'riŋ
   'to Turin' [Turin]

Non-verbal predication is also found in sequences of words without a Verb. Leaving aside the common cases of lists, titles, and the like, this is of course possible in conversation:

(7) a. *còs tim conte?*
   koz ti=m='kuɲt-e   ↗
   what SBJ.2S=OBJ.1S=count-PRS.2S Q
   'what do you tell me?' ('what's the news?')

b. *gnun-a bon-a neuva*
   'ɲyŋ-a   'buŋ-a   'nøv-a
   nobody-F good-F news-S
   'no good news'

It is important to stress the fact that non-verbal predication is not limited to replies to "normal" (verbal) questions: one may well imagine them being uttered in isolation or as orders.

A special type of bare non-verbal predication is introduced by the Subordinator *che* /ke/ ("SUB;" 14.4.) and is detailed in 15.5.

15.1.2 *Non-verbal Predication with a Copula*

Apart from bare non-verbal predication, the copula *esse* /'ese/ 'to be' is used. The following categories may act as non-verbal predicates:
– Nouns and Noun phrases ((8) and (9))
– Adjectives ((10))
– Independent and Possessive Pronouns ((11) and (12))
– numerals and other Quantifiers ((13))
– prepositional clauses ((14))
– locative and temporal Adverbs ((15))

(8) *it ses **la poesìa ch'am acontenta**, it ses **la mia pitura a l'aquarel***
    it=sez   la=pue'zi-a   k=a=m=akuŋ'tæŋt-a
    SBJ.2S=be\PRS.2S DET=poetry-S SUB=SBJ.3=OBJ.1S=satisfy-PRS.3S
    it=sez   l-a=mj-a=pi'tyr-a   a=l=akwa'rel
    SBJ.2S=be\PRS.2S DET-F=POSS1-F=painting-S ADE=DET=watercolour
    'you are the poetry that satisfies me, you are my watercolour painting'
    (Nicòla 2007: 252)

(9) *a l'é **n'anvìa che am serca***
    a=le   n=aŋ'vi-a   ke=a=m='særk-a
    SBJ.3=be\ PRS.3S DET=desire-S SUB=SBJ.3=OBJ.1S=seek PRS.3S
    'it is a desire that seeks me' (Dorato 1998: 59)

(10) *s'a fussa **possìbil**, am piasrìa guernelo an conserva*
     s=a='fysa   pu'sibil   a=m=piaz'ria
     if=SBJ.3=be\SUBJ.IMPF.3S possible SBJ.3=OBJ.1.S=like\COND. 3S
     gwer'n-e=l-u   aŋ=kuŋ'særv-a
     keep-INF=OBJ.3-M   INE=preserves-S
     'if it were possible I would like to keep it canned' (Frusta 1969: 5)

(11) *a sarà stait **chiel***
     a=sa'ra   stajt   kjæl
     SBJ.3=be\DUB.3S be\PTCL IDP.3M
     'it should have been him'

(12) *a l'é tut **mè**, mach **mè**!*
     a='le   tyt me /   mak me
     SBJ.3=be\PRS.3S all POSS.1S only POSS.1S
     'everything is mine, just mine!'

(13) *a son bele, brute, **vaire**, pòche*
     a='suŋ   'bel-e / 'bryt-e / 'vajre / 'pok-e
     SBJ.3=be\PRS.3P nice-F.P ugly-F.P several few-F.P
     'they are fine, bad, (there are) many (of them) (or) (too) few'
     ("Vëndëmmia;" https://pms.wikipedia.org/wiki/V%C3%ABnd%C3%AB
     mmia)

(14) *problema che a son **ant l'aria**, combin che a sìo nen afrontà ëd propòsit*
     pru'blema ke=a='suŋ   aŋt=l='arj-a   kum'biŋ
     problem   SUB=SBJ.3=be\PRS.3P INE=DET(-F)=air-S although

ke=a='siu   næŋ afruŋ't-a   d=pru'pozit
SUB=SBJ.3=be\SUBJ.3P NEG face-PTCL ATT=purpose
'Problems that are in the air, although they are not addressed on purpose'
(Pacòt 1956)

(15) a l'é **ambelessì**, it ses bòrgno?
      a='le   ambe'lesi / it='sez   'borɲu ↗
      SBJ.3=be\PRS.3S here   SBJ.2S=be/PRS.2S blind   Q
      'it is right here; are you blind?'

Non-verbal predications may cover a range of meanings and values:
– proper inclusion, as in (8) above, and, strictly linked to it
– ascription, as in (10) and (13), and
– identity, as in (9);
– quantification, as in the use of *vaire* 'several' in (13);
– location, as in (15);
– possession, as in (12)

In existential non-verbal predication the copula is preceded by the Indirect Pronoun in its locative value (☞ 7.4.), yielding *a-i é* /a='j=e/ ("SBJ.3=IND=be\PRS.3S") 'there is,' *a-i era* /a='j=era/ ("SBJ.3=IND=be\IMPF.3S") 'there was,' etc.

(16) *a-i é gnun ch'av òbliga a ocupé 'n pòst an sla navëtta*
      a ='j=e   'ɲyŋ   k=a='v=oblig-a
      SBJ.3=IND=be\PRS.3S nobody SUB=SBJ.3=OBJ.2P=oblige-SUBJ.3S
      a=uky'p-e   [a]ŋ='post aŋ=s=l-a=na'vətt-a
      ADE=occupy-INF IND=place INE=SUP=DET-F=shuttle-S
      'there is nobody [there is nobody who is] forcing you to take a seat on the shuttle' (Tuberga and Antonel 2021)

Apart from the use of a non-verbal predication, the use of the Possessives (☞ 8.4.) and the Attributive *ëd* (☞ 13.5.), the most common verbal strategy for the expression of possession involves the possessor coded as the agent of a transitive Verb and the possessee coded as a patient. The transitive auxiliary Verb *avèj* /a'væj/ 'to have' (☞ 10.2.4.3.) is most typically in use:

(17) *s'i l'eve 'l cheur afrì 'd malinconìa, fërmeve sì, trames a sti gognin*
      s=i='leve   l='kør   af'ri   d=maliŋku'ni-a
      if=SBJ.2P=have\PRS.2P DET=heart afflicted\PTCL ATT=melancholy-S
      fər'm-e=ve   'si   tra'mæz a=st-i=gu'ɲiŋ
      stop-IPV.2P=OBJ.2P here among ADE=PROX-P=little_boys

'If your heart is afflicted with melancholy, stop here among these little boys' (Costa 1982b [1938]: 66)

15.2 Declarative Clauses

Declarative clauses show agreement with the subject both through the person affixes on the Verb and Preverbal Subject clitics (☞ 7.3.); they further show agreement with an Indirect Object via the IND clitic (☞ 7.4.; cf. also Cerruti 2008: 17):

(18) *i l'hai dajlo a Gioann*
i='laj   'da=j=l-u   a=dʒu'an
SBJ.1=have\PRS.1S give\PTCL=IND=OBJ.3-M ADE=G.
'I gave it to Gioann'

(18') **i l'hai dalo a Gioann*
i='laj   'da=l-u   a=dʒu'an
SBJ.1=have\PRS.1S give\PTCL=OBJ.3-M ADE=G.

(19) *a Tòjo a-j pias bèive*
a='toju a=j='pjaz   'bæjv-e
ADE=T.   SBJ.3=IND=like\PRS.3S drink-INF
'Tòjo loves to drink (*scil.*: alcohol)'

(19') **a Tòjo a pias bèive*
a='toju a='pjaz   'bæjv-e
ADE=T.   SBJ.3=like\PRS.3S drink-INF

The indirect object is mostly a [+animate] entity[1] and generally a beneficiary or a recipient, and is eventually coreferenced with a PP phrase headed by Adessive *a*.

The positioning of clitics follows the rules outlined in 7.10., i.e.

{SBJ}={IND}={OBJ} {ATTR.PRO}=V$_{/\text{SIMPLE}}$
(Subject—Indirect Object—Object—Attributive—simple verbal form)

---

[1] Agreement with [– animate] beings is possible but less frequent.

{SBJ}=V/COMPOUND= {IND/}={OBJ} {ATTR.PRO}
(Subject—compound verbal form—Indirect Object—Object—Attributive)

and, if Interrogative Subject clitics are used:

(SBJ)={IND}={OBJ} {ATTR.PRO}=V=INT/SIMPLE
(Subject—Indirect Object—Object—Attributive—simple verbal form—Interrogative)

(SBJ)=V=INT/COMPOUND= {IND}={OBJ} {ATTR.PRO}
(Subject—compound verbal form—Indirect Object—Object—Attributive)

Pronominalization leads to variation in the basic SVO sentence word order insofar as pronominal clitics come to precede the Verb with tensed non-compound verbal forms:

(20) *i lo faso*
　　i=l-u=ˈfazu
　　SBJ.1=OBJ.3-M=do\PRS.1S
　　'I do it'

(21) *i-j chërdo*
　　i=j=ˈkərdu
　　SBJ.1=IND=believe\PRS.1S
　　'I believe him/her/them'

An Indirect object precedes the direct object both in preverbal and postverbal position.

(22) *i-j lo diso*
　　i=j=l-u=ˈdizu
　　SBJ.1=IND=OBJ.3-M=say\PRS.1S
　　'I say it to him/her/them'

The positioning of the object clitics after the participle in compound forms (☞ 10.) may be seen as restoring the SVO order even with pronominalization.

(23) *i l'hai beivulo*
　　i=ˈlaj　　　　　bæjˈvy=l-u
　　SBJ.1=have\PRS.1S drink\PTCL=OBJ.3-M
　　'I drank it'

Apart from pragmatic factors, variation in word order may occur when a human non-subject participant is placed after the Verb:

(24) *am pias ël cafè*
    a=m=ˈpjaz   əl=kaˈfæ
    SBJ.3=OBJ.1S=like\PRS.3S DET=coffee
    'I like coffee' [coffee is likable to me]

(25) *am fa scheur*
    a=m=ˈfa   skør
    SBJ.3=OBJ.1S=do\PRS.3S horror
    'it makes me sick' [it makes disgust to me]

15.3 Introducing the Ubiquitous *che*

The Non-Main-clause marker *che* /ke/ (SUB) is pervasive in Piedmontese: while it is certainly for the most part a generalized subordination and relative-clause marker (as the label "SUB" implies), it also appears in certain independent clauses, provided they are not asseverative, and could be more aptly called a "generalized non-declarative marker."

Che is always cliticized to a following clitic and loses its final vowel. The cliticized form is often written *ch'*.

Overall, *che* enters into the following configurations:
– alone ("bare *che*;" ☞ 15.4.)
– in relative clauses (☞ 15.5.)
– in object and subject subordinate clauses
– in immediative clauses with the Verb 'to do' (☞ 11.9.)
– in exhortative clauses (☞ 15.7.)
– virtually always, preceded by a question word (*wh-* word) but also alone, in constituent questions (☞ 15.9.4.)
– virtually always, preceded by another subordinator in adverbial subordinate clauses (see also Berruto 2009)
– in clefts (☞ 18.2.)

While the extension of an element similar (and etymologically related) to *che* to question words and subordinate clauses is widespread in all the Romance varieties of Northern Italy (Benincà 1994, 1995, Bonato 2006), the spread of this phenomenon and the concomitant loss of any pragmatic value to it in Piedmontese is probably unparalleled elsewhere.

15.4 Bare *che* in Non-verbal Predication

15.4.1 *Exclamative* che

As anticipated, *che* may introduce a non-verbal predication, and both with an exclamative function and with a quantificational value. In many cases it also gives rise to fixed collocations. When followed by a bare Noun or an Adjective it has an exclamatory value:

(26) *che sgiaj!*
    ke   zdʒaj
    SUB disgust
    'how disgusting!'

(27) *che bel!*
    ke   bel
    SUB nice
    'so nice!'

The Noun may further be subcategorized by Attribuive *ëd* (☞ 13.5.9.):

(28) *che (rassa d') amis!*
    ke   ('ras-a d=)a'miz
    SUB (race-S ATTR=) friend
    'what a kind of friends!; such friends!' (ironic)

These non-verbal predications may be supplemented through a relative clause:

(29) *che amis ch'it l'has!*
    ke   a'miz   k=it='laz
    SUB friend SUB=SBJ.2S=have\PRS.2S
    'what a kind of friends you have!'

The use of a relative clause headed by a Noun introduced by *che* must be distinguished by its use with a general interrogative *che* (☞ 14.9.4.), as in:

(30) *che temp ch'a fa?*
      ke   tæmp k=a='fa   ↗
      SUB time   SUB=SBJ.3=do\PRS.3S Q
      'what is the weather like?'

15.4.2 Quantificational *che ëd*

When followed by Attributive *ëd* it often takes on a quantificational value:

(31) *che 'd bordel!*
    ke   d=bur'del
    SUB ATTR=noise
    'what a noise!'

Note in the following the quantificational value imparted to an exclamatory clause by the use of the Attributive on (29) above:

(29') *che d'amis ch'it l'has!*
    ke   d=a'miz   k=it='laz
    SUB ATTR=friend SUB=SBJ.2S=have\PRS.2S
    'so many friends you have!'

15.5 Relative Clauses

When *che* modifies a NP it introduces a relative clause, either restrictive or appositive. As there is no separate relative verbal paradigm, *che* is the subordinator for relative clauses. The syntactic role of the head Noun is marked independently from its role in the main clause; i.e., the subject of the relative clause will be marked in the same way irrespective of its role in the main clause:

(32) [*la fija* [*ch'a l'ha salutame*]$_{Subject}$ *a l'é ëd Biela*]$_{Subject}$
    l-a='fi-a   k=a='la   saly't-a=me
    DET-F=girl-S SUB=SBJ.3=have\PRS.3S greet-PTCL=OBJ.1S
    a='le   əd='bjela
    SBJ.3=be\PRS.3S ATTR=B.
    'the girl who greeted me is from Biela'

(33) *i conòsso pa* [*la fija* [*ch'a l'ha salutame*]$_{Subject}$]$_{Object}$
    i=ku'nosu   pa   l-a='fi-a   k=a='la
    SBJ.1=know\PRS.1S NEG.EMPH DET-F=girl-S SUB=SBJ.3=have\PRS.3S
    saly't-a=me
    greet-PTCL=OBJ.1S
    'I do not know the girl who greeted me'

In no case is *che* omissible:

(32′) *la fija a l'ha salutame a l'é ëd Biela

(33′) *i conòsso nen la fija a l'ha salutame

The next two examples show the use of *che* in relative clauses where the relativized Noun is subject and object, respectively, of the relative clause:

(34) *la dòna che a la sèira am provocava*
l-a=ˈdon-a   ke=a=l-a=ˈsæjr-a
DET-F=woman-S SUB=ADE=DET-F=evening-S
a=m=pruvuˈk-ava
SBJ.3=OBJ.2S=provoke-IMPF.3S
'the woman who provoked me in the evening' (Ferrero 1970: 71)

(35) *un romanz che a les e arles*
aŋ=ruˈmaɲz   ke=a=ˈlez   e=arˈles
INDEF=novel SUB= SBJ3=read\PRS.3S AND=re-read\PRS.3S
'a novel that he reads and rereads' (Menietti 2021: 8)

The distinction between restrictive and non-restrictive relatives bears no syntactic difference, with the exception of relatives on Direct Objects, where pronoun retention may be used in non-restrictive relatives—and in some dialects, e.g. in Cairese (Parry 2005: 243–244) is even obligatory—but is instead always barred in restrictives (Cennamo 1997b: 191):

(36) *ël fieul che it l'has conossù ier a l'é mè frel*
əl=ˈfjøl   k=it=ˈlas   kunuˈsy   ˈjer
the=boy SUB=SBJ.2S=have\PRS.3S know\PTCL yesterday
a=ˈle   me=ˈfrel
SBJ.3=be\PRS.3S POSS.1S=brother
'the boy that you met yesterday is my brother' (restrictive; Cennamo 1997b: 191)

(37) *a l'é mortje Carlo ch'a l'avio vist(lo) pròpe ier a l'ospidal*
a=ˈle   ˈmort=je   ˈkarlu k=a=laˈviu
SBJ.3=be\PRS.3S die\PTCL=IND C.   SUB=SBJ.3=have\IMPF.3P
ˈvist(=l-u)   ˈpropi jer   a=l=uspiˈdal
see\PTCL(=OBJ.3-M) just   yesterday ADE=DET=hospital
'Carlo, whom they saw just yesterday in hospital, has died' (non-restrictive, Cennamo 1997b: 191, modified)

Pronoun retention is obligatory with relatives on the Indirect objects:

(38) *la nòrma ch'a j'han daje*
    l-a='norm-a k=a=j='aŋ   'da=je
    DET-F=rule-S SUB=SBJ.3=IND=have\PRS.3P give\PTCL=IND
    'the rule they gave them' (Calvo 1816: 14)

The Indirect object is expressed twice in the early 19th-century text quoted under (38) (Parry 1993, 1994, Tuttle 1992). In the example, the Indirect clitic *j(e)* is found first before the form of the Verb 'to have' and then after the participle. Modern Piedmontese has generalized the use of *l'* before the auxiliaries 'to be' and 'to have' (Tosco 2002a) and reserved the Indirect clitic to the post-participial position. The modern form would be *la nòrma ch'a l'han daje*.

Other syntactic roles may be expressed by other coreferential devices (e.g. Possessives for Relatives on the Genitive):

(39) *cola fija ch'i conòsso sò pare a studia da avocat*
    'kul-a 'fi-a k=i=ku'nosu   so   'pare
    DIST-F girl-S SUB=SBJ.1=know\PRS.1S POSS.3 father
    a='stydi-a   da=avu'kat
    SBJ.3=study-PRS.3S ABL=lawyer
    'that girl whose father I know studies to become a lawyer'

Other relativization words are much more common in written registers.

Dont /duŋt/ "ATTR.SUB" is used in the same range of collocations of its nominal phrasal counterpart *ëd* "ATTR," such as the attribution of membership in a group, property, substance, source, etc.:

(40) *la sità dont a son partì ij coridor*
    l-a=si'ta duŋt   a='son   par't-i   i=kuri'dur
    DET-F=city ATTR.SUB SBJ.3=be/PRS.3P start-PCTL DET\P=runners
    'the city where runners started [from]' (Villata 1997: 143)

Qual /kwal/, always preceded by the Determiner and glossed "REL," is a relative clause marker used in order to relativize syntactic roles other than the Subject, Object (which are commonly reserved to *che*) or Attributive (for which *dont* is used). The relevant Preposition precedes the Determiner. It has a Feminine form *quala* /'kwal-a/ "REL-F," a Masculine Plural form *quaj* /kwaj/ "REL\P" and a Feminine Plural form *quale* /'kwal-e/ "REL-F.P" It is rather typical of the written registers and rarely used in the spoken language. Thus, while (41) is typical of the spoken language, (42) and (43) are archetypically written texts:

(41) *la fija che Carlin a-j parla (**ansema**)*
    l-a=ˈfi-a   ke=karˈliŋ   a=j=ˈparl-a   (aŋˈsema)
    DET-F=girl-S SUB=C.   SBJ.3=IND=speak-PRS.3S (together)
    'the girl Carlin is talking with (i.e., is courting)'

(42) *un recint fortificà andrinta **al qual** as trovavo le ca costruìe dai vàire sgnor*
    aŋ=reˈtʃiŋt   furtifiˈk-a   aŋˈdriŋta a=l=ˈkwal
    INDET=enclosure fortify-PTCL inside   ADE=DET=REL
    a=s=truˈv-avu   l-e=ˈka   kustryˈi-e
    SBJ=REFL.3=find-IMPF.3P DET-FP=house build\PTCL-F.P
    da=i=ˈvajre   ˈɲur
    ABL=DET\P=many Lord
    'a fortified enclosure inside which were the houses built by the different lords' (Lachello 2022)

(43) *la fija giovo Barbara, la blëssa e la generosità 'd cheur **ëd la quala** a l'avìo sùbit fàit colp sël capitani*
    l-a=ˈfi-a   ˈdʒuvu ˈbarbara / l-a=ˈbləss-a
    DET-F=daughter-S young Barbara / DET-F=beauty-S
    e=l-a=dʒeneruziˈta   dˈkør   əd=l-a=ˈkwal-a
    and=DET-F=generosity ATTR=heart ATTR=DET-F=REL-F
    a=laˈviu   ˈsybit   ˈfajt   ˈkulp
    SBJ.3=have\IMPF.3P immediately make\PTCL blow
    s=əl=kapiˈtani
    SUPER=DET=captain
    'the young daughter Barbara, whose beauty and generosity of heart had immediately impressed the Captain' (Lachello 2021a)

There are no syntactic differences between restrictive and appositive clauses, but the latter are always preceded and, in case, followed, by an intonation pause:

(44) *ëdcò 'l prim fieul, **al qual** Vitòrio Medeo a vorìa tanta bin, a l'era mòrt*
    ədˈko l=ˈprim   fjøl / a=l=ˈkwal   viˈtorju meˈdeu
    also   DET=first son / ADE=DET=REL V.   A.
    a=vuˈria   ˈtant-a biŋ / a=ˈlera   mort
    SBJ.3=want\IMPF.3S much-F good / SBJ.3=be\IMPF.3S dead
    'also (his) first son, whom Victor Amadeus loved so much, had died' ("Carl Emanuel III;" https://pms.wikipedia.org/wiki/Carl_Emanuel_III)

Occurences of *qual* and the like for Subject and Objects are extremely rare, even in written texts:

(45) *deve nen neghene sto favor, / 'L qual a costa a voi pòch o pavaire*
'deve   næŋ ne'g-e=ne   stu=fa'vur əl='kwal
must\PRS.2P NEG deny-INF=OBJ.1P PROX=favor DET=REL
a='kust-a   a=vuj   pok o pa='vajre
SBJ.3=cost-PRS.3S ADE=IDP.2P little or NEG.EMPH=several
'you must not deny us this favor, which costs you little or not much' (Calvo 1816: 16, verses 38–39)

15.6 Imperative Clauses

No Subject clitics are found in Imperative clauses. Other clitics are found after the Verb:

$V_{/IPV}$= {IND}={OBJ}
(Imperative verbal form—Indirect Object—Object)

(46) *damlo*
    'da=m=l-u
    give\IPV.S=OBJ.1S=OBJ.3-M
    'give it to me'

Like in Declarative clauses, a nominal Indirect object is coreferenced as a clitic:

(47) *dajlo a Magna Neta*
    'da=j=l-u   a='maɲ-a   'neta
    give\IPV.S=IND=OBJ.3-M ADE=aunt-S N.
    'give it to Aunt Annie'

(47′) **dalo a Magna Neta*

Imperatives to persons other the addressee(s), i.e, Exhortative or jussive clauses, use forms of the Main Present without Subject clitics:

(48) *andoma*
    aŋˈduma
    go\PRS.1P
    'let's go'

15.7 Exhortative Clauses

Preceding a clause with a Subjunctive verbal form, *che* is used in order to express a jussive or exhortative:

(49) *ch'as na vada!*
    k=a=s=na=ˈvada
    SUB=SBJ.3=REFL=ATTR.PRO=go\SUBJ.PRS.3S
    'let him go!'

(49') **as na vada!*
    a=s=na=ˈvada

The Exhortative may be preceded by an adverbial in a limiting function:

(50) *mach ch'it lo sapie!*
    mak k=it=l-u=ˈsapje
    only SUB=SBJ.2S=OBJ.3-M=know\SUBJ.2S
    'just be aware of it!'

Lexicalized constructions are common:

(51) *che mi i sapia*
    ke mi i=ˈsapja
    SUB IDP.1S SBJ.1=know\SUBJ.PRS.1S
    'as far as I know'

(52) *ch'a sia com ch'a sia*
    k=a=ˈsia   **kum k=a=ˈsia**
    SUB=SBJ.3=be\SUBJ.PRS.3S as SUB=SBJ.3=be\SUBJ.PRS.3S
    'let it be as it can be; whatever will be will be'

(53) *ch'a costa lòn ch'a costa*
 k=a='kust-a   loŋ   k=a='kust-a
 SUB=SBJ.3=cost-PRS.3S DIST.PRO SUB=SBJ.3=cost-PRS.3S
 'at whatever price' [let it cost what it costs]²

(54) *basta ch'a sia*
 'basta   k=a='sia
 enough   SUB=SBJ.3=be\SUBJ.PRS.3S
 'anyway' [let it be enough]

As a question, this construction may express doubt:

(55) *ch'a-i sia nen?*
 k=a=j='sia   næŋ ↗
 SUB=SBJ.3=IND=be\SUBJ.PRS.3S NEG Q
 'maybe he is not in?' (e.g., after repeatedly knocking at somebody's door)

(56) *ch'a ven-a a pieuve?*
 k=a='væŋa   a='pjøve   ↗
 SUB=SBJ.3=come\SUBJ.PRS.3S ADE=rain\INF Q
 'maybe it will rain?' (e.g., looking at a cloudy sky)

15.8   Mirative and Exclamative Clauses

Mirative and Exclamative clauses are most commonly marked via intonation only.

A peculiar expression involves the presence of an element *se* /se/ from Latin SIC 'so' (Domokos 1998) but as of today homophonous with the conditional marker *se* 'if' (☞ 15.2.9.–10.) and interpreted as such (and therefore glossed 'if'). The only very common instance of this construction in the spoken language of today (apart from popular songs, where it is still common) seems to be the following:

---

2   Being the motto of the Aosta Battalion of Alpine Infantry, the sentence is found in different Italianizing orthographies (such as *ca custa lon ca custa*) on many monuments to this military corps. The most notable and imposing example is found on a bridge near Asmara (Eritrea).

(57) *s'a l'é vera!*
  s=a='le   'ver-a
  if=SBJ.3=be\PRS.3S true-F
  'it is true indeed!' (an emphatic confirmation to a preceding statement)

The persistence of this expression through time may be seen in its occurrence in mid-19th-century texts, such as in Act 1, Sc. 14 of the successful play *Le miserie 'd Monsù Travet* ("Mr. Travet's miseries") by Vittorio Bersezio (☞ 1.7.3.), first staged in 1863. The same offers other examples that nowadays sound odd:

(58) MADAMA TRAVET: *A l'é che gnente.*
  TRAVET: (*S'a l'é lòn! Am lassa mai parlé*)
  a='le   ke   'ɲæŋte / s=a='le   loŋ /
  SBJ.3=be\PRS.3S SUB nothing / if=SBJ.3=be\PRS.3S DIST.PRO /
  a=m='las-a   maj   par'l-e
  SBJ.3=OBJ.1S=let\.PRS.3S never speak-INF
  'Mrs. Travet: "It is nothing."
  Travet: "(It is exactly that, actually! She never lets me speak)"' (Bersezio 1980 [1863]; Act 1, Scene 8)

Abundant examples are provided in literature at least until the early 20th century. The following is from a popular novel published in 1902:

(59) A: ... *mi im sento a meuire* ...
  B: *S'a l'é pa gnente, diasne; ch'a staga alegher* ...
  mi   i=m='sænt-u   a='møjre   s=a='le
  IDP.1S SBJ.1=OBJ.1S=feel-PRS.1S ADE=die\INF if=SBJ.3=be\PRS.3S
  pa   'ɲæŋte / 'djazne //   k=a='staga
  NEG.EMPH nothing / what_devil // SUB=SBJ.3=stay\SUBJ.PRS.3S
  a'leger
  happy
  'A: "I feel like dying ..."
  B: "It is really nothing, what the hell! Just be happy!"' (Mania Reida 1995 [1902]: 29)

Overtly exclamative sentences can also be built with the Subordinator *che* and parallel the use of bare *che* in similar verbless contexts (☞ 15.4.1.):

(60) *ch'it ses furb!*
 k=it='se(z)   fyrb
 SUB=SBJ.2S=be\PRS.2S smart
 'you (s) are so smart!' (ironic)

15.9 Questions

Polar, tag and content questions are distinguished. Negative questions have no peculiarities of their own. Questions may be marked through question words, intonation and dedicated subject markers, or a combination of all these.

15.9.1 *Polar Questions*

Polar questions are essentially expressed though a dedicated rising intonation, orthographically expressed by ⟨?⟩:

(61) *it ses andait*
 it='sez   aŋ'dajt
 SBJ.2=be\PRS.2S go\PTCL
 'you (s) went'

(61') *it ses andait?*
 it='sez   aŋ'dajt ↗
 SBJ.2=be\PRS.2S go\PTCL Q
 'did you (s) go?'

Rising intonation may be accompanied by the use of the Interrogative Subject Pronouns:

(62) *ses-to andait?*
 'ses=tu   aŋ'dajt ↗
 be\PRS.2S=INT.2S go\PTCL Q
 'did you (s) go?'

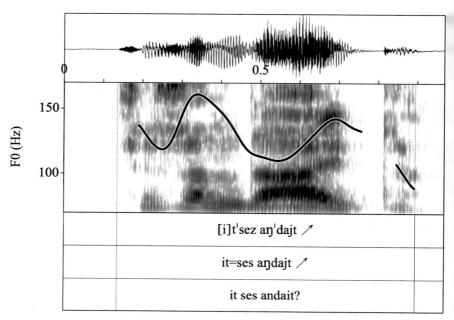

FIGURE 23 *it ses andait?* ('did you (s) go?;' male speaker born in Turin in 1956)

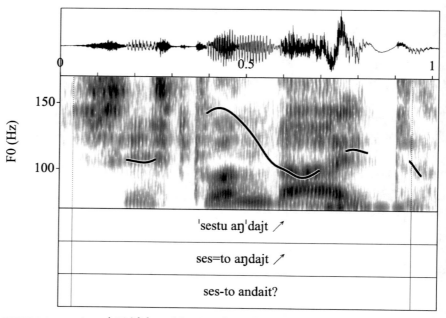

FIGURE 24 *ses-to andait?* ('did you (s) go?;' male speaker born in Turin in 1956)

15.9.2 Tag Questions

Tagging is only partially grammaticalized, and tag questions use a variety of means in clause-final position, paramount among them *nè/neh* /næ/ ("TAG"; ☞ 18.3) and *é-lo vera* /'e=l-u 'vera/ ("be/PRS.3S=INT.3-M") 'is it true?' The former is so common in both Piedmontese and the variety of Italian spoken in Piedmont that it has become a shibboleth of Piedmontese speech; the latter is maybe more typical of formal registers. The sequence preceding the tag bears declarative intonation and an intonational break occurs before the tag:

(63) *i son pròpi contenta, neh, che tò òm a l'abia arpijasse*
    i=suŋ   'propi kuŋ'tæŋt-a / næ / ke   to='om
    SBJ.1=be\PRS.1S really happy-F   TAG SUB POSS.2S=man
    a='labja   ar'pj-a=se
    SBJ.3=have\SUBJ.3S regain-PTCL=REFL
    'I am really happy, aren't I?, that your husband recovered' (overheard in ël Mondvì, Feb. 21, 2017)

(64) *it ses content, neh?*
    it='sez   kuŋ'tæŋt / næ
    SBJ.2=be\PRS.2S happy /   TAG
    'you (S) are happy, aren't you?' (Mottura 2009: 29)

15.9.3 Negative Questions

The reply to negative questions answers the contents of the question and not the negation (see also 18.3):

(65) *has-to pa vistlo?*
    'as=tu   pa   'vist=l-u   ↗
    have\PRS.2S=INT.2S NEG.EMPH see\PTCL=OBJ.3-M Q
    'haven't you (S) seen him/it?'

(65') *é (, i l'hai vistlo)*
    e /   (/ i='laj   'vist=l-u)
    (yes) / SBJ.1S=have\PRS.1S see\PTCL=OBJ.3-M
    'yes (, I saw him)'

(65″) *nò (, i l'hai pa vistlo)*
    no / (/ i='laj   pa   'vist=l-u)
    no / SBJ.1S=have\PRS.1S NEG.EMPH see\PTCL=OBJ.3-M
    'No (, I didn't)'

15.9.4 Constituent Questions

Constituent questions make use of dedicated fronted question-words, irrespective of their syntactic role.

A human/non-human distinction is instantiated, while syntactic roles have no bearing on the choice of the question word.

The question words are often (and usually) followed by the Subordinate marker *che* /ke/ (SUB) with no change in meaning nor in pragmatic value.

(66) *chi a-i é?*
    ki   a='j=e   ↗
    who SBJ.3=IND=be\PRS.3S Q
    'who is there?'

(66′) *chi ch'a-i é?*
    ki   k=a='j=e   ↗
    who SUB=SBJ.3=IND=be\PRS.3S Q Q
    'who is there?'

In a similar way, each of the following questions may be replaced by its corresponding sentence with or without *che*:

(67) *còs a l'é?*
    koz   a='le   ↗
    what SBJ.3=be\PRS.3S Q
    'what is it?'

(68) *còs ch'it veule?*
    koz   k=it='vøle   ↗
    what SUB=SBJ.2S=want\PRS.2S Q
    'what do you (s) want?'

(69) *anté ch'a l'é?*
    aŋ'te   k=a='le   ↗
    where SUB=SBJ.3=be\PRS.3S Q
    'where is it?'

(70) *andoa ch'it ses andait?*
    aŋ'dua k=it='sez   aŋ'dajt ↗
    where SUB=SBJ.2S=be\PRS.2S go\PTCL Q
    'where have you (s) gone?'

(71) *quand ch'as ancamin-a?*
 kwaŋd k=a=s=aŋka'miŋ-a ↗
 when SUB=SBJ.3=REFL=start-PRS.3S Q
 'when do we start?'

(72) *com as fa?*
 kum a=s='fa ↗
 how SBJ.3=REFL=do\PRS.3S Q
 'how is it done?'

(73) *com ch'i foma?*
 kum k=i='foma ↗
 how SUB=SBJ.1=do\PRS.1P Q
 'how will we do?'

(74) *vaire ch'i n'oma ancheuj?*
 'vajre k=i=n='uma aŋ'køj ↗
 several SUB=SBJ.1=ATTR.PRO=have\PRS.1P today Q
 'what is the date today?' [how many do we have of them today?]

A selection among many possible items may be introduced by *che* followed by an ungrounded Noun:

(75) *che liber ch'it lese?*
 ke='liber k=it'lese ↗
 SUB=book SUB=SBJ.2S=read\PRS.2S Q
 'what book are you (S) reading?'

(76) *an che manera ch'it farie?*
 aŋ=ke =ma'ner-a k=it=fa'rie ↗
 INE=SUB=way-F SUB=SBJ.2S=do\COND.2S Q
 'which way would you (S) do?'

Selection may also be expressed by the Distal deictic *col* /kul/ 'that' (DIST) followed by the Subordinator *che*:

(77) *col ch'at pias?*
 kul k=a=t='pjaz ↗
 DIST SUB=SBJ.3=OBJ.2S=like\PRS.3S Q
 'which one do you (S) like?'

or explicitly through an interrogative clause expressing the choice

(78) *it veule cost-sì o col-là?*
    it='vøle   kust='si   o   kul='la   ↗
    SBJ.2S=want\PRS.2S PROX=here or DIST=there Q
    'do you (S) want this one or that one?'

as well as, with deletion of the Verb, through non-verbal predication:

(78') *cost-sì ò col-là?*
    kust='si   o   kul='la   ↗
    PROX=here or DIST=there Q
    'this one or that one?'

15.10 The Expression of Atmospheric Events

Atmospheric events are expressed by Verbs; the clauses in which they appear are subjectless and the Verb is in the 3rd person Singular:

(79) *a tron-a e a lòsna*
    a='truŋ-a   e   a='lozn-a
    SBJ.3=thunder-PRS.3S and SBJ.3=thunder-PRS.3S
    'it's thunder and lightning'

(80) *a ven a pieuve*
    a='væŋ   a='pjøve
    SBJ.3=come\PRS.3S ADE=rain\INF
    'it is going to rain'

(81) *a l'ha fiocà tut ël di*
    a='la   fju'k-a   tyt əl='di
    SBJ.3=have\PRS.3S snow-PTCL all DET=day
    'it has been snowing the whole day'

(82) *sta neuit a l'ha nen giassà*
    st-a='nøjt   a='la   næŋ dʒa's-a
    PROX-F=night SBJ.3=have\PRS.3S NEG freeze-PTCL
    'yesterday night it did not freeze'

Equally subjectless are other clauses reporting atmospheric events through the use of a generic Verb and an Adjective or an object expressing respectively a state or event:

(83) *a fa sempe pì caud*
 a=ˈfa   ˈsæmpe pi   kawd
 SBJ.3=do\PRS.3S always more warm
 'it is hotter and hotter'

(84) *a l'é torna nivol*
 a=ˈle   ˈturna ˈnivul
 SBJ.3=be\PRS.3S again cloudy
 'it is cloudy again'

(85) *a tirava un vent dël diav*
 a=ˈtir-ava   aŋ=ˈvæŋt   d=əl=ˈdjaw
 SBJ.3=pull-IMPF.3S INDEF=wind ATTR=DET=devil
 'a hell of a wind was blowing'

CHAPTER 16

Linkage

The traditional, but far from universal (Cristofaro 2003, Haspelmath 2004) opposition between coordination and subordination in clause linkage finds some validation in Piedmontese: while coordinated structures are formally expressed either asyndetically (i.e., without segmental marking) or syndetically (though one out of several connectives), subordination is mainly the domain of a single word (and often clitic), the Subordinator *che* /ke/.

16.1 Coordination

Phrases and clauses may be segmentally juxtaposed. This is the strategy commonly used when more than two phrases or clauses are listed: the last element only is usually preceded by a connective, while the preceding ones are linked asyndetically ((1)).

The category of connectives is represented in Piedmontese by a few independent words; some of them may be used with both phrases and clauses, while others are reserved to clause linkage.

16.1.1 *Conjunction*
Simple conjunction between Nouns ((1) and (2)), Noun phrases ((3)) and clauses ((4)) is expressed with *e* /e/ 'and:'

(1) *pan, bross e sòma d'aj*
 paŋ ˈbrus e=ˈsom-a d=aj
 bread and=fermented_cheese and=bruschetta-S ATTR=garlic
 'bread, fermented cheese and garlic bread'

(2) *pas a l'é slòira e beu, arsigneuj e lumin*
 paz a=ˈle ˈzlojr-a e=ˈbø / arsiˈɲøj e=lyˈmiŋ
 peace SBJ.3=be\PRS.3S plough-S and=oxen / nightingale\P and=firefly
 'peace is plough and oxen, nightingales and fireflies' (Bodrie 2000: 168)

(3) *un pòpol costumà a gropé d'idèje, ëd religion e d'origin diferente*
aŋ=ˈpopul kustyˈm-a a=gruˈp-e d=iˈdæj-e / əd=reliˈdʒuŋ
INDEF=people use-PTCL ADE=tie-INF ATTR=idea-P / ATTR=religion
e d=uˈridʒiŋ difeˈrænt-e
and ATTR=origin different-F.P
'a people well used to put together different opinions, religions and origins' (Sandron 2005)

(4) *an cost sens a registra e a crea nen la crisi*
aŋ=ˈkust sæŋs a=reˈdʒistr-a e a=ˈkre-a næŋ
INE=PROX sense SBJ.3=record-PRS.3S and SBJ.3=create-PRS.3S NEG
l-aˈkrizi
DET-F=crisis
'in this sense, it (just) records—it does not give rise to the crisis' (Vielmin 2005)

16.1.2 Disjunction

Disjunction is expressed with *o* /o/ ((5)),[1] *o pura* (or *opura*) /o=ˈpyra/ ((6)), or—more rarely—*o purament* /o=pyraˈmæŋt/ 'or:'

(5) *a l'avria podù fé torné a ca o fé ritiré al Bon Pastor soa fija*
a=lavˈria puˈdy ˈfe turˈn-e a=ˈka
SBJ.3=have\COND.3S can\PTCL make\INF come.back-INF ADE=home
o ˈfe ritiˈr-e a-l=buŋ=pasˈtur
or make\INF withdraw-INF ADE-DET=Good=Shepherd
su-a=ˈfi-a
POSS3S-F=daughter-S
'he could have sent his daughter home or have her withdrawn at the Good Shepherd' (Ferrero 1981 [1888], p. 100)

(6) *a son-ne soe parente ... o ... o pura soe sorele?*
a=ˈsuŋ=ne ˈsu-e paˈræŋt-e / o / oˈpyra
SBJ.3=be.PRS.3P=INT.3P POSS.2HON-F.P relative-P or or_even
ˈsu-e suˈrel-e ↗
POSS.2HON-F.P sister-P Q
'are they Your relatives ... or ... or even Your sisters?' (Pietracqua 1973 [1871], Act 3, Scene 12)

---

1 Written without any accent mark but still pronounced /o/.

In disjunction, the connective may be repeated before each item ((7)), but is more commonly found only before the last element:

(7) *amparentà con j'Ibérich, **o pura** na branca indoeuropenga amparentà con j'Itàlich e ij Selt, **o pura** bele che na branca dij Selt*
 amparæŋˈt-a kuŋ=j=iˈberik /   o=ˈpyra n-a=ˈbraŋk-a
 relate-PTCL COM=DET\P=Iberian or_even INDEF-F=branch-S
 indewruˈpæŋg-a amparæŋˈt-a kuŋ=j=iˈtalik   e   i=ˈsælt /
 Indeuropean-F relate-PTCL COM=DET\P=Italic and DET\P=Celt
 oˈpyra   ˈbele ke=n-a=ˈbraŋka   d=i=ˈsælt
 or_even even=SUB=NDEF-F branch ATTR=DET\P=Celt
 'related to the Iberians, or else an Indoeuropean branch related to the Italics and the Celts, or still a branch of the Celts' ("Ligurin;" https://pms.wikipedia.org/wiki/Ligurin)

16.1.3 *Contrast*

Contrast (i.e., adversative) relations may be divided in three types, namely relation encoding opposition, correction, and denial of expectation (Mauri 2008).

The conjunction *e, mentre (che)* /ˈ**mæŋtre(=ke)**/ and *antramentr(e che)* /aŋtraˈ**mæŋtr(e=ke)**/ may be used to encode oppositive contrast. The latter elements have been grammaticalized in this function from their original temporal meaning (☞16.2.5):

(8) *chiel as ciama Mario e mi Felicita*
 kjæl   a=s=ˈtʃam-a   ˈmarju e=ˈmi   feˈlitʃita
 IDP.3M SBJ.3=REFL=call-PRS.3S M.   and=IDP.1S F.
 'his name is Mario whereas mine is Felicita'

Other elements, such as *anvece* /aŋˈvetʃe/ (also ☞ 12.5.), may appear along with *e* in order to stress the contrast between coordinated clauses:

(9) *Chiel as cred d'avej fait un bel sonet, e **anvece** a l'ha fait na porcheria!*
 ˈkjæl   a=s=ˈkræd   d=aˈvæj   fajt
 IDP.3M SBJ.3=REFL=believe\PRS.3S ATTR=have\INF do\PTCL
 aŋ=ˈbel suˈnæt/   e=aŋˈvetʃe   a=ˈla   fajt
 INDEF=nice sonnet and=instead SBJ.3=have\PRS.3S do\PTCL
 n-a=purkeˈri-a
 INDEF-F=rubbish-S
 'he thinks he wrote a good sonnet, but he actually wrote garbage' (Pietracqua 1859b Act 2, Scene 3)

Corrective contrast can be encoded by *ma* /ma/ 'but' only:

(10) *as ciama pa Franca, ma Felicita*
 a=s=ˈtʃam-a   pa   ˈfraŋka ma=feˈlitʃita
 SBJ.3=REFL=call-PRS.3S NEG.EMPH F.   but=F.
 'her name is not Franca, but Felicita'

Ma is the most used connective for counterexpectative contrast ((11)):

(11) *a 'ndasìa nen bin sta machina, mi acelerava, ma chila a 'ndasìa nen*
 a=ŋd-aˈzi-a   næŋ biŋ st-a=ˈmakin-a/ mi   atʃeleˈr-ava/
 SBJ.3=go\IMPF.3S NEG well PROX-F=car-S IDP.1S accelerate-IMPF.3S
 ma ˈkila   a=ŋd-aˈzia   næŋ
 but IDP.3FS SBJ.3=go\IMPF.3S NEG
 'that car didn't work well, I pushed to accelerate, but it did not work' (Bonato 2003–2004: 195)

Ma can coordinate NPs also:

(12) *i veuj na bota ëd vin, ma ëd col bon*
 i=ˈvøj   n-a=ˈbut-a   əd=ˈviŋ / ma əd=ˈkul
 SBJ.1=want\PRS.1S INDEF-F=bottle-S ATTR=wine / but ATTR=DIST
 buŋ
 good
 'I want a bottle of wine, but the good one'

Other connectives conveying counterexpectative contrast are *però* /peˈro/ and *tutun* /tyˈtyŋ/. Their checkered history and usage are discussed at length in Miola (2012). *Però*'s attestations in Piedmontese date only from the first half of the 18th century. It is widely used in both oral and written registers. *Tutun*, which acquired its contrastive value from an earlier adverbial meaning only in the early 19th century, is nowadays rampant in written Piedmontese for obvious reasons of Ausbauization: *però* is both phonologically and graphically too similar to Italian *però* and tends therefore to be shunned in puristic writing. Interestingly, while Miola (2012) found that the ratio of *però* vs. *tutun* in the Piedmontese Wikipedia was 45% *però* vs. 55% *tutun*[2]—which certainly does not reflect the spoken usage:

---

2 A further check (August 2020), based upon a larger number of entries, had *però* down to 41% and *tutun* up to 59%.

(13) *vedend che con soa fòrsa e soa sapiensa | a l'ha però mancà d'previdensa*
  ved'ænd ke kuŋ='su-a 'fors-a e 'su-a sa'pjæŋs-a
  see-GER SUB COM=POSS.3-F strength-S and POSS.3-F wisdom-S
  a='la pe'ro maŋ'k-a d=previ'dæŋs-a
  SBJ.3=have\PRS.3S still lack-PTCL ATTR=foresight-S
  'realizing that, even with his strength and knowledge, still he lacked foresight' (Calvo 1845: I, 63)

(14) *a l'ha sempe mantnù un caràter unitari. A l'é **tutun** possìbil arconòss-ne vàire setor*
  a='la 'sæmpe mant'ny aŋ=ka'rater yni'tari /
  SBJ.3=have\PRS.3S always preserve\PTCL INDEF=character unitary /
  a='le ty'tyŋ pu'sibil arku'noss=ne 'vajre
  SBJ.3S=be\PRS.3S still possible recognize\INF=ATTR.PRO several
  se'tur
  sector
  'it always preserved a unitary character, but it is still possible to recognized several areas' ("Matemàtica;" https://pms.wikipedia.org/wiki/Matem%C3%A0tica)

16.1.4 Correlatives

As for correlatives, correlative conjunction mostly uses pairs of connectives in each member clause or phrase, such as *tant ... che* /taŋt ... ke/ or *sia ... che* /sia ... ke/, *e ... e* /e ... e/:

(15) *a-j piasìa **tant** a gieughe al fotbal **che** a core an bici*
  a=j=pia'zia taŋt a='dʒøge a=l='futbal
  SBJ.3=IND.3=like\IMPF.3S both ADE=play\INF ADE=DET=football
  ke=a='kure aŋ='bitʃi
  SUB=ADE=run\INF INE=bike
  'he enjoyed both playing football and riding a bike' (Villata 1997: 251)

Negative disjunction is expressed with *ni ... ni* /ni ... ni/ 'neither ... nor.' Other negative markers may appear before the first *ni*:

(16) *a l'é pa nì piemontèis nì ositan*
  a='le pa 'ni pjemuŋ'tæis ni usi'taŋ
  SBJ.3=be\PRS.3S NEG.EMPH neither Piedmontese nor Occitan
  'it is neither Piedmontese nor Occitan' (Bonato 2003–2004: 201)

16.2 Subordination

The distinction between asyndetic and syndetic coordination with connectives finds a parallel in subordination, where both untensed and tensed verbal forms are used. Subordination with tensed verbal forms always implies the use of the Subordinator *che*. In many instances, moreover, *che* directly follows a connective (this use of *che* is called "double complementizer" in some grammatical traditions). With untensed verbal forms the distinction between different semantic values of the subordinate clause is often vague, although here again connectives may be used.

16.2.1 *Untensed Subordination*
Provided it shares the same subject of its main clause, an untensed verbal form may be used in subordination. The Gerund is often (especially in the formal registers) preceded by Inessive *an* in a gerundive construction (☞ 10.5.7.).

(17) *quand che la capital dle stat da Turin, **passand** për Fiorensa, a l'era diventà Roma.*
 kwaŋd ke=l-a=kapiˈtal d=lə=sˈtat da=tyˈriŋ/ paˈs-aŋd
 when SUB=DET-F=capital ATTR=DET=State ABL=T. pass-GER
 pər=ffjuˈræŋsa / a=ˈlera diveŋˈt-a ˈruma
 BEN=F. / SBJ.3=be\IMPF.3S become-PTCL R.
 'when the State capital from Turin, passing through Florence, had become Rome' (Pacòt 2000: 363)

(18) *Leibniz as trasferiss, **an passand** prima për l'Olanda*
 l. a=s=trasfeˈris / aŋ=paˈs-aŋd ˈprima pər=l=uˈlaŋda
 L. SBJ.3=REFL=move\PRS.3S / INE=pass-GER firstly BEN=DET=N.
 'Leibniz moves, passing first through the Netherlands' ("Gottfried Leibniz;" https://pms.wikipedia.org/wiki/Gottfried_Leibniz)

The Infinitive, either in its simple or compound (i.e., preceded by an auxiliary) form is likewise in wide use:

(19) *dòp d'avej travajà tut 'l santo dì a l'ufissi am faria tant sangh na bona sana 'd col bon*
 dop d=aˈvæj travaˈj-a tut əl=ˈsaŋtu di a=l=yˈfisi
 after ATTR=have\INF work-PTCL all DET=saint day ADE=DET=office
 a=m=faˈria taŋt saŋg n-a=ˈbuŋ-a ˈsaŋ-a
 SBJ.3=OBJ.1S=make\COND.3S a_lot blood INDEF-F=good-F glass-S

əd='kul=buŋ
ATTR=DIST=good
'after having worked all day, I'm so longing for a nice glass of good wine'
(Bersezio 1980 [1863], Act 3, Scene 2)

The use of the Participle in subordination overlaps with its use as an Adjective in phrases:

(20) *e da lì a pòchi di 'l fieul pi giovo,* **butà** *ansema tyt col ch'a l'avia tirà dij sò beni, s n'é andassne*
 e da='li a='pok-i di əl='fjøl pi 'dʒuvu / by't-a
 and ABL=there ADE=few-M.P day DET=boy more young / put-PTCL
 aŋs'ema tyt loŋ k=a=la'via ti'r-a
 together all DIST.PRO SUB=SBJ.3=have\IMPF.3S pull-PTCL
 d=i='so 'beni s=n=e
 ATTR=DET\P=POSS.3 wealth REFL=ATTR.PRO=be\PRS.3S
 aŋ'da=s=ne
 go\PTCL=REFL=ATTR.PRO
 'not long after that, the younger son, after he got together all he had of his wealth, set off' [Luke 15:13] (Biondelli 1853: 505)

16.2.2 *Subordination with* che *and Use of Tenses*
In every syndetic subordinate clause, with the notable exception of conditional clauses, the connective may (and often must) be followed by *che* without any difference in meaning. The use of *che* is more common than its absence.

A general rule (usually going under its Latin name *consecutio temporum* 'sequence of tenses'—although with very different rules than was the case in Latin) accounts for the match of tenses between different clauses within a sentence. Given the progressive weakening of the future tense, which has been more or less changed into a (present) Dubitative mood (☞ 10.5.3.), a threefold opposition between a retrospective, present or prospective time reference has been replaced by a twofold contrast past vs. non-past. Still, the retrospective, present or prospective time reference of the event in the subordinate clause relative to the one expressed in the main one has a major bearing on the paradigm of the subordinate Verb.

A simplified temporal system opposing antecedent and not-antecedent only in the independent clause applies in untensed subordinates ((25), (26)).

It is to be noted that in the subordinate clauses (but not in Conditionals; ☞ 16.2.11.) the Dubitative mood has (or rather preserves) a temporal, rather than modal meaning ((22‴), (24‴)).

TABLE 54   Time and tense in subordinate clauses

Dependent	Subordinate		
	Retrospective	Present	Prospective
...t	Pluperfect	(Main/Subjunctive) Imperfect	Conditional Past
...-past	Past	(Main/Subjunctive) Present	Dubitative
...st, non-past)	(untensed, non-compound) INF	(untensed, compound) INF	

(21) *Pero **a lo savìa** che 'l vendior ...*
  'peru a=l-u=sa'via   ke=l=væŋ'djur
  P.   SBJ.3=OBJ.3-M=know\IMPF.3S SUB=DET=salesman
  'Pero knew that the salesman ...'

(21') *... **a l'avìa vorsulo ciolé**[3]*
  a=la'via   vur'sy=l-u   ʧu'l-e
  SBJ.3=have\IMPF.3S want\PTCL=OBJ.3-M have_sex-INF
  '... had wanted to cheat him'

(21") *... **a volìa ciolelo***
  a=vu'lia   ʧu'l-e=l-u
  SBJ.3=want\IMPF.3S have_sex-INF=OBJ.3-M
  '... wanted to cheat him'

(21''') *... **a l'avrìa vorsulo ciolé***
  a=lav'ria   vur'sy=l-u   ʧu'l-e
  SBJ.3=COND\IMPF.3S want\PTCL=OBJ.3-M have_sex-INF
  '... will have wanted to cheat him'

(22) *Pero **a lo sa** che 'l vendior ...*
  'peru a=l-u='sa   ke=l=væŋ'djur
  P.   SBJ.3=OBJ.3-M=know\PRS.3S SUB=DET=salesman
  'Pero knows that the salesman ...'

---

[3] The first meaning of the Verb *ciolé* /ʧu'l-e/ is 'to have sexual intercourse.' It is gender-neutral (at least nowadays) as to subject and object when transitive, and has a reciprocal reading when used with a plural subject and no object. It is not as vulgar as corresponding verbs in other languages and is largely desemanticized into 'to cheat, trick.' English 'to fuck up' and 'to fuck with' are instead covered by different Piedmontese Verbs.

(22′) ... *a l'ha vorsulo ciolé*
    a=ˈla   vurˈsy=l-u   tʃuˈl-e
    SBJ.3=have\PRS.3S want\PTCL=OBJ.3-M have_sex-INF
    '... wanted to cheat him'

(22″) ... *a veul ciolelo*
    a=ˈvøl   tʃuˈl-e=l-u
    SBJ.3=want\PRS.3S have_sex-INF=OBJ.3-M
    '... wants to cheat him'

(22‴) ... *a vorerà ciolelo*
    a=vureˈra   tʃuˈl-e=l-u
    SBJ.3=want\DUB.3S have_sex-INF=OBJ.3-M
    '... will want to cheat him'

(23) *Pero a l'avìa l'impression che 'l vendior ...*
    ˈperu a=laˈvia   l=impreˈsjuŋ   ke=l=væŋˈdjur
    P.   SBJ.3=have\IMPF.3S DET=impression SUB=DET=salesman
    'Pero got the impression that the salesman'

(23′) ... *a l'aveissa vorsulo ciolé*
    a=laˈvæjsa   vurˈsy=l-u   tʃuˈl-e
    SBJ.3=have\SUBJ.IMPF.3S want\PTCL=OBJ.3-M have_sex-INF
    '... wanted to cheat him'

(23″) ... *a voreissa ciolelo*
    a=vuˈræjsa   tʃuˈl-e=l-u
    SBJ.3=want\SUBJ.IMPF.3S have_sex-INF=OBJ.3-M
    '... wanted to cheat him'

(23‴) ... *a l'avrìa vorsulo ciolé*
    a=lavˈria   vurˈsy=l-u   tʃuˈl-e
    SBJ.3=have\SUBJ.IMPF.3S want\PTCL=OBJ.3-M have_sex-INF
    '... wanted to cheat him'

(24) *Pero a l'ha l'impression che 'l vendior ...*
    ˈperu a=ˈla   l=impreˈsjuŋ   ke=l=væŋˈdjur
    P.   SBJ.3=have\PRS.3S DET=impression SUB=DET=salesman
    'Pero gets the impression that the salesman ...'

(24') ... *a l'abia vorsulo ciolé*
  a='labja   vur'sy=l-u   tʃu'l-e
  SBJ.3=have\SUBJ.3S want\PTCL=OBJ.3-M have_sex-INF
  '... wanted to cheat him'

(24") ... *a veuja ciolelo*
  a='vøja   tʃu'l-e=l-u
  SBJ.3=want\SUBJ.3S have_sex-INF=OBJ.3-M
  '... wants to cheat him'

(24''') (= (22")) ... *a vorerà ciolelo*
    a=vure'ra   tʃu'l-e=l-u
    SBJ.3=want\DUB.3S have_sex-INF=OBJ.3-M
    '... will want to cheat him'

(25) *Pero a lo sa / a lo savìa ëd ...*
  'peru a=l-u='sa /   a=l-u=sa'via   əd
  P. SBJ.3=OBJ.3-M=know\PRS.3S SBJ.3=OBJ.3-M=know\IMPF.3S ATTR
  'Pero knows /new that he ...'

(25') ... *nen avèj podù ciolé 'l vendior*
  næŋ a'væj pu'dy tʃu'l-e   l=væŋ'djur
  NEG have\INF can/PTCL have_sex-INF DET=salesman
  '... could not cheat the salesman'

(25") ... *nen podèj ciolé 'l vendior*
  næŋ pu'dæj tʃu'l-e   l=væŋ'djur
  NEG can\INF have_sex-INF DET=salesman
  '... cannot / will not be able to cheat the salesman'

(26) *Pero a l'ha / a l'avia l'impression ëd ...*
  'peru a='la /   a=la'via   l=impre'sjuŋ
  P. SBJ.3=have\PRSF.3S SBJ.3=have\IMPF.3S DET=impression
  ke=l=væŋ'djur
  SUB=DET=salesman
  'Pero gets / got the impression that ...'

(26') = (25') ... *nen avèj podù ciolé 'l vendior*
    næŋ a'væj pu'dy tʃu'l-e   l=væŋ'djur
    NEG have\INF can/PTCL have_sex-INF DET=salesman
    '... could not cheat the salesman'

(26″) = (25″) ... *nen **podèj** ciolé 'l vendior*
    næŋ pu'dæj ʧu'l-e   l=væŋ'djur
    NEG can\INF have_sex-INF DET=salesman
    '... cannot / will not be able to cheat the salesman'

While (21), (23), (25) and (26) exemplify the use of the Imperfect in the main clause, the same rules obtain of course with a Past:

(27) *Pero **a l'ha capilo** che 'l vendior **a volìa** ciolelo*
    'peru a='la   ka'pi=l-u
    P.   SBJ.3=have\PRS.3S understand\PTCL=OBJ.3-M
    ke=l=væŋ'djur   a=vu'lia   ʧu'l-e=l-u
    SUB=DET=salesman SBJ.3=want\IMPF.3S have_sex-INF=OBJ.3-M
    'Pero understood that the salesman wanted to cheat him'

Likewise, the selection of a Dubitative (or, for that matter, a Subjunctive) in the main clause does not affect the Verb of the subordinate clause, which depends exclusively upon the reference time (for the selection of Main or Subjunctive ☞ 10.5.2.):

(28) *Pero **a lo savrà** che 'l vendior **a veul** ciolelo*
    'peru a=l-u=sav'ra   ke=l=væŋ'djur
    P.   SBJ.3=OBJ.3-M=know\DUB.3S SUB=DET=salesman
    a='vøl   ʧu'l-e=l-u
    SBJ.3=want\PRS.3S have_sex-INF=OBJ.3-M
    'Pero would/should know that the salesman wants to cheat him'

(28′) *che Pero **a lo sapia** che 'l vendior **a veul** ciolelo!*
    ke   'peru a=l-u='sapja   ke=l=væŋ'djur
    SUB P.   SBJ.3=OBJ.3-M=know\SUBJ.3S SUB=DET=salesman
    a='vøl   ʧu'l-e=l-u
    SBJ.3=want\PRS.3S have_sex-INF=OBJ.3M
    'may Pero know that the salesman wants to cheat him!'

In the following examples a Present and Imperfect Main tense in the main clause are matched by a Present Subjunctive or a Past Subjunctive tense in the subordinate clause:

(29) *më smija ch'a sìa fin-a [...] ant la Region Piemont*
mə =ˈzmi-a   k=a=ˈsia   ˈfiɲa aɲt=l-a=reˈdʒuŋ
IND.1S=look_like-PRS.3S SUB=SBJ3=be\SBJ.3S even INE=DET-F=region
pjeˈmuɲt
Piedmont
'it seems to me that he is even in the Piedmont Regional Council' (Bonato 2003–2004: 205)

(30) *a smija ch'a fussa ël confin ossidental*
a=ˈzmi-a   k=a=ˈfysa   əl=kuŋˈfiŋ
SBJ.3=look_like-PRS.3S SUB=SBJ.3=be\SUBJ.PST.3S DET=border
usidæŋˈtal
western
'it seems probable that it was the Western border' ("Ël Mondvì," https://pms.wikipedia.org/wiki/%C3%8Bl_Mondv%C3%AC)

(31) exemplifies a "future in the past," i.e., a state of affairs that would take place in a subsequent moment in the past:

(31) *Giòna a cherdìa che lor a sarìo mai arpentisse e cambià stra, ma sò apel a sarìa stàit arseivù bin*
ˈdʒona a=kərˈdia   ke=ˈlur   a=saˈriu   maj
J.   SBJ.3=believe\PRS.3S SUB=IDP.3P SBJ.3=be\COND.3P never
arpæŋˈti=se   e   kamˈbj-a   stra / ma so=aˈpel
repent\INF=REFL and change-PTCL street but POSS.3=appeal
a=saˈria   stajt   arsæjˈv-y   biŋ
SBJ.3=be\COND.3S be\PTCL receive-PTCL well
'Jonah thought that they could never repent and change course, but [that] his appeal could (still) be well received' (https://www.tempodiriforma.it/bibiapiemonteisa/2021/01/20/duminica-24-d-gene-2021-leture-bibliche-an-piemonteis/Duminica 24 'd Gené 2021—Leture bìbliche an piemontèis | La Bibia piemontèisa (tempodiriforma.it))

(32) further exemplifies an untensed subordinate clause:

(32) *a s'é contentasse 'd mostreje la lenga*
a=ˈs=e   kuŋteŋˈt-a-se   d=musˈtr-e=je
SBJ.3=REFL.3=be\PRS.3S please-PTCL=REFL ATTR=must-INF=IND
l-a=ˈlæŋg-a
DET-F=tongue-S

'he contented himself with sticking his tongue out' (Mania Reida 1995 [1902]: 99)

16.2.3 *Subject and Object Clauses*

Subject and object clauses are always argumental (differently from all other clauses) and may use either a tensed or an untensed mood. In the latter case the clause is generally preceded by the Attributive *ëd* (ATTR), although Subject clauses may also be expressed by a bare Infinitive:

(33) *a l'é belfé* [*('d) trové 'd masnà che a parlo italian*]_s
    a=ˈle   bel'fe d=truˈv-e   əd=maˈzna
    SBJ.3=be\PRS.3S easy ATTR=find-INF ATTR=child
    k=a=ˈparl-u   itaˈljaŋ
    SUB= SBJ.3=speak-PRS.3P Italian
    'it is easy to find children who speak Italian'

(34)=(32)   *a s'é contentasse* [*'d mostreje la lenga*]_o
                a=ˈs=e   kuŋteŋˈt-a=se
                SBJ.3=REFL3=be\PRS.3S please-PTCL=REFL
                d=musˈtr-e-je   l-a=ˈlæŋg-a
                ATTR=must-INF=IND DET-F=tongue-S
                'he contented himself with sticking his tongue out' (Mania Reida 1995 [1902]: 99)

When tensed, Subject and Object Clauses are preceded by the Subordinator *che*:

(35) *a smijava* [*che a-i fussa pì gnun-a speransa*]_s
    a=zmiˈ-ava   ke=a=j=ˈfysa   pi
    SBJ.3=look-like-IMPF.3S SUB=SBJ.3=IND=be\SUBJ.IMPF.3S more
    ˈɲyŋ-a speˈraŋs-a
    none-F hope-s
    'it looked like there was no hope anymore' ("Valensan-a Fòtbal;" https://pms.wikipedia.org/wiki/Valensan-a_F%C3%B3tbal)

(36) *A diso tuti* [*ch'a sìa 'n torolo*]_o
    a=ˈdizu   ˈtyti   k=a=ˈsia   n=tuˈrulu
    SBJ.3=say\PRS.3P everybody SUB=SBJ.3=be\SUBJ.3S INDEF=daft
    'everybody says he's a daft' (Villata 1997: 276)

16.2.3.1 Indirect Clauses

When question words are used as heads of subordinate subject or object clauses they are usually followed (as in questions; ☞ 15.9.) by the Subordinator *che*:

(37) *ciameje **chi** ch'a l'ha rangiaje la màchina*
tʃaˈm-e=je   ki   k=a=ˈla   raŋˈdʒ-a=je
ask-IPV.2P=IND who SUB=SBJ.3=have\PRS.3S fix-PTCL=IND
l-a=ˈmakin-a
DET-F=car-S
'ask her/him who fixed her/his car' (Villata 1997: 275)

This is not the case of *se* /se/ 'if,' that finds its prototypical use in conditional clauses (☞ 16.2.10.) and is never followed by *che*. *Se* is used when the indirect subordinate clause contains a 'yes-no' question:

(39) *mi adess i-j ciamo a chila **s'**a l'é nen fortunà*
mi   aˈdes   i=i=ˈtʃam-u   a=ˈkila   s=a=ˈle
IND.1S now SBJ.1=IND=ask-PRS.1S ADE=IDP.3F if= SBJ.3=be\PRS.3S
næŋ furtyˈna
NEG lucky
'now I ask her if she is not lucky' (Pietracqua 1871: 206)

16.2.4 Temporal Clauses

Temporal clauses are most commonly marked by *quand* /kwaŋd/ 'when' ((40)) or its local variant *cand* /kaŋd/ ((41)):

(40) *a circondo 'l sol **quand** ch'a nass*
a=tʃirˈkuŋdu   l=sul   kwaŋd k=a=ˈnas
3S=surround\PRS.3P DET=sun when SUB=SBJ.3=be_born\PRS.3S
'they surround the sun when it's sunrise' (Pietracqua 1859b, Act 1, Scene 1)

(41) ***cand** che quaidun a fa dle ròbe come anciochésse*
ˈkaŋd ke=kwajˈdyŋ   a=ˈfa   d=l-e=ˈrob-e   ˈkume
when SUB=somebody SBJ.3=do\PRS.3S ATTR=DET-F.P=thing-P like
aŋtʃuˈk-e=se
get_drunk-INF=REFL
'when someone does a thing like get completely drunk' (https://www.facebook.com/amprendomalalengapiemonteisa/photos/a.1209717215708827/1266351543378727/)

16.2.4.1 Concomitant Temporal Clauses

Concomitant temporal clauses are expressed with *mentre* /ˈmæŋtre/, very rarely *mentr* /mæŋtr/ or more commonly *antramentr(e)* /aŋtraˈmæŋtr(e)/ 'while' (the latter lit. 'in between while'), and also with *antant* /aŋˈtaŋt/ 'while' (lit.: 'in (so) much'):

(42) *se la sartòjra a ven **mentre** ch'i-i son nen, fela speté*
se=l-a=sarˈtojr-a   a=ˈvæŋ   ˈmeŋtre
if=DET-F=seamstress-S SBJ.3=come\PRS.3S while
k=i-j=ˈsuŋ   næŋ ˈfe=l-a   speˈt-e
SUB=SBJ.1=IND=be\PRS.1S NEG do\IPV.2P=OBJ.3-F wait-INF
'if the seamstress arrives while I am not there, let (P) her wait' (Bersezio 1980 [1863], Act 1, Scene 11)

(43) *e a l'é stait pròpi un bel vëdde la gòj dël publich **antramentr** che a scotava stòrie*
e   a=ˈle   stajt   ˈpropi aŋ=ˈbel ˈvədde
and SBJ.3=be\PRS.3S be\PTCL really nice   see\INF
l-a=ˈgoj   d-əl=ˈpyblik   aŋtraˈmæŋtr
DET-F-happiness ATTR-DET=audience while
ke=a=skuˈt-ava   ˈstorj-e
SUB=SBJ.3=listen-IMPF.3S tales-P
'and it was really nice to see the happiness of the audience as they listened to the tales' (Siròt 2004)

(44) ***antant** che a mostrava a l'ha aussà la vos*
aŋˈtaŋt ke   a=musˈtr-ava   a=ˈla   awˈs-a
while   SUB SBJ.3=teach-IMPF.3S SBJ.3=have\PRS.3S raise-PTCL
l-a=ˈvuz
DET-F=voice
'While he was teaching, he called out' [John 7, 28] (Brero 1984: 34)

Some of these connectives have grammaticalized a contrastive meaning and may also be used in coordination (☞ 16.1).

16.2.4.2 Antecedent Temporal Clauses

When the Subordinate clause is temporally antecedent to the Main clause, especially in narratives, it is possible to have this relation coded on the subordinate via the dislocation of the Participle of the Verb to the extreme left of the sentence and the insertion of *che* after the Participle:

(45) *calmà ch'a l'é staita la pì gròssa, a s'é durbisse 'l capitol dle confidense*
   kal'm-a   k=a='le   'stajt-a   l-a='pi   'gros-a /
   calm-PTCL SUB=SBJ.3=be/PRS.3S be/PTCL-F DET-F=more big-F /
   a='s=e   dyr'bi=se   l=ka'pitul
   SBJ.3=REFL=be/PRS.3S open\PTCL=REFL DET=chapter
   d=l-e=kuɲfi'dæŋs-e
   ATTR=DET-F.P=confidence-P
   'as soon as the greatest part of it was over, it was the turn of the "Confidense Chapter"' (Mania Reida 1995 [1902]: 100)

The Subjunctive mood may appear in alternative to the Main in these clauses whenever the main sentence's paradigm is Present or Dubitative.

16.2.5 Clauses Expression Location and Movement

Subordinate clauses expressing location or movement are introduced by *andoa* /aŋ'dua/, *andova* / aŋ'duva/, *anté* / aŋ'te/ 'where' (for phrases expressing location and movement ☞ 13.4.):

(46) *l'han-ne 'l dirit ëd serni sò doman ant la tèra anté ch'a vivo*
   'laŋ=ne   əl='drit   əd='serni   so=du'maŋ
   have\PRS3P=INT.3P DEF=right ATTR=choose\INF POSS3=tomorrow
   aŋt=l-a='tær-a   aŋ'te   k=a='vivu
   INE=DET-F=land-S where SUB=SBJ.3=live\PRS.3P
   'do they have the right to choose their tomorrow in the land where they live?' (Sautabachëtte 2006)

16.2.6 Phrases and Clauses Expressing Similarity

Phrases expressing similarity involve one of the three phonological and orthographical variants *com* /kum/, *coma* /'kuma/, *come* /'kume/, all meaning 'as, like:'

(47) *a l'é come lavé la testa a j'aso*
   a='le   'kume la'v-e   l-a='testa   a='j=azu
   SBJ.3=be\PRS.3S like   wash-INF DET-F=head ADE=DET\P=donkey
   'it is like washing the donkey's head'

16.2.7 Causal and Final Phrases and Clauses

Phrases and clauses expressing the cause or the goal of some state of affairs may be expressed with the same elements; the clauses are always introduced by at least one *che*.

In phrases and in untensed clauses as well the Benefactive *për* (BEN) is used both for causes and goals:

(48) *për teni an fòra ij malufissi a bërdocavo mincasòrt ëd dësmentiure*
pər=ˈtæɲi aŋ=ˈfora i=malyˈfisi a=bərduˈk-avu
BEN=keep\INF INE=out DET\P=curse SBJ.3=stutter-IMPF.3P
miŋkaˈsort əd=dəzmeŋˈtjyr-e
every.type ATTR=spell-P
'to keep the curses out they stammered all sorts of spells' (Cosio 1980: 34)

(49) *i veuj pa gnanca meuire d'inedia për ij fastidi dj'autri*
i=ˈvøj pa ˈɲaŋka ˈmøjre d=iˈnedj-a
SBJ.1=want\PRS.1S NEG.EMPH neither die\INF ATTR=starvation-S
pər=i=fasˈtidi ˈd=j=awtr-i
BEN=DET\P=annoyance ATTR=DET\P=other-P
'I don't even want to starve from other people's annoyances' (Garelli 1874b, Act 2, Scene 1, p. 39)

In tensed clauses *përchè* /pərˈkæ/ 'since, because, in order to' is used. *Përchè* may be followed by the Subordinator *che*:

(50) *na grafia che mi i definiss "sarvaja", përchè a smija scrita sensa la pi cita régola*
n-a=graˈfi-a ke=mi i=defiˈnis sarˈvaj-a /
INDEF-F=orthography-S SUB=IDP.1S SBJ.1=define\PRS.1S wild-F /
pərˈkæ a=sˈmia ˈskrit-a ˈsæŋsa l-a=pi
because SBJ.3=look_like-PRS.3S write\PTCL-F without DET-F=more
ˈt͡ʃit-a ˈregul-a
small-F rule-S
'an orthography [that] I call "wild," as it looks written without even the tiniest rule' (Eandi 2006: 18)

(51) *e a bsògna nen chërdsse, përchè ch'i son na pòvra fia, ëd podejme mal pressié*
e a=ˈbzoɲ-a næŋ ˈkərd=se / pərˈkæ
and SBJ.3=must-PRS.3S NEG believe\INF=REFL / because
k=i=ˈsuŋ n-a=ˈpovr-a ˈfi-a / əd=puˈdæj=me
SUB=SBJ.1=be\PRS.1S INDEF-F=poor-F girl-S / ATTR=can\INF=OBJ.1S
mal preˈsj-e
badly appreciate-INF

'one must not think that, since I'm a poor girl, one can despise me' (Bersezio 1980 [1863], Act 1, Scene 6)

When used to express cause, *përchè* may be followed by a Verb in the Main mood, more rarely in the Subjunctive or Conditional mood.

Përchè is also used in order to express goal. In such sentences, however, the Verb always displays the Subjunctive mood:

(52) *it lo diso **përchè** ch'it lo sapie*
 i=t=l-u=disu pərˈkæ
 SBJ.1=OBJ.2S=OBJ.3-M=say\PRS.1P because
 k=it=l-u=ˈsapje
 SUB=SBJ.2S=OBJ.3-M=know\SUBJ.IMPF.3P
 'I tell you so that you know' (Villata 1997: 278)

It is noteworthy that in negative final clauses the negative Adverb *nen* occurs before the Subordinator *che*:

(53) *për nen che a l'abio da trovesse malsoà*
 pər næŋ k=a=ˈlabju da=truˈv-e-se malˈswa
 BEN NEG SUB= SBJ.3=have\SBJV.3P ABL=find-INF=REFL unease
 '[he taught what the next day he might bring them] so that they would not be uncomfortable' (Brero & Musso 2011: 39)

Strictly causal is instead *da già* /da=ˈdʒa/, lit. 'from already,' always followed by *che*:

(54) *e **da già** ch'i son si sul brondolé [...] Scassé l'òssi ch'a regna ant quaich quarté*
 e da=ˈdʒa k=i=ˈsuŋ ˈsi sy=l=bruŋˈdul-e
 and ABL=already SUB=SBJ.1=be\PRS.1S here SUP=DET=grumble-INF
 skaˈs-e l=ˈosi k=a=ˈɲ-a ant=ˈkwajk
 drive_out-INF DET=laziness SUB= SBJ.3=reign-PRS.3S INE=some
 kwarˈte
 neighborhood
 'and since I'm already grumbling, get rid of the laziness that reigns in some places' (Ferrua-Chierico 1871: 56)

16.2.8 Concessive Phrases and Clauses

Concessive clauses, both tensed and untensed, are introduced by various connectives, among which the most used is without any doubt *bele* /ˈbele/, notably in untensed clauses (55). In tensed clauses, *bele che* /ˈbele ke/, *contut che* /kuŋˈtyt ke/ 'even if,' or, more rarely, *conbin che* /kuŋˈbiŋ ke/ 'although,' *ëdcò se* /ədˈko se/ 'even if,'[4] *malgré* /malˈgre/ 'despite:'[5]

(55) *bele an seghitand a mostré filosofìa, a l'é anteressasse dzortut a la pedagogìa*
ˈbele aŋ=segiˈt-aŋd a=musˈtr-e filusuˈfi-a / a=ˈle
even INE=follow-GER ADE=teach-INF philosophy-S / SBJ.3=be\PRS.3S
aŋtereˈs-a=se dzurˈtyt a=ˈl-a=peda guˈdʒi-a
interest-PTCL=REFL most_of_all ADE=DET-F=pedagogy-S
'even if he kept teaching philosophy, he became interested most of all in pedagogy' ("John Dewey;" https://pms.wikipedia.org/wiki/John_Dewey)

(56) *a vòlta da l'àutra, bele che për andé a sò ufìssi a sia pi longh*
a=ˈvolt-a da=ˈl-awtr-a /ˈbele ke=pər=aŋˈde
SBJ.3=turn-PRS.3S ABL=DET=other-F / even SUB=BEN=go\INF
a=so=yˈfisi a=ˈsia pi luŋg
ADE=POSS.3=office SBJ.3=be\SBJV.3S more long
'turn on the other side even if it takes longer to get to his office' (Bersezio 1980 [1863], Act 1, Scene 1)

(57) *bele che an vàire region coste lenghe a son ancora bastansa spantià*
ˈbele ke=aŋ=ˈvajre reˈdʒuŋ ˈkust-e ˈlæŋg-e a=ˈsuŋ
even SUB=INE=several region PROX-F.P language-P SBJ.3=be\PRS.3P
aŋˈkura basˈtaŋsa spaŋˈtj-a
still enough spread-PTCL
'even if in several regions these languages are still rather widespread' ("Lenga italian-a;" https://pms.wikipedia.org/wiki/Lenga_italian-a)

---

4 *Anche se/che* may also be used as concessive connectives. Both are Italianisms.
5 *Con tut* (lit. 'with all/every') is developing, or has already developed, a sense akin to that of 'despite:' *con tut lòn* 'with all that/despite that;' *con tut jë stent, I l'oma pijalo* 'with all the hardships, we got it/ despite all the hardships, we got it.' In the latter case the concessive reading might also be invited by the meaning of *stent* 'hardships.'

TABLE 55   Combinations of *se* and a Subject Clitic

		i		s'i	/s=i/	'if=SBJ.1, 2P'
se	+	it	=	s'it	/s=it/	'if=SBJ.2S'
		a		s'a	/s=a/	'if=SBJ.3'

(58)   ma la mòrt, **con tut che** a smija na ròba bruta, a l'ha nen riessù a dëstache-ne
ma l-a='mort   kuŋ='tyt ke=a=z'mia
but DET-F=death   COM=all SUB=SBJ.3=seem-SUBJ.PRS.3S
n-a='rob-a   'bryt-a a='la   næŋ rje'sy
INDEF-F=thing-S ugly-F SBJ.3=have\PRS.3S NEG manage\PTCL
a=dəsta'k-e=ne
ADE=detach-INF=OBJ.1P
'but death, although it is a bad thing, could not separate us' (Ravizza 2004)

(59)   ëdcò se a pieuv i surtirai l'istess
əd'ko se a='pjøv   i=syrti'raj   l=istes
also if SBJ3=rain\PRS.3S SBJ.1=go_out\DUB.1S DET=same
'even if it rains, I'll go out anyway' (Villata 1997: 279)

16.2.9   Conditional Clauses

Conditional clauses are the province of the connective *se* /se/ 'if.'

Se is a clitic whose presence, as already mentioned in 16.2.3.1. excludes the use of the Subordinator *che*, and which is subject to the same assimilation rules to a following Subject clitic (most often expressed in writing, too; see Table 55).

As other subordinate clauses, conditionals may be used with untensed verbal forms, although a tensed verbal form is much more common:

(60)   a smija ëdcò che, se beivù con moderassion, a l'abia n'efèt anti-ossidant
a=z'mij-a   əd'ko ke / se bæj'vy   kuŋ=mudera'sjuŋ /
SBJ.3=look_like-PRS.3S also   SUB if drink\PTCL   COM=moderation /
a='l-abja   n=e'fet   aŋti=usi'daŋt
SBJ.3=have\SUBJ.PRS.3S INDEF=effect anti-oxidant
'it looks like it can also have an anti-oxidant effect, if drunk with moderation' ("Vin;" https://pms.wikipedia.org/wiki/Vin)

With conditional clauses, the truth of the main clause is conditional on the dependent, the conditional clause.

Implicative and predictive conditional clauses have a Main or Dubitative verbal form in both the condition (the antecedent, or protasis) and the subsequent (the apodosis) of a conditional clause:

(61) *s'a l'é nen vnua a vnirà*
s=a='le næŋ 'vny-a a=vni'ra
if=SBJ.3=be\PRS.3S NEG come\PTCL-F SBJ.3=come\DUB.3S
'if she has not come she will come' (Garelli 1874b, Act 1, Scene 3, p. 13)

The verbal form of the conditional clause may be Main, with the usual rules pertaining to the sequence of tenses rules applying. In the following sentence the main clause is not declarative and an Imperative verbal form is used:

(62) *s'it lo sas dimlo!*
s=it=l-u='sa(z) 'di=m=l-u
if=SBJ.2S=OBJ.3-M=know\PRS.2S say\IPV.S=OBJ.3-M
'if you know, tell me!'

Irrealis or countefactual conditional clauses express unfulfilled conditions and are typically marked by the use of the Subjunctive in the condition (the antecedent, protasis), with the Conditional mood being found in the subsequent (the apodosis) of a conditional clause (☞ 10.5.4.):

(63) *s'a s'emendeissa 'd col difet, chiel a saria un d'ij fieui i pi amabij*
s=a=s=emeŋ'dejsa d=kul di'fet kjæl
if=SBJ.3=REFL=amend\COND.3S ATTR=DIST defect IDP.3MS
a=sa'ria yŋ d=i='fjøj pi=a'mabij
SBJ.3=be\COND.3S one ATTR=DET\P=boy\P more=lovable\P
'if he were to correct that defect he would be one of the most lovable boys' (Bersezio 1980 [1863], Act 1, Scene 6)

(64) *s'a l'aveissa vëddulo a saria staita fiera 'd sò marì*
s=a=la'væjsa vəd'dy=l-u a=sa'ria
if=SBJ.3=have\COND.IMPF.3S see\PTCL=OBJ-M SBJ.3=be\COND.3S
'stajt-a 'fjer-a əd='so ma'ri
stay\PTCL-F proud-F ATTR=POSS.3 husband
'if you had seen him you would have been proud of your husband' (Bersezio 1980 [1863], Act 5, Scene 4)

Occasionally, a Main Imperfect replaces the Conditional:

(65) *s'a savìa prima ëd l'esistensa ëd Weeds, a l'avrìa lassà perde l'idèja*
    s=a=saˈvia   ˈprima d=l=esisˈtæŋs-a   əd=ˈwids /
    if=SBJ.3=know\IMPF.3S firstly ATTR=DET=existence-S ATTR=W.
    a=l=avˈria   laˈs-a   ˈpærde   l=iˈdæj-a
    SBJ.3=have\COND.3S let-PTCL lose\INF DET=idea-S
    'if he had known of Weeds' existence before he would have given up (his) idea' ("Breaking Bad;" https://pms.wikipedia.org/wiki/Breaking_Bad)

or, probably more common:

(65) *s'a l'avèissa savù ...*
    s=a=laˈvæjsa   saˈvy
    if=SBJ.3=have\COND.IMPF.3S know\PTCL

Rarely, *se* is omitted altogether:

(66) *i l'aveisso mangià, i l'avrio nen fam*
    i=laˈvæjsu   maɲˈdʒ-a i=lavˈriu   næŋ fam
    SBJ.1=have\ SUBJ.IMPF.1P eat-PTCL SBJ.1=have\COND.1P NEG hunger
    'had we eaten we would not be hungry'

(67) *un pòch ch'i andeisso ancor anans i andasio a finì ant la sabia*
    aŋ=ˈpok   k=i=aŋˈdæjsu   aŋˈkur anaŋs /
    INDEF=bit SUB=SBJ.1=go\COND.IMPF.1P still   ahead /
    i=aŋdaˈziu   a=fiˈni   aŋt=l-a=ˈsabj-a
    SBJ.1=have\IMPF.1P ADE=end-INF INE=DET-F=sand-S
    'had we gone still a bit ahead we would have ended up in the sand'

CHAPTER 17

Negation

17.1 Overview

Negation is not expressed via verbal morphology through dedicated negative paradigms, but syntactically. Generally, negation is positioned after the finite verbal forms and is expressed by the negator *nen* /næŋ/ (NEG). In compound tenses, *nen* is placed after the inflected form.

(1) *i capisso **nen***
 i=kaˈpisu næŋ
 SBJ.1=understand\PRS.1S NEG
 'I do not understand' (Rohlfs 1969: 305)

(2) *l'hai **nen** sentilo a soné*
 laj næŋ sæŋˈti=l-u a=suˈn-e
 have\PRS.1S NEG hear\PTCL=OBJ.3-M ADE=ring-INF
 'I did not hear the bell-tower clock strike it [=noon]' (Garelli 1874b, Act 1, Scene 1)

Piedmontese is a negative-concord language, i.e., the co-occurrence of more than one negative item in the clause does not (necessarily) affirms. However, in sentences with multiple negative items, *nen* /næŋ/ must be dropped under certain conditions, or else the sentence would take on a marked positive reading (☞ 17.5.).

17.2 Sentence Negators

The unmarked sentence negator is *nen* /næŋ/. It comes from Latin NE(C) ENT(EM) 'nor a thing.'[1] In simple finite verbal forms, *nen* appears postverbally. In compound finite Verbs, it is placed after the inflected form (see (1) and (2) above). When the Verb is an Infinitive, *nen* is mandatorily placed before the

---

1 Rohlfs (1968: 218) prefers NE(C) GENTE(M) 'not people' to NEC ENTE(M) as etymon for *nen*, *gnente*, Italian *niente* and the like.

Verb (3). With Gerunds, *nen* may appear either preverbally or postverbally. The latter strategy, however, is usually preferred (see also Miola 2017: 148–149):[2]

(3) *la prima vitura ëd Segment B con carosserìa zincà për **nen** fela dësvërnisé*
l-a='prim-a vi'tyr-a d=əl=seg'mænt   bi kuŋ=karuse'ri-a
DET-F=first-F car-S   ATTR=DET=segment B COM=car_body-S
ziŋ'k-a   pər=næŋ   'f-e=l-a   dəzvərni'z-e
zinc-PTCL   BEN=NEG   do\-INF=OBJ.3-F remove_paint-INF
'the first B-Segment car with a zinc-coated body in order to avoid loss of varnish' ("Fiat Punto I;" http://pms.wikipedia.org/wiki/Fiat_Punto_I)

(4) *pensand **nen** a la possibilità 'd na cariera an costa dissiplin-a*
pæŋ's-aŋd næŋ a=l-a=pusibili'ta   d=n-a=ka'rjer-a
think-GER NEG ADE=DET-F=possibility   ATTR=INDEF-F=career-S
aŋ='kust-a   disip'liŋ-a
INE=PROX-F   discipline-S
'Without thinking to the possibility of an academic career in this field' ("Stefan Banach;" http://pms.wikipedia.org/wiki/Stefan_Banach)

(5) ***nen** avend d'arzultà, a scriv na litra an sij prinsipi dla mecànica*
næŋ a'væŋd   d=arzyl'ta / a=s'kriw   n-a='litr-a
NEG have\GER   ATTR=result / SBJ.3=write\PRS.3S   INDEF-F=letter-S
aŋ=s=i=priŋ'sipi   d=l-a=me'kanik-a
INE=SUP=DET\P=principle   ATTR=DET-F=mechanics-S
'Since he could not get any results, he writes a letter regarding the principles of mechanics' ("Pierre Simon de Laplace;" http://pms.wikipedia.org/wiki/Pierre_Simon_de_Laplace)

Postverbal *nen* is used also for prohibition, i.e., for negating imperative and exhortative clauses (☞ 15.6.–7.).

(6) *schersa **nen**!*
'skærs-a   næŋ
joke-IPV.2S   NEG
'do not goof around!'

---

2 As shown below, some Adverbs may separate the Verb form from *nen*.

(7) *esageroma **nen**!*
ezadʒeˈr-uma   næŋ
exaggerate-PRS.1P NEG
'let's not go over the top'

Pa /pa/ (NEG.EMPH) is used as an intensifying negator ((8) and (9)) and/or as a counter-expectational negator ((10) and (12)):

(8) *i son **pa** bel*
i=ˈsuŋ   pa   bel
SBJ.1=be\PRS.1S NEG.EMPH nice
'I am not beautiful (at all)' (Aly-Belfàdel 1933: 280)

(9) *fumé **pa***
fyˈm-e   pa
smoke-IPV.PL NEG.EMPH
'no smoking; do not smoke!' (a sticker in Turin)

(10) [TRAVET *A m'rincress ricevlo ant costa tnua, ma j'heu apena finì adess 'd feme la barba.*]
GIACHËTTA *I guardo **pa** cole stòrie-lì, mi.*
i=ˈgward-u   pa   ˈkul-e   storj-e=ˈli /   mi
SBJ.1S=look-PRS.1S NEG.EMPH DIST-F.P story-F.P=there / IDP.1S
'[Travet—I am sorry to receive you in such an attire, but I just finished shaving.]
Giachëtta—Actually, I don't care about those silly things (contrary to what you expect)' (Bersezio 1980 [1863], Act 1, Scene 2)

(11) *a cor **nen***
a=ˈkur   næŋ
SBJ.3=run\PRS.3S NEG
's/he does not run'

(12) *a cor **pa***
a=ˈkur   pa
SBJ.3=run\PRS.3S NEG.EMPH
's/he does not run (contrary to what you expect)'

If *nen* and *pa* co-occur, *pa* precedes *nen*. This sequence is grammatical only for a minority of today's speakers:

(13) *?a cor pa nen*
 a=ˈkur   pa   næŋ
 SBJ.3=run\PRS.3S NEG.EMPH NEG
 's/he does not run (at all)'

but it is nonetheless attested in 18th- and 19th-century Piedmontese texts:

(14) *mi 'v la peuss pa nen dëscrive*
 mi v=l-a=ˈpøs   pa   næŋ   dəsˈkrive
 IDP.1S OBJ.2P=OBJ.3-F=can\PRS.1S NEG.EMPH NEG describe\INF
 'I can't describe it to you' (Pipino 1783: 130)

With transitive Verbs, *nen* may be (marginally) interpreted as the Pronoun 'nothing.' More frequently, albeit uncommon in today's Piedmontese, the [*pa+ nen*] construction functions as an emphatic negator even with transitives:

(15) *col ch'a l'ha pa nen*
 kul k=a=ˈla   pa   næŋ
 DIST SUB=SBJ.3=have\PRS.3S NEG.EMPH NEG
 'the one who has not/the one who has nothing' (*L'evangeli secound Matteo* 1861 [1834], 13:12)

(16) *fa pa nen lolì*
 fa   pa   næŋ lu=ˈli
 do\IPV.S NEG.EMPH NEG DIST.PRO=there
 'don't (S) do that!' (Berruto 1990: 14, fn. 25; cf. Zanuttini 1997: 75)

Negators can be modified and even intensified, typically by *franch* /fraŋk/ 'indeed,' *dël tut* /d=əlˈtyt/ (ATTR=DET=all) 'at all,' or *pròpi* /ˈpropi/ 'indeed,' which are placed before the negator (for further discussion ☞ 12.3.):

(17) *se la montagna a'l l'ha nen dël tut*
 se l-a=muɲˈtaɲ-a   a=l=ˈla   næŋ d=əlˈtyt
 if DET-F=mountain-S SBJ.3=OBJ.3=have\PRS.3S NEG ATTR=DET=all
 'if the mountain does not have it at all'

(18) *a-i vintra pròpi pa*
 a=j=ˈviɲtr-a   ˈpropi pa
 SBJ.3=IND=enter-PRS.3S really NEG.EMPH
 'it really does not fit in'

As for the position of *pa* and *nen* in relation to other temporal Adverbs (☞ 12.2.2.) that might be present in the sentence, Zanuttini (1997: 70–72), along the lines of Cinque (1994, 1999), showed that *nen* follows *già* 'already' and *pi* '(no) more' (with the former in turn preceding the latter), and is followed by *semp(r)e* 'always.' On the other hand, *pa* precedes *già* and *pì*, but is followed by *sempre*. Thus, the linear order of the aforementioned five elements is as follows:

pa > *già* > *pì* > *nen* > *semp(r)e/mai*
(NEG.EMPH > already > (no) more > NEG > always/never).[3]

17.2.1 *Other Sentence-Negating Constructions*

Some constructions have grammaticalized, or are on the verge of grammaticalizing, as sentence negators in Piedmontese. Notably, [*si+che+*Verb] /'si k(e)/+Verb 'yes that'+Verb is nowadays used only with a negative meaning, such as in the following example:

(19) *si ch'i l'hai mangià!*
     si   k=i=ˈlaj   maɲˈdʒ-a
     yes SUB=SBJ.1=have\PRS.1S eat-PTCL
     'I (actually) did not eat!'

[*si+che+*Verb] took on its negative meaning from a preceding ironic reading ('of course I did that' (ironic) > 'I did not do that'). The same holds for the (less-grammaticalized as a negation) construction [*già+che+*Verb] /ˈdʒa=k(e)/+Verb 'yeah that'+Verb.

17.2.2 *Other Intensifying Negators*

Other than *pa*, sometimes *gnente* may be used as an intensifying negator, taking the meaning of 'not at all:'

(20) *sté adòss a le përson-e l'é **gnente** civiltà!* ...
     ste   aˈdos a=le=pərˈsuŋ-e   l=e   ˈɲæŋte tʃivilˈta
     stay\INF upon ADE=DET-P=person-P be\PRS.3S nothing civilization
     'standing too close to other people is not polite at all' (Pietracqua 1871, Act 1, Scene 2)

---

3 Note that the construction [*pa+pi*] cannot be focalized/intensified by *pròpe* and the like (Zanuttini 1997: 75–76).

7.3 Negation with Scope over Smaller Units

When the scope of the negation is not over the entire clause but over one of its constituents, such as a Noun phrase, an adjectival phrase or an adverbial phrase, the negator is *nen*.[4] This usage is normal in contrastive and corrective contexts:

(21) *nen ti, ma un dij tò*
    næŋ ti   ma yŋ d=i=ˈto
    NEG IDP.2S but one ATTR=DET\P=POSS.2S
    'not you, but one from your family' (San Giovann Bòsch; quoted in Cerrato 1981: 28)

(22) *a l'é nen cit, ma grand*
    a=ˈle   næŋ tʃit ma graŋd
    SBJ.3=be\PRS.3S NEG small but big
    'it's not small, but big'

(23) *i parlo ëd lòn che a-j riva ant ël mond, e nen mach an tra Coni e Ast*
    i=ˈparl-u   ëd=ˈloŋ   ke=a=j=ˈriv-a
    SBJ.1=talk-PRS.1S ATTR=DIST.PRO SUB=SBJ.3=IND=happen-PRS.3S
    ant=əl=ˈmuŋd e næŋ mak ˈaŋtra ˈkuni e ast
    INE=DET=world and NEG only INTER C. and A.
    'I am talking of what happens in the world, and not only between Coni and Ast' (Tosco 2004: 3)

Other constituent negators are *gnanca* /ˈɲaŋka/ 'not even', *manch* /maŋk/ 'not even', and the negative coordinative conjunction *ni ... ni* /ni ... ni/ 'neither ... nor' (the latter correlatives may appear also in the Italianized form *né ... né* /ne ... ne/). They may occur in a clause that already has a negative polarization:

(24) *i conòsso (pa) gnanca sò frel*
    i=kuˈnosu   pa   ˈɲaŋka soˈfrel
    SBJ.1=know\PRS.1S NEG.EMPH not_even POSS.3=brother
    'I do not even know his brother'

---

4 *Pa* may sometimes appear instead of, or together with, *nen* when the intended meaning is more clearly counter-expectative (Villata 1997: 228).

(25) *i l'hai (nen) vist **ni** ti **ni** tò frel*
      i=ˈlaj   næŋ vist   ni   ti   ni   to=ˈfrel
      SBJ.1=have\PRS.1S NEG see\PTCL nor IDP.2S nor POSS.2S=brother
      'I did not see either you or your brother'

17.4 Other Negative Items

Other negative words are *mai* /maj/ 'never,' *pì* /pi/ '(no) more,' *gnun* /ɲyŋ/ 'nobody' (as a Pronoun) and 'no' (as an Adjective), *gnente* /ˈɲænte/ 'nothing.' *Gnun* and *gnente* repeat among the negative words the human/non-human opposition found in interrogative *chi* /ki/ 'who' vs. *còs(a)* /koz(a)/ 'what' (☞ 15.9.4.). These negative words may occur alone to convey a negative meaning to the sentence, but may also, under special conditions, co-occur with *nen* (☞ 17.5.):

(26) *ij gròss antra lor-aitri as mangio (*nen) **mai***
      i=ˈgros   ˈaŋtra luˈrajtr-i   a=s=ˈmaŋdʒ-u   maj
      DET\P=big INTER IDP.3P.EXCL-M SBJ.3=REFL=eat-PRS.3P never
      'big fish never eat each other' (Calvo 2003 [1816]: 87; *Faula* VI, *'L can e l'òss*, v. 34)

(27) *ës telefonin-sì, che adess i treuvo **pì***
      ës=telefuniŋ=ˈsi /   ke aˈdes i=ˈtrøw   pi
      DEICT=cellphone=here / SUB now SBJ.1=find.PRS.1S more
      'this cellphone, that now I can't find' (DjSnorcKeey 2017, *Nen tante bale*; https://youtu.be/KOHcvYmd8mw)

(28) *l'hai (*nen) **gnanca** un sòld, bon fieul!*
      laj   ˈɲaŋka n=ˈsold /   buŋ fjøl
      have\PRS.1S not_even INDEF=coin / good boy
      'I don't [even] have a dime, good boy!' (Pietracqua 1871; Act 1 scene 8)

17.5 Negative Concord

Piedmontese is a negative concord language, that is, multiple negative words may occur in the same sentence without necessarily affirming:

(29) *mai gnun a l'ha capì 'l përchè 'd costa solussion*
 maj ɲyŋ a='la   ka'pi l=për'kæ
 never nobody SBJ.3=have\PRS.3S understand\PTCL DET=why
 d='kust-a suly'sjuŋ
 ATTR=PROX-F solution
 'nobody ever understood the reason behind this decision' (Burzio 2003: 1)

(30) *decis a nen lassesse sofié sota ij barbis da gnun*
 de'tʃiz   a='næŋ la's-e=se   su'fj-e 'suta
 decide\PTCL ADE=NEG let-INF=REFL blow-INF under
 i=bar'biz   da='ɲyŋ
 DET\P=moustache ABL=nobody
 'determined not to be picked on by anybody' (Pietracqua 1974 [1891]: 66; cf. Bruno Villata: https://www.piemunteis.it/studi/cum-dis-bun-piemunteis-espressiun-idiomatiche-ant-ij-rumanz-ed-luis-pietracqua)

(31) *i l'hai pa mai tocà gnente*
 i='laj   pa   maj tu'k-a   'ɲæŋte
 SBJ.1=have\PRS.1S NEG.EMPH never touch-PTCL nothing
 'I never touched anything (at all)'

(32) *mai pì ch'as finissa d'ancheuj*
 maj pi   k=a=s=fi'nisa   d=aŋ'køj
 never more SUB=SBJ.3=REFL=finish\SUBJ.3S ATTR=today
 'we could never finish by today' [(it could) never more (be the case) that we finish by today]

With the exception of *pì*, the negative words discussed below cannot display negative concord if they occur immediately after *nen* in simple tenses, as in these examples, where capital letters indicate possible prosodic emphasis:

(33) *i vëddo NEN gnun*
 i='vəddu   næŋ ɲyŋ
 SBJ.1S=see\PRS.1S NEG nobody
 'I do *not* see nobody (i.e., I actually see someone)' (*I do not see anybody)

(34) *a marcia NEN mai: quaich vòlta a marcia pro*
 a='martʃ-a   næŋ mai /   kwajk 'volt-a a='martʃ-a
 SBJ.3S=walk-PRS.3S NEG never / some time-s SBJ.3S=walk-PRS.3S
 pru
 actually
 'it does not *never* work [walk]: sometimes it does' (*it never works)

Pì /pi/ '(no) more,' on the other hand, can be optionally used with *nen* either in compound or simple tenses, conveying a negative concord meaning:

(35) *falo pi (nen)*
 'fa=l-u   pi
 do\IPV.S=OBJ.3-M more
 'do not do (s) it anymore'

When *gnente*, *mai* or *gnun* are in preverbal position, the co-occurrence of *nen* (and *pa*) is ungrammatical (cf. Zanuttini 1987). However, some speakers may judge grammatical sentences with *gnun* in preverbal position and *nen* in postverbal position. Moreover, with *gnun*, the occurrence of *pa* as a negator is always grammatical.

(36) *gnente a-j pias (*nen/*pa)*
 'ɲæŋte   a=j='pjaz
 nothing   SBJ.3=IND= like.PRS.3S
 's/he does not like anything' (Zanuttini 1987: 156)

(37) *gnun a l'ha (*nen) dime lòn*
 ɲyŋ   a='la   'di=me   loŋ
 nobody   SBJ.3= have\PRS.3S say\PTCL=OBJ.1S DIST.PRO
 'nobody told me that'

(38) *gnun a ven pi (nen)*
 ɲyŋ   a='væŋ   pi
 nobody   SBJ.3S=come\PRS.3S   more
 'no one is coming anymore'

With compound tenses, *nen* may co-occur with others negative words maintaining a negative-concord reading. However, even in clauses with compound Verbs, *nen* cannot appear immediately before another negative word. According to Ricca (2016) "[t]he cooccurrence may even become the better choice if the separation is greater."

(39) *i l'hai (nen) vist gnun*
 i=ˈlaj   vist   ɲyŋ
 SBJ.1=have\PRS.1S see\PTCL nobody
 'I have not seen anybody'

(40) *gnun a l'ha (*nen) mai savune gnente*
 ɲyŋ   a=ˈla   maj   saˈvy=ne   ˈɲæŋte
 nobody SBJ.3=have\PRS.3S never know\PTCL=ATTR.PRO nothing
 'nobody has ever known anything about it'

Contrary to what happens with *nen* (☞ 17.2.), the co-occurrence of all negative words with *pa*, conveying a negative-concord meaning, is always possible (Parry 2013: 96).

17.6 Holophrastic Negation

Holophrastic negation is expressed by *nò* /no/ 'no' (☞ 18.3. for the functions of *nò* as a discourse marker). *Nò* may be a negative answer to both a positive polar question and/or a negative polar question:

(41) Sablin:—*J'é-lo madama?* Giovanin:—*Nò, sgnora.*
 ˈj=e-lu   maˈdam-a ↗ no / ˈzɲur-a
 IND=be\PRS.3S=INT.3M madam-S Q no / miss-S
 'Sablin:—Is Milady here? Giovanin:—No, Madam' (Pietracqua 1859: Act 2, Scene 2)

(42) Madlen-a: *Nò! Adess i son mi ch'i lo dio: Gigin a bala nen*
 Agata: *A bala nen?*
 Madlena e Gigin: *Nò!*
 no / aˈdes i=ˈsuŋ   mi   k=i=l-u=ˈdiu
 no / now SBJ1=be\PRS.1S IDP.1S SUB=SBJ1=OBJ.3-M=say\PRS.1S
 dʒiˈdʒiŋ a=ˈbal-a   næŋ // a=ˈbal-a   næŋ ↗ no
 G.   SBJ.3=dance-PRS.3S NEG // SBJ.3=dance-PRS.3S NEG Q no
 'Madlen-a:—No! Now I am talking: Gigin will not dance! Agata:—She will not dance?
 Madlena and Gigin:—No!' (*i.e.*: Gigin will not dance) (Pietracqua 1859, Act 3, Scene 5)

Nò may sometimes be used as a positive answer to a negative polar question, but in these cases it must be followed by a clause in which the affirmation is made explicit, as in the following exchange:

(43) *it lo conòsse nen?*
    it=l-u=ku'nos-e   **næŋ** ↗
    SBJ.2S=OBJ.3-M=know-PRS.2S NEG Q
    'don't you know him?'

(43') *nò, i lo conòsso benissim*
    no / i=l-u=ku'nos-u   **be'nisim**
    no / SBJ.1=OBJ.3-M=know-PRS.1S very_well
    'no, I (actually) know him very well'

Nò can also function as a holophrastic negation in contrastive elliptic coordinated clauses. In such clauses, along with the contrastive marker (e.g., *ma*), a contrasted topic is present before *nò*:

(44) *mi i l'hai beivù, ma chiel nò*
    mi   **i='laj**   **bej'v-y /**   **ma kjæl**   **no**
    IDP.1S SBJ.1=have\PRS.1S drunk-PTCL / but IDP.3M no
    'I drank, but he didn't'

In disjunctive coordinated elliptic clauses, holophrastic negation can be realized either by *nò* (sometimes also pronounced as /nu/) or by *nen*.

(45) *é-lo permes dë paghé l'impòst a Cesare, o nò?*
    'e=lu   **pər'mæs**   **əd=pa'g-e**   **l=im'post**   **a='ʧezare**
    be\PRS.3S=INT.3M permit\PTCL ATTR=pay-INF DET(-F)=tax ADE=C.
    o no ↗
    or no Q
    'is it lawful to pay taxes to Caesar, or not?' (*L'Evangeli secound Matteo* 1861 [1834], 22:17)

(46) *che a sio bele o nen, a fa gnente*
    ke   **a='siu**   **'bel-e**   **o næŋ / a='fa**   **'ɲæŋte**
    SUB SBJ.3=be\SBJV.3P nice-F.P or NEG / SBJ.3=do\PRS.3S nothing
    'be they (F) pretty or not, it does not matter'

A resumptive negator

In various parts of Piedmont, *no* /nu/ is used for a resumptive negation, i.e., a negator that "originally represented the 'comment' in the form of an 'afterthought' of the preceding negative sentence" (Bernini and Ramat 1996: 43, see also Jespersen 1917). Parry (2005: 259–260) attests this phenomenon for elder Southern Piedmontese speakers from Còiri, co-occurring with the discountinuous negation *n ... pa*. Berruto (1974: 34) notes that in some Monferrine varieties *pano* /ˈpanu/ or /ˈpano/, clearly from *pa* and a resumptive *nò*, may be sometimes used as an unmarked sentence negator (with *pa* as the most common alternative):

(47) *sì, ma duminica a n'é pa vnù-no*
 ʃi mɑ dyˈminik-a u=ˈn=æ pɑ
 yes but Sunday-s SBJ.3S.M=NEG=be\PRS.3S NEG.EMPH
 vˈny=nu
 come\PTCL= NEG.RES
 'yes, but on Sunday he did not come (not)' (Parry 2005: 259)

CHAPTER 18

Pragmatics and Discourse

This chapter will be devoted to how Piedmontese speakers structure their linguistic utterances in relation to the speakers' and hearers' mental representation of the information, its context and co-text, and the referents of the discourse.

In the following sections, we will address in particular the issues related to information structure and sentence word order (☞ 18.1 and 18.2.), and to the meaning and function of the most frequently used Piedmontese discourse markers (☞ 18.3.).

18.1 Information Structure and Sentence Word Order

Basic word order for out-of-the-blue assertive active-voice sentences in Piedmontese is Subject—Verb—Object (henceforth, S, V, and O)—Other Complements, see (1) and (2) (also ☞ 15. and 19.):

(1) *Mama l'ha vendù ij cochèt.*
    'mama la   væn'dy   i=ku'kæt
    mom   have\PRS.3S sell\PTCL   DET\P=cocoon
    S   V   O
    'Mom sold the cocoons' (Autelli 1983 [1937]: 77–79; 1st sentence of the short story)

(2) *la Menabrea dovrèissa fé na ròba parègg përchè, a l'é la méj*
    l-a=mena'brea   duv'r-æjsa   fe   n-a='rob-a   pa'rædʒ
    DET-F=M.   must-COND.IMPF.3S   do\INF   INDEF-F=thing-S   so
    S   V   O
    pər'kæ   a='le   l-a='mej
    because   SBJ.3=be\PRS.3S   DET-F=better
    'Menabrea should make a thing like that, because it's the best one' (conversation in Lissandria; Bonato 2003–2004: 191; discussing advertising, no previous mention of Menabrea[1])

---

1 The most famous brewery in Piedmont.

It is worth noting that with compound Verb forms even the Object clitic (☞ 7.4.) appears to the right of the Verb. This feature is almost unparalleled in other Romance languages:

(3) [madama l'òsta] *A grata 'l formagg! E l 'formagg? Ël gat a l'ha mangialo!*

    a=ˈgrat-a   l=furˈmadʒ   e   l=furˈmadʒ ↗
    SBJ.3=grate\PRS.3SG   DET=cheese and DET=cheese   Q
    əl=ˈgat   a=ˈla   maɲˈdʒ-a=l-u
    DET=cat SBJ.3=have\PRS.3SG   eat-PTCL= OBJ.3-M
    ⎣___S___⎦ ⎣_____V_____⎦ ⎣_____O_____⎦

'(the landlady) is grating the cheese! And the cheese? The cat ate it!' (traditional nursery rhyme)

In thetic sentences, especially with unaccusative Verbs but also with some unergatives, the NP functioning as a subject may, and normally does, appear in postverbal position (the Subject clitic remains in preverbal position). In such sentences, the Verb form always exhibits a 3S inflection, and the Subject clitic *a* is mandatorily accompanied by a non-argumental Indirect clitic *j(e)* /j(e)/ (☞ 7.4.), that is thus grammaticalized, in these constructions, as a marker of presentativity.[2] The latter form may be proclitic or enclitic according to the syntactic rules described in Ch. 7.

(4) *a-i é truch e branca 7000 lenghe vive*

    a=ˈj=e
    SBJ3=IND=be\PRS.3SG
    ⎣_____V_____⎦

    tryk=e=ˈbraŋk-a   setˈmila   ˈlæŋg-e   ˈviv-e
    bump=and=span-S seven_thousand language-P   alive-F.P
    ⎣_____S_____⎦

'there are, very roughly, 7000 living languages' (Miola 2015c).

(5) *A metà 'd luj a l'é mancaje Guido Amoretti*

    a=meˈta   d=lyj   a=ˈle   maɲˈk-a=je   ˈgwido amoˈretːi
    ADE=half ATTR=July SBJ.3=be\PRS.3S lack-PTCL=IND G.   A.
    ⎣_____V_____⎦ ⎣_____S_____⎦

'Guido Amoretti passed away mid-July' (*Tron e Lòsna* 2008: 14)

---

2 In those dialects where there are different 3rd person Singular Masculine and Feminine clitic forms, the Masculine form is used in thetic sentences.

(6) a-i nass 'd sospet
   $\underbrace{\text{a=j='nas}}_{V}$ $\underbrace{\text{əd=sus'pet}}_{S}$
   SBJ.3=IND=be_born\PRS.3SG ATTR=suspicion
   'suspicions arise' (Pierluigi Barbano, *La bola dël misteri*; quoted in Parry 1998: 79)

Parry (1998: 79) observes that the "lack of agreement was the norm in earlier stages of the language [...], but it now seems optional and less common than agreement." This is arguably due to contact with Standard Italian, where agreement is obligatory.

Impersonal or passive constructions with the Pronoun =s(e) (REFL; ☞ 7.6.) normally display a VS order (ex. (7)), although SV is by no means ungrammatical. Such constructions may lack agreement between the Verb and the postverbal nominal ((8)). Even in these cases, however, there are good arguments in favor of considering the postponed nominal as a subject: for instance, "[i]t is logical to assume that the nominals involved in [...] rhematic structure (with and without *se*), had (originally at least) the same grammatical function, namely that of (postposed) subject" (Parry 1998: 80; see also Parry 2000).

(7) *as tosonavo ij cavaj lassandje mach la còma [...] an sla testa*
   $\underbrace{\text{a=s=tuzu'n-avu}}_{V}$ $\underbrace{\text{i=ka'vaj}}_{S}$ la's-aŋd=je mak
   SBJ.3=REFL=clip-IMPF.3P DET\P=horse\P leave-GER=IND only
   l-a='kom-a aŋ=s=l-a='test-a
   DET-F=mane-S INE=SUP=DET-F=head-S
   'the horses were clipped, leaving only the mane on their head' (Pro Piemonte (eds), *Sudor antich*; quoted in Parry 1998: 78)

(8) *as frava ij beu*
   $\underbrace{\text{a=s='fr-ava}}_{V}$ $\underbrace{\text{i='bø}}_{S}$
   SBJ.3=REFL=shoe-IMPF.3S DET\P=ox
   'the oxen were shod/they shod the oxen' (Pro Piemonte (eds), *Sudor antich*; quoted in Parry 1998: 80)

Left and right dislocations are other devices that give rise to non-basic word orders. As in other Romance and non-Romance languages, in Piedmontese they are exploited to topicalize constituents of the sentence other than the subject, and to focus the attention on them.

In left dislocations the topic, consisting in a full Noun phrase, a Pronoun or a prepositional phrase, is put to the immediate left of a sentence and is copied (or, in other words, doubled) by a coreferential clitic in the remaining of the sentence.

Object left dislocation is the preferred construction in the array of passive constructions (Cennamo 1997: 147). In these constructions, the Direct Object is promoted in first position and the Subject usually follows the Verb:

(9) *Costa conta i l'oma butala giù mi, Gianfranco, e mia fomna*
 'kust-a 'kuŋt-a i='luma by't-a=l-a dʒy
 PROX-F tale-S SBJ.1=have\PRS.1P put-PTCL-F=OBJ.3-F down
 ⎣_____O_____⎦ ⎣_____V_____⎦
 mi / dʒiaŋ'fraŋku e 'mi-a 'fumn-a
 IDP.1S G. and POSS.1S-F woman-S
 ⎣_____S_____⎦

'this tale was written by me, Gianfranco and my wife (lit.: this tale, I, Gianfranco, and my wife wrote it down)' (Novero s.d.; beginning of the 1st paragraph)

(10) *Sta stòria-sì a la contava Roseta*
 st-a=storj-a='si a=l-a=kuŋ't-ava ru'zeta
 PROX-F=IND=story-S =here SBJ.3=OBJ.3-F=count-IMPF.3S R.
 ⎣_____O_____⎦ ⎣_____V_____⎦ ⎣__S__⎦

'it was Roseta who used to tell this story [this story, Roseta used to tell it]' (Novero s.d.; beginning of the 2nd paragraph)

In (9) and (10) also postverbal S are focalized. With an indefinite 3P Subject the phrase containing the Agent may be suppressed:

(11) *mi, am chërdo cativ*
 mi a=m='kərd-u ka'tiw
 IDP.1S SBJ.3=OBJ.1S=believe-PRS.3P evil
 'I am thought to be evil/They think me evil [I, they believe me evil]' (Aly-Belfàdel 1933: 207; quoted in Cennamo 1997: 147)

In right dislocations the topicalized and focalized constituent (again, a NP, a Pronoun or a prepositional phrase) is put on the right of the sentence, with the copying clitic serving in these cases as a cataphoric element. Therefore, for instance, when the S is right-dislocated it is focalized and the sentence word order is VOS:

(12) (Travet): *J'eu spasgiala mi tuta la neuit*
$\underbrace{\text{j=ø}}_{\text{SBJ.1=have}\backslash\text{PRS.1S}}$ $\underbrace{\text{spaz'dʒ-a=l-a}}_{\text{walk-PTCL =OBJ.3-F}}$ $\underbrace{\text{mi}}_{\text{IDP.1S}}$ $\underbrace{\text{'tyt-a l-a='nøjt}}_{\text{all-FS DET-F=night}}$
V$$OS

'(Travet): "It was me who took her out for a walk all night"' (Bersezio 1980 [1863]: 5; Act I, Scene 1)

Before the dislocated constituent, a pause in the prosody may occur (in writing, it is frequently indicated by a comma). When present, the pause seems to give some relevance to the immediately preceding phrase, which is somewhat contrasted with other elements of the context or co-text. In (13), a focus reading is intended for the constituents *tute le duminiche an piassa*, preceding the right-dislocated *sta predica*, which is the topic of the discourse.

(13) [*Vnì tuti sì, che i veui feve un tòch ëd prédica dzora sta bestia feròce.*] *E la fareu tute le duminiche an piassa sta prédica.*
$\underbrace{\text{e}\text{l-a=fa'rø}}_{\text{and OBJ.3-F=do}\backslash\text{DUB.1S}}$ $\underbrace{\text{'tyt-e l-e=dy'minik-e}}_{\text{all-F.P DET-F.P=Sunday-P}}$ $\underbrace{\text{aŋ='pjas-a}}_{\text{INE=square-S}}$
V$$Time$$Space
$\underbrace{\text{st-a='predik-a}}_{\text{PROX-F=preach-S}}$
O

'[come here, you all, I want to preach a little piece of sermon to you about this ferocious beast.] And I will repeat all Sundays in the square this sermon' (Faldella 1974 [1868]: 23; Act I, Scene 6)

18.2 Hanging Topics and Clefts

Hanging topics are also frequent in Piedmontese, especially in (allegro) speech. Hanging topics (also called *nominativi pendentes* or *Freie Themen*) are evident when the extraposed phrase is not a direct object, since they appear in their bare form, i.e., without any role marker (such as prepositions and the like).[3]

---

3 Obviously, it is not easy to distinguish between a hanging topic and a left or right dislocation if the detached constituent is a direct object.

(14) *ma ti co' 't 'n anfà se mi l'hai plissa da òmo adòss?*
　　ma　ti　　　ko=t=n=aŋˈfa　　　　　　　　　se　mi　　laj
　　but IDP.2S what=OBJ.2S=ATTR.PRO=care\PRS.3S if IDP.1S have\PRS.1S
　　pˈlis-a　da=ˈomu　aˈdos ↗
　　fur-S　ABL=man　upon　Q
　　'but why do you care if I wear a man's fur? [but you, what does it mat-
　　ter to you if I wear a man's fur?]' (conversation in Colègn;[4] from Bonato
　　2003–2004: 196)

Clefts are used in the written as well as in the oral register. Clefts are constructed with the focalized constituent of the sentence put to the left, preceded by a form of the Verb *esse* 'to be' and followed by *che* (☞ 15.3.). Often the intended reading is that of a contrastive focus:

(15) (*un liber che as fa lese. Bele che a sio 700 pàgine a l'é malfé chité.*) *Ma a l'é dël messagi che i veuj parlé.*
　　ma　a=ˈle　　　　　　d=əl=meˈsadʒi　　　　　ke=i=ˈvøj
　　but SBJ.3=be\PRS.3S ATTR=DET=message SUB=SBJ.1=want\PRS.1S
　　parˈl-e
　　talk-INF
　　'(a book that one can read with pleasure. Even though it's 700 pages it is difficult to stop reading it.) But it is its message I want to talk about' (Tosco 2006: 10)

(16) Giorgio: [...] *a l'ha dame apontament për des ore e a l'é 'ncora racoman-dasse che i fèissa pontual.*
　　Censo: *A l'é chiel che purtròp a l'é mai pontual*
　　a=ˈle　　　　　kjæl　　　ke　pyrˈtrop　　　　　a=ˈle　　　　　maj
　　SBJ.3=be\PRS.3S IDP.3M SUB unfortunately SBJ.3=be\PRS.3S never
　　puŋˈtwal
　　punctual
　　'(Giorgio: He gave me an appointment at 10 am and even insisted with me not to be late.)
　　Censo: It is he who unfortunately is never on time' (Oddoero 1989: 43)

A new, rhematic constituent may be introduced in the discourse via a "*there-cleft*" (Lambrecht 2001) constructed with a presentational *a-i é* ('there is') fol-

---

4　Colègn /kuˈlæɲ/, Italian Collegno /kolˈleɲo/ (45°05′N 07°35′E).

lowed by the Subordinator *che*,⁵ and by a (pseudo-)relative sentence. Here all the information is focalized, but it is distributed on two different clauses, so that it is easier to codify and understand:

(17) *a-i é Mario ch'at ciama*
 a=ˈj=e   ˈmarju k=a=t=ˈtʃam-a
 SBJ.3=IND=be-PRS.3S M.   SUB=SBJ.3=OBJ.2S=call-PRS.3S
 'Mario is calling you'

18.3 Discourse Markers

Huge amounts of ink have been spilled over the classification and precise differentiation of discourse markers, on the one hand, and modal particles, on the other. In what follows, however, we subsume modal particles under the label "discourse markers," as do, e.g., Fraser (1996) and Aijmer (2007; but compare, a.o., Degand, Cornillie and Pietrandrea 2013).

Discourse markers (henceforth, DMs), then, may be defined as a heterogeneous class of items (Schriffin 1987, Fraser 1999, 2009, Fedriani and Sansò 2017, among many others) that

- do not have a fixed position in the utterance, although they usually appear in initial or final position in the sentence;
- can be cancelled from their host utterance without changing its propositional meaning, since they play an intersubjective and procedural role, operating at the discourse-level and guiding the hearer in relation to the interpretation of the discourse itself, and
- have a characteristic intonation contour.

According to Bazzanella (2006), three different functions of DMs can be distinguished: interactional/conversational, meta-textual, and cognitive.

Interactional DMs are used to signal particular moments of the interaction between the communicative dyad, such as turn-taking and giving, backchanneling, attention getting and the like. They may also have face-saving, face-threatening and similar (un)politeness-related uses. Meta-textual DMs have three main meta-discursive functions:

1. "organizing the different parts of the message (structuring function);"
2. taking "a distance from previous formulations" (the so-called "reformulative function;" Pons Bordería 2006: 89–90);

---

5 In some rural dialects, (*o-*)*i ha* [(**u=**)ˈj=a] ("(SBJ.3=)IND=have\PRS.3S") might be used instead of *a-i é*.

3. focusing: focus particles and exemplifiers are included in this category.

Finally, cognitive DMs are utilized to modify the illocutionary force of an utterance, but also to signal commitment and agreement and/or disagreement in relation to a previous utterance.

Note however that, given the polyfunctionality of DMs (Bazzanella 1995, 2006; Sansò 2020: 19–40), a DM may have different functions with different co(n)texts, and even in the same context.

In the followings, without any claim to exhaustiveness, some examples for each type of DMs from Piedmontese books and corpora will be offered and briefly commented upon.

An example of interactional DM is found in (18), and taken from a conversation held in two languages (Italian and Piedmontese): all participants are bilingual, as becomes evident also from the code-switching they produce in other turns of the same conversation.

(18) A: e quanto fai d'infusione?
B: *alora / lòn ch' i faso mi / quat bote n'oma fait,* [xxx]*?*
a'lura / loŋ   k=i='fazu   mi /   kwat 'but-e
then   DIST.PRO SUB=SBJ.2=do\PRS.1S IDP.1S four bottle-P
'n=oma   fajt   ↗
ATTR.PRO=have\PRS.1P do/PTCL Q
C: non mi ricordo
B: *eh devo trové # s'i treuvo ël feuj 't lo dio*
e   'devu   tru'v-e / s=i='trøv-u   əl='føj
uh must\PRS.1S find-INF if=SBJ.1=find-PRS.1S DET=sheet
(i)t=l-u='diu
OBJ.2S=OBJ.3-M=say\PRS.1S
('A:—And how long is the infusion time?)
B:—Well, what I do / four bottles, we did / [xxx]?
(C:—I can't remember.)
B:—Uh, I must find out / if I find the paper I'll tell you' (conversation in Turin; ParlaTO corpus, PTB026; non-italicized turns are in Italian and are not transcribed nor glossed)

After being asked for information, B takes his turn with *alora*. *Alora*'s origin may lie in a shortened form of the temporal Adverb *an(t)lora* meaning 'at that time' (from Latin *in illam horam* or *ad illam horam*; Ghezzi and Molinelli 2020, REP s.v. *anlora*) or in a phonetically adapted loan from Italian *allora*, with which it shares most discourse functions. These functions range from the formulation of the relationship between the speaker and the utterance, to the highlighting of the common knowledge of the dyad of communication and the content of the utterance, to the management of the turns of conversation (Molinelli 2018). However, in today's Piedmontese, while both *an(t)lora* and *alora* may function as temporal Adverbs, *alora* is widely preferred when it comes to (more) pragmatic readings, especially in informal speech (see Stolz 2007, Retaro 2010, Fiorentini 2017: 178 for similar conclusions about *allora* and its cognates in other minority languages of Italy). As it has been said, *alora* in (18) signals that B intends to take the floor from now on, after A gives up his turn.

Piedmontese interactional discourse markers sometimes heard also in the spoken Italian of Piedmont are *voilà* /vwaˈla/ 'here it is' (an obvious loan from French), as well as the deictics (☞ 8.3.3.) *sà* /sa/ 'here, around here' (sometimes also written *sàh* when used as a Discourse Marker and glossed DM below) and *là* /la/ 'there.' *Sà* is an attention getter and is also utilized to introduce a predication ((19)), while *là* usually follows the predication and functions as an insistence marker ((20)).

(19) *sàh, l'amis: cimpoma, e al diav la malinconia*
 sa / l=aˈmiz / ʧimˈp-uma e=a=l=ˈdjaw
 DM DET=friend guzzle-PRS.1P and=ADE-DET=devil
 l-a=maliŋkuˈni-a
 DET-F=melancholy-S
 Lorenzo [taking a glass]: 'So, my friend, let's have a drink and to hell with melancholy' (Garelli 2001 [1874]: 121; Scene 8)

(20) *sta un pòch ciuto, là!*
 sta aŋ=ˈpok ˈʧytu / la
 stay\IPV.2S INDEF=little silent there
 'just shut up a sec, will you?'

Other frequent interactional Discourse Markers are *nè/neh* /næ/, as well as *dì* /di/ and *é* /e/. The first is the most typical tag (☞ 15.9.2.); it is a phatic expression that usually marks a confirmation check of a shared knowledge between the speaker and the hearer/s. In the following Nina asks Menica for a confirmation of the Count's talents as a speaker:

(21) [CONT: *Son informà 'd tut, mè bon vej, e i son sentume a strassé l'anima a la vista 'd tanti malheur. Ma a-i é un Ente Supremo ch'a peisa tut e a rend giustissia a tuti.*]

PRAGMATICS AND DISCOURSE

NINA (piano a Menica): *Coma ch'a parla bin! neh?*
'kuma k=a='parl-a   biŋ / næ ↗
how   SUB=SBJ.3=speak-PRS.3S well / TAG Q
['The Count:—I am aware of everything, my good old fellow, and my soul was torn apart by seeing so much suffering. But there is a Supreme Being who weights everything and gives justice to all.']
Nina (whispering to Menica):—He speaks so well, does not he?' (Garelli 1873: 95; Act 3, Scene 5)

Dì /di/, the Imperative Plural form of the Verb 'to say,' is an attention getter:

(22) GIOBERT:—*Ma dì! Gnanca Giobert a l'era pà un sëbber ëd vòlte, che ti 't chërdèisse. (A l'ha scrit le* Primissie d'Italia, *e se l'avèissa conossù 'l nòstr amis a l'avrìa butalo ant ël* Gesuita moderno)
ma di   'ɲaŋka G. a='lera   pa   aŋ='səbber
but say\IPV.2S not_even G. SBJ.3=be\IMPF.3S NEG.EMPH INDEF=tub
əd='volt-e   ke   ti   (i)t=kər'd-æjse
ATTR=time-P SUB IDP.2S SBJ.2S=believe-SUBJ.IMPF.2S
'but look, even Giobert[6] was not sometimes/perhaps the moron [tub] you think. [He wrote *Firstfruits of Italy* and if he had known our friend he'd have put him in the *Modern Jesuit*.]' (Faldella 1974 [1868]: 6; Act I, Scene 1)

Note that in this example *dì* is used to get the attention of a single person (the only other character on stage is Brofferio), notwithstanding the fact that it is originally the *plural* form of the Imperative of 'to say.' *Dì* is also devoid of its original lexical meaning, since Giobert begins his turn with *dì*, but does not really want to let the hearer say something, and actually keeps the floor after having got the hearer's attention.

The back-channel *é* /e/ is also utilized as an affirmative holophrase, with the meaning of 'yes' (from Latin *est*, 3rd singular of the present indicative of 'to be', see Clivio 1970: 74). Along with *é, si* /si/, and (especially among elders) *eui* /øj/, *ui* /yj/, *òj* /oj/ and *é é* /e=e/ (Clivio 1970), all roughly meaning 'yes,' are DMs that signal agreement with some or the whole information of one of the preceding turns. Disagreement is usually expressed by *nò* /no/ (☞ 17.6.). Interestingly, *nò* is also used to check for the hearer's attention and comprehension, and to highlight shared knowledge, especially in narratives:

---

6 Reference is made to Vincens Giobert (Italian Vincenzo Gioberti; Turin, April 5, 1801—Paris, October 26, 1852), a leading political thinker of the *Risorgimento*.

(23) *La stra peu a la fasien⁷ tuit ansema, nò, përchè a s'era un grup [...].*
Ël Nero a l'é un pais visin a Alpëtte, nò.
l-a=ˈstra   a=l-a=faˈziəŋ   tyjt aŋˈsema / no / pərˈkæ
DET-F=street SBJ3=OBJ3-F=do\IMPF.3P all together / no / because
a=ˈs=era   aŋ=ˈgryp   əl=ˈneru a=ˈlera
SBJ.3=REFL=be\IMPF.3S INDEF=group DET=N. SBJ.3=be\IMPF.3S
aŋ=paˈiz   vi'ziŋ a=alˈpətte / no
INDEF=village near ADE=A. / no
'they all walked the road together, you see, because they were a group of friends [...]. Nero was a village near Alpette, you see' (Conversation recorded in Corgné⁸ by Zörner 1998: 119–120)

(A)*donch/donc(r)a* /(a)ˈduŋk, ˈduŋk(r)a/ may display various meanings, but most frequently it functions as an inferential marker (see (24)), especially in writings. In colloquial speech, (a)*donch/donc(r)a* may signal the introduction of a new topic (as in (25), from an article mimicking the author's inner dialogue), or the taking of the speaker's turn. For the latter functions also the Italianism *donque* /ˈduŋkwe/ is used.

(24) *Costa-sì a l'era na veja cesa romànica dël 1207 e donca un-a dle pi antiche 'd Turin*
ˈkust-a=si   a=ˈlera   n-a=ˈvej-a   ˈʧez-a
PROX-F=here SBJ.3=be\IMPF.3P INDET-FS=old-F church-S
ruˈmanik-a   d-əl=miladuzeŋteˈsæt e=ˈduŋka   ˈyŋ-a
Romanesque-F ATTR=DET=1207   and=therefore one-F
d=l-e   pi   aŋˈtik-e   əd=tyˈriŋ
ATTR=DET-F.P more ancient-F.P ATTR=T.
'This was an old Romanesque church built in 1207 and therefore one of the oldest in Turin' (Carle and Ricossa 2021: 4)

(25) [*Gnente ëd fòra via [...].*] *Contut ... Donca: an Piemont a-i é na lege [...] che a guerna la lenga piemontèisa*
ˈɲæŋte   əd=foraˈvia   kuŋˈtyt/ ˈduŋka aŋ=pjeˈmuŋt
nothing ATTR=exceptional anyway   so   INE=P.
a=ˈj=e   n-a=ˈledʒe   ke=a=ˈgwærn-a
SBJ.3=IND=be\PRS.3P INDEF-F=law SUB=SBJ3=protect-PRS.3P

---

7 Canavzan and archaic variant of *fasio*.
8 Corgné /kurˈɲe/, Italian Cuorgné /kwɔrˈɲe/ (45°23'N 07°39'E).

l-a=ˈlæŋg-a   pjemuŋˈtæjz-a
DET-F=language-S Piedmontese-F
'[Nothing exceptional.] Anyway ... So: in Piedmont there's a law protecting Piedmontese' (Siròt 2004b)

The commitment of the speaker towards the truth of the utterance may be lowered by DMs such as *miraco* /miˈraku/, *magara* /maˈgara/, *peudesse* /pøˈdese/, *fòrsi* /ˈforsi/, all roughly meaning 'maybe.' The Adverb *mach* /mak/, originally meaning 'only, just', can be used as a focus particle, but also as a booster to intensify an order:

(26) *Gaute* [sic: *gavte*] *mach da sota*
ˈgaw=te   mak da=ˈsuta
remove\IPV.2S=OBJ.2S only ABL=below
'Just get out of the way!' (M**bun's advertisement in Turin; quoted in Favaro and Goria 2019: 227)

Other focus particles that may exhibit also a connective meaning (see Andorno 2000: 99 ff.) are *pròpe/pròpi* /ˈprope/propi/ 'indeed,' *bele* /ˈbele/ 'even,' *dabon* /daˈbuŋ/, roughly 'actually, really,' and *(ëd)cò* /ədˈko/ 'also.' *Già* /dʒa/ is an *Erinnerungsfragepartikel* used to ask for the repetition of information that has been just said or that is part of the previous knowledge shared by the speaker and their interlocutor(s), although the speaker does not remember it at the time of speaking, as is for English *again* in such utterances as *What's your name, again?* (Fedriani and Miola 2014).

As can be seen in (18), Discourse Markers may be borrowed from other languages.

As further examples, compare the reformulation Discourse Marker in (27) and (28):

(27) (*Ròbe dl'autr mond! a sclama tra lë stupì e l'arsentì 'l cavalier. Përchè, pòch da fé,*) *cola ròba a rivava pròpe da n'autr mond, visadì da l'Egit*
ˈkul-a ˈrob-a a=riˈv-ava   ˈprope da=n=ˈawtr
DIST-F thing-S SBJ.3=come-IMPF.3S indeed ABL=INDEF=other
muŋd / vizaˈdi da=l=eˈdʒit
world / i.e. ABL=DET=E.
'(those things are out of this world! — shouts the knight, amazed and resentful. Because, you can say it,) those things were really coming from another world, that is from Egypt' (https://www.youtube.com/watch?v=zZ7tz7Ad9sk)

(28) *Mi anlora i j'era an Italia, cioè lò*[9] *che i dio adess? ... an Lombardìa.*
    mi   aŋˈlura   i=ˈj=era   an=iˈtalj-a   tʃuˈæ   lo
    IDP.1S   then   SBJ.1=IND=be\IMPF.1S   INE=Italy-S   i.e.   DIST.PRO
    ke=i=ˈdiu   aˈdes   aŋ=lumbarˈdi-a
    SUB=IND=say\PRS.3P   now   INE=Lombardy-S
    'at that time I was in Italy, I mean—how do they call it now?—in Lombardy' (Faldella 1974 [1868], Act 1, Scene 1)

(27) is in a very regimented register, and the reformulation marker is the inherited *visadì* (possibly from Germanic *wisa* 'way' + Latin *de dicere* 'of say\INF,' 'by way of saying,' see REP s.v.), scarcely used in everyday speech.[10] With *visadì*, the speaker explains what is the 'other world' she is talking about, clarifying that she intends another cultural world linked to a nation-state, the culture and the nation-state of Egypt. In (28), the speaker ironically corrects himself since after the Unification of Italy, that occurred only four years before the first draft of the piece, he is in Italy too, and wants to reformulate his assertion by modifying its last word to 'Lombardy.'[11] The occurrence of *cioè* in Piedmontese confirms that reformulation Discourse Markers, and the Italian Discourse Marker *cioè* in particular, are borrowed only when both the source language and the target language are employed in everyday-life interactions by bilinguals that usually engage in language alternation practices (Dal Negro and Fiorentini 2014; for a few notes on the Piedmontese sociolinguistic situation ☞ 20.1.–3.).

---

9   Quite possibly a reduced form of *lòn* /loŋ/ (☞ 8.3.6.).
10 This is confirmed, for instance, by the fact that *visadì* is absent from Bonato's (2013–2014) corpus, while it has 377 occurrences on the Piedmontese edition of Wikipedia.
11 *Cioè* appears once in the Piedmontese Wikipedia. Interestingly, this single occurrence is a quotation from a sonnet published in 1876 by Fulbert Alarni.

CHAPTER 19

Piedmontese in a Typological Perspective

19.1 Genealogy and Overview

As seen in Chapter 1, Piedmontese is a Romance language belonging to the Western Romance subgroup. The insertion of Piedmontese in this subgroup should line it up a fortiori with other Gallo-Romance varieties such as French or Occitan. However, it has also been seen that Piedmontese and other Gallo-Italic languages have been treated as part of the Italo-Romance *Sprachraum*,[1] where Italo-Romance means a variety that descends from Latin and that is spoken today in the territory of Italy. Italo-Romance varieties belong to so-called Eastern Romance languages.

Nonetheless, Gallo-Italic languages, and Piedmontese in particular, are frequently mentioned as "a bridge between Gallo- and Italo-Romance" (Bossong 2016: 68; see also Bossong 2000 and Villata 2010; this idea dates back at least to Denina 1804), by virtue of their linguistic features. A deep, although brief typological overview might be of some help in shading light on the position of Piedmontese between Gallo-Romance and Italo-Romance languages.

As far as areal typology is concerned, however, Piedmontese has to be regarded as one of the languages belonging to Standard Average European (☞ 19.5.).

Due to the regrettable use—even in scientific and academic works—of the label *dialect* for defining the Piedmontese language (☞ 1.2.–3.), it is mentioned just once, in relation to (the absence of) distributive numerals, in the World Atlas of Language Structures (WALS), with the glottonym 'Italian (Turinese).'[2] The following alternative names are listed on the WALS webpages: Italian (Ruhlen), Italian (Routledge), Piemontese (Ethnologue).[3] All in all, it does not seem easy to grasp from the WALS that Piedmontese is a full-blown language, independent and most of all, from the linguistic viewpoint, horizontally diverse (as opposed to vertically diverse, see Grandi 2020) from Italian, with

---

1 Since Gallo-Romance and Italo-Romance have been used unconsistently in the literature, alternatively as a cultural-linguistic, as a sostratic, and as a geographical label, Regis (2020: 33) puts forward the proposal to call Italo-Francoromance, or Franco-Italoromance, the Romance branch Piedmontese (and other languages) belong to.
2 https://wals.info/languoid/lect/wals_code_itu.
3 https://www.ethnologue.com/language/pms.

the result of erasing, to some extent, language diversity in Italy. No sources are given for Italian (Turinese) data in the WALS. This chapter will at least try and fill this gap in the literature.[4]

19.2 Phonology

The koine, i.e., the variety of Piedmontese described in this volume, has nine vocalic phonemes (☞ 2.1.). This system is skewed, insofar as it has two mid front vowels /e/ and /æ/ vs a single mid back /o/. Six vowels are peripheral, while three, namely /ø/, /ə/ and /y/, are internal. Therefore, Piedmontese has a large vowel quality inventory, since the average number of vowels in a language is five to six (Maddieson 2013b). Besides contemplating the three phonemes /i/, /u/ and /a/, which are identified by Crothers (1978) as the three basic vocalic phonemes, Piedmontese inventory also displays /y/ together with /i/ and /ø/. As Maddieson (1984, 2013a) details, cross-linguistically the presence of an internal vowel in the inventory implies the presence of the co-articulated peripheral vowel (/y/ ⊃ /i/), while the presence of an open/close mid front rounded vowel implies the existence of a phonemic /y/, i.e., of a high front rounded vowel (/ø—œ/ ⊃ /y/). The absence of /y/ in Southern (Monfrà and Langhe) varieties of Piedmontese (☞ 2.1.) aligns these varieties to the very small number of languages (only six in the WALS sample, none of them in Europe) having a close-mid front rounded vowel /ø/ without a corresponding high /y/ (Maddieson 2013a).[5] Schmid (1999: 258) argues that the mid central /ə/ rarely enjoys phonemic status in the varieties of languages spoken in Italy, Piedmontese being a notable exception.

As for consonantal phonemes, they are twenty and such an inventory size is considered more or less average with respect to the inventory of the world's languages (Maddieson 2013c).

The canonical syllable structure, (C)(C)(C)V(C)(C), is complex from a typological point of view, since it "allow[s] three or more consonants in this onset position, and/or two or more consonants in the position after the vowel" (Maddieson 2013d).

---

4 A brief typological note in relation to the writing system (☞ 3.): Piedmontese has always been written using the Latin alphabet, except for the use of Hebrew writing in the so-called *Glossario di Alba* or *Glossary A*, a Judeo-Piedmontese text from 1567 (Berenblut 1949; Terracini 1956; Duberti, Milano and Miola 2015).
5 Schmid (1999: 260) discusses two Ladin varieties that are other apparent counterexamples to the former universal, since they have a phonemic /ø/ without /y/.

19.3 Morphosyntax

As it applies to all other Romance languages, the morphology of Piedmontese is *fondamentalmente flessiva con una marcata tendenza all'analiticità* ('basically fusional with a strong tendency to analyticity,' Berruto 1990: 13). Nominal morphology is relatively poor, while verbal morphology is rich.

For most Nouns, plurality is normally encoded via a Grounder (☞ 8.1.), or via other Determiners that may occur before the Noun. In other words, Piedmontese Nouns usually do not inflect for number, with the exception of few Masculines and Feminines. In this respect, then, Piedmontese sides with French in contrasting the most frequent European strategy of encoding nominal plurality, i.e., suffixation (Dryer 2013).

Some peripheral dialects, and ancient varieties, of the language mark nominal plurals via stem change, exhibiting metaphony (Parry 1997: 239). Whereas in some dialects (e.g., Bielèis and Canavzan varieties) this pluralization strategy is widespread on all nominal paradigms (Berruto 1974: 27, 30; Parry 1997: 241; Di Stefano 2017: 73–75), in others it is no longer productive and it is limited to a restricted set of items (Duberti 2014: 7–8; Tonso 2017: 111–115; see also Forner 1988 in relation to the Monregalèis dialect spoken in Stralussi, one of the hamlets of Frabosa Sovran-a[6]).

Among Grounders, Piedmontese exhibits what in traditional terms are called a definite and an indefinite article (☞ 8.2., referred to as Determiners and Classifiers). The Attributive grounder *ëd*, i.e., the "plural indefinite article," more traditionally called partitive article, is obligatory and the obligatoriness of this feature usually correlates with the absence in Piedmontese of prepositional accusatives (i.e., direct objects marked with a preposition such as *a(d)* or *pe(r)*). According to Bossong's (2016: 69) classification, obligatoriness of *de* combined with the definite article as a "partitive article" before all Nouns is a characteristic of Modern French. Central dialects of Occitan exhibit the same conditions as Piedmontese koine, while articulated *de* is also found, albeit not obligatorily, in Italian, in the northernmost dialects of Occitan, and in some varieties of Piedmontese.

Pronominal Possessives are always introduced by Grounders. In the written variety, Adnominal Possessives are not preceded by articles if they are Singulars and Feminine Plurals, but articles are obligatory with Masculine Plurals:

---

[6] Stralussi /stra'lysi/, Italian Straluzzo /stra'luttso/; Frabosa Sovran-a /fra'buza suv'raŋa/, Italian Frabosa Soprana /fra'boza so'prana/ (44°17′14.48″N 07°48′25.36″E).

(1) *mè can*   'my dog'
me=ˈkaŋ
POSS.1S=dog
mia idèja   'my idea'
mi-a=iˈdæj-a
POSS.1S-F=idea-S
mie idèje   'my ideas'
mi-e=iˈdæj-e
POSS.1S-F.P=idea-P

but

(1') *ij mè can*
i=me=ˈkaŋ
DET\P=POSS.1S=dog
'my dogs'

TABLE 56   Independent personal Pronouns

Person	M.S	F.S	M.P	F.P
1	*mi*	*mi*	*noi*	*noi*
2	*ti*	*ti*	*voi*	*voi*
3	*chiel*	*chila*	*lor*	*lor*

Dialectal variation may be high in this connection. This behavior puts Piedmontese "mid-way" between Italian, Modern Greek, Romanian and the like, where the article is always needed in a Possessive Phrase; and French, English, German and such languages, where the article must be absent.

Neither Nouns nor Independent personal Pronouns are inflected for case. With the exception of the 3S and the augmented Plural forms (☞ 7.2.), no gender opposition operates in the Independent Pronouns.

Varieties from the Monregalèis area and the Bormia Valley maintain a more complex system, with *chiej* for Masculine 3P and *chile* for Feminine 3P Pronoun (Parry 1997: 241; 2005; Miola 2013). Synchronically, the Pronouns of 3rd person are different from Demonstratives. However, *chiel* and *lor* are etymologically related to Latin ECCU ILLE, 'here+distal demonstrative' and (IL)LOR(UM), genitive plural of the distal demonstrative, respectively. (EC)CU ILL(E) is also the etymon of the contemporary distal Demonstrative *col* (see REP, s.v.).

In relation to demonstratives, Ledgeway (2015: 76 ff., 92) classifies the Piedmontese's system as binary (i.e., marking a distinction between two distances). This type of demonstrative system is "widespread across northern Italy" (Ledgeway 2015: 77) and is also the system of contemporary spoken Italian. However, in the adnominal system, the two distances may be expressed by three different exponents: *cost* and *ës*, usually encoding proximity to speaker-hearer dyad, and the aforementioned distal *col*.[7]

Piedmontese is a split-intransitivity language (Burzio 1986). In the koine, split intransitivity manifests itself morphosyntactically via auxiliary selection (and with the so-called *ne*-cliticization, see Burzio 1986; Bentley 2004).

The Adverb formation rule with *-ment* < Lat. MENTE is still slightly productive in the contemporary language (☞ 12.1., 12.2.1.) and this induces to group Piedmontese with those Romance languages in which this derivational strategy is present (e.g., Italian, French, Spanish etc.) and not with those in which it is absent or virtually unproductive (e.g., Friulian, Romanian, Sardinian, and other languages spoken in Southern Italy, see Ramat and Ricca 1998: 245; Virdis 2003: 2; Putzu 2017: 310). In the literature, the presence of a formation rule for manner Adverbs such as the suffixation of *-ment* "is closely tied to the development of the written standard" (Hummel 2014: 37): this confirms the at least moderate grade of standardization and Ausbauization of Piedmontese.

Hummel (2014) calls Type B the Adverbs formed with the aforementioned strategy, and Type A "the unmarked or neuter form of the Adjective for adverbial functions" (Hummel 2014: 36). Type C Adverbs are those manner Adverbs that may have an independent form, such as Piedmontese *bin* and its English counterpart *well* or French and Piedmontese *mal* 'badly.' Finally, periphrastic adverbials (such as *ëd vòte* 'sometimes,' and *dël tut* 'completely'),[8] are labelled Type D. Piedmontese, as well as other Romance and Germanic languages, is a language where "flexibility" (the existence of one word-class for Adverbs and Adjectives, where by and large only of Type A are found) competes and coexists with "specialization" (the existence of two different word-classes: one for

---

7 Some dialects of Piedmontese can be classified as ternary systems because the basic system "can be readily expanded into a strict ternary system through its combination with one of the three spatial Adverbs *sì* 'here,' *lì* 'there' (near the addressee) and *là* 'yonder' (Lombardi Vallauri 1995: 219)" (Ledgeway 2015: 84).
8 The difference between Type C and D is not actually clear-cut, since doublets (or triplets!) like Piedmontese *dël tut* (Type D), *dëltut* and *dautut* (belonging to Type C would speakers be unable to recognize their etymology) are by no means rare in standard and non-standardized languages.

Adjectives and the other for manner Adverbs); in Piedmontese, as seen above, all three types of Adverb formation strategy are used. However, "traditional Adverbs" deriving from Latin *bene* and *male* cannot be substituted by a Type A Adverb (i.e., *bon* and *gram/cativ* respectively) even in sub-standard and dialectal varieties: *a va bin / mal;* ***a va bon/gram* 'it's going well/badly.' Interestingly, this holds true also for Italian (*va bene/male;* ** *va buono/cattivo*), but not for French (*ça va mal; ça va moche*) and Spanish.

Taking into consideration evaluative morphology, Piedmontese has various suffixes for diminutives and one, possibly productive, suffix for augmentatives. The typological implication according to which if a language has a morphological marker for augmentatives then it has one also for diminutives (Grandi 2003) is therefore satisfied. It is however noteworthy that, according to REP: XLV the suffix *-in* (< -INUM) in Piedmontese only originally had a diminutive meaning (conveyed, e.g., in *taulin* 'little table' < *tau(la)* 'table,' see also *madamin* < 'little woman, young woman, Miss' < *madama* 'woman, madam;' other *-in*-ending Nouns may be borrowings from Italian). Nowadays it is used to derive *nomina instrumenti* or *nomina agentis* (*ciavatin/savatin* 'shoe maker' < *ciavata/savata* 'slipper;' *tabachin* 'tobacconist' < *tabach* 'tobacco'). Apart from Italian borrowings and Italianized forms, more used as diminutive suffixes are *-el, -èt, -òt, -inòt*. *-on* (< -ONEM) is not productive as an augmentative (*panson(-a)* 'big belly' < *pansa* 'belly'), and may be marginally used also to name young or baby animals (*levron* 'little hare' < *levr* 'hare'). Diminutives and augmentatives may also be encoded juxtaposing to the Noun the Adjectives *cit* 'small' and *gròss* 'big,' respectively.

With regard to verbal morphosyntax, according to the traditional terminology, Piedmontese, at least in its learned, written variety, should be labelled a non-pro-drop language, since a Subject clitic must always be put before the verbal form. However, following the revised typology of Subject expression and indexing on Verbs proposed by Haspelmath (2018), one should more correctly say that in Piedmontese the Subject can be expressed by up to two indexes and one coreferential nominal (i.e., a conominal, traditionally called a Noun phrase or a Pronoun, see Haspelmath 2013: 217). This type seems to be quite infrequent in the languages of the world, to the extent that Haspelmath (2018) does not list it as a possible type of its typology, which includes

1. Spanish-type languages, where the Subject may be expressed with a coreferential nominal and an index; or only with a verbal index:
   a. *Marta lleg-ó* "Marta arrived-3S"
   b. *Lleg-ó* "arrived-3S;"
2. Swedish-type: "Marta arrived; she arrived;"
3. German-type: "Marta arrived-3S; she arrived-3S;"

4. Japanese-type: "Marta arrived; arrived" (in the last case, no coreferential nominal nor index are used).

Piedmontese sentences, on the other hand, exhibits a fifth type, namely [Maria 3S-arrived-3S] and [3S-arrived-3S] (see the examples below, where subscript numbers signal indexes and coreferential nominals):

(2) a. *Marta a l'é rivà*
    'marta₁ a₂='le₃ ri'v-a   (Main Past tense)
    M.   SBJ.3=be\PRS.3S come-PTCL

   b. *Marta a riva*
    'marta₁ a₂='riv-a ₃   (Main Present tense)
    M.   SBJ.3=come-PRS.3S

(3) a. *a l'é rivà*
    a₁='le₂ ri'va   (Main Past tense)
    SBJ.3=be\PRS.3S come-PTCL

   b. *a riva*
    a₁='riva₂   (Main Present tense)
    SBJ.3=come-PRS.3S

Both the Subject clitic and the inflectional morpheme of the Verb are indexes of the Subject and may co-occur (and in fact in learned and written registers must co-occur) also in the presence of nominal Subjects (☞ 7.3.; Bossong 2000, 2016: 67). This very rare fifth type is also attested in Tuscan, at least until the beginning of the 20th century (Renzi 1983), but not in Italian.

Piedmontese leaves Subject and Direct object nominals unflagged, and indexes the Subject alone on the finite verb through affixation and cliticization (see 2–3 above, for the term "flagging" see Haspelmath 2013). Moreover, like in many varieties of Northern Italy (Ricca and Ramat 2016: 60), also animate Indirect objects are obligatorily indexed on the Verb with a morpheme traditionally regarded as a clitic dative pronoun (☞ 7.4.); whereas nominal Indirect objects are flagged by means of the Adessive preposition *a*:

(4) *chiel a prësta un liber*
    kjæl_i a_i='prəst-a_i aŋ='libær
    IDP.3M SBJ.3=lend-PRS.3S INDEF=book
    'he lends a book'

(4′) *chiel a_j prëst-a un liber a Maria*
kjæl_i   a_i=j_j='prəst-a_i   aŋ='libær   a=ma'ria_j
IDP.3M   SBJ.3=IND=lend-PRS.3S   INDEF=book   ADE=M.
'he lends Maria a book'

Interestingly, however, when verbal agreement is controlled by unaccusative Subjects, it displays double indexation, with the expected Subject clitic and an originally locative clitic (-*j*- preverbally; -*je* postverbally), which is crucially homophonous with the 3S Indirect object clitic. Therefore, monoargumental unaccusatives are encoded in the same way as ditransitives, when all their three arguments are saturated:

(5) *a-i cala Mario*
a=j='kala   'marju
SBJ.3=IND=go_down\PRS.3S   M.
'Mario comes down / is coming down'

(6) *a-j dà na man a Mario*
a=j='da   n-a='maŋ   a='marju
SBJ.3=IND=give\PRS.3S INDEF-F=hand   ADE=M.
's/he gives Mario a hand'

Due to split intransitivity, the past participle of compound Verbs agrees with the Subject of unaccusatives in both gender and number where they are overtly marked (i.e., in 2nd Class Verbs). Very rarely, in some peripheral dialects, notably in Ormea, the slot of 3S of the Main Present of 'to have' agrees with the gender of the Subject (☞ box in 10.2.).

The verbal paradigm presents the so-called preterite decay, i.e., "the loss of the old preterite and its replacement by the former present perfect" (Haspelmath 2001: 1504; ☞ 10. for more details)

The expression of the agent is allowed in the passive, whose canonical construction is formed with a copula or copula-like verb (the already mentioned *esse* 'to be,' or *vnì* 'to come') plus a passive participle.

The basic word order in affirmative sentences is Subject—Verb—Direct Object. This order, in turn, correlates with the presence of prepositions and with postponed genitives in the Noun phrase. As for clitic syntax, a very peculiar feature of the Piedmontese variety at issue is the mandatory postverbal positioning of all non-subject clitic Pronouns in compound tenses. This feature seems to be unparalleled in Romance languages and is exceptionally found in Romanian, only with the feminine singular accusative *o*, which actually "occurs after the participial part of the compound tense" (Joseph 1999: 232).

Negation is expressed with a postverbal morpheme *nen* (postponed to the auxiliary part in compound verbal forms). Verbal negation usually does not co-occur with negative Pronouns, giving rise to sentences of the type [Verb + negative indefinite] (*a-i ven gnun*, 'nobody comes,' lit. 'comes nobody') as opposed to [negated Verb + negative indefinite], as in Italian *non viene nessuno*, lit. 'doesn't come nobody.'

The relative clause appears postnominally. In everyday speech, the relative clause is introduced by a subordinative morpheme (SUB) *che* and a resumptive clitic Pronoun that encodes the gender, number and syntactic function of the head of the subordinate clause. In written Piedmontese, we find also the strategy of an inflecting relative Pronoun—signaling the head's role within the relative clause (☞ 14.5.). Other subordinate clauses are generally introduced by a preposition, often co-occurring with *che* (☞ 15.3.).

VO languages tend to put grammatical markers before nominal and verbal heads, while OV languages usually do the opposite. The shape of Piedmontese's Noun and Verb phrases is located in a transition point between Latin OV and the fully grammaticalized VO order of Romance. However, Piedmontese stands very near to the latter pole. Consistently with the VO language type, Piedmontese has Prepositions, postnominal Adjectives and genitives. Furthermore, again consistently with VO order (Lehmann 1973, Carlier and Lamiroy 2014), in Noun phrases grammatical morphemes (marking gender and number) are put before the head and other lexical morphemes (e.g., *IJ can* 'the dogs;' grammatical morphemes are capitalized in this and in the following two examples). Likewise, in compound Verb forms the morpheme(s) encoding person, tense and mood appear before the verbal head. In non-compound forms, person is encoded twice, once before and once after the Verb, tense and mood morphemes, on the other hand, follow the lexical part of the Phrase (see examples (2) and (3) above). Diachronically, the grammatical part of the words seems to move constantly towards the beginning of the Phrases: for instance, while Latin and 17–18th century Piedmontese exhibited grammatical morphemes only or also at the end of Past Tenses forms (Latin *laudavERUNT*, Ancient Piedmontese *A laudERO*), in present-day Piedmontese these morphemes are positioned before the lexicon (*A L'HAN laudà*).

Taking into account major Romance languages, French developed more than Piedmontese the positioning of grammatical markers before nominal and verbal heads. In contrast, Spanish and Italian strongly maintain verbal and nominal morphology at the end of words and phrases (Carlier and Lamiroy 2014).

19.4 Lexical Typology

The semantics of specific lexemes of Piedmontese often points to the North and West rather than to Italian and generally Romance. For instance, the Piedmontese lexeme *bòsch* /bosk/ 'wood' covers both a substance and a collective (in a spatial sense, denoting the place where a sizable number of entities of that substance are found), while the entity itself is expressed by a different lexeme. This is the same pattern of metonymical polysemy found, e.g, in English and French, where *wood* and *bois* denote both the substance and an area where the substance itself is more typically (or naturally) found. Italian, as most Romance, resorts instead to different lexemes, namely *legno* /'leɲo/ 'wood' (the substance), and *bosco* /'**bosko**/ 'wood' (a place where many trees are found).[9]

Piedmontese aligns to most European languages in its color terminology. Dedicated color terms are Adjectives and there are separate basic color terms[10] for GREEN and BLUE; the latter, *bleu* /**blø**/, is originally a Germanic loan but has been fully incorporated in the language, as its (optional) Feminine form *bleuva* /'**bløv-a**/ shows.

Other basic color terms include:
- *bianch* /**bjaŋk**/ 'white'
- *nèir* /**næjr**/ 'black'
- *ross* /**rus**/ 'red'
- *giaun* /**dʒawn**/ 'yellow'
- *verd* /**værd**/ 'green'
- *gris* /**griz**/ 'grey'

The next three
- *maròn* /**ma'roŋ**/ 'brown; chestnut'
- *reusa* /'**røza**/ 'rose'
- *viòla* /'**vjola**/ 'violet'

fail a morphological test for basicness (they do not agree in gender and number with their head); moreover, although they have been conventionalized as color terms, they also witness one and the same metonymical process (as they still also mean a fruit or flower).[11] Other color terms seem to be more or less con-

---

9   Other patterns are of course possible. The polysemy WOOD/TREE is found in Russian and many other languages, in and out of Europe (Koch 2000: 104). Gawwada, an East Cushitic language of Ethiopia (Tosco 2021b), adds to WOOD/TREE the value STICK, all covered by *kaarko*. The Piedmontese word for 'tree' is *erbo* /'ærbu/.

10   These notes and the use of the "basic color terms" are merely descriptive and not intended as either an endorsement or a critique to the influential—and highly contested—tradition of studies inaugurated by Berlin and Kay (1969).

11   Cugno and Cusan (2018, 2019) consider the equivalents of all these terms, plus ORANGE, as basic in Romance.

ventionalized analogic terms, while still others, such as *biond* /bjuŋd/ 'blonde' or *brun* /bryŋ/ 'brown-haired, brunet(te),' are restricted to specific semantic fields.

In accordance with a tendency to reduce evaluative morphology, Piedmontese sparingly and not productively uses suffixes in order to express shades of color, such as *-iss* /-is/ in *giauniss* /dʒawˈnis/ 'yellowish' and *-ass* /-as/ in *neirass* /næjˈras/ 'blackish.' In its shunning of derivational morphology, also in this area Piedmontese seems to align rather with French than with Occitan (Bach, Kopecka and Fagard 2019).

Kinship terminology follows the Eskimo (or Inuit) system found in European languages; it has both classificatory and descriptive terms and distinguishes between gender, generation and both lineal and collateral relatives. It is worth mentioning that Piedmontese aligns again with French rather than, e.g., Italian in a few lexicalization patterns where Piedmontese and French are underspecified:

- *fieul* /fjøl/ and French *garçon* 'son; boy' vs. Italian *figlio* 'son' and *ragazzo* 'boy'
- *fija* /ˈfi-a/ and French *fille* 'daughter; girl' vs. Italian *figlia* 'daughter' and *ragazza* 'girl'
- *fomna* /ˈfumn-a/ and French *femme* 'woman; wife' vs. Italian *donna* 'woman' and *moglie* 'wife'
- *òm(o)* /ˈom(u)/ and French *homme* 'man; husband' vs. Italian *uomo* 'man' and *marito* 'husband'

19.5 Piedmontese, Standard Average European, and Other Romance Languages

As evident from previous paragraphs, Piedmontese exhibits almost all the features that identify Standard Average European (SAE) as defined by van der Auwera (1998) and Haspelmath (2001) among others. Within the major SAE features enumerated by Haspelmath (2001), only the type of relative clause with a relative Pronoun is not common in contemporary Piedmontese (albeit not unknown to written usage). In addition to the features discussed above, Piedmontese displays also other SAE or SAE-like features: intensifier-reflexive differentiation, Verb fronting in yes/no interrogatives (albeit in regression), syncretism of comitative and instrumental, "A and-B" conjunction, suppletive second ordinal, dedicated construction for negative coordination, use of particles related to the relative Pronoun in comparative constructions, not obligatory identification of agent and Subject, and many others. Despite not being a fully-Ausbauized language, Piedmontese shares with the major languages of Europe a great number of typological features, in particular those relevant in defining the SAE area. This has led scholars to include it amongst the "core European languages" (Haspelmath 2001: 1493), defining, along with German, Dutch, French and other (non-national) languages spoken in northern Italy, the so-called Charlemagne *Sprachbund* (van der Auwera 1998: 824).

Many other features discussed in the paragraphs above confirm that Piedmontese is typologically very similar to French and Gallo-Romance varieties, if, besides SAE features, one takes into account also the presence of front rounded vowels (a typologically marked feature, typical, within the realm of Romance langueges, of French, Occitan, Gallo-Italic and part of Rhaeto-Romance varieties, Bossong 2016: 71), of the unmarked strategy of nominal plurality marking, the postverbal position of the negative morpheme in negative sentences (proper of colloquial French, Piedmontese and Lombard, along with German), the obligatoriness of the attributive Grounder, the pro-drop parameter (although Piedmontese's indexing on the Verb is peculiar to the language to a large extent). As for some of these features, French is usually regarded as the fastest in the grammaticalization paths (see Carlier, De Mulder and Lamiroy 2012), but when one looks at non-national languages, it turns out that Piedmontese and Gallo-Italic varieties (e.g., Lombard) are usually on a par with, or even faster than, French (Miola 2017a, b). The only morphosyntactic feature for which Piedmontese sides with Italian and other central-southern languages of Italy and contrasts French seems to be the auxiliary selection for unaccusatives and unergatives. Thus, the typological physiognomy of Piedmontese puts it more akin to Gallo-Romance varieties than to Italo-Romance, therefore confirming the classical positioning of Piedmontese and other Gallo-Italic varieties within Western Romance, as part of Gallo-Romance, proposed e.g., by Bec (1970–1971: II, 316).

CHAPTER 20

Use, Contact, and Care: Endangerment, Loss, Enrichment and Standardization

Is Piedmontese a dialect or a "real" language? This is probably the gist of any laypeople's talk on the subject. "It changes from place to place," but "It is written" come next—sometimes uttered by the same individual. The people's (be them speakers or not, and linguists included) relation to Piedmontese is conflicting and far from settled. No wonder that, as for any contested language (Tamburelli 2014; Tamburelli and Tosco 2021 and different articles therein, especially Miola 2021 and Dołowy-Rybińska and Soria 2021), the answer to the question is manifold—again, for laypeople and linguists alike.

As anticipated in Chapter 1 and as this grammar has abundantly shown, Piedmontese is such an obvious example of an *Abstand* language, in Kloss' (1987) terms, that no further discussion is needed on the subject. But as an inescapable consequence of its contestedness, its standing as an *Ausbausprache* is far from optimal and has led Muljačić (1997: 390) to speak of Piedmontese as a "middle language" (see also Tosco 2008, 2012, and Ricca 2016).

The following pages address the actual use of the language and some timid steps taken in the direction of its elaboration or Ausbauization (Tosco 2008).

20.1 Language Ideology through Language Use

As stated in Chapter 1, Piedmontese is certainly a highly endangered language. Many speakers use it only in codeswitching with Italian, others sprinkle their Italian with *some* Piedmontese; other *can* speak Piedmontese but don't. Much of the younger generation simply cannot, although many claim to be able to understand it. Apart from the meagre data on speakers provided in Chapter 1 (with 700,000 speakers being just a rough approximation), not much is available on language transmission. It can be assumed to be fairly limited (although some still learn Piedmontese *alongside* Italian, or later in life).

Moreover, it is common opinion that minoritzed languages such as Piedmontese may be used only in informal and "low," or less serious domains. In the following excerpt, Piedmontese gives place to Italian only when dealing with names of foreign towns. The text is a funny joke from Facebook in which a

Piedmontese voice is dubbed over a scene from a James Bond movie; the secret agent answers a phone call and after a moment says in protest:

(1) *i peule nen, i peule nen mandeme a **Londra**, a **Parigi** e peui ciameme d'andé a **Condove**!*
i=ˈpøle næŋ / i=ˈpøle næŋ
SBJ.2P=can\PRS.2P NEG / SBJ.2P=can\PRS.2P NEG
maŋˈd-e=me a=⟨ˈlondra⟩ cs / a=⟨paˈridʒi⟩ cs e pøj
send-INF=OBJ.1S ADE=L. / ADE=P. and then
tʃaˈm-e=me d=aŋˈde a=⟨konˈdove⟩ cs
ask-INF=OBJ.1S ATTR=go\INF ADE=C.
'you cannot, you cannot send me to London, to Paris and then ask me to go to Condòve!' (https://www.facebook.com/1661028661/posts/10222245574 962564/?sfnsn=scwspwa; last accessed on Dec. 11, 2020)

Note that the whole joke is in Piedmontese. The Italian forms for London (Londra /ˈlondra/), Paris (Parigi /paˈridʒi/) and Condòve[1] (Condove /konˈdove/) are used instead of the corresponding (and in common use) Piedmontese forms (Londra /ˈluŋdra/, Paris /paˈriz/—or /paˈris/ with final devoicing)—and Condòve /kuŋˈdove/—the last one in Italian possibly as an automatic follow-up to the two preceding, international towns, or maybe due to the Italian graphization, which is very similar to the Piedmontese pronunciation of the toponym. The mildly funny effect is given by the use of Piedmontese on the part of James Bond and the idea of him going to Condòve, but most of all by the juxtaposition of London and Paris to Condòve (where the total population—less than 5,000 in 2019—is distributed between a town and more than 70 mountain hamlets).

While in real life dialogues very rarely involve each party speaking in a different language, this is often resorted to in jokes posted on the net. In one case, somebody consistently answers in Piedmontese to a call-center assistant who tries to sell him a new cellphone contract using stereotypical, well-rehearsed lines in Italian. In the end, the increasingly baffled saleswoman gives up.

In another, Santa Claus offers gifts and his good wishes in Italian to a farmer speaking Piedmontese (with a thick rural accent). In a similar sketch, the same actor confronts trick-or-treating children on Halloween. Always talking in Piedmontese and not understanding what the children want, he finally treats them with homemade cheese and a glass of red wine.

---

1 Condòve /kuŋˈdove/, Italian Condove /konˈdove/ (Francoprovençal Coundove, French Condoue; 45°07′02.71″N 07°18′34.04″E) is a mountain town in Piedmont.

The reactionary (for what concerns Ausbauization) ideology lying behind the jocular use of Piedmontese in this example is that Piedmontese is conveyed as something certainly "original," but also belonging to the past, to "our roots." In a word, something to "be preserved," not to "develop." In the end, such a mind-frame adheres to and actually reinforces the linguistic *status quo*.

All considered, in such a situation a language is doomed.

20.1.1 *Codeswitching and Borrowing*

To disentangle codeswitching from borrowing is notoriously difficult. Many (such as Matras 2009) embrace a "fuzzy" approach and claim that such a distinction is not possible and is even misleading. We maintain that difficulty is not a reason not to try and reach a clear-cut distinction, and that a distinction *is* possible, at least in most cases. Take the following example: two ladies waiting at a bus-stop are discussing a pair of slippers one of them just bought. The buyer comments:

(2) mach ch'a sio mòrbide
 mak k=a='siu 'morbid-e
 only SUB=SBJ.3=be\SUBJ.PRS.3P soft-F.P
 'let them just be soft!' (overheard conversation in Chér, 2011)

The Adjective *mòrbid* /ˈmorbid/ 'soft' is a loan from Italian *morbido* /ˈmorbido/. Still, the realization /ˈmorbid-e/ for the Feminine Plural gives it out as an instance of codeswitching with Italian, because the local variety of Piedmontese would have /ˈmorbid-i/, with the closing of final unstressed /e/ (☞ 2.4.1.4.). (2) is therefore to be analyzed as

(2′) mach ch'a sio mòrbide
 mak k=a='siu ⟨'morbid-e⟩ cs
 only SUB=SBJ.3=be\SUBJ.PRS.3P soft-F.P

And yet, in any variety (the koine included) without final raising of unstressed /e/ the matter would be impossible to settle.[2]

Still, in most cases loans are easy to take apart from codeswitching. In the following excerpt a fourth-generation Piedmontese Argentinian born in 1946 and living in San Francisco (Córdoba, Argentina)[3] talks about the introduction of *mate*:

---

[2] In principle, one would have to further exclude the possibility that the speaker was from out of town and speaking a "non-raising" variety, or simply the koine.
[3] The data from Argentina are courtesy of Eugenio Goria.

(3) e l'òm da sì a l'ha mostraje ai piemontèis a pijé ël **mato**
 e   l='om   da='si   a='la   mus'tr-a=je
 and DET=man   ABL=here SBJ.3=have\PRS.3S   show-PTCL=OBJ.3P
 a=i=pjemuŋ'tæjz a='pj-e   əl='matu
 ADE=DET\M.P=P. ADE=take-INF   DET=mate
 'and the man from here showed the Piedmontese how to drink *mate*.'[4]

Apart from the use of *da sì* for 'from here' (in Piedmont it could possibly be more colloquial *da ambelessì*, ☞ 8.3.3.), the sentence perfectly fits "normal" Piedmontese. *Mate* has been integrated as a /u/-ending Masculine Noun in the Piedmontese of Argentina.

20.1.2 *Language Attrition*

Maybe the first step in language crisis, attrition may be defined as the loss of language features as a result of encroachment from another language. The language continues to be spoken but in a less distinctive way, while at the same time getting closer to the encroaching language.

As well-known and already mentioned, discourse markers (☞ 18.2.) are particularly prone to borrowing. Although the matrix language (in line with Myers-Scotton's 1993, 2001 framework) of the following example is certainly Piedmontese, among Argentinian Piedmontese the dominating language at the societal level is Spanish, which makes its only lexical appearance here in the discourse marker *entonces*, but is evident also in the construction with the Comitative Preposition *con* and the Infinitive, unknown in Piedmontese (here *con vardé*, calqued upon Spanish *con mirar*):

(4) *però i ngh'eu nent ij sòd për felo **entonces** im confòrt **con vardé** cartoline*
 pe'ro   i='ŋg=ø   næŋt i='sot
 but   SBJ.1S=NEG= have\PRS.1S   NEG   DET=money
 pər='fe-l-u   en'tonses i=m=kuŋ'fort
 BEN=do\INF=OBJ.3-M   DM   SBJ.1S=OBL.1S=confort\PRS.1S
 kuŋ=var'd-e   kartu'lin-e
 COM=look_at-INF   postcard-F.P
 'but I don't have the money to do that, so I comfort myself by looking at the postcards' (Grassi and Pautasso 1989: 116)

---

4   The traditional South American infused drink made from *yerba mate* (*Ilex paraguariensis*).

Note also that in (4) the discontinuous negation *ngh ... nent*, typical of ancient and Eastern Piedmontese varieties, is present.

Morphosyntactic change as a result of external influence is possibly the next step: in the following example, interference from Spanish is evident in the use of the prepositional accusative (or, in other words, of the Differential Object Marker *a*) with humans and animated entities:[5]

(5) *i vëddo a mia mare*
 i=ˈvəddu   a=ˈmi-a   ˈmare
 SBJ.1S= see\PRS.1S ADE=POSS.1S-F mother
 'I see my mother' (Giolitto 2000: 15; cf. also Cerruti and Regis 2015: 24)

No varieties of European Piedmontese exhibit such a feature.

For other features, such as the spread of the Auxiliary *avej* to the expenses of *esse* ((6)), the interference of Spanish might have played a role, along with other factors, e.g., normal drift towards the loss of Auxiliary *esse*; different Auxiliary choice's rules in the variety spoken by the first-generation of Piedmontese immigrants, etc. (Cennamo 2008, Goria 2015: 145, Miola 2017: 149–153):

(6) *euj andait al pais*
 øj   aŋˈdajt   a=l=paˈiz
 have\PRS.1S go\ PTCL ADE=DET=village
 'I went to the village' (Goria 2015: 149)

Apart from the absence of Subject clitics ((*i*) *l'euj andait* would be expected here)—again, possibly a feature of the original dialect used in the area or by the ancestors of the speaker—and the "mixed" form of First person Singular of the Auxiliar *avèj* (due to the merging of peripheral/archaic *eu* /œ/ and koine's *hai* /aj/), what is noteworthy here is the choice of the auxiliary 'to have' rather than 'to be' with the unaccusative Verb 'to go:' *i son andait* /i=suŋ aŋˈdajt/ is expected here; further compare Spanish *yo he ido*.

20.1.3 *Codeswitched Piedmontese*

Codeswitching often involves the insertion of a limited amount of Piedmontese material into Italian. The simplest case is provided by the frequent use of inter-

---

5 The ongoing ERC-funded project *Microcontact. Language Variation and Change from the Italian heritage perspective*, coordinated by Roberta D'Alessandro is another rich mine of data on Piedmontese and other minority languages and Italian dialects spoken in the Italian diaspora (https://microcontact.sites.uu.nl/).

phrasal codeswitching between a dominating and dominated variety. This is probably very common among many minority and endangered languages, and Piedmontese is no exception.

The following excerpt is from an interview in Piedmontese. The speaker, a retired worker from the countryside who moved to Turin in his youth, talks about his life. In this excerpt he mocks the current fears of fine dust and talks about the fog and the cold winters of the past, asking his wife for confirmation:

(7) altro che polveri sottili *a-i era, professor ... ciamje a chila, quand i andasio a spass, a fé ... ëd passegiate për ël Piemont. Për la stra chila con la testa fora për vëdde ij cartej e tut. [I]t s-ciairave niente, còse, còse. Ma tut l'invern, nen mach un meis o doi. Temperatura meno quindes, meno disdeut.*[6]

altro che polveri sottili **a=i=era** / **prufesur** //
                            SBJ.3=IND=be\IMPF.3S / professor //
ˈtʃam=je   **a=ˈkila** /   **kwaŋd i=aŋdaˈziu**
ask(-IPV.2S)=IND ADE=IDP.3F / when SBJ.1=go\IMPF.1P
a=ˈspas /   **a=ˈfe** /   **əd=paseˈdʒate pər=əl=pieˈmuŋt** //
ADE=pastime / ATTR=do\INF / ATTR=walk-F.P BEN=DET=P. //
pər=l-a=ˈstra   **kiˈla**   **kuŋ=l-a=ˈtesta**   **ˈfora**   **pər=ˈvədde**
BEN=DET-F=road IDP.3F COM=DET-F=head outside BEN=see\INF
i=karˈtej   **e**   **tyt** / **it=stʃajˈr-ave**   **ˈɲæŋte** /
DET\P=billboard\P and all / SBJ.2S=discern-IMPF.2S nothing
ˈkoz-e / **ˈkoz-e** / **ma tyt l=iŋˈværn** / **næŋ mak aŋ=ˈmæjz** **o**
thing-F.P thing-F.P but all DET=winter / NEG only INDET=month or
duj / **temperaˈtyra ˈmenu ˈkwiŋdez** / **ˈmenu dizˈdøt**
two / temperature minus ftfteen/   minus eighteen

'Forget about [other than] fine particles (my dear) professor ... Ask her, when we used to go around, take trips around Piedmont. Along the road she kept her head out (the window), so she could see street signs and anything. You couldn't see anything ... you can't imagine [(such) things ... (such) things]. And the whole winter, not just a month or two. Temperature: -15°, -18°' (corpus ParlaTO, PTB026)

The excerpt is instructive in many ways: apart from the Italian phrase "altro che polveri sottili" (something like 'forget about fine dust,' a topic that had just been mentioned in Italian), there is no codeswitching (which does occur in the

---

6 Examples from (7) to (16) included are from the oral corpus *ParlaTO* collected in Turin (www.corpusparlato.com). The Piedmontese data have been re-transcribed according to the standard orthography. In our examples Piedmontese only (in italics) is transcribed and glossed.

conversation and will be exemplified later on). Likewise, there is no attempt at any adaptation of Italian loans; thus, 'temperature' is *temperatura* /tempera'tyra/, where the only sign of adaptation is the automatic process whereby Italian /u/ is changed into /y/ in Piedmontese, but without intervocalic voicing of stops (*temperadura* /tempera'dyra/ is expected); likewise, Italian *passeggiate* /passedʒ'dʒate/ 'walks' is adapted simply as *pasegiate* /pase'dʒate/ with the loss of gemination and against expected *spassëggiade* /spasə'dʒade/. Finally, *còse* /koze/ 'things' stands for the more "genuine" *ròbe* /robe/ with the same meaning.

A few minutes later, the speaker interrupts his narration by translating into Italian the Piedmontese word for 'plumber,' and after that he continues in Italian until a shift in topic occurs (from how and when he started working to a comparison of working conditions now and then). All this intersentential codeswitching is well signaled also prosodically:

(8) com i son surtì da ... da le scòle, subit a travajé; trovà un parent, a l'ha dime: "Ven con mi, ven con mi. A fé 'l tolé." L'idraulico. E così ho iniziato. A far l'idraulico, nei cantieri ... Ma anlora nen com adess ...
kum i='suŋ syr'ti da=l-e='skol-e
as SBJ.1=be\PRS.1S come_out\PTCL ABL=DET-F.P=school-F.P /
'sybit a=trava'j-e // tru'v-a aŋ=pa'rænt/
immediately ADE=work-INF // find-PTCL INDEF=relative /
a='la 'di=me / væŋ kuŋ='mi /
SBJ.3=have\PRS.3S say\PTCL=OBJ.1S / come\IPV.2S COM=IDP.1S /
væŋ kuŋ='mi / a='fe l=to'le //
come\IPV.2S COM=IDP.1S / ADE=do\INF DET=plumber //
< L'idraulico. E così ho iniziato. A far l'draulico, nei cantieri > // **ma**
but
aŋ'lura næŋ kum a'des
then NEG like now
'as I finished ... school, I immediately started working. I came by a relative, he told me: "Come with me, come with me. To be a plumber." *The plumber. This way I started, to be a plumber, on the building sites.* But at that time (it was) not like today ...' (corpus ParlaTO, PTB026)

Another very common pattern involves the use of both intrasentential and intersentential codeswitching. Intersentential codswitching may appear as a whole clause in Piedmontese within a conversation basically in Italian, as in the following uttered by an old interviewee towards the end of a conversation:

(9) trovomse n'auta vòlta.
    tru'v-um=se   n='awt-a   'volt-a
    find-PRS.1P=REFL   INDET=other-F time-S
    'let's meet another time' (corpus ParlaTO, PTB014)

Intrasentential codeswitching is very common and has been thoroughly investigated (Berruto 1985, Cerruti and Regis 2005, Regis 2005). In the following excerpt, basically in Italian, the speaker of examples (7) and (8) complains about foreign immigrants getting too much welfare and social benefits:

(10) come quelli sotto il ponte di corso Marche // ah sì / *a l'han daje ël për-mess* di farsi una casetta un piano // *han fane doi tre pian* // son tanti // *han tuti ij* Mercedes / BMW // (Wife: e la luce la paghiamo noi) // e l'acqua la *pagoma noi* // il comune // però *i é* il pullmino per i bambini *ch'a dev porteje a scòla*. Giusto?
come quelli sotto il ponte di corso Marche // ah sì **a='laŋ**
                                                    SBJ.3=have\PRS.3P
'da=je   əl=pər'mes / *di farsi una casetta / un piano*
give-PTCL=IND   DET=permit /
[a=l]aŋ   'fa=ne   duj træ   pjaŋ /
[SBJ.3=]have\PRS.3P do\PTCL=ATTR.PRO two three floor /
sono tanti // **[a=l]aŋ   'tyt-i ij='m. /   B.** /
              [SBJ.3=]have\PRS.3P all-P   DET\P=M. B.
e la luce la paghiamo noi / e l'acqua la / **pa'g-uma   nuj** /
                                            pay-PRS.1P IDP.1P /
il comune però / **[a=]i='e**   *il pullmino per i bambini*
                   [SBJ.3=]IND=be\PRS.3S
k=a='dev   pur't-e=je   a='skol-a /   Giusto?
SUB=SBJ.3=must\PRS.3S take-INF=IND ADE=school-F /
'like the ones (living) under the bridge in Marche Avenue: oh yes, *they gave them the authorization* to build a small house, one floor. *They made two or three floors.* They are many. *They all drive* Mercedes, BMWs. (Wife: and we (have to) pay for their electricity). And we *(have to) pay* for their (tap) water. But the Townhall ... there is a minibus for the children, *to take them to school.* Right?' (corpus ParlaTO, PTB026)

Still different is the case where language change is linked to quotes. Talking about the massive immigration of Southern Italians starting in the 1960s, the speaker uses Italian when he mockingly imitates their speech. Conversely, in an interview another speaker quotes in Piedmontese within a stretch in Italian:

(11) C'era il piemontese di Porta Pila [...] quello guardato / dall'alto in basso negli alti quartieri [...] / *chila chiel lì a parla ëd Pòrta Pila* / C'era il piemontese di Porta Pila [...] quello guardato / dall'alto in basso negli alti quartieri [...] /
'kila / kjæl='li   a='parla   əd='porta 'pila
IDP.3F / IDP.3M=there SBJ.3=speak-PRS.3S ATTR=P. P.
'there was the Piedmontese (variety) from Porta Pila[7] [...] the one looked down on uptown ... *She, he speaks Pòrta Pila*' (corpus ParlaTO, PTD004)

20.1.4 Piedmontese in Other Languages

Language contact is often non-unidirectional, and all languages involved give each other items from the lexical, morphological and/or syntactic level. Therefore, even when Piedmontese has been the less prestigious language—which has not always been the case—loans from Piedmontese entered the grammar and lexicon of other languages and other language varieties. The Piedmontese origin of several items might still be hidden, but, since etymological studies sometimes disregard minor or less studied languages, it may happen that an originally Piedmontese word in Italian is considered a French loan, or a Piedmontese word in Spanish is erroneously treated as Italian.

20.1.4.1   Piedmontese in the Regional Italian of Piedmont

Among dormant or rusty speakers codeswitching leaves the place to the occasional insertion of words from the minority (and, for these speakers, moribund) language into their only active language.

Moreover, no bilingualism nor any active use of Piedmontese is involved in the very frequent use of single words or idioms within the Italian speech of people born or living in Piedmont: these can be safely assumed to be instances of (individual, family, local or regional) loans in Italian, and may be learned without much exposure to Piedmontese at all.

Obviously, the same applies to such instances of syntactic loans such as the inherent reflexive *osarsi* 'to dare' (rather than standard Italian transitive *osare*), calqued upon Piedmontese *ancalesse* (☞ 10.1.), the regional Italian "corrective"

---

7   Pòrta Pila (Porta Pila in Italian) is a neighborhood in the old part of Turin and the area where the greatest open-air market (Piedmontese Pòrta Palass; Italian Porta Palazzo "Palace Gate") and flea market (ël Balon; no Italian toponym) are located. Originally a working- and low-class neighborhood, it has become a symbol of "old Turin" (although in its present form it basically dates from the 19th century only and its largely multiethnic nowadays).

clauses with *fare che*, calqued upon Piedmontese *fé che* (☞ 11.8.), or loans of discourse markers such as the *Erinnerungsfragepartikel già* (see below and ☞ 18.).

Piedmontese *fòra via* /ˈfora=ˈvia/ 'weird, strange, unusual' (lit. "out [of the] way") is very much used by Piedmontese speakers also in codeswitching with Italian, which does not have a literal translation (*fuori via does not exist). It is no wonder to see it cropping up in the following excerpt from a conversation that is otherwise fully in Italian:

(12) *tutto ciò che va / che è **fòra via** come si dice in piemontese / tutto cio che è fuori da ...*
'whatever goes ... (whatever) is *weird*, as we say in Piedmontese, whatever is out of ...' (corpus ParlaTO, PTD017)

Another example, maybe less common, is *moschin* /musˈkiŋ/ 'gnat' but usually a metaphor for somebody who easily takes offense, a touchy person. The metaphor is unknown in Italian (where the literal translation *moscerino* /moʃeˈrino/ could, if anything, be used for somebody who buzzes around, and therefore annoys—not somebody who *gets* annoyed).

What is worse, all Italian translations (*permaloso, suscettibile, irritabile* ...) feel literary and belonging to a high register, or still not expressive enough. In a passage characterized by quite a good amount of codeswitching, and looking for an appropriate word in Italian, the speaker of examples (7), (8) and (10) asks for an Italian word and the interviewer offers Piedmontese *moschin*. Unconvinced, he finally settles for Italian *permaloso*:

(13) *i peuss nen neghelo.* Non si può negare. Aut[r]e teste. Com as dis quandi uno, quando uno se la prende ... (*Interviewer:* **Moschin**). Nen **moschin**. (*Interviewer and wife:* Permaloso). Permaloso. A-i ero molto permaloso. Però a l'han giutà tant përchè ... a ruscavo eh ...
i=ˈpøs   næŋ neˈg-e=lu / /   Non si può negare > //
SBJ.1=can\PRS.1S NEG deny-INF=OBJ.3M /
ˈawt-e   ˈtest-e // kum a=s=ˈdiz   kwaŋdi /
other-F.P head-F.P how SBJ.3=REFL=say\PRS.3S when
/ uno ... quando uno se la prende // **musˈkiŋ** // næŋ musˈkiŋ /
                                       touchy   // NEG touchy /
permaloso / permaloso / a=ˈjeru   molto permaloso / **peˈro**
                         SBJ.3=be\IMPF.3P   but
a=ˈlaŋ   dʒyˈt-a   taŋt pərˈkæ /
SBJ.3=have\PRS.3P help-PTCL much because /

a=rys'k-avo æ
SBJ.3=work_hard-IMPF.3P yeah
'I cannot deny it. *One cannot deny it. Different heads. How do you say when one ... when one takes offense? (Interviewer: Moschin). Not moschin ... (Interviewer and wife: Touchy). Touchy. They were *very touchy*. But they helped a lot because ... they worked hard, yeah ...' (corpus ParlaTO, PTB026)

The same speaker who in example (11) introduced a clause in Piedmontese in an Italian text resorts to Piedmontese *gargagnan* /garga'ɲaŋ/ 'pimp' when he has to talk about prostitution:

(14) *fatti di sangue erano i regolamenti tra / **gargagnan** / eh, questo sì*
'bloody events were the settling of scores among pimps. Oh, yes indeed' (corpus ParlaTO, PTD004)

Along the same lines, swear words or jocular and familiar expressions are likely to be preserved and activated. The following excerpt is entirely in Italian with a strong Southern accent except for *coto* /'kutu/, a familiar and not vulgar Piedmontese word for 'halfwit:'

(15) *comunque mi son trovato bene; e poi ho ... si capisce impari a fare qualche cosa no? Dopo tanti anni se ... se sei un **coto** non capisci niente*
'anyhow, I found myself well. And then I have ... of course, you learn to do something, right? After so many years ... if you are a halfwit you do not learn anything' (corpus ParlaTO, PTB002)

It is also no wonder that a swear word like *picio* /'pitʃu/, lit. the male sexual organ but also a very vulgar expression used for males[8] is often found in Italian speech but only in its derived metaphorical meaning 'stupid.'[9]

---

8   Its Feminine form *picia* /'pitʃa/ is instead a very derogatory word for 'prostitute.'
9   Conversely, single Italian swear words may be inserted with a functional value, as in the following example, where the Italian swear word *cazzo* /'kattso/ for the male sexual organ (preceded by the Indefinite) is used as a negator (☞ 16.2.2.):

   i. *I capisse*   *'n cazzo*
       i=ka'pis-e   ⟨un cazzo⟩_CS
       SBJ.2P=understand\ PRS.2P ⟨un cazzo⟩
       'you (P) don't fucking understand' (https://www.facebook.com/esclamazioniinpiemontese/videos/1018581291540625/, 2017).

The presence of toponyms is another instance in which the original, Piedmontese name of a place can accompany (generally following) its official Italian form in an otherwise Italian-only conversation:

(16) Speaker 1: *Mia nonna era di Montiglio //*
Speaker 2: *Ah, Montiglio è vicino a Passerano //*
Speaker 1: **Montij, Montij**, *certo*
'Speaker 1: My grandma was from Montiglio.
Speaker 2: Montiglio is close to Passerano.[10]
Speaker 1: *Montij, Montij*, of course' (corpus ParlaTO, PTB025)

The presence of Piedmontesisms in texts that are otherwise in Italian is well attested in 19th-century documents written not only by illiterates and semi-literates (so-called speakers of *italiano popolare* 'popular Italian;' see Testa 2014 and references therein), but also by cultivated writers. For instance, in Italian writings by the 19th-century Turinese priest and theologician Giovanni Bosco (1815–1888; proclaimed Saint by the Catholic Church in 1934), adapted borrowings such as *arciere* 'cop' (Braido 1988; from Piedmontese *arcé*, see Gribaudo 1996: s.v.) can be found; *arciere* in Standard Italian means only 'archer.'[11]

Non-adapted loans are also very frequent in the private letters of 19th-century Piedmontese politician Massimo D'Azeglio:

(17) *Un po' di lezione di disegno alle **tote*** [Piedm. orthography *tòte*]
Un po' di lezione di disegno alle 'tot-e
                                      young_lady-F.P
'A little bit of drawing lesson to the young ladies' (D'Azeglio 1989; quoted in Toso 1999: 512)

Piedmontesisms surface also in surveilled, journalistic prose from more recent years:

(18) *Come si chiamava **già** quel pittore famoso ...?*[12]
Come si chiamava dʒa   *quel pittore famoso ...*
                    already
'what was the name of that famous painter, again?' (Gambarotta 2003: 47)

---

10   Montiglio /mon'tiʎo/ and Passerano /passe'rano/ are the Italian denominations of, respectively, Montij /muŋ'tij/ (45°04′N 08°06′E) and Passeiran /pasæj'raŋ/ (45°03′N 08°01′E), small towns in Piedmont.
11   Giovanni Bosco also wrote poetries and homilies in Piedmontese, cf. Cerrato (2006).
12   *Già* must be a borrowing from Piedmontese since no other Regional varieties of Italian

20.1.4.2 Piedmontese in Different Varieties of Italian and Other Languages

Loans from Piedmontese are by no means exclusive of the regional variety of Italian spoken in Piedmont. Many Piedmontese words and idioms have made it to the Standard variety of Italian. Around 200 Piedmontesism are lemmatized in the GRADIT, and suffice it to mention here *battere la fiacca* (< *bate la fiaca* /'bate l-a='fjak-a/ or *batla fiaca* /'bat=l-a 'fjak-a/), originally a military slang idiom meaning 'to beat a sluggish rhythm (on the battle drum),' and which entered everyday speech as 'to slack off' (Renzi 1966).

Two words usually considered peculiar of the "Romanesco" or *italiano de Roma* (Italian of Rome) and of Neapolitan, respectively, are in fact Piedmontese borrowings. On the one hand, Romanesco *piotta* '100 Liras' or '100,000 Liras,' nowadays '100 Euros,' is arguably a borrowing from argots and cants ultimately connected to Piedmontese *piòta* /'pjota/ 'paw,' through the well-attested semantic shift 'body part' > 'type of coin' (Ferrero 1991; D'Achille and Giovanardi 2001: 100); on the other hand, De Blasi (2018) defends the provenance of Neapolitan (and local regional Italian) *scugnizzo* 'young boy, apprentice,' originally 'rascal, little thief,' as possibly a corruption of Piedmontese *gognin* /guˈɲiŋ/ 'little boy,' since in the years immediately after unification (1861) when the word *scugnizzo* first appeared, the policemen dealing with young boys and children belonging to criminal gangs often were from Turin (the first capital city of Italy).

Piòla /'pjola/ 'tavern,' a term used in several argotic varieties beyond Piedmontese, has reached Argentinian and Uruguayan Spanish, where *piola* is attested with the meaning of 'nice, friendly, cunning' (https://dle.rae.es/piola). It probably entered the colloquial register through the mediation of the Argentian argot called Lunfardo (Domingo 2016).

As a final example, Piedmontese is one of the superstratum languages of Sardinian, since Piedmont and Sardinia were united in the Kingdom of Sardinia under the Savoy's crown during the 18th century. Direct contact between Sardinians and Piedmontese architects, workers and laypeople in the island gave Sardinian *lóbiu* 'closet' (from Piedmontese *lòbia* /'lobja/ 'balcony'), *tamàtiga* 'tomato' (from *tomatica* /tuˈmatika/), *buttu* 'wheel hub' (from *but* /byt/ 'sprout, wheel hub'), *baròne* 'pile of gravel' (< from *baron* /baˈruŋ/ 'pile'), *dróllu, drólle* 'sloppy, awkward' (from *dròlo* /'drolu/ 'weird'), and many other words (Dettori 2017).

---

display an *Erinnerungsfrage* discourse marker, and the French correspondent discourse marker is *déjà*, which would have been automatically translated as *di già* in (Piedmontese Regional) Italian (see Fedriani and Miola 2014 and ☞ 18.3.).

20.1.5 Language Attrition in a Written Dialect

Despite the above-mentioned influences it had, at least at the lexical level, on a number of languages, most written material in Piedmontese falls within the typical repertoire of a dialect.

What passes for "serious prose" in Piedmontese is mostly made up of belletristic prose (short stories, to a lesser extent novels, also in translation—and not only from Italian) and poetry.

Kloss' (1967: 33) reminder that "it is not so much by means of poetry and fiction that a language is reshaped (and perhaps salvaged) but by means of non-narrative prose" has obviously not come a long way among Piedmontese activists and writers.

In the past, non-literary documents written in Piedmontese are confined to the Medieval period, but from the 18th century onward published poetry and theatrical plays are abundant. In the 19th century the circulation of the satirical weekly *'L Birichin* peaked to 12,000 copies (Clivio 2002: 359) and, among many other Piedmontese writers, even Carolina Invernizio, "one of the most popular writers [of Italy] of her time amongst the working classes," whose "writings have become the object of a new interest, both as a document for sociology of culture and as valuable examples of a literary genre" only in recent years (Lepschy 1979: 93fn), published in her mother tongue the feuilleton *Ij delit d'na bela fia* ['The crimes of a beautiful girl;' original orthography].

Still, nowadays "serious" prose and scientific divulgation are certainly more common than in many other minority languages. To take a few examples, *torinosette*, the weekly insert of the Turin newspaper *La Stampa*, ran, until 2021, a regular column *An Piemontèis* ('In Piedmontese') authored by Albina Malerba (Director of the Regional Center for Piedmontese Studies) and Giovanni Tesio (University of Eastern Piedmont) and mainly dealing with literary criticism.[13] Many articles in the proceedings of the annual *Rëscontr Antërnassional dë studi ans la lenga e la literatura piemontèisa* (international scholarly meeting(s) on Piedmontese language and literature), held until the mid-1990s and organized by Gianrenzo P. Clivio, are written in Piedmontese. The bimonthly *é!* (2004–2006) was specially devoted to topics ranging from local politics to foreign affairs and economy.[14]

The linguistic landscape presents a gloomy picture: as the goal is to make a language invisible, official, government billboards and signs carefully avoid the

---

13   Partially accessible online at https://www.lastampa.it/torinosette/rubriche/an-piemonteis.

14   An almost complete collection is available online at http://www.maurotosco.net/an-piemonteis.html.

USE, CONTACT AND CARE   515

use of unrecognized minority languages (and most recognized ones, for that matter); this does not arguably negatively affect the language much, given their general ineffectiveness. Private enterprises use local languages more and more, but again essentially in the name of shops, sometimes products; in a few fortunate cases also in advertisements, and the trend is growing (on these topics, see Goria 2012).

20.1.6 *Piedmontese in the World Wide Web*

As a result of the diffusion and democratization of the World Wide Web, that "allows large numbers to publish, and they can do so in their own language variety" (Wright 2006: 209), Piedmontese is today consistently used online.[15]

At the beginning of the 21th century, Patrucco (2002: 142) found it in so-called "folkloric [...] websites where idioms or proverbs are collected" and the language was "only exhibited as a series of crystallised expressions, like relics preserved by an antiquar" (Miola 2013b: 126). These uses show very low vitality of the language.

In some cases, however, more vital content is found. The Piedmontese Wikipedia (largely quoted all along this grammar), with its 64,871 entries,[16] ranks second among the minority languages of Italy,[17] and easily leaves behind many national, official and well-recognized minority languages (Gobbo and Miola 2015, Miola 2013b). The Wikipedia is of course a living testimony to the use of Piedmontese in highly formal domains and therefore the whole project could be categorized as symbolic or ideological—aiming to elaborate and ultimately *Ausbauize* a variety that is eminently used orally and for informal topics. The impact of this material (i.e., how much is actually read) remains unknown but is certainly very limited. Italianisms and even more Frenchisms are rampant in the Piedmontese Wikipedia.

Actual/real use of Piedmontese may be found on newsgroups and on social networks' discussion groups. Here the variety used is more likely the one spoken in the speech community and this denotes a vital use of the language. The following excerpt is taken from a newsgroup message from the first decade of 2000s:

---

15 Kornai (2013) mentions instead Piedmontese as a typical example of language spoken by a fairly large community "without any significant digital presence." For a critic to this view, see Gobbo and Miola (2015: 297).
16 This and following data last accessed on Nov. 22, 2020.
17 It is preceded by Venetan with 66,991 entries and followed by Lombard with 44,313 entries.

(19) *e cume't fase a scrive en piemounteis?! Mi, en mancu sinc o ses tast en'sla tastiera per pudei scrive ... ;-) Ciao Michele*

e	ˈkume	it=ˈfaze	a=sˈkrive	aŋ=pjemuŋˈtæjz ↗
and	how	SBJ.2S=do\PRS.2S	ADE=write\INF	INE=Piedmontese Q

mi	a=m=ˈmaŋk-u	siŋk	o	ses	tast
IDP.1S	SBJ.3=OBJ.1S=miss-PRS.3P	five	or	six	key

aŋ=s=l-a=tasˈtjer-a	pər=puˈdæj	ˈskrive
INE=SUP=DET-F=keyboard-S	BEN=can\INF	write\INF

'and how can you write in Piedmontese?! I need five or six more keys on my keyboard in order to write properly. Bye from Michele' (mygate.mailgate.org/mynews/italia/italia.torino.internet, quoted in Patrucco 2003: 166)

As can be seen, Italianization (e.g., *come 't fase* instead of *comA CHE it fase*, *tastiera* instead of *tastadura*) and codeswitching (*Ciao Michele* is an Italian greeting formula) are frequent.

Orthography is virtually never the conventional one, since such messages are obviously the product of illitterate (in Piedmontese) speakers or semi-speakers but *not* of language activists. Miola (2021) is a detailed study of their orthographies. The content of Facebook groups and of other social networks mainly deals with jokes (often accompanied by video) but also proverbs and the like. Real exchange of data and news and, most of all, "serious" topics are generally absent, although much more abundant than for scores of other minorities.

In this connection, one can also find private enterprises, such as whole treatises on the mathematical foundations of physics, optics, mechanics and thermodynamics,[18] and it must also be mentioned the world-famous Egyptian Museum in Turin, which ran in 2020 on its Youtube channel a series of videos in Piedmontese (with Italian subtitles) on the forerunners of its long history.[19]

All considered, however, given the reduction of intergenerational transmission, a very real risk for Piedmontese today is to become a language only written, with no use outside the World Wide Web.

---

18   Carlo Demichelis' website is maybe the richest in this regard: https://digilander.libero.it/dotor43/ind30.html.
19   https://www.youtube.com/channel/UCuoNN4cZekeB2KKha2XwYyQ.

20.2 The Long Road toward Resurgence

It would be wrong to infer, from examples of spoken discourse in 20.1.3, that codeswitching is the usual or even the only way to use Piedmontese; it would likewise be far from the truth to conclude that amatorial poetry and Facebook jokes make up the totality of written Piedmontese.

Still, the language is certainly under great stress. This section will explore a few tentative steps undertaken in language revitalization and expansion in recent years.

20.2.1 *The Orthography: A Resource and a Problem*

The presence of a historically rich koine is a powerful tool in Ausbauization. But it can also become a burden, as in the case of the orthography (☞ 3.), where an Italianizing attitude makes written Piedmontese look *less* different from Italian than the spoken language (the thorny issue of the orthographic expression of vowels being here the clearest example). It is obvious that the orthography was conceived with other goals in mind than language elaboration and "guarding the borders:" quite to the contrary, it was devised under the false assumption that using when possible the same spelling rules of Italian would help spreading written Piedmontese.

Specifically, many problems are generously provided by the pedantic insistence on writing down allophonic variation: the use of apostrophes is widespread in the orthography of Western Romance languages, which are faced with an abundance of sandhi phenomena. Still, in Piedmontese "apostrophese" is sometimes almost pathological. As detailed in 8.2.3., the (Masculine Singular) Determiner *ël* receives the following orthographic expressions:

- *l'* before a vowel-initial word (as in *l'aso* /'l=azu/ 'the donkey')
- *lë* before a cluster (as in *lë sbaruv* /lə=zba'ryw/ 'the fright')
- *'l* after a vowel (as in *dovré 'l martel* /duv'r-e l=mar'tel/ 'to use the hammer')
- *ël* elsewhere

Similar rules apply to its allomorphs, to the Attributive *ëd* and, *ceteris paribus*, to many other clitics.

The third allograph (*'l*) is probably the most pernicious in matters of language teaching and writing, as it involves not just the control of the following Noun, which the Determiner grounds and with which it forms a phonological unit, but of *any* preceding last word, be it a part of the same phrase or not.

Just as French, Piedmontese uses the hyphen in its orthography and here as there it is the source of many mistakes. An extreme example of orthographic overdifferentiation mainly due to the "curse of the hyphen" is the writing of the string /aj/:

- *a-i*, as in *a-i é* /a='j=e/ ("SBJ.3=IND=be\PRS.3S") 'there is'
- *a-j*, as in *i-j diso* /a=j='diz/ ("SBJ.3=IND=tell\PRS.3S") 's/he tells her/him/them'
- *ai*, as in *ai fieuj* /a=i='fjøj/ ("ADE=DET\P=boy\P") 'to the boys'
- and, finally, simply *aj* /aj/ 'garlic'

While this is duly noted and carefully detailed in Brero's (1975: 22–23) pedagogical grammar, it is no wonder that much writing, either out of practical considerations or sheer ignorance, often dispenses with such niceties—even without taking into account the casual (but very common) writing of illitterate (in Piedmontese) people, as studied in Miola (2021).

20.2.2 Ausbauization: Between Tradition, Enrichment, and Standardization

The history of the various attempts to recognize Piedmontese and use it in education has been sketched many times and is immaterial here (the curious reader is referred to Duberti and Tosco 2021 for an overview).

Whatever role Piedmontese and other minority languages of Italy (even many of those recognized by National Law no. 482 of 1999) may find in education is usually limited to a few hours per week or supplementary afternoon courses (as has been the case for Piedmontese). It is generally restricted to primary schools and often has a folkloric content (traditional songs, riddles, and the like). Italian remains the medium of instruction.

In the absence of any status planning at the public level, the efforts of language activists and passionate had to concentrate on the corpus.[20]

Lexical and phraseological enrichment go hand in hand, but often with conflicting results: with lexicon, where the degree of "control" is higher because higher is the consciousness of loss and interference, the "golden rule" of Ausbauization (Tosco 2008) reigns: "maximize internal uniformity and be as much different as possible from thy neighbours." This should imply, on the one hand, a stubborn reliance on the koine and a parallel refusal of as much Italianization as possible. In practice, being based upon the dialect of the Regional administrative center, Turin, the koine itself is quite often more Italianizing than scores of local dialects. On the other hand, as a spoken medium, Turinese is arguably the most endangered variety of Piedmontese, while, as a written, literary medium, its prestige is much lower than in the past—if not altogether vanishing—while writing in the local varieties (again, with a "dialectal" content) is more widespread than ever (Regis 2012a).

---

20 The regional government actually lacks any real power—not only in matters of education and language use in the administration, but even for more trivial matters such as place names.

The lexical modernization of Piedmontese has not received any comprehensive treatment so far. The following brief notes will be taken in part from Tosco (2011a, 2012).

A tendency to orthographic de-Italianization is visible in the restoration of consonant clusters that have been reduced in Italian (and often in spoken Piedmontese, too), but are widely attested in the languages of Europe. One can read, i.e., *monarchia constitussional(a)* /munar'kia kuŋstitysju'nal(a)/ 'constitutional kingdom' with the cluster *-nst-* /nst/, rather than *costitussional* /kustitysju'nal/ (after Italian *costituzionale* /kostitutsjo'nal-e/, with the shift of Latin cluster *-nst-* to *-st-*).

As maybe everywhere, reliance on the "original" lexicon is of course the language activist's first concern. What is "original" is not always clear—and may lead to shunning words that, although amply attested in Piedmontese since centuries, have the misfortune of looking too similar to their Italian translation; this is beacuse, as in any *bona fide* Ausbauization, the goal is to be (and look) as different as possible from the dominating language. Even a small amount of phonological and spelling distance is enough. Identity in spelling must be avoided: while everyday Piedmontese is happy with /'trenu/ 'train'—by now an old borrowing from Italian /'treno/—the problem is that both are spelled *treno*. A possible solution is to resort to the old, less frequent form *tren* /træŋ/. The matter is far from settled (in the Wikipedia both have approximately the same number of entries, with a slight prevalence for *treno*).

Semantic extension is the next step.

The Italian word *gruppo* /'gruppo/ 'group' is adapted into Piedmontese as *grup* /gryp/. Another solution is to use an unrelated word and semantically extend its use. E.g., *strop* /strup/ 'herd, pack (of animals)' is used for an algebraic group in the Piedmontese Wikipedia:

(20) *L'ansema ëd tute le posission possìbij dël Cubo 'd Rubik a forma në* **strop**
l=aŋ'sema əd='tyt-e l-e=puzi'sjuŋ pu'sibij d=əl='kybu
DET=set ATTR=all-F.P DET-F.P position possible\P ATTR=DET=cube
d=r. a='furm-a nə='strup
ATTR=R. SBJ3=form-PRS.3S INDEF=group
'the set of all possible positions of a Rubik's Cube makes up a group'
("Strop;" https://pms.wikipedia.org/wiki/Strop)

The following preserves its original meaning, although metaphorized in the following excerpt about the Church as a herd:

(21) *Gesù a la presenta tanme mia Cesa (Maté 18,18), a veul në **strop** ùnich, un sol bërgé (Gioann 10,14–16)*

ʤeˈzy a=l-a=preˈzænt-a   ˈtaŋme ˈmi-a   ˈʧeza [...] /
J.   SBJ.3=OBJ.3F=present-PRS.3S as   POSS.1S-F Church /
a=ˈvøl   nə=ˈstrup   ˈynik /   aŋ=ˈsul   bərˈʤe
SBJ.3=want\PRS.3S INDEF=herd unique / INDEF=alone shepherd

'Jesus presents it (: the Church) as one (Mt 18,18), he wants a single herd, just one shepherd (John 10,14–16)' ("Cesa;" https://pms.wikipedia.org/wiki/Cesa)

The process starts with the simple extension of use to "exotic" animals, as in the Wikipedia articles for mustangs and bisons, passes through its generalization (as when describing the selection of *a group* of animals in the article on domestication), and finally reaches groups of painters (as in the article on Leon Battista Alberti's *De Pictura*) and armed groups.

Still, the great majority of its 50 entries[21] refer to mathematics and are probably the work of a single, anonymous contributor or a small ... *strop* of them. It is clearly no match for *grup* and its 1,400 entries. The much wider range of uses of the latter ranges from ethnic to language groups to the translation of Italian *Gruppo* in the name of commercial and industrial groups.

We can say that, in the long fight for the Ausbauization of Piedmontese, the less radical choice has here been the winner, at least so far.

Neologisms fare better—after all, they do not have competitors by definition, or at least not an established one. The modernization of tradition plays again a great role, but to evaluate the success of many neologisms is simply impossible due to sheer lack of data. E.g., *fusëtta* /fyˈzətta/ is recorded since the 18th century for the type of firework known with the Italian name of 'girandola' or French 'girandole.' Its use for 'rocket, missile' is certainly an interesting solution, but so far it has just three entries in Wikipedia and a few others elsewhere.

Taja /ˈtaja/, attested again since the 18th century, is fairly consistently used in the written language for 'tax.' Its only competitor is the Piedmontese adaptation of Italian *tassa* /ˈtassa/ as *tassa* /ˈtasa/—which not only has the fatal flaw of being homographous with its Italian source, but it is also homonymous with the word for 'cup' (compare Italian *tazza* /ˈtattsa/, French *tasse* /tas/).

Both *fusëtta* and *taja* look like "natural" winners. But will they actually be? Again, their very semantic field requires a modicum of official or formal use in society (e.g., in education, broadcasting, etc.).

---

21   Number of entries for all words in this section as of Dec. 26, 2020.

While everyday lexicon is therefore the object of great care in using a supposedly "original" (i.e., less Italianized) vocabulary, Frenchization plays a major role in lexicon enrichment in the high domains, and both in the lexical and phraseological domains.

Frenchization, i.e, using French as the source of neologisms, calques and, in some cases, French look-alikes, is the most exploited tool in the Ausbauization of Piemontese.

Frenchization and the desire to "look different" conspire even in phonology. Thus, Italian *costituire* /kostitu'ire/ 'to constitute, to form' has been regularly loaned in Piedmontese as *costituì* /kustity'i/, but it nowadays faces the competition of *constituì* /kuŋstity'i/, where the etymological /n/ lost in Italian (but retained in French and other languages) has been restored. Examples can be multiplied at will.

A preliminary investigation of Frenchization was carried out in Tosco (2012), where the use of French-like derivational affixes was examined.

Frenchization is easy because Piedmontese is already extremely rich in French loans, while many other words, without being directly French, can easily *pass* for French. The French influence in Piedmontese has never been properly analyzed, let alone quantified: the ultimate cause is probably to be found in the same 19th-century old linguistic nationalism so pervasive in Italian academia (☞1.2.) and that even today hinders any real recognition of the country's language situation and language diversity (and even linguistic classification). Another reason has to do with a deep-rooted academic hostility toward language management and enrichment—a subversion of the supposed "naturalness" of historical and social processes.

Frenchization is extremely useful and has been widely successful. It provides not only the mold for making neologisms, more specifically in the choice of derivational affixes or simply for the use of a derivational affix where Italian uses a zero suffix (a few examples are discussed in Tosco 2012), but is also used with proper names.

Proper names are maximally referential and must be understandable without much reference to context. At the same time, they are often very similar across languages, especially if referring to foreign entities. Innovation in this area must be applied with care. *Alman* /al'maŋ/ is the traditional word for 'German' and is consistently used, at least in the Wikipedia (1,525 entries) against its more modern Italian-derived counterpart *tedesch* /te'desk/ (from Italian *tedesco* /te'desko/; 21 entries only). At the same time, *Germania* /dʒer'manja/ 'Germany' (identical in spelling in Italian) is widely preferred to *Almania* /al'manja/, which has a single occurrence. *Polonèis* /pulu'næjz/ 'Polish' is obviously calqued on French *polonais* /pɔlɔnɛ/. It has 31 occurrences in the Wikipedia, while *polach* /puˈlak/, from Italian *polacco* /polakˈko/, has four. By the way, the country is *Polònia* /puˈlonja/ (cf. Italian *Polonia* /poˈlonja/), not a theoretically possible **Pològna* /puˈloɲa/ (cf. French *Pologne* /pɔlɔɲ/).

Instead, *Bèlgica* /ˈbældʒika/ for 'Belgium,' from French *Belgique* /bɛlʒik/ has not taken on, and *Belgi* /ˈbældʒi/ is used—more similar to and borrowed from Italian *Belgio* /ˈbeldʒo/.

Other instances of failed or questionable Frenchization are offered by an analysis of the following excerpt:

(22) *A l'é franch sa condission ëd tampa gravitassionala, pì che l'anvironament estrem, ch'a fà bëstenté tut proget ëd dësanvlupé n'economìa spassiala*
a=ˈle   frank s-a=kuɳdiˈsjun   əd=ˈtampa
SBJ.3=be\PRS.3S really PROX-F=condition ATTR=pit
gravitasjuˈnal-a / pi   ke   l=aɳvirunaˈmæɳt   esˈtrem /
gravitational-F / more SUB DET=environment extreme /
k=a=ˈfa   bəsteɳˈt-e   tyt pruˈdʒet əd=dəzaɳvlyˈp-e
SUB=SBJ.3=do\PRS.3S struggle-INF all project ATTR=develop-INF
n=ekunuˈmia   spaˈsjal-a
INDEF(-F)=economy spatial-F
'it is precisely this condition of gravitational pit, more than the extreme environment, the reason why [that makes] any project for the development of a spatial economy struggles' (Sandrone 2004: 12)

For 'environment,' *anvironament*, obviously borrowed from French *environnement*, is used here. This is a good example of both Frenchization and "Europeization," as both the English and French counterparts of *anvironament* suggest: its use conveys the idea that Piedmontese is a European language, much more European than Italian—where 'environment' is *ambiente* /amˈbjente/, which, in its turn, is the source of "plain" (not-*Ausbauized*) Piedmontese *ambient* /amˈbjæɳt/. Still, *anvironament* has only 13 entries in the Wikipedia, *ambient* 2,793.

'To develop' and 'development' are another case in point: *svilup* /zviˈlyp/, simply adapted from Italian *sviluppo* /zviˈluppo/, is the first possibility. A more radical solution is to calque French *développement* using the prefix *dë-* but adding it, as it were, to Italian *sviluppo* /zviˈluppo/, thereby getting *dësvilup* /dəzviˈlyp/. Actually, the Italian and French words and also Piedmontese *dësvilup* all hark back to a root (ultimately of uncertain origin, see REP, s.v. *vlupé*) which is found with no prefixes in the Piedmontese Verb *vlupé* /vlyˈp-e/ 'to wrap.' Scarcely used, it is usually provided with a prefix and yields *anvlupé* /aɳvlyˈp-e/ with the same meaning (and with cognates in both French *envelopper* /ãvlɔpe/ and Italian *avviluppare* /avvilupˈpare/).

USE, CONTACT AND CARE   523

In the case of 'develop(ment)' the prefix added to the same root is *s-* in Italian, *dé-* in French and *dës-* in Piedmontese. *Dësvilup* would certainly be the "natural" outcome had a Piedmontese word autonomously developed. So here comes the third, most radical solution for 'develop(ment)' and the one exemplified in (18): *dësanvlupé* /dəzaŋvly'p-e/ 'to develop,' *dësanvlup* /dəzaŋv'lyp/ 'development.' Here, once again the same root is the starting point, but already provided with the prefix *an-* and further extended with *dës-* /dəz/. The end result is a form dissimilar from Italian.

The Piedmontese Wikipedia has instances of both *svilup* and *dësvilup* with no clear preference, but no *dësanvlup, dësanvlupé*; (22) remains quite possibly a *hapax legomenon*. While reminding us that Frenchization, successful as may be, should not be overused, it witnesses once again the inventiveness and efforts deployed in trying to keep at bay an encroaching, dominating language.

20.2.3   *Phraseology, Ausbau and Language Policy*

Phraseology is the great absent in any treatment of language enrichment. It escapes the attention of activists and it is where the influence of a dominating language is more pervasive—maybe even unavoidable.

A common word such as *erbo* /'ærbu/ 'tree' may be semantically extended and give rise to *erbo a ghëmmo* /'ærbu a='gəmmu/ 'crankshaft,' built around the model of Italian *albero a gomiti* (lit. 'elbows tree') and *schema a erbo* /'skema a='ærbu/ 'tree diagram' following the pattern of Italian *schema ad albero*.

"Traditional," everyday Piedmontese used to have *cassia* /'kasja/ for 'box' but also Italian *cassa* /'kassa/ adapted as /'kasa/ (but still written *cassa*, as per the Piedmontese spelling) for abstract and metaphorical uses, as in *cassa ëd risparmi* /'kasa əd=ris'parmi/ 'savings bank' (Italian *cassa di risparmio*). "Ausbauized" Piedmontese shuns the use of Italian-derived and Italian-looking *cassa* (which by the way is homophonous with the word for 'hunting;' cf. Italian *caccia* /'kattʃa/ and French *chasse* /ʃas/): *cassia* is employed throughout and its use extended in according to Italian lexicalizations. We thus find *cassia d'arsonansa* /'kasja d=arsu'naŋsa/ calqued upon Italian *cassa di risonanza*, lit. 'resonance box,' and just as its Italian source both a 'sound box' and a 'sounding board' (also figuratively).

Examples can be multiplied, but the end result is that Italian, consciously or not, is the source of semantic extensions (and this notwithstanding the role of French in modern Piedmontese).

On the other hand, as Italian is the language of education and the preferred (often the only) reading language for most speakers, too much a distance from the semantic pattern of Italian could again endanger comprehensibility.

Età ëd Mes /e'ta d=mez/, lit. precisely "Middle Age" is an easy target: Italian 'Medioevo' /medjo'evo/ is less transparent than its translations in other languages, as it derives directly from Modern Latin *medium aevum* 'middle age.' Its literal translation as *Età ëd Mes* brings again Piedmontese closer to other European languages without being too difficult to the reader.

Example (22) above has a few other interesting stories to tell us: its very title ("The space of the private sector in the space") shows the use of *ëspasse* /əs'pase/ 'space' in both its everyday meaning of a (metaphorical) dimensional extent and in astronomy as the region beyond the earth's atmosphere. In the text itself one also finds a *tampa gravitassionala* 'gravitational pit.' Here, it is of course not so much the use of *tampa* which may strike the casual reader, but its association with *gravitassional*: after all, *tampa* is just a pit in the ground, natural or man-made (and, if anything, evokes the countryside and the past, certainly not spaceflights).

Tampa is not cognate with any of its possible Italian translations (actually, it is isolated, attested since 1564 and of unknown origin, possibly—it has been suggested—even Pre-Indo-European; REP s.v.): it perfectly fits the bill for being used and provided with new meanings in modern Piedmontese.

In short: what is strange to talk about in Piedmontese is gravitation, not pits. But, of course, to make a *tampa gravitassionala* less unusual, even weird, is a matter of status planning, or, to cut it short, of language policy: minority language education, advertisement, publishing, broadcasting—all of which is out of reach for speakers and activists alike. The obvious objection that, minority-language education or not, gravitational pits are hardly the matter of everyday talk, in Piedmont or elsewhere, is immaterial to the point: lexical enrichment cares about gravitation, not holes in the ground.

The lack of official recognition—which, *per se*, has more symbolic than practical effects—has a damping effect on private initiatives: in Piedmont as elsewhere, the heavy dependance of culture from public financial support is a major cause of the dearth of grassroot activities—just another facet of the negative influence of states and governments on culture and diversity (Tosco 2011b, 2021b).

20.3 Envoi

Bedeviled by century-old dialectization, barely visible in the linguistic landscape, shunned by intellectuals, forgotten by politicians of any persuasion (we kindly assume here that they *do* have persuasions), and—worst of all for intergenerational transmission (the only thing that matters for language survival, after all)—traditionally an object of shame and scorn among the speakers themselves, Piedmontese may at times look just another dying minority language.

Still, there are glimmers of hope even in an ocean of tears. There is debate. There is a growing perception of language endangerment and much, at times chaotic, activism. Among older and younger speakers alike. Possibly more than ever.

APPENDIX

Text

Censin Pich, *Otogn a Turin* ("Fall in Turin," 1978; from: Pich and Pasé 1996: 68)[1]

Malinconia dl'otogn. La sità a chita ij sò color e a smija ch'a chërsa 'l ciadél e 'l trafen e 'l gas ch'at intra ant ij polmon, fasendte tëmme con ësgiaj che un di 'dcò lor a-i la faran pi nen a travonde tut col tòssi.
A fussa tansipòch mia sità ... Ma a 'l l'é-lo ancor? Nò, miraco a 'l l'é pi nen da un péss,
5. *con tut che im iludèissa dël contrari fin-a tant ch'a vivìo ij testimòni 'd soa stòria 'd jer.*
Doi agn fà a l'é mancaje Armando. Adess a l'ha lassane nòst pare e an nòsta ca a smija ch'a sia mòrtje 'dcò la paròla. Bele se ant j'último agn assè pi silensios visavì 'd prima, sempe pi c[h]inà an sël baston e pì trist—che 'd magon a-j dasìa la gramissia
10. *dël mond!—a restava sensa comparision nòst prim magìster ëd lenga piemontèisa. A scotelo bin, nòsta parlada a arsonava nuansà an tuta soa natura fòrta e genita.*
E adess? Sparìa na sorgiss parèj, i vad për la sità an serca 'd cheicòsa che i treuvo pa pì. Anté ch'a l'é fini 'l pòpol turinèis? A l'era 'l pòpol dël comersi e dij mësté. Ore ij negossiant a l'han përdú sò bél deuit e sò ghëddo tradissionaj e intré ant una botega,
15. *se it ses nen ëd ca da vàire, a l'é scasi parèj ëd trovesse ant un gran magasin. E ij mësté? Costi a son mòrt da temp. A l'é da ani giumai che i sento pi nen ël crij dlë strassé o dël vedrié. I chërdo ch'a l'abio fàit la fin ëd l'últim viturin.*
I l'avia mai scrivú 'd paròle tant amère, ma i chërdo pròpi che la partensa 'd nòst pare a l'abia s-ciancame andrinta ij seugn che im portava dapress da tant temp. Darmagi
20. *përchè, sognand, im mantnìa seren e alégher e i s-ciairava tanta lus d'antorn, bele ant ij di pì fumos.*
Mej, se possìbil, torné a sugné, ëdcò përchè ij seugn an dan la fòrsa d'andé anans e, seghitand a pensé e a travajé, cheicòsa a cambia, cheicòsa as combin-a 'd bon. O tansipòch i chërdoma ch'a sia parèj e a basta sòn, chèich vire, a fene content.
25. *Foma pura tuti ij cont, la speransa ch'an resta a son le masnà. Ma i savroma deje nòste bon-e antension e 'l bagage 'd nòsta esperiensa?*
J'ani passà, chèich fërvaja a l'é pro bogiasse ant le scòle e ant le famije, ma a venta ch'as fasa viaman ëd pì, dësnò soma dabon a la fin. A giuta pa l'arvangia cost caràter

---

[1] Censin Pich (1930–2021) was a well-known figure on the Piedmontese cultural scene. An author of short stories and a regular contributor to the literary journal *La Slòira*, he was also an organizer of cultural and scientific events.

528 APPENDIX

30. *piemontèis, sarà, genà fin-a a l'arnonsia, portà a travonde bërbotand an silensi o trames a pòchi, decis autërtant a fé nen d'autut.*
A j'é da auguresse che ij pòchi apòstoj, bele se combatú, criticà, pijàit an gir, lassà tròp soj, a sapio trové la fòrsa pér ëspataré ancor sò mëssagi an sla miseria coltural e moral ch'a serca dë stenzje. A son-ne coste paròle mach ëd malinconie dl'otogn?

maliŋku'ni-a d=l=u'tuɲ /   l-a=si'ta   a='kit-a
melancholy-s ATTR=DET=fall / DET-F=city SBJ.3=quit-PRS.3S
i=so=ku'lur   e   a=z'mi-a   k=a='kərsa
DET\P=POSS.3=color and SBJ.3=looks_like-PRS.3S SUB=SBJ.3=grow\SUBJ.3S
l=tʃa'del   e   l=tra'fæŋ   e   l=gaz   k=a='t=iŋtr-a
DET=NOISE and DET=turmoil and DET=gas SUB=SBJ.3=OBJ.2S=enter-PRS.3S
aŋt=i=pul'muŋ /   fa'zæŋd=te   təmm-e kuŋ=z'dʒaj   ke   aŋ='di
INE=DET\P=lung / do\GER=OBJ.2S   fear-INF COM=disgust SUB INDEF=day
əd'ko lur   a=j=l-a=fa'raŋ   pi   næŋ a=tra'vuɲde   tyt
also   IDP.3P SBJ.3=IND=OBJ.3-F=do\DUB.3P more NEG ADE=swallow\INF all
kul   'tosi //   a='fysa   taŋsi'pok 'mi-a   si'ta //   ma
DIST venom //   SBJ.3=be\SUBJ.IMPF.3S at_least   POSS.1S-F town // but
a=l='le=lu   aŋ'kur ↗ no / m'iraku a=l='le
SBJ.3=OBJ.3=be\PRS.3S=INT.3M still   Q no perhaps SBJ.3=OBJ.3=be\PRS.3S
pi   næŋ da=ŋ='pes   kuŋ='tyt
more NEG ABL=INDEF=piece COM=all

5. ke=i=m=ily'dæjsa   d=əl=kuŋ'trari   fiɲa='taŋt
SUB=SBJ.1=OBJ.1S=delude\SUBJ.IMPF.1S ATTR=DET=contrary until=much
k=a=vi'viu   i=testi'moni   əd='sua   'storj-a
SUB=SBJ.3=live\IMPF.3P DET\P=witness ATTR=POSS.3F history-S
d=jer //   duj aɲ   fa   a='le   maŋ'k-a=je
ATTR=yesterday // two year\P ago SBJ.3=be\PRS.3S miss-PTCL=IND
ar'maŋdu // a'des a=la   la's-a=ne   nost   'pare //   e
A.   now SBJ.3=have\PRS.3S leave-PTCL=OBJ.1P POSS.1P father // and
aŋ='nost-a   ka   a=z'mi-a   k=a='sia
INE=POSS.1P-F house SBJ.3=look_like-PRS-3S SUB=SBJ.3=be\SUBJ.3S
'mort=je   dko l-a=pa'rol-a //   'bele se aŋt=i='yltim   aɲ   a'se
die\PTCL=IND also DET-F=word-S // even if INE=DET\P=last year\P much
pi   silæŋ'sjuz viza'vi d='prima /   'sempe pi   ki'n-a
more silent   versus ATTR=first / always more bend-PTCL
aŋ=s=əl=bas'tuŋ   e   pi   trist //   ke=d=ma'guŋ
INE=SUP=DET=stick and more sad // SUB=ATTR=blues
a=j=da'zia   l-a=gra'misj-a   d=əl='muŋd //
SBJ.3=IND=give\IMPF.3S DET-F=wickedness-S ATTR=DET=world //

TEXT 529

```
     a=res't-ava                 'sæŋsa   kumpari'zjuŋ  nost       prim  ma'dʒistær
     SBJ.3=remain-IMPF.3S        without  comparison    POSS.1P    first  teacher
     əd='læŋg-a                  pjemuŋ'tæjz-a //  a=sku't-e=l-u             biŋ /
     ATTR=language-S             Piedmontese-F  //  ADE=listen-INF=OBJ.3-M   well /
10.  'nost-a     par'lad-a   a=arsu'n-ava                   nyaŋ's-a    aŋ='tyt-a   'sua
     POSS.1P-F   speech-S    SBJ.3=reverberate-IMPF.3S      tint-PTCL   INE=all-F   POSS.3F
     na'tyr-a    'fort-a     e     dʒe'nit-a //    e    a'des ↗    spa'ri-a
     nature-S    strong-F    and   genuine-F //    and  now   Q    vanish-PTCL.F
     n-a=sur'dʒis        pa'ræj /    i='vad             pər=l-a=si'ta        aŋ='særka
     INDEF-F=spring      such /      SBJ.1S=go\ PRS.1S  BEN=DET-F=city       INE=search
     d=kæj'koza          ke=i='trøv-u                pa              pi //   aŋ'te
     ATTR=something     SUB=SBJ.1S=find-PRS.1S       NEG.EMPH        more // where
     k=a='le                fi'n-i           l='popul       pjemuŋ'tæjz ↗
     SUB=SBJ.3=be\PRS.3S    end\PTCL         DET=people     Piedmontese Q
     a='lera            l='popul          d=əl=ku'mærsi           e         d=i=məs'te //
     SBJ.3=be\IMPF.3S   DET=people        ATTR=DET=business       and       ATTR=DET\P=job //
     'ure   i=negu'sjaŋt              a='laŋ          'pərd-y            so       bæl'døjt    e
     now    DET\P=shopkeeper          SBJ.3=have\PRS.3P  lose-PTCL        POSS.3   politeness  and
     so         'gəddu   tradisju'na-j   e      iŋ'tr-e          aŋt=yn-a=buteg-a /        se
     POSS.3     style    traditional\P   and    get_in\INF       INE=INDEF-F=shop-S /      if
     it='sez                 næŋ   əd='ka          da='vajre /          a='le                 'skasi
     SBJ.2S=be\PRS.2S        NEG   ATTR=home       ABL=several /        SBJ.3=be\PRS.3S       almost
     pa'ræj  əd=tru'v-e=se               aŋt=yŋ='gran      maga'ziŋ //      e=i=məs'te        ↗
     so      ATTR=find-INF=REFL         INE=INDEF=big      store //          and=DET\P=job    Q
     'kust-i          a='suŋ              mort        da='tæmp /      a='le
     PROX.PRO-P      SBJ.3=be\PRS.3P     die\PTCL    ABL=time         SBJ.3=be\PRS.3S
     da='an-i
     ABL=year-P
15.  dʒu'maj   ke=i='sænt-u            pi       næŋ    əl='krij    d=lə=stra'se         o
     by_now    SUB=SBJ.1S=hear-PRS.1S  more     NEG    DET=cry     ATTR=DET=ragman      or
     d-əl=ve'drje //             i='kərd-u              k=a='labju
     ATTR=DET.MS=glazier //      SBJ.1S=believe-PRS.1S  SUB=SBJ.3=have\SUBJ.3P
     'fajt       l-a='fiŋ         əd=l='yltim          vity'riŋ //      i=la'via              maj
     do\PTCL     DET-F=end        ATTR=DET=last        coach_driver //  SBJ.1=have\IMPF.1S    never
     skri'v-y         d=pa'rol-e       taŋt   a'mær-e        ma    i='kərd-u                   'propi
     write-PTCL       ATTR-word-P      so     bitter-F.P     but   SBJ.1S=believe-PRS.1S       actually
     ke=l-a=par'tæŋs-a              d=nost             'pare        a='labja
     SUB=DET-F=departure-S          ATTR=POSS.1P       father       SBJ.3=be\SUBJ.3S
     stʃaŋ'k-a=me              aŋ'driŋta   i='søɲ           ke=i=m=pur'tava
     tear-PTCL=OBJ.1S          inside      DET\P=dream      SUB=SBJ.1S=IND1S=bring-IMPF-1S
```

da'pres   da='taɲt   'tæmp //   dər'madʒi pər'kæ / su'ɲ-and /
alongside from=much time //   too_bad because dream-GER
i=m=maɲ'tnia   se'ræŋ e   a'læger e   i=stʃaj'r-ava
SBJ.1=OBJ1S=stay\IMPF.1S calm   and cheerful and SBJ.1=behold-IMPF.1S
'taɲt-a   'lyz daŋ'turn / 'bele aɲt=i='di   pi   fy'mus //
much-F light around /   even INE=DET\P=day more obscure //

20. mej se pu'sibil tur'n-e   a=sy'ɲ-e/   əd'ko pər'kæ
     better if possible come_back-INF ADE=dream-INF / also because
     i='søɲ   a=n=daŋ   l-a='fors-a   d=aŋ'd-e
     DET\P=dream SBJ.3=OBJ.1P=give\PRS.3P DET-F=strength-S ATTR=go\INF
     a'naɲs/ e=segi't-aɲd   a=sy'ɲ-e   kej'koza a='kambj-a/
     forward and=go_on-GER ADE=dream\INF something SBJ.3=change-PRS.3S
     kej'koza   a=s=kuŋ'biɲ-a   əd=buŋ//   o=taŋsi'pok
     something SBJ.3=REFL=arrange/PRS.3S ATTR=good // or=at_least
     i=kər'd-uma   k=a='sia   pa'ræj /
     SBJ.1=believe/PRS.1P SUB= SBJ.3S=be/PRS.3S so /
     e=a='basta   soŋ   kæjk='vir-e
     and=SBJ.3=be_enough-PRS.3S PROX.PRO some=time-F.P
     a='fe=ne   kuŋ'tæŋt //   'fuma   'pyra   'tyti=i='kuɲt/
     ADE=make/INF=OBJ.1P happy //   make/SUBJ.1P as_well all=DET/P=count
     l-a=spe'raɲs-a k=a=n='rest-a   a=suŋ
     DET-F=hope-S SUB=SBJ.3=OBJ.1P=remain-PRS.3S SBJ.3= be\PRS.3P
     l-e=maz'na//   ma i=sa'vruma   d-e=je   'nost-e   'buŋ-e
     DET-F.P=child but SBJ.1=know\DUB.1P give/INF=IND POSS.1P-F.P good-F.P
     ateŋ'sjuŋ e=l=ba'gadʒe   əd='nost-a   espe'rjæŋs-a ↗
     attention and=DET=luggage ATTR=POSS1P-F experience-S Q

25. j='an-i   pa's-a   kæjk fər'vaja a='le   pru
     DET\P=year-P pass-PTCL some crumb SBJ.3=be\PRS.3S indeed
     bu'dʒ-a=se   aɲt=jə='skol-e   e=aɲt=l-e=fa'mi-e/
     move-PTCL=REFL INE=DET\P=school-P and= INE=DET/F.P=family-P
     ma=a='vaɲt-a   k=a=s='faz-a   vja'maŋ əd=pi/
     but=SBJ3S=need\PRS.3S SUB=SBJ.3=REFL=make=SUBJ.3S vja'maŋ ATTR=more/
     dəs'no   'suma   da'buŋ a=la=fiŋ //   a='dʒyt-a   pa
     otherwise be\PRS.1P indeed ADE=DET-F=end // SBJ.3=help-PRS.3S NEG.EMPH
     l=ar'vaɲdʒ-a   kust ka'rater pjemuŋ'tæjz/ sa'r-a /   dʒe'n-a
     DET=revenge-S PROX character Piedmontese/ close-PTCL / embarrass-PTCL
     'fiɲa a=l=ar'nuŋsj-a/   pur't-a   a=tra'vuɲde
     until ADE=DET(-F)=renunciation-S bring-PTCL ADE=swallow\INF
     bərbu't-aɲd   aŋ=si'læŋsi o=tra'mɛz a='pɔki/   de'tʃiz awtər'taɲt
     grumble-GER INE=silence or=between ADE=few-P resolute as_much

TEXT

```
       a='fe           næŋ daw'tyt //   a='j=e                  da=awgy'r-e=se            ke
       ADE=do\INF     NEG at_all //     SBJ3=IND=be\PRS.3S     ABL=wish-INF=REFL         SUB
       i='poki         a'postuj /      bele='se kuŋba't-y /    kriti'k-a /         pj-ajt
       DET\P=few-P    apostle\P /      even=if fight\PTCL /    criticize\PTCL /    take\PTCL
       aŋ='dʒir /     la's-a           trop            suj /
       INE=round /    leave\PTCL      too_much         alone\P /
30.    a='sapju              tru'v-e    l-a='fors-a         pər=əspata'r-e      aŋ'kur
       SBJ3=know\SUBJ.3P    find\INF   DET-F=strength-S    BEN=spread-INF      still
       so=me'sadʒi           aŋ=s=la=mi'zerj-a           kulty'ral  e=mu'ral
       POSS.3=message       INE=SUP=DET-F=misery-S       cultural   and=moral
       k=a='særk-a                  də='stæŋz=je //              a='suŋ=ne
       SUB=SBJ.3S=look_for\PRS.3S   ATTR=suffocate=OBJ.3P //     SBJ.3=be\PRS.3P=INT.3P
       'kust-e     pa'rol-e    mak     əd=maliŋku'ni-e     d=l=u'tuɲ          ↗
       PROX-F.P   word-P      only    ATTR-melancholy-P   ATTR=DET=fall      Q
```

Melancholy in Fall. The city sheds its colors it looks like only the noise, the turmoil, and the gas entering your lungs grow, so that you fear in horror that someday even they won't be able to swallow all the poison.

Were it even my town! But is it still? No, perhaps it is not, and since long, even
5. though I was deluding myself of the contrary as far as the witnesses of yesterday's history were alive.

Two years ago Armando died. Now our father left us and it seems that in our home even the Word has died. Sure in his last years he was much quieter than before, more and more bent over his stick and sadder—such was his grief for all
10. the world's evil!—and still he was our first, unparalleled teacher in the Piedmontese language. When you listened to him with care, our speech rang, nuanced in all its strong and genuine nature.

So, now? After such a source ran out, I roam the city looking for something I can no longer find. Where is the people from Turin gone? They were a people of trade and craft. Nowadays, the shopkeepers have lost their politeness and traditional good manners, so that to step into a shop, unless you are at home there, and since long,
15. it is almost the same as being in a shopping center.

And the crafts? They have been dead since a long time. It is years nowadays that I do not hear the ragman's or the glazier's call. I guess they met the same fate of the last cabman.

I had never written such a bitter words, but I sincerely believe that the departure
20. of our father tore inside me all the dreams I was carrying around since long.

Such a pity, because by dreaming I kept myself in peace and joy, and I could see light all around me, even in the most foggy days.

Better, if possible, to dream again, also because the dreams give us the strength to go ahead, so that, keeping with the thought and work, something really happens.

25. Or, at least, we think it is so, and this is enough, sometimes, to make us happy. Let's just consider everything: the children are the only hope we have. But will we be able to provide them with our good wills and the heritage of our experience? Actually, these past years something, very little, moved in schools and families, but much more must be done, otherwise we are really at the end. This Piedmontese
30. character of ours does not help: reserved, awed to the point of defeatism, prone to swallow down and grumble in silence or among a few who are just the same resolute ... in doing nothing.

We may only wish that those few apostles—even if battled, criticized, made fun of, left alone—all too alone—may find the strength to spread the news about the cultural and moral misery that's trying to choke them.

Are these words maybe just a Fall melancholy?

References

Adams, Larin. 2015. Case Studies of Orthography Decision Making in Mainland Southeast Asia. In: *Developing Orthographies for Unwritten Languages*, edited by Michael Cahill and Keren Rice, 231–250. Dallas: SIL International.

Aijmer, Karin. 2007. The meaning and functions of the Swedish discourse marker *alltså*—Evidence from translation corpora. *Catalan Journal of Linguistics* 6: 31–59.

AIS = Jakob Jud and Karl Jaberg. 1928–1940. *Sprach- und Sachatlas Italiens und der Südschweiz*, 8 vols. Zofingen: Ringier u. C.

Allasino, Enrico. 2007. La diffusione delle parlate in Piemonte. In: *Le lingue del Piemonte*, edited by Enrico Allasino, Consuelo Ferrier, Sergio Scamuzzi and Tullio Telmon, 61–98. Torino: IRES Piemonte.

Aly-Belfàdel, Arturo. 1933. *Grammatica piemontese*. Noale: Guin.

Andorno, Cecilia. 2000. *Focalizzatori tra connessione e messa a fuoco. Il punto di vista delle varietà di apprendimento*. Milano: Franco Angeli.

Ascoli, Graziadio Isaia. 1882–1885. L'Italia dialettale. *Archivio Glottologico Italiano* 8: 98–128.

Bach, Xavier, Anetta Kopecka and Benjamin Fagard. 2019. Complex color denomination in French and Occitan. In: *Lexicalization patterns in color naming: A cross-linguistic perspective*, edited by Ida Raffaelli, Daniela Katunar and Barbara Kerovec, 213–234. Amsterdam: John Benjamins.

Bazzanella, Carla. 1995. I segnali discorsivi. In: *Grande grammatica italiana di consultazione, vol. III*, edited by Lorenzo Renzi, Gianpaolo Salvi and Anna Cardinaletti, 225–257. Bologna: il Mulino.

Bazzanella, Carla. 2006. Discourse Markers in Italian: towards a 'compositional' meaning. In: *Approaches to discourse particles*, edited by Karen Fischer, 449–464. Amsterdam: Elsevier.

Bec, Pierre. 1970–1971. *Manuel pratique de philologie romane*. Paris: Picard.

Bellert, Irena. 1977. On Semantic and Distributional Properties of Sentential Adverbs. *Linguistic Inquiry* 8/2: 337–351.

Bentley, Delia. 2004. Ne-Cliticisation and Split Intransitivity. *Journal of Linguistics* 40/2: 219–262.

Bentley, Delia. 2016. Split intransitivity. In: *The Oxford Guide to the Romance Languages*, edited by Adam Ledgeway and Martin Maiden, 821–832. Oxford and New York: Oxford University Press.

Berenblut, Max. 1949. *A Comparative Study of Judaeo-Italian Translations of Isaiah*. PhD thesis, New York: Columbia University.

Benincà, Paola. 1994. *La variazione sintattica. Studi di dialettologia romanza*. Bologna: il Mulino.

Benincà, Paola. 1995. I dati dell'ASIS e la sintassi diacronica, in.—Iliescu M. (a cura di), *Italia Settentrionale: crocevia di idiomi romanzi*, edited by Emanuele Banfi, Giovanni Bonfandini, Patrizia Cordin and Maria Iliescu, 133–143. Tübingen: Niemeyer.

Benincà, Paola, Mair Parry and Diego Pescarini. 2016. The dialects of Northern Italy. In: *The Oxford Guide to the Romance Languages*, edited by Adam Ledgeway and Martin Maiden, 185–205. Oxford and New York: Oxford University Press.

Berenblut, Max. 1949. *A Comparative Study of Judaeo-Italian Translations of Isaiah*. PhD thesis, New York: Columbia University.

Berizzi, Mariachiara. 2012. *Toccare* come verbo deontico nei dialetti italiani. *Quaderni di Lavoro ASIt* 14: 191–208.

Berlin, O. Brent and Paul Kay. 1969. *Basic Color Terms: Their Universality and Evolution*. Berkeley, CA: University of California Press.

Bernini, Giuliano and Paolo Ramat (eds.). 1996. *Negative sentences in the languages of Europe: a typological approach*. Berlin: Mouton de Gruyter.

Berruto, Gaetano. 1974. *Piemonte e Valle d'Aosta* ("Profilo dei dialetti italiani 1"). Pisa: Pacini.

Berruto, Gaetano. 1990. Note tipologiche di un non tipologo sul dialetto piemontese. In: *Studi di sociolinguistica e dialettologia italiana offerti a Corrado Grassi*, edited by Gaetano Berruto and Alberto A. Sobrero, 3–24. Galatina: Congedo.

Berruto, Gaetano. 1990/91. Review of: 1. III Rëscontr antërnassional dë studi an sia lenga e la literatura piemontèisa, Alba 10–11 magg 1986. Alba: Famija Albèisa: 1987; 2. IV Rëscontr antërnassional dë studi an sia lenga e la literatura piemontèisa, Alba 9–10 magg 1987. Alba: Famija Albèisa: 1988; 3. V Rëscontr antërnassional dë studi an sia lenga e la literatura piemontèisa, Alba 7–8 magg 1988. Alba: Famija Albèisa: 1989; 4. VI Rëscontr antërnassional dë studi an sia lenga e la literatura piemontèisa, Alba 6–7 magg 1989 (a cura 'd Gianrenzo P. Clivio e Censin Pich). Alba: Famija Albèisa: 1990. *Vox Romanica* 49/50: 496–497.

Berruto, Gaetano. 2002. Parlare dialetto in Italia alle soglie del Duemila. In: *La parola al testo*, edited by Gian Luigi Beccaria e Carla Marello, 33–49. Alessandria: dell'Orso.

Berruto, Gaetano. 2006. Quale dialetto per l'Italia del Duemila? Aspetti dell'italianizzazione e risorgenze dialettali in Piemonte (e altrove). In: *Lingua e dialetto nell'Italia del duemila*, edited by Alberto A. Sobrero and Annarita Miglietta, 101–127. Galatina: Congedo.

Berruto, Gaetano. 2009. Περί συντάξεως. Sintassi e variazione. In: *Sintassi storica e sincronica dell'italiano. Subordinazione, coordinazione, giustapposizione, Atti del X° Congresso della Società Internazionale di Linguistica e Filologia italiana (Basilea, 30 giugno–3 luglio 2008)*, 3 voll., edited by Angela Ferrari, 21–58. Firenze: Cesati.

Berruto, Gaetano. 2018. The languages and dialects of Italy. In: *Manual of Romance Sociolinguistics*, edited by Günter Holtus and Fernando Sánchez Miret, 494–525. Berlin: de Gruyter.

Bertinetto, Pier Marco and Mario Squartini. 2016. Tense and aspect. In: *The Oxford Guide to the Romance Languages*, edited by Adam Ledgeway and Martin Maiden, 939–953. Oxford and New York: Oxford University Press.

Bertolino, Remigio and Nicola Duberti. 2007. *Petite anthologie de la poésie de Mondovi*. Mondovì: Ël Pèilo.

Bertoni, Giulio. 1916. *L'Italia dialettale*. Milano: Hoepli.

Bertoni, Giulio. 1940. *Profilo linguistico d'Italia*. Modena: Società Tipografica Modenese.

Bhat, Darbhe Narayana Shankara. 1999. *The Prominence of Tense, Aspect and Mood*. Amsterdam: John Benjamins.

Biber, Douglas, Stig Johansson, Geoffrey Leech, Susan Conrad, and Edward Finegan. 1999. *The Longman Grammar of Spoken and Written English*. London: Longman.

Billò, Ernesto et al. 2003. *Paròle nòstre. Il dialetto ieri e oggi nei paesi del Monregalese*. Mondovì: CEM.

Biondelli, Bernardino. 1853. *Saggio sui dialetti gallo-italici*. Milano: Bernardoni (reprint: Bologna: 1988).

Bollati, Emanuele and Antonio Manno. 1878. Documenti inediti in antico dialetto piemontese. *Archivio Storico Italiano* 4/2: 375–388.

Bonato, Massimo. 2003–2004. *Tratti variabili nella sintassi del piemontese parlato contemporaneo*. Turin: University of Turin MA thesis.

Bonato, Massimo. 2006. "Quand ch'it ven-e?". Il doppio introduttore nelle frasi interrogative del piemontese parlato contemporaneo. *LIDI-Lingue e idiomi d'Italia* 2: 36–66.

Bossong. Georg. 2000. Écrire dans une langue régionale. L'expérience piémontaise vue de l'extérieur. In: *II Convegno internazionale sulla lingua e la letteratura del Piemonte*, edited by Sergio Gilardino and Bruno Villata, 159–193. Vercelli: VercelliViva.

Bossong, Georg. 2016. Classifications. In: *The Oxford Guide to the Romance Languages*, edited by Adam Ledgeway and Martin Maiden, 63–72. Oxford and New York: Oxford University Press.

Bottasso, Enzo. 1953. Introduzione. In: *L'opera piacevole di Giovan Giorgio Alione*, VII-LXXIX. Bologna: Palmaverde.

Brasca, Lissander. 2021. Mixing methods in linguistic classification: a hidden agenda against multilingualism? The contestedness of Gallo-"Italic" languages within the Romance family. In: *Contested Languages: The Hidden Multilingualism of Europe* ("Studies in World Language Problems 8"), edited by Marco Tamburelli and Mauro Tosco, 59–86. Amsterdam: John Benjamins.

Brero, Camillo. 1967. *Gramàtica piemontèisa*. Turin: Musicalbrandé.

Brero, Camillo. 1971. *Gramàtica piemontèisa. Sconda tiradura dla sconda edission arvëddùa e slargà con la gionta 'd na sèrnia 'd leture*. Torino: Ij Brandé.

Brero, Camillo. 1972. Presentassion. In: Gianfranco Gribaudo, Pinin Seglie e Sergio Seglie, *Dissionari piemontèis A–B*. Turin: Ij Brandé: vii–viii.

Brero, Camillo. 1975a. *Gramàtica piemontèisa. Quarta edission arvëddùa e soagnà con nòte 'd leteratura e na sèrnia antològica*. Torino: A l'ansegna dij Brandé.
Brero, Camillo. 1975b. *Le Magnifiche Vos dla Leteratura Piemontèisa*. Torino: Piemonte in Bancarella.
Brero, Camillo. 1981. *Storia della letteratura piemontese. Primo Volume (da Sec. XII a Sec. XVIII)*. Torino: Piemonte in Bancarella.
Brero, Camillo. 1982a. *Storia della letteratura piemontese. Secondo volume (Sec. XIX)*, Torino: Editrice Piemonte in Bancarella.
Brero, Camillo. 1982b. *Vocabolario piemontese-italiano*. Torino: Piemonte in Bancarella.
Brero, Camillo. 1983. *Storia della letteratura piemontese. Terzo volume (Sec XX)*. Torino: Editrice Piemonte in Bancarella.
Brero, Camillo. 1994. *Sintassi dla lenga piemontèisa*. Sconda edission. Turin: Edission «Piemont/Europa».
Brero, Camillo. 2008. *Grammatica e sintassi della lingua piemontese. Gramàtica e sintassi dla lenga piemontèisa*. Torino: Il Punto-Piemonte in Bancarella.
Brero, Camillo and Remo Bertodatti. 2000. *Grammatica della lingua piemontese*. Savigliano: L'Artistica.
Brero, Camillo and Renzo Gandolfo (eds.). 1967. *La letteratura in piemontese dalle origini al Risorgimento*. Torino: Casanova.
Burdet, Carlo A.M. 2012. Padre Ignazio Isler (1699–1778) schwytzerdütsch subalpino. *Studi Piemontesi*: xli/1: 153–162.
Burzio, Luigi. 1986. *Italian syntax*. Dordrecht: D. Reidel Publishing Company.
Cahill, Michael. 2015. Non-Linguistic Factors in Orthographies. In: *Developing Orthographies for Unwritten Languages*, edited by Dallas Michael Cahill and Keren Rice, 9–26. Dallas, TX: SIL International.
Calosso, Silvia. 1973. Osservazioni sui microsistemi morfologici di alcune parlate galloitaliche occidentali. *Archivio Glottologico Italiano* 58/2: 142–154.
Canepari, Luciano. 1979. *Introduzione alla fonetica*. Torino: Einaudi.
Canepari, Luciano. 1980. *Italiano standard e pronunce regionali*. Padova: Cleup.
Canini, Renato. 2007. *Ël gran rimari ëd la lenga piemontèisa*. Cuneo: Primalpe.
Capello, Renata *et alii* 2001. *Piemontèis d'amblé. Avviamento modulare alla conoscenza della lingua piemontese*. Torino: Gioventura Piemontèisa.
Carlier, Anne, Walter De Mulder and Béatrice Lamiroy (eds). 2012. The pace of grammaticalization in Romance [Special issue]. *Folia Linguistica* 46/2.
Carlier, Anne and Lamiroy, Béatrice. 2014. The Romance partitive. In: *Partitive Cases and Related Categories*, edited by Silvia Luraghi and Tuomas Huumo, 477–518. Berlin: Mouton-De Gruyter.
Cennamo, Michela. 1997a. Passive and impersonal constructions. In: *The Dialects of Italy*, edited by Martin Maiden and Mair Parry, 145–161. London: Routledge.

Cennamo, Michela. 1997b. Relative clauses. In: *The Dialects of Italy*, edited by Martin Maiden and Mair Parry, 190–201. London: Routledge.

Cennamo, Michela. 2001. L'Inaccusatività in alcune varietà campane: Teorie e dati a confronto. In: *Dati empirici e teorie linguistiche: Atti del XXXIII Congresso Internazionale della Società di Linguistica Italiana, Napoli, 28–30 ottobre 1999*, edited by Federico Albano Leoni, Rosanna Sornicola, Eleonora Stenta Krosbakken and Carolina Stromboli, 427–453. Roma: Bulzoni.

Cennamo, Michela. 2016. Voice. In: *The Oxford Guide to the Romance Languages*, edited by Adam Ledgeway and Martin Maiden, 967–980. Oxford and New York: Oxford University Press.

Cerrone, Pietro C. and Emanuele Miola. 2011. La selezione degli ausiliari in un'area del Piemonte nordorientale. *Atti del Sodalizio Glottologico Milanese* 6 n.s.: 196–207.

Cerruti, Massimo. 2007. Sulla caratterizzazione aspettuale e la variabilità sociale d'uso di alcune perifrasi verbali diatopicamente marcate. *Archivio Glottologico Italiano* 92/2: 203–247.

Cerruti, Massimo. 2008. Condizioni e indizi di coniugazione oggettiva: I dialetti italiani settentrionali tra le lingue romanze. *Rivista Italiana di Dialettologia* 32: 13–38.

Cerruti, Massimo. 2011. Note sulla grammaticalizzazione di perifrasi aspettuali. *Quaderni di lavoro ASIt* 13: 71–93.

Cerruti, Massimo. 2012. Dialetto, italiano regionale, italiano neo-standard: un confronto sullo stadio di grammaticalizzazione di perifrasi verbali consimili. In: *Coesistenze linguistiche nell'Italia pre- e postunitaria. Atti del XLV Congresso Internazionale della Società di Linguistica Italiana (Aosta-Bard-Torino, 26–28.09.2011)*, edited by Tullio Telmon, Gianmario Raimondi and Luisa Revelli, 605–619. Roma: Bulzoni.

Cerruti Massimo and Riccardo Regis. 2005. Code switching e teoria linguistica: la situazione italo-romanza. *Italian Journal of Linguistics* 17/1: 179–208.

Cerruti Massimo and Riccardo Regis. 2015. Dal discorso alla norma: prestiti e calchi tra i fenomeni di contatto linguistico. *Vox Romanica* 74: 20–45.

Cerruti, Massimo and Riccardo Regis. 2020. Partitive determiners in Piedmontese: A case of language variation and change in a contact setting. *Linguistics* 58/3: 651–677.

Cinque, Guglielmo. 1994. Sull'ordine relative di alcune classi di avverbi in italiano e in francese. In: *Teoria del linguaggio e analisi linguistica: XX Incontro di Grammatica Generativa*, edited by Gianluigi Borgato, 163–177. Padova: Unipress.

Cinque, Guglielmo. 1999. *Adverbs and Functional Heads*. Oxford and New York: Oxford University Press.

Clivio, Gianrenzo P. 1964. *Piedmontese. A short basic course*. Waltham: Brandeis University.

Clivio, Gianrenzo P. 1970a. Brevi prose in volgare piemontese del Quattrocento: i testi carmagnolesi. In: *Essays in honor of Louis Francis Solano*, edited by Raymond J. Cormier and Urban T. Holmes, Jr., 54–64. Chepel Hill: University of North Carolina Press:

Clivio, Gianrenzo P. 1970b. The *volgare* in Piedmont from the Middle Ages to the end of the Sixteenth Century. *Romanische Forschungen* 82/1–2: 65–93.

Clivio, Gianrenzo P. 1970c. Le particelle affermative in piemontese. *Forum Italicum* 4/1: 70–75.

Clivio, Gianrenzo P. 1971. Avertiment. In: Brero 1971: X.

Clivio, Gianrenzo P. 1972. Language Contact in Piedmont: Aspects of Italian Interference in the Sound System of Piedmontese. In: *Studies for Einar Haugen*, 119–131. The Hague: Mouton. Now in: Gianrenzo P. Clivio. 1976. *Storia linguistica e dialettologia piemontese*, 91–106. Torino: Ca dë Studi Piemontèis.

Clivio, Gianrenzo P. 1974. Il dialetto di Torino nel Seicento. Parte I. Testi, Glossario. *L'Italia dialettale* 37: 18–120.

Clivio, Gianrenzo P. 1975. Su alcune vicende lessicali del gallo-italico occidentale. In: *Civiltà del Piemonte. Studi in onore di Renzo Gandolfo nel suo settantacinquesimo compleanno*, edited by Gianrenzo P. Clivio and Riccardo Massano, 29–46. Torino: Centro Studi Piemontesi/Ca dë Studi Piemontèis.

Clivio, Gianrenzo P. 1976. *Storia linguistica e dialettologia piemontese*. Torino: Centro Studi Piemontesi/Ca dë Studi Piemontèis.

Clivio, Gianrenzo P. 1984. Aspetti linguistici del Piemonte settecentesco. In: *Teorie e pratiche linguistiche nell'Italia del Settecento*, edited by Lia Formigari, 263–279. Bologna: Il Mulino.

Clivio, Gianrenzo P. 1988. Dal latin al piemonteis. A l'arserca dla stòria 'd la nòsta lenga. In: *IV Rescontr sla lenga e la literatura piemontèisa*, 125–136. Alba: Famija albeisa.

Clivio, Gianrenzo P. 2001. Debat sla grafia piemontèisa. *La Lòsna* (March 15). www.piemont.org, now accessible via http://web.archive.org; last accessed on Nov. 24, 2020.

Clivio, Gianrenzo P. 2002a. Il Piemonte. In: *I dialetti italiani*, edited by Manlio Cortelazzo, Carla Marcato, Nicola De Blasi and Gianrenzo P. Clivio, 151–195. Torino: UTET.

Clivio, Gianrenzo P. 2002b. *Profilo di storia della letteratura in piemontese*. Turin: Ca dë Studi Piemontèis.

Clivio, Gianrenzo P. 2003a. Giovan Giorgio Alione. In: *La letteratura in piemontese dalle origini al Settecento. Raccolta antologica di testi*, edited by Giuliano Gasca Queirazza, Gianrenzo P. Clivio and Dario Pasero, 133–232. Torino: Centro Studi Piemontesi/Ca dë Studi Piemontèis.

Clivio, Gianrenzo P. 2003b. Il Settecento. In: *La letteratura in piemontese dalle origini al Settecento. Raccolta antologica di testi*, edited by Giuliano Gasca Queirazza, Gianrenzo P. Clivio and Dario Pasero, 167–276. Torino: Centro Studi Piemontesi/Ca dë Studi Piemontèis.

Clivio, Gianrenzo P. and Dario Pasero (eds.). 2004. *La letteratura in piemontese dalla stagione giacobina alla fine dell'Ottocento. Raccolta antologica di testi*. Centro Studi Piemontesi/Ca dë Studi Piemontèis.

REFERENCES

Cognasso, Francesco. 1969. *Vita e cultura in Piemonte dal Medioevo ai giorni nostri.* Centro Studi Piemontesi/Ca dë Studi Piemontèis.

Cordin, Patrizia. 1997. Tense, mood and aspect in the verb. In: *The Dialects of Italy*, edited by Martin Maiden and Mair Parry, 87–98. London: Routledge.

Corbett, Greville. 1991. *Gender.* Cambridge: Cambridge University Press.

Cornagliotti, Anna. 1993. Parlate provenzali del versante orientale delle Alpi. In: *Atti del Secondo Congresso Internazionale della "Association Internationale d'Etudes Occitans" Torino 31 agosto–5 settembre 1987. Volume 2*, edited by Giuliano Gasca Queirazza, 954–967. Torino: AIEO/Dipartimento di Scienze Letterarie e Filologiche.

Coulmas, Florian. 2003. *Writing Systems.* Cambridge: Cambridge University Press.

Coveri, Lorenzo. 1996. Dialetto rock! *Italiano & Oltre* 11: 134–142.

Cristofaro, Sonia. 2003. *Subordination.* Oxford: Oxford University Press.

Crothers, John. 1978. Typology and Universals of Vowel Systems. In: *Universals of language. Vol. II: Phonology*, edited by Joseph Greenberg, Charles A. Ferguson and Edith A. Moravcsik, 93–152. Redwood City, CA: Stanford University Press.

Cugno, Federica and Federica Cusan. 2018. La designazione delle aree cromatiche del blu e del rosso nei dialetti italiani. *Bollettino dell'Atlante Linguistico Italiano* 3/42: 1–33.

Cugno, Federica and Federica Cusan. 2019. Dialectal words for colour: an analysis of data from the *Atlante Linguistico Italiano* (ALI). *Quaderni di Semantica* 5: 261–286.

Cuzzolin, Pierluigi, Ignazio Putzu, and Paolo Ramat. 2006. The Indo-European Adverb in diachronic and typological perspective. *Indogermanische Forschungen* 111: 1–38.

'd Min, Franco [Crotta, Franco]. 2015. *Abecedari dël ciavraneiss.* Ciavran: Youcanprint.

Dal Negro, Silvia. 2013. Variazione dialettale e tipologia. *Vox Romanica* 72/1: 138–150.

Dal Negro, Silvia and Ilaria Fiorentini. 2014. Reformulation in bilingual speech: Italian *cioè* in German and Ladin. *Journal of Pragmatics* 74: 94–108.

Danesi, Marcel. 1976. *La lingua dei "Sermoni Subalpini."* Torino: Centro Studi Piemontes/Ca dë Studi Piemontèis.

Danesi, Marcel. 1991. The language of the "Sermoni Subalpini" revisited. A reply to Wolf. *Atti del VII Rëscontr Antërnassional dë Studi an sla Lenga e la Literatura Piemontèisa*, 255–262. Alba: Famija Albèisa.

Degand, Liesbeth, Bert Cornillie and Paola Pietrandrea (eds). 2013. *Discourse markers and Modal particles. Categorization and Description.* Amsterdam: Benjamins. doi: 10.1075/pbns.234

Dell'Aquila, Vittorio and Gabriele Iannàccaro. 2004. *La pianificazione linguistica.* Roma: Carocci.

Dell'Aquila, Vittorio and Gabriele Iannàccaro. 2008. Per una tipologia dei sistemi di scrittura spontanei in area romanza. *Estudis Romànics* 30: 311–331.

De Mauro, Tullio. 1963. *Storia linguistica dell'Italia unita.* Roma-Bari: Laterza.

Denina, Carlo. 1804. *La clef des langues.* Berlin: Mettra, Umlang & Quien.

Devoto, Giacomo and Gabriella Giacomelli. 1972. *I dialetti delle regioni d'Italia.* Firenze: Sansoni.

Diessel, Holger. 1999. *Demonstratives. Form, function and grammaticalization.* Amsterdam: John Benjamins.

Diringer, David. 1968 [1948]. *The Alphabet: A Key to the History of Mankind.* 2 vols. 3rd edition, completely revised with the collaboration of Rheinold Regensburger. London: Hutchinson.

Di Stefano, Andrea. 2017. *Leĝe e scrive 'l Piemontèis. Gramàtica e antologia dla lengua Piemontèisa e dël dialët ëd Bièla. Grammatica ed antologia della lingua Piemontese e del dialetto di Biella.* Biella: Lineadaria.

Dixon, R.M.W. 2004. Adjective Classes in Typological Perspective. In: *Adjectives. A Cross-Linguistic Typology*, edited by R.M.W. Dixon and Alexandra Y. Aikhenvald, 1–49. Oxford: Oxford University Press.

DOC = Dizionario di Occitano Medievale. https://www.dizionariodoc.unisa.it/

Dołowy-Rybińska, Nicole and Claudia Soria. 2021. Surveying the ethnolinguistic vitality of two contested languages: The case of Kashubian and Piedmontese. In: *Contested Languages: The Hidden Multilingualism of Europe* ("Studies in World Language Problems 8"), edited by Marco Tamburelli and Mauro Tosco, 125–142. Amsterdam: John Benjamins.

Domingo, Javier Marcelo. 2016. *Una lingua piola. Il lunfardo argentino.* Unpublished MA Thesis. Venice: Ca' Foscari University.

Domokos, György. 1998. Appunti sulla morfologia e sulla sintassi delle opere di Bonvesin de la Riva. *AEVUM—Rassegna di Scienze Storiche, Linguistiche e Filologiche* 72/3: 619–631.

Dressler, Wolfgang U. *et alii* 2003. Le classi di coniugazione in italiano e francese. In: *Il verbo italiano. Studi diacronici, sincronici, contrastivi, didattici. Atti del XXXV congresso internazionale di studi SLI (Società di Linguistica Italiana), Parigi, 20–22 settembre 2001*, edited by Mathée Giacomo-Marcellesi and Alvaro Rocchetti, 397–416. Roma: Bulzoni.

Dryer, Matthew S. 2013. Coding of Nominal Plurality. In: *The World Atlas of Language Structures Online*, edited by Matthew S. Dryer and Martin Haspelmath. Leipzig: Max Planck Institute for Evolutionary Anthropology (Available online at http://wals.info/chapter/33; last accessed on Nov. 24, 2020).

Duberti, Nicola. 2010. Trin kamlé tikné. Studenti sinti a Rocca de' Baldi (CN). *Bollettino dell'Atlante Linguistico Italiano.* III serie, 34: 37–78.

Duberti, Nicola. 2012. Desinenze e desistenze. Una prima analisi di alcuni dati di coniugazione verbale desunti dalle inchieste ALEPO nelle valli meridionali del Piemonte. In: *Alpi del Mare tra lingue e letterature. Pluralità storica e ricerca di unità*, edited by Nicola Duberti and Emanuele Miola, 43–65. Alessandria: Dell'Orso.

REFERENCES

Duberti, Nicola. 2013. Ignazio Isler. Un nuovo manoscritto. *Studi Piemontesi* 42/1: 229–249.

Duberti, Nicola. 2014. *I costrutti causativi in una varietà galloitalica pedemontana: il dialetto di Rocca de' Baldi*. München: Lincom Europa.

Duberti, Nicola. 2016. *Appunti di piemontese*. https://www.academia.edu/27623977/Appunti_di_piemontese.pdf

Duberti, Nicola. 2018. Il tredicesimo manoscritto. Nuove testimonianze sul canone piemontese. In: *Atti del XXVIII Congresso internazionale di linguistica e filologia romanza (Roma, 18–23 luglio 2016). Volume 2*, edited by Roberto Antonelli, Martin Glessgen, and Paul Videsott, 172–184. Strasbourg: Editions de Linguistique et de Philologie.

Duberti, Nicola, Emanuele Miola and Maria Teresa Milano. 2015. A linguistic sketch of Judeo-Piedmontese and what it tells us about Piedmontese Jews' origins. *Zeitschrift für Romanische Philologie* 131/4: 1042–1064.

Duberti, Nicola and Mauro Tosco. 2021. Teaching Piedmontese: a challenge? In: *Contested Languages: The Hidden Multilingualism of Europe* ("Studies in World Language Problems 8"), edited by Marco Tamburelli and Mauro Tosco, 199–207. Amsterdam: John Benjamins.

Eandi, Enrico 2008. *Ortografia della lingua piemontese: sistema standard e sistemi fonetici*. http://www.piemunteis.it/lese-e-scrive/ortografia-della-lingua-piemontese-sistema-standard-e-sistemi-fonetici; retrieved on Jul. 20, 2016.

Fagard, Benjamin, Jordan Zlatev, Anetta Kopecka, Massimo Cerruti and Johan Blomberg. 2013. The expression of motion events: A quantitative study of six typologically varied languages. *Annual Meeting of the Berkeley Linguistics Society* 39/1: 364–379.

Favaro, Marco and Eugenio Goria. 2019. Effetto del contatto sullo sviluppo di particelle modali. Il caso di *solo*. In: *Le tendenze dell'italiano contemporaneo rivisitate. Atti del LII Congresso Internazionale di Studi della Società di Linguistica Italiana (Berna, 6–8 settembre 2018)*, edited by Bruno Moretti, Aline Kunz, Silvia Natale and Etna Krakenberger, 221–238. Milan: Officinaventuno.

Fedriani, Chiara and Emanuele Miola. 2014. French *déjà*, Piedmontese Regional Italian *già*: A case of contact-induced pragmaticalization. In: *Discourse and Pragmatic Markers from Latin to the Romance languages*, edited by Chiara Ghezzi and Piera Molinelli, 166–189. Oxford: Oxford University Press.

Fedriani, Chiara and Andrea Sansò. 2017. Pragmatic Markers, *Discourse* Markers and Modal Particles. What do we know and where do we go from here? In: *Pragmatic Markers, Discourse Markers and Modal Particles: New perspectives*, edited by Chiara Fedriani and Andrea Sansò, 1–33. Amsterdam: John Benjamins.

Ferrarotti, Lorenzo. 2022. *I dialetti del Piemonte orientale. Contatto e mutamento linguistico*. Berlin: de Gruyter.

Fiorentini, Ilaria. 2017. *Segnali di contatto*. Milano: Franco Angeli.

Forner, Werner. 1988. Metafonesi roiasca nel ligure alpino. In: CSDI, *Elementi stranieri nei dialetti italiani*, vol. 2, 157–168. Pisa: Pacini.

Fraser, Bruce. 1996. Pragmatic markers. *Pragmatics* 6: 167–190.

Fraser, Bruce. 1999. What are discourse markers? *Journal of Pragmatics* 31: 931–952.

Fraser, Bruce. 2009. An account of discourse markers. *International Review of Pragmatics* 1/2: 293–320.

Garuzzo, Sergio. 2011. *Poeti in piemontese della provincia di Alessandria. 1861–2010*. Torino: Ca dë Studi Piemontèis.

Garvin, Paul L. 1951. Review of *Phonemic analysis of the word in Turinese: An analysis of the phonemic structure of the word in Turinese* by James Peter Soffietti. *Language* 27/2: 192–194.

Gasca Queirazza, Giuliano. 1965. *Documenti di antico volgare in Piemonte. Fascicolo I: Le "Recomedaciones" del Laudario di Saluzzo*. Torino: Bottega d'Erasmo.

Gasca Queirazza, Giuliano. 1966a. *Documenti di antico volgare in Piemonte. Fascicolo II: Gli Ordinamenti dei Disciplinati e dei Raccomandati di Dronero*. Torino: Bottega d'Erasmo.

Gasca Queirazza, Giuliano. 1966b. *Documenti di antico volgare in Piemonte. Fascicolo III: Frammenti vari da una Miscellanea Grammaticale di Biella*. Torino: Bottega d'Erasmo.

Gasca Queirazza, Giuliano. 1967. Il «Promptuarium» di Michele Vopisco (Mondovì 1564). In: *Vita e cultura a Mondovì nell'età del Vescovo Michele Ghislieri (San Pio V)*: 185–195. Torino: Deputazione Subalpina di Storia Patria.

Gasca Queirazza, Giuliano. 1971. Per una onomasiologia diacronica: documentazioni medievali per la regione piemontese. In: *Atti del VII Convegno per gli studi dialettali italiani (Torino-Saluzzo, 18–21 maggio 1970)*, Torino: Ca dë Studi Piemontèis, 174–179. Reprinted in: Giuliano Gasca Queirazza. 2010. *Saggi minimi di storia del volgare piemontese (1970–2009)*, edited by Alda Rossebastiano, Elena Papa and Daniela Cacia, 29–38. Alessandria: dell'Orso.

Gasca Queirazza, Giuliano. 1996. Un'ipotesi sulla localizzazione dei *Sermoni subalpini*. *Studi piemontesi* 25: 105–110.

Gasca Queirazza, Giuliano. 2002. Pagine di grammatica del piemontese I. *Studi Piemontesi* 31: 67–70. Reprinted in: Giuliano Gasca Queirazza. 2010. *Saggi minimi di storia del volgare piemontese (1970–2009)*, edited by Alda Rossebastiano, Elena Papa and Daniela Cacia, 285–288. Alessandria: Dell'Orso.

Gasca Queirazza, Giuliano. 2003a. Pagine di grammatica del piemontese II. *Studi Piemontesi* 32: 389–392. Reprinted in: Gasca Queirazza, Giuliano (2010), *Saggi minimi di storia del volgare piemontese (1970–2009)*, edited by Alda Rossebastiano, Elena Papa and Daniela Cacia, 289–292. Alessandria: Dell'Orso.

Gasca Queirazza, Giuliano. 2003b. Pagine di lingua e di esperimentazioni letterarie dai secoli XI–XII al Quattrocento. In: *La letteratura in piemontese dalle origini al Settecento. Raccolta antologica di testi*, edited by Giuliano Gasca Queirazza, Gianrenzo P. Clivio and Dario Pasero, 7–132. Torino: Centro Studi Piemontesi/Ca dë Studi Piemontèis.

Gasca Queirazza, Giuliano. 2003c. Il secondo Cinquecento e il Seicento. In: *La letteratura in piemontese dalle origini al Settecento. Raccolta antologica di testi*, edited by Giuliano Gasca Queirazza, Gianrenzo P. Clivio, and Dario Pasero, 233–301. Torino: Centro Studi Piemontesi, Ca dë Studi Piemontèis.

Gasca Queirazza, Giuliano. 2005. Il sistema verbale del piemontese. In: *Actes du 11ème Colloque des Langues Dialectales. Monaco, 27–28 novembre 2004*. Monaco: Académie des Langues Dialectales: 157–166. Reprinted in: Giuliano Gasca Queirazza. 2010. *Saggi minimi di storia del volgare piemontese (1970–2009)*, edited by Alda Rossebastiano, Elena Papa and Daniela Cacia, 299–308. Alessandria: Dell'Orso: 299–308.

Gasca Queirazza, Giuliano, Gianrenzo P. Clivio and Dario Pasero. 2003. *La letteratura in piemontese. Dalle origini al Settecento*. Turin: Ca dë Studi Piemontèis and Regione Piemonte.

Gentile, Lorenzo. 1911. *Frasario piemontese-italiano, o, Raccolta di frasi e proverbi piemontesi aventi riscontro in italiano*. Ast: Tipografia legatoria popolare astigiana.

Ghezzi, Chiara and Piera Molinelli. 2020. Connectives and cyclicity. From the Latin temporal phrase *illa hora* to the Italian discourse marker *allora*. *Journal of Historical Pragmatics* 21/2: 209–236.

Gibbon, Edward. 1840. *The life of Edward Gibbon, with selection from his correspondence. Volume 1*. Paris: Baudry's European Library.

Giacalone Ramat, Anna. 1995. Sulla Grammaticalizzazione di verbi di movimento: *andare* e *venire* + gerundio. *Archivio Glottologico Italiano* 80: 168–203.

Girardin, Sergi. 1989. Art satìrica e umanità ant la poesìa d'Ignassi Isler. In: *Atti del VI Rëscontr antërnassional dë studi an sla lenga e la literatura piemontèisa*, 15–66. Alba: Famija Albèisa.

Girardin, Sergi. 1995. Pan ëd pròsa, alvà 'd poesìa: l'art ëd Nino Autelli. In: *At dël X Rëscontr antërnassional dë studi an sla lenga e la literatura piemontèisa. Quinsnè 8–9 magg 1993*, edited by Gianrenzo P. Clivio, Dario Pasero, and Censin Pich, 21–44. Ivrea: Ferraro

Goria, Eugenio. forthcoming. Il piemontese in Argentina. Preliminari per un'indagine sociolinguistica. In: *Plurilinguismo e Pianificazione linguistica: esperienze europee ed extraeuropee*, edited by Gabriele Iannaccaro, Barbara Turchetta and Simone Pisano. Alessandria: Dell'Orso.

Grandi, Nicola. 2003. *Morfologie in contatto. Le costruzioni valutative nelle lingue del Mediterraneo*. Milano: Franco Angeli.

Grandi, Nicola. 2020. La diversità inevitabile. La variazione linguistica tra tipologia e sociolinguistica. *Italiano LinguaDue* 12/1: 416–429.

Grassi, Corrado and Tullio Telmon. 1990. Sulla trasferibilità di morfemi tra sistemi linguistici: il caso dei microsistemi dei possessivi in contatto nell'Italia nordoccidentale. In: *Parallela 4*, edited by Monica Berretta, Piera Molinelli and Ada Valentini, 193–205. Tübingen: Gunter Narr.

Grassi, Corrado, Alberto A. Sobrero and Tullio Telmon. 1997. *Fondamenti di dialettologia italiana*. Roma-Bari: Laterza.

Grevisse, Maurice. 1993. *Le bon usage. Grammaire française refondue par André Goosse*. Treizième edition. Paris: Duculot.

Gribaudo, Gianfranco. 1996. *Ël Neuv Gribàud dissionari piemontèis. Tèrsa Edission*. Torino: Daniela Piazza.

Griva, Guido. 2007. *Grammatica della lingua piemontese*. Torino: Viglongo (1st ed. 1980).

Grosso, Michela. 2000. *Grammatica essenziale della lingua piemontese*. Torino: Litoart.

Grosso, Michela. 2002. *Grammatica della lingua piemontese. Nozioni di grafia e morfologia*. Torino: Nòste Rèis—Libreria Piemontese.

Hall, Robert Anderson. 1976. *Proto-Romance phonology*. New York and Amsterdam: Elsevier.

Hull, Geoffrey. 1982. *The Linguistic Unity of Northern Italy and Rhaetia*. PhD Thesis, University of Sidney. Published in 2017 (Sydney: Beta Crucis Editions).

Harley, Heidi and Elizabeth Ritter. 2002. Person and number in pronouns: A feature-geometric analysis. *Language* 78: 482–526.

Haspelmath, Martin. 2001. The European Linguistic Area: Standard Average European: In: *Language Typology and Language Universals. An International Handbook, vol. 2*, edited by Martin Haspelmath et al., 1492–1510. Berlin/New York, Mouton de Gruyter.

Haspelmath, Martin. 2004. Coordinating constructions: An overview. In: *Coordinating Constructions*, edited by Martin Haspelmath, 3–39. Amsterdam: John Benjamins.

Haspelmath, Martin. 2013. Argument indexing: a conceptual framework for the syntactic status of bound personal forms. In: *Languages across Boundaries: Studies in Memory of Anna Siewierska*, edited by Dik Bakker and Martin Haspelmath, 197–226. Berlin: De Gruyter.

Haspelmath, Martin. 2017. Equative constructions in world-wide perspective. In: Yvonne Treis and Martine Vanhove (eds.), *Similative and equative constructions: A cross-linguistic perspective*, 9–32. Amsterdam: John Benjamins.

Haspelmath, Martin. 2018. Cross-indexing is the most common type of subject expression in the world's languages. https://dlc.hypotheses.org/1340; last accessed on Nov. 24, 2022.

Heap, David. 2000. *La variation grammaticale en géolinguistique: les pronoms sujet en roman central*. München: Lincom Europa.

Herslund, Michael. 2003. Articles et classificateurs. *Cahiers Ferdinand de Saussure* 56: 21–33.

Herslund, Michael. 2008. Articles, definite and indefinite. In: *Essays on Nominal Deter-*

mination, edited by Henrik Høek Müller and Alex Klinge, 27–43. Amsterdam: John Benjamins.

Herslund, Michael. 2012. Grammaticalisation and the internal logic of the indefinite article. *Folia Linguistica* 46/2: 341–357 (Special Issue: "The pace of grammaticalization in Romance").

Hummel, Michail. 2014. The adjective-adverb interface in Romance and English. In: *Adjectives in Germanic and Romance*, edited by Petra Sleeman, Freek Van de Velde and Harry Perridon, 35–72. Amsterdam: John Benjamins.

Iannàccaro, Gabriele. 2005. *La scrittura della lingue*. Milano: CUEM.

Irvine, Judith T. and Susan Gal. 2000. Language ideology and linguistic differentiation. In: *Regimes of language: Ideologies, polities and identities*, edited by Paul V. Kroskrity, 35–83. Oxford: James Currey.

Izre'el, Shlomo. 2018. Unipartite clauses: A view from spoken Israeli Hebrew. In: *Afroasiatic: Data and Perspectives*, edited by Mauro Tosco, 235–259. Amsterdam: John Benjamins.

Jackendoff, Ray. 1972. *Semantic Interpretation in Generative Grammar*. Cambridge, MA: M.I.T. Press.

Jochnowitz, George. 1981. Religion and Taboo in Lason Akodesh (Judeo-Piedmontese). *International Journal of Sociology of Language* 30: 107–117.

Jochnowitz, George. No date/a. The Absence of Northern Features in the Judeo-Italian of Lombardy and Emilia, http://www.jochnowitz.net/Essays/JudeoItalian.html; last accessed on Nov. 24, 2022.

Jochnowitz, George, No date/b. From Judeo-Provençal to Judeo-Piedmontese and Western Yiddish, http://www.jochnowitz.net/Essays/from-judeo-provencal-to-judeo-piedmonteseand-western-yiddish.html; last accessed on Nov. 24, 2022.

Joseph, Brian D. 1999. Romanian and the Balkans: Some Comparative Perspectives. In: *The Emergence of the Modern Language Sciences. Studies on the transition from historical-comparative to structural linguistics in honour of E.F.K. Koerner*, edited by Sheila M. Embleton, John E. Joseph and Hans-Josef Niederehe, 217–234. Amsterdam: John Benjamins.

Jungbluth, Konstanze. 2003. Deictics in the Dyad of Conversation. In: *Deictic conceptualisation of space, time and person*, edited by Friedrich Lenz, 13–40. Amsterdam: John Benjamins.

Karan, Elke. 2015. Standardization: What's the Hurry? In: *Developing Orthographies for Unwritten Languages*, edited by Dallas Michael Cahill and Keren Rice, 107–138. Dallas, TX: SIL International.

Kayne, Richard S. 1975. *French Syntax. The Transformational Cycle*. Cambridge, MA: M.I.T. Press.

Klima, Edward S. 1972. How alphabets might reflect language. In: *Language by eye and by ear*, edited by James F. Kavanagh and Ignatius G. Mattingly, 57–80. Cambridge, MA: M.I.T. Press.

Kloss, Heinz. 1967. "Abstand Languages" and "Ausbau Languages." *Anthropological Linguistics* 9/7: 29–41.

Koch, Peter. 2000. Indirizzi cognitivi per una tipologia lessicale dell'italiano. *Italienische Studien. Jahreszeitschrift* 21: 99–117.

Koch, Peter. 2001. Lexical typology from a cognitive and linguistic point of view. In: *Language Typology and Language Universals, Vol. 2*, edited by Martin Haspelmath, Ekkehard König, Wulf Oesterreicher and Wolfgang Raible: 1142–1178. Berlin: de Gruyter.

Koenig, Ekkehard. 2018. Beyond exophoric and endophoric uses: Additional discourse functions of demonstratives. Paper presented at the Workshop *Discourse Functions of Demonstratives*, Uio, Oslo, June 14–15, 2018.

Laenzlinger, Christopher. 2000. French adjective ordering: perspectives on DP-internal movement types. *GG@G (Generative Grammar in Geneva)* 1: 55–104.

La Fauci, Nunzio. 1991. La continuità nella diversità formale: aspetti di morfosintassi diacronica romanza. In: *Innovazione e conservazione nelle lingue*, edited by Vincenzo Orioles, 135–158. Pisa: Giardini.

Lambrecht, Knud. 2001. A framework for the analysis of cleft constructions. *Linguistics* 39: 463–561. DOI: 10.1515/ling.2001.021.

Lane, Pia. 2015. Minority language standardisation and the role of users. *Language Policy* 14/3: 263–283.

Langacker, Ronald W. 1987. *Foundations of Cognitive Grammar. Volume 1: Theoretical Prerequisites*. Stanford, California: Stanford University Press.

Langacker, Ronald W. 1992. The symbolic nature of cognitive grammar: The meaning of *of* and of *of-* periphrasis. In: *Thirty Years of Linguistic Evolution: Studies in Honour of René Dirven on the Occasion of his Sixtieth Birthday*, edited by Martin Pütz, 483–502. Amsterdam: John Benjamins.

Lausberg, Heinrich. 1963. *Romanische Sprachwissenschaft*. Zweite, durchgesehene Auflage. Berlin: de Gruyter (first edition 1956).

Laver, John. 1994. *Principles of phonetics*. Cambridge: Cambridge University Press.

Lazard, Gilbert. 1990. Characteristiques actancielles de l'Européen moyen type. In: *Toward a typology of European languages* ("Empirical Approaches to Language Typology 8"), edited by Johannes Bechert, Giuliano Bernini and Claude Buridant, 241–253. Berlin: Mouton de Gruyter.

Ledgeway, Adam. 2009. *Grammatica Diacronica Del Napoletano*. Tubingen: Niemeyer.

Ledgeway, Adam. 2012. *From Latin to Romance*. Oxford: Oxford University Press.

Ledgeway, Adam. 2016. Varieties in Italy1. In: *Manual of Deixis in Romance Languages*, edited by Federica Da Milano and Kostanze Jungbluth, 5–114. Berlin: de Gruyter.

Ledgeway, Adam. 2020. The north-south divide: Parameters of variation in the clausal domain. *L'Italia Dialettale* 81: 29–78.

Lehmann, Winfred P. 1973. A Structural Principle of Language and Its Implications. *Language* 49/1: 47–66.

REFERENCES

Levinson, Stephen C. 2003. *Space in Language and Cognition: Explorations in Cognitive Diversity*. Cambridge: Cambridge University Press.

Lenker, Ursula. 2010. *Argument and rhetoric: adverbial connectors in the history of English*. New York/Berlin: de Gruyter.

Lombardi Vallauri, Edoardo. 1995. Il sistema dei pronomi dimostrativi dal latino al piemontese (varietà torinese), una catena di trazione morfologica. In: *Dialetti e lingue nazionali. Atti del XXVVII congresso della società di linguistica italiana, Lecce, 28–30 ottobre 1993*, edited by Maria Teresa Romanello and Immacolata Tempesta, 209–225. Roma: Bulzoni.

Lonzi, Lidia. 1991. Il sintagma avverbiale. In: *Grande grammatica italiana di consultazione*, edited by Lorenzo Renzi and Giampaolo Salvi, 341–412. Bologna: il Mulino.

Loporcaro, Michele. 2007. On triple auxiliation in Romance. *Linguistics*, 45/1: 173–222.

Loporcaro, Michele. 2009. *Profilo linguistico dei dialetti italiani*. Bari: Laterza.

Loporcaro, Michele. 2016. Auxiliary selection and participial agreement. In: *The Oxford Guide to the Romance Languages*, edited by Adam Ledgeway and Martin Maiden, 802–818. Oxford and New York: Oxford University Press.

Loporcaro, Michele and Maria Teresa Vigolo. 2002–2003. Accordo per genere del verbo finito in italo-romanzo: l'arco alpino orientale. *Italia Dialettale* 63–64: 7–32.

LRL = Günter Holtus, Michael Metzeltin and Christian Schmitt (eds.). *Lexikon der Romanistischen Linguistik*, 8 vols, Tübingen: Max Niemeyer.

Luraghi, Silvia. 2011. Human landmarks in spatial expressions: From Latin to Romance. In: *Case, Animacy and Semantic Roles*, edited by Seppo Kittilä, Katja Västi and Jussi Ylikoski, 209–234. Amsterdam: John Benjamins.

Luraghi, Silvia. 2014. Plotting diachronic semantic maps: The role of metaphors. In: *Perspectives on Semantic Roles*, edited by Silvia Luraghi and Heiko Narrog, 99–150. Amsterdam: John Benjamins.

Lyons, Christopher. 1999. *Definiteness*. Cambridge: Cambridge University Press.

Maddieson, Ian. 1984. *Patterns of Sounds*. Cambridge University Press.

Maddieson, Ian. 2013a. Front Rounded Vowels. In: *The World Atlas of Language Structures Online*, edited by Matthew S. Dryer and Martin Haspelmath. Leipzig: Max Planck Institute for Evolutionary Anthropology (available online at http://wals.info/chapter/11; last accessed on Nov. 24, 2020).

Maddieson, Ian. 2013b. Vowel Quality Inventories. In: *The World Atlas of Language Structures Online*, edited by Matthew S. Dryer and Martin Haspelmath. Leipzig: Max Planck Institute for Evolutionary Anthropology (available online at http://wals.info/chapter/2; last accessed on Nov. 24, 2020).

Maddieson, Ian. 2013c. Consonant Inventories. In: *The World Atlas of Language Structures Online*, edited by Matthew S. Dryer and Martin Haspelmath. Leipzig: Max Planck Institute for Evolutionary Anthropology (available online at http://wals.info/chapter/1; last accessed on Nov. 24, 2020).

Maddieson, Ian. 2013d. Syllable Structure. In: *The World Atlas of Language Structures Online*, edited by Matthew S. Dryer and Martin Haspelmath. Leipzig: Max Planck Institute for Evolutionary Anthropology (available online at http://wals.info/chapter/12; last accessed on Nov. 24, 2020).

Maiden, Martin. 2009. "From pure phonology to pure morphology. The reshaping of the Romance verb". *Recherches linguistiques de Vincennes* 38: 45–82.

Maiden, Martin. 2016. Inflectional morphology. In: *The Oxford Guide to the Romance Languages*, edited by Adam Ledgeway and Martin Maiden, 497–512. Oxford and New York: Oxford University Press.

Manzini, Maria Rita and Leonardo Maria Savoia. 2005a. *I dialetti italiani e romanci. Morfosintassi generativa, vol. I*. Alessandria: dell'Orso.

Manzini, Maria Rita and Leonardo Maria Savoia. 2005b. *I dialetti italiani e romanci. Morfosintassi generativa, vol. II*. Alessandria: dell'Orso.

Manzini, Maria Rita and Leonardo Maria Savoia. 2005c. *I dialetti italiani e romanci. Morfosintassi generativa, vol. III*. Alessandria: dell'Orso.

Marazzini, Claudio. 1984. *Piemonte e Italia. Storia di un confronto linguistico*. Torino: Centro Studi Piemontesi.

Marazzini, Claudio. 1992. *Il Piemonte e la Valle d'Aosta*. In: *L'italiano nelle regioni. Volume I. Lingua nazionale e identità regionali*, edited by Francesco Bruni, 1–44. Torino: UTET.

Marazzini, Claudio. 1994. *Il Piemonte e la Valle d'Aosta*. In: *L'italiano nelle regioni. Volume II. Testi e documenti*, edited by Francesco Bruni, 1–54. Torino: UTET.

Masini, Francesca. 2012. Costruzioni verbo-pronominali "intensive" in italiano. In: *Language and the brain—Semantics (Proceedings SLI42), Vol. 2*, edited by Pier Mario Bertinetto et al. Roma: Bulzoni [cd-rom].

Masini, Francesca. 2015. Idiomatic verb-clitic constructions: lexicalization and productivity. In: *Morphology and Semantics—MMM9 On-line Proceedings*, edited by Jenny Audring, Jenny et al., 88–104.

Masini, Francesca. 2016. Binominal constructions in Italian of the N1-di-N2 type: towards a typology of Light Noun Constructions. *Language Sciences* 53: 99–113.

Matras, Yaron. 2009. *Language Contact*. Cambridge: Cambridge University Press.

Mauri, Caterina. 2008. *Coordination Relations in the Languages of Europe and Beyond*. Berlin: Mouton de Gruyter.

Mauri, Caterina, Silvia Ballarè, Eugenio Goria, Massimo Cerruti and Francesco Suriano. 2019. KIParla corpus: a new resource for spoken Italian. In: *Proceedings of the 6th Italian Conference on Computational Linguistics CLiC-it* (http://ceur-ws.org/Vol-2481/), edited by Raffaella Bernardi, Roberto Navigli and Giovanni Semeraro (eds.), http://ceur-ws.org/Vol-2481/paper45.pdf; last accessed on Nov. 24, 2022.

Merlo, Clemente. 1936. *Lingue e dialetti d'Italia*. In: *Terra e nazioni. XV. L'Italia. Caratteri generali*, edited by Assunto Mori, 257–280. Milano: Vallardi.

REFERENCES

Merlotti, Andrea. 2017. I sonetti piemontesi di Vittorio Alfieri (1783). Lingua di corte e "nazione piemontese" nell'età di Vittorio Amedeo III. *Studi piemontesi* 46/2: 397–410.

Metzeltin, Michael. 1990. La formazione linguistica di un piemontese del Settecento. In: *Studi di sociolinguistica e dialettologia italiana offerti a Corrado Grassi*, edited by Gaetano Berruto and Alberto A. Sobrero, 97–105. Galatina: Congedo.

Migliorini, Bruno. 1978. *Storia della lingua italiana*. Fifth edition. Firenze: Sansoni.

Miller, Philip. 1992. *Clitics and constituents in Phrase Structure Grammar*. New York: Garland.

Miola, Emanuele. 2012. Birth, Death and Resurrection of Connectives in today's online Piedmontese. *Journal of Historical Linguistics* 2/2: 208–238.

Miola, Emanuele. 2013a. *Innovazione e conservazione in un dialetto di crocevia. Il kje di Prea*. Milano: Franco Angeli.

Miola, Emanuele. 2013b. A Sociolinguistic Account of WikiPiedmontese and WikiLombard. *Sociolinguistica* 27: 116–131.

Miola, Emanuele. 2015a. La tirannia della tastiera. Il caso dell'ortografia piemontese. *Language Problems & Language Planning* 39/2: 136–153.

Miola, Emanuele. 2015b. Per una grammatica del piemontese di oggi: gli aggettivi dimostrativi. *Studi Piemontesi* 44/2: 109–117.

Miola, Emanuele. 2017a. The position of Piedmontese on the Romance grammaticalization cline. *Folia linguistica* 51: 133–167.

Miola, Emanuele. 2017b. Quali fattori accelerano il passo della grammaticalizzazione? Un'indagine su quattro varietà romanze non-standardizzate. *Archivio Glottologico Italiano* 102/2: 108–138.

Miola, Emanuele. 2021. Contested orthographies: a closer look at spontaneous writing in Piedmontese. In: *Contested Languages: The Hidden Multilingualism of Europe* ("Studies in World Language Problems 8"), edited by Marco Tamburelli and Mauro Tosco, 143–162. Amsterdam: John Benjamins.

Molinelli, Piera. 2018. Different Sensitivity to Variation and Change: Italian Pragmatic Markers *dai* vs. Discourse Marker *allora*. In: *Beyond Grammaticalization and Discourse Markers*, edited by Salvador Pons Bordería and Óscar Loureda Lamas, 271–303. Leiden: Brill.

Monachesi, Paola. 1999. *A lexical approach to Italian cliticization*. Stanford: CSLI Publications.

Moseley, Christopher (ed.). 2010. *Atlas of the World's Languages in Danger*. 3rd edn. Paris: UNESCO Publishing. http://www.unesco.org/languages-atlas/index.php?hl=en&page=atlasmap; last accessed on Nov. 24, 2022.

Musso, Giancarlo. 2003. *Gramática astesan-a*. Asti: Gioventura Piemontèisa.

Pacotto, Giuseppe. 1930. La grafia piemontese. Norme per la pronuncia e altri scritti esplicativi. In: Edoardo I. Calvo, *Tutte le poesie piemontesi*. Torino: SELP: 11–15.

ParlaTO, www.corpusparlato.com; last accessed on Nov. 24, 2022.

Parry, Mair. 1991. Le système démonstratif du cairese. In: *Actes du XVIIIe Congrès International de Linguistique et de Philologie Romanes, Université de Treves (Trier), 1986*, edited by Dieter Kremer, 626–631. Tubingen: Max Niemeyer.

Parry, Mair. 1993. Subject clitics in Piedmontese. *Vox Romanica* 52: 96–116.

Parry, Mair. 1994. Posizione dei clitici complemento nelle costruzioni verbali perifrastiche del piemontese. In: *VIII Rëscontr antërnassional dë studi an sla lenga e la literatura piemontèisa: Alba 4–5 magg 1991*, 247–259. Alba: Famija Albèisa.

Parry, Mair. 1995. Costruzioni impersonali in piemontese. In: *At dël XI Rëscontr anternassional dë studi an sla lenga e la literatura piemontèisa, Quinsné, 14–15 magg 1994*, edited by Gianrenzo P. Clivio, Dario Pasero and Censin Pich, 111–123. Turin: Centro Studi Piemontesi / Ca dë Studi Piemontèis.

Parry, Mair. 1997. Piedmont. In: *The dialects of Italy*, edited by Martin Maiden and Mair Parry, 237–244. London: Routledge.

Parry, Mair. 1998. The reinterpretation of the reflexive in Piedmontese: 'impersonal' SE constructions. *Transactions of the Philological Society* 96/1: 63–116.

Parry, Mair. 2005. *Sociolinguistica e grammatica del dialetto di Cairo Montenotte. Parluma 'd Còiri*. Savona: Società Savonese di Storia Patria.

Parry, Mair. 2009. Mutamento linguistico e grammaticalizzazione: uno sguardo sul piemontese. In: *"Quem tu probe meministi". Studi e interventi in memoria di Gianrenzo P. Clivio*, edited by Albina Malerba, 153–176. Turin: Ca dë Studi Piemontèis.

Parry, Mair. 2013. Negation in the history of Italo-Romance. In: *The History of Negation in the Languages of Europe and the Mediterranean*, edited by David Willis, Christopher Lucas, and Anne Breitbarth, 77–118. Oxford: Oxford University Press.

Pasero, Dario. 2011. La grafia dei manoscritti di padre Ignazio Isler e di altri autori del Settecento. In: *La grafia della Lingua Piemontese nei secoli*, 71–89. Vercelli: Vercelli-Viva.

Pasero, Dario. 2013. Il P. Ignazio Isler e la sua opera. In: *Ignazio Isler. Canzoni piemontesi*, edited by Dario Pasero, xi–xlvi. Ivrea: Associazione Culturale «I luoghi e la storia».

Paterson, Linda. 2008. Joan d'Albuzon ~ Nicolet de Turin. En: Nicolet, d'un sognie qu'ieu sognava (BdT 265.2 = 310.1). *Lecturae tropatorum* 1, 2008 http://www.lt.unina.it/Paterson-2008.pdf; last accessed on Nov. 24, 2022.

Patrucco, Elisa. 2002. Dialetto online. *Italiano e oltre* 17: 140–144.

Pellegrini, Giovan Battista. 1975. I cinque sistemi dell'italo-romanzo. In: *Saggi di linguistica italiana. Storia, struttura, società*, edited by Giovan Battista Pellegrini, 55–87. Torino: Boringhieri. First published in: *Revue roumaine de linguistique* 1973/18.2: 105–129.

Pellegrini, Giovanni Battista. 1977. *Carta dei dialetti italiani*. Pisa: Pacini.

Pellegrini, Giovan Battista. 1992. Il 'cisalpino' e l'italo-romanzo. *Archivio Glottologico Italiano* 77: 272–296.

Pennacchietti, Fabrizio A. 2015. The Fuzzy Boundary between Verb and Preposition. The Case of Serial Instrumental Verbs in Chinese. In: *Fuzzy Boundaries: Festschrift für Antonio Loprieno. Vol. 1*, edited by Hans Amstutz, Andreas Dorn, Matthia Müller, Miriam V. Ronsdorf and Sami Uljas, 119–129. Hamburg: Widmaier.

Perrini, Gianluca. 2011. La grafia del piemontese alla Restaurazione fino alla fine dell'Ottocento. In: *La grafia della Lingua Piemontese nei secoli*, 131–142. Vercelli: VercelliViva.

Peyron, Vincenzo Andrea. 1830. *Opere piemontèise*. Turin: Tipografia'd Vittorio Picco.

Pipino, Maurizio. 1783a. *Gramatica Piemontese*. Torino: Reale Stamparia.

Pipino, Maurizio. 1783b. *Vocabolario piemontese* del medico Maurizio Pipino, A sua Altezza Reale Maria Adelaide Clotilde Saveria di Francia, Principessa del Piemonte. Torino: Reale Stamparia.

Poletto, Cecilia and Christina Tortora. 2016. Subject clitics: syntax. In: *The Oxford Guide to the Romance Languages*, edited by Adam Ledgeway and Martin Maiden, 772–785. Oxford: Oxford University Press.

Pons Bordería, Salvador. 2006. A functional approach to discourse markers. In: *Approaches to discourse particles*, edited by Karen Fischer, 77–99. Amsterdam: Elsevier.

Ponza, Michele. 1838. *Donato piemontese-italiano*. Torino: Tipografia Baglione, Melanotte e Pomba.

Priale, Giuseppe. 1973. *Il parlare del "kie" nell'Alta Valle dell'Ellero*. Unpublished thesis, University of Turin.

Putzu, Ignazio. 2017. Tipologia del sardo. In: *Manuale di linguistica sarda*, edited by Eduardo Blasco Ferrer, Peter Koch and Daniela Marzo, 303–319. Berlin and New York: De Gruyter.

Quer, Josep. 2016. Mood. In: *The Oxford Guide to the Romance Languages*, edited by Adam Ledgeway and Martin Maiden, 954–966. Oxford and New York: Oxford University Press.

Quirk, Randolph, Sidney Greenbaum, Geoffrey Leech, and Jan Svartvik. 1985. *A comprehensive grammar of the English language*. London: Longman.

Rainer, Franz. 2016. Derivational morphology. In: *The Oxford Guide to the Romance Languages*, edited by Adam Ledgeway and Martin Maiden, 513–523. Oxford and New York: Oxford University Press.

Ramat, Paolo. 2011. Adverbial grammaticalization. In: *The Oxford Handbook of Grammaticalization*, edited by Bernd Heine and Heiko Narrog, 502–510. Oxford: Oxford University Press.

Ramat, Paolo. 2016. What's in a word? *Skase—Journal of Theoretical Linguistics* 13/2 (Special Issue: Selected papers from the Word-Formation Theories conference, Košice, 26–28 June, 2015. Guest editors: Aleksandra Bagasheva and Jesús Fernández-Dominguez): 106–119.

Ramat, Paolo and Davide Ricca. 1994. Prototypical Adverbs: On the Scalarity/radiality of the Notion of ADVERB. *Rivista di linguistica* 6/2: 289–326.

Ramat, Paolo and Davide Ricca. 1998. Sentence adverbs in the languages of Europe. In: *Adverbial Constructions in the Languages of Europe, Part 1*, edited by Johan van der Auwera: 187–276. Berlin: de Gruyter.

Ramat, Paolo and Ricca, Davide. 2016. Romance: a typological approach. In: *The Oxford Guide to the Romance Languages*, edited by Adam Ledgeway and Martin Maiden, 50–62. Oxford and New York: Oxford University Press.

Ramello, Laura. 2004. La lessicografia piemontese: profilo storico. *Bollettino dell'Atlante Linguistico Italiano*, III serie 28: 27–65.

Regis, Riccardo. 2002. Commutazione di codice e italianizzazione del dialetto in una canzone di Gipo Farassino. *Rivista italiana di linguistica e di dialettologia* 4: 83–92.

Regis, Riccardo. 2005. *Appunti grammaticali sull'enunciazione mistilingue*. München: Lincom.

Regis, Riccardo. 2012a. Verso l'italiano, via dall'italiano: le alterne vicende di un dialetto del Nord-ovest. In: *Coesistenze linguistiche nell'Italia pre- e postunitaria. Atti del XLV Congresso Internazionale della Società di Linguistica Italiana (Aosta-Bard-Torino, 26–28.09.2011)*, edited by Tullio Telmon, Gianmario Raimondi and Luisa Revelli, 263–274. Roma: Bulzoni.

Regis Riccardo. 2012b. Centro/periferia, Torino/Mondovì. In: *Alpi del mare tra lingue e letterature*, edited by Nicola Duberti and Emanuele Miola, 97–118. Alessandria: dell'Orso.

Regis, Riccardo. 2012c. Koinè dialettale, dialetto di koinè, processi di koinizzazione. *Rivista Italiana di Dialettologia* 35: 7–36.

Regis, Riccardo. 2012d. Su pianificazione, standardizzazione, polinomia: due esempi. *Zeitschrift für Romanische Philologie* 128/1: 88–133.

Regis, Riccardo. 2013. I suffissi agentivi in piemontese. Fattori esterni e fattori interni. *Lingua e Stile* 49/2: 249–284.

Regis, Riccardo. 2014. Può un dialetto essere standard? *Vox Romanica* 72–2013: 151–169.

Regis, Riccardo. 2015. Dal dialetto di koinè al dialetto rustico: itinerari (socio)linguistici nella poesia di Remigio Bertolino. *Rivista Italiana di Linguistica e Dialettologia* 17: 71–95.

Regis, Riccardo. 2020. Italoromanzo. *Revue de Linguistique Romane* 84: 5–39.

Renzi, Lorenzo. 1983. Fiorentino e italiano: storia dei pronomi personali soggetto. In: *Italia linguistica. Idee, storia, strutture*, edited by Federico Albano Leoni et al., 223–239. Bologna: il Mulino.

Renzi, Lorenzo, Giampaolo Salvi and Anna Cardinaletti (eds.). 2001. *Grande grammatica italiana di consultazione. II. I sintagmi verbale, aggettivale, avverbiale. La subordinazione*. New edition. Bologna: Il Mulino.

Renzi, Lorenzo and Laura Vanelli. 1983. I pronomi soggetto in alcune varietà romanze. In: *Scritti linguistici in onore di Giovan Battista Pellegrini, 1*. Pisa: Pacini: 121–145.

REP = Cornagliotti, Anna (ed.). 2015. *Repertorio etimologico piemontese*. Torino: Centro Studi Piemontesi/Ca dë Studi Piemontèis.

Retaro, Valentina. 2010. Usi e funzioni di 'allora' e 'ahera' nel parlato arbëresh di Greci. *Bollettino Linguistico Campano* 17: 204–235.

Ricca, Davide. 1993. *I verbi deittici di movimento in Europa: una ricerca interlinguistica*. Firenze: La Nuova Italia.

Ricca, Davide. 1998. Una perifrasi continua-iterativa nei testi piemontesi dal Cinquecento all'Ottocento: TENERE + participio passato. In: *Sintassi Storica. Atti del XXX congresso della Società di Linguistica Italiana*, edited by Paolo Ramat and Emanuele Roma, 345–368. Roma: Bulzoni.

Ricca, Davide. 2001. "Facciamo che andare": sulla semantica di una tipica perifrasi dell'italiano regionale piemontese. In: *La parola al testo. Scritti per Bice Mortara Garavelli*, edited by Carla Marello and Gian Luigi Beccaria, 355–371. Alessandria: Dell'Orso.

Ricca, Davide. 2006. Sulla nozione di dialetto italianizzato in morfologia: il caso del piemontese. In: *Lingua e dialetto nell'Italia del Duemila*, edited by Alberto A. Sobrero and Annarita Miglietta, 129–149. Galatina: Congedo.

Ricca, Davide. 2007. *Morfemi, allomorfie, partizioni: uno sguardo ai paradigmi verbali di latino, italiano e torinese*. Handout pro manuscripto, Zurich January 15, 2007.

Ricca, Davide. 2016. *Piedmontese: A sketch*. Handout of a course held at the Summer School *Linguistics and Language of the Mediterranean*, Cagliari, 20 June 2016.

Ricca, Davide. 2017. Morfomi, allomorfie, partizioni: uno sguardo ai paradigmi verbali del torinese. In: *Di tutti i colori. Studi linguistici per Maria Grossmann*, edited by Roberta D'Alessandro, Gabriele Iannàccaro, Diana Passino and Anna M. Thornton, 257–282. Utrecht: Utrecht University.

Rijkhoff, Jan. 2000. When can a language have adjectives? An implicational universal. In: *Approaches to the Typology of Word Classes*, edited by Petra M. Vogel and Bernard Comrie, 217–257. Berlin: Mouton de Gruyter.

Rijkhoff, Jan. 2002. *The Noun Phrase*. Oxford: Oxford University Press.

Rivoira, Matteo. 2020. Lingue, dialetti e religione nelle aree occitane e francoprovenzali. *Language Problems and Language Planning* 44/3: 320–345.

Rohlfs, Gerhard. 1968. *Grammatica storica della lingua italiana e dei suoi dialetti, vol. II. Morfologia*, Turin: Einaudi (Italian translation of: *Historiche Grammatik der italienischen Sprache und ihrer Mundarten*. Bern: A. Franke A. G. Verlag. Band II Formenlehre und Syntax. 1. Teil: 1950).

Rohlfs, Gerhard. 1969. *Grammatica storica della lingua italiana e dei suoi dialetti, vol. III. Sintassi e formazione delle parole*. Turin: Einaudi. Italian translation of: *Historiche Grammatik der italienischen Sprache und ihrer Mundarten*. Bern: A. Franke A. G. Verlag. Band III Formenlehre und Syntax. 2. Teil 1954.

Ronco, Giovanni. 2015a. La situazione linguistica del Piemonte. In: *Repertorio Etimo-*

logico Piemontese, edited by Anna Cornagliotti, xxxiii–xxxiv. Torino: Centro Studi Piemontesi/Ca dë Studi Piemontèis.

Ronco, Giovanni. 2015b. Caratteristiche principali del piemontese. In: *Repertorio Etimologico Piemontese*, edited by Anna Cornagliotti, xxxv–xliii. Torino: Centro Studi Piemontesi/Ca dë Studi Piemontèis.

Rosenkvist, Henrik and Sanna Skärlund. 2013. Grammaticalization in the present—The changes of modern Swedish *typ*. In: *Synchrony and diachrony: a dynamic interface*, edited by Anna Giacalone Ramat, Caterina Mauri and Piera Molinelli, 313–338. Amsterdam: John Benjamins.

Rossebastiano, Alda and Elena Papa. 2011. Osservazioni sulla grafia dei testi piemontesi delle origini. In: *La grafia della Lingua Piemontese nei secoli*, 21–70. Vercelli: VercelliViva.

Rubat Burel, Francesco, Mauro Tosco and Vera Bertolino. 2006. *Il Piemontese in tasca*. Chivasso: Assimil Italia.

Russi, Cinzia. 2008. *Italian clitics. An empirical study*. Berlin/New York: Mouton de Gruyter.

Salminen, Tapani. 2007. Endangered Languages in Europe. In: *Language Diversity Endangered*, edited by Matthias Brenzinger, 210–232. Berlin: Mouton de Gruyter.

Salvi, Giampaolo and Laura Vanelli. 2011. *Nuova grammatica italiana*. Bologna: Il Mulino.

Salvioni, Carlo. 1886. Antichi testi dialettali chieresi. In: *Miscellanea in onore di Napoleone Caix e Ugo Canello*, 345–355. Firenze: Le Monnier.

Salvioni, Carlo. 1919. Sul dialetto Milanese arcaico. *Rendiconti dell'istituto lombardo di scienze e lettere*, serie II 52: 517–540.

Sanga, Glauco. 1990. La lingua lombarda. Dalla koinè alto-italiana delle Origini alla lingua cortegiana. In: *Koinè in Italia dalle Origini al Cinquecento. Atti del convegno 25–26 settembre 1987*, edited by Glauco Sanga, 79–163. Bergamo: Lubrina.

Sansò, Andrea. 2020. *I segnali discorsivi*. Roma: Carocci.

Savoia, Leonardo. 1997a. Inflectional morphology of the verb. In: *The Dialects of Italy*, edited by Martin Maiden and Mair Parry, 75–86. London: Routledge.

Savoia, Leonardo. 1997b. The geographical distribution of the dialects. In: *The Dialects of Italy*, edited by Martin Maiden and Mair Parry, 225–234. London: Routledge.

Scala, Andrea. 2015. Dal sinto piemontese al piemontese sinto: sulle tracce di una lingua mista. In: *Plurilinguismo e sintassi. Atti del XLVI congresso internazionale di studi della società di linguistica italiana (SLI)—Siena, 27–29 settembre 2012*, edited by Simone Casini, Carla Buno, Francesca Gallina and Raymond Siebetcheu, 255–267. Roma: Bulzoni.

Schiffrin, Deborah. 1987. *Discourse markers*. Cambridge: Cambridge University Press.

Schmid, Heinrich. 1956. Über Randgebiete und Sprachgrenzen. *Vox Romanica* 15/2: 19–80.

Schmid, Stefan. 1999. Per un'analisi del vocalismo italo-romanzo in chiave tipologica. In: *Fonologia e morfologia dell'italiano e dei dialetti d'Italia. Atti del XXXI congresso della Società di Linguistica Italiana*, edited by Paola Benincà, Alberto Mioni and Laura Vanelli, 249–267. Roma: Bulzoni.

Sebba, Mark. 2015. Iconisation, attribution and branding in orthography. *Written Language & Literacy* 18/2: 208–227.

Serianni, Luca. 1989. *Grammatica italiana. Italiano comune e lingua letteraria. Con la collaborazione di Alberto Castelvecchi*. Torino: UTET.

Sgall, Petr. 1987. Towards a Theory of Phonemic Orthography. In: *Orthography and Phonology*, edited by Philip A. Luelsdorff, 1–31. Amsterdam: John Benjamins.

Sheehan, Michelle. 2016. Complex predicates. In: *The Oxford Guide to the Romance Languages*, edited by Adam Ledgeway and Martin Maiden, 981–993. Oxford and New York: Oxford University Press.

Siegel, Jeff. 1985. Koines and Koineization. *Language in Society* 14: 357–378.

Siewierska, Anna. 2004. *Person*. Cambridge: Cambridge University Press.

Smalley, William A. 1963. *Orthography studies: Articles on new writing systems*. London: United Bible Society.

Soffietti, James P. 1949. *Phonemic Analysis of the Word in Turinese*. New York: Columbia University.

Sorace, Antonella. 2000. Gradients in auxiliary selection with intransitive verbs. *Language* 76: 859–890.

Squartini, Mario. 2015. *Il verbo*. Second edition. Roma: Carocci.

Stolz, Thomas. 2007. 'Allora'. On the recurrence of function-word borrowing in contact situations with Italian as donor language. In: *Connectivity in grammar and discourse*, edited by Jochen Rehbein, Christiane Hohenstein, Lukas Pietsch, 75–99. Amsterdam: John Benjamins.

Strik Lievers, Francesca and Miola, Emanuele. 2019. Lì ('there') and là ('over there') in Italian phrasal verbs. *Archivio Glottologico Italiano* 103/1: 75–97.

Talmy, Leonard. 2000. *Toward a Cognitive Semantics. Volume 1: Concept Structuring Systems*. Cambridge, Massachusetts: The MIT Press.

Tamburelli, Marco. 2014. Uncovering the 'hidden' multilingualism of Europe: an Italian case study. *Journal of Multilingual and Multicultural Development* 35: 252–270.

Tamburelli, Marco and Mauro Tosco (eds.). 2021. *Contested Languages: The Hidden Multilingualism of Europe*. Amsterdam: John Benjamins.

Telmon, Tullio. 1988a. Italienisch: Areallinguistik II. Piemont. Aree linguistiche. II. Piemonte. In: *Lexicon der Romanistischen Linguistik*, Band/Volume IV *Italienisch, Korsisch, Sardisch / Italiano, Corso, Sardo*, 469–485. Tübingen: Max Niemeyer.

Telmon, Tullio. 2001. *Piemonte e Valle d'Aosta*. Bari: Laterza.

Telmon, Tullio. 2006. La recente lessicografia amatoriale in Piemonte. In: *Lessicografia dialettale. Ricordando Paolo Zolli*, edited by Francesco Bruni and Carla Marcato, 25–44. Editrice, Roma and Padova: Antenore.

Terracini, Benvenuto A. (ed.). 1924. *Esercizi di traduzione dai dialetti del Piemonte. Torinese*. Torino: Paravia and Firenze: Bemporad.
Terracini, Benvenuto A. (ed.). 1925. *Esercizi di traduzione dai dialetti del Piemonte. Parte terza per la quinta classe*. Torino: Paravia and Firenze: Bemporad.
Terracini, Benvenuto A. 1938. Due composizioni in versi giudeo-piemontesi del secolo XIX. *Rassegna Mensile di Israel* 12: 164–183.
Terracini, Benvenuto A. 1956. Review of Max Berenblut, Max, *A Comparative Study of Judaeo-Italian Translations of Isaiah*, PhD thesis, New York, Columbia University, 1949; *Romance Philology* 10: 243–258.
Tesio, Giovanni. 1991. *Piemonte letterario dell'Otto-Novecento. Da Giovanni Faldella a Primo Levi*. Roma: Bulzoni.
Tesio, Giovanni. 2014. *La poesia ai margini. Novecento tra lingua e dialetto*. Novara: Interlinea.
Tesio, Giovanni. 2016. An Piemonteis. *Torino Sette* n. 1370, weekly insert of *La Stampa* (October 21): 36.
Tesio, Giovanni and Albina Malerba (eds.). 1990. *Poeti in piemontese del Novecento*. Torino: Ca dë Studi Piemontèis.
Thornton, Anna Maria. 2005. *Morfologia*. Roma: Carocci.
Timberlake, Alan. 2007. Aspect, Tense, and Mood. In: *Language Typology and Syntactic Fieldwork, 3: Grammatical Categories and the Lexicon*, edited by Timothy Shopen, 280–333. Cambridge: Cambridge University Press.
Tonso, Livio. 2017. *Le parlate del Canavese*. Alessandria: dell'Orso.
Tosco, Mauro. 2002a. When Clitics Collide: On 'to have' in Piedmontese. *Diachronica* 19/2: 367–400.
Tosco, Mauro. 2002b. N'ortografìa pi "democratica" për ël piemontèis? *Assion Piemontèisa* 9/9 (September 15): 6.
Tosco, Mauro. 2007. Feature-geometry and diachrony: The development of the subject clitics in Cushitic and Romance. *Diachronica* 24/1: 119–153.
Tosco, Mauro. 2008. *Ausbau* is everywhere! *International Journal of Sociology of Language* 191: 1–16.
Tosco, Mauro. 2011a. Between endangerment and Ausbau. In: *Language Contact and Language Decay. Socio-political and linguistic perspectives*, edited by Emanuele Miola and Paolo Ramat, 227–246 [maps: 284–285]. Pavia: IUSS Press.
Tosco, Mauro. 2011b. The Nation-State and Language Diversity. In: *Multilingualism. Language, Power, and Knowledge*, edited by Paolo Valore, 87–101. Pisa: Edistudio.
Tosco, Mauro. 2012. Swinging back the pendulum: French morphology and de-Italianization in Piedmontese. In: *Morphologies in contact*, edited by Martine Vanhove, Thomas Stolz, Aina Urdze and Hitomi Otsuka, 247–262. Berlin: Akademie.
Tosco, Mauro. 2021a. Democracy: a threat to language diversity? In: *Contested Languages: The Hidden Multilingualism of Europe* ("Studies in World Language Problems

REFERENCES

8"), edited by Marco Tamburelli and Mauro Tosco, 41–56. Amsterdam: John Benjamins.

Tosco, Mauro. 2021b. *A Grammar of Gawwada*. Köln: Köppe.

Tosco, Mauro, Francesco Rubat Borel and Vera Bertolino. 2006. *Piemontèis lenga svicia. Lìber ëd travaj për ij giovo*. Torino: Nòste Rèis.

Treis, Yvonne. 2018. Comparative constructions: An Introduction. *Linguistic Discovery* 16/1: i–xxvi.

Tressel, Yvonne. 2004. *Sermoni subalpini: studi lessicali con un'introduzione alle particolarità grafiche, fonetiche, morfologiche e geolinguistiche*. Darmstadt: Wissenschaftliche Buchgesellschaft.

Tuttle, Edward F. 1992. Del pronome d'oggetto suffisso al sintagma verbale. In calce ad una nota salvioniana del 1903. *L'Italia Dialettale* 55: 13–63.

Tuttle, Edward F. 1997. The Veneto. In: *The Dialects of Italy*, edited by Martin Maiden and Mair Parry, 263–270. London: Routledge.

van der Auwera, Johan. 1998. Phrasal adverbials in the languages of Europe. In: *Adverbial Constructions in the Languages of Europe, Part 1*, edited by Johan van der Auwera: 25–146. Berlin: de Gruyter.

van der Auwera, Johan. 1998c. Conclusion. In: *Adverbial Constructions in the Languages of Europe, Part 1*, edited by Johan van der Auwera, 20–23. Berlin: Mouton de Gruyter.

Van Valin, Robert D. and Randy J. LaPolla. 1997. *Syntax: Structure, Meaning, and Function*. Cambridge: Cambridge University Press.

Vendler, Zeno. 1957. Verbs and Times. *The Philosophical Review* 66/2: 143–160.

Villata, Bruno. 1996. *I Sermoni Subalpini e la lingua d'oe*. Montreal: Lòsna e Tron.

Villata, Bruno. 1997. *La lingua piemontese. Fonologia Morfologia Sintassi Formazione delle Parole*. Montréal: Lòsna & Tron.

Villata, Bruno. 2001. Na grafia ùnica për un piemontèis pi fòrt. *La Lòsna* (March 14). www.piemont.org, now accessible at http://www.piemunteis.it/lese-e-scrive/na-grafia-unica-per-un-piemunteis-pi-fort; last accessed on Nov. 24, 2020.

Villata, Bruno. 2009. La lingua piemontese. *Savej*, Torino, http://www.piemunteis.it/gramatica; last accessed on Nov. 24, 2020.

Villata, Bruno. 2010. La grafìa antërnassiunal, përchè? *Ël buletin ëd l'academia* 21: 1–5.

Villata, Bruno. 2010b. Il piemontese lingua ponte tra il francese e l'italiano. https://www.piemunteis.it/studi/villata-bruno/il-piemontese-lingua-ponte-tra-il-francese-e-litaliano#bibliografia; last accessed on Nov. 24, 2020.

Villata, Bruno. 2013. Ël Sessent. *Ël Buletin ëd l'Academia* 26: 1–4.

Villata, Bruno. s.d. Cum as dis an bun piemunteis: espressiun idiomàtiche ant ij rumanz ed Lüis Pietracqua, http://www.piemunteis.it/studi/cum-dis-bun-piemunteis-espressiun-idiomatiche-ant-ij-rumanz-ed-luis-pietracqua; last accessed on Nov. 24, 2020.

Vincent, Nigel. 2016. A structural comparison of Latin and Romance. In: *The Oxford*

Guide to the Romance Languages, edited by Adam Ledgeway and Martin Maiden, 37–49. Oxford and New York: Oxford University Press.

Virdis, Maurizio. 2003. Tipologia e collocazione del sardo tra le lingue romanze. *Ianua: revista philologica romanica* 4: 1–9.

Vitale Brovarone, Alessandro. 1978. La *Passione* di Vercelli: documenti di uso letterario piemontese nel tardo Quattrocento. In: *Lingue e dialetti nell'arco alpino occidentale. Atti del Convegno Internazionale di Torino 12–14 aprile 1976*, edited by Gianrenzo P. Clivio and Giuliano Gasca Queirazza, 39–52. Torino: Ca dë Studi Piemontèis.

Voghera, Miriam. 2013. A case study on the relationship between grammatical change and synchronic variation: The emergence of $tipo_{[-N]}$ in Italian. In: *Synchrony and diachrony: a dynamic interface*, edited by Anna Giacalone Ramat, Caterina Mauri and Piera Molinelli, 283–311. Amsterdam: John Benjamins.

Vv.Aa. 2000. *Piemontèis ëd Biela. Abecedare, gramàtica e sintassi, literatura bielèisa, glossare*. Biella: Ieri e oggi.

Wartburg, Walther von. 1950. *Die Ausgliederung der RomanischenSprachräume*. Bern: Verlag Francke.

Wolf, Heinz Jurgen. 1991. La langue des "Sermoni Subalpini". In: *Atti del VII Rëscontr Antërnassional dë Studi an sla Lenga e la Literatura Piemontèisa*, 237–254. Alba: Famija Albèisa.

Zamboni, Alberto. 1998. Dal latino tardo al romanzo arcaico: aspetti diacronico-tipologici della flessione nominale. In: *Sintassi storica. Atti del XXX Congresso Internazionale della Società di Linguistica Italiana (Pavia, 26–28 settembre 1996)*, edited by Paolo Ramat and Elisa Roma, 127–146. Roma: Bulzoni.

Zanchi, Chiara. 2018. On the Italian demonstratives with attitude: a cognitive intersubjective account. *Archivio Glottologico Italiano* 103/2: 98–128.

Zanuttini, Raffaella. 1987. Negazione e concordanza negativa in italiano e piemontese. *Rivista di Grammatica Generativa* 12: 153–172.

Zanuttini, Raffaella. 1997. *Negation and Clausal Structure*. New York and Oxford: Oxford University Press.

Zörner, Lotte. 1996. Neues zur oberitalienischen Personalendung der 4. Person Präsens -úma. *Vox Romanica* 55: 33–37.

Zörner, Lotte. 1998. *I dialetti canavesani di Courgné, Forno e dintorni*. Cuorgné: CORSAC.

References

Primary Sources

Aime, Marco, Adriano Favole e Maria Teresa Milano. 2013. Trelilu. *Opera buffa alla piemontese*. Boves: Araba Fenice.

Alion, Giovan Giorgio. 1953 [1521]. *Farsa de Pero e Cheirina jugalli, chi littigoreno per un petto*, In: *L'opera piacevole di Giovan Giorgio Alione*, edited by Enzo Bottasso. Bologna: Palmaverde.

Alion, Giovan Giorgio. 2003 [1521]. *Farsa de Zoan Zavatino e de Biatrix soa mogliere e del prete ascoso soto el grometto*. In: *La letteratura in piemontese dalle origini al Settecento. Raccolta antologica di testi*, edited by Giuliano Gasca Queirazza, Gianrenzo P. Clivio and Dario Pasero, 141–188. Torino: Centro Studi Piemontesi/Ca dë Studi Piemontèis.

Anonymous. 1969 [1800–1802]. *Le ridicole illusioni. Un'ignota commedia piemontese dell'età giacobina*. Introduzione, testo, note e glossario a cura di Gianrenzo P. Clivio. Torino: Centro Studi Piemontesi/Ca dë Studi Piemontèis.

Arnolfo, Bartolo. 2021. Ël cunij bianch. *Piemontèis Ancheuj* 39/6: 2.

Artuffo, Carlo. 1960. *I pompista 'd me pais*. Odeon dischi.

Autelli, Nino. 1985 [1931]. *Pan d'coa. Leggende e racconti popolari piemontesi*. Introduzione di Giuseppe Pacotto. Xilografie originali di Pino Stampini. Torino: Edizioni Viglongo [Torino: SELP Studio Editoriale Librario Torinese].

Autelli, Nino. 1983 [1937]. *La muda neuva*. In: Camillo Brero, *Storia della letteratura piemontese*. Terzo volume (Sec XX). Torino: Editrice Piemonte in Bancarella: 77–79 [original in: *Masnà*. Turin: A l'ansëgna dij Brandé].

Barba Sergin. 2021a. Ël pòst ësbalià. *Piemontèis Ancheuj* 39/10: 5–6.

Barba Sergin. 2021b. Tiroma doe note … *Piemontèis Ancheuj* 39/7–8: 8.

Barba Sergin. 2022. A l'é temp d'aniversari. *Piemontèis Ancheuj* 40/4: 2.

Baron, Gianfranch. 2021. Un sachèt ëd caramele. *Piemontèis Ancheuj* 39/9: 15.

Bersezio, Vittorio. 1980 [1863]. *Le miserie 'd Monsù Travet*. Critical edition by Gualtiero Rizzi and Albina Malerba. Torino: Centro Studi Piemontesi/Ca dë Studi Piemontèis.

Bertolino, Remigio. 1986. *L'eva d'ënvern*. Mondovì: Amici di Piazza/Edizioni "Ël Pèilo."

Bertolino, Remigio. 2006. *Stanse d'ënvern*. With an introduction by Elio Gioanola. Genova: Edizioni San Marco dei Giustiniani.

Bodrero, Antonio. 2011. *Opera poetica occitana*. Milano: Bompiani.

Bodrié, Tòni [Antonio Bodrero]. 2000. *Dal prim uch a l'aluch*. Turin: Ca dë studi piemontèis.

Bonavero, Michele [Bonavé, Michel dij]. 2018. *Stòrie d'ordinaria portierìa. Monòlogh an lenga piemontèisa*. https://pms.wikisource.org/wiki/Michel_dij_Bonav%C3%A9/St%C3%B2rie_d%27ordinaria_portier%C3%ACa/P%C3%A0gina_2

Bonavero, Michele [Bonavé, Michel dij]. 2020. Le paròle con le bestie e le bestie con le paròle. *Corriere AVIS Torino*. 3/2020: 33.

Bré, Milo. 2019. *An mes a l'erba*. https://pms.wikisource.org/wiki/Milo_Br%C3%A9/An_mes_a_l%27erba

Brero, Camillo. 1972. *Amor polid e àutre conte*. Turin: Ij Brandé.

Brero, Camillo. 1978. *Arsetari dla cusin-a piemontèisa*. Torino: Piemonte in bancarella.

Brero, Camillo. 1984. *Evangeli ëd San Gioann*. Turin: Piemontèis Ancheuj.

Bré, Milo and Barba Guido (eds). 2011. *Fàule, conte e legende dla tradission popolar piemontèisa*. Torino: Piemonte in Bancarella.

Burat, Tavo. 1990. La storia del «Gran Fumé a l'Aramé». In: *Ij Brandé. Armanach ëd poesìa piemontèisa*. https://pms.wikisource.org/wiki/Tavo_Burat/Na_st%C3%B2ria_%27d_Sord%C3%A8ivo

Burzio, Beppe. 2003. "Televendite con ël trocion," *Assion piemontèisa* 10/1 (January 2003): 1. https://pms.wikisource.org/wiki/Beppe_Burzio/Televendite_con_%C3%ABl_trocion

Buzzati, Dino. 2000. San Gancil (I Santi). In: *La boutique del mistero*. Milano: Mondadori. Unpublished Piedmontese translation by Renato Agagliate. https://giannidavico.it/gopiedmont/files/2014/01/San-Gancil.pdf

Calvo, Ignassi Edoard. 2003 [1816]. *Fàule moraj con le stanse a Mëssé Edoard*, edited by Fransesch Rubat Borel. Turin: Nòste Rèis Associassion Coltural Piemontèisa.

Calvo, Edoardo Ignazio. 1803. *Petission dij can a l'Ecelensa Ministr dla Poliss*. In: *La letteratura in piemontese dalla stagione giacobina alla fine dell'Ottocento. Raccolta antologica di testi*, edited by Gianrenzo P. Clivio and Dario Pasero. 2004: 64–69. Torino: Centro Studi Piemontesi/Ca dë Studi Piemontèis: 64–69. https://www.europacristiana.com/anche-i-Anche i giacobini dicono la loro in piemontese: Edoardo Ignazio Calvo (1773–1804)—1—Europa Cristiana.

Calvo, Edoardo Ignazio. ³1816. *Poesie scritte in dialetto piemontese*. Turin: Pomba.

Calvo, Edoardo Ignazio. 1845. *Follie religiose. Poema in dialetto piemontese di Edoardo Calvo*. Brusselle: Vimargy.

Carle Anna Maria and Olinto Ricossa. 2021. Le cese 'd Turin. *Piemontèis Ancheuj* 39/2: 4.

Castellina, Paolo. 2021. *Dumìnica 24 'd Gené 2021. Leture bìbliche an piemontèis*. Dumìnica 24 'd Gené 2021—Leture bìbliche an piemontèis | La Bibia piemontèisa (tempodiriforma.it)

Cerrato, Natale. 1981. *Car ij me fieuj. Miei cari figlioli. Il dialetto piemontese nella vita e negli scritti di don Bosco*. Foreword by Gaetano G. di Sales. Roma: Libreria Ateneo Salesiano.

Chessa, Fernando. 2005. A-i era na vira la Fiat. *é!* 7: 5.

Chessa, Fernando. 2006. Monsù Chirac e la liberta 'd religion. *é!* 1: 5–6.

Chiapetto, Mario and John Hajek. 2012. *Pipì a va a spass (Chicken Little goes for a walk)*. Melbourne, Victoria (Australia): RUMACCC. https://arts.unimelb.edu.au/__data/assets/pdf_file/0006/1821669/cl-piedmontese-bw_0.pdf

Clivio, Gianrenzo P. 1972. *Un di marcc-rai da sol*. In: Renzo Gandolfo, *La Letteratura in Piemontese dal Risorgimento ai giorni nostri*. Torino: Centro Studi Piemontesi/Ca dë Studi Piemontèis: 393–394. https://pms.wikisource.org/wiki/Gianlorenzo_Clivio/Un_d%C3%AC_marcc-rai_da_sol

Coccio, Carlo. 1966. *Rime infilssà*. Mondovì: Tipografia Fracchia.

Comollo, Adriana. 2005. Doe vache a tiro anans na cassin-a. *é!* 4: 5–6.

Cosio, Tavio. 1975. *Pere gramon e lionsa. Conte an piemontèis ëd Vilafalet e dj'anviron. Con prefassion ëd Tòni Bodrìe*. Torino: Centro Studi Piemontesi/Ca dë Studi Piemontèis.

Cosio, Tavio. 1980. *Sota ël chinché. Conte piemontèise*. Presentazione di Giuliano Gasca Queirazza. Torino: Centro Studi Piemontesi/Ca dë Studi Piemontèis.

Costa, Nino. 1982a. [1928]. *Brassabòsch. Poesie piemontèise*. Torino: Andrea Viglongo & C. [Torino: Libreria Editrice F. Casanova & C.].

Costa, Nino. 1982b [1938]. *Ròba nòstra*. Torino: Viglongo.

Costa, Nino. 2014. *Cento poesie piemontesi*. Prefazione di Albina Malerba e Giovanni Tesio. Milano: La Civiltà Cattolica/Corriere della Sera.

Davico, Gianni. 2016. *A tuta cana*. https://giannidavico.it/gopiedmont/2016/11/30/a-tuta-cana/

D'Azeglio, Massimo. 1989. *Epistolario (1841–1845)*. Edited by Georges Virlogeux. Torino: Centro Studi Piemontesi/Ca dë Studi Piemontèis.

Demichelis, Carlo. No date. *Coma a fonsion-a ël Conteur Geiger-Müller*. Cita nòta ëd Carlo Demichelis. conteurg.pdf (libero.it).

dij Bonavé Michel [Michele Bonavero]. 2022. Un sécol ëd dosseur. *Piemontèis Ancheuj* 40/7–8: 13.

Donna, Sergio. 2015. *Salut a Tòjo*. Testo dell'intervento in lingua piemontese tenuto da Sergio Donna alla «Vijà» in memoria dell'amico Vittorio Fenocchio (Tòjo Fnoj) sabato 26 settembre. https://www.civico20news.it/sito/articolo.php?id=17419.

Donna, Sergio. 2021. Riflession sla lenga piemontèisa. *Piemontèis Ancheuj* 39/4: 10.

Donna, Sergio. 2022. *Cerea. Archeujta 'd poesìe piemontèise*. Turin: Ël Torèt-Monginevro Cultura.

Dorato, Bianca. 1990. *Drere 'd lus*. Mondovì: Amici di Piazza/Edizioni "Ël Pèilo."

Dorato, Bianca. 1998. *Fiòca e òr*. Mondovì: Amici di Piazza/Edizioni "Ël Pèilo."

Duberti, Nicola. 1996. *Varsci*. Mondovì: Il salice dorato.

Eandi, Enrico. 2006. La question dla grafìa. *é!* 14: 18.

Ellena, Carlo. 2022. N'alba 'n sl'Albergian. *Piemontèis Ancheuj* 40/4: 10.

Faldella, Giovanni. 1974 [1868]. *Un bacan spiritual*. Inedita commedia in piemontese. A cura di Caterina Benazzo. Torino: Centro Studi Piemontesi/Ca dë Studi Piemontèis.

Ferrero, Alfonso. 1970. *Létere a Mimì e àutre poesìe*. Turin: Ca dë Studi Piemontèis.

Ferrero, Carlo Bernardino. 1981 [1888]. *La cracia. Romans dal ver*. Torino: Andrea Viglongo & C.

Ferrero, Anna, Fulvia Lupo and Marina Lupo. 2006. *Prima Mignin*. Torino: Ca dë Studi Piemontèis and Regione Piemonte.

Ferrua-Clerico, G. Odoardo. 1871. *Pamparato*. Mondovì: Fracchia.

Frusta, Arrigo. 1969. *Fassin-e 'd sabia. Pròse piemontèise*. A cura di Gianrenzo P. Clivio. Torino: Centro Studi Piemontesi/Ca dë Studi Piemontèis.

Gambarotta, Bruno. 2003. Storie di Città. *La Stampa. Torino Sette*, October 17, 2003.

Garelli, Federico. 1873. *Un neuv Giòb o La cabana dël re galantòm*. In: Federico Garelli. 1873–1876. *Teatro comico in dialetto piemontese*. Volume Secondo. Torino: Stamperia Gazzetta del Popolo.

Garelli, Federico. 1874a. *Chi romp a paga. Commedia brillante in tre atti*. In: Federico Garelli. 1873–1876. *Teatro comico in dialetto piemontese*. Volume Quinto. Torino: Stamperia Gazzetta del Popolo.

Garelli, Federico. 1874b. *Delfina l'ovriera. Commedia popolare in tre atti*. In: Federico Garelli. 1873–1876. *Teatro comico in dialetto piemontese*. Volume Quinto. Torino: Stamperia Gazzetta del Popolo.

Garelli, Federico. 2001 [1874]. *La vos dl'onor*. Turin: Gioventura Piemontèisa.

Garuss, Sergi. 2004a. Lòn che a-i càpita. *é!* 2: 4.

Garuss, Sergi. 2004b. Gipo a buta le scòle a scòla ëd piemontèis. *é!* 4: 4–5.

Geymet, Enrico. 1834. *'L Testament Neuv de Noussëgnour Gesù-Crist tradout in lingua piemonteisa*. London: dai torchi di Moyes.

Girardin, Sergi. 2016. Lus e top: deje 'n nòm a le nuanse dl'ànima: un prim tentativ an sla poesìa 'd Bianca Dorato. *La slòira* 86: 12.

Girardin, Sergi. 2020. Dissionari dla lenga piemontèisa a usagi literari. *Piemontèis Ancheuj* 38/12: 10–12.

Giovannini, Pietro. 2017. *Piemontèis*, September 17, 2017. http://anviagi.it/26/piemonteis.

Goria, Giusep. 2000. *Serman e poesie*. Ivrea: Ferraro.

Il vangelo di San Matteo volgarizzato in dialetto piemontese. 1861. Londra: Strangeways and Walden.

Invernizio, Carolina. 1976 [1890]. *Ij delit d'na bela fia*. Turin: Viglongo.

Isler, Ignazio. 2013 [1799]. *Canzoni piemontesi*. A cura di Dario Pasero. Ivrea: Associazione Culturale "I Luoghi e la Storia."

Lachello, Beppe. 2021a. Ij castej minor dël Piemont: Olesc Castel. *Piemontèis Ancheuj* 39/3: 4.

Lachello, Beppe. 2021b. Ij castej minor dël Piemont: Soris. *Piemontèis Ancheuj* 39/7, 8: 5.

Lachello, Beppe. 2022. Ij castej minor dël Piemont: Cangia. *Piemontèis Ancheuj* 40/7, 8: 8.

La slòira. 2002. December.

Leoni, Mario. 1986 [1877]. *'L sàut dla bela Auda. Romans piemontèis*. Torino: Viglongo [1877: Libreria Editrice della Famiglie].

REFERENCES

Malerba, Albina (edited by). 1979. *La Cichin-a 'd Moncalé*. Torino: Ca dë Studi Piemontèis.

Malerba, Albina. 2015. An piemontèis. *La Stampa. Torino Sette*, January 22, 2015. https://www.lastampa.it/torinosette/rubriche/an-piemonteis/2015/01/22/news/an-piemonteis-1.37672666

Mania Reida, Cap. 1995 [1902]. *Le straodinarie aventure 'd Martin Cassul a n'Africa*. Torino: Viglongo.

Menietti, Piergiuseppe. 2022. Ël teatro roman. *Piemontèis Ancheuj* 40/7,8: 5.

Mottura, Armando. 2009. *Rossòt. Stòria d'un pòvr diav. Bossèt ant un at*. In: Armando Mottura. *Teatro*. Edizione critica delle commedie a cura di Dario Pasero. Premessa di Giovanni Moretti. Ivrea: Ca dë Studi Piemontèis-La Slòira: 25–52.

Nicòla, Alfredo. 2007. *Poesìe*. Ivrèja: La Slòira-Ca dë Studi Piemontèis.

Nigra, Costantino. 1888. *Canti popolari del Piemonte*. Torino: Loescher.

Oddoero, Luigi. No date. *Na portiera ficapocio*. Commedia brillante in tre atti in lingua piemontese. https://www.ateatro.info/copioni/na-portiera-ficapocio/

Oddoero, Luigi. 1989. *Tant fracass për niente*. Commedia brillante in dialetto piemontese. http://www.piccolovarieta.com/copioni/TANTFRACASSPERNIENTE.pdf

Oddoero, Luigi. 2012. *Na tòta sfaragià*. Commedia brillante in tre atti in dialetto piemontese. http://www.piccolovarieta.com/copioni/NATOTASFARAGIA.pdf

Pacòt, Pinin. 1956. Teatro'd Motura. *Ij Brandé* 234–235: 930.

Pacòt, Pinin. 1967. *Poesìe e pàgine 'd pròsa*. Torino: Centro Studi Piemontesi/Ca dë Studi Piemontèis.

Pansoya, Giovanni Ignazio. 1827. *Ricreassion d' l'Autôn*. Turin: Sylva.

Pasquero, Dino and Giorgio Salvaja. 1992. *Sudor antich: stisse pressiose cujìe e smonùe da vajant ëscritor*, con tërdes taule ëd Pino Pasquero e fòto scatà o bele mach sernùe da Giorgio Salvaja. Turin: Pro Piemonte.58

Pich, Censin and Dario Pasé. 1996. *Sapej. Pròse piemontèise*. Ivrea: Tipografia Ferraro.

Pietracqua, Luigi. 1859a. *Gigin a bala nen: misteri'd na soffiëtta*. Commedia in tre atti. Torino: Stamperia Gazzetta del Popolo.

Pietracqua, Luigi. 1859b. *Sablin a bala. Misteri d'un pruché*. Torino: Stamperia Gazzetta del Popolo.

Pietracqua, Luigi. 1871. *Spatuss e debit*. Torino: Luigi Mattirolo.

Pietracqua, Luigi. 1974 [1891]. *La bela panatera ëd Pòrta Palass*. Torino: Andrea Viglongo & C.

Pietracqua, Luigi. 1979 [1877]. *Lucio dla Veneria. Stòria dij temp 'd na vòlta*. Testo riveduto corretto e integrato nella grafia moderna unificata. Annotato ed illustrato. Torino: Andrea Viglongo & C.

Pipino, Maurizio. 1783. *Poesie piemontesi*. Torino: Stamperia Reale.

Rabia, Candida. 2022. Nòst salut a un grand dël Pì-a-mont: ël magìster Angelo. *Piemontèis Ancheuj* 40/2–3: 8.

Ravizza, Luciano. 2004. An ricòrd. *é* 5: 21.
Regis, Carlo. 1960. Agost '44. In: *Cantoma pian*, edited by Ernesto Billò et al., 110. Torino: Edizioni del Cenacolo. https://www.facebook.com/unionemonregalese/photos/ma ce-%C3%ABd-sangh-su-la-piassa-stamatinan-sle-pere-grise-sul-murajon-scrost% C3%A0doi-p%C3%B3vr/1259159650910021/
Ronco, Umberto Luigi. 1968. Partisan con folar ensangonà. *Armanach dij Brandé*: 30–31. https://www.studipiemontesi.it/tag/umberto-luigi-ronco/
Saint-Exupéry, Antoine de. 2005 [1946]. *Ël Cit Prinsi*. Con j'aquarele dl'Autor. Version piemontèisa d'Adriana Chiabrando. Turin: Gioventura Piemontèisa. [*Le Petit Prince*. Paris: Gallimard].
Saint-Exupery, Antoine de. 2016. *Il piccolo principe*, transl. by Franco Perini. Milano: Liberi Pomi.
Sandron, Silvio [Sandrone, Silvio]. 2005. Pì nen d'ëstrangé. *é!* 4: 9.
Sandrone, Silvio. 2004a. L'ëspasse dij privà ant l'ëspasse. *é!* 1: 10–13.
Sandrone, Silvio. 2004b. Në statù tròp coragios. *é!* 3: 7.
Sandrone, Silvio. 2004c. Barba John: leture da gabinet. *é!* 1: 20.
Sandrone, Silvio. 2006. Ël Piemont che an pias nen. *é!* 11: 3.
Sané, Bepe. 2006. I soma pront për ël web 2.0? *é!* 14: 20.
Sapino, Silvana. 2021. *Ciapa lì!* Ivreja: Priuli & Verlucca.
Sautabachëtte. 2006. Dai partì dla drita e dla gàucia. *ALP* 55/1: 1.
Siròt, Paolin. 2004a. Pòche teste ... tante idèje. *è!* 2: 17
Siròt, Paolin. 2004b. "Sagrin e Speranse" ... Fantasma. *é!* 4: 19.
Soldati, Mario. 2010. *Le due città*. Milano: Mondadori [First edition: Milano: Garzanti: 1964].
Solferini, Amilcare. 1923. *Mentre la tera a gira*. Torino: Pasta.
Tana, Carlo Giambattista. 1784. *Il conte Pioletto*. Torino: Briolo.
Tesio, Giovanni. 2017. *Vita dacant e da canté*. Turin: Ca dë Studi Piemontèis.
Tosco, Mauro. 2004. Ij përchè d'"é!" *é!* 1: 3.
Tosco, Mauro. 2006. Quand l'amor (për l'ambient) a massa. *é!* 13: 10.
Tron e Lòsna. 2008. A metà 'd luj a l'é mancaje Guido Amoretti. *Tron e Lòsna* 46: 14.
Tuberga, Eleonora and Franco Antonel. 2021. Un pòst da setesse. *Piemontèis Ancheuj* 39/9: 10.
Tuberga, Eleonora and Franco Antonel. 2022. Ël pedigrì, salvacondòt për ij pardon. *Piemontèis Ancheuj* 40/4: 8–9.
Vaira, Luigi Lorenzo. 2020. Ij brichèt ëd montagna. *Piemontèis Ancheuj* 38/10: 13.
Vaira, Luigi Lorenzo. 2021. Farinel. *Piemontèis Ancheuj* 39/12: 9–10.
Vielmin, Fabrissi. 2005. Le reis ëd la cris ëd l'Euròpa. *é!* 9: 6.

Videos, Multimedia and Websites

https://youtu.be/KOHcvYmd8mw, Il Piemontese moderno, *Nen tante bale*; last accessed on Nov. 24, 2022.

https://www.youtube.com/watch?v=leTHdhbQ1kw, La Lionetta, *Prinsi raimund—1978*; last accessed on Nov. 24, 2022.

https://vimeo.com/42639684, Nuzweb.tv, *Chej-si vard-je*; last accessed on Nov. 24, 2022.

https://www.youtube.com/watch?v=CnhuKyxf134, Trelilu, *Tersilla*; last accessed on Nov. 24, 2022.

Miola, Emanuele. 2015c. *Piemontèis e tipologia. Il Piemontese tra le lingue d'Europa*; https://www.studipiemontesi.it/il-piemontese-tra-le-lingue-deuropa/; last accessed on Nov. 24, 2022.

Novero, Gianfranco. No date. *Ël gatin e la volp*. https://pms.wikisource.org/wiki/Gianfranco_Novero/Ël_gatin_e_la_volp; last accessed on Nov. 24, 2022.

Piedmontese Wikipedia: https://pms.wikipedia.org/wiki/Intrada; last accessed on Nov. 24, 2022.

Index of Subjects

Adjectives
    Classes   151–155
    degrees of comparison   158–161
    derivation   162–167
    semantic categories   149–151
    stem allomorphy   155–158
Adverbs
    functional classification   356
    morphological classification   357
Approximants
    Approximant alveolar   61–62
    Delateralization   76
    Deletion   76
    Gliding   75–76
Articles ☞ Determiners; Indefinite
Ausbauization   166, 281, 445, 493, 501, 503, 517–524

Back /a/   64

Clefts   480–482
Clusters
    Gemination   93–94
    Cluster Reduction   81
    Three-consonant clusters   91–94
    Word-final   92
    Word-initial   87–92
    Word-internal   92–94
    Word-internal with identical consonant   92–93
Codeswitching   1, 501, 503–504, 506–510, 516
Colors   150, 155, 498–499
Contact
    Piedmontese in different regional varieties of Italian and other languages   513
    Piedmontese in the regional Italian of Piedmont   509–512

Demonstratives
    local variation   224–225
Determiners:
    allomorphy   210–213
Dialects
    classification   18–19
    orthography   64–65, 103–104

Dubitative
    as a marker of future tense   311–313

Endangerment   1, 501, 506, 518
Exhortative   179, 186, 283, 316–317, 352, 431–433

Focus   169, 412, 480–481, 483, 487
Frenchization   521–523
Future ☞ Dubitative

Glides ☞ Approximants
Gliding   75–76

Homophones   14n23, 62, 66, 122–123, 133n5, 179, 212, 261, 308, 371, 372n12, 433, 496, 523
Homographes   122

Immediative   351–353
Indefinite   199–200, 203, 208–210, 212–214
Italianization, Italianisms   6, 10, 31, 66, 152, 159, 321–320, 460 n., 486, 515–516, 518

Jespersen's cycle   475, 497
Juxtaposition
    in adjectives   167
    in adverbs   216
    in clauses and phrases   442–443

Main:
    Imperfect   296–299
        local variation   298–299
Main:
    Past   299–300
Main:
    Pluperfect   300–303
Main:
    Present   293–296
Medio-palatal phonemes   65
Metaphors
    AGENTS ARE SOURCES   381
    BENEFICIARIES ARE DESTINATIONS   375
    INSTRUMENT IS A COMPANION   385
    POSSESSORS ARE SOURCES   394
Music   54–57

INDEX OF SUBJECTS 567

Nasals
   Develarization 80–81
Newspapers 46–47, 106, 514
Nouns
   inflectional classes 129–131
   semantics 128–129
Numerals
   gender in numerals 230–231
      local variation in gender 233–234
   old forms 232–233
Possessives:
   local variation 226–227
Pronouns
   Personal Pronouns:
      categories 168–169
   Independent Pronouns: 176–177
      as markers of politeness 173
      dialect variation 168, 171–173
      exclusive vs. inclusive
   Indirect Object pronoun for locative 183–185
   Reflexive pronoun as an impersonal 188
   Subject Clitic pronouns:
      dialect variation 180
      feature geometry 177–178
      variation and obligatoriness 177–179
Topic 169, 479–480, 486
Verbs
   agreement 249–250
      local variation in gender agreement 250
   auxiliaries 251–255

      local variation 259–263
      paradigms 261–263
      prefixal element in the tensed forms 252–253
   classes 251–252
   early treatment of the system
   Infinitive 252–253
      local variation
   irregular verbs 256–257
      First Class 256–259
      Second Class 246–248
   labile
   local variation in person marking 316
      in the Conditional 316
      in the First person Singular 279–282
      in the Second person Singular 279–282; 334
   neologisms 245–246
   semantic categories
Vowels
   Centralization 71–73
   Delateralization 76
   Deletion 75–76
   Epenthesis 73
   Closing 75
   Back Raising 74–75
   Dropping 74
   Gliding 75
   length 94

Word order 417, 476–480

Index of Languages, Varieties and Language Groups

Corsican 6

Daco-Romance 5
Dalmatian 5
Danish 28
Dutch 28, 500

Emilian 1, 3 Map, 4, 9–11, 19
English 109, 110 n., 114–115, 140, 146, 204, 215–216, 358, 362, 449 n., 487, 492–493, 498, 522

Franco-Provençal 2–3, 5, 8–10, 20, 23, 26
French 2, 5–7, 10–11, 13, 17, 22–30, 33, 53, 61, 66, 71, 73, 103, 131, 140–141, 150, 154, 156, 183, 204, 233, 251, 261, 283, 286, 313, 322, 326–327, 337, 339, 370376, 399, 406–407, 484, 489–491–494, 497–500, 509, 517, 520–552

Gallo-Italic 1, 4–7, 10, 61, 250, 283, 489, 500
German 28, 492, 494, 500
    Swiss 2
Greek (Modern) 492

Ibero-Romance 5

Italian 2, 4–7, 9, 20, 22–32, 34, 37–38, 45, 59, 65–69, 72–73, 79–82, 98 n., 109, 112–113, 116, 131, 134, 141–142, 154–155, 159, 163, 183, 191, 204–206, 209, 236, 242, 246, 251, 261, 281, 284–286, 289, 292, 311, 313, 320–322, 326–328, 330, 334, 338, 344, 348–349, 351 n., 352 n., 358, 365, 369, 371–372, 375, 381, 388, 390, 392, 395, 398–399, 411, 437, 445, 460 n., 464 n., 469, 478, 483–484, 486, 488, 490–491–495, 497–503, 505–514, 516–524

Italo-Romance 5–6, 489, 500

Kje 103, 233, 252

Latin 5, 7–8, 13, 17, 22–23, 25–27, 29, 33, 65, 67, 101, 103, 110–112, 122, 138, 173, 183, 232, 251–255, 260, 282, 284, 322, 328, 331, 354 n., 357, 359, 371–372, 374, 377, 392, 433, 448, 464, 484486, 489490, 492, 494, 497, 519, 524
Ligurian 1n2, 3 Map, 4, 9–11, 13, 19, 57, 62, 103, 233, 284, 316, 354
Lombard 1–4, 9–11, 13, 19, 23, 25, 207, 212, 233, 316, 354, 500, 515n.

Neapolitan 371, 513

Occitan 2–3, 5, 8, 10–11, 13, 17, 20, 22–24, 26, 33, 38, 45, 49, 51–52, 54, 61, 65, 80, 103, 141, 180, 207, 233, 279, 282, 284, 286, 489, 491, 499–500

Portuguese 28, 285–286, 354n8

Rhaeto-Romance 5, 500
Roman, Romanesco 513
Romanian 71, 492–493, 496

Sardinian 5, 493, 513
Standard Average European 489, 499–500
Swedish 28, 494

Turinese 5
Tuscan ☞ Italian

Walser 2–3

Index of Towns, Villages, and Geographical Terms in Piedmont

Piedmontese/Italian denomination

Alba / Alba   57
Alpëtte / Alpette   413, 486
Aron-a / Arona   50
Assèj / Acceglio   282
Ast / Asti   13 f., 25, 28, 37, 225

Biela / Biella   14, 52, 103, 104, 212, 225, 326, 340, 427–428
Bormia / Bormida   11, 492

Canavzan / Canavese   9, 11–14, 19, 107, 212, 252, 283–284, 299, 316, 486, 491
Carù / Carrù   307
Casal Monfrà / Casale Monferrato   33, 111
Castel d'Anon / Castello di Annone   49
Castelmagn / Castelmagno   282
Castelneuv Brusà / Castelnuovo Calcea   44
Cavlimor / Cavallermaggiore   57
Chér / Chieri   38, 71, 111, 503
Cheuri / Corio   282
Chison / Chisone   22
Ciusèila / Chiusella   9
Colègn / Collegno   481
Condòve / Condove   502
Coni / Cuneo   9, 28, 45, 51, 54, 180, 208, 326, 380
Corgné / Cuorgné   486
Crava / Crava ☞ La Ròca / Rocca de' Baldi

Druent / Druento   51

Entrèive / Entracque   38

Favria / Favria   39
Frabosa Sovran-a / Frabosa Soprana   491
Frasso / Frassino   51

Garess / Garessio   17
Germanasca / Germanasca   22é
Gess / Gesso   9
Giaven / Giaveno   338

Ivreja / Ivrea   47, 54

Langhe / Langhe   9, 14, 63, 103–104, 107, 279, 281, 490
Lans / Lanzo   23, 279, 281
La Ròca / Rocca de' Baldi   294
Limon / Limone Piemonte   282
Lissandria / Alessandria   13, 14, 24, 51, 53, 208, 476
(ël) Mango / Mango   50

Massran / Masserano   182
(ël) Mel / Melle   53
Moncalé / Moncalieri   283
Moncalv Monfrà / Moncalvo Monferrato   50
(ël) Mondvì / Mondovì   9, 13, 20, 23–24, 45, 52–53, 104, 208, 236, 282–283, 290–291, 300 303, 311, 316, 340, 437
Monfrà / Monferrato   13–14, 23, 44, 50–51, 61, 63, 69, 107, 281, 316, 490
Montanar / Montanaro   338
Montàud dël Mondvì / Montaldo di Mondovì   52
Montij / Montiglio   512
Moross / Morozzo   302

Neuve / Novi Ligure   282, 299
Noara / Novara   14, 26

Orméa / Ormea   250, 284, 496

Pamparà / Pamparato   51
Pancalé / Pancalieri   338
Passeiran / Passerano   512
Pelis / Pellice   22
Pianëssa / Pianezza   51
Pinareul / Pinerolo   225, 317
Pivron / Piverone   181, 182
Povragn / Peveragno   45

Rocafòrt dël Mondvì / Roccaforte Mondovì

354

INDEX OF TOWNS, VILLAGES, AND GEOGRAPHICAL TERMS IN PIEDMONT

Salusse / Saluzzo   23, 26, 279–281, 304
Seraval Scrivia / Serravalle Scrivia   233
Sesia, Valsesia / Sesia, Valsesia   10, 12, 14, 65
Séssera / Sessera   10
Seva / Ceva   23
Sijé / Cigliè   326
Stralussi / Straluzzo ☞ Frabosa Sovran-a / Frabosa Soprana   491
Stron-a / Strona   10
Susa / Susa   23, 44, 284

Tani / Tanaro   9
Turin / Torino   9, 14, 20, 24, 26, 29–34, 36–41, 44–45, 48–56, 130, 136, 178, 216, 219, 227, 279, 283, 316, 338, 483, 485, 506, 509, 513, 518

Valansengh / Vallanzengo   326
Valàuria / Valloriate   65
Valensa / Valenza   26
Vaudié / Valdieri   282
Vërsèj / Vercelli   14, 26, 33, 111
Vian-a / Avigliana   44
Vilafalèt / Villafalletto   53, 321
Vilastlon / Villastellone   51
Vinàj / Vinadio   282
Viola / Viola   208, 233, 284–286, 289–290, 306

Printed in the United States
by Baker & Taylor Publisher Services